Praise for the First Edition

"*Welcome, Holy Spirit* should be welcome in the libraries of all Christians interested in the Charismatic renewal. Written by and for Lutherans, it will nevertheless constitute a standard theological work for Pentecostals and Charismatics in all of the churches.
The publication of this foundational volume marks a milestone in the development of the Charismatic movement in our time. Well-written and researched, it gives well-balanced answers to most of the questions usually raised about the modern Pentecostal/Charismatic movement."

Vinson Synan, Pentecostal

"This book makes it clear that the renewal is not Gospel tinsel, a peripheral adornment, a passing enthusiasm of the religious adolescent. *Welcome, Holy Spirit* is an ecumenically sensitive presentation of what God has been doing in the Charismatic renewal in Lutheran churches. To the process of theological discernment the international team brings academic credentials, pastoral experience, and a worldwide contact with the Lutheran renewal. From this global perspective, it faces the issues of justification, the cross, Christ alone, grace alone, faith alone, Scripture alone."

Kilian McDonnell, Roman Catholic

"We've waited for years for someone to chronicle the acts of the Holy Spirit in this generation. This is history, systematic theology, and inspiration combined in a practical, how-to volume."

Jamie Buckingham

Welcome, Holy Spirit

Charismatic Renewal in the Global Church:
Experience, Doctrine and Practice,
in Biblical and Missional Perspective

REGNUM STUDIES IN MISSION

Welcome, Holy Spirit

Charismatic Renewal in the Global Church:
Experience, Doctrine and Practice,
in Biblical and Missional Perspective

New, revised, updated and expanded edition by
Tormod Engelsviken (2023)

First edition edited by
Larry Christenson (1987)

This edition published 2023 by Regnum Books International

Regnum is an imprint of the Oxford Centre for Mission Studies
St. Philip and St. James Church, Woodstock Road
Oxford, OX2 6HR, UK
www.regnumbooks.net

Published in cooperation with Oase, Norway

British Library Cataloguing in Publication Data
A catalogue record for this book is available from the British Library

ISBN: 979-8-8898-3319-2
eBook ISBN: 979-8-8898-3320-8

Typeset by Words by Design
Cover image © Daoudi Aissa www.unsplash.com

Library of Congress Cataloging-in-Publication Data
Welcome. Holy Spirit
BX8065.5.W45 1987 284.1 87-14565
ISBN 0-8066-2273-3

Distributed by Fortress Press in the US, Canada, India, and Brazil

Being therefore exalted at the right hand of God, and having received from the Father the promise of the Holy Spirit, Jesus has poured out this which you see and hear.

Acts 2:33

Contents

Part Four: Taught by the Holy Spirit
Doctrinal Concerns in the Charismatic Renewal

Part Five: Led by the Holy Spirit
Practical Concerns in the Charismatic Renewal

Introduction to the First Edition in 1987: A View from Within

The Charismatic renewal has been around for more than a quarter of a century. It has evoked a variety of reactions, and still does. Some people personally identify with the movement and talk about the blessings they have received. Others point out problems that the movement has caused, and raise critical questions. The movement has been the occasion for considerable controversy in the church.

Yet the Charismatic renewal has not become a breakaway movement. It has generally remained in the churches. This is a special grace of God. In the past, the encounter between renewal movements and the church has often resulted in separation. One thing that can help prevent separation is for members to speak honestly and openly with each other, and to continue to listen to one another.

This book is an invitation to think together about Charismatic renewal in the church, with particular reference to the Lutheran church. It is not an official position of the church. It is a statement on behalf of a group within the church, those members whom we have come to call "charismatics". In a sense, it is a response to such oft-repeated questions as: "Who are these charismatics? What do they believe?"

This book is the product of a consultation that was initiated at an International Lutheran Charismatic Renewal Leaders' Conference held in Finland in the summer of 1981, with about 100 people from 12 different countries in attendance. Members of the consultation were chosen on the basis of long-term pastoral experience and theological training in the Lutheran tradition. In addition, they represented a broad range of first-hand experiences in the Charismatic renewal.

In 1981–1982, several members prepared papers based on an overall outline of the projected work. The group held its first meeting at Schloss Craheim in Bavaria, Germany, 15th–22nd July 1982. The prepared papers were thoroughly discussed. Generous time was also given to prayer, worship, and fellowship; this was felt to be an essential aspect of the undertaking.

Further writing assignments were handed out to members of the consultation. Larry Christenson was asked to be overall editor of the work. A second meeting was held at Lögumkloster Refugium in Denmark, 6th–13th October 1983. The format of the meeting was similar to the first: discussion of the document, prayer, worship, fellowship. In addition, a considerable amount of new material, drawn from the broad experience of the group, was introduced and discussed.

Overall evaluation of the work continued during the following three years, as subsequent drafts of the work were sent to members of the consultation. Although various members contributed first drafts for major sections of the book, the final work is the product of the group as a whole, working together with one another in the fellowship of the Holy Spirit.

The meetings and correspondence were lively. Members exchanged views freely, and they were not always in agreement with one another. Indeed, the final result – the book now before you – would probably still evoke some good discussions, including some disagreements, if the consultation were to meet again.

This book is presented with the prayer that the Lord may use it to help strengthen and unify his body, the church, so that it may better accomplish his purposes in the world.

Introduction to the Revised, Updated and Expanded Edition in 2022: A View after 36 More Years

More than 36 years have elapsed since the first publication of *Welcome, Holy Spirit. A Study of Charismatic Renewal in the Church.* Both the world and the world church have experienced great changes during this time and are now confronted with several new challenges. What have we learned about the work of the Holy Spirit in the Charismatic renewal from its beginning in the 1960s until now? How do we meet the new global challenges under the guidance of the Holy Spirit? How can the church in the whole world experience the renewing work of the Holy Spirit in a way that is conducive to spiritual growth, doctrinal maturity and world mission? These are some of the questions that we want to address in this new edition of the book.

An initiative was taken among leaders in the Evangelical Lutheran church in India to produce a revised, updated and expanded edition of the book that might address some of the new developments in church and mission, and at the same time remain faithful to the original vision and contribution of the International Lutheran Charismatic Theological Consultation. The Indian Christian leaders approached the *Oasis Movement* in Norway to assist them in this endeavour.

Before his death in 2017, the editor of *Welcome, Holy Spirit*, the American Lutheran pastor Larry Christenson, had given two of the original Norwegian contributors, Professor Tormod Engelsviken and Professor Asbjørn Simonnes, full freedom to translate and revise the book. This resulted in an edited Norwegian translation, *Velkommen, Hellige Ånd: Karismatisk fornyelse i kirken,* that was published in 2018 in co-operation with the *Oasis Movement.* This book has been widely distributed in Norway and has been well-received. Based on this experience, the *Oasis Movement* agreed to assist in the revision and publication of a *new English edition.* It asked Professor Dr Tormod Engelsviken to take responsibility for editing, revising, and expanding a new and updated version of the book.

For historical and practical reasons, the participants in the original consultations to produce the first edition of the book were drawn almost exclusively from the Western world, that is, from North America and Europe. However, a significant number of them were or had been cross-cultural missionaries working in countries other than their homeland. Therefore, they brought with them important experiences and insights also from non-Western contexts. See to this the list of participants in the Appendix.

The editor of this revised edition, Tormod Engelsviken, has been a missionary to Ethiopia and has had a global perspective and a particular interest in the concerns and contributions of the church in the Global South, with a special emphasis on areas such as Ethiopia, China, India, and Malaysia, in addition to his own context of Europe and North America in both his academic studies and practical ministry as a professor of missiology. Several of his contributions in the field of missiological and charismatic studies deemed especially relevant for this book are referred to or even partly included in this book.

The book has been abbreviated or rewritten in sections that contained highly specialised theological language, required an advanced Lutheran theological expertise, or were deemed to have less relevance for the world church today. The footnotes have also been reduced. In Part Two on Biblical Foundations, chapter 18 has been significantly expanded, and almost the whole of chapter 19 has been added by the editor, thus making the biblical section more comprehensive. In Part Three, more material on Luther's understanding of the Holy Spirit has been written and added as well as chapters 30 and 31 on Lutheran Pietism and some significant Lutheran precursors of the Charismatic Movement in the 19th and 20th centuries. In Part Five, Chapter 53 has been added and Chapter 56 expanded. Particular topics of importance have been dealt with in four excursus.

While the editor and the authors of the first edition were particularly concerned with answering criticism coming from the Lutheran churches, especially in the West, and therefore gave the book a certain apologetic character, the present edition is less defensive and more ecumenical and global in orientation, acknowledging the fact that the Pentecostal/Charismatic Movement today has grown to encompass and influence almost all Christian churches, Protestant, Orthodox and Catholic, including small and large Lutheran churches in the Global South. The number of "conversation partners" of this book has therefore become larger and more diverse, a fact that is reflected in the discussion of the various issues related to the Charismatic renewal.

The attentive reader will notice some repetitions in the text of the book. This may in some respects represent an advantage since it has been said that "repetition is the mother of learning". However, the main reason for such repetition is that some of the same subjects are dealt with under different perspectives: *historical* and *experiential* in Part One, *biblical* in Part Two, *Lutheran-confessional* in Part Three, *doctrinal* in Part Four, and *practical* in Part Five.

This revised edition with its abbreviations, amendments and additions has been reviewed and approved by an advisory group of leaders and theologians within the leadership of the *Oasis Movement* in Norway, consisting of Senior Pastor Jan Gossner, Assistant Professor Jens-Petter Jørgensen, Senior Pastor Trond Løberg and Professor Asbjørn Simonnes (see the Appendix).

It is the hope and prayer of the editor and the advisory group that this book may function as a comprehensive presentation of the work of the Holy Spirit from both a Lutheran and ecumenical perspective and may be used by theological students and church leaders, as well as reflecting believers, as a biblical, historical, doctrinal and practical exposition of the global Charismatic renewal, and thus further the spiritual renewal and mission of the worldwide church in our time.

Part One

Renewed by the Holy Spirit

The History and Experience of the Charismatic Renewal

He saved us, not because of deeds done by us in righteousness, but in virtue of his own mercy, by the washing of regeneration and renewal in the Holy Spirit, which he poured out upon us richly through Jesus Christ our Saviour, so that we might be justified by his grace and become heirs in hope of eternal life. The saying is sure.

Titus 3:5-8

(1) The History and Scope of the Charismatic Renewal

Present Status

What we call the Charismatic renewal is a Christian movement that began around 1960. In the span of its first two decades, the movement spread to every continent of the globe and into every major Christian denomination. No other movement in the history of Christianity has spread so fast and so extensively. It has continued to spread and today is a significant Christian movement in churches around the world, including mainline churches such as the Roman Catholic Church, the Anglican Church and the Lutheran Church, as well as most other churches. It has been especially important in churches in the Majority World,[1] among them the largest Lutheran churches in the world in Ethiopia, Tanzania and Madagascar. There are vibrant and growing Pentecostal/Charismatic movements and churches in the continents of Latin America with countries like Brazil and Argentina, in Asia with countries like China, India, South Korea, Indonesia, the Philippines and Malaysia, and in Africa with countries like Nigeria, Ethiopia, Kenya, Tanzania, Ghana, Cameroun, South Africa, and Madagascar as well as in many other large and small countries around the world.

It is common to divide what we call the Pentecostal/Charismatic movement into three major streams: firstly, the *Classical Pentecostal movement* dating back to the first decade of the 20th century, having formed *independent* churches and denominations in most parts of the world; secondly, the *Charismatic movement* which started around 1960 and is a movement *within* denominations of various traditions, Catholic, Orthodox, and Protestant; and, thirdly, the *Independent Charismatics* represented by independent churches and ministries around the world. Many of these have arisen in the Majority World and are independent of both the historical mainline denominations and the Classical Pentecostal movement.

Here are some recent statistics gathered and published by independent and recognised researchers in the *Center for the Study of Global Christianity* at *Gordon-Conwell Seminary* in Boston, USA:

The total number of Christians in the world doubled from about 560 million in 1900 to about 1 230 million in 1970, and it almost doubled again to about 2 480 million in 2017. In the year 1900, Pentecostals/Charismatics constituted 0.18% of all Christians; that is less than 1 million. In 1970, they

---

[1] By this term, we mean the world outwith Europe, North America, Australia and New Zealand; the world where most people on earth live.

constituted about 5% of all Christians; that is about 62 million. In 2017, they constituted about 27% of the total number of Christians; that is about 670 million.[2]

Although Christianity as a world religion has grown rapidly, especially in the Majority World, Pentecostal/Charismatic Christianity has grown even faster, increasing the percentage of Pentecostal/Charismatic Christians in the global church by more than 20% over the last 50 years. Pentecostal/ Charismatic Christians now represent the second largest block of Christians after Roman Catholicism. In recent statistics, 86% of all Pentecostals/Charismatics live in the Global South or the Majority World. "The growth of Pentecostal/Charismatic Christianity is more conspicuous than that of any other Christian group."[3]

If one takes into consideration that the total number of baptised Christians in the world today contains a large number of nominal Christians; that is, Christians who are Christians in name only, and do not have a personal Christian faith or practice Christianity, the percentage of Pentecostal/Charismatic Christians, who for the most part are believing, practicing Christians, is even higher, maybe as high as 50%. The Pentecostal/Charismatic movement of the past 120 years is thus by far the largest and fastest growing movement within the Christian church, and also the fastest growing major religious movement in the world compared with any world religion in the past or the present. It is therefore of enormous significance for the local church, for the global church and for the world at large.[4]

Characteristics and Definition

The Charismatic movement, as one major part of the larger Pentecostal/ Charismatic movement, has, like most Christian movements in history, some distinguishing characteristics. As the Protestant Reformation in the 16th century focused on justification by faith, and the Methodist revival in the 18th century on sanctification and a new life, the Charismatic renewal has emphasised the person, work and gifts of the Holy Spirit. It has important similarities to the Classical Pentecostal movement that came into being at the beginning of the 20th century, although it is historically distinct from it. It

[2] Todd M. Johnson, Gina A. Zurlo, Albert W. Hickman and Peter F. Crossing, "Christianity 2017: Five Hundred Years of Protestant Christianity", *International Bulletin of Mission Research,* 41(1), (January 2017), p. 8.

[3] Younghoon Lee, "Pentecostal Mission in the Third Christian Millennium: An Introduction", in Younghoon Lee and Wonsuk Ma (eds), *Pentecostal Mission and Global Christianity* (Oxford: Regnum, 2018), pp. 1-9.

[4] These figures are based on a recent statistical survey of the world church and of each country, see Todd M. Johnson and Gina A. Zurlo (eds), *World Christian Encyclopedia,* Third Edition (Edinburgh: Edinburgh University Press, 2020).

includes the practice of some spiritual gifts that have not been commonly experienced or practiced in the mainline churches since the first few hundred years of the Ancient Church,[5] but for the last 120 years have been part of classical Pentecostal spirituality, notably, speaking in tongues, prophecy, and healing. Another major emphasis of the Charismatic movement, also shared with the Pentecostal movement, has been on world mission and evangelism in the power of the Holy Spirit.

The focus on spiritual gifts has given the movement its distinctive name: "charismatic", which comes from the Greek word *charis* ("grace") and its derivative *charisma* (in plural: *charismata*), which means "outworkings of grace", "gifts of grace" or, more commonly, "spiritual gifts" (see 1 Cor. 12:1, 4)). According to Scripture, every Christian could be called a "charismatic" (see 1 Cor. 12:7, 11).

That is, however, not what most people mean when they use the word "charismatic" today. Although it is a biblical term, it is often used in a *secular sense* about a person with a personality that inspires enthusiasm or devotion, whether a politician, an artist or another kind of popular figure. "Charismatic" leadership in this secular sense can be for good or bad, but it has *nothing to do with Christian charisms*. Hence, this is *not* what we mean by charismatic in this book.

The dictionary definition of a charismatic is simply "a member of a charismatic religious group or movement." It is primarily in this practical sense that we will be using the term. When we speak about charismatics, we mean persons who participate in the experience and fellowship of the Charismatic renewal; who generally tell other people what it has meant in their lives; who listen to the teachings, read the literature, and share the sense of mission of this widespread renewal movement. In short, *charismatics are people who personally identify with the Charismatic renewal.* This is what most Christians mean when they use the word.

Early Formative History

Many factors contribute to the occurrence and growth of religious movements. Before they surface as identifiable movements, their shape and direction are already being affected by many forces. Yet, movements are often dated from a particular event that symbolises the meaning of that movement and its outbreak into the public arena. We usually date the Reformation from the day Luther nailed his 95 Theses to the door of the castle church in Wittenberg, Germany, in 1517, or Methodism from the meeting in

---

[5] For the understanding and practice of spiritual gifts in the ancient church, see e. g. Kilian McDonnell and George T. Montague, *Christian Initiation and Baptism in the Holy Spirit. Evidence from the First Eight Centuries* (Collegeville, MN: The Liturgical Press, 1991).

Aldersgate Street, London, England, in 1738 when John Wesley felt his heart "strangely warmed". The present-day Charismatic renewal is usually dated from a Sunday morning in April 1960, when pastor Dennis Bennett (1917–1991) announced to his Episcopalian (Anglican) congregation in Van Nuys, California, USA, that he had been baptised in the Holy Spirit and spoke in tongues.[6]

In little more than a year, similar events were occurring in a variety of Protestant congregations in the United States – Baptist, Church of Christ, Methodist, Presbyterian and Lutheran. Lutherans in California, Montana, and Minnesota began testifying to charismatic experiences in 1961–1962. As early as 1970, the religion editor of the large American newspaper *The New York Times* referred to it as the most vital movement in American religion.[7] By 1980, more than 29 million people in the United States were calling themselves Pentecostal or charismatic Christians.[8]

Within two years of its beginnings in the United States, the renewal was spreading to mainline Protestant churches in other countries. By 1970, the movement was present and growing on every continent. Every major denomination numbered charismatics among its members. "There is nothing quite like it in the history of the church," said Presbyterian historian Robert Whitaker. "Earlier renewal movements have been limited geographically and denominationally. This one has penetrated every denomination and is present on every continent of the globe – and all within a space of about 15 years."[9]

In 1967, the Charismatic renewal broke out in the Roman Catholic Church in the United States, where it experienced its most remarkable growth. By the 1980s, Catholics in 120 countries were actively involved. Roman Catholic participants in the Charismatic renewal, worldwide, were conservatively estimated at twenty million, and the movement showed no signs of abating.[10]

The Charismatic renewal is still growing; although in some areas, especially in the West, there have been some setbacks. The following chapters are not offered as a comprehensive or exhaustive study of the Charismatic renewal; they present an "underway perspective". It is our hope

---

[6] See Dennis Bennett, *Nine O'Clock in the Morning*, Newberry, FL: Bridge Publishing, 1970.

[7] Edward Fiske, "Pentecostals gain Among Catholics," *The New York Times*, 3rd November 1970.

[8] Kenneth Kantzer, "The Charismatics Among Us," *Christianity Today*, 11th February 1980, p. 25.

[9] Robert Whitaker, Presbyterian pastor and church historian, in a lecture in San Pedro, California, March 1980. From notes taken by Larry Christenson.

[10] Tom Forrest, past director of the International Catholic Charismatic Renewal Office, in a report made at a meeting of representatives of the World Council of Churches and Anglican, Lutheran, and Roman Catholic charismatic leaders in England, September 1985. From notes taken by Larry Christenson.

that this work may contribute to a greater understanding what is taking place throughout the global church today and that will strongly affect the lives of believers in Christ for years to come.

(2) The Questions and The Quest of the Charismatic Renewal

In the 13th century, the Catholic monk Francis of Assisi asked how the church of Christ, which had fallen into corruption, could be restored. In the 16th century, the German reformer Martin Luther's basic question was, "How can I find a gracious God?" In the 18th century, John Wesley's quest was for holiness of life.

What kind of questions did people ask in the latter half of the 20th century and what do they ask in the first half of the 21st? What are the questions asked by people in the Minority World of the Global North and what are the questions of the people in the Majority World of the Global South?

Questions in the Minority World

When the Lutheran World Federation met in Helsinki, Finland, in 1963 under the theme "Christ Today", they recognised that people were asking different questions:

> The man of today no longer asks, "How can I find a gracious God?" His question is more radical, more elementary: he asks about God as such, "Where is God?" He suffers not from God's wrath, but from the impression of his absence; not from sin, but from the meaninglessness of his existence; he asks not about a gracious God, but whether God really exists.[1]

A young American missionary, reflecting on his seminary training, described his own experience, and his frustration, in rather similar terms:

> Luther's question was not my question at all. For myself, there was the question of meaning and direction in life. I was active in confirmation and the church's youth group, but other than the fun times with friends who gave me a lot of social support (which shouldn't be underestimated), there was no real spiritual seeking within the context of that group. "Is God real?" was one of the questions that I struggled with. Another question that was on my mind was, "What difference does it make whether I believe in God or not?" The answer for me became clear when God revealed himself as being personally concerned for me. *The central issue of my quest was that of personal experience.* The meaning of my existence was thoroughly wrapped up in the question of God's existence and his concern for me as an individual. You can imagine the kind of

---

[1] "Message of the Lutheran World Federation Fourth Assembly," a two-page statement handed out to the Assembly participants (July 1963), p. 1.

> problems that arose when I came up against astute theologians who were sceptical of personal experience. For which reason, of course, I became sceptical of all theological activity, formally speaking. It all seemed totally irrelevant. The basic problem was that their questions were not my questions and my questions were not their questions, and there was no sensitivity on either side for the questions of the other. So all they could offer me was answers to questions that I never asked.[2]

The world views of secular people in Western countries are heavily influenced by the modern religious, philosophical and scientific traditions since the Enlightenment in Europe, and people have to a large extent succumbed to atheism (denying that there is a god) and agnosticism (not knowing whether there is a god). In the so-called post-modern period over the last 50 years or so, people in the West have also been exposed to philosophical doubt and the deconstruction of nearly all major truths, resulting in extreme individualism and relativism both with regard to truth claims and morality. This has led to a deep uncertainty with regard to religion.

Also Christians have been exposed to this modern and post-modern culture which has resulted in liberal theology, a compromise with biblical doctrine and ethics, as well as widespread nominal Christianity, when people keep up membership in the church, without having a personal relationship with God or belonging to a Christian fellowship where they regularly participate in listening to preaching, Bible study, prayer, praise, ministry and mission.

Questions in the Majority World

While the modern Western world views are also influencing some people among the educated elites in the Majority World, the general population is in a different situation.

In a famous article from 1982 with the title "The Flaw of the Excluded Middle", the American anthropologist and missionary to India, Paul G. Hiebert, argues that the Western worldview has a blind spot that makes it difficult for many Western missionaries to understand or answer problems related to spirits and similar phenomena.[3] When attempting to apply Jesus' words about his power to heal the sick and cast out evil spirits to mission today, Hiebert had a sense of uneasiness. He recounts how non-Christian people in India brought their problems related to misfortune, sickness, spirit possession, witchcraft and black magic to *sadhus* and various kinds of

---

[2] Private correspondence between Larry Christenson and a missionary of the American Lutheran Church, January-March, 1985.

[3] Paul G. Hiebert, "The Flaw of the Excluded Middle", *Missiology*, X(1), (January 1982), pp. 35-47.

healers, while the Christian missionaries from the West had no answers to these existential questions.

Hiebert argues that Western theology largely has ignored what he calls the "middle level", that part of reality that is not the transcendent creator God outside the created world, nor the immanent, created and visible world of nature, but the *unseen spiritual reality that exists in this world.* In this reality, one finds spiritual beings and forces, among them demons, who influence the daily lives of people. He says that Christianity in its Western form by denying this reality, actually has contributed to secularisation.

Agreeing with another famous missionary to India, Lesslie Newbigin, Hiebert says that the answer to this denial is "holistic theologies that deal with all the areas of life" including divine guidance, provision, healing, ancestors, spirits, invisible powers of this world, suffering, misfortune and death. This will involve the "doctrine of the Holy Spirit to show God's active involvement in the events of human history". "Many of the most successful missions," says Hiebert, "have provided some form of Christian answer to the middle level questions".

At the same time, Hiebert warns the church against becoming a new kind of magic, where human beings try to control their destiny by turning prayer into a formula in order to force God to do their own will by saying or doing the right things. Christian worship places the worshipper in the power and at the mercy of God, seeking God's will, he who knows what is best for us. The answers to prayer are those that give glory to God, not those that satisfy our immediate desires.

In this book, we want to take this challenge seriously, dealing with both the physical and the spiritual world in the power of the Holy Spirit, yet leaving the answers to God, not trying to force him to do our bidding which is another form of magic.

In many parts of the world, people experience a deep need for *liberation;* from spiritual, religious, political or economic forces that bind and oppress them. We do not pretend to have all the answers, but want to point to the evil forces that stand behind the oppression and injustice, that can only be fought in the power of the Holy Spirit and with spiritual weapons (Eph. 6:10-18), yet without neglecting the concrete social, political and economic actions that are called for to solve the many problems of the world today.

The Common Quest

As we have pointed out, people in the world today, both in the North and the South, are asking different questions from those asked in earlier centuries, and they are also asking different questions in different religious, political, social, and economic contexts. Behind these differences, however, is a common quest: the *desire to relate to God.*

Luther's question about a gracious God was not an abstract theological inquiry. It was a personal, existential quest. The reformers of the 16th century recognised that people looking on from the outside regarded "justification by faith" with contempt as a mere teaching; but for the reformers themselves it was a profound experience of God.[4]

The same concern motivates people today. When they ask whether God is real, and whether he can be experienced in their personal lives, it is not to satisfy intellectual curiosity. They want to know whether there is a God to whom they can relate and respond and who responds to them.

The questions that people ask change precisely because the quest remains the same. Experience tends to evolve into tradition. The questions and answers of one generation become the doctrines of later generations. This can enrich the church's understanding of the faith, but it also runs the danger of blunting the quest for a genuine relationship with God. People may learn about God and talk about God, rehearsing the traditions of the past, without experiencing the reality of a relationship with God today. Recitation of truth, even heartfelt acceptance of a doctrine, does not necessarily involve a personal relationship with God. That is a gift of God, and it often comes only as people wrestle with the particular questions that God sets before their generation.

In 1985, the *International Lutheran Renewal Center* in St Paul in the USA conducted a survey of people with varying degrees of involvement in the Charismatic renewal, to determine the nature of their spiritual quest and the kind of basic religious questions that they were asking. The survey indicated that these people were not asking the modern question, "Does God exist?" Nor were they asking: "How can I find a gracious God?" For them, the existence of God and the mercy of God were not in question. The reality of spiritual life was in a sense taken for granted. Their questions dealt rather with the quality of their life as Christians. They expressed discontent with a merely perfunctory expression of faith. They asked practical questions about living the Christian life more deeply and effectively.

A pastor from the United States wrote: "The question is not, 'Is God real?' but rather, 'How can I be real to God?'"

The relationship between church membership and spiritual life was the concern of a woman from the same country: "Is there spiritual life beyond

---

[4] That justification by grace alone through faith is not only a doctrine or a theory but a deep personal *experience* is expressed clearly in the "Augsburg Confession" (CA) of the Lutheran Church in Art. XX, 15, which states: "Although this teaching is despised by inexperienced men, God-fearing and anxious consciences *find by experience* that it offers the greatest consolation because the consciences of men cannot be pacified by any work but only by faith when they are sure that for Christ's sake they have a gracious God." Theodore G. Tappert (ed), *The Book of Concord* (Philadelphia, PA: Fortress Press, 1959), p. 43.

church membership? If you educate the mind, does this have the same result as spiritual conversion? I want to know the fullness of God in my life."

The response of a man from Canada was typical of various people who noted the lack of correspondence between church ritual and genuine spiritual life in their own experience:

> I was brought up in a Lutheran church, baptised as an infant, and confirmed at age 14, but had never received Jesus as my Lord and Saviour. I believed in God and knew about Jesus but had never experienced his love, until I surrendered my life to him. I was filled with the Holy Spirit, and my new life began. Since my life began, God has opened many doors of ministry to me."

A pastor from Norway expressed concern about the apathy of many church members: "There is so little joy in the churches and prayer fellowships. People know the right doctrine of salvation, but it doesn't show in their lives. One of the main things that the Charismatic renewal has to offer, it seems to me, is to give people joy in their faith."

Side by side with testimonies of revitalised faith came questions about the daily struggle to live more effectively as Christians. Their understanding of experience was not static, but involved a continuing response to the initiatives of the Spirit.

"The Lord seems to be prodding me to witness. I want to be a more effective witness, but how?"

"How can I pray more effectively?"

"How do I develop relationships with other people in the body of Christ so that we move and work in unity and harmony?"

"Why do we make such a limited impact on the non-Christian world?"

"Why are we [the church] seemingly so powerless over the powers of sin, sickness, Satanic tyranny, and godless thinking?"

"The non-Christians seem to make all the noise, draw big crowds, make more decisive moves, and influence the world and society more than the church does. How come? Where is the power?"

"How can I hear the Lord's voice more clearly? Many times, I have experienced his guidance specifically and many other times I see it in hindsight. Still, I long for more."

The Charismatic renewal has raised the question of *personal religious experience*, and it has given particular shape to the question; it has moved the central focus from the human individual to the Holy Spirit – from psychology to *pneumatology. Personal religious experience is rooted primarily in what the Holy Spirit says and does*; the human response is secondary and derivative. This is a fundamental conviction that lies behind what is presented in this book. The Charismatic renewal has arisen in response to a sovereign move of the Spirit of God in the latter half of the 20th century. *No evaluation of the movement that ignores God's sovereign initiative will come to a balanced understanding of its true significance.*

This does not mean that everything associated with Charismatic renewal should be approved and accepted out of hand. Human response to an initiative of God often involves a mixture of flesh and Spirit. We need to be as attentive to any word that the Holy Spirit would address *to* the Charismatic renewal as we are to the word that he wants to speak *through* the renewal. Where criticism or correction of the Charismatic renewal is needed, we shall call attention to it. A renewal that is truly of the Holy Spirit can only be strengthened when it honestly faces its own weaknesses and failures. Indeed, this is a simple necessity if a renewal is to be taken seriously and fulfil God's purpose.

(3) The Meaning of Charismatic Experience

Charismatic Experience and the Lordship of Christ

The Charismatic renewal understands itself as a renewal of biblical faith and experience. The central feature of this experience is a profound encounter with the triune God who has revealed himself in the Scriptures, his inspired Word. Thus, charismatic experience in a real sense stems from the Word of the Lord. It has this Word both as its basic impulse and as its final norm. It is from this perspective that we speak of charismatic experiences.

If Scripture is the supreme authority for understanding and evaluating charismatic experience, the centre of that authority is the lordship of Jesus Christ. Every aspect of the Charismatic renewal must be seen in relationship to Christ's lordship – over his church first and foremost, then also over the world and all creation.

The Charismatic renewal has not been called into being by the Holy Spirit simply to promote an experience, or spiritual gifts, or particular doctrines. It stands as a particular witness to the lordship of Christ.

If we speak about charismatic experience, it is because we understand that this is something Christ wants to be said in his church (cf. 1 Pet. 4:10-11). If we call for a more radical dependence on the Holy Spirit, it is because we understand that Jesus Christ himself wants to call attention to the ministry of the Holy Spirit. If we have emphasised certain parts of Scripture, such as those dealing with the fullness and power of the Holy Spirit, and his gifts, it is because we understand this to be a present priority of the Lord.

The Charismatic renewal has sometimes been dubbed a "speaking in tongues movement", as though that designation fully accounted for its significance. This would be like dismissing the people of Israel as a "silent marching people" because that was a feature of their behaviour at the battle of Jericho (Joshua 6). We know, however, that behind the marching was a command of the Lord, who wanted his people to carry out a particular strategy. The reality of his lordship, not a technique of marching in silence, was the central issue. If the Charismatic renewal gives particular attention to some spiritual gifts, it is because we believe that the restoration of the full spectrum of spiritual gifts to the church is part of the Lord's present strategy.

The lordship of Christ is the central issue that the Charismatic renewal raises in the church, and it is by this issue that it wishes to be judged. "For we do not preach ourselves, but Jesus Christ as Lord, and ourselves as your servants for Jesus' sake" (2 Cor. 4:5).

The Character of Charismatic Experience

Religious experience has often been equated with subjectivity or, even more narrowly, with mere interiority or feelings.[1] It is understood in terms of what goes on inside a person's consciousness.

In the Charismatic renewal, there exists a broader and more objective understanding of experience. It is a *comprehensive term* embracing every aspect of an *action of God that touches a person and creates in them a consciousness of God's reality.* Experience is thus a conscious *encounter with God* himself through an *action or word of God*, having tangible, observable results in the lives of individuals and communities and sometimes also in the outward physical world.

Authentic charismatic experience is God-given evidence of God's reality and power. This does not mean that it is always scientifically verifiable, for science is not its frame of reference. Verification of empirical data must be appropriate to a particular frame of reference: verification of temperatures requires different instruments and procedures than verification of musical pitch. The verification of historical events is generally not done by scientific proofs; although it may be confirmed by archaeological finds and by other sciences. It is, however, most often based on the study of empirical data, such as eyewitness accounts.

One of the great attractions of the Charismatic renewal is exactly that it does not only involve interior experiences – important as they are – but also outward experiences and manifestations of the Spirit of God, observable not only to Christians but also to everybody else.

The most important evidence of the work of the Holy Spirit through the Charismatic renewal is renewed, empowered, and transformed personal lives, churches, and ministries, which are in some respects invisible and in other respects quite visible for all. Yet, some of the spiritual gifts that are in common use in the Charismatic renewal are (more than in most other church traditions before it[2]) tangible and visible evidence of God's intervention in the lives of people. Prophecies that are fulfilled, sick people who are miraculously healed through prayer, demons that are cast out, even dead that

---

[1] See, for example, Carter Lindberg, *The Third Reformation? Charismatic Movements and the Lutheran Tradition* (Macon, GA: Mercer University Press, 1983). Lindberg sees Pietism defining "experience" primarily in terms of subjectivism and interiority (pp. 159), and he lumps the Charismatic renewal together with this tradition (pp. 183, 187).

[2] There are many examples of e.g. healing by prayer in church history before or apart from the Pentecostal/Charismatic movement, but this movement has been the first to make healing and miracles a major and normal part of its theory and practice. Any church or individual Christian who believes in the Bible and God's supernatural intervention in answer to prayer may experience divine healings and other miracles. But the Charismatic renewal has strengthened both the belief in healing and the experience of it.

are raised, and other miracles have been witnessed by numerous trustworthy people, Christians as well as non-Christians.

The highly respected New Testament scholar Craig S. Keener, who has documented that there are in fact millions of Christians in our time who have been eyewitnesses to healings and other miracles, argues that the eyewitness accounts of the miracles and signs of Jesus in the New Testament and those today are similar and that they may in many cases be irrefutable evidence of supernatural causation.[3] The data of charismatic experience must be tested and verified within the framework of God's Word and the community of faith, but some of the claims of supernatural signs may also be verified by science, particularly medical science, provided the scientists are Christians or at least has a worldview that does not *a priori* exclude a spiritual dimension or a divine intervention.

Scripture instructs us to confirm prophetic words and supernatural experiences, test and distinguish the spirits, prove all things, and beware of falsehood and deception (Mt. 24:11; Acts 13:6-12; 1 Cor. 12:2, 10; 14:29; Col. 2:18; 1 Thess. 5:19-21; 1 Jn 4:1-3). This kind of instruction is not aimed at developing psychological profiles of people who have had religious experiences, but at verifying the objective truth or falsity of their reports.

When charismatics talk about "experience", they may therefore have in mind something visible and concrete, such as a healing. They would draw no significant distinction between this and an inner perception or change of attitude; both would be attributed to the intervention and working of the Spirit, the only difference being that one took place publicly and the other took place in the privacy of the inner life. The focus is on the empirical reality behind the experience – the intervention of God – not simply on one's subjective response.[4]

---

[3] Keener has documented this in two major works. One is Craig S. Keener, *Christobiography: Memory, History, and the Reliability of the Gospels* (Grand Rapids, MI: Eerdmans, 2019); the other the more than 1000 pages two volume work, Craig S. Keener, *Miracles: The Credibility of the New Testament Accounts*, Vols. 1 and 2 (Grand Rapids, MI: Baker Academic, 2011). In the latter books, Keener has collected, documented, evaluated, and discussed an enormous amount of eyewitness testimonies to healings, raisings of the dead, exorcisms of evil spirits and other suprahuman or supernatural events. Keener argues that in many of these cases divine causation is the only possible, or the most likely explanation. For a shorter presentation, see Tormod Engelsviken, "Deliver Us From Evil: Evangelism, Spiritual Conflict, Signs and Wonders", in *Pentecostal Mission & Global Christianity. An Edinburgh Centenary Reader*, edited by Younghoon Lee and Wonsuk Ma (Oxford: Regnum, 2018), pp. 193-206.

[4] Marc D. McLean, "Toward a Pentecostal Hermeneutic", in *Toward a Pentecostal/Charismatic Theology of Baptism in the Holy Spirit*, edited by J. Rodman Williams (Bound Volume of Papers from the Fourteenth Annual Meeting of the Society for Pentecostal Studies, 1984), pp. 21-25. He says, "We have experienced the divine person directly acting in our lives, not only by internal

Charismatic experience may affect a person's inner life, or the world they live in, or both. In the Charismatic renewal, people refer as readily to the objective action of God as to their own subjective response. To illustrate this, we quote some testimonies: words like "The Lord healed her…", "The Spirit guided us…", are as common as, "God forgave me…", "I felt his love and forgiveness…", "I knew a joy I had never known before…", "I sensed his presence." Whichever the focus, the *experience arises out of something that God has done.* The action of God is objective and primary; the human response is derivative and secondary.

Two Aspects of Charismatic Experience

In the Charismatic renewal, experience does not follow a rigidly uniform pattern. One sees some diversity both at the individual and the corporate level. Nevertheless, millions of Christians who identify with the Charismatic renewal (Lutherans among them) tend to speak of their encounter with God the Holy Spirit in *two major ways*.

First, this encounter usually represents an *initiation into a new dimension of Christian living.* This is true whether it occurs at the beginning of a person's life as a consciously committed Christian, or at a later stage. As an *initiation* experience, it is often called "baptism with the Holy Spirit" or "spiritual renewal."

Second, such experience has *far-reaching consequences* for most aspects of one's Christian life. This *continuing dimension* is frequently called "life in the Spirit" or a "renewed life."

Most people who enter into charismatic experience associate it with an initiation event, although this is not always the case. Some people who have had no clearly identifiable initiatory experience may become deeply involved in the renewal and move into a life of ongoing charismatic spirituality.

In the early years of the Charismatic movement, "being baptised with the Holy Spirit" or "being filled with the Spirit" as an *initiation event*, captured major attention for the simple reason that many Protestants and Catholics were rather ignorant with regard to charismatic experience. By the mid-1960s, however, the overall emphasis had already begun to shift more toward the value of charismatic experience for spiritual growth, for the formation of Christian community, and for ministry. The emphasis on initiation experience remains an integral part of the renewal, for the movement continues to draw in new people, but it has less overall prominence than it did when the movement first broke on the scene.

---

renewal, but external experiences such as healings, not merely "religiously sensitive reflections", but as an infilling of the Holy Spirit… we proclaim that God acts and speaks today just as he did in biblical times."

What remains at the centre of the renewal, however, is the conviction that *charismatic experience is a normal, indeed an indispensable, part of Christian life* – which is simply another way of saying that God's intervention in our lives, according to the pattern and teaching of Scripture, is an objective reality. Without it, our witness will be weak and impoverished.

(4) The Reception and Content of Charismatic Experience

How do people actually come into charismatic experience? How does it affect their faith?

Although charismatic experience is essentially personal, it is not an individualistic experience. Sometimes, people come into charismatic experience in the quiet of their own devotions, but usually it takes place through *communal relationships*; the prayer group or the praying community plays a distinctive role in the Charismatic renewal. These may vary considerably in size – from two or three persons to thousands! They form a fellowship with social and spiritual functions that are interrelated.

The group or community provides a *loving, caring, and praying fellowship* in which one may learn about charismatic experience, and in which charismatic experience can be received, sustained and deepened. In this fellowship, through observation and instruction, one acquires a certain biblical and doctrinal framework that makes charismatic experience normal, meaningful, relevant, and attractive. It serves as a guideline for the person's own search and experience. One then goes on to actually desire and seek such experience in expectant faith.

Opening up to charismatic experience in practice may often – but not always – include such things as confessing sins and receiving forgiveness (absolution); setting aside theological and emotional doubts and passivity; active, personal prayer for the Holy Spirit; and a readiness to yield to the exercise of charismatic gifts that are one result of the sought experience.

The charismatic fellowship provides a framework for such experience. It serves as a supportive fellowship, praying for the seeker to receive an expanded awareness and experience of the Holy Spirit. Frequently this happens through *the laying on of hands* by fellow Christians who themselves have had a charismatic experience and who exercise their gifts within the fellowship.

The fellowship is also the setting where the spiritual gifts are used, and where charismatic worship and spirituality are encouraged and practiced. Charismatic fellowships are strongly oriented toward personal participation and individual freedom of religious expression, although in a structured way under responsible leadership. In the Charismatic renewal, freedom and authority, spontaneity and ritual, improvisation and preparation do not appear as contradictory terms. They all find expression in charismatic fellowships.

The *content* of charismatic experience has several aspects to it. Essentially, it is an *encounter with God the Father through Jesus Christ the*

Son that results in being filled with the Holy Spirit. It involves also a heightened confidence in the Spirit's continuous presence. The underlying common feature of people's diverse experiences seems to be a conscious awareness that the indwelling Holy Spirit is affecting the whole person. It may or may not be an instantaneous experience, but it sets the recipient on a fresh course, with a new and conscious dependence on the presence and power of the Holy Spirit.

The *testimonies of ordinary Christians* to their charismatic experience are very frequent and important in the Charismatic renewal. This is the testimony of a businessman,

> The Lord has blessed me with a renewal of the Holy Spirit. Many of the blessings are not yet completed, but only in the process, and many of the blessings I am probably still unaware of. However, I do have the confidence that I am growing in the Spirit and in God's will. The gift of speaking in tongues came to me only after I had witnessed the effect it was having on my wife. It then was given to me after I sought it in confession, prayer, and release. The gift came to me in song, and I still most often express it in this way.
>
> Of course, spiritual renewal and conformity to God's will are possible without the gift of speaking in tongues. They can be fruit of a dedicated Christian life. However, I must confess that until I experienced this gift, they were not very evident in my life. I was, and had been, active in church activities, and undoubtedly many would have said that I was living a truly Christian life. I can assure you I was trying, but there was something missing: *I* was trying to do God's work. There is now within me a new joy, a new vitality, a new desire and urgency. It is not I, but Christ in me. I am aware of this continually, and I thank God for it in prayers of tongues and in prayers of my understanding.
>
> As to the overall effect, I would say this renewal of the Holy Spirit has awakened within me an awareness of the true blessing of Christ: his ministry, his death, his resurrection – our salvation. I have found a new desire to read God's Word, a new understanding as I read and hear it preached. I have found a greater conviction of sin – mine and others'. I have felt much more the urge to witness to others, and the ability to do so seems to be increasing. I believe that more and more my desire is to put God's work first and to be truly dedicated to Christ."[1]

Charismatic experience is signally an encounter with God. The individual Christian has a perception of being directly and personally faced with divine reality. God is encountered both in his majestic power and in his loving nearness. God is real, present, and personal. The intense and positive awareness of God's immediate presence brings a "here and now" quality into one's personal testimony of faith.

---

[1] Larry Christenson, *The Charismatic Renewal Among Lutherans* (Minneapolis, MN: International Lutheran Renewal Center, 1976, rev. ed. 1985), pp. 22-23.

Frequently, the experience has a pronounced *trinitarian* structure as it unfolds in a person's life, involving each of the persons of the Godhead in a particular way.

Jesus Christ is experienced as the *living Lord, present with his people*, to be loved and obeyed. This realisation may involve an awareness of his saving power, a deep knowledge of forgiveness of sin and deliverance from the power of Satan that are experienced presently and personally by the believer. The continuing experience tends to focus on the lordship of Christ, both in terms of one's own life and the establishment of God's kingdom. In its fundamental structure, charismatic experience is thus as Christ-centred as it is Spirit-centred.

The Holy Spirit is experienced as a distinct person who grants supernatural power, equipping the believer both for ministry and for holy living. Another way of putting it is that the Holy Spirit brings the living, redeeming, ministering, and present Christ into vital union with the believer. The experience of the Spirit is not simply equated with receiving the person of Christ and his saving work in faith. The focus of charismatic experience is different from an initial experience of conversion and salvation, although the two may occur at the same time. Charismatic experience brings a more conscious awareness of the presence and work of the Holy Spirit that enables Christ to express his life in the life of a believer. By the Spirit, Christ lives in and through the believer.

Finally, *God* is experienced as the *loving, caring Father*. The experience of being a *loved child of God* is often related to the first person of the Trinity. The encounter with God the Father, who in charismatic experience meets the believer so personally and immediately, often brings with it a sense of being overwhelmed by love and grace, a *new assurance* of being a child of God and a wish to address him as *Abba*, Father (Rom. 8:15-16).

At the concluding service of a charismatic conference in Germany, one of the participants stood up and said, "All my life I have known Jesus as my Saviour. By God's grace, I have led many people to personal and saving faith in Christ. But in these days, for the first time in my life, I have been able to say, *Lieber Vater* (Dear Father)."[2]

---

[2] Arthur Richter, executive secretary of the Marburger Kreis, in a closing statement at a charismatic conference, Enkenbach, Germany, July 1963. Reported by Larry Christenson.

(5) The Effects of Charismatic Experience

Charismatic experience is greater than any of its effects. In a certain sense, the subjective effects are secondary to the content of the experience as described in the previous chapters. A distinction must be maintained between the God who is experienced and the effects of this experience in the lives of individuals and communities. Yet, the results of an experience do contribute to our understanding of its purpose and add vitality to our Christian witness.

Assurance of God's Reality and Personal Salvation

For many, a desire for greater spiritual power, enabling them to live and serve more effectively as Christians, has led them to seek charismatic experience. The encounter with God in charismatic experience frequently brings about a keen sense of *assurance*, both with regard to the objective reality of God and the more personal question of one's own salvation and ministry. There is a close connection between experiencing the power of God and experiencing the love and grace of God. The power that is received through charismatic experience heightens one's awareness of God's holy and loving presence; such awareness renews the spiritual life both in its ethical and in its ministry dimensions. Knowledge made alive through subjective and objective experience produces a personal and profound certainty not arrived at through teaching alone.

Power for Witness and Mission

The *power* received in connection with charismatic experience equips one to live more effectively as a Christian. Since the commencement of the classical Pentecostal movement at the beginning of the 20th century, a major reason for seeking charismatic experience has been the quest for spiritual power and authenticity, especially regarding mission. There is both theological and historical evidence, particularly from the Majority World, that charismatic power is a necessary ingredient for effective mission and evangelism.[1]

---

[1] This has been documented by many studies. See for example Philip Jenkins, *The Next Christendom: The Coming of Global Christianity* (Oxford: Oxford University Press, 2002); Wonsuk Ma, "The Theological Motivations for Pentecostal Mission", in Younghoon Lee and Wonsuk Ma (eds), *Pentecostal Mission and Global Christianity* (Oxford: Regnum, 2018), pp. 25-39. The Malaysian Methodist scholar and bishop Hwa Yung concludes after a thorough discussion of the contribution of Pentecostals and Charismatics to contextual mission in Asia, that contextual theology "would necessarily involve the practice of 'power encounters' in the

Both biblically and experientially, the outpouring of the Holy Spirit's power produces noticeable results. For example, Christians gain a deeper personal conviction that God's Word is truth, a heightened awareness of the Spirit's indwelling presence, a boldness to proclaim the gospel even in the face of widespread indifference or stiff opposition and persecution, a divine confirmation of the spoken message through "signs and wonders", and greater results from evangelistic ministry, as people are convinced and convicted by the proclamation of the gospel by charismatically empowered ministers.

Although the *gospel itself* "is the power of God for the salvation of everyone who believes" (Rom. 1:16), the power given by the Holy Spirit is also a power that accompanies and empowers the *witness* to the gospel. It is a power given to *witnessing persons*, anointing and equipping them for ministry (Acts 1:8). It is not something added to their life in Christ. It is a release of the power of that life through the Holy Spirit, working actively in and through them for the salvation and upbuilding of others.

Use of Spiritual Gifts

When we focus on the dynamics and power of the Holy Spirit, we see another essential characteristic of charismatic experience: the *gifts of the Spirit, the charisms*, come into active use. As the Spirit fills believers, bringing home to them the reality and presence of the triune God, the Spirit is manifested in the individual and in the community. One way that this is experienced is in the variety of charisms.

The charisms have played such a prominent role in the movement that they have provided it with its most widely accepted name, "charismatic". Practical and realistic emphasis on the charisms is a prominent characteristic of the Charismatic renewal. On theological grounds, one may affirm that there is no basic difference between those inside and outside the movement since every Christian has received the Spirit and in this sense is a charismatic (cf. 1 Cor. 12:11-13; 1 Pet. 4:10-11). What one encounters in the Charismatic renewal, however, is a *more conscious expectation and experience of the*

---

healing and exorcism ministries, and serious attention being given to inculturation... It must be able to empower the Asian church in apostolic cross-cultural missions to other people". Hwa Yung, *Mangoes or Bananas? The Quest for an Authentic Asian Christian Theology* (Oxford: Regnum, 1997), pp. 71-76. Hwa Yung also has a challenge to Asian churches: "Many Asian Christians have been led by God to discover afresh the gifts of the Holy Spirit for themselves. They have learned to appropriate his power in addressing the vital issues of Hiebert's "excluded middle" [...] This, together with other factors, has contributed to the vitality of much of Asian Christianity. Surely it is time for Asian Christians to dare to begin to formulate their own biblically-informed understanding of the dynamics of the Holy Spirit's work!" (p. 239).

entire range of spiritual gifts that we find in Scripture. The gifts are earnestly *desired and sought after* (cf. 1 Cor. 12:31; 14:1). They are seen as indispensable for the building up of the body of Christ, the church (Eph. 4:7-12)

The conviction that the Spirit manifests his divine presence through observable gifts underlies charismatic experience. *The charisms are seen as vehicles through which the Spirit comes to visibility in the body of Christ*: "To each one the manifestation of the Spirit is given for the common good" (1 Cor. 12:7). The heightened awareness of God's presence that one finds in the Charismatic renewal contributes decisively to the operation of the gifts. Although all the charisms may not be evident in the life of a given community, there will be openness for, expectation of, and seeking after the *full range of spiritual gifts*.

Since spiritual gifts are given to all regardless of gender, age, status or ethnicity, they have also led to an increase in bold and fruitful ministry by *lay people, women and young people* in the church, and have challenged traditional hierarchical structures that have restricted ministry and leadership to a few.

Recognition of the Supernatural

Closely related to the awareness of God's concern for all areas of human life is an increased appreciation of the *biblical worldview*, especially the recognition of the *supernatural dimension.* A common result of charismatic experience is an awakening to the spiritual dimensions of the universe such as the good "powers of the age to come" (Heb. 6:5), the existence of evil powers such as Satan and other demons and the reality of spiritual conflict and deliverance (Mt. 12:28). It also includes a conviction of Christ's victory over the evil powers on the cross (Col. 2:15) and boldness in confronting and defeating Satan in the name of Jesus (Eph. 6:10-18; 1 Pet. 5:8-9; Acts 16:18).[2]

Worship and Prayer

In response to God's manifestation through his Word and in the lives and ministries of his people, charismatic fellowships break forth in Spirit-inspired *praise and worship.* New songs and melodies, spontaneous speech (prayer, speaking in tongues, prophecy, testimony), and expressive bodily actions

---

[2] To the theme of the supernatural and spiritual conflict, see the results of a Lausanne consultation in Nairobi in the year 2000 in Tormod Engelsviken, *Spiritual Conflict in Today's Mission*. Lausanne Occasional Paper, No. 29 (Monrovia, CA: MARC, 2001). See also the full consultation report with all the written contributions in A. Scott Moreau et al. (eds), *Deliver Us From Evil: An Uneasy Frontier in Christian Mission* (Monrovia, CA: MARC, 2002).

(kneeling, upraised hands, clapping, prostration) have come to characterise many gatherings in the Charismatic renewal.

An assembled worshiping community may break into loud praise or remain in prolonged periods of expectant silence. The popular image of charismatic meetings is more associated with praise than with silence. Where the renewal matures, however, the value of silent waiting on the Lord is increasingly appreciated.

Together with the emphasis on praise and worship, there is also an enhanced awareness of the value and necessity of *prayer*. The charismatic experience opens up depths of freedom in prayer and intercession. For many, prayer ceases to be a heavy obligation and becomes a joyous and refreshing event, both individually and communally.

The Authority of the Bible

The impact of the *Bible as the authoritative Word of God* is strengthened. Traditional doctrines may take on fresh meaning and become relevant in unexpected ways. Bible study, both in private and in the fellowship, becomes more exciting and renewing as it strengthens held beliefs and opens up a deeper understanding of God's revelation. In theological terms, the Holy Spirit *illuminates* the Word in an ongoing way.

Ethics and Attitudes

Although more difficult to measure in an objective way, charismatic experience does produce *noticeable ethical effects in the lives of people.* Charismatics frequently testify that the intense experience of God's love kindles in them *a new love for God and for others* (cf. Rom. 5:5). This is evidenced in the Charismatic renewal by close, deeply committed relationships between people, by a sense of oneness and unity within the fellowship, by a genuine appreciation for Christians of other traditions and denominations leading to practice of Christian unity (*ecumenism*), especially among charismatics of various traditions, and by social ministries (*diakonia*) that reach out to the suffering and deprived, with attention to various human needs.

Along with love, charismatic experience often enhances the believers' sense of *joy and peace*, both individually and corporately. Joy may be expressed in exuberant praise, or in peaceful contentedness that waits quietly on the Lord. All of the *fruit of the Spirit* may become a reality in people's lives through the work of the Holy Spirit (cf. Gal. 5:22-23). This has traditionally been called *sanctification* and has often been seen as a long process in the lives of Christians. In the Charismatic renewal, this fruit may appear as an immediate result of the initial experience. This does not mean, however, that it is granted once for all. Like the gifts of the Spirit, the fruit of the Spirit has to be renewed in the lives of believers as they repeatedly pray for the coming of the Holy Spirit anew.

Charismatic experience tends to have a broad rather than a narrow impact on a person's life. Where one experiences a release of power in ministry, more than likely there will also be noticeable changes in attitude and behaviour that affect daily life. Charismatic experience is consistent with the purpose and strategy of the Holy Spirit, which is to vitalise and demonstrate the fullness of the life of Christ which has been given us.

(6) The Tasks of the Charismatic Renewal

For the most part, the Charismatic movement has been a renewal movement occurring within historical denominations. It is both similar and dissimilar to previous revival and renewal movements. It is *similar* in its emphasis on confession and forgiveness of sin, conversion and a personal relationship with Jesus Christ, new life and a changed lifestyle, reading and obeying the Bible, prayer and worship, Christian unity and fellowship, personal testimony and missionary fervour. It has, however, a *distinctive emphasis* on the person, work, experience and gifts of the Holy Spirit, which it shares with Pentecostalism. But it is *unique* in the history of the church by virtue of its worldwide scope and its penetration of virtually every denomination of the Christian church.

The Apologetic Task

As is true for all movements within the church that claim to be initiated by the Holy Spirit, the teachings and practices of those who speak for the movement *must be tested.* They must be examined relative to the whole of the biblical message, the ecumenical creeds, historical theological understanding, and church tradition. Thus, there is an *apologetic* theological task required of leaders and theologians within a renewal movement in answer to the question: Are the teachings and practices of this movement consistent with the biblical, historical, classical Christian faith?

This is one part of our task in this book: we wish to present and evaluate the Charismatic renewal in the light of the classical biblical Christian faith, and with particular reference to the Lutheran tradition.

The Prophetic Task

There is, however, also a *prophetic* task characteristic of a renewal movement initiated by the Holy Spirit. In its prophetic role, a renewal movement will *challenge, correct, redirect, and perhaps even help redefine* the church's character and mission. By definition, God-initiated renewal breaks in to challenge prevailing practices in the church, to cause reassessment of traditional expressions of the gospel, to renew loyalties to essential doctrines, and to foster the kind of change necessary to accomplish in the present time the unvarying purpose of the Spirit: to bring people into relationship with the living Christ, and to extend his kingdom. Seen from this perspective, a renewal movement does not bring something "new" in an absolute sense. On the contrary, it seeks to bring the church in line with a truth older than that by which it is presently living. It applies unchanging truth to a changed time. It is a corrective, not a new norm.

Periodically, the church must redefine itself in contrast to non-Christian values and practices that have crept into the church, or with reference to forces outside the church against which the church must stand in judgement. Here, too, renewal movements may exercise a prophetic role.

As a prophetic presence within the church, the Charismatic renewal must pose some timely and straightforward questions:

- Is the church in the 21st century charismatic in a practical, realistic sense? Are the person and power of the Holy Spirit evident in the church today, or has a mere doctrine of him as the third person of the Trinity replaced him as a living reality?
- Does prevailing biblical interpretation, often dominated by Western exegetical and hermeneutical methodology, strengthen or weaken belief in the living God who is presented in Scripture?
- How clearly is the biblical call to holy living being sounded in the church today?
- Does traditional teaching on certain biblical themes need to be restated and, where necessary, expanded for our day (for example, the biblical worldview, baptism, justification, sanctification, the doctrine of the means of grace, the spiritual gifts, worship and praise, the nature and government of the church, the doctrine of evil, the ministry of the laity, mission and evangelism)?
- Are the Lutheran Confessions generally used to limit or to release the full dynamic of the biblical revelation? Are there biblical doctrines and practices that the Confessions do not deal with that should be emphasised anew today?
- Is the Holy Spirit redirecting the church, including the Charismatic renewal, to greater dependence on the Spirit – to brokenness, humility, and servanthood rather than to power, organisation, and program?

The Theological Task

Almost from the outset, Lutherans addressed themselves to some of the *theological questions raised by the renewal.* This found expression in articles and books written by Lutherans who had become personally involved in the renewal. To begin with, these centred on certain aspects that the renewal shared with classical Pentecostalism: personal experience of the baptism or fullness of the Holy Spirit and the catalogue of spiritual gifts in 1 Corinthians 12. Then other issues began to be addressed, for example, family and congregational life, ethical and social issues, spiritual formation and pastoral care, and not least world mission and evangelism.

Beginning in 1962, Lutheran church bodies began to produce theological statements, position papers, study documents, and pastoral guidelines that sought to deal with the Charismatic renewal.[1] Looked at as a whole, they present a moderate or positive stance toward the Charismatic renewal.[2] For the most part, these documents were written by people not personally involved in the Charismatic renewal. While this offered the advantage of some measure of objectivity, it also had certain built-in limitations. It is hard to get a truly objective view of a widespread renewal movement from the outside. It is like attempting to write a mission report without the participation of any missionaries.

While the understanding of the charismatic experience during the first years of the Charismatic renewal in the mainline churches was strongly influenced by the terminology and theology of the Classical Pentecostal movement, there was a growing concern and conviction that theological reflection on the charismatic experience as well as charismatic practice could and should be developed within the traditions of the various denominations and without introducing to much "baggage" from other traditions. This book is thus an attempt to *reflect theologically on the charismatic experience within the Lutheran tradition, without ignoring what we may learn from other traditions*, including the Pentecostal. It is therefore both *Lutheran and ecumenical*. This Lutheran perspective does not, however, mean that we cannot be critical of aspects of the Lutheran tradition – in particular, some of its omissions or shortcomings in doctrine and practice with regard to the experience and gifts of the Holy Spirit. The renewal can be seen as a theological *enrichment* of the Lutheran church.

Conclusion

A renewal must take seriously its responsibility to be faithful and consistent regarding the historical teaching of the church. It must have ears to hear what the church has said and is saying. That is the *apologetic task*. The other task, *the prophetic*, is equally important, and here the church also must exercise responsibility: it must set aside defensiveness and have ears to hear a word that calls for change, a word that calls it to break free from bondages and enter into the freedom of the Spirit. The prophetic task must be combined with the *theological* task. The church must hear and reflect on a calling for

---

[1] Many of these Lutheran statements from churches in various parts of the world are found in the three-volume work by Kilian McDonnell (ed), *Presence, Power, Praise – Documents of the Charismatic Renewal* (Collegeville, MN: The Liturgical Press, 1980).

[2] In Norway, for example, the Lutheran bishops approved of a document produced by a group of theologians that recommended the renewal. They said that it "might give valuable impulses for a richer life of the congregations and a richer spiritual life for the individual", see Tormod Engelsviken, Ove Conrad Hanssen, Kjell Olav Sannes, *Den Hellige Ånd i kirkens liv* (The Holy Spirit in the Life of the Church) (Oslo: Luther Forlag, 1981), p. 8.

radical dependence on the Holy Spirit in every area of its life and mission. If this were not needed, the Lord would not have graced the churches with the Spirit's demonstrative, unsettling presence in our day.

The study by the international group of Lutheran charismatic leaders and theologians which led to this book reflects not only knowledge and training in the Lutheran theological tradition, but also a broad range of first-hand experience in the Charismatic renewal. It is written with charismatics in mind – to help them articulate as accurately as possible the meaning and importance of their experience, so that they can share it more effectively with others. It is written for those who want to gain a better understanding of what God is saying through this renewal. This book is written with the "priesthood of all believers" in mind – the ministers who sit in the pews as well as those who stand in the pulpits.

Part Two

Inspired by the Holy Spirit

Biblical Foundations

All Scripture is God-breathed and is useful for teaching, rebuking, correcting and training in righteousness, so that the man of God may be thoroughly equipped for every good work.

2 Timothy 3:16-17

(7) Biblical Interpretation in the Charismatic Renewal

The Authority of Scripture

In the preceding chapters, we have maintained that charismatic experience grows out of an encounter with the triune God according to God's self-revelation in Scripture. It is true, however, that although various denominational expressions of the worldwide Charismatic renewal see the Bible as the primary source and norm for the interpretation of their experience, biblical interpretations vary, depending on one's biblical methodology and theological tradition.

No interpretation of the Scriptures takes place in a historical vacuum. We come to the study of Scripture from our own personal backgrounds, often with strong denominational and theological traditions, in the midst of a contemporary situation that to a considerable degree determines the impetus and framework for our study. Those of us who have prepared this book stand in a Lutheran tradition, with certain presuppositions, emphases, and concerns that belong to our Lutheran heritage. We treasure this heritage. We recognise its value for our theological endeavour. At the same time, we recognise the Holy Spirit's call to humility. No one tradition in the body of Christ has a monopoly on understanding. While we, as Lutherans, have gifts to share, we must also have the humility to receive and learn from others. Above all, we must be willing to be taught and led by the Spirit as the Spirit sheds light on the Word of God.

Charismatics have no uniform *view of the Bible*. But all Pentecostals and Protestant charismatics belong to the *evangelical* tradition in the world church. Classical Pentecostals have traditionally had a so-called *fundamentalistic* view of the Bible (not to be confused with political, violent fundamentalism!). This means that they have believed in the *inerrancy* of Scripture in *all areas*, including history and nature, and have seen this as a result of God's verbal inspiration of Scripture. More recent Pentecostal scholarship has moved away from this understanding of inerrancy toward an understanding that emphasises the historical *trustworthiness* of Scripture, yet admitting errors and incompatibilities in minor areas. The same would apply to most charismatics. All Protestant[1] charismatics, both fundamentalist and

[1] Charismatics who belong to the Catholic and Orthodox churches mostly share the views of their own churches that give equal authority to the Bible and the tradition of the church. These churches claim that a continued revelation by the Holy Spirit in the church has led the church to new theological insights that are not found in the Bible, for example, the doctrine of the virgin Mary or the papacy. Although,

non-fundamentalist, would probably agree with Article 2 in the Lausanne Covenant (1974) on the authority and power of the Bible:

> We affirm the divine inspiration, truthfulness and authority of both the Old and the New Testament Scriptures in their entirety as the only Written Word of God, without error in all that it affirms, and the only infallible rule of faith and practice […] Through it the Holy Spirit still speaks today. He illumines the mind of God's people in every culture to perceive its truth freshly through their own eyes and thus discloses to the whole church ever more of the many-coloured wisdom of God.[2]

Charismatic Hermeneutics

Hermeneutics (in this case, the principles and methodology of biblical interpretation) depends, like everything else in the Christian life, on the Holy Spirit in order to produce good fruit. Lutheran charismatics build their hermeneutics outward, from the centre of Scripture, which is the *lordship of Christ*, pre-eminently revealed through his person, life, words, acts, death, resurrection, ascension, and being seated at the right hand of the Father.

Lutheran hermeneutics distinguishes between two basic motifs of Scripture's redemptive message: *the law (what God demands, including his judgement) and the gospel (what God gives, including his forgiveness).* It does not assume, however, that distinguishing between law and gospel is a simple matter of categorising texts of Scripture. To properly distinguish between law and gospel is only possible in the experience realised by the Spirit. It is easy enough logically to distinguish between law and gospel as the demanding and the giving word. But in practice, when the question regarding the interpretation of Scripture is: what is demanded of me by the law? or, what does God give me by his grace? it is not always easy to differentiate. Then the gospel easily becomes a law. For everything is law and demand without the Holy Spirit. The real distinction between law and gospel is not made in theology, but in the experience of the Holy Spirit himself.[3]

---

according to their view, not all doctrines have to be based on the Bible, doctrines which conflict with the Bible are in principle not accepted. "The Church does not derive her certainty about all revealed truths from the Holy Scriptures alone. Both Scripture and Tradition must be accepted and honoured with equal sentiments of devotion and reverence." "Thanks to the assistance of the Holy Spirit, the understanding of both the realities and the words of the heritage of faith is able to grow in the life of the Church", *The Catholic Catechism.* Second edition (Citta del Vaticano: Libreria Editrice Vaticana, 2019), pp. 26 and 29.

[2] John Stott (ed), *Making Christ Known. Historic Mission Documents from the Lausanne Movement 1974-1989* (Carlisle: Paternoster Press, 1996), p. 13.

[3] According to Luther, see Regin Prenter, *Spiritus Creator*, translated by John M. Jensen (Philadelphia, PA: Fortress Press, 1953), pp. 208-209. This book by the well-

Doctrinal and Exegetical Work in the Pentecostal/Charismatic Movement

In the Charismatic renewal, hermeneutics has served primarily the task of practical or applied theology. Regarding systematic theology, it has adopted essentially the traditional or conservative position within each of the confessions in which the renewal has found expression. As a movement, it has not developed *one* comprehensive or unique systematic theology of its own, although several books have been written in recent years which try to explore a distinctive Pentecostal or charismatic comprehensive theology.[4]

Its distinctive contribution has been a lively sense of how the Holy Spirit applies Scripture to present situations. It views hermeneutics as a dynamic interplay of Scripture, believers, and the Holy Spirit.

Exegetical work in the Charismatic renewal tends to reflect the range and diversity of the movement itself. In addition to a significant number of Pentecostal theologians in recent years, Lutherans Arnold Bittlinger and Tormod Engelsviken, and the Catholic George T. Montague, have produced competent exegetical work, using the basic skills of scholarly exegesis.[5] Most

---

known Danish professor in Systematic Theology is regarded as the most authoritative study of Martin Luther's view of the Holy Spirit.

[4] Some of the most important and influential systematic theologians who are writing from a Pentecostal or Charismatic perspective, include the Finnish Lutheran, Veli-Matti Kärkkäinen: *Pneumatology: The Holy Spirit in Ecumenical, International, and Contextual Perspective*, 2nd ed. (Grand Rapids, MI: Baker Academic, 2018) and *Spirit and Salvation: A Constructive Christian Theology for the Pluralistic World,* Vol. 4 (Grand Rapids, MI: Eerdmans, 2016); the Malaysian Pentecostal, Amos Yong's *The Spirit Poured out on All Flesh: Pentecostalism and the Possibility of a Global Theology* (Grand Rapids, MI: Baker Academic, 2005), *Spirit of Love: A Trinitarian Theology of Grace* (Waco, TX: Baylor University Press, 2012) and *Renewing Christian Theology: Systematics for a Global Christianity* (Waco, TX: Baylor University Press, 2014); and the American Pentecostal Steven Land, *Pentecostal Spirituality: A Passion for the Kingdom* (Cleveland, TN: CPT Press, 2010). Their views may not always agree with those expressed in this book, but the enormous number of books and articles on Pentecostal and charismatic theology indicates how the Pentecostal/Charismatic movement have contributed to and even renewed theology as a whole. Discussing their various views here would, however useful, go beyond the scope of this book which is a comprehensive theological contribution from a charismatic Lutheran perspective.

[5] See, for example, Arnold Bittlinger, *Gifts and Graces* (Grand Rapids, MI: Eerdmans, 1968); Tormod Engelsviken, *The Gift of the Spirit: An Analysis and Evaluation of the Charismatic Movement from a Lutheran Theological Perspective,* unpublished Ph.D. dissertation (Dubuque, IA: Aquinas Institute of Theology, 1981); and George T. Montague, *First Corinthians*. Catholic Commentary on Sacred Scripture (Grand Rapids, MI: Baker Academic, 2011). We should also mention Pentecostal contributions such as Roger Stronstad, *The Charismatic Theology of St Luke*, (Peabody, MA: Hendrickson, 1984) and *Spirit, Scripture and Theology: A Pentecostal Perspective*, 2nd ed. (Eugene, OR: Wipf and Stock, 2019); and not least

of the speaking and writing in the renewal, however, has taken place at conferences and in publications aimed at the broad cross-section of a grassroots movement. It has been expressed at a popular rather than an academic level, with a strong emphasis on practical application. This is not to say that exegesis and interpretation in the renewal is inadequate or poorly grounded, but simply that it has been pressed more into the service of proclamation than of scholarly writing.[6]

The fruit of biblical interpretation in the Charismatic movement cannot be reduced to a catalogue of doctrinal conclusions; the movement is too broad and diverse. Among those who identify with the Charismatic renewal, interpretation of the Bible still varies considerably on a number of issues, such as baptism, holy communion, eschatology, ecclesiology including church order, the roles of men and women – and even on things that are part of the particular focus or emphasis of the renewal, such as baptism with the Holy Spirit, speaking in tongues, exorcism, and prophecy. The Charismatic movement has not produced a monolithic or stereotyped interpretation, which would lead to a quick, detailed, doctrinal consensus.

The Point of Concurrence: Worldview

The Charismatic renewal does not raise major questions in the field of hermeneutics at the point of methodology or research. Charismatic biblical students, like everyone else, must use sound scholarship to help unpack the original sense of the text. Full weight must be given to the historical background, to the social and literary context, to differences in literary form and style, and to the authors' audience and intentions. Allegorical interpretations or generalisations must be drawn with caution. All of this is part of the task of the Spirit-led interpreter of Scripture.

The place where charismatic hermeneutics raises questions is at the point of *presuppositions*. At this point, the Charismatic renewal has involved an intellectual renewal for many people. What one sees throughout the renewal is a certain *worldview* (German: *Weltanschauung*) that has been produced both by Scripture and experience, and in turn affects one's approach to Scripture. One aspect of this has been to question the assumptions of *naturalism* and to take a more realistic stance toward what is generally termed the "supernatural". This has practical implications for biblical interpretation when we deal with the question of epistemology, that is: How do we arrive at accurate knowledge? In effect, a new epistemology is being developed which is significantly at variance with the accepted wisdom of our time, and

---

the monumental work by American Pentecostal Craig S. Keener, *Acts: An Exegetical Commentary*, 4 vols. (Grand Rapids, MI: Baker Academic, 2013-2014).

[6] See, for example, McDonnell (ed), *Presence, Power, Praise – Documents of the Charismatic Renewal,* Vol. 2, p. 116.

which has been variously characterised as "biblical realism", "radical orthodoxy", or "supernaturalism".[7]

The effect of this epistemological shift is that one begins to treat the biblical material more realistically. Miraculous events are no longer embarrassing "myths" that must somehow be explained (away!) or "demythologised" before modern people will take the Bible seriously. Prophetic passages that contain a predictive element do not need to be historically repositioned. Moral standards and practical instructions for the community of faith are not lightly dismissed as mere cultural transmissions or additions; a heightened sense of the transcendent appears to carry with it a sense also for the transcultural, perhaps because it is accompanied by awe.

The churches have made attempts to relate themselves to the *experience* and *spirituality* of the Charismatic renewal, but another challenge, one that has scarcely been recognised, is the substantial *intellectual challenge* that this movement presents to the church. It poses a challenge to the naturalism and rationalism that have dominated much of the contemporary theological scene, in practice if not wholly in theory, by offering the church a vital, worldwide movement in which biblical presuppositions as well as present experience consciously shape theological methodology and practical ministry.

Historical-critical Studies

Martin Luther was definitely a biblical theologian. On the one hand, he held the traditional view that everything in the Bible was the Word of God, including its cosmological and historical presuppositions.[8] On the other hand, he did not equate the Bible and God's Word in a simplistic way. The purpose of the Bible, and that which governs the interpretation of it, is that it promotes

---

[7] The Lutheran theologian Bengt Hoffman has challenged the contemporary antipathy within the theological community toward the term *supernaturalism* in his book *Luther and the Mystics* (Minneapolis, MN: Augsburg, 1976). In various published works, Morton Kelsey has offered an alternative to an epistemology that rules out *a priori* the possibility of direct encounter with the divine. To express this line of thinking more directly as it relates to hermeneutics, the term "biblical realism" has been used with some frequency in charismatic circles, which differs from a strict literalism, on the one hand, and from a skeptical rationalism, on the other. To the question of worldview and supernaturalism, see Morton Kelsey, *Encounter with God: A Theology of Christian Experience* (Minneapolis, MN: Bethany, 1972), Paul G. Hiebert, *Missiological Implications of Epistemological Shifts: Affirming Truth in a Modern/Postmodern World* (Harrisburg, PA: Trinity Press International, 1999); Hiebert, "Excluded Middle"; Hiebert, *Anthropological Insights*; Keener, *Miracles.*

[8] Paul Althaus, *The Theology of Martin Luther*, translated by Robert C. Schultz (Philadelphia, PA: Fortress Press, 1966), pp. 5-51.

Christ and his gospel.[9] Rightly used, the Scriptures are God's intended instrument for the proclamation of Christ. Luther asserted with vigour: "And what is the New Testament but a public sermon and proclamation of Christ?"[10] In the same text, he wrote of the Old Testament, "Here you will find the manger and swaddling cloths in which Christ lies [...] meagre raiment it is, but precious is Christ, the Treasure which lies within." With this sentence, Luther staked out his perimeter for "biblical criticism." Biblical criticism has to do with "the manger" and "the sort of material it is made of." Most important for those who read and hear the biblical texts, however, is whether they have personally gained access to Christ and are ready to worship him as did the Wise Men from the East.

Charismatics would insist on the classic understanding and use of the historical-critical method of biblical interpretation, that is, the attempt to interpret Scripture according to the way it was meant by those who wrote it, and the way it was understood by those to whom it was addressed. They are critical of the tendency to impose present-day presuppositions or concerns on the text. Charismatics take seriously the truth claims, and therefore the authority, of biblical presuppositions.

While charismatics and some historical-critical scholars would essentially agree on what Scripture says, they might apply it in quite different ways. Charismatics would accord more cross-cultural significance to the Bible than some historical-critical scholars. They would be less likely to relativise a teaching of Scripture simply because it comes out of another culture. Beneath obvious differences in culture and ways of thinking, they would be more inclined to see themes and truth that are independent of culture, true for all time.

Charismatics might also be more cautious about historical judgements than some historical-critical scholars. Historical research from literary sources does not yield the kind of objective and verifiable data that we normally associate with the word science. We encounter no little difficulty understanding accurately what people in our own time think and mean – to say nothing of thinking our way back into a culture separated from ours by 2000 years – as C. S. Lewis so clearly demonstrated in his essay, "Modern Theology and Biblical Criticism."[11] That fact alone should give us some humility when we attempt to reconstruct the thought world of the New Testament. Our attempt to be "historically realistic" must be seen as just that, an attempt. Also in this intellectually demanding enterprise, we must look to the Holy Spirit to guide us.

---

[9] Althaus, *Theology*, pp. 35,74,79-81.

[10] *Preface to the Old Testament*, 1523, WADB 8, p. 11.

[11] C. S. Lewis, *Christian Reflections* (Grand Rapids, MI: Eerdmans, 1971), pp. 152-166.

What charismatics most strongly take issue with in historical-critical studies, however, is not its methodology as such, but precisely an uncritical use of this method, whereby one imposes on the text a presupposition, such as an anti-supernatural bias, that is basically alien to the biblical world.

A typical example of the way in which the so-called historical-critical method imposes an anti-supernatural bias on a text is the following commentary on Mark 6:45-52, of Jesus coming to his disciples walking on the water. The explanation of this text concludes:

> We must conclude that homiletical and doctrinal interests have left their mark upon an original tradition coloured from the first, in which the action of Jesus in *wading through the surf near the hidden shore* was interpreted as a triumphant progress across the waters [italics added].[12]

This kind of interpretation would be widely discounted in the Charismatic renewal – not because charismatics are wooden literalists or anti-intellectual, nor because they are simply ready to believe anything, but rather because they have a fundamentally different *worldview.* Aside from the patent absurdity of the disciples mistaking a hidden shore for deep water on a lake which they had plied for years as professional fishermen, the interpretation does not realistically consider the possibility that the point the story means to convey – that Jesus exercised supernatural power – was in fact true. That possibility is ruled out *a priori*, and a naturalistic interpretation is laid on the text under the guise of "scientific exegesis". Charismatics would approach the text more realistically, not because they hold to a particular theory of biblical inspiration (there would be some variety on this point among charismatics), but rather because the event, while unusual, is not fundamentally incredible within the framework of their worldview.

Generally speaking, Charismatics are also on guard against attempts to read present-day ideologies back into the New Testament: casting Jesus, for instance, in the role of a political revolutionary, or pressing apostolic testimony into the service of concrete and controversial political solutions.

Practical Application of Scripture

It is a frequent experience in the Charismatic renewal that new light is shed on well-known biblical passages, or that neglected and forgotten passages come alive with present-day meaning. Charismatic hermeneutics takes seriously both the historical character of the Scriptures and their present relevance and application, for the other side of understanding Scripture in its historical setting is *applying it in the present situation.*

---

[12] Vincent Taylor, *The Gospel According to St Mark: The Greek Text with Introduction, Notes, and Indexes* (London: Macmillan, 1955), p. 327.

The scholarly study of Scripture does not exclude a personal, edifying use of Scripture as the Holy Spirit lets the words speak into a person's contemporary situation, although this will not necessarily become a basis for general teaching.

The Holy Spirit is the source of Scripture (2 Tim. 3: 16) and he is also the source of sound interpretation (2 Pet. 1:20-21). Prayer for the guidance of the Spirit is the indispensable companion to serious Bible study. Belief in the Bible, separated from the active intervention of the Holy Spirit, withers into mere formalism. Only the Spirit can bring into us the living, redemptive presence of Christ whereby we "have the mind of Christ" and are able therefore to "understand the gifts bestowed on us by God" (1 Cor. 2:12-16).

Lutheran Theological Heritage

A Lutheran perspective on charismatic experience involves two points of reference: the biblical revelation and the theological confessions and traditions of the Lutheran church.

Scripture is, according to the Lutheran Confessions, the highest norm by which all teachings and teachers must be evaluated.[13] It is called *norma normans* (the "norming norm") in Latin. It is the source for Christian doctrine and life. This is a fundamental Reformation principle, called *sola scriptura* ("Scripture alone"). Contemporary charismatic teaching and experience must therefore be shown to lie within the boundaries of Scripture, consistent with the experience and doctrine of the Holy Spirit as set forth in the Word.

The *Lutheran Confessions*[14] are in essence an interpretation of Scripture. Their authority is *derived* from Scripture and therefore subject to evaluation and confirmation on the basis of Scripture. They are *norma normata* ("normed norm"). Our attempt to evaluate charismatic experience from a particular place in the body of Christ called "Lutheran", therefore, is not being undertaken in a narrow, sectarian spirit. Rather, it is our response to a worldwide visitation of the Holy Spirit that sets before every body of Christians the apostolic injunction: "Test everything. Hold on to the good" (1 Thess. 5:21). In this, we want humbly to heed the wisdom and instruction that the Lord brings through our Lutheran heritage, yet also boldly challenge

---

[13] "We pledge ourselves to the prophetic and apostolic writings of the Old and New Testaments as the pure and clear fountain of Israel, which is the only true norm according to which all teachers and teachings are to be judged and evaluated", *The Formula of Concord*, in Tappert, *The Book of Concord*, pp. 503-504, cf. also p. 464.

[14] Different Lutheran denominations may not all have exactly the same confessional writings. While all Lutheran churches have the *three ecumenical creeds* (the Apostolic, Nicene and Athanasian Creeds) from the ancient church, the *Augsburg Confession* (1530) and *Luther's Small Catechism* (1529), some include the other writings in the *Book of Concord* (1580), including the *Formula of Concord* (1577), see Tappert, *The Book of Concord.*

Lutheran tradition or contemporary practice when these would lead us to distort or restrict the Holy Spirit's work.

The prominent features of charismatic experience that we have described in previous chapters are certainly laden with biblical and theological content. Yet, charismatic Christians from different denominations have not reached biblical consensus concerning all aspects of biblical interpretation and validation of charismatic experience. This means, among other things, that charismatic experience is not self-validating or self-explanatory.

We shall outline the fundamental biblical message that pertains to charismatic thought and experiences. Although this can only be a summary statement, it is based on accepted principles of biblical interpretation and reflects both historical and contemporary biblical scholarship. *It is our conviction that the Bible in its plain, historical sense gives a clear and adequate basis for establishing the validity of charismatic experience. Upon reflection, it also shows the need for and the effect of a movement of charismatic renewal in the Lutheran church today.*

Interpreting the Biblical Witness

The books of the Old and New Testament are, as we have seen, normative for the church. This does not mean that one can directly apply every part of Scripture to present-day life. Certain Old Testament practices and doctrines have been superseded in the New Testament as a result of the progressive character of salvation history. There is also development within the New Testament itself, as the events of salvation history unfold. What happened in the life of Jesus may not necessarily be transferred to the era of the church. Certain events of salvation history are *unique*, such as the birth and baptism of Jesus, his death and resurrection, his ascension, and the sending of the Holy Spirit on the day of Pentecost. What is *repeatable* in history and what is not, can only be determined by a thorough analysis of the texts themselves.

Classical Pentecostal theology draws heavily on Luke-Acts for its interpretation of charismatic experience. Without denying the central role of Luke-Acts in interpreting and validating charismatic experience, we would emphasise the *totality of the biblical witness*. On the other hand, we must be on guard against the tendency to let our reading of other New Testament writers, primarily Paul and John, colour our reading of Luke. Some interpreters downgrade the theological significance of Luke's two books, and especially Acts, asserting that "the purpose of God in Scripture should be sought in its didactic, rather than its historical parts."[15] This kind of distinction, however, is alien to the New Testament. Luke stands in the tradition of Old Testament historiography that sees divine revelation

---

[15] John R. Stott, *The Baptism and Fullness of the Holy Spirit* (Downers Grove, IL: InterVarsity Press, 1964), p. 8.

imbedded in the understanding of historical events.[16] The biblical message expressed in narrative form is an indispensable part of the scriptural revelation, with profound significance for the church today. While narrated events may not be repeatable, nor meant as invariable patterns for the church today, their theological significance and meaning are still normative.

Biblical doctrine that is valid and normative for the charismatic movement within the Lutheran church today is set forth in a simple and general way in the chapters that follow.

---

[16] Stronstad, *The Charismatic Theology of St Luke*, pp. 5-9.

(8) The Holy Spirit in Creation and Redemption

The Holy Spirit as God's Life-giving Power and Presence

The concept of "spirit", most often rendered by the Hebrew term *ruach* in the Old Testament and by the Greek term *pneuma* in the New Testament, is not easily defined or described. In its concrete material connotations, it denotes air in motion: wind and breath. On another level, it denotes breath of life, the human spirit, good or evil spirits, and, finally, God's Spirit. Even in this use, it may frequently have very concrete connotations, as the imagery of wind and breath when describing the Spirit of God indicates (see Gen. 2:7; Ez. 37:9, 10, 14; Jn 3:8; 20:22; Acts 2:2).

The common distinction between the visible and the invisible reality, between the material and the spiritual realm, does reflect a biblical viewpoint (see, for example, 2 Kings 6:15-17; 2 Cor. 4:18; Eph. 6:10-12). Yet, if we think of the Holy Spirit simply in relation to the "spiritual realm", we miss the essential point in the biblical understanding of the Spirit. *Throughout the Bible, the Spirit is God personally and powerfully present in the world, mysterious and inexplicable in rational terms, yet having tangible and visible effects in the created world, both in nature and in human experience.* Although the Spirit is present in the created world, he is at the same time transcendent and *beyond the control of human beings*. He expresses the sovereignty of God. Any attempt to limit or control the freedom of the Holy Spirit, which is the freedom of God himself, is futile: "The wind blows where it wills" (Jn 3:8).[1]

Although the term "spirit" may be used in several different senses in the Scriptures, *God's Spirit is qualitatively and fundamentally different* from all that may be called "spirit" in the created world. The weakness of human beings and the created order stands in contrast to the creative power of the Spirit of God (Is. 31:3). The Spirit of God as the breath of God is the life-giving force granting existence to human beings (Gen. 2:7; Job 33:4).

This life-giving force, however, is not limited to human beings, but permeates the whole creation, all "living things both large and small" (Ps. 33:6; 104:24-25). The creation, preservation, and renewal of all life depend on the activity of the Spirit of God. "When you send your Spirit, they are

---

[1] This freedom and sovereignty of the Holy Spirit are expressed in the Augsburg Confession Art. V regarding the means of grace and justifying faith: "To obtain such faith God instituted the office of the ministry, that is provided the Gospel and the sacraments. Through these, as through means, he gives the Holy Spirit, who works faith, *when and where he pleases*, in those who hear the Gospel" (italics added), Tappert, *The Book of Concord*, p. 31.

created, and you renew the face of the earth" (Ps. 104:30). If God withdraws his Spirit, *all humans*, and we might add *all life*, would perish (Job 34:14-15; Ps. 104:29). Life comes from God and remains dependent on God's Spirit. As hinted to in the creation story, the Spirit is God's agent in creating and ordering the universe (Gen. 1:2).

Human beings have come into being and received life by the power of the Spirit of God. They are therefore dependent on God and his Spirit in all areas of life. And God has reserved the divine right to revoke this gift of life (Gen. 6:3; 2:17).

It is primarily in the Old Testament that the role of the Holy Spirit in the creation, preservation and renewal of the world is emphasised. This creative work of the Holy Spirit is related to the whole world, and is therefore universal. It applies to all people regardless of their faith. The universal natural mysteries of human conception, birth, growth, strengthening in weakness, and healing in sickness are in a profound sense attributable to the power of God's Spirit. In this sense, all people – whether they accept it or not –have a relationship to God and his Spirit because they are created and sustained by God.

The Holy Spirit as God's Redemptive Power

Because of the disobedience of the first human beings created in the image of God – in his likeness – and their rebellion against God and his will for human life, all human beings became sinners and were cut off from the source of life (Gen. 3:1-24). They came under the judgement of God that ultimately led to death: physically, spiritually, and eternally. "All have sinned and fall short of the glory of God" (Rom. 3:23). "Sin entered the world through one man, and death through sin, and in this way death came to all men, because all sinned" (Rom. 5:12, cf. Eph. 2:1-3). The fall affected human beings in all their relationships: their relationship to God, to other human beings, to themselves and to creation. The image of God in human beings (Gen. 1:26) was not lost, however, but seriously damaged.

The Bible promises that all that was lost through the fall will be restored. This is the promise of *redemption.* Redemption is the great theme of the story of the biblical revelation from the election of Abraham and the people of Israel in Genesis 12 to the new heaven and earth revealed in Revelation 21. In this story, the Holy Spirit plays a decisive role, both in the Old and the New Testament. The work of the creative, life-giving Spirit is also seen in the promise of redemption, of a future *spiritual renewal and rebirth* of the people of God. "I will put my Spirit in you, and you will live" (Ez. 37:14; see also Is. 32:15-20; 44:3-5).

Endowment with Spiritual Power and Gifts in the Old Covenant

In the Old Testament, the Holy Spirit is primarily given as an *endowment or power for ministry to certain individuals* in the people of God, such as artists (Ex. 31:2-5); Moses and the elders (Num. 11:16-17), judges (Judg. 6:34), anointed kings (1 Sam. 10:6-7,10; 16:13; 2 Sam. 21:1-3), priests (2 Chron. 24:20), and prophets who speak the word of God (Num. 22-24; Mic. 3:8; Is. 61:1). The last prophet in the old covenant who spoke the word of the Lord filled with the Holy Spirit was John the Baptist (Lk. 1:15-17). In the Old Testament, God also promises a future *universal outpouring* of the Spirit on all his people:

> I will pour out my Spirit on all people. Your sons and daughters will prophesy, your old men will dream dreams, your young men will see visions. Even on my servants, both men and women, I will pour out my Spirit in those days (Joel 2:28-29).

The Promises of the Coming of Messiah and the Pouring out of the Spirit

The Old Testament predictions and promises of a perfect kingdom, an eschatological time of salvation, centre equally on the *pouring out of the Spirit of God and the coming of the anointed Davidic king, the Messiah.* King David was anointed with the Spirit (1 Sam. 16:13), and thus equipped with power from God for his kingly reign. Likewise, the future anointed king, the Messiah, will usher in a time of divine blessings comparable to the first creation, because the Spirit of God rests permanently on him:

> The Spirit of the Lord will rest on him, the Spirit of wisdom and of understanding, the Spirit of counsel and of power, the Spirit of knowledge and of the fear of the Lord (Is. 11:2).

The Messiah's endowment with the Spirit is also related to his authority as a righteous judge. He punishes the evil and saves the suffering (Is. 11:3-9). The effects of the Spirit of God resting on the Messiah will be felt in all areas of human life, in the religious and ethical as well as in the political and social spheres.

In the famous "Songs of the Servant of the Lord," in the Book of Isaiah, the coming Servant (who in light of the New Testament is Jesus Christ) is depicted as a prophet endowed with the Spirit of God. The servant has a universal role to fulfil: as one *sent by God,* he has a missionary assignment to bring a new covenant and be a *light to the nations* (Is. 42:6-7). The Spirit is here understood both as the means of inspiration and as the power for carrying out this great task: "I will put my Spirit on him, and he will bring justice to the nations" (Is. 42:1, 4).

Jesus and the Holy Spirit

Redemption is not universal in the same way as creation. It depends on a reconciled, saving relationship with God, a reconciliation that comes about through God's historical *saving acts* in Jesus Christ (his incarnation, life, death, resurrection and ascension), the *message* about these acts and their significance (the preaching of the Gospel), and *faith* in this message on the part of the hearers (cf. 2 Cor. 5:18-21). This redemption is realised through a *history of salvation that takes place in world history* without being identical with it.

In the New Testament, the Old Testament promises concerning the Messiah and the Spirit come to fulfilment in the divine person of Jesus Christ and his redemptive ministry. The *incarnation of the Son of God* comes about by a direct intervention by the Spirit of God. Jesus as both human and divine is the result a unique, creative act by God through the Spirit: the angel said to Mary, "*The Holy Spirit will come upon you, and the power of the Most High* will overshadow you. So the holy one to be born will be called the Son of God" (Lk. 1:35; see also Mt. 1:18-23).

The *birth narratives* not only describe the Spirit in terms of the Old Testament concept of the creative force of God, they also address themselves to the question of the relationship between Jesus and the Spirit. Jesus' uniqueness as the Son of God and Saviour from sin are closely associated with his miraculous conception: Jesus was the Son of God incarnate by his miraculous conception by the Spirit and his birth of a virgin. He did not later become the Son of God by his endowment with the Spirit at his baptism, nor by his resurrection from the dead, although these events did serve to designate or reveal him as the Son of God (Mt. 3:17; Rom. 1:4).

Jesus *proclaimed and manifested the kingdom of God in the power of the Holy Spirit* (Mk 1:15; Lk. 4:18-21). He brought to visibility the powers of the age to come. He overcame the power of Satan and his demons (Mt. 12:28). He granted people forgiveness of sins (Mk 2:5), deliverance from demons (Mk 1:21-28), healing (Mk 1:33-34; 2:1-12), food (Lk. 9:10-17), eternal life (Jn 3:16), and fullness of life (Jn 10:10). He was *anointed with the Spirit at his baptism* (Lk. 3:21-22). He was permanently filled with the Spirit and exercised his ministry in word and deed by the power of the Spirit (Lk. 4:1, 14). *Jesus was a charismatic person.*

Of course, Jesus was more than a charismatic prophet and healer; some Old Testament figures would also be included in that category. He was the only begotten Son of God who made the Father known (Jn 1:18). He was more than a charismatic, more than a prophet. He was – and is – divine *and* human, *the unique God-man.* He transcends all human categories.

A Christology that interprets Jesus' earthly ministry solely in terms of his deity or solely in terms of his endowment with the Holy Spirit, is an unbiblical Christology. Jesus did not sometimes act as the divine Son of God, and at other times as a human being empowered by the Spirit. He did everything as the unique God-man. There was a clearly Trinitarian character of his ministry. As Son of God, he was fully dependent on his Father in heaven (Jn 5:17, 19-23) as he spoke and acted in the power of the Spirit. Jesus' charismatic ministry was also meant to be an encouragement to his disciples. With the coming of the Holy Spirit, they would do the same kind of things (Jn 14:12). Yet, as being God and one with the Father, Jesus' relationship with the Holy Spirit is unique (Jn 16:14-15).

According to the unanimous testimony of the four Gospels, Jesus did not begin his public ministry until after he had been *baptised by John the Baptist*. Two important elements conspicuously distinguished Jesus' baptism from the "baptism of repentance" that John administered to others: the voice from heaven and the descent of the Holy Spirit. The heavenly voice identified Jesus as the divine Son of God (Mt. 3:17; Mk 1: 11; Lk. 3:22); closely related was his identification as the Lamb of God who, by his sacrificial death, "takes away the sin of the world" (Jn 1:29). The descent of the Spirit as a dove testified to Jesus' messianic calling (cf. Lk. 3:16-17); by his permanent possession of the Spirit, he is authorised and endowed by God to carry out his mission.

Jesus' endowment with the Spirit brought him into *conflict with the enemy, Satan*. Immediately after he was empowered by the Spirit, Jesus was led or driven by the Spirit into a confrontation with Satan (Mt. 4:1; Mk 1:12; Lk. 4:1), but he overcame the temptations, defeated the enemy, and returned to his ministry "in the power of the Spirit" (Lk. 4:14).

It is noteworthy that the Spirit-filled *Christ used the Word of God* in the Old Testament as he resisted Satan. At every point, Jesus took his stand on Scripture. According to the view of the biblical authors, the Scriptures are inspired (or "God-breathed") by the Holy Spirit (2 Tim. 3:16; 1 Pet. 1:10-11; 2 Pet. 1:21), and as such they are also a vehicle for the Spirit. This becomes clear both in the proclamation of the gospel, which is often tied to Old Testament texts, and pre-eminently in the conflict with Satan. The admonition of the apostle Paul for spiritual warfare against Satan is, "And take [...] the sword of the Spirit, which is the word of God" (Eph. 6:17).

Another important feature of Jesus' response to temptation is that he *submitted absolutely to the will of God.* The redemptive work of Christ involved obedience to the Father's will, even to death on a cross (Phil. 2:8; Heb. 2:14-15; Col. 2:15). The temptation in the desert and the struggle in Gethsemane (Mt. 26:30-46), in which Jesus obeyed the Father, although it meant suffering and death, stand as a constant reminder that suffering and death lie along the pathway of obedience. Although Jesus himself bore the sins of the world, his disciples cannot claim a life free from suffering. Their destiny is bound up with that of their Master (Phil. 3:10-11).

Yet another aspect of Jesus' victory over Satan is seen in his *deliverance of those* who *were oppressed by demons*. The expulsions of evil spirits by Jesus are not isolated events. They belong to the bedrock of the gospel tradition and are a central part of Jesus' ministry. They have salvific and eschatological significance: "But if it is by the Spirit of God that I cast out demons, then the kingdom of God has come upon you" (Mt. 12:28). Deliverance from bondage to Satan is one of the gifts granted to all who enter the kingdom of God. The vanquishing of Satan and the freeing of those who are oppressed by demons are signs that the time of salvation has come. The driving out of evil spirits also shows who Jesus is: the Son of God, the "stronger" one (Lk. 11:22).

The *healing of people* suffering from various forms of illness, although different from deliverance, is also done in the power of the Spirit (Mt. 12:15-21). Both the healing of the sick, the raising of dead and the deliverance from the power of Satan make the kingdom of God visible in the present, and are at the same time a sign and a foretaste of the perfect kingdom that will come with power at the return of Christ (Mk 9:1). In Matthew, the word about sinning against the Holy Spirit is set in the context of Jesus' miracles. It is a warning to those who render prejudiced and cynical judgements against his miracles, attributing to Satan that which is the work of the Spirit; it implies a hardening of the heart against the evident work of the Holy Spirit (Mt. 12:24, 31-32).

The *authority* to preach the kingdom, to heal the sick and expel demons was given by Jesus both to the twelve apostles and to other disciples whom Jesus sent out on his behalf (Mt. 10:1; Lk. 9:1-2; 10:1, 9, 16-17). However, there was a significant difference between the healing ministry of Jesus and that of his disciples: *Jesus healed on his own authority*; he was himself the healer. The disciples healed and expelled demons *in the name of Jesus*. Jesus was therefore the real author both of his own healings and of those of his disciples (Lk. 10:17; Acts 3:6). Jesus rejoiced in the Holy Spirit when his disciples returned from a successful healing mission, and he specifically related their success to the authority that he had given them and which they had successfully exercised (Lk. 10:19).

The Holy Spirit empowered Jesus for his ministry. This is evident both in Jesus' words and in his acts (Lk. 4:18-21; Jn 14:11). In the Bible, the Spirit of God is manifested in both word and deed (Rom. 15:18-19; 1 Cor. 12:7-11). Jesus spoke with authority: "For the one whom God has sent speaks the words of God, for God gives the Spirit without limit" (Jn 3:34). In his conflict with Satan, the decisive issue was Jesus' authority (Mk 1:27).

Jesus' Promise of the Holy Spirit to his Followers

Jesus' own anointing with the Holy Spirit at his baptism in the Jordan has paradigmatic significance: he is the one who baptises with the Holy Spirit (Jn 1:33). God has sent his Son, his Messiah, and equipped him with the Spirit according to the Old Testament promises. The Spirit of God was now poured out on the Messiah. This was a unique event of salvation history, a change of times. The time of salvation was at hand, the eschatological era had begun. The anointing of the Messiah ("the anointed one") marked the beginning of his ministry. The apostle Peter says about Jesus' earthly ministry in his speech to Cornelius:

> You know what has happened throughout Judea, beginning in Galilee after the baptism that John preached – how God anointed Jesus of Nazareth with the Holy Spirit and power, and how he went around doing good and healing all who were under the power of the devil, because God was with him (Acts 10:36-38).

This kind of a ministry would be shared by Jesus' followers, his disciples, on whom God would also pour out his Spirit.

Both in the wonder of the incarnation and in the events associated with the baptism of Jesus, God the Father, God the Son, and God the Holy Spirit are seen carrying out the redemption of humanity through their divine interrelationship: the Father sent the Son to serve and save; the Spirit conceived him; the Father testified to him and endowed him with the Holy Spirit.

During his earthly ministry, Jesus was the sole bearer of the fullness of the Spirit. In the power of the Spirit, he proclaimed the coming of the time of salvation, the kingdom of God (Lk. 4:14, 18-19). When he ascended back to the Father, he and the Father poured out the Spirit on Jesus' followers, baptising them in the Spirit, as John the Baptist has prophesied (Mt. 3:11) and Jesus himself had promised (Jn 20:22; Lk. 24:49: Acts 1:5; 2:33).

Jesus' uniqueness as the incarnate Son of God does not rule out a continuity between his ministry and that of the Christian church. Jesus is not only the unique *bearer of the Spirit*; he is also the Lord who together with the Father *bestows the Spirit* (Jn 14:16; 16:7; 20:22).

After the ascension of Jesus and the day of Pentecost, when they had received the Holy Spirit, his followers continued Jesus' ministry of powerful proclamation of the gospel, healing the sick, delivering the possessed, and prophetic speech. Thus, the ministry of Jesus has paradigmatic significance for the ministry of the church; it serves as a model and a pattern. The mission commission with the power and authority to carry it out was given to the disciples by Jesus after his resurrection:

> Again, Jesus said, "Peace be with you! As the Father has sent me, I am sending you." And with that he breathed on them and said, "Receive the Holy Spirit. If you forgive anyone his sins, they are forgiven; if you do not forgive them, they are not forgiven" (Jn 20:21-23, cp. Mt. 28:18-20: Lk. 24:47-49: Acts 1:8; Mk 16:15-18).

The Holy Spirit who at Jesus' baptism descended on him and empowered him for his ministry is the same Spirit who later was given as a gift to the disciples. *The continuity and similarity between the Spirit's work in the earthly ministry of Jesus and in the ministry of the post-Pentecost Christian church is part of the scriptural validation of the present-day Charismatic renewal in the church.*

A Strategic View of the Coming of the Holy Spirit

In considering the coming and the working of the Holy Spirit in the post-Pentecost Christian community, it can be instructive to study the New Testament, especially the historical sections, from a perspective of the Spirit's strategy. There are a number of basic factors or elements that Scripture links to the coming of the Spirit. The way that they occur, however, suggests a varied use of the different factors – sovereign and often surprising strategies – that the Holy Spirit employs to accomplish particular objectives. This approach offers a fresh way of not only looking at the biblical material but also at some of the traditional systematic approaches to the topic.

Three systematic approaches to the coming of the Holy Spirit are prominent in the church today: the sacramental, the evangelical, and the Pentecostal. Simply stated, the sacramental approach teaches that the Holy Spirit is given in baptism and primarily works through the spoken word and the sacraments. The evangelical approach links the gift of the Spirit to regeneration and the new life: you receive the Holy Spirit when you are born again through faith. The Pentecostal approach distinguishes between a reception of the Spirit in regard to regeneration, and a baptism with the Spirit, understood as a charismatic reception of the Spirit that empowers one for witness and ministry, and which happens subsequent to regeneration. Although these three approaches involve some overlap and do not altogether exclude one another, they nevertheless stand in considerable tension. Historically, they have been sources of controversy and division.

We are not necessarily suggesting an alternative systematic theology, but simply a more flexible way of looking at the reality of the Spirit's coming – a way that gives perhaps greater attention to the sovereignty of the Spirit in varying situations.

In his coming and working, the Holy Spirit may not always bind himself to one particular way of doing things. He is goal-oriented and may come up with unexpected strategies to deal with particular situations. This causes us always to be dependent on the Holy Spirit for the kingdom of God to continue to grow.

The Holy Spirit is concerned with advancing the cause of Christ. He wants to communicate not merely correct ideas about Christ but the very life of Christ in all its fullness. That requires more than a clear and accurate statement of truth. It requires application of the truth that is appropriate to a given situation – a strategy that can move successfully against powers that actively oppose the kingdom of Christ.

A strategic approach to the coming of the Spirit is consistent with the realistic way in which the New Testament presents the kingdom of God and the kingdom of this world in conflict with one another. It helps identify fundamental truths in the scriptural revelation, yet recognises that the Spirit is sovereign in applying these truths to specific situations.

Such a strategic approach can help us make sense of both the consistencies and the seeming irregularities that we observe in the early church's experience of the Holy Spirit. And because the same Spirit is still at work today, it may also help us understand and open ourselves to present strategies that the Spirit wants to employ in our own lives, or in the lives of fellow believers.

In the next eleven chapters, we will look at a variety of actions or concepts that the New Testament links closely to the coming of the Holy Spirit – basic factors that we must take into account if we are to understand his coming and working among us. At the same time, we want to acknowledge the Spirit's sovereignty in applying these factors to life situations, whether in Scripture or in the ongoing life of the church.

(9) The Promise and the Coming of the Holy Spirit

Let us repeat: In the New Testament, the promise of a coming of the Holy Spirit in power was prophesied by John the Baptist and repeated by Jesus. John the Baptist administered a baptism of repentance. He contrasted this with the ministry that Jesus would perform: "I baptise you with water, but he will baptise you with the Holy Spirit" (Mk 1:8; also Mt. 3:11; Lk. 3:16; Jn 1:33).

Jesus returned to this promise before his ascension: "I am going to send you what my Father has promised; but stay in the city until you have been clothed with power from on high" (Lk. 24:49). "John baptised with water, but in a few days, you will be baptised with the Holy Spirit" (Acts 1:4-5). Jesus had taught his disciples to pray for the Holy Spirit (Lk. 11:13). Between Jesus' ascension and Pentecost, the disciples were gathered together in praise and prayer, waiting for the fulfilment of the promise (Lk. 24:53; Acts 1:14).

The Coming of the Holy Spirit

On the day of Pentecost, Jesus fulfilled the promise: his followers were filled with the Holy Spirit (Acts 2:4). What the disciples experienced was the manifest fulfilment of "what my Father has promised" (Lk. 24:49; Acts 1:5).

Although the historical event of Pentecost was not repeated, the personal experience of being filled with the Holy Spirit was. The personal experience of believers being filled or empowered with the Holy Spirit is recorded repeatedly throughout Acts. Often this takes place in connection with people coming to faith and being baptised (Acts 2:38-39; 9:17-18; 10:44, 47; 19:5-6). The gift of the Spirit was not intended for the first disciples alone. It is a reality promised to everyone who hears, believes, and is baptised in the name of Jesus for the forgiveness of sins (Acts 2:38-39).

Forgiveness, Baptism, and the Gift of the Holy Spirit

The apostle Peter's exhortation and promise at the close of his sermon on the day of Pentecost – and the response of the people – gives us insight into how the early church experienced and understood the coming of the Holy Spirit. *The following text sets a lasting pattern for the relationship between the various aspects of Christian initiation*:

> Therefore let all Israel be assured of this: God has made Jesus, whom you crucified, both Lord and Christ. When the people heard this, they were cut to the heart, and said to Peter and the other apostles, "Brothers, what shall we do?"

> Peter replied, "Repent and be baptised, every one of you, in the name of Jesus Christ for the forgiveness of your sins. And you will receive the gift of the Holy Spirit. The promise is for you and your children and for all who are far off – for all whom the Lord our God will call" (Acts 2:36-39).

In this passage of Scripture, the *promise of the gift of the Spirit* is connected to the preceding part of Peter's statement in verse 38 by a consecutive "and". This "and" is important because it shows that what Peter (and Luke) meant by the gift of the Spirit cannot be simply equated with baptism or forgiveness of sins. The gift of the Holy Spirit is not identical with receiving forgiveness of sins, although it is related to it. Likewise, baptism in water is not identical with baptism in the Spirit, although the two are related and may occur simultaneously.

It is true that the Holy Spirit is active in bringing people to repentance and salvation. This is done through the convincing and convicting work of the Holy Spirit (Jn 16:8-11). It takes place through preaching the word of God. It was the Holy Spirit, who through the sermon of the Spirit-filled Peter on the day of Pentecost, touched the hearts of the hearers and caused them to repent (repentance always includes faith, Mark 1:15). It was through the Holy Spirit's work that the apostle Paul was able to bring people to faith by word and deed (Rom. 15:18-20). In Scripture, the Spirit's work is also seen in cleansing from sin (see, for example, Ez. 36:25-27; Ps. 51:7-12; Tit. 3:5-6).

However, it is not the Spirit's role in creating faith in the gospel or cleansing people from sin that Luke is referring to by the term "the gift of the Holy Spirit". His focus is more precisely on the empowerment of the Holy Spirit for evangelism and Christian life in the church. This is clearly seen by his description of the life and ministry of the early Christian church in Acts 2:41-47 and 4:31-35, since both passages follow immediately after words about the disciples being filled with the Holy Spirit and describe the concrete results of being filled.

Manifest Demonstrations of the Holy Spirit

In Acts, Luke emphasises another significant aspect of receiving the gift of the Holy Spirit: it is normally accompanied by *tangible, visible or audible manifestations* of the Spirit. Acts tells about believers in various circumstances and with various backgrounds who received the gift of the Holy Spirit with demonstrable manifestations. Here are some examples:

The day of Pentecost. The gift of the Holy Spirit to all the assembled disciples was accompanied by a "sound like the blowing of a mighty wind", "tongues of fire", and speaking in "other tongues" (Acts 2:2-4). Although the experience on the day of Pentecost was unique in that it was the *first general outpouring of the Spirit* on the community of believers, the audible sign of speaking in other tongues was not. It was repeated later.

The apostle Paul. The apostle Paul was baptised, filled with the Holy Spirit and *healed from blindness* when he was converted and ministered to by Ananias (Acts 9:17-18).

The household of Cornelius. A crucial step in the Christian mission was taken, under the evident guidance of the Holy Spirit, when Gentiles in the household of Cornelius were received into the church without the obligation of circumcision or adherence to the Mosaic Law (Acts 10:1–11:18; 15:7-11). It was the Gentiles' demonstrable reception of the Spirit that forced Peter and the other apostles to accept them as fellow believers. The exceptional circumstances under which this took place do not detract from the narrative's enduring theological significance.

In the case of Cornelius and his household, the pattern of the day of Pentecost was followed with an important variation. The word of salvation through Christ was preached, and forgiveness of sins was offered (Acts 10:43). Cornelius and his household repented, believed, and on believing received forgiveness of sins and eternal life (Acts 11:15-18; 15:9). What was outwardly noticeable to Peter and the other Jews, however, was not their faith, but the effects of their reception of the Spirit: "They heard them speaking in tongues and praising God" (Acts 10:46).

The irregular aspect of the event was the fact that the Gentiles were *not baptised before they received the Spirit.* Peter commanded that they be baptised, thereby providing for their full inclusion in the church (Acts 10:47-48; cf. 11:18). Although baptism in water normally precedes the gift of the Holy Spirit in Acts, in this instance, the Spirit was given prior to baptism in water. It happened when Cornelius and his household received the gospel in faith. The Cornelius case may not be as unique as is sometimes imagined. The missionary experience of the church testifies to similar occurrences.[1]

The Samaritans. The narrative of the Samaritans' reception of the Holy Spirit (Acts 8:4-25) seems to present an opposite kind of situation. The Samaritans heard the gospel preached by Philip in the power of the Spirit. They believed and were baptised. Yet the Holy Spirit did not fall on any of them. They received the Spirit at a later time, when the apostles Peter and John came down from Jerusalem and prayed for them and laid hands on them.

As we have seen, where the Holy Spirit is mentioned in Acts, the focus is on manifest demonstrations of his presence. It was this dimension of the Spirit's working that was not apparent in the initiation of the new converts in Samaria. The fact that the apostles came down from Jerusalem to pray for

---

[1] An interesting case is the conversion of some *felashas* or so-called "black Jews" to Christianity in Ethiopia many years before the Charismatic movement. A convert said, "We have not yet been baptised with the water of the Abyssinian church (the Ethiopian Orthodox Church), but we have been baptised with the Holy Spirit in our inner man." Recorded in Gustaf Arén, *Evangelical Pioneers in Ethiopia* (Stockholm: EFS-förlaget, 1978), p. 245.

them suggests that the situation was somewhat irregular. The normal experience in the apostolic community was that new converts would receive and manifest the Holy Spirit. When this did not happen, the apostles took special steps to rectify the situation.

There have been different theories about the irregularity of this event. One is that the initial faith of the Samaritans was somehow flawed as Christian faith. It is unusual that it is said that the Samaritans "believed Philip" (v. 12). Does this mean that they put their trust in a man or his miraculous power (cp. Simon's spurious "belief" in vv. 13, 18-23) rather than in Christ and the gospel?[2] Another theory is that Philip's mission was not part of the apostles' mission, and that therefore the coming of the Holy Spirit by the laying on of hands by the apostles Peter and John indicates that the mission and the new believers in Samaria were incorporated into the church led by the apostles in Jerusalem. Regardless of explanation, the main point is that the *gift of the Spirit belongs to Christian initiation.*[3] The Holy Spirit is received when people become Christians. Also, this time, there were manifestations of the Spirit for all to see, even for Simon (Acts 8:18).

The Ephesians. In Ephesus, the apostle Paul encountered a situation that at first glance seemed to resemble what had happened in Samaria (Acts 19:1-7). He found some disciples and asked them, "Did you receive the Holy Spirit when you believed?" As it turned out, they were disciples of John the Baptist and had not yet received Christian instruction or Christian baptism, and were therefore ignorant of even the existence of the Holy Spirit. They had been baptised with John's baptism of repentance that did not include faith in Jesus or the reception of the Holy Spirit.

When they were told about John's words about Jesus, and – presumably – heard the gospel, they were baptised with Christian baptism in the name of Jesus. When Paul laid hands on them in connection with their baptism, they received the gift of the Holy Spirit, and also with tangible manifestations: They spoke in tongues and prophesied.

---

[2] This is the interpretation offered by e.g. James D. G. Dunn, *Baptism in the Holy Spirit* (Naperville, IL: Allenson, 1970), p. 65, and others.

[3] See McDonnell and Montague, *Christian Initiation*, pp. 34-35. The Catholic Church has argued that the laying on hands in connection with Christian initiation could only be done by apostles, and later by their successors, the bishops. This, in turn, developed into the sacrament of confirmation, performed by a bishop, often years after baptism, see Kilian McDonnell, *The Baptism in the Spirit as an Ecumenical Problem* (Notre Dame, IN: Charismatic Renewal Services, 1972), p. 42. The Catholic New Testament scholar Montague does not see the Catholic view of confirmation supported by the text in Acts 8, which he sees as an irregularity emphasising the need to bring Philip's mission under the authority of the twelve apostles (McDonnell and Montague, *Christian Initiation*), pp. 31 and 35.

The Importance of Luke as a Theologian

Luke the historian has sometimes been downgraded as a theologian. Prominent expositors of Scripture have said that in shaping our doctrine of the Holy Spirit, we must look to the Epistles, not to Acts.[4] The Epistles tend to highlight the Holy Spirit's work of bringing people to faith and salvation. Paul, for example, testified to the fact that every Christian is indwelt by the Spirit: "You, however, are controlled not by the sinful nature but by the Spirit, if the Spirit of God lives in you. And if anyone does not have the Spirit of Christ, he does not belong to Christ" (Rom. 8:9). In writing to the Corinthian church, Paul presupposed that all the believers had received the Holy Spirit (1 Cor. 12:13; see also Gal. 3:2, 5). John, likewise, spoke of receiving the Spirit in the context of salvation (John 7:37-39).

There is, however, a renewed appreciation among New Testament scholars for Luke as a theologian of the Holy Spirit in his own right.[5] He did not contradict what was taught by Paul or John. But he added a significant dimension to our understanding of the work of the Holy Spirit with his emphasis on receiving the Holy Spirit in terms of power for mission. This may open the way for dealing more effectively with some of the disagreements that have plagued discussions about receiving the Holy Spirit.

The danger of reading Luke through Pauline glasses was pointed out by Larry Christenson in one of his contributions to the book *Practical Christianity*:

> The New Testament writers spoke of receiving the Holy Spirit in different contexts. Paul talked about receiving the Spirit of adoption into God's family: "for you did not receive a spirit that makes you a slave [...] but you received the Spirit of sonship" (Rom. 8:15.) Luke, on the other hand, spoke about receiving or being filled with the Holy Spirit primarily in terms of power for ministry: "You will receive power when the Holy Spirit comes on you" (Acts 1:8) [...] Luke used the word receive in a particular way when he referred to the coming of the Holy Spirit. We should not attempt to impose Paul's usage on the writings of Luke. That would distort the meaning, and it would rob us of the unique emphasis the Spirit wants to bring through Luke.
>
> Is receiving the Spirit different from receiving Christ? In Paul's writings, these concepts run very close to each other, yet the element of the Spirit's charismatic manifestation is not absent. In Galatians 3:1-5, he spoke of the Holy Spirit coming in power, complete with miracles. He asked, "Did you receive the Spirit by observing the law, or by believing what you heard? [...] Does God give his Spirit and work miracles among you because you observe the law, or because you believe what you heard?" The Galatians had experienced the power of the Spirit in miraculous manifestations, and Paul pointed to this as confirming the

---

[4] Stott, *The Baptism and Fullness of the Holy Spirit*, p. 8.

[5] I. Howard Marshall, *Luke. Historian and Theologian* (Grand Rapids, MI: Zondervan, 1970), p. 75.

> reality of the saving faith by which they received Christ. In Luke, however, the focus is somewhat different. Receiving the Holy Spirit is the way that those who already believe in Christ are empowered to serve him.
>
> People receive the Holy Spirit, in Luke's meaning of the term, in different ways. Some people receive the Spirit more or less spontaneously; for others, the response is quite conscious and deliberate; some experience dramatic manifestations of the Spirit; for others, the manifestations are more subdued. The way in which a person receives the Spirit will be determined, to some extent, by the situation and by the person (their personality type, age, station in life, church environment). More important than the particular way in which we receive the Spirit, however, is what we do after having received.
>
> It's important that we receive the power of the Spirit for living the Christian life: Luke's message needs to come through loud and clear. But when it comes to the question of how, it's more important to focus on how one lives the Spirit-filled life than on a rigid formula for receiving it.
>
> Receiving the Spirit in the Lukan sense is not a one-time event, but an ongoing way of life. It is needed every day; some occasions may call for a special filling of the Spirit (see Acts 4:31; 7:55). The effects of the Spirit's filling may be dramatic, accompanied by supernatural signs; they may open up a new area of witness or ministry; they may issue in a quiet growth of the fruit of the Spirit. When the Spirit controls us, we are moved to accomplish God's will in God's way. Luke's emphasis on receiving the Spirit to empower us for ministry is a needed emphasis today, when one thinks of the enormous missionary challenge facing the church – three billion people who haven't heard the gospel. We need to move beyond past misunderstandings and get on with the task![6]

In Acts, several expressions are used to describe the manifest coming of the Spirit. The expression, "to be baptised with the Spirit" is used on two occasions. In both cases, it is an initial reception and manifestation of the Spirit that is in view (Acts 1:5; 11:16). The phrase, "filled with the Spirit" is used both of initial and subsequent experiences of the Spirit's coming (Acts 2:4; 4:31). On occasion, several expressions can be used more or less interchangeably to denote nuances of the same experiential reality: "the Holy Spirit fell (or came) on" (Acts 10:44; 11:15), "the gift of the Holy Spirit was poured out or given" (Acts 10:45; 11:17), "they have received the Holy Spirit" (10:47), "[they were] baptised with the Holy Spirit" (11:16).

A careful exegetical study shows that "Luke gives pride of place to the term filled with the Holy Spirit."[7] Other terms add nuance, but his foundational term for describing the coming of the Spirit is "filled". Luke's

---

[6] Larry Christenson, "Receiving the Holy Spirit," *Practical Christianity* (Wheaton, IL: Tyndale, 1987), pp. 63-65.

[7] Roger Stronstad, "'Filled With the Holy Spirit' Terminology in Luke-Acts," in *Toward a Pentecostal/Charismatic Theology of the Holy Spirit*, edited by J. Rodman Williams (Bound volume of papers from Fourteenth Annual Meeting of the Society for Pentecostal Studies, 15th–17th November 1984), p. 21.

preference for this term is important for understanding his theology of the Holy Spirit: it puts the primary focus not on a single, initiatory experience of receiving the Spirit, but on a coming of the Spirit that may be repeated from time to time in a believer's life.

Jesus had promised his disciples that the Holy Spirit would come and be with them forever; he would indwell them (Jn 14:15-17). According to John, the reception of the Holy Spirit is connected with Jesus' breathing on them on Easter evening (Jn 20:22). According to Acts, Jesus baptised them with the Holy Spirit on Pentecost, 50 days later (Acts 1:5; 2:4). Sometime later, they were again filled with the Holy Spirit (Acts 4:31).

Stephen provides a particularly vivid example of a believer in whom the abiding, indwelling presence of the Holy Spirit was clearly evident. He is introduced to us as a man "full of faith and of the Holy Spirit [...] full of God's grace and power" (Acts 6:5, 8). Yet at his martyrdom, he is described as full of the Holy Spirit, "not in the sense of an abiding endowment, as in Acts 6:3-8, but as a rapture granted at that moment by which he saw Jesus standing at the right hand of God (Acts 7:55-56)".[8]

The community of believers that grew up around the apostles, that was filled individually and corporately by the Holy Spirit, expected fresh anointings of the Holy Spirit. They looked for the manifest presence of the Spirit to be seen in new converts (Acts 8:16; 10:44-46; 11:15-17; 19:2-6). Believers continued to experience new infillings of the Spirit (Acts 4:8, 31; 13:9-11, 52) – a renewing of the gift of the Holy Spirit that was given to all believers (Acts 5:32) – as they faced new difficulties and challenges.

The Taking Away and the Renewal of the Holy Spirit

As we record many instances in the Bible of people being filled with the Spirit of God, we should also be aware that the Holy Spirit is not like a "thing" that Christians possess and can control and use at will. There are serious warnings in the Bible that it is possible to grieve, quench and even lose the Holy Spirit. Spirit-filled Christians may sin and grow weary and need to repent and pray for a new fullness of The Holy Spirit. Let us look at some biblical examples.

King David, who at his anointing had experienced that "the Spirit of the Lord came upon him in power" (1 Sam. 16:13), fell deeply in sin and committed both adultery and indirect murder (2 Sam. 11). "The thing David had done displeased the Lord" (v. 27). When the prophet Nathan rebuked David for his sin, David repented and was forgiven (2 Sam. 12:1-14). This experience is reflected in one of the most gripping prayers in the Book of Psalms where David confesses his sin and pleads for God's mercy:

---

[8] Fritz Rienecker, *Sprachlicher Schlüssel zum Griechishen Neuen Testament* (Giessen-Basel: Brunnen Verlag, 1952), p. 266.

> Have mercy on me, O God, according to your unfailing love, according to your great compassion blot out my transgressions. Wash away all my iniquity and cleanse me from my sin (Psalm 51:1-2).

This prayer of confession and plea for forgiveness with reference to God's love and mercy, is followed by a prayer for renewal of his own spirit by the Spirit of God,

> Create in me a pure heart, O God, and renew a steadfast spirit within me. *Do not cast me from your presence or take your Holy Spirit from me.* Restore to me the joy of your salvation and grant me a willing spirit, to sustain me (vv. 10-12).

This is maybe the most illustrious example in the Bible of a person who had experienced the power of the Spirit of God and yet fallen in sin.

The Bible is very realistic regarding human sinfulness and frailty, even as it applies to Spirit-filled leaders in God's people. The Spirit-filled Moses – the greatest prophet in Israel (Dt. 34:10-12) – at a certain time did not believe God, was disobedient, and therefore was not allowed to enter the promised land (Num. 20:7-12).

John the Baptist, who according to Jesus was the greatest born by women (Mt. 11:11) and was filled with the Holy Spirit from his birth (Lk. 1:15-17), doubted – when he was in prison – whether Jesus was the Messiah, and had to be comforted by the news of the ministry of Jesus (Mt. 11:2-6).

The leading apostle, Peter, to whom it was revealed by God that Jesus was the Messiah, the Son of God, became an instrument of a Satanic temptation of Jesus (Mt. 16:16-17, 22-23). Even during his Spirit-empowered apostolic ministry after Pentecost, he was rightfully criticised by Paul because of hypocrisy (Gal. 2:11-13).

Paul and Barnabas, both Spirit-filled missionaries sent out by the Holy Spirit himself (Acts 9:17; 11:24; 13:4), ended up in a sharp disagreement that made them part company (Acts 15:36-40). Paul also openly acknowledged his own weakness and suffering (2 Cor. 12:7-10: 4:7-11; 6:3-10). He got a special word from the Lord "My grace is sufficient for you, for my power is made perfect in weakness" (2 Cor. 12:9-10). A charismatic Christian is not only a Christian with gifts of grace (*charisms*), but also a Christian who always needs the grace of God (*charis*).

If the most outstanding leaders of the people of God both in the Old and the New Testament showed sinfulness and weakness, and needed forgiveness and a renewed filling with the Spirit, this also applies to more ordinary members of the congregation.

The believers in the church at Corinth who were "sanctified in Jesus Christ and called to be holy" (1 Cor. 1:2), did "not lack any spiritual gift" (1 Cor. 1:7), and were "all baptised by one Spirit" and "given the one Spirit to drink"

(1 Cor. 12:13), suffered nevertheless from deep moral and spiritual flaws that Paul had to condemn and correct (1 Cor. 5-11). He had to encourage them to desire and seek both love and the spiritual gifts (1 Cor. 12:31, 14:1). By despising the spiritual gifts, for example prophecy, Christians may quench or "put out the Spirit's fire" (1 Thess. 5:19).

In connection with Paul's exhortations to the Christians in Ephesus to live lives "in true righteousness and holiness" (Eph. 4:24) he also warns them, "Do not grieve the Holy Spirit of God, with whom you were sealed for the day of redemption" (Eph. 4:30). They are rather encouraged to be "filled with the Spirit" which results in praise and prayer (Eph. 5:18-20).

The most serious warning against apostasy and the hardening of the heart against God's Word and the Holy Spirit's work is found in Hebrews 6:4-6: "It is impossible for those who have one been enlightened, who have tasted the heavenly gift, who have shared in the Holy Spirit, who have tasted the goodness of the word of God and the powers of the coming age, if they fall away, to be brought back to repentance, because to their loss they are crucifying the Son of God all over again and subjecting him to public disgrace." To "deliberately keep on sinning after we have received the knowledge of the truth" is like "insulting the Spirit of grace" (Heb. 10:26-29). This warning should probably be seen in connection with Jesus' warning against blasphemy against the Holy Spirit (Mt. 12:31-32). It is possible both for those who have never believed in Christ and for those who have come to faith in him and experienced salvation and the gift of the Holy Spirit to persist in sin and disobedience and thus harden their hearts against the Spirit's work in such a way that this hardening cannot be reversed and ultimately will lead to eternal judgement. Therefore, it is of utmost importance for Christians who have been filled with the Holy Spirit to continue to walk in the light, continue to confess their sins, and continue to receive forgiveness and be purified from all unrighteousness (1 Jn 1:5-10).

(10) The Holy Spirit and the Word of God

The Sovereignty of the Holy Spirit

From the day of Pentecost onward, the coming of the Holy Spirit has been inseparably linked with *telling people* what God has done, is doing, and will do through Christ and the giving of the Holy Spirit. The spreading of the Word of God and the activity of the Spirit are so intimately linked with one another that we speak about the Word as a "means of grace" that is, a God-appointed vehicle through which his grace enters into a person's life.

There is some danger if we conceive of this in a simplistic, causal sense, whereby the recitation of the Word becomes the cause, and the giving of the Spirit a necessary and invariable result. That would run the danger of making the New Testament a book of word-magic: if we simply recite or teach the right words, we will get an assured result. This assumption can easily creep into theological and catechetical traditions.

Charismatics hold to a high view of the power and authority of Scripture (this is dealt with in some detail in chapters 7, 23, 33 and 34), but they take issue with any doctrine or use of Scripture that does not recognise the sovereignty of the Holy Spirit. It is one thing to recognise the "means of grace" (the Word and the sacraments) as the Lord's gracious provision for his people. It is something else to think of the means of grace as something that we can use or control to obtain the Spirit, or to teach the doctrine in a way that dismisses any working of the Spirit that is not immediately and directly linked with hearing the Word or receiving the sacraments. A theology of the Word should also express a profound sense of dependence on the work of the Holy Spirit. *Both Scripture and experience confirm the Holy Spirit's sovereign authority to come to us when and where and how he pleases, never at variance with the Word, but also sovereign over the Word and our proclamation of it.*

The Holy Spirit Works through the Word

The relationship between the Word of God and the work of the Holy Spirit is extremely close. The Spirit exercises creative and redemptive power through the Word.

Already in the Old Testament, we read that God the Father sovereignly created the world by his Spirit and by his word. While this connection is implicit in the creation story (Gen. 1:2-26), it is explicit elsewhere: "By the word of the Lord were the heavens made, their starry host by the breath of his mouth" (Ps. 33:6). In the prophecy of Ezekiel, the Word and the Spirit bring new life to the dry bones. The Spirit of God will renew the people religiously and ethically through the Word of God (Ez. 37:1-14). Words spoken in the Spirit of God are effective words, words of power (Num. 23:19-20; 24:2-4, 16).

The notion of the Holy Spirit using the Word as an instrument to accomplish God's purpose is carried over into the New Testament. The gospel of John, especially, emphasises that the life-giving quality of Jesus' words is due to the Spirit: "The *words* that I have spoken to you are *spirit and life*" (Jn 6:63). In the church's mission, the preaching of the gospel is of central importance, "And this gospel of the kingdom will be *preached* in the whole world as a testimony to all nations, and then the end will come" (Mt. 24:14, Mk 16:15). The Holy Spirit brings salvation through the proclamation of the Word:

> Repentance and forgiveness of sins will be *preached* in his name to all nations, beginning in Jerusalem. You are *witnesses* of these things. I am going to send you what my Father has promised, but stay in the city until you have been clothed with *power from on high* (Lk. 24:47-49, cp. Acts 1:8)).

On the day of Pentecost, 3000 people were saved (Acts 2:36-41). Prior to their conversion, baptism, gift of the Spirit, and inclusion in the church, Peter *preached the gospel* to them. His words, spoken in the power of the Spirit, convicted them of their sin and convinced them that Jesus was Lord and Messiah (v. 36). The Holy Spirit both empowered and inspired the *messenger*, Peter, as well as working through his *message*, the Word, to bring the hearers to repentance and faith. The apostle Paul taught that *saving faith comes through hearing the gospel* (Rom. 10:17, cf. Rom. 1:15-17; Gal. 3:2, 5).

The Holy Spirit Makes the Word Effective

The Holy Spirit inspires and reveals the words that are spoken, making them effective for salvation in the hearers. The Word is the Spirit's instrument in creating faith. Paul writes,

> My speech and my message were not in plausible words of wisdom, but in demonstration of the Spirit and power, that your faith might not rest in the wisdom of men but in the power of God (1 Cor. 2:4-5).

The Holy Spirit is the power behind and in the proclaimed Word. When we speak about the Word as a means of grace, we mean that the Holy Spirit uses the Word as a vehicle of his presence and power. Spirit and Word must be understood in relation to one another. Especially in relation to the missionary situation, Paul emphasised how the Spirit and the Word are united in bringing about saving faith:

> God chose you from the beginning to be saved, through sanctification by the Spirit and belief in the truth. To this he called you through our gospel (2 Thess. 2:13-14; see also 1 Thess. 1:4-6).

The Holy Spirit inspires the message. It is "not in words taught us by human wisdom but in words taught by the Spirit, expressing spiritual truths in spiritual words" (1 Cor. 2:13), and through the hearing of this message the Spirit creates the faith that receives salvation (Eph. 3:5; 2:8).

Word and Deed

Paul's own apostolic ministry to the Gentiles illustrates that there is a necessary connection between words, deeds and the Holy Spirit. He may speak of his ministry as the "priestly duty of *proclaiming the gospel* of God, so that the Gentiles might become an offering acceptable to God, *sanctified by the Holy Spirit*". It is Christ himself who has led the Gentiles to obey God. It has happened through the ministry of Paul, "by *word and deed*, by the power of *signs and wonders,* by the *power of the Holy Spirit*" (Rom. 15:16-19). According to this text, the Word of the gospel was not alone in Paul's ministry: Word (Greek: *logos*) and deed (Greek: *ergon*) went together.

The *deed* referred to by Paul here are the *miracles*, the "signs and wonders", that accompanied the preaching of the Word. These miracles, for instance healings, are seen as divine confirmation by the Holy Spirit of the spoken message. One instance of this is what happened in Iconium on one of Paul's missionary journeys: "Paul and Barnabas spent considerable time there, speaking boldly for the Lord, who *confirmed the message* of his grace *by enabling them to do miraculous signs and wonders*" (Acts 14:3).

In the same way, Jesus' own ministry had consisted of preaching, healing and expulsion of evil spirits in the power of the Holy Spirit (Acts 10:38; Luke 4:18-19; 5:15). It was this ministry that was to be continued by the disciples in the power of the Spirit. "As the Father has sent me, I am sending you [...] Receive the Holy Spirit" (Jn 20:21-22).

Although miracles had and still have an important role to play in convincing people of the truth of the gospel, also *works of mercy* that are not miraculous but expressions of *Christian love and compassion*, can testify to the truth of Christianity. The church's *diakonia,* or service for suffering, sick, poor, oppressed and marginalised people should always accompany the preaching of the gospel. Jesus' parable of the Good Samaritan is an exemplification of the message of love for one's neighbour. It is not a miracle story, but a story of compassion and practical concern for a person in need. As such, it is a *model for the disciples of Jesus* then and now (Lk. 10:25-37).

The Holy Spirit Uses the Word to Apply Christ's Redemptive Work to the Individual

The objective basis of salvation, Christ's redemptive work carried out in history has universal validity. Christ's incarnation and birth, earthly life and ministry, passion and death, resurrection and ascension all belong to the events of salvation that happened once for all 2000 years ago. "He has appeared once for all at the end of the ages to do away with sin by the sacrifice of himself" (Heb. 9:26). All of humanity was included in Christ's redemptive work. He died for all (2 Cor. 5:14) as he carried the sins of the whole world on the cross (Jn 1:29). God has made Jesus Lord and Christ (Acts 2:36). That is the fundamental truth which is universal.

However, only the Holy Spirit can make this truth a personal confession: "No one can say 'Jesus is Lord' except by the Holy Spirit" (1 Cor. 12:3). *The Holy Spirit applies to individuals what Christ has secured for all.* But the Spirit does not do this simply by a divine command. He does it in such a way that people may respond freely through faith. He makes this application through the Word. God who has laid the basis for reconciliation of human beings with himself in Christ, still needs ambassadors who on Christ's behalf implore people: "*Be* reconciled to God" (2 Cor. 5:20).

The fruit of God's redemptive work in Christ – forgiveness of sins, reconciliation with God and eternal life – has to be appropriated personally by each individual through the Holy Spirit's working. It is the unanimous testimony of the New Testament that the Holy Spirit uses the proclamation of the gospel to accomplish this. Personal faith, the subjective side of salvation, is created by the Spirit when the gospel is proclaimed.

The Holy Spirit is Sovereign in Using the Word

The link between the Word and the coming of the Holy Spirit cannot be locked into one predictable pattern. Nevertheless, the happening of Pentecost does provide something of a paradigm, for throughout the New Testament the proclamation of the gospel is the primary means by which the Holy Spirit initiates people into new life in Christ. In the book of Acts, wherever the Spirit is received for the first time, the preaching of the *gospel precedes it* (Acts 2:14-36; 8:5, 14-17; 10:34-43; 19:4-5). The only significant exception is the apostle Paul who received a direct revelation from Jesus (Acts 9:5, 17)

Furthermore, the Holy Spirit is linked to an *ongoing revelation* of God's purpose in Christ. The apostle Paul prayed that God might give the believers "the Spirit of wisdom and revelation so that you may know him better" (Eph. 1:17; see also Col. 1:9; Phil. 1:9). Jesus promised his disciples that the Holy Spirit "will teach you all things and will remind you of everything I have said to you" (Jn 14:26). "When he, the Spirit of truth, comes, he will guide you into all truth (Jn 16:13). The Spirit guides the church in its understanding and proclamation of the Word in order that people's experience of Christ will be accompanied by clear and ever-growing knowledge and understanding.

The Holy Spirit Inspires Prophecy

The Word is sometimes oriented toward the future, through prophetic utterance. This is in accordance with Jesus' promise: "When he, the Spirit of truth, comes, he will guide you into all truth. He will not speak on his own, he will speak only what he hears, and *he will tell you what is yet to come*" (Jn 16:13).

This statement by Jesus indicates that the Spirit will inspire predictive prophecy in the church. At the same time, the words provide a safeguard against error by emphasising that the Spirit speaks on Christ's authority; he speaks only what he hears, and his aim is to glorify Christ (Jn 16:14).

In the three basic revelatory functions of the Holy Spirit – witnessing, teaching, and prophesying – we see the intimate connection between the Spirit and the Word.

The Word is the Criterion for the Work of the Holy Spirit

Those who seek or desire the Spirit must recognise that he links himself to the proclamation of the Word. We should be wary of any alleged experience of the Spirit that is not rooted in the Word. This does not mean that the Word will in every case precede an activity of the Spirit, in a simplistic causal sense. People were often initially drawn to the New Testament community by the demonstration of supernatural power, as the famous theologian Emil Brunner correctly pointed out:

> People draw near to the Christian community because they are irresistibly attracted by its supernatural power. They would like to share in this new dimension of life and power, and they enter the zone in which the Spirit operates before they have heard a word about what lies behind it as an ultimate transcendent-immanent cause. There is a sort of fascination which is exercised mostly without any reference to the Word, comparable rather to the attractive force of a magnet or the spread of an infectious disease.[1]

This is seen already in the story of Pentecost when Peter's sermon was in response to the people's questions caused by curiosity about speaking in tongues (Acts 2:6-7, 12).

When the apostle Paul was put ashore on the island of Malta, people were moved by a demonstration of the Spirit's power before there was any

---

[1] Emil Brunner, *The Misunderstanding of the Church*, translated by Harold Knight (London: Lutterworth, 1952), p. 52.

proclamation of the Word (Acts 28:3-6). The Spirit is sovereign; he moves when and where he pleases (cf. Jn 3:8). Whether the Word precedes, coincides with, or occurs subsequent to an action of the Spirit is a matter of his particular determination. *But it is only the Word that can explain the Holy Spirit's actions and lead to salvation.* Only, as Paul explained the healing of a lame man in Lystra by the words of the gospel, could he prevent the people from misunderstanding the miracle and worship him and Barnabas as pagan gods (Acts 14:8-18). Deeds without the Word may be misunderstood and even lead to idolatry.

Where the Word is neglected, we may infer that the activity of the Holy Spirit will be thwarted, for in neglecting the Word we grieve the Spirit who has linked himself to the Word. For the same reason, where some part of the biblical revelation is neglected, the Holy Spirit's activity in that area of truth will be diminished. The Spirit's strategy may then call for special attention to that neglected area. *Renewal often comes at a point where the Holy Spirit stirs up response to some aspect of truth that has been neglected in the church.*

Many people in the Charismatic movement testify to a more vital experience of the Holy Spirit than they have ever known before. This has been accompanied by widespread teaching on the subject of receiving the Holy Spirit and his gifts, and for many this has been new. More than mere superficial charismatic enthusiasm lies behind the common statement, "We never heard about this in our church!" It says something about the lack of space that the Holy Spirit has traditionally held in our everyday expressions of the faith. In many churches and even in evangelical circles, there has been little, and sometimes no specific teaching on receiving the Holy Spirit and his gifts. Other truths have been emphasised, but not this one.

This raises an important question about the work of the Holy Spirit: Does the Spirit come with his gifts on the basis of a doctrinal position that assumes his coming without our specifically proclaiming it or asking for it? The sacramental tradition says, "You receive the Holy Spirit when you are grafted into Christ in baptism." The evangelical tradition says, "You receive the Holy Spirit when you are born again." Assuming that both of these traditions teach something important about receiving the Spirit, we still have to ask: to what degree will a charismatic work of the Spirit actually happen, if a clear word about this part of receiving the Spirit is not part of the proclamation and teaching? Is the Holy Spirit's work in fact linked to a proclamation of the Holy Spirit that is specific? Would people, for example, experience the reality of forgiveness of sins if the word of forgiveness was not specifically proclaimed, and God only was presented and believed in as Creator? Would people experience guidance, healing, or spiritual gifts if these were seldom or never mentioned? Would people do mission work if the biblical words about mission were never referred to or explained? Would people be empowered as witnesses by the Holy Spirit if they were never told that such a thing is possible?

Each of the three main positions – sacramental, evangelical, and Pentecostal/ charismatic – has something to teach the others about the coming of the Spirit; their doctrinal differences are not irreconcilable or mutually exclusive. *But it is not likely that people will be led into a charismatic experience of the Holy Spirit and his gifts without a clear and energetic proclamation of this particular biblical truth. The Holy Spirit comes and works where and when the Word is clearly presented.*

(11) Faith, Repentance and Obedience

Two Aspects of Faith: Gift and Response

The Holy Spirit's objective is to unite the lives of human beings with the life of Christ. Faith involves making this connection, bringing about and maintaining the union of Christ's life and our life.

Faith describes the whole action by which the Holy Spirit brings the living, redeeming presence of Christ into a living union with a human being. The initiative and the power to accomplish this lie with the Holy Spirit. In this sense, *faith is a gift.* That is the understanding that lies behind the comment by Peter about the coming of the Spirit to the Gentiles: "God, who knows the heart, showed that he accepted them (the Gentiles) by giving the Holy Spirit to them just as he did to us. He made no distinction between us and them, for he purified their hearts by faith" (Acts 15:8-9, cf. Eph. 2:9). Faith, in this context, was an action accomplished by God that was clearly manifested by the coming of the Spirit.

Faith, however, also involves a human response, and Scripture usually views it from this perspective: Jesus' main message was an invitation and an exhortation *to people to believe*, "The kingdom of God is near. Repent and *believe* the gospel" (Mk 1:15). It is the response in faith to this invitation that saves a person: "that whoever *believes* in him (Jesus) shall not perish but have eternal life" (Jn 3:16). This is also what people did in response to the message: "Those who *accepted* his [Peter's] message were baptised, and about three thousand were added to their number that day" (Acts 2:41). "Many who heard the message *believed*, and the number of men grew to about five thousand" (Acts 4:4). It is human beings who are the subjects of faith; it is people who believe, not God. "We have heard of *your faith* in Christ Jesus" (Col. 1:4). In Scripture, the grammar of faith is weighted overwhelmingly toward the side of human response. "Believe" is something we are told to do; "faith" is something we are exhorted to have.

The emphasis on human response, however, is set in the context of divine action: the Word has been proclaimed; God has cleansed their hearts; God has *granted them repentance* unto life. God wants to bring us into a union with Christ; not by coercion, but freely offered and freely received. The Holy Spirit takes the initiative and demonstrates through the gospel that the basis for new life in Christ has been established by God. The Holy Spirit presents the invitation to receive this new life, and grants to us the will and ability to reach out and receive it: *faith.*

Even though God's initiative and action are *primary* in the matter of faith, Scripture gives *more emphasis* to the side of human response. God's will in the matter is already a settled issue. He does not need to be convinced. The work of the Holy Spirit is aimed at creating a *response from us*. He holds before us the invitation to enter into a life of faith, to receive what God has prepared and now offers.

In establishing faith, the way the Holy Spirit does it will vary from one individual to another. In one person, he may create the reality of faith through a message that is preached. Another person may come to faith as the result of a personal testimony that someone has shared. Faith may be sparked by something that is read in the Bible or another book, by an act of kindness, by an exhortation to believe, by a struggle of conscience, by a charismatic demonstration of the Spirit, by a miracle of healing or a power encounter where Satan is defeated. Yet *coming to saving faith in Christ will always involve a knowledge of the saving acts of Christ as expressed in the gospel* (Rom. 1:16; 10:17).

The entire action of establishing and maintaining a reconciled personal relationship between God and the believer is included in the biblical meaning of faith, both the side of God's gift and the side of human response. In individual cases, however, the Holy Spirit may focus on one side or the other. If we labour under the notion that faith is a "work" that we ourselves must "do", he may point out that faith is a gift. If we turn faith into an intellectual belief system, he may turn our attention to the practical results of a life of faith: "faith expressing itself through love" (Gal. 5:6). If he has amply demonstrated God's provision for life in Christ, he may command us to believe with such vehemence that the whole issue of faith seems to hang on our will and decision.

In Ephesus, the apostle Paul met a small group of disciples and asked them, "Did you receive the Holy Spirit when you believed?" (Acts 19:2). The shape of his question illustrates the fact that, in the early church, believing in Jesus was closely linked to receiving the Holy Spirit, although the two were not identical. Their answer showed that the problem, in this case, did not stem from a lack of faith but from a deficient proclamation: "We have not even heard that there is a Holy Spirit". When Paul corrected the matter by sharing the Christian message, they promptly responded with faith, were baptised and received the Holy Spirit with demonstration of spiritual gifts (Acts 19:3-6). The episode began with an inquiry about faith and ended with a manifestation of the Spirit.

This incident illustrates that faith is always faith *in Jesus*. It is a condition for the saving union between Jesus and the believer and for the reception of the gift of the Holy Spirit. The invitation to receive and be filled with the Holy Spirit is not about something that has to be added to one's faith in Jesus, as though faith in Jesus were not enough. It is, rather, a part of one's life in Jesus, which, like every manifestation of that life, calls for a response of faith.

Repentance unto Life

Repentance (Greek: *metanoia*, literally: change of mind) is the other side of faith; it involves that which we *cease* to believe and do. In repentance, we *turn away* from that which prevents us from entering into a saving union with Christ. The groundwork for repentance, like that of faith, is laid by the Holy Spirit. It is the coming of the Spirit that makes repentance possible and opens the gateway to salvation.

The Spirit of God was a redemptive power in the history of Israel. It was prophesied that the Spirit would be instrumental in the future salvation of the people, as a *means of judgement and cleansing.* A purified and sanctified people would remain when the Spirit had carried out his work:

> Those who are left in Zion, who remain in Jerusalem, will be called holy [...] The Lord will cleanse the bloodstains from Jerusalem by a Spirit of judgement and a Spirit of fire (Is. 4:3-4).
>
> I will sprinkle clean water on you, and you will be clean; I will cleanse you from all your impurities and from all your idols. I will give you a new heart and put a new spirit in you; I will remove from you your heart of stone and give you a heart of flesh. And I will put my Spirit in you and move you to follow my decrees and be careful to keep my laws (Ez. 36:25, 27).

Repentance comes to expression first and foremost in sincere *confession of sins with the intent of turning away from them* (Mt. 3:2, 6-10). Jesus' parable of the lost son illustrates what repentance and faith are (Lk. 15:11-32). It is *leaving* a life of sin and rebellion against and away from our heavenly Father, then *returning* to him, *confessing* our sins to him (v. 18-19, 21), and *receiving* from him a new reconciled and joyous *relationship as his child* (v. 22-24). The father said to his other son, "We had to celebrate and be glad, for this brother of yours was dead and is alive again; he was lost and is found" (v. 32). Repentance and confession of sins are not a one-time event for the believers, but a practice that continues throughout life, since we continue to be sinners,

> If we claim to be without sin, we deceive ourselves, and the truth is not in us. If we confess our sins, he is faithful and just and will forgive us our sins and purify us from all unrighteousness. If we claim we have not sinned, we make him out to be a liar and his word has no place in our lives (1 Jn 1:8-10).

John presents salvation in terms of "life": life in the kingdom of God (Jn 3:3); eternal life (Jn 3:16); abundant life (10:10); life lived in communion with the Father and the Son (Jn 14:6; 17:3). Jesus sent his disciples, in the power of the Holy Spirit, to proclaim this salvation and the forgiveness of sins by which one enters into it (Jn 20:20-23, 31).

Repentance unto life lies at the very heart of the Holy Spirit's work. In order to bring us into a saving union with Christ, he must lead us through repentance, for "all have sinned and fall short of the glory of God" (Rom. 3:23). When the Holy Spirit was given on the day of Pentecost, Peter's first admonition to his hearers was, "Repent and…!" (Acts 2:38).

When the Holy Spirit came on the Gentiles in the household of Cornelius, there were some dramatic manifestations of his presence: speaking in tongues and praising God (Acts 10:44-46). The central issue for the apostles, however, was that of salvation or life. When Peter later reported the incident to the apostles back in Jerusalem, their comment was telling: "So then, God has granted even the Gentiles *repentance unto life*" (Acts 11:18). At the later Council of Apostles in Jerusalem, Peter again referred to this incident, and with the same emphasis: God "purified their hearts by faith" (Acts 15:9).

It is a mark of wisdom and maturity to give first importance to the issue of salvation or life, even though it may be less noticeable than other workings of the Spirit. Jesus said to his disciples, "Do not rejoice in this, that the spirits are subject to you; but rejoice that your names are written in heaven" (Lk. 10:20). The kingdom of God which includes all the gifts of salvation is described by Paul in this way, "The kingdom of God is not a matter of eating or drinking, but of righteousness, peace and joy in the Holy Spirit" (Rom. 14:17).

Evangelical Christianity has given first importance to the issue of salvation or life, and that has given strength and endurance to its witness. Evangelicals have recognised that repentance unto life is basic to the work of the Holy Spirit. It is important to keep this in mind as we consider certain other aspects of the Spirit's work.

Repentance and Faith

The preached gospel is always either being received or rejected by its hearers. The basic call to those who receive it is the call to repentance. In his call for repentance, Peter stood in the tradition of the Old Testament prophets, John the Baptist, and Jesus himself (see, for example, Ez. 14:6; Mt. 3:1-2; 4:17).

The term repentance denotes a complete change of relationship to God with serious ethical consequences. It consists, as we have seen, of a twofold movement: a turning away from one's unbelief and sins and a turning to God in faith and obedience.

Repentance and faith in God are therefore two sides of the same coin. In Christian repentance, turning *from sin is always at the same time a turning to Christ* (Acts 2:38; 26:18; 20:21). Wherever repentance is called for, faith is implied, and vice versa. Peter, therefore, in a situation similar to that of Pentecost, could call for faith without explicitly mentioning repentance, yet repentance was implied (Acts 10:43; cp. 11:18).

Although the motivation to repent is a result of the working of God's Spirit, repentance is nevertheless a person's own response. We are the subject of the action of repentance and the ones who are commanded to repent (Acts

17:30). Thus, repentance is a person's first step in becoming a Christian. *There can be no salvation without repentance and faith.*

Obedience

Peter said that God *gives the Holy Spirit to those who obey him* (Acts 5:32). Paul said that his ministry was aimed at producing "the obedience that comes from faith" (Rom. 1:5; cp. Rom 16:26; 15:18). Obedience to God and his Holy Spirit, the obedience of faith, involves more than adherence to general principles. It means being obedient to the whole message of Scripture, to pay attention to the work and the promptings of the Spirit; it means being under the lordship of the living and indwelling Christ, with whom we are united through faith. Obedience expresses itself not only in our belief concerning the basic truths of the gospel, but also in a life of following Christ and in our readiness to follow the Holy Spirit's guidance for implementing the will of God.

But this obedience is not attainable by human beings by themselves. It involves not only obedience *to* the Holy Spirit, but obedience *in* the Holy Spirit. *It is the result of the Spirit's own work in our lives* (Rom. 8:4-6; Phil. 2:12-13; 2 Cor. 3:5-6).

Pentecostal and charismatic Christianity is sometimes faulted for emphasising the Holy Spirit at the expense of Christ or of the Father. However, a fair response is whether the emphasis on the Holy Spirit does not in fact restore the balance, especially in some of the churches of the Reformation that have virtually developed a kind of Christomonism, a one-sided emphasis on Christ. Jesus Christ spoke at some length with his disciples about the coming of the Holy Spirit. It was important not only that the Spirit would come, but that they would know he was coming and would then recognise and welcome him when he came. Reading about the church after Pentecost in Acts, the Epistles and Revelation, one is struck by the frequency with which the Holy Spirit is mentioned and the centrality of the Spirit in the life and ministry of the church. The "Apostolic Benediction" in 2 Corinthians 13:13 spells out both the equality and central features of the three persons of the triune Godhead: the love of God, the Father, the grace of the Jesus Christ, the Lord, and the fellowship of the Holy Spirit (2 Cor. 13:13).

When Christ is preached and people are urged to "believe", what results all too often is an acceptance of a Christian belief system followed by moral striving rather than a living faith. "To believe" is often understood simply in human terms, something people must do in order to be saved. It is precisely a dependence on the Holy Spirit that helps keep faith and obedience from becoming an exercise in human achievement. The Holy Spirit is Scripture's answer to words of God that are impossible to obey. Therefore, the prayer: "Come, Holy Spirit! Make *Christ* to be my wisdom from God, that is, my righteousness, holiness and redemption" (cf. 1 Cor. 1: 30).

No believer can bypass the fundamental importance of obedience: the work of the Holy Spirit makes no provision for cheap grace. Yet neither can one undertake obedience apart from the Holy Spirit: his work rules out sanctification by self-effort. Any preaching of holy obedience without dependence on the Holy Spirit will miss the mark. Obedience is not a product of my own effort: it is a gift of grace. Its appropriate accompaniment is not human willpower, but loving and thankful confidence in the Holy Spirit who unites me with Christ, he who obeys the Father in all things. As Paul says, "Therefore I glory in Christ Jesus in my service to God. I will not venture to speak of anything except what Christ has accomplished through me [...] through the power of the Holy Spirit" (Rom 15:18-19).

> If *by the Spirit*, you put to death the misdeeds of the body, you will live, because those who are *led by the Spirit* of God are sons of God (Rom. 8:13-14).

(12) The Indwelling of the Holy Spirit

The Holy Spirit's desire is to come and dwell within the believer. This was laid down in the prophetic word: "I will put my Spirit in you, and move you to follow my decrees and be careful to keep my laws" (Ez. 36:27). Jesus promised the fulfilment of the prophecy when he said,

> I will ask the Father, and he will give you another Counsellor to be with you forever – the Spirit of truth. The world cannot accept him, because it neither sees him nor knows him. But you know him, for he *lives with you and will be in you* (John 14:16-17).

The redemptive plan of God comes to reality when the Holy Spirit indwells the believers and brings the living, redeeming presence of Christ into their lives, and from that indwelling proceeds to work God's purpose in and through them.

The Spirit as Down Payment on Life in the Kingdom to Come

The Spirit indwells the person who has been forgiven and justified by faith (Acts 11:17; 15:7-9; Gal. 2:16; 3:2, 5, 14). He comes to those who have been adopted into divine sonship. The *internal testimony* of the Spirit gives *assurance* of this sonship and of the fatherhood of God.

> Because you are sons, God sent the Spirit of his Son into our hearts, the Spirit who calls out, '*Abba*! Father!' (Gal. 4:6).

> For you did not receive a spirit that makes you a slave again to fear, but you received the Spirit of sonship. And by him we cry "Abba, Father". The Spirit himself testifies with our spirit that we are God's children"(Rom. 8:15-16).

Our divine sonship is completed in eternity (Rom. 8:21-23); in the meantime, the Spirit serves as the guarantee or down payment on the coming salvation in the consummated kingdom of God.

Closely associated with the inner testimony of the Spirit is what Scripture calls sealing with the Holy Spirit. "When you believed, you were marked in him with a *seal, the promised Holy Spirit*, who is a *deposit guaranteeing our inheritance* until the redemption of those who are God's possession" (Eph. 1:13-14; also 2 Cor. 1:22).

The biblical terms "seal", "guarantee", or "deposit" (2 Cor. 1:22; 5:5; Eph. 1:13-14), and first fruits (Rom. 8:23) all denote the indwelling Holy Spirit as both *experiential and eschatological* – as a present divine gift guaranteeing a future reality. The experiential possession of the Spirit in the present is a foretaste guaranteeing that the Christian will also have the full future salvation. *We know by experience that we have the Holy Spirit, therefore* we also *know that we shall be saved into God's coming kingdom.* "And *hope* does not disappoint us, because God has poured out his *love* into our hearts by the Holy Spirit, whom he has given us" (Rom 5:5).

Eastern Orthodox theology, together with the early church fathers, identifies "sealing" with the practice of chrismation following baptism; this parallels later Roman Catholic confirmation practice.[1] It is closely identified with the scriptural precedent of baptism with the Holy Spirit on the day of Pentecost, described by Peter as a promise "for you and your children and for all who are far off – for all whom the Lord our God will call" (Acts 2:39).

Life in Union with Christ

Christians are indwelt by the living Christ through the working of the Holy Spirit. This is a reality so dizzying that the human tongue stutters to express it. But it is clearly taught in the Bible:

> I have been crucified with Christ and I no longer live, but *Christ lives in me.* The life I live in the body, I live by faith in the Son of God, who loved me and gave himself for me (Gal. 2:20).

It is no patching up of the old creation, but a new beginning. Mortal human life is superseded by eternal life: "If anyone is in Christ, he is a new creation; the old has gone, the new has come" (2 Cor. 5:17). The newness lies not simply in the fact that human nature has been forgiven and cleansed. That is, in a sense, preparation. The newness goes deeper: a person now lives in union with the risen Christ. That which has been created, the "new creation," is precisely this reality of the indwelling Spirit establishing and maintaining the union between the risen Christ and the believer. *Christ lives in us and we live in him.*

Paul relates this new life to baptism, when he says,

> We were therefore buried with him through baptism into death in order that, just as Christ was raised from the dead through the glory of the Father, we too may live a new life. If we have been *united* with him like this in his death, we

---

[1] E.C. Whitaker, *Documents of the Baptismal Liturgy* (London: SPCK, 1977), pp. 13-17; J.D.C. Fisher, *Confirmation, Then and Now* (London: SPCK, 1978). See also the study by one of the participants in the consultation that produced this book, Theodore Jungkuntz, *Confirmation and the Charismata* (Lanham, MD: University Press of America, 1983), pp. 33-35.

will certainly also be *united* with him in his resurrection (Rom. 6:4-5, see also Phil. 3:9-10).

Every believer should experience the reality of the indwelling Christ and the indwelling Spirit (Rom. 8:9-11). And this is a truth that must be rehearsed again and again – not least by those who have experienced dramatic manifestations of the Spirit in the midst of a charismatic renewal movement. A steady and consistent spiritual walk does not happen automatically.

When we ask the practical question: how then is this life of the indwelling Spirit sustained, the apostle Paul points to the relationship between what we do and what we think:

> Those who live according to the sinful nature (or the flesh) have their minds set on what that nature desires, but those who live in accordance with the Spirit have their *minds set on what the Spirit desires*. The mind of sinful man is death, but the *mind controlled by the Spirit is life and peace*: the sinful man is hostile to God. (Rom. 8:5-7; see also Rom. 12:2; Col. 3:2; Phil. 4:8-9; Eph. 5:17-20).

The mind transformed by the Holy Spirit is able to discern what pleases God so that the believer may be able to live out the life in the Spirit that is according to the will to God.

The Outpouring of the Holy Spirit

The Spirit indwells believers in order that Christ may live his life through them. The outpouring of the Spirit may therefore be broadly understood as a means to that end. The Spirit is poured out in order that the indwelling presence of Christ might be established, strengthened, or released in power and ministry.

Pentecostals have laid special stress on the outpouring of the Holy Spirit, and in this they have assessed accurately the present work of the Spirit. An emphasis on the outpouring of the Spirit may be necessary when the awareness of the indwelling of Christ is at low ebb among his people, or when they face formidable opposition or new challenges. Mainline churches have frequently made the mistake of opposing a *theology of indwelling and the accompanying emphasis on gradual growth* to a *theology of outpouring demonstrated by experience and signs,* as though the two were in competition, or one obviated any need for the other.

Francis Sullivan, a Jesuit scholar, makes the interesting observation that Catholic theologian Thomas Aquinas saw the two motifs rather as complementary to one another: Aquinas asks the question whether one can speak of a sending of the Holy Spirit to a person in whom he is already dwelling, and if so, how this is to be understood. His answer is as follows: "There is an invisible sending of the Divine Person not only in the initial gift of grace but also with respect to an advance in virtue or an increase of grace [...] as for example when a person moves forward into the grace of working miracles, or prophecy."[2]

Discussions between different segments of the body of Christ have sometimes become a sterile restatement of positions when they have focused simply on the question: how do you receive the Holy Spirit? We may make more progress by shifting the ground of the question and ask: *how is the Holy Spirit employing these two basic truths – permanent indwelling and new outpouring – in the present situation in the church?*

[2] Francis Sullivan, *Baptism in the Holy Spirit: A Catholic Interpretation of the Pentecostal Experience* (Rome: Gregorian University, 1974) pp. 52-53. Also, Jungkuntz, *Confirmation and Charismata*, pp. 33-35.

(13) The Holy Spirit and Baptism

In the early church, the initial coming of the Holy Spirit to an individual was closely associated with baptism. It was a basic component in the missional task of the church and the work of the Holy Spirit which the apostles remembered from Jesus' own instructions (Mt. 28:19; Mk 16:16), and which they recognised in the Spirit-led life of the witnessing community. When the Holy Spirit fell on those who heard the Word in the household of Cornelius, Peter's first thought was for their baptism (Acts 10:47). When Paul spoke with some believers in Ephesus and discovered that they had not even heard about the Holy Spirit, the first thing he inquired about was their baptism (Acts 19:3).

Apostolic teaching makes a strong link between faith, baptism and the believer's union with Christ (Rom. 6:4-5; Gal. 3:26-27). Sometimes the church has had difficulty thinking in any terms other than an almost mechanical understanding of cause and effect, and this may be part of the problem when we consider the sacramental tradition. This mind-set drives sacramentalists toward a virtually automatic view of baptism: the rite of baptism is the cause; union with Christ is the result. The same thinking drives those on the other end of the theological spectrum toward a purely symbolic view of baptism: since faith is the efficient cause of spiritual life, baptism can be allowed no higher role than that of a symbol or confirming witness.

We would propose approaching baptism from another direction: the Holy Spirit himself is responsible for spiritual life. Baptism is an indispensable part of his work of uniting a believer with Christ.

The Holy Spirit's Activity in Baptism

The activity of the Holy Spirit in the work of salvation has a particular focus in Jesus' words to Nicodemus: "No-one can enter the kingdom of God unless he is born of water and the Spirit" (Jn 3:5). This evident allusion to Christian baptism indicates that baptism is an integral part of the Holy Spirit's work of bringing about the new birth, which is necessary for entering the kingdom of God and receiving salvation.

A similar understanding of baptism is found in the Pauline writings:

> He [God] saved us, not because of righteous things we had done, but because of his mercy. He *saved us through the washing of rebirth and renewal by the Holy Spirit,* whom he poured out on us generously, through Jesus Christ our Saviour (Titus 3:5).

> You were washed, you were sanctified, you were justified in the name of the Lord Jesus Christ and by the Spirit of our God (1 Cor. 6:11).

The "washing" of baptism in these texts is linked to regeneration, justification, and sanctification, by the working of the Holy Spirit. This does not mean that the performance of the baptismal rite of itself brings about salvation. The salvific effect of baptism cannot be viewed apart from the activity of the Spirit himself, and the response that he works in the heart of people. It does mean, however, that in a sovereign way the Holy Spirit links new life with the water of baptism. *Baptism is used as a means of grace by the Spirit in regeneration.*

To avoid the impression that baptism works automatically, simply by virtue of being performed, it is necessary to point out that the New Testament also links regeneration to *faith*:

> Yet to all who *received* him, to those who *believed* in his name, he gave the *right to become children of God* – children born not of blood, nor of the will of the flesh nor of the will of man, but born of God (Jn 1: 12-13).

> Whoever *believes and is baptised will be saved*, but whoever does not believe will be condemned (Mk 16:16).

Going through the ritual of baptism does not in itself guarantee salvation unless there is a corresponding reception of Jesus by faith. Paul writes that the Christians have "been buried with him in baptism and raised with him *through faith* in the power of God" (Col. 2:12). The Holy Spirit makes the necessary connection between the outer means: the water and the word, and the inner reception: faith.

Paul even warns against taking salvation for granted because of baptism, just as the people of Israel were not guaranteed salvation by merely having been led through the waters or being under the cloud at the exodus from Egypt (1 Cor. 10:1-4).

In Baptism the Holy Spirit Unites the Believer with Christ

Those who have heard the gospel, repented of their sins, and believed in Jesus as their Saviour and Lord (Acts 2:21, 36) are exhorted to be *baptised in the name of Jesus* for the forgiveness of sins (Acts 2:38). Baptism is integral to the Spirit's work of uniting a new believer with Christ. Scripture links the promise of life in Christ and the Spirit, as well as Christian discipleship, to the event of baptism (for example, Mt. 28:19: Acts 22:16; 1 Cor. 6:11; Col. 2:12-14; Titus 3:5-7; 1 Pet. 3:21).

The ministry of baptising, like that of proclamation, is carried out by human agents, and those who are baptised submit voluntarily to baptism.

Nevertheless, as in the proclamation of the Word, the Spirit is at work. Baptism is not simply a rite entered into by a man or woman in order to express their faith and commitment. It is a means that the Spirit uses, together with the promises of the gospel connected with baptism, to wash away sins, and unite the believer with Christ in dying with him for the old sinful nature and rising to a new life based on his resurrection (Rom. 6:3-4; Gal. 3:26-27; Phil. 3:10-11).

Mere water and ritual could never grant the blessings that Scripture promises in connection with baptism. Jesus Christ himself acts in baptism, for it is carried out in his name. When the New Testament community prayed and acted in the name of Jesus, the crucified and risen Saviour – now the living and exalted Lord – was present in power among his people. As surely as they expected the Holy Spirit to come in charismatic power, they expected him to move powerfully through the water of baptism. *Lutheran charismatics, then, have a sacramental view of baptism – that is, they believe the Triune God acts through it as a means of salvation – yet, they are not sacramentalists believing that salvation takes place automatically by baptism, regardless of faith.*

We shall later deal with the question of *infant baptism*, and the situation which occurs when the child does not have a conscious faith at the time of baptism. The understanding and preaching of baptism in the church today – as in New Testament times – must, however, have the "normal" missionary situation as its point of departure: baptising adults who have come to personal faith in Christ.

(14) Baptism with the Holy Spirit

John the Baptist prophesied that Jesus would baptise his followers with the Holy Spirit (Lk. 3:16). Jesus confirmed this (Acts 1:5). Believers in the early church experienced it (Acts 2:4; 11:16-17). The phrase "baptised with the Holy Spirit", in Acts, is used in reference to two events: the outpouring of the Holy Spirit initially on the disciples at Pentecost and later on the household of Cornelius.

Systematic explanations of the coming of the Spirit come to sharp disagreement here. The Pentecostal view sees baptism with the Spirit as a "second blessing" by which someone who has already received salvation is empowered for service. The sacramental and evangelical views both take exception to this interpretation. They hold that baptism with the Spirit is either identical with or invariably happens along with baptism or salvation respectively. Thus, every believer has been baptised with the Spirit. This also seems to be in accord with what Paul writes, when he uses the term, "We were all baptised with one Spirit into one body" (1 Cor. 12:13).

On purely exegetical grounds, the case is hard to resolve: neither in the Gospels, where the expression is used prophetically, nor in Acts where it is used descriptively, nor in Paul where it is used didactically, is baptism with the Holy Spirit precisely defined; and its use in Acts is somewhat ambiguous. It is difficult to make Pentecost out to be a salvation event for the disciples. Jesus' words to them in Acts 1:4-8 do not concern their salvation but rather their need of power for witness. Jesus' expression, "You shall be baptised with the Holy Spirit" (Acts 1:5) was not a reference to baptism with water, since the disciples were not baptised on the day of Pentecost when the promise was fulfilled. It was rather a metaphorical expression denoting the experience that the disciples would have of being filled with the Holy Spirit and manifesting that reality in a demonstrable way. That was exactly what happened to those who were gathered together at Pentecost: "All of them were filled with the Holy Spirit and began to speak in other tongues, as the Spirit enabled them" (Acts 2:4). On the other hand, the primary interpretation that the apostles in Jerusalem put on the occurrence in the household of Cornelius was that it was a testimony to the fact that they had been saved by faith (Acts 10:17-18; 15:7-9).

Despite its presence in the New Testament, "baptised with the Holy Spirit" is not a terminology that has been much used in the history of the church until the advent of the Holiness and Pentecostal movements in the 19th and 20th centuries. Even in the writings of the New Testament it seldom occurs. Luke himself, as we noted earlier, gives greater weight to the phrase "filled with the Spirit."

In the 20th century, however, through the Pentecostal and Charismatic movements, the term "baptism with the Holy Spirit" has broken on the scene with dramatic results. To give disproportionate emphasis to a teaching or a term that has relatively little biblical or historical weight could lead to distortion. However, this does not mean that we should altogether abandon or neglect the term "baptism with the Holy Spirit." We should seek to understand it more clearly.

It has been common in some mainline churches with venerable theological traditions to acknowledge the vitality and growth of Pentecostal Christianity, while at the same time belittling its exegesis and theology in general, and its doctrine of baptism with the Holy Spirit in particular. It is possible, of course, that the Holy Spirit could enliven the life, worship and witness of Pentecostals, and prosper their missionary endeavours in an unprecedented way, yet make little headway with them in regard to their understanding of Scripture and theology. *Authentic experience may be inaccurately assessed and explained.* That is a reminder to us all.

We should, however, be very cautious about making a harsh theological judgement regarding a movement with the scope and significance and history of worldwide Pentecostalism. It might be that the Holy Spirit wants to correct some aspects of traditional Pentecostal teaching. The Charismatic movement may be the Spirit's occasion for addressing some questions to Pentecostal theology. But it may equally be the Spirit's occasion for Catholics and Protestants alike to give more respectful consideration to the substance and the contribution of the exegesis and theology of Pentecostals.

If we consider the content and effects of "baptism with the Spirit", it seems to answer the need for an outpouring of the Spirit's power to initiate or renew witness and ministry. In the book of Acts, every time the term occurs it describes a dramatic *initial outpouring* of the Spirit. The history of the Pentecostal and Charismatic movements tends to echo this: a *key factor in the spread of the movements has been the widely shared personal experience of an outpouring of the Spirit.* For many, perhaps most, *this has initiated a new sense of the Spirit's presence and power for life and ministry.*

This experience has commonly been accompanied by a manifest demonstration of the Spirit's presence through charismatic gifts, and this is also consistent with the scriptural witness. In the theology of Luke, the experience of being filled with the Holy Spirit consistently results in a manifest demonstration of the Spirit's presence, usually in the form of inspired or empowered speech – they spoke in tongues (Acts 2:4; 10:46; 19:6), prophesied (Acts 19:6), praised God (Acts 10:46) – and spoke the Word of God with boldness (Acts 4:31); or it was accompanied by a supernatural sign of healing (Acts 9:17-18), a divine judgement (Acts 13:9-11), or a heavenly vision (Acts 7:55).

To state that such events – or such charisms – are "not necessary" is to miss the point. It goes without saying that an outpouring of the Holy Spirit with the manifestation of spiritual gifts is not "necessary" in a strict sense for either salvation or ministry. One could argue the case both from Scripture and history by mentioning prominent and universally respected movements or ministers outside the Pentecostal/Charismatic movement. Nevertheless, there are also many examples of people *before and outside* the Pentecostal/Charismatic movement who have had strong experiences of being empowered and equipped by Holy Spirit in connection with a personal renewal or call to ministry.[1]

Given the worldwide spread and witness of the Pentecostal and Charismatic movements since the beginning of the 20th century, the church as a whole must consider questions not only of exegesis and systematic theology but also of what the Holy Spirit actually is doing in the church in our time. This emphasis on a personal Pentecost – the experience of an outpouring of the Holy Spirit in one's life, a baptism or filling with the Holy Spirit – and its key role in the amazing spread of Pentecostal and Charismatic Christianity is well documented. Then, how are we to understand it? It may be that some Pentecostals and Charismatics have over-systematised their own perception and experience of the Holy Spirit. If so, that would be an understandable response to other systematisations of the working of the Holy Spirit that have produced deficient results. Any attempt to systematise the working of the Holy Spirit, however, will be a helpful approximation at best. We may not agree with some aspects of the Pentecostal way of explaining the coming of the Spirit, but we will not be far off if we acknowledge that they have accurately perceived the Spirit's work: he is calling believers to receive a personal outpouring of the Holy Spirit; he is calling them to be filled with the Holy Spirit in a way and to a degree that they have not experienced before.

The Holy Spirit is calling the church to *experience* more of what the doctrines talk about – to go beyond a mere belief in the third person of the Trinity to a demonstration of the Holy Spirit and his power (see 1 Cor. 2:4), to extend the expectation of the Spirit's working to the horizons of Scripture. This will not happen simply by asserting doctrines of the Holy Spirit. It calls for an obedient response to the prompting of the Spirit: a personal encounter with Jesus, who fills his followers with the Holy Spirit.

---

[1] One remarkable example is the Norwegian lay evangelist Hans Nielsen Hauge (1771–1824), who in 1796 had such an overwhelming experience of the Holy Spirit while plowing the fields that his whole life was transformed. It made him the most important Christian preacher and leader in Norway, leaving a deep and lasting impact on Norwegian church life. His experience was actually called "baptism with the Spirit", independently of the Pentecostal movement. Although his revival ministry drew opposition from the official Norwegian Lutheran state church and caused him to be imprisoned for several years, he nevertheless remained faithful to that church until his death. See also chapter 31.

Whether one understands this broadly speaking as an *experiential appropriation* of something already received in baptism/confirmation (sacramental), or in conversion/ salvation (evangelical), or a *reception of something promised to people who already are believers* (Pentecostal), *the plan of the Holy Spirit will be served: the Spirit will be poured out; believers will talk about the Holy Spirit with a new sense of reality; they will walk in a new dimension of power; and the Lord's people will register gains against the powers that oppose the gospel.*

(15) Praying for the Holy Spirit

Jesus taught his disciples that the Father would give the Holy Spirit *in response to prayer* (Lk. 11:13). The outpouring of the Spirit on the day of Pentecost, and elsewhere in the book of Acts, took place in the context of prayer (Acts 1:14; 2:1, 42; 4:29-31; 7:55, 59; 8:15-17; 19:6).

Kilian McDonnell, a leading Roman Catholic authority on the Charismatic renewal, has observed that, seen from the outside, the renewal could almost be taken for a prayer movement. Especially in the movement's early years, the prayer meeting was the major gathering place for the nurture and spread of the renewal. Over and over, the pattern was repeated: a handful of people would decide to gather for prayer, and the word would get around. Soon, people would be coming from miles away to study the Bible together, hear a speaker, and pray. Prayer groups sprang up all over. In metropolitan areas, one could find prayer groups to visit almost any time of day, every day of the week. It was a springtime of prayer, Bible study, testimony, and personal experience of the Holy Spirit. Some of the prayer groups continued only for a few months or years; others are still going.

Here, we come very close to the practical centre of the working of the Holy Spirit, vividly described in the New Testament and fulfilling the promise of Christ himself. Prayer is the activity *par excellence* that bridges the gap between an intellectual belief system and a living faith. *In prayer, we move from talking about God to talking to God.* When prayer ceases to be a ritual formality and becomes a genuine encounter with God, then the central focus of life begins to shift away from self and back to God. *The Holy Spirit equips believers to demonstrate a life that proceeds in every regard from a radical dependence on God; and for that, prayer is indispensable.*

Prayer and Laying on of Hands

There are many forms of prayer. One of them is *intercessory prayer*; believers praying to God for others. Intercession may take place together with *laying on of hands.* In the book of Acts, the Holy Spirit is sometimes given through the laying on of hands (Acts 9:17; 19:6); or, to state it negatively, the Spirit is not given until hands have been laid on (Acts 8:17). In these cases, it functioned as part of Christian initiation, performed in close relationship to baptism.

Laying on of hands is also used in other contexts: in the healing of the sick (Mt. 9:18; Mk 6:5; Acts 9:12; 28:8), in the blessing of children (Mt. 19:13-15), in dedicating people to special ministries of diakonia and mission (Acts 6:6; 13:3). Charisms also were given through laying on of hands (1 Tim. 4:14;

2 Tim. 1:6). Only in one place, however, is a *promise* directly tied to laying on of hands: "They will place their hands on sick people, and they will get well" (Mk 16:18).

There are no promises that the gift of the Holy Spirit will be granted, or granted exclusively, through the laying on of hands. The promise of the gift of the Spirit, as we have seen, is linked quite simply to becoming a Christian.

Jesus did, however, *promise the Spirit to those who pray* (Lk. 11:13). This is the essential significance of the laying on of hands. It is a form of prayer, and, as such, it is of great significance. God's promises are tied to prayer. Prayer is faith in action: it reaches out for what is promised. In this sense, the laying on of hands is an act of faith. It should be seen in the light of passages like Matthew 18:19-20: "I tell you that if two of you on earth agree about anything you ask for, it will be done for you by my Father in heaven. For where two or three come together in my name, there am I with them."

We cannot exclude the possibility that the act of laying on of hands serves as a channel for God's power, but we cannot tie God to this act. There are cases in which God grants his Holy Spirit without laying on hands (Acts 2:4; 10:44). However, according to the biblical testimony, laying on of hands seems to be used quite regularly in connection with Christian initiation, with dedication of individual Christians for special ministries, and with healing. Being filled with the Spirit and manifesting the gifts of the Spirit are sometimes associated with this action. It may therefore be used with expectation as a form of earnest prayer. *Through laying on of hands fellow Christians pray concretely and personally that a particular individual may receive the gifts that God wants to grant in a particular situation.*

Somewhat akin to the laying on of hands would be the practice of *anointing with oil*. In Eastern Orthodox churches in connection with baptism, as well as in Roman Catholic confirmation, this is done, as we have already seen, with reference to the biblical concept of being "sealed" with the Holy Spirit (2 Cor. 1:22; Eph. 1:13).[1] The use of oil in connection with prayers for healing, based on James 5:14, is found in both ancient and contemporary

---

[1] Anointing with oil and/or laying on of hands of those who receive Christian initiation, as they emerge from the baptismal waters, was a practice included in almost all the liturgies of initiation in the ancient church, and has continued in various forms until today, especially in the Orthodox and Catholic traditions. In most Protestant churches, the laying on of hands is practiced when people are baptised. The early church knew therefore *two outward actions* combined with the prayer for the coming of the Holy Spirit: laying on of hands and anointing with oil. See, for example, "The Apostolic Tradition of St Hippolytus", in C. Whitaker, *Documents of the Baptismal Liturgy* (London: SPCK, 1977), pp. 13-19; Jungkuntz, *Confirmation and the Charismata*, pp. 22-23, and Montague and McDonnell, *Christian Initiation and Baptism in the Holy Spirit*, pp. 33-39, 238. It should also be noted that, in most mainline churches, a prayer for a coming of the Holy Spirit takes place in connection with the Lord's Supper, the so-called *Epiclesis*.

liturgies of the church. In the Charismatic renewal, it is also a practice that frequently is followed in more informal prayers for healing or blessing.

Paradoxically, radical dependence on the Holy Spirit goes hand in hand with a high regard for such external means as the laying on of hands or anointing with oil. Believers are also anointed by the Spirit in a metaphorical sense, "you have no need that any one should teach you; as his anointing teaches you about everything" (1 Jn 2:27). Nevertheless, they are told to "teach and admonish one another in all wisdom" (Col. 3:16); and elders who labour in preaching and teaching are considered worthy of double honour (1 Tim. 5:17).

There is, however, no biblical basis for a doctrine about a special anointing given to certain preachers that elevate them above ordinary believers or grant them immunity against being tested by the community based on Scripture and sound doctrine. Even the Spirit-filled apostles were rightly tested on the Scriptures (cf. Acts 17:11, also 1 Thess. 5:21).

Lest we become spiritually self-sufficient, or fail to recognise the significance of the body of Christ – or when faith needs special encouragement – the Holy Spirit may call us to humble ourselves and receive his guidance, wisdom, power and gifts through such special ministrations as the prayers of fellow believers, including the laying on of hands or anointing with oil.

(16) Manifestations of the Holy Spirit and Their Meaning for Mission

According to the book of Acts, the *coming of the Holy Spirit was tangible*. In writing a report of these early days in the church, Luke observed that the working of the Holy Spirit apparently did not include any coming so quiet and unobserved that one would not know whether he had come or not. If new believers did not experience a manifest outpouring, the Holy Spirit took further initiatives to correct the matter.

This is a point at which the Holy Spirit may help us avoid unprofitable arguments about who "has" the Holy Spirit. When the apostles heard that people in Samaria had accepted the Word of God (Acts 8:14), they made a practical observation: "The Holy Spirit had not yet come upon any of them" (Acts 8:16). There had been no manifestations of the Spirit, although this normally happened when the Holy Spirit came on new believers.

What the apostles did, and how Luke reported it, is best understood in relation to the issue of the Holy Spirit's working in this particular situation: they "placed their hands on them, and they received the Holy Spirit" (Acts 8:17). The new believers needed to receive the Holy Spirit – and the apostles needed to see that they had received him – in this demonstrable sense, and therefore the apostles took steps to bring it about. If the Holy Spirit calls for manifest demonstrations of his presence, then we need to talk about "receiving" him in this specific sense with the simplicity and directness that Scripture itself employs. The doctrine of having or receiving the Holy Spirit in terms of salvation or new life is important in itself, but *if it is used to deny or diminish the need for a demonstrable presence of the Holy Spirit, it could hinder the working of the Holy Spirit.*

Pentecostals and charismatics have been faulted for making too much of spiritual gifts, especially the gift of tongues. If an emphasis on particular manifestations of the Spirit is implicitly linked to the issue of salvation or to one's status as a believer, the criticism is needed and helpful. But if the working of the Holy Spirit in empowering and endowing believers for a fruitful Christian life and ministry is the point at issue, then an emphasis on manifestations of the Spirit is probably long overdue. Pentecostals and charismatics are bearing a clear, even a stern, communique: "Do not neglect the gifts! God has provided them for a purpose. Learn about them, pray for them, use them". Manifestations of the Holy Spirit are not accidental or optional. *They are equipment that every Christian is expected to receive and use – an integral part of the working of the Holy Spirit for advancing the cause of Christ* (1 Cor. 12:7).

Spirit-empowered Life and Ministry

The outpourings of the Spirit in Acts focus on the Holy Spirit as an endowment for Christian life and ministry, granted to Christians as a gift. It is the manifest demonstration of the Spirit, which is primarily in view, rather than his work of bringing people to salvation. The strong *missional emphasis of the whole book of Acts* (cf. Acts 1:8) brings to special focus the Holy Spirit's work of empowering believers for ministry.

One sees this clearly in the story of Philip and the Ethiopian eunuch (Acts 8:26-39). The Holy Spirit's working is not mentioned in direct connection with the eunuch's conversion. It is simply recorded that the eunuch requests baptism; some manuscripts include also his profession of faith. The references to the Holy Spirit do not focus on his working with the eunuch (although we may assume that he did that too), but rather on his charismatic manifestations in Philip: the Spirit gives *specific guidance* that brings Philip in contact with the eunuch, and when the task is accomplished he supernaturally takes Philip away (vv. 29, 39).

It is the special concern of Acts to present the Holy Spirit as the one who is poured out on believers to empower them for their missional task. The connection between the gift of the Spirit and power to carry out the mission of the church as witnesses to Christ to the ends of the earth is made explicit when Jesus said, "You will receive power when the Holy Spirit comes on you: and you will be my witnesses in Jerusalem, and in all of Judea and Samaria, and to the ends of the earth" (Acts 1:8).

When Acts speaks of "receiving the Holy Spirit", "being baptised with the Holy Spirit", "being filled with the Holy Spirit", "being full of the Holy Spirit", and "receiving the gift of the Holy Spirit", the primary issue being addressed is not that of salvation, but of empowerment for Christian life and ministry. This is seen most clearly in the descriptions of the life of Spirit-filled Christian community (Acts 2:42-47; 4:32-35) and the mission of the church through Spirit-filled apostles, deacons, evangelists, elders, and ordinary Christians. We enumerate here some of the great number of instances in Acts of this connection between, on the one hand, the fullness of the Holy Spirit, his power and guidance, and, on the other, the ministry of mission, inspired speech and church leadership, with regard to apostles (Acts 4:8, 29-31); deacons (6:3-6); Stephen (6:8; 7:55-56); Philip (8:4-8, 29); the church (9:31); Paul (9:17-20; 13:2-4, 9; 14:3; 16:6; 20:22-23; 28:31); Peter (10:19-20; 11:12); Gentile believers (10:44-46); Barnabas (11:23-24; 13:2-4; 14:3); Ephesian believers (19:6); elders (20:28), and the prophet Agabus (21:10-11).

The Witness of the Pauline Epistles

An important question at this point is whether the way that Acts presents the coming of the Spirit and his manifestations finds confirming evidence in the Pauline epistles.

Do letters such as Galatians and Romans, the rich soil out of which the Reformation experience grew, provide corroborating or contradictory material?

Galatians 3:1-5 provides helpful insight into Paul's teaching and ministry concerning Christian initiation and the Spirit as gift. In the verses immediately preceding (2:15-21), Paul revealed his self-understanding as a Christian and what conversion meant in his own experience. Contrary to the assertions of the Jewish legalists, who argued that one had to observe the Mosaic law to be saved, Paul knew that justification comes through faith in Christ by grace. By the work of the indwelling Holy Spirit (Gal. 5:18; cf. Rom. 8:9-10), Paul experienced an altogether new kind of existence: "I have been crucified with Christ and I no longer live, but *Christ lives in me*" (Gal. 2:20). Therefore, he realised that he was a new creation before God and had a new life, even though this reality was "hidden with Christ in God" (Col. 3:3).

Paul went on to develop his argument for justification by faith: it was through hearing and believing the gospel that they had experienced a specific, clear, and undeniable change. What is interesting to note, however, is that he pointed to the gift of the Holy Spirit, coming in power to the Galatian Christians, replete with miracles, as a confirmation of his argument for justification by faith against living by the law:[1]

> You foolish Galatians! Who has bewitched you? Before your very eyes, Jesus Christ was clearly portrayed as crucified. I would like to learn just one thing from you: Did you *receive the Spirit* by observing the law, or *by believing what you heard*? Are you so foolish? After beginning with the Spirit, are you now trying to attain your goal by human effort? Have you suffered so much for nothing – if it really was for nothing? Does God *give you his Spirit* and *work miracles* among you because you observe the law, or *because you believe what you heard*? (Gal. 3:1-5, italics added).

Historically, Paul's argument for justification has won the day. Justification by faith is the secure foundation stone of the Reformation heritage. The way that Paul built his case, however, reveals an understanding of the Holy Spirit similar to what we find in Acts. He pointed to manifest demonstrations of the Spirit – coming not through observing the law, but in response to faith in the gospel message they had heard – as confirming evidence for the doctrine of justification by faith. The experience of being

---

[1] Hans Dieter Betz, *Galatians*. Hermeneia – A Critical and Historical Commentary on the Bible (Philadelphia, PA: Fortress, 1979.

empowered by the Spirit, including miraculous manifestations, provided an instructive parallel for understanding justification. It happens in exactly the same way: through hearing and believing, by grace, not works of the law (Gal. 2:21).

Any attempt to set an objective doctrine of justification against a subjective experience of the Spirit as gift and power would be unthinkable for the apostle Paul. For him, the experience of the Holy Spirit, received by faith, was a confirmation of the preaching of the cross. Furthermore, the gift of the Holy Spirit is absolutely necessary to live out the new existence as Christians (Gal. 5:16-18).

The parallelism of Galatians 3:8 and 3:14 is also telling: the blessing of the nations that was promised through Abraham is exactly the justification by faith that brings with it the gift of the Holy Spirit. The coin on which is stamped justification by faith has on its other side the gift of the Holy Spirit.

In 1 Corinthians 12-14, Paul confirms and explains that manifestations of the Spirit are given to each believer for the common good (1 Cor. 12:7), and then goes on to enumerate several of the gifts, services and workings of the Spirit, "the spiritual gifts" (1 Cor. 12:1, 4-11, cp. Rom. 12:6-8; Eph. 4:7, 11-13). Among these gifts are some of the same manifestations of the Spirit as those we read about in Acts, including healing, speaking in tongues and prophecy. *Paul teaches that the basis for the many and various gifts granted by the Spirit, the charismata, is the one gift of the Spirit himself, the baptism with the Spirit* (1 Cor. 12:12-13).

He tells the Christians in Rome, whom he had not yet seen, about his own apostolic mission and how Christ had worked through him in "leading Gentiles to obey God" (that is, the obedience of *faith*, cp. Rom. 10:10-15)). This he has done in *word* (Greek: *logos*) and *deed* (Greek: *ergon*), "by the power of signs and miracles, through the power of the Spirit" (Rom. 15:17-19, cp. 2 Cor. 12:12*). Manifestations of the Holy Spirit were part and parcel of his apostolic ministry as they were in the churches.*

There is full correspondence between the witness of Acts and the witness of the Pauline epistles regarding the manifestations of the Spirit in the life and mission of the church.

(17) The Fullness of the Holy Spirit

In the New Testament, believers in a variety of situations are *described* as being "filled with the Holy Spirit". Believers are also *exhorted* to be filled with the Spirit (Eph. 5:18). The will of the Holy Spirit calls for Spirit-filled believers.

"Filled" is essentially a quantitative concept. The exhortation to be filled makes sense only if the one spoken to is less than full. Here, we see clearly that the work of the Spirit is dynamic, rather than static. It does not focus primarily on what we are. In a sense that is taken for granted, a given: we are disciples of Christ. The Holy Spirit looks rather to where we are going and how we are to get there. When that comes into focus, the coming of the Spirit will be an expectation of what is yet to be.

Life in the Holy Spirit

The new life is characterised by the fulfilment of the law of God (Rom. 8:4). Power for ethical living comes through the Spirit's indwelling. The believers experience the power of the Holy Spirit, giving both a new desire and a new ability to live according to the will of God (Phil. 2:13). Those who are indwelt by the Spirit are enabled to go on to lead lives of active holiness and effective ministry (1 Cor. 6:11; 1 Thess. 4:3-8; 2 Cor. 3:3-6).

Since the Spirit is the Spirit of Jesus, the Holy Spirit by his indwelling conforms the Christian to the image of Christ. Conformity to Christ is the goal of the transforming work of the Holy Spirit (2 Cor. 3:17-18; Rom. 8:29).

The Holy Spirit, however, does not change the lives of Christians into holiness and conformity to Christ against their own wills. Believers must respond to the Spirit, and are encouraged and exhorted to do so. As they do this, Christ communicates his heart and will so that they may fulfil the commandments of God (Phil. 2:13; Rom. 8:4; 12:1-2). This does not mean that Christians are perfect or sinless. They are keenly aware of their own weakness and sinfulness (2 Cor. 4:7; 12:7-10; Rom. 7:18). They are involved in a deep conflict between the old sinful nature (the flesh, Greek: *sarx*) and the Spirit. According to the flesh, they are sinners, yet according to the Spirit, they are a new and righteous creation (Rom. 7:13-25; Gal. 5:16-18; 2 Cor. 5:17).

Christians are called to side with the Spirit and live accordingly: "Live by the Spirit, and you will not gratify the desires of the sinful nature [...] Since we live by the Spirit, let us also walk by the Spirit" (Gal. 5:16, 25; see also Rom. 8:2-4, 12-14). *Christians are called to become, by the power of the Spirit, in actual life what they already are in Christ.*

The Fruit of the Holy Spirit

The expression "fruit of the Spirit" can be seen as a comprehensive metaphor for how the gift and indwelling of the Holy Spirit affects the believer's relationships both to God and to other people:

> But the fruit of the Spirit is love, joy, peace, patience, kindness, goodness, faithfulness, gentleness and self-control. Against such things, there is no law (Gal. 5:22).

First and foremost, among the fruit is *love* (Greek: *agape*). Love is a divine gift that comes along with the reception of the Holy Spirit: it is "poured out into our hearts by the Holy Spirit, whom he has given us" (Rom. 5:5). Both in terms of living our personal Christian life and in carrying out our spiritual ministry, love is seen as the highest expression of the Holy Spirit's work in a believer, the "most excellent way", without which we are or gain nothing (1 Cor. 12:31; 13:1-13). Christian love is not determined by the lovability or likability of the person being loved; it comes from the inside of the person who loves, as a divine miracle. It extends even to persecutors and enemies (Mt. 5:43-47; Rom. 12:14), and it involves practical acts of love (Rom. 12:20). Love is to be sought by Christians above all else and is the necessary foundation for the exercise of all the spiritual gifts (1 Cor. 12:31; 13:1-3, 13; 14:1).

This love is united with *joy* (Greek: *chara*) and *peace* (Greek: *eirene*). Although these concepts do have a psychological dimension, they should not be limited to expressing merely emotional experiences. Deep joy may exist in the midst of sorrow and afflictions (2 Cor. 6: 10; Col. 1:24; 1 Thess. 1:6). It is a quality of existence in the kingdom of God. So also is the peace of God: "For the kingdom of God is not a matter of eating or drinking, but of righteousness, peace and joy in the Holy Spirit" (Rom. 14:17). Joy and peace are the realities of salvation appropriated by faith, and made into real experience by the Holy Spirit.

Reconciliation with God by faith through Christ brings about peace with God and with other people: "Since we have been justified through faith, we have peace with God through our Lord Jesus Christ" (Rom 5:1). "He himself (Christ) is our peace, who has made the two (believing Jews and Gentiles) one and has destroyed the barrier, the dividing wall of hostility" (Eph. 2:14). "He came and preached peace to you who were far away and peace to those who were near. For through him we both have access to the Father by the Spirit" (Eph. 2:17-18).

Joy and peace are a foretaste of the salvation to come, granting an *assured hope of salvation*: "May the God of hope fill you with all joy and peace in believing, so that by the power of the Holy Spirit you may abound in hope!" (Rom. 15:13).

The other fruits of the Holy Spirit mentioned in Galatians 5:22, “patience, kindness, goodness, faithfulness, gentleness and self-control” are virtues and attitudes that are created by the indwelling Spirit and practical results of love, joy and peace (1 Cor. 13:4-7).

The Relationship between the Gifts and the Fruit of the Holy Spirit

One frequent misunderstanding must be corrected: by overemphasising the metaphor of “fruit”, which in the natural world grows slowly, some have thought that the fruit of the Holy Spirit also is a result of slow growth. However, the fruit, or the result, of the fullness of the Holy Spirit may be *instantaneous, and be present in new believers as well as in old.* In Acts, there are several examples of the fruit of the Spirit – such as love, joy and peace – existing in and among new believers (Acts 2:44-46; 8:39; 13:52). Love is poured out *with the Holy Spirit* and should therefore *coexist* with the gifts of the Spirit. *Although empowerment by the Holy Spirit and sanctification by the Holy Spirit should be distinguished, they should not be separated.* They belong together. The fruit should determine and characterise how the gifts are used. Paul moves in 1 Corinthians 13, as he does in Romans 12, directly from the Spirit’s gifts to the Spirit’s fruit: “*Love* must be sincere [...] be devoted to one another in brotherly *love* [...] be *joyful* in hope, *patient* in affliction, *faithful* in prayer. Share with God’s people who are in need [...] If it is possible, as far as it depends on you, live at *peace* with everybody [...] Overcome evil with *good*” (Rom. 12:9-21, our italics).

Living in the Fullness of the Holy Spirit

We have already pointed out that the term “to be filled with the Spirit”" may denote either an initial, manifest reception of the Spirit or subsequent receptions of the Spirit in the lives of Christians.

Although all Christians are indwelt by the Spirit, there is a place in Christian life for new experiences of being filled with the Spirit. This may happen to individual Christians or to whole Christian communities. Some Christians may be characterised as “full of the Spirit”, in obvious contrast to others who are less subject to the influence of the Spirit in their lives and ministry.

The fullness of the Spirit may come about as the result of experiences in which the Spirit is poured out (Acts 4:8, 31; 13:9, 52). The relation between the Holy Spirit dwelling in believers and the Holy Spirit being poured out on believers may be explained by reference to the nature of the Holy Spirit himself. The Holy Spirit who indwells believers is a divine person, alive and active. He is never at our disposal, as if owned or controlled by us. His indwelling presence is effective only as we give ourselves ever anew to the

Spirit's leading (Rom. 8:13-14). The Spirit may be sinned against (Acts 5:3; 1 Thess. 4:8) and withdraw. There is no guarantee that Christians, who are the temple of the Spirit (1 Cor. 3:16; 6:19), will continue to live and serve in the Spirit. Therefore, Paul warned against grieving (Eph. 4:30) or quenching the Spirit (1 Thess. 5:19). He encouraged Christians to be filled with the Spirit (Eph. 5:18), take "the sword of the Spirit, which is the word of God" (Eph. 6:17), and "pray in the Spirit on all occasions with all kinds of prayer and requests" (Eph. 6:18).

According to the New Testament, the Christian life should be one of expectancy, openness, preparedness, and prayer for the repeated and continuous coming of the Holy Spirit (Lk. 11:13). *There are no significant differences in the testimony of the Scripture between the effects of the Spirit's first outpouring on a believer and his later comings. The term "filled with the Spirit" may be used in either case. The experiential reality is essentially the same.*

(18) Witnessing in Word and Deed in the Power of the Holy Spirit

As we have seen earlier, one strand of biblical testimony presents the *creative and life-giving activity* of the Holy Spirit; the Spirit is the divine *agent* who accomplishes God's work of creation and redemption. Another major strand presents the Holy Spirit as a divine *gift or endowment*, the one whom believers receive in an experiential and personal way. We have called this the *charismatic* work of the Holy Spirit. It is this charismatic endowment by the Holy Spirit that is primarily in view when we consider the Spirit's work of empowering the church for its mission. Luke is the principal New Testament spokesman in this regard, and he stands in a well-established Old Testament and gospel tradition.

Charismatic Endowment in the Old Testament

In the Old Testament, the charismatic Spirit came on select individuals for specific tasks of service among the people of God. These tasks included military, political, and religious leadership through powerful words and deeds. Outstanding leaders such as Moses, the seventy elders in Israel, the judges, and the kings Saul and David were all equipped for their tasks by possessing the Spirit of God (Num. 11:16-30; Dt. 34:9; Judg. 3:10; 6:34; 1 Sam. 10:5-7, 10-11; 16:13).

The reception of the Spirit was often sudden and unexpected, sometimes even violent and irresistible (for example, Num. 24:2; 1 Sam. 10:10). It was never merited, often contrary to human expectations or qualifications, and always a free gift.

The charismatic Spirit granted power and courage to carry out heroic feats and to perform miracles. Through the words and deeds of charismatically equipped leaders, the people were directly confronted with the power of God and liberated from their enemies.

The visible and tangible effects of the possession of the God's charismatic Spirit served as a divine confirmation of leadership and ministry among the people. The outward evidence of the presence of the Spirit could be prophecy, miracles, or even some form of trance. However, spirit possession in itself was no unambiguous proof of the presence of *God's Spirit.* Since there were also *other spirits and false prophecy*, the Spirit of God would be recognised on the basis of the *truth of the word spoken and the correspondence of the ministry of the prophet to the will of God revealed in the covenant* (Dt. 18:22; 1 Kings 22:21-25). This was the criterion according to which spiritual phenomena had to be judged. The claims of charismatic persons should be backed up by the genuineness of their message and the moral integrity of their life.

Closely related to the charismatic Spirit is the *prophetic* Spirit. In the prophets, the charismatic endowment with the Spirit of God served primarily their ministries of *proclaiming the Word of God with power*:

> But as for me, I am filled with *power*, with the *Spirit of the Lord*, and with justice and might, *to declare* to Jacob his transgression, to Israel his sin" (Mic. 3:8).

Powerful deeds also accompanied the ministries of the prophets and supported their prophetic calling (for example, 1 Kings 18:25-40).

In the Psalms and the Chronicles, the priests and the Levites are included among the charismatically equipped leadership, leading the congregation of Israel in *worship and praise* as well as *speaking the word of God to the people* (1 Chr. 25:1; 2 Chr. 20:14; 24:20). The priests in Israel had a *double function*: representing the people before God in sacrifice, prayer and praise and representing God before the people in proclaiming God's word and will. This is a ministry similar to the priesthood of all believers in the New Testament, with the exception of the task of offering sacrifice (1 Pet. 2:9; Rev. 1:6; Rom. 15:16). The sacrifice of our high priest Jesus Christ for the sins of the world happened once for all and makes all other sacrifices preliminary and superseded (Heb. 7:26-27; 10:19-22).

In Psalm 51, we read about King David, a man of God who had committed adultery, murder, and falsehood (2 Sam. 11-12), but who confessed his sins and asked forgiveness (Ps. 51:3-11). Following the re-establishment of a right relationship to God, he asked for a renewal of his human spirit: "Create in me a pure heart, O God, and renew a steadfast spirit within me" (v. 10). Then he prayed that he might remain in God's gracious presence and that the Holy Spirit might remain with him. The result of the Holy Spirit's sanctifying work in the penitent sinner's heart was a restoration of the joy of salvation, a willing spirit, and the desire to teach repentance and faith to other sinners (vv. 12-13). *Prayer for the Holy Spirit* thus had its place also in the lives of Old Testament believers, although the gift of the fullness of the Spirit was not yet given to all.

The Promise of a Future Outpouring of the Holy Spirit

The Spirit of God was never granted in the Old Testament as a gift to the people as a whole. It was limited to select individuals or groups. However, there was a *vision of a future, general outpouring of the Spirit on all the people of God.* The charismatic, prophetic Spirit, characterised by prophetic revelation in dreams and visions, would be poured out on all the people. They would have direct access to the Lord. He would put his words in their mouths, words of witness to the saving acts of God in history (Joel 2:28-29; Is. 59:21). God's blessing would rest on his people, resulting in ethical and religious transformation (Is. 44:3-5; 32:15-17). They would receive a new heart that would make them God's people and cause them to live according to his will (Ez. 36:26-28).

This general outpouring of the Spirit will be initiated and accompanied by the coming *Servant of the Lord* who will have the Spirit of God, bring justice to the nations and a time of salvation to the whole earth (Is. 42:1-4; 49:6: 61:1-2). In light of the prophetic Isaiah 52:13–53:12 graphically depicting the salvific work of the servant as he atones for the sins of the world by taking on himself the punishment for sins and dying in our place for us to have peace (v.5), healing (v.5) and justification (v.11), we understand that this servant is no other than our Lord Jesus Christ.

The Holy Spirit as it rests on Jesus Christ (Lk. 4:18-19) is also clearly an endowment with power for his ministry of proclaiming a time of salvation and his acts of mercy. Through his own ministry and that of his disciples, he will "bring justice to the nations" (Is. 42:1). It is an endowment for mission (Latin: *missio* = sending), since Christ is both himself sent by God and the sender of his disciples to the whole world (Jn 20:21; Acts 1:8).

The Holy Spirit Glorifies Jesus Christ and Gives New Life through Faith

The *Christocentric nature of the Holy Spirit's witness* is particularly noticeable in Jesus' farewell discourse: the Father would send the Spirit in response to the Son's prayer (Jn 14:16) and in his name (Jn 14:26), or the Son would send him from the Father (Jn 15:26; 16:7). *The Holy Spirit is sent by the Father and the Son.* The Holy Spirit carries the features of Jesus Christ, the incarnate Son of God. When believers experience the Holy Spirit, they encounter Jesus Christ. Therefore, the Holy Spirit represents the risen and exalted Jesus Christ on earth, both in relation to the church and to the world. He glorifies Jesus Christ by making the gospel about about Jesus' person, words, acts, death and resurrection convincing and convicting. "He will bring glory to me by taking what is mine and making it known to you" (Jn 16:14). "The Holy Spirit [...] will teach you all things and will remind you of everything I have said to you" (Jn 14:26).

The Holy Spirit will mediate salvation, granting *new birth* and life through *faith* in Jesus: "No-one can enter the kingdom of God unless he is born by water and the Spirit. Flesh gives birth to flesh, but the Spirit gives birth to spirit" (Jn 3:5-6). In his explanation to Nicodemus about this new birth, and how this salvation will come about, we find the famous saying of Jesus that summarises the whole gospel, "For God so loved the world that he gave his one and only Son, that whoever *believes in him* shall not perish but have *eternal life* (Jn 3:16). In his words to the disciples after his resurrection, Jesus connects the sending of the disciples and the reception of the Holy Spirit with *forgiveness of sins* (20:21-22). The Holy Spirit also makes believers into credible witnesses who glorify Christ through their life and ministry and by that bring forgiveness and salvation. "He (the Holy Spirit) will testify about me. And you also must testify (Jn 15:26-27, cp. 7:37:41).

The Holy Spirit as Witness, Teacher and Prophet

In Jesus' farewell discourse to his disciples, he called the Holy Spirit the Counsellor (Greek: *parakletos*). A "Paraclete" is someone called to help, an attorney, someone speaking on another's behalf in court, as a counsel for the defendant, or even as a prosecutor. The Spirit will be the counsellor of the disciples, speaking on behalf of the Father and Christ, both with regard to them and with regard to the world (Jn 14:15-17, 25- 26; 15:26-27; 16:5-15).

He is the *Spirit of truth* (Jn 14:17; 15:26; 16:13) who will reveal to the disciples and the church the things of Christ. It will not be a new revelation, but rather a revelation of Christ, who himself is the truth (Jn 14:6). *The Spirit will act as a witness, a teacher, and a prophet to them.*

As a *witness*, the Spirit is a witness to Christ: "But when the Counsellor comes [...] the Spirit of truth [...] he will testify about me; and you also must testify, for you have been with me from the beginning" (Jn 15:26-27). Concretely, the testimony of the Holy Spirit takes place in and through the testimony of the disciples. The content of the witness includes the historical facts of Jesus' earthly ministry, atoning death, and victorious resurrection; who Jesus was as the Messiah and Lord and the significance of his work for our redemption. It is always followed by an *exhortation to the listeners to believe in Jesus*. The testimony aims at showing that "God has given us eternal life, and this life is in his Son" (1 Jn 5:11). The testimony that the Holy Spirit gives the disciples is precisely this inner awareness of who Christ is and what he has done. Because he is the Son of God incarnate, his life, death and resurrection have saving significance. Through this testimony – as we have seen already – the Spirit brings about faith:

> It is the Spirit who testifies, because the Spirit is the truth. For there are three that testify: the Spirit, the water and the blood; and the three are in agreement. We accept man's testimony, but God's testimony is greater because it is the testimony of God, which he has given about his Son. Anybody who believes in the Son has this testimony in his heart [...] And this is the testimony: God has given us eternal life and this life is in his Son (1 Jn 5:7-11).

The *teaching* ministry of the Holy Spirit will enable the disciples to grasp the full significance of Jesus' own teaching: "But the Counsellor, the Holy

Spirit, whom the Father will send in my name, will *teach* you all things and will remind you of everything I have said to you" (Jn 14:26). He makes the words of Jesus clear, relevant, and personal.

The Holy Spirit also has a *prophetic* ministry. "But when he, the Spirit of truth, comes, he will guide you into all the truth. He will not speak on his own; he will speak only what he hears, and *he will tell you what is yet to come*" (Jn 16:13).

Looking back on the *writing of the New Testament*, we may say that Jesus' words about the Holy Spirit, the Counsellor, the Spirit of truth, was fulfilled in the ministries of those who wrote the New Testament, both in terms of testimony, teaching, and prophecy. The New Testament authors were aware of the work of the Spirit in their speaking and writing:

> We have not received the spirit of the world but the Spirit who is from God, that we may understand what God has freely given us. This is what we speak, not in words taught us by human wisdom but in words taught by the Spirit, expressing spiritual truth in spiritual words (1 Cor. 2:6-16, vv. 12-13, see also Rom. 8:16, 26).

The whole book of Revelation is a prophecy inspired by the Holy Spirit, and so are the words to the seven churches: "He who has an ear let him hear *what the Spirit says to the churches*. To him who overcomes, I will give the right to eat from the tree of life, which is in the paradise of God" (Rev. 2:7, see also Rev. 22:16-18).

The witnessing, teaching and prophesying work of the Holy Spirit did not cease, however, when the New Testament had been written, but continues through the history of the church. The Holy Spirit does not bring any new revelation but *illumines the already given Word of God and provides new insight in how it is to be understood, applied and practiced by the church in different contexts in a changing world.*

The Holy Spirit Convicts the World

Through the disciples' testimony, the Holy Spirit also *confronts the world.* The role of the Spirit in this respect is that of a prosecuting attorney. Jesus said of the Spirit's work towards the world:

> When he (the Counsellor) comes, he will convict the world of guilt in regard to sin and righteousness and judgement: in regard to sin, because men do not believe in me: in regard to righteousness, because I am going to the Father, where you can see me no longer; and in regard to judgement, because the prince of this world now stands condemned (Jn 16:8-11).

The Holy Spirit is not given to the world, but his role is to convict, showing the world its sin and calling it to repentance. The concept of conviction does not necessarily include the notion that the world actually turns to God. Some people do; others do not. The basic sin that the Spirit exposes is unbelief: the rejection of the gospel of Christ (see also Mt. 11:20-24). The righteousness that the Spirit testifies to is God's vindication and justification of Christ by raising him from the dead (see also Rom.1:4; 2 Tim. 3:16). The judgement is Jesus' defeat of Satan (see also Mt. 12:28-29; Col. 2:15; Lk. 10:18; Rom. 16:20).

The Holy Spirit Gives Power and Inspires Speech in Situations of Resistance and Persecution

The era of the church is the era of mission to the ends of the earth. As the Father sent the Son, the Son sent the disciples (Jn 20:21). The Holy Spirit was given in order to enable them to carry out their missionary task, to be witnesses for Christ (Jn 20:22; Lk. 24:47-49; Acts 1:4-5, 8; 5:32).

Wherever missionary proclamation of the gospel takes place, it also provokes *opposition and persecution.* The Holy Spirit gives strength to Christians both against inner temptations and demonic attacks (Luke 4:1-2, 13; 1 Cor. 10:13; Eph. 6:17-18). He also gives them power and inspires their words to help them resist and conquer external pressure, opposition, and persecution. In his eschatological discourses, Jesus said that Christians should expect suffering and persecution as they carried out their mission work. He encouraged them to trust in the presence and inspiration of the Spirit: "And the gospel must first be preached to all nations. Whenever you are arrested and brought to trial, do not worry beforehand about what to say. Just say whatever is given you at the time, for it is not you speaking, but the Holy Spirit" (Mk 13:10-11).

The fulfilment of this promise was often seen in the apostolic church. The apostles spoke with a *boldness* after Pentecost that was very different from their fear and timidity prior to Pentecost (Acts 4:12-13, 29-31; 28:31 compared to Mk 14:50; Mt. 26:69-75; Jn 20:19). They were filled with the Holy Spirit and spoke words that could strike the consciences of their hearers, silence their critics, provoke their persecutors, and judge their opponents (Acts 2:37; 4:8, 13-14; 7:54-60; 13:8-11; 26:19-20,28-32).

The same promise has been fulfilled in the lives of persecuted Christians and martyrs down through the history of the church, not least in the ancient church and in the last two centuries. As Christians are faithful to the missional calling of God, they must be prepared to face opposition and persecution but also depend on the power and inspiration of the Holy Spirit to meet suffering with boldness, humility and even love (Mt. 5:11, 44: Rom. 12:14; Jn 15:20; 1 Cor. 4:12; 2 Tim. 3:12). In the early church, martyrs were seen as possessing a special charism that gave added authority to their words.

The Proclamation of the Gospel in the Power of the Holy Spirit

It is inherent in the universal scope of the redemption wrought by Christ that the good news of this redemption be proclaimed to people everywhere. Because Christ died and rose to bring forgiveness of sins and righteousness to all, the *salvation message must be brought within reach of all.* The Holy Spirit gives believers power and boldness in proclaiming the gospel. He equips and empowers them in such a way that the gospel will be heard and believed in all the earth, and a people of God from all nations will be established (Mt. 28:18-20; Acts 15:14). Thus, the oral proclamation of the gospel carries with it the convincing and convicting power of the Spirit, although it may take different outward forms depending on the situation and the people to whom the message is directed – such as personal witness, public preaching, dialogical conversation, private counselling, intellectual debate, legal defence, biblical study, Bible distribution, Christian literature, etc.

Churches that are created by the gospel – preached by evangelists and missionaries in the power of the Holy Spirit – become themselves churches from which the gospel spreads out to other areas, as the new believers follow the example of the missionaries and are impelled by the gospel message itself and the Holy Spirit to share it with others. The church in Thessalonica may exemplify this. The apostle Paul writes to this church, which he had founded, in his first letter:

> Our gospel came to you not simply with words, but also with power, with the Holy Spirit and with deep conviction. You know how we lived among you for your sake. You became imitators of us and of the Lord; in spite of severe suffering you welcomed the message with the joy given by the Holy Spirit. And so you became a model to all the believers in Macedonia and Achaia. The Lord's message rang out from you not only in Macedonia and Achaia – your faith in God has become known everywhere (1 Thess. 1:5-8).

Surprisingly, the New Testament epistles do not contain many direct exhortations to Christians to engage in mission and evangelism. A reason for this is probably the fact that the obligation to witness for Christ and give a public account of one's faith were so deeply ingrained in the spirituality of the early Christians that it was not necessary to emphasise it. Still the apostle Peter encourages the believers,

> Always be prepared to give an answer to everyone who asks you to give the reason for the hope that you have. But do this with gentleness and respect, keeping a clear conscience, so that those who speak maliciously against your good behaviour in Christ may be ashamed of their slander (1 Pet. 3:15-16).

This is a main text justifying the need for *Christian apologetics* both on the intellectual and personal level, and for leading a life of "good behaviour in Christ".

The Witness of "Signs and Wonders" Performed in the Power of the Holy Spirit

A basic characteristic of the Holy Spirit both in the Old Testament and in the New Testament is that of divine power that makes possible inspired speech and miraculous deeds. From the day of Pentecost, the gift of the Spirit came with power. It is exactly in terms of this power that Jesus promised the coming of the Holy Spirit: "But you will receive power when the Holy Spirit comes on you; and you will be my witnesses in Jerusalem, and in all Judea and Samaria, and to the ends of the earth" (Acts 1:8; see also Lk. 24:49). In what ways is this witness expressed? We have already looked at the oral witness of the apostles and other believers, and the written witness in the New Testament and other writings. But does this witness also include various kinds of *works, actions and behaviours*? In the following, we will look at the witness of the Holy Spirit through the performance of "signs and wonders", both through the community of believers, the church, and through the life of individual Christians.

We will start with the witness of "signs and wonders". To elucidate the biblical material, we will begin with the ministry of Jesus. The most common form of wonders in the New Testament are healings and expulsion of evil spirits. At this point, we want to include an excerpt of an article written by Tormod Engelsviken about the role of "signs and wonders" in the mission of the church:[1]

> While the Great Commission in Matthew 28:18-20 does not explicitly mention deliverance or healing ministries as part of the mission of the apostles, this silence cannot be used as an argument for the view that there was a deliberate change in the apostles' task from the one they received from the earthly Jesus when he sent them out to the people of Israel, a task that included expulsion of evil spirits and healing (Mt. 10:1, 6-8).
>
> Luke emphasises the *preaching* of repentance and forgiveness to all nations and the *witness* of the apostles to the ends of the earth, without mentioning exorcism and healing (Lk. 24:47; Acts 1:8). His *narrative* of the mission of the early church in Acts, however, includes several accounts of healing and exorcism (e.g. Acts 3:1-10; 8:6-7; 14:8-18; 16:16-18). Sometimes these events are simply summarised as "wonders and signs" (Greek: *terata kai semeia,* Acts 2:43). The role of these in the mission of the apostles is succinctly expressed in Acts 14:3: "Paul and Barnabas spent considerable time there [at Iconium], speaking boldly for the Lord, who confirmed the message of his grace by enabling them to do miraculous signs and wonders". The term that is translated "confirmed" is the Greek *martyreo* which means "to give testimony" or "to witness". Here *God*

[1]Tormod Engelsviken, "Deliver Us From Evil: Evangelism, Spiritual Conflict, 'Signs and Wonders'", in Younghoon Lee and Wonsuk Ma (eds) *Pentecostal Mission & Global Christianity*, pp. 193-206. The text is slightly edited by the author.

himself gives corroborating evidence to the apostles' preaching of the Gospel by enabling them to perform signs and wonders. This is a most significant statement on how Luke values the role of signs and wonders for the mission of the church.[2]

The mission commission in John 20:21-22, "As the Father sent me, so I send you. Then he breathed on them and said, 'Receive the Holy Spirit'", has become very important in missiology over the last fifty years or so. There are at least two reasons for this:

Firstly, the text lays the basis for an understanding of mission as *God's mission*: the Father sends the Son, the Father and the Son send the Holy Spirit, and the Son sends the church with the Spirit to the world.[3] The nature and identity of the church as being sent to the world by the Triune God as a witness to the Gospel is central in recent missiology, not least in the "missional church" movement.

Secondly, there is a *holistic* understanding of mission that is based on Jesus and his earthly ministry as a model or pattern for mission. The "as" in John 20:21 is not only understood as a reference to the fact *that* the church is sent by Jesus, but also as a reference to *how* and for *what purpose* the church is being sent. Just as Jesus' ministry included a ministry of the *word* in preaching and teaching the gospel of the kingdom of God, it also included a ministry in *deed*, a demonstration of the character and power of the kingdom seen in his healings, expulsion of evil spirits, caring for the needs of the hungry, recognising and raising up the downtrodden and despised, such as poor people, leprosy sufferers, publicans, sex workers and Samaritans. The programme of Jesus according to Luke 4:18-19 was to preach the good news of God's salvation in the power of the Spirit, which meant liberty for captives, recovery of sight for the blind, and freedom from oppression. Whether these words are taken mainly metaphorically or literally, they still indicate the comprehensiveness of Jesus' mission in meeting the needs of people…

If we accept this comprehensive nature of the church's missionary task, it is the more surprising that the ministry of Jesus as healer and exorcist so often is ignored or denied as a model for the church's ministry today. Especially in the theology of western post-Enlightenment Protestantism, both in its more conservative and liberal forms, it seems to have caused some embarrassment that Jesus in the gospels is portrayed as a miracle worker, and that this was

---

[2] The secondary ending of Mark 16:9-20 places great emphasis on the signs that will accompany the believers, including exorcism and healing of the sick through laying on of hands (Mk 16:17-18). Although this was not originally written by the author of Mark's gospel, it nevertheless may faithfully reflect the view and experience of the early church.

[3] To various understandings of the concept of God's mission or *Missio Dei,* see Tormod Engelsviken, "Missio Dei: the Understanding and Misunderstanding of a Theological Concept in European Churches and Missiology". *International Review of Mission,* 92(367), (2003), pp. 481-497.

central to his ministry and even to his proclamation of the coming of God's kingdom.

The *kingdom of God* (Greek: *basileia tou theou*) is a comprehensive expression for everything that God's redemption includes. The church is the *people of the kingdom* who believe in, follow, serve and proclaim Jesus Christ as Saviour and Lord... The kingdom has *already* arrived with Jesus (Mk 1:14), but it is *not yet* fulfilled. This "already" and "not yet" distinction is important because it raises the question about which of the gifts of salvation have already been given and may be experienced here and now, and which are still future and will not be realised until the return of Christ and the redemption of God's creation. Among the gifts that are given *in the present* to those who enter the kingdom of God through *faith in Jesus* are forgiveness of sins, a new and right relationship with God our father and Jesus the Messiah, freedom from Satan's power, a fellowship of believers (Greek: *koinonia*), eternal life, the gift of the Holy Spirit, righteousness, peace and joy (Rom. 14:17).

In the gospels, healings and exorcisms are signs (Greek: singular *semeion,* plural: *semeia*). It is especially in John's Gospel that we find the term "sign" frequently used about Jesus' miracles (e.g. Jn 2:11; 20:30). It may also be used in a negative sense when people *demand* signs in order to believe (Mt. 12:38-39). The signs have various meanings. We may discern at least *four dimensions*: A Christological, an eschatological, a diaconal and a missiological.

The *Christological* dimension points to *who Jesus is*. Jesus did, in fact, refer to the miracles and his preaching of the gospel when asked who he was (Mt. 11:4-6). There is an ongoing debate, prompted by some charismatic teachers, whether Jesus did his miracles as a human being anointed with the Spirit or in his capacity as the Son of God. The Gospels and Acts present Jesus both as endowed with the Spirit and doing his mighty deeds by the power of the Spirit (e.g. Lk. 4:14, 18; Mt. 12:28; Acts 10:38). Yet, there is something *unique* about Jesus' ministry. His healings and exorcisms were performed through his word and *on his own authority* without invoking any other power. The disciples, however, both in the Gospels and Acts healed and expelled evil spirits *in the name of Jesus*, which implies that it was *Jesus*, not the disciples, who actually healed and expelled the spirits. After Pentecost, it was God or the risen and ascended Christ who performed the signs and wonders through the ministry of the disciples. The earthly Jesus had the *authority as God both to forgive sins and to heal diseases* (Mk 2:6-12). We also notice that Jesus is never said to have faith in God, while the disciples are encouraged to believe in God and in Jesus (Mt. 17:19-20; Jn 13:14). There is therefore a fundamental difference between the healings and exorcisms done by the earthly Jesus and those done by the disciples in the name of Jesus, although both Jesus and the disciples were empowered by the Holy Spirit for their ministries.

The *eschatological* dimension is primarily expressed by the fact that the mighty deeds were *signs of the coming of the kingdom of God.* We have mentioned above that the kingdom had *already* arrived with the coming of Jesus and his message of repentance and faith in the Gospel (Mk 1:14; 4:17). Further evidence of the kingdom is the expulsion of evil spirits from people who are possessed: "If I cast out evil spirits by the Spirit of God, then the kingdom of God has come to you" (Mt. 12:28; Lk. 11:20). The defeat of Satan and the liberation of those who were possessed or oppressed by him or his demons were one of the central features of Jesus' earthly ministry. Together with the healing ministry, they represent a foretaste or anticipation of the kingdom that will come in power at the end of time. Then the devil and his evil powers will be finally defeated and all disease will be gone forever through the resurrection of the body to eternal life.

There is, however, a *basic difference between the healings and the exorcisms.* In the healings, there are two persons involved, Jesus and the sick person; and Jesus speaks words of comfort and encouragement to the sick person, who is then healed. In the exorcisms, however, there are three subjects involved: Jesus, the possessed and the demon(s). It is the demon(s) that is spoken to and driven out by a strict command from Jesus, while the possessed person is fully restored to life. The expulsions demonstrate that the kingdom of Satan loses its power in the encounter with Jesus and kingdom of God, and that those who have been bound by Satan are set free (Mt. 12:24-29).

Especially significant is what we have called the *diaconal* dimension. The wonders and the exorcisms are motivated by *Jesus' love and compassion for people who suffer or have deep needs*, whether they are sick, marginalised or possessed by evil spirits (e.g. Mt. 20:34). Matthew 9:36 portrays Jesus as being "moved with compassion" for "sheep without a shepherd". This attitude of love and compassion has correctly been used as a foundation for the church's diaconal ministry, yet it should be pointed out that it is Jesus' (and the apostles') preaching of the gospel and miraculous healing ministry which constitute the context of Matthew 9:36 (Mt. 9:35-10:1).

Finally, the miracles of Jesus *presuppose faith or imply* a *call to faith.* This is the *missiological* dimension. This faith may be that of the suffering person, the faith of others, or, in the case of the disciples, of those who perform the miracle. Faith, on the part of the suffering person, is not demanded, neither is it seen as a prerequisite for healing. Nevertheless, Jesus encourages people to believe, and performs some of his miracles in response to faith. *It is not the strength of the person's faith but its direction towards Jesus that is decisive.* In the story of the boy with an evil spirit (Mk 9:17-29), Jesus rebuked the lack of faith (v. 19). When the father of the boy asked for Jesus' help, Jesus answered that "everything is possible for the person who has faith" (v. 23). The father confessed his lack of faith: "I believe, help my unbelief" (v. 24), yet Jesus threw out the evil spirit and healed the boy. The story ends with Jesus' word about the need for prayer in the ministry of exorcism (v. 29).

The wonders of Jesus may also lead to *praise of God and faith in Jesus*, both among those who are helped and those who witness the healing or the exorcism (Mt. 9:8; 15:30-31; Jn 2:23; 4:53) This is one of the purposes of Jesus' miracles (Jn 20:31). There are, however, also texts that warn against demanding signs, or making faith dependent on them (see e.g. Mt. 12:38-39; Jn 4:48; 20:29).

We have looked at some central features of Jesus' earthly ministry that may be carried forward by the church as it emulates the ministry of Jesus, according to

Jesus' word in John 20:21. In the early church as described in Acts, the healing and exorcism ministry of Jesus is continued by the apostles and other Christians in the Jesus' name and with some of the same dimensions as in Jesus' own ministry – particularly the Christological, diaconal and missiological dimensions. There are general references to "signs and wonders" (Acts 2:43; 4:30; 5:12; 8:6-7; 14:3) and specific references to healing (Acts 3:6-8, 16; 4:14, 16; 5:15-16; 8:7: 9:34-42; 19:12; 28:8-9) and deliverance from evil spirits (Acts 5:16; 8:7; 16:16-18; 19:12). The high number of references to these signs and wonders show the importance that Luke attributes to them in the early mission of the church.

A *warning* is, however, needed here since the *healings in themselves are not unambiguous signs.* The story of Paul and Barnabas' healing of a lame man in Lystra (Acts 14:8-18) shows that Christian healing without the accompanying word may be interpreted within the religious worldview of the observers. In this case, Paul and Barnabas were seen as Greek gods rather than representatives of the living God (vv. 11-12, 15). The lesson to be drawn from this incident is that the *preaching of the Gospel and the healing ministry should always go together.*

The significance of signs and wonders is also corroborated by Paul himself in his epistles. Paul could refer to the experience of the churches in Galatia (Gal. 3:5) and Corinth (1 Cor. 2:4; 12:9-10). When Paul in Romans 15:15-21 presents his missionary programme and method, he includes "signs and wonders":

> I will not venture to speak of anything except what Christ has accomplished through me in leading the Gentiles to obey God by *what I have said and done* – by the *power of signs and miracles*, through the *power of the Spirit* (vv.18-19).

It is common in current missiology to speak of mission in word and deed,[4] and rightly so. It should be noted, however, that the deeds that Paul refers to here are not the more common diaconal ministry but the signs and wonders that are a result of the Spirit's power that accompanies Paul's preaching of the Gospel. When this text is used correctly as an argument for *holistic ministry*, it should not be forgotten that *it includes "signs and wonders" and the "power of the Spirit".*

In 1 Corinthians 12:9, Paul includes gifts of healing by the Spirit among the charisms that are in operation in the church. In the introductory statement in 12:4-5, the gifts are called charisms and services (Greek: *diakonia* = service). The Greek term *diakonia* may be used for any kind of service, yet it is significant that all the gifts that are mentioned in 1 Corinthians 12:6-11 are called "services". They are supposed to be permanent features of the ministry of the church in the power of the Holy Spirit.[5]

---

[4] See e.g. Michael W. Goheen, *Introducing Christian Mission Today* (Downers Grove, IL: IVP Academic, 2014), pp. 227-263.

[5] Cp. the list of charisms in Romans 12:6-8 which includes a charism called *diakonia* (v. 6).

The New Testament text which has most influenced the church's *practice* of healing is found in James 5:14-16 which describes a simple rite of anointing and prayer:

> Is one of you ill? Let him send for the elders of the church to pray over him and anoint him with oil in the name of the Lord; the prayer offered in faith will heal the sick man, the Lord will restore him to health and if he has committed sins they will be forgiven. Therefore, confess your sins to one another, and pray for one another, that you may be healed (James 5:14-16).

This text is the foundation for the Catholic and Orthodox sacrament of anointing of the sick, and it has also been widely used in Protestant churches in connection with a healing ministry. This is the closest that we come to an institutional form of healing ministry in the New Testament. It does not, however, exclude more spontaneous and individual forms of healing with or without anointing or the laying on of hands.

Overcoming the Enemy in the Power of the Holy Spirit

In addition to the four dimensions of Jesus; healing ministry, we will add a fifth that specifically pertains to the *expulsion of evil spirits*. As we saw above, this ministry involved a third party, namely the evil spirit(s). Jesus' relation to the evil spirits (not to the possessed or demonised!) is one of enmity and judgement. We can speak of an *antagonistic or conflict dimension* in this ministry. Jesus did not want any testimony from the demons, even though they knew that he was the Son of God before anybody else did (e.g. Mk 1:23-26; Mt. 8:29). He drives them out with an authoritative word of command, and the possessed persons are completely restored to normalcy. This action demonstrates that Jesus is stronger than Satan and therefore can free those who are kept in bondage by Satan and his demons (Mt. 12:28-29). Jesus' explanation of his exorcisms makes it impossible to reduce spirit possession to a form of mental disease. There are real demonic powers involved.

In the history of mission, one has spoken of *power encounters* when Christian missionaries are challenged by evil forces. There are some examples of such encounters in Acts, where the Holy Spirit and Satan are opposed to each other, and Satan or evil acts or thoughts are judged in a dramatic way (Acts 5:1-11; 8:18-24; 13:6-11). Many more examples from mission history in many parts of the world might be added.

Exorcisms and power encounters may lead to fear (Mk 5:15; Mt. 9:34; Acts 5:11; 8:24), joy (Acts 8:8), or faith in Jesus as people witness his liberating power (Acts 13:12; 19:11-20).

The strategy of the Holy Spirit is indeed devised with a view to a spiritual opponent:

> Finally, be strong in the Lord and in his mighty power. Put on the full armour of God so that you can take your stand against the devil's schemes. For our struggle is not against flesh and blood, but against the rulers, against the authorities, against the powers of this dark world and against the spiritual forces of evil in the heavenly realms (Eph. 6:10-12).

The kingdom of God opposes the kingdom of Satan (Acts 26:18; Col. 1:13). The Holy Spirit's strategy unites us with Christ and with one another; it fills us with the Holy Spirit, so that together we may move forward in the cause of Christ. "Take the helmet of salvation and the sword of the Spirit, which is the word of God. And pray in the Spirit on all occasions with all kinds of prayers and requests" (Eph. 6:17-18).

The Guidance of the Holy Spirit in Mission

The wonders and signs that were performed by the apostles and others contributed significantly to the *growth of the early church* (Acts 5:12-16; 8:6-7, 12; 9:35, 42; 13:12; 14:3-4; Rom. 15:18-19).

The signs and miracles that are mentioned in Acts are of various kinds. They include most frequently healings and deliverance from evil spirits. But there were also occurrences of other supernatural events, such as visions containing calls and other messages from God (Acts 9:3-6, 10-16; 10:3-6, 9-20; 16:9; 22:6-11; 26:13-19), concrete prophecies that were later fulfilled (Acts 11:28; 21:10-11; Acts 13:1-2; 27:21-26), discernment of secret thoughts (Acts 5:3-4), divine guidance of the apostles and other gospel witnesses (Acts 8:26, 29; 10:19-20; 11:12,17; 13:2-4; 16:6-10; 15:7-9, 28-29; 22:17-21), and direct insight into God's will and purpose (Acts 10:19-20).

The importance of divine, supernatural events can hardly be overestimated in looking at the mission and growth of the early church. *All the major changes and new initiatives in the mission* of the church were due to *direct divine guidance.* Let us mention them briefly in chronological order: the *establishment of the church and the first mission* on the day of Pentecost (Acts 2); the mission outside of Jerusalem in *Samaria* (Acts 8), the conversion of the *Gentile Ethiopian* (Acts 8); the conversion and call of the *apostle Paul* (Acts 9; 22; 26); the conversion and inclusion in the church of the *first Gentile believers* (Acts 10; 11), the decision of the Jerusalem Council to *include Gentiles* in the church on a par with Jewish believers, without circumcision and keeping the Jewish law (Acts 15), the sending out of the *first missionaries* Paul and Barnabas from the church in Antioch (Acts 13), and, finally, the mission to *Europe* (Acts 16).

As we have already seen, these supernatural signs and wonders in various forms are testified to or alluded to in all parts of the New Testament (for example: Rom. 15:18-19; Rom. 12:6-8; Gal. 3:5; 1 Cor. 12-14; 2 Cor. 12:12;

1 Thess. 1:5; Heb. 2:4). *There is no evidence that these signs were limited to the apostles.* They were also part of and confirmed the *ministry of other believers and ministers* in the early church (see Acts 8:6-7; 9:17-18; Mk 16:14-20), and *they are also part of the church's mission in the power of the Holy Spirit today.*

Are the Biblical "Signs and Wonders" Historically True?

Important questions may be raised regarding the many examples of miracles and divine interventions both in the gospels, Acts and the other New Testament writings: are they historically true? Did they actually happen the way they are described?

Some Christians argue that, since the Bible is inspired, all that is told in it must be true. End of discussion! However, this line of reasoning does not convince those who do not believe in the inspiration of the Bible in the first place, and more importantly, this was not the way the New Testament authors argued. Luke, our main source of information about the early church, did not claim inspiration for himself when he wrote the gospel about Jesus but referred to his painstaking research based on eyewitness accounts:

> Many have undertaken to draw up an account of the things that have been fulfilled among us, just as they were handed down to us by those who from the first were eyewitnesses and servants of the word. Therefore, since I myself have carefully investigated everything from the beginning, it seemed good also to me to write an orderly account for you, most excellent Theophilus, so that you may know the certainty of the things you have been taught (Lk. 1:1-4, cp. Acts 1:1).

Luke's second book, Acts, is also based on *eyewitness accounts*, and Luke was probably himself a companion of Paul and an eyewitness to some of the events on Paul's journeys (see Acts 16:10; 20:5; 21:1; 27:1). But can eyewitness accounts be trusted? Or have New Testament authors invented stories, handed down untrustworthy tradition or exaggerated and embellished what took place historically?

The church owes a debt of gratitude to the highly respected New Testament scholar, Professor Craig S. Keener, who has devoted much work both to the question of the trustworthiness of the gospels and Acts, and to the question of miracles in biblical times and today. Based on the study of other written sources from the same period in the history of the Roman Empire as the New Testament writings, he has shown that Luke and the other evangelists wrote historical biographies of Jesus based on eyewitnesses who shared their accounts of what they had seen and heard within what is called "living memory", in most cases less than 40 years after the events took place. He has also showed that ancient biographers had a certain freedom in writing to stress their particular concerns but they were not free to invent stories or go against the eyewitness accounts, especially since many of the eyewitnesses were still alive and could control the text. This explains both the variations and the similarities in the synoptic gospels. Details could vary, but the main stories would remain the same, as is the case in true, unrehearsed testimonies.[6]

In a second two-volume work of more than 1000 pages, Keener has discussed the New Testament miracle stories in particular.[7] In Western New Testament studies, especially during the middle of the 20th century, many scholars were very critical of the miracle accounts and claimed that they were unhistorical legends and myths. The German theologian Rudolf Bultmann and his followers, for example, called for a "demythologisation" of the Bible since modern people cannot believe that supernatural events occur and can therefore not believe in the miracles of the Bible.

Keener and others have shown that much of the scepticism towards the supernatural is based on a Western cultural prejudice since the time of the Enlightenment in the 18th century. The English philosopher David Hume, for example, wrote an essay against the possibility of miracles that has had great influence. His argument is built on an *a priori* (beforehand) view that excludes miracles in principle – since miracles cannot occur, no testimony to miracle experiences can be trusted. This is obviously a circular argument since it presupposes the answer; it has already been stated that no miracles occur, therefore testimonies about them must be false. But what would happen if the researcher had a more open mind? If one believes in a God who *does* intervene in the present world, having a so-called *theistic* view of the world, is there any *evidence* of supernatural events? *They should not, as in much modern thinking following Hume, be excluded beforehand for philosophical or ideological reasons.*

Keener has collected thousands of eyewitness accounts of healings, exorcisms, even raisings of the dead, in our time or in the immediate past. He raises two fundamental questions. The first: are there witnesses today in the worldwide church who can tell about healings and other supernatural events similar to those found in the New Testament? His answer is an unequivocal *yes* and he expects *everybody to accept this conclusion* since these *witness accounts are historical facts.* Statistically, there are millions of people who claim to have witnessed healings in response to prayer!

His second question is: if at least a large number of these healings cannot be explained by reference to known natural causes, is it possible that the best explanation is *divine causation*? He does not expect everybody to say yes to this second question because it presupposes faith in God and not everybody has that. Yet, the fact remains: *if one allows for a God who has created the*

---

6 Craig S. Keener, *Christobiography.*
7 Craig S. Keener, *Miracles.*

world and still intervenes in it, then divine intervention, often in answer to prayer, may be the most probable cause of those healings and other seemingly supernatural events that cannot be explained by nature or reason.

Granted that God sometimes intervenes miraculously, he may also intervene in events and gifts that are not inexplicable in scientific terms, but occur in the lives of the church and of individual Christians, often in answer to prayer, such as for example dreams, visions, guidance, and prophecy. They may also have a divine source, because we cannot assume that God has chosen to intervene in the lives of people only in ways that are contrary to nature or are inexplicable. God may also use the natural abilities of people when he intervenes for his own purposes.

One major conclusion that can be drawn from Keener's studies is that there is no reason to be sceptical of the New Testament stories about healing during the ministry of Jesus and in the early church based on the view that, because these events cannot occur, the stories about them must be historically untrustworthy and therefore be made up by people. We must rather accept the fact that people, *both believers and non-believers, experienced and witnessed these seemingly supernatural events as they are recorded in the New Testament, because trustworthy witnesses tell us about the same kinds of events in our time.* Then we may leave it to the readers or listeners to make up for themselves whether or not they believe the biblical claim that these events are caused by divine power. People in the Charismatic movement as well as most Christians in the world today believe that they are, and for good reasons! Fortunately, there is also a greater openness to the inexplicable and to non-natural explanations in many circles in the scholarly world today as the dogmatic and unfounded faith in naturalism and rationalism is becoming weaker.

What about Those Who Are Not Healed or Live with Disability?

We shall close this section on "signs and wonders" by stating what is singularly important and should be obvious: *supernatural healing is the exception* – although it may happen more often than people expect – while *healing through the natural healing abilities of the human body* – which also are God-created – and through the *use of natural medical knowledge* are the *normal ways of healing*, also among Christians. Healing through prayer *should not replace* the use of the service of medical doctors or medicines. People in the healing profession work on the basis of God's creation and as such fulfil a divine task, whether they are Christians or not.

We should also remember that some diseases and disabilities are incurable from a human and medical perspective. Millions of people have to live with *permanent diseases* and *disabilities*, such as blindness, deafness, mental illness or physical disability. *These people should be treated with respect and concern as having the same human value and rights as others.* Their disability is not their own fault, nor is it punishment for sin. Because human beings are vulnerable, some may have to live their whole lives with serious diseases or disabilities. Some have called these people "differently abled", not disabled. They are of course also invited to be filled with the Holy Spirit, receive the gifts and fruit of the Spirit, and exercise important ministries in the church. Some of the greatest servants of God have had some disease or disability (perhaps, for example, Paul's "thorn in the flesh", 2 Cor. 12:7) that have not disappeared, even after repeated prayer. *We should also not assume that all people want to get rid of their disability when they have been reconciled with it and used to live and minister with it.*[8] The famous German theologian Jürgen Moltmann formed the following poignant statement: "A church without disabled people is a disabled church".[9]

In Chapter 44, we shall discuss in more detail the *practice* of the healing ministry as a charism in the church. Here, we have dealt primarily with its *biblical basis*. At this point, we include a short excursus that may be helpful for understanding the ministries of healing and exorcism in the history of the church.

---

[8] For those who want to pursue further the important topic of how Christians with permanent disease or disability and other vulnerable people can live, serve and be served in the church, we recommend the books by the Lausanne Associate for people with disability *Joni Eareckson Tada*, and the ecumenical document *The Gift of Being: Called to be a Church of All and for All* (Geneva: The World Council of Churches, 2016).

[9] Reported by Tormod Engelsviken from a large international charismatic conference in Brighton, England, in 1998.

Excursus 1: Healing and Exorcism in the Ancient Church

By Tormod Engelsviken

It is not possible to follow the long history of healing and exorcism in the church down through the ages but a few observations may be yet useful. Contrary to the assumptions of some theologians in the past, these ministries did not disappear after the apostolic age. Regarding exorcism, the Norwegian patristic scholar Oskar Skarsaune has, based on extensive textual evidence from church fathers such as Tertullian, Justin Martyr, Origen and Athanasius, shown that a particular set of thought was consistent throughout the ancient church.[1]

Firstly, the Christians were convinced that the gods of the Gentiles in reality were demons. The Gentiles were seen as relating to real powers in their religious cults but these powers were demonic idols (cf. Ps. 96:5 and 1 Cor. 10:19-20).

Secondly, when people worshipped these demons in the pagan cults, they risked possession by them. The ancient church placed possession in a pagan context and denied that baptised Christians could be possessed, except if they lapsed from faith. A pre-baptismal exorcism had as its purpose to get rid of demonic forces before the seal of baptism. This did not mean that all non-Christians were seen as possessed by evil spirits. But it did mean that, at the same time as the baptisands confessed their allegiance to Christ and the Christian faith, they also *renounced the enemy*. An effect of this pre-baptismal rite is today found in the renunciation of Satan in the form of a question that is answered in the affirmative by the baptisands or their sponsors at baptism: "Do you renounce the devil and all his works and all his ways?" This or a similar renunciation is still practiced in most historical churches, including the Lutheran churches.

Thirdly, the context of possession and exorcism in the ancient church was for people outside the church. Most of the evidence occurs in apologetic and

---

[1] Oskar Skarsaune and Tormod Engelsviken, "Possession and exorcism in the history of the church", in Moreau, *Deliver Us From Evil,* 2002, 65-90; Engelsviken, *Spiritual Conflict,* 2001, 18-20. To the question of healing and exorcism in the New Testament and the ancient church, see also the studies by Andrew Daunton-Fear, *Healing in the Early Church. The Church's Ministry of Healing and Exorcism from the First to the Fifth Century* (Milton Keynes: Paternoster, 2009) and Amanda Porterfield, *Healing in the History of Christianity* (Oxford: Oxford University Press, 2005).

missionary literature. It happened at the *border between church and paganism*. Exorcism is seen as a sign demonstrating that Christ has conquered Satan and his hosts. It was also taken as a *proof of the resurrection of Jesus Christ because only a living Lord could exercise authority over demonic powers*. The exorcisms made great impressions on people and contributed to the attraction and growth of the church.

Fourthly, the church was of the conviction that Christian exorcism could be performed by any Christian. Both Christian and pagan authors confirm that Christians were recognised as effective exorcists without the use of complicated incantation techniques. Exorcisms were so impressive because they functioned as "miracles of confrontation", where demons had to openly admit who Jesus was, and recognise his superiority and power.

In connection with *Christian initiation* in the ancient church, those who were baptised expected to receive the gift of the Holy Spirit and charisms of the Spirit such as healing and prophecy. The Catholic scholar Kilian McDonnell has shown how widespread the expectation and experience of the charisms were in different parts of the church, especially during the first three hundred years. The charisms that are mentioned by the church fathers in relation to Christian initiation include *prophecy, healing, miracles, and in general "all the divine gifts"*.[2] Several of the fathers saw the baptism of Jesus as a model for Christian baptism. The Spirit came upon Jesus at his baptism and he then began his public ministry in which healings and miracles were an integral part.[3] McDonnell and Montague conclude regarding the normativity of the charisms,

> We believe [...] that the prophetic gifts must continue until the final coming. In some way, the charisms, including the prophetic ones, structure the church. If the church is built upon the apostles and the prophets (Eph. 2:20) the charisms are in some way essential.[4]

The reason why we have put such a strong emphasis on the evidence of the New Testament and the ancient church, is the need to lay a biblical, historical and theological foundation for the practice of healing and deliverance as part of the church's *diakonia* today, and also to show the inadequacy of the so-called "cessationist" position where signs and wonders are seen as having ceased after the period of Jesus and the first apostles. Both the New Testament writers and the ancient church believed in and practiced Christian healing and exorcism without in any way assuming that these practices were not supposed to accompany the church at all times. Among the mainline churches, it is the Roman Catholic Church that has been most

---

[2] McDonnell and Montague, *Christian Initiation*, p. 309.
[3] McDonnell and Montague, *Christian Initiation*, p. 319.
[4] McDonnell and Montague, *Christian Initiation*, p. 333.

faithful to the Bible and early Christian history in this regard, having an office of exorcist in every diocese and a sacrament of healing based on James 5:14-16.

(19) The Church in the Power of the Holy Spirit

In the modern Western Christian tradition, there has been a tendency toward individualism, an undue emphasis on the individual and a neglect of the Christian fellowship. The Charismatic renewal wants to correct this. The reception of the gift of the Holy Spirit or the experience of being filled with the Holy Spirit, is a both a *personal* and a *communal* experience. On the day of Pentecost, we note that the tongues of fire "rested on *each* of them" and that they "were *all* filled with the Holy Spirit". It happened when they were together and simultaneously for all (Acts 2:3-4).

Pentecost marks 1) the *coming of the Holy Spirit* to every believer in Christ, 2) the *beginning of mission* in the power of the Holy Spirit, and 3) the *beginning of the church* as a fellowship of believers. The church as portrayed in the New Testament is not an institution or an organisation, but a *fellowship* (Greek: *koinonia*). Today, most Christian churches, including the Roman Catholic Church, hold to an understanding of the church which is called "koinonia-ecclesiology" (from Greek: *ekklesia* = church). This fellowship has two major forms: the *universal* church including all Christians in the world, and the *local* church consisting of the Christians in a specific place, for example in a city or even a home. A church may consist of as few as two believers coming together in Jesus' name. They have the promise that Jesus will be with them (Mt. 18:20). The basis of the church, the "rock" on which it is built, is the confession made by Peter to Jesus as "Christ, the Son of the living God" (Mt. 16:16-18, cp. Eph. 2:20). The confession of Jesus as Lord is also the confession that the Holy Spirit elicits in believers (1 Cor. 12:3, cp. 1 Cor. 8:6; 1 Jn 4:2-3).

While the Holy Spirit dwells in each believer, he also dwells in the church as a whole, as a fellowship. The church is God's people, God's household, a holy temple in the Lord, a *dwelling in which God lives by his Spirit* (Eph. 2:19-22). The relationship between the individual Christians with their specific gifts or charisms and the fellowship of the church is expressed by the image of the church being the *body of Christ* and the individual Christians with their various gifts are *members of that body* (1 Cor. 12:12-13, 27-28).

Jesus' promise of a baptism with the Holy Spirit that would give power for witness was not only given to individual disciples but also to their fellowship, the church (Acts 1:5, 8). We should therefore not only focus on the effects of the gift of the Spirit on individuals as seen in their various ministries after Pentecost, but also on the effects of this gift on the *fellowship* of believers. Both in Acts 2:42-47 and 4:32-35, Luke describes *the rich life of the early church as an immediate result of the indwelling of the Holy Spirit.* Just as Acts 2:38 in a programmatic way describes *Christian initiation into the church of God for the individual*, including repentance (and faith), baptism in the name of Jesus, forgiveness of sins and the gift of the Holy Spirit, the following section in Acts 2:42-47 in an equally programmatic way describes the *life and mission of the newly established church*. Both texts are *normative* for the church at all times, thus in our own time. We agree with Max Thurian, who writes:

> These verses (Acts 2:42-47) epitomise the *whole life of the Church* through the ages. The Church will assume different forms through the centuries but only if these fundamental elements are found within it will it truly be the Church of Christ. We have here *the model by which it will be able to measure this fidelity* in the course of history. *All periods of renewal in the Church will be due to the return to these original springs* (italics added).[1]

What are then, according to this text, the *main characteristics of the church* as a fellowship of believers giving witness to the gospel in the power of the Holy Spirit?

The Apostles' Teaching

Firstly, the Christians "devoted themselves to the apostles' teaching" (v. 42). The church's coming together for worship was in many ways influenced by the Jewish synagogue worship. In this, a large place was given to the *reading and exposition of the Scriptures* (see Lk. 4:16-21). This was also practiced in the Christian church. In addition, *teaching about the Christian faith and life* were central parts of the Christian worship service – as we can see from the New Testament gospels and epistles. Right and rich teaching of Christianity based on the prophetic and apostolic witness was essential for the life and mission of the church (Eph. 2:19-22). Paul told the elders in the church of Ephesus that he had proclaimed to them the "whole will of God" (Acts 20:27). The church should not proclaim a truncated gospel but the full gospel of Jesus Christ, including the work and gifts of the Holy Spirit.

Fellowship and Unity

Secondly, the believers were not only devoted to Jesus Christ. They were also *devoted to his body, the church.* It is especially John who in his writings emphasises the *mutual love* between the Christians. This love is of the same

---

[1] Max Thurian is a leading ecumenist and is commenting on the ecumenical document *Baptism, Eucharist and Ministry* (BEM) produced by the World Council of Churches (WCC) Commission on Faith and Order in 1982. All the member churches of the WCC and the Roman Catholic Church stand behind this important document. The document and Thurian's own comments are found on the website of the WCC.

kind as God's love. It is not motivated by the lovability of others but by an inner disposition of the one who loves. It is a work of the Holy Spirit (Gal. 5:22; Rom. 5:5). This love extends to all human beings, but is especially related to Christian brothers and sisters. In one of his last words to his disciples, Jesus told them:

> A new command I give you: *Love one another.* As I have loved you, so you must love one another. By this all men will know that you are my disciples, if you love one another (Jn 13:34-35; cp. 15:12, 17).
>
> And this is his command: to believe in the name of his Son, Jesus Christ, and to love one another as he commanded us. Those who obey his commands live in him, and he in them. And this is how we know that he lives in us: We know it *by the Spirit he gave us* (1 Jn 3:23-24).

This love is a testimony to the world about Jesus and his love for us. It is *attractive.* It was said about the first Christians, "See, how they love one another". It was a visible love that was expressed both by the very fact that the Christians frequently *came together* for worship and fellowship and by *the way they viewed and treated each other.*

In this fellowship, a *common meal* was shared, a so-called "meal of love" or *agape-meal* (Acts 2:42, 6). In most cultures, the shared meal is a deep expression of fellowship with and acceptance of one another. Therefore, the betrayal of Judas was seen as an especially serious sin since he shared the last meal with Jesus and the other apostles (Jn 13:18, 26-27: Lk. 22:21; Mk 14:18; Mt. 26:23).

The fellowship demonstrated the *unity of the church.* "All the believers were one in heart and mind" (Acts 4:32). In his prayer for all believers, Jesus prayed especially for their unity:

> My prayer is not for them alone, I pray also for those who will believe in me through their message, *that all of them may be one*, Father, just as you are in me and I am in you. May they also be in us *so that the world may believe* that you have sent me [...] May they be brought to complete unity to let the world know that you sent me and I have loved them even as you have loved me (Jn 17:20-21, 23).

The mutual love and the unity of the disciples have their source and model in the mutual love and unity between the Father and the Son and have also a *missionary effect:* "that the world may believe". This unity among the disciples is also a *result of the work of the Holy Spirit*:

> Make every effort to keep the *unity of the Spirit through the bond of peace.* There is one body and one Spirit – just as you were called to one hope when you were called – one Lord, one faith, one baptism, one God and Father of all, who is over all and through all and in all (Eph. 4:3-6).

Unity and peace belong together. Peace is a fruit of the Spirit in the individual (Gal. 5:22; Rom. 14:17) but it is also a reality in the church when the reconciliation and peace that are established between God and human beings through the cross of Christ lead to reconciliation and peace between people of different identities and backgrounds in the church.[2]

> His [Christ's] purpose was to create in himself *one new man out of the two* (Jews and Gentiles), thus making peace, and in this one body to reconcile both of them to God through the cross, by which he put to death their hostility [...] For, through him, we *both have access to the Father by one Spirit* (Eph. 2:15-18).
>
> There is neither Jew nor Greek, slave nor free, male nor female, for *you are all one in Christ Jesus* (Gal. 3:28, cp. Col. 3:11).

This love, unity and peace are to be lived out in the fellowship of the church by the power of the Spirit and as a witness to the world.

The Eucharist

Thirdly, when the believers came together in unity as a church, they shared in the "breaking of the bread", the *Eucharist* (from Greek: *eucharistia* = thanksgivings), also called *the Lord's Supper* or *Holy Communion,* which was originally practised as a part of the agape-meal.

Although the risen Lord Jesus Christ always is present when Christians gather in his name, in the Eucharist, he is *present in the bread and wine* in a concrete way as expressed by Jesus' words of institution: "Take and eat; this is my body". "This is my blood of the new covenant which is poured out for many for the forgiveness of sins" (Mt. 26:26-27, cp. Mk 14:22-24; Lk. 22:19-20; 1 Cor. 11:23-26). Based on these texts, we may state that the Eucharist was celebrated in *remembrance of Jesus* (Greek: *anamnesis* = memory), as a memorial of his sacrificial, atoning death and his victorious resurrection (Lk. 22:19; 1 Cor. 11:25), that it brought about *forgiveness of sins, participation* in the body and blood of Christ (1 Cor. 10:16), and expressed both the *unity* of the church with Christ and the unity of the believers with one another (1 Cor. 10:17). It also had a clearly *missional purpose*: "For whenever you eat this bread and drink this cup, *you proclaim the Lord's death* until he comes" (1 Cor. 11:26).

This celebration of the Eucharist will continue in the church until the return of Christ, and it has an *eschatological significance* as an expression of

---

[2] To the relationship between reconciliation with God, reconciliation between people in the church, the church's ministry of reconciliation, and its work for reconciliation in the world, see Tormod Engelsviken, "Mission and Reconciliation", *International Review of Mission*, 109(2), (November 2020), pp. 163-179.

the hope and anticipation of the perfect meal in the coming consummated kingdom of God (Lk. 22:18). The Eucharist is a unique form of witness to the gospel, and – like baptism –rightly called a *sacrament* because it conveys the grace of God to those to partake of it in faith.

From the very beginning of the history of the church, a *eucharistic prayer* has been a major part of the eucharistic liturgy (from Greek: *leitourgia* = service by the people). This prayer goes back to Jesus' own *prayers of thanksgiving* before the Last Supper (Lk. 22:17, 19; 1 Cor. 11:24), and was developed in the church into a prayer that was improvised and prayed extemporaneously by the leader of the congregation. The term "liturgy" suggests a service by the *people*, the *laos*, and not necessarily led by an ordained minister. Neither does it imply a rigid order or fixed formulas.[3] In the New Testament, there is great flexibility and freedom in the worship services of the congregation, with the use of both previously formulated confessions and hymns (for example 2 Cor. 13:13; Phil. 2:6-11; 1 Tim. 3:16) and informal, spontaneous and extemporaneous speech and prayers (1 Cor. 14:26-33). The Charismatic renewal has also be characterised by this freedom in worship where traditional ecclesiastical liturgies have been combined with open time for the exercise of spiritual gifts, free testimonies, spontaneous prayer and praise, and individual ministry – as the Spirit leads.

The eucharistic prayer that developed into various fixed forms during the history of the church, included two forms of *praying for the coming of the Holy Spirit,* called with the Greek term *epiclesis.* The first prayer was for the coming of the Spirit *on the bread and wine* to transform them into the body and blood of Christ, the second prayer was for the coming of the Spirit *on the congregation.* An example of the second epiclesis is the following:

> Leader: 'As we partake of Christ's body and blood, fill us with the Holy Spirit that we may become one single body and one single spirit in Christ, a living sacrifice to the praise of your glory'. The congregation: '*Veni, Creator Spiritus!*' [Come, Creator Spirit!].[4]

---

[3] See Allan Bouley, *From Freedom to Formula: The Evolution of the Eucharistic Prayer from Oral Improvisation to Written Texts* (Washington, D.C.: Catholic University of America Press, 1981).

[4] This is taken from the so-called "Lima Liturgy" which is a liturgy formulated by the World Council of Churches Commission on Faith and Order in Lima, Peru, in 1982, in connection with the acceptance of the ecumenical document *Baptism, Eucharist and Ministry.* One of its main authors, Max Thurian, writes about the *Eucharistic liturgy* and the *epiclesis*: "In the Eucharist, the whole people of God are united with Christ's unique priesthood, each member in accordance with the charism and ministry received." "A second epiclesis then invokes the Holy Spirit on the whole congregation, a fresh outpouring consequent of communion in the Body and Blood of Christ". "This effusion of the Spirit rallies together the body of Christ, the Church, and inspires it to spiritual unity; it makes the congregation a living

Both the leader and the congregation thus ask for a fresh outpouring of the Holy Spirit. In this way, it comes to expression that the unity and life of the church are wholly dependent on the Holy Spirit and his indwelling of the church as the body of Christ.

Prayer and Praise

Fourthly, the early church as depicted in Acts as a result of the coming of the Spirit also devoted itself to *prayer and praise* (Acts 2:42, 47). The believers' relationship to God was expressed not only by individual prayer, but also by *common* prayer, *praying to and praising God together as a fellowship.* The prayers would include Old Testament psalms as well as improvised prayers and intercessions. The intimate relation between the Holy Spirit and prayer is seen when Paul admonishes the believers to pray incessantly for all Christians in general and for himself and his ministry in particular:

> And *pray in the Spirit* on all occasions with all kinds of prayers and requests. With this in mind, be alert and always *keep praying for all the saints. Pray also for me*, that whenever I open my mouth, *words may be given me* so that I will fearlessly make known the mystery of the gospel, for which I am ambassador in chains. Pray that I may *declare it fearlessly, as I should* (Eph. 5:18-19).
>
> I urge you, brothers, by our Lord Jesus Christ and by the *love of the Spirit*, to join me in my struggle by *praying to God* for me (Rom. 15:30, see also Col. 4:2-4, 12; Acts 4:24-31; 13:3; 20:36).

The mission of the church cannot be accomplished without prayer for all believers and for all missionaries. All revival and renewal movements in the church have been preceded and accompanied by fervent prayer both by individuals and by fellowships![5]

Praising and worshipping God would also be a central part of the believers' gatherings. Again, the Old Testament psalms were used, for example Psalm 22 that was quoted by Jesus on the cross: "My God, my God, why have you forsaken me? Yet you are holy, enthroned on the praises of

---

offering to the glory of God, it anticipates the coming of the Kingdom". The BEM documents and Thurian's very insightful expositions are found on the WCC website. See also Louis Bouyer, *Eucharist: Theology and Spirituality of the Eucharistic Prayer* (Notre Dame, IN: University of Notre Dame Press, 1968). *We may hope that the invocation of the Holy Spirit in the Eucharistic Prayer will become a real prayer for a fresh outpouring of the Holy Spirit on the assembled congregation in our time. The title of this book, "Welcome, Holy Spirit", is inspired by this prayer and the expectation of a new coming of the Holy Spirit.*

[5] The greatest scholarly authority on revivals in the history of the church, the Irish-born professor at Fuller Seminary, USA, J. Edwin Orr (1912–1987), is famous for the saying: "No great spiritual awakening has begun anywhere in the world apart from united prayer – Christians persistently praying for revival".

Israel [...] I will declare your name to my brothers; in the congregation, I will praise you. You who fear the Lord, praise him" (Ps. 22:1, 3, 22-23).

Also, this great Psalm gives the same admonition to praise God:

> Come, let us sing for joy to the Lord: let us shout aloud to the Rock of our salvation. Let us come before him with thanksgiving, and extol him with music and song. For the Lord is the great God, the great king above all gods [...] Come let us bow down in worship. Let us kneel before the Lord our Maker; for he is our God, and we are the people of his pasture, the flock under his care (Ps. 95:1-7).

The *presence of God may be experienced in a special way* through sessions of praise and thanksgiving where God in his glory, greatness and grace is proclaimed and lifted up. It may fill the believers with a sense of awe (Acts 2:43). The praise of God by the church on earth reflects the praise of the angelic hosts in heaven (Is. 6:1-3; Lk. 2:13-14). Serving God and the Lamb on the throne by worship and praise will be the main occupation throughout eternity of the great multitude of redeemed people from all nations who "have washed their robes and made them white in the blood of the Lamb" (Rev. 7:9-17). So important is the praise of God that it can be seen as a main motivation for mission and as its ultimate goal: "so that the Gentiles may glorify God for his mercy, as it is written: 'Therefore I will praise you among the Gentiles: I will sing hymns to your name'" (Rom. 15:9; cp. Ps. 18:49).[6]

Praise of God may be expressed in spoken form or in song, in understandable language or in tongues (1 Cor. 14:15-17). In different forms of speech, song and music, praise is one of the most common and immediate effects of being filled with the Holy Spirit (Eph. 5:18-20; Acts 10:46). It has accompanied the church everywhere throughout its history but has been renewed in a special way the world over through the Charismatic renewal.

---

[6] Especially among evangelical Christians with a Reformed background, the *glory of God* has been a main motivation for mission. In his commentary on the Lausanne Covenant from 1974, its main author, John Stott, writes about its first article, called "The Purpose of God", that there are three aims of mission: to extend Jesus' kingdom, to build up Christ's body and to glorify God's name. The last is "*the ultimate aim of mission, and what we all are created for*, e.g. Psalm 115:1; Eph. 1:6, 12, 14". See John Stott: *For the Lord We Love: Your Study Guide to the Lausanne Covenant* (The Lausanne Movement, 2009, first published in 1975). In Ephesians 1:13-14, the *role of the Holy Spirit* in this connection is emphasised: "Having believed, you were marked in him with a seal, the *promised Holy Spirit*, who is a deposit guaranteeing our inheritance until the redemption of those who are God's possession – *to the praise of his glory*".

Signs and Wonders

Fifthly, the church experienced "many signs and miraculous wonders" performed by the apostles (v. 43). We have above pointed out the significance of the "signs and wonders" in the mission of the church, and will not repeat this here. However, we have to emphasise a significant *difference* between the other characteristics of the church and the "miraculous wonders". While the other traits describe what the believers, inspired by the Holy Spirit, are doing, and the words and actions therefore are under the control of human beings, "the miraculous wonders" cannot be performed or controlled by the people: *they are sovereign acts of God himself, although communicated through his servants. "Signs and wonders" are no "method" to be used by the church. They can only be recognised, expected and prayed for.* This is obvious in Acts 4:29-35, similar to Acts 2:42-47, where the *church's prayer* for "miraculous signs and wonders" is explicit:

> Now, Lord, consider their threats and *enable your servants to speak your word* with great boldness. *Stretch out your hand to heal and perform miraculous signs and wonders* through the name of your holy servant Jesus. After they prayed, the place where they were meeting was shaken. And they were all filled with the Holy Spirit and spoke the word of God boldly (Acts 4:29-31).

The experience of miraculous answers to prayer was *normal* in the New Testament church, and should also be so today, yet we are in no position to demand, or even less produce, such answers by human efforts. They belong to the sovereign work of the Holy Spirit. He performs them where and when he pleases.

Joy

Sixthly, the common life of the early Spirit-filled church was characterised by *joy*. "They ate together with *glad and sincere hearts*, praising God" (Acts 2:46-47). Joy and praise are closely connected since praise often grows out of joy and gratitude (Col. 3:16). "Is anyone of you in trouble? He should pray. Is anyone happy? Let him sing songs of praise" (James 5:13).

This joy is not a superficial and fluid emotion determined by external or internal circumstances. It is deeply *anchored in the experience of salvation and the gift of the Spirit*. It is the *joy of being right with God* (Lk. 10:20), having *fellowship with the risen Christ* (Jn 16:20-22, 24), and *hope of eternal life* (Mt. 25:21; Rom. 15:13). It should be a constant quality of Christian life (Phil. 4:4). It can therefore persist in trials (2 Cor. 7:4; 8:2) and in suffering: "In spite of severe suffering, you welcomed the message with the *joy given by the Holy Spirit*" (1 Thess. 1:6; cf. 2 Cor. 7:4; 1 Pet. 4:12-14). It is present in weakness (2 Cor. 13:9), and, paradoxically, even in sorrow: "sorrowful, yet always rejoicing" (2 Cor. 6:10, see also vv. 4-10). Just like peace, joy is a gift of salvation made real by the Holy Spirit (Rom. 14:17). Joy is both an individual fruit of the Spirit and a communal experience (Acts 13:52).

Caring and Sharing

Seventhly, the fellowship of love and unity in the church led to *concrete action* by the Spirit-filled believers: "All the believers were together and had everything in common. Selling their possession and goods, they gave to anyone as he had need" (Acts 2:44-45, cp. Acts 4:32-35). The main point here is that the believers exercised a *practical solidarity and mutual care* that extended also to the economic area. We are not bound today by a communitarianism that involves common ownership of everything – although some Christians may still want to establish such communities – since sharing of property was voluntary (Acts 5:4), and some Christians kept it and used it for the benefit of the church (Acts 12:12). However, the love and *solidarity between the believers made it impossible to accept a situation where some believers had enough while others were needy.* Those who are able to, are obligated to share their resources with those who are poor, hungry, or in other ways in need of help. We see this principle at work both in the early church as described in Acts and in the Pauline congregations.

In Acts 6:1-6, the apostles solved the difficult question of discrimination in the daily distribution of food to poor widows. In the Greek text, this distribution of food is called "diakonia" (= service, v. 1) and waiting on the tables is called "serving" (from Greek: *diakoneo* = serve, v. 2). The term "diakonia" may be used for any kind of service, but is often used for service of the needy or waiting on tables, as it is here. However, in this same section, the apostles' "ministry" of the Word is also called "diakonia". *Serving the poor and preaching the word of God belong equally* to the "services" (Greek: *diakoniai*), "gifts" (Greek: *charismata)* and "workings" (Greek: *energemata*) that are given by the Holy Spirit to the church (1 Cor. 12:4).

The apostles' solution of the problem was to establish a special ministry with responsibility for serving the poor (v. 4). The spiritual qualification for this ministry was the same as for other ministries in the church: "Choose seven men from among you who are known to be *full of the Spirit and wisdom*" (v. 3). Whether these ministers should be called "deacons" (Greek: *diakonoi*) or something else, is a matter of choice. What is *not* a matter of choice, however, is that *the church should have a ministry of caring for the poor and needy, empowered by the Holy Spirit.*

The apostle Paul writes with great passion about the collection of funds for the poor in the church at Jerusalem in 2 Corinthians 8-9. He lauds the churches in Macedonia because, "out of the most severe trial, their overflowing joy and their extreme poverty welled up in rich generosity. For I testify that they gave as much as they were able, and even beyond their ability" (2 Cor. 8:2-3). One does not have to be rich or have enough to be able to share and give. Even those who are poor participate in giving – as we see today in many of the poorer nations of the world. Generous giving and showing mercy are also gifts of grace, charisms, mentioned among other charisms in Romans 12:6-8: "If it is *contributing to the needs of others*, let him give generously [...] if it is *showing mercy*, let him do it cheerfully" (cp. 2 Cor. 8:7). The basic principle is that there should be *equality*:

> Our desire is not that others might be relieved while you are hard pressed, but that there might be *equality*. At the present time your plenty will supply what they need, so that in turn their plenty will supply what you need. Then there will be equality as it is written: "He who gathered much did not have too much, and he who gathered little did not have too little" (2 Cor. 8:13-15).

In the global family of the church today, it is shameful that some Christians are rich while others are needy even to the point of starving. As we sit at God's world-wide table, Paul's stern rebuke in 1 Corinthians11, 21-22 against the fact that "one remains hungry, another gets drunk [...] or do you despise the church of God and humiliate those who have nothing?" may apply to rich Christians, particularly in the West, who ignore the plight of their poor brothers and sisters, especially in parts of the Global South.

Some Christians complain about all the "talk about money" in the church or about the regular collection of offerings at church services. This depends, however, on a serious misunderstanding. While the gospel is free, ministry is not. It is costly. The church needs money both for its own work and for the work among the needy in the world. It is part of Christian stewardship to contribute generously according to one's ability to the work of the Lord, and it holds a promise of great blessing. "God loves a cheerful giver" (2 Cor. 9:7).

> And God is able to make all grace abound to you, so that in all things at all times, having all that you need, you will abound in every good work (2 Cor. 9:8).

The blessing is not for one's own selfish enjoyment but for the service of God and other people: "You will be made rich in every way so that you can be generous on every occasion [...] This service that you perform is not only supplying the needs of God's people but also overflowing in many expressions of thanks to God" (2 Cor. 9:11-12).[7]

---

[7] God's reward for giving generously should not be understood, as it is often done in the so-called "prosperity gospel", as a law or a right that forces God to always materially and in other ways prosper the giver. *The blessing is always dependent upon God's free grace* (2 Cor. 9:8). Also, generous givers may experience suffering as they are people living in a fallen and broken world, and they cannot expect to totally avoid poverty, disease and other hardships. Yet, they will experience God's abundant grace, love and care in the midst of their sufferings.

The texts that we have looked at, deal primarily with sharing with the *needy in the church.* What about *people outside the church*? Do Christians have an obligation to serve them in their needs? The Bible tells us to have a primary responsibility for our own families (1 Tim. 5:8). Since the church is the "family of God" and is one loving and committed fellowship, there should be a special concern for fellow believers. "Therefore, as we have opportunity, let us do good to all people, especially to those who belong to the family of believers" (Gal. 6:10). But, as Paul says here, we should *do good to all people,* regardless of who they are.

The commandment of love for the neighbour, which Jesus exemplified with the Parable of the Good Samaritan (Lk. 10:27-37), shows that Christian love and ministry to the needy should extend to everybody, even the enemy: "If your enemy is hungry, feed him; if he is thirsty, give him something to drink [...] Do not be overcome by evil, but overcome evil with good" (Rom. 12:20-21).

From the beginning, the history of the church shows that this loving ministry to the needy has been one of the characteristic marks of the church. It has set the church apart from society as a whole where it has been common only to take care of one's own. It was particularly through its ministry to the sick and dying that the ancient church showed its love for all and gained favour among the common people.

This ministry of the church to the needy, whether it is called *diakonia or social responsibility,* may take many forms, depending on the needs of people. In our time, it may also involve the struggle for peace, justice and the integrity of creation, in addition to fighting oppression, discrimination, marginalisation, poverty, disease and lack of education. It is part of the *holistic mission* of the church in the power of the Holy Spirit, according to Christ's model of ministry shown in his own life, in word and deed (Jn 20:21-22).

The Reaction of the People: Favour and Growth

Eighthly, the last characteristic of the early church as depicted in Acts 2:42-47 is the fact that it enjoyed "the *favour* of all the people. And the Lord *added to their number* daily those who were being saved" (v. 47). Here, we move from the life and ministry of church to the *reaction and response of the world,* the people, to the life and ministry of the church.

Let us state an obvious, yet nevertheless very important, fact: the *church is being observed by the world* around it. This is because the church is an *open and transparent* community, not a closed cult or sect. This openness is demonstrated in the practice of the believers to meet both in *public* where other people also met, "in the temple courts", and also in *private,* "in their homes" (v. 46). The church was also open in the sense that *it invited people to join,* to be "added" to its number. The people outside the church observed *what* the church did: its reading, teaching, fellowship, prayers, praise, meals, miracles, and ministry to the poor. They also observed *how* the church did it: in love and unity, with awe, joy, and generosity, as described in Acts 2:42-46.

The reaction of the people to what they observed was *positive*. The church was "enjoying the favour of all the people". This may seem strange in light of the history of persecution and resistance suffered by the early church. But this persecution came mainly from the religious and – later – the political leaders, not from the people (cf. Acts 4:2, 5, 18; 6:12). It illustrates the fact that the Christians often were slandered and criticised by people at a distance, but those who came to know them personally got a different impression and came to love them. Peter writes:

> Live such good lives among the pagans that, though they accuse you of doing wrong, they may see your good deeds and glorify God on the day he visits us (1 Pet. 2:12).

This corresponds to Jesus' own words: "You are the light of the world [...] Let your light shine before men, that they may see your good deeds and praise your father in heaven" (Mt. 5:14, 16). Nobody would want to join a community of people whom they do not like. The persons, lives and deeds of the Christians should therefore be so *likable* that people would want to join them. But this "likability" should not come at the expense of truth and justice: "Let your conversation be always full of grace, seasoned with salt, so that you may know how to answer everybody" (Col. 4:6; cp. Mt. 5:13; Mk 9:50). Christians should be both light and salt!

The life and ministry of the fellowship of believers led to *church growth* as new people were added daily. In understanding the mission of the church, it has been common to distinguish between centripetal and centrifugal mission on the basis of texts both in the Old and New Testaments.

Centripetal mission is based on the *attraction* of the church, the "pull-factor" that draws people to Christ and his church. It is foretold in Old Testament prophecies (e.g. Is. 2:2-3; 66:18-21), and realised in New Testament times as we see it in this and other texts, especially in those texts in the gospels that describe how the multitudes were attracted to Jesus and his ministry and therefore *came to him* in order to hear him and be served by him (see for example Mk 3:7-8. 10, 20: 4:1).

Besides the attractiveness of the church, there is also another factor that is important for the growth of the church, but that is hard to define. Both the ministry of Jesus and that of the early church put people in a situation of *awe* (Greek: *fobos* = awe, fear). "Everyone was filled with awe" (Acts 2:43). Awe is the numinous, overwhelming experience of being intensely aware of the presence of the holy and almighty God in our midst (see Is. 6:1-8: Lk. 5:8; 7:16; 8:37). This awe might have been experienced by both believers and other people as they witnessed the great things that God was doing in and through the church (cp. also 1 Cor. 14:24-25). There are many testimonies from the history of the church about how the sense of God's presence in the fellowship of believers has made people open to faith in thc gospel and led them to join the church. There is therefore no reason to be modest about what God can do through the worship service and the ministry of the church.

Centrifugal mission is the *sending of messengers* or *going out* with the gospel, as exemplified by the Jesus' mission commissions in John 20:21 ("send"); Matthew 28:19 ("go", also Mark 16:15)), Luke 24:47 ("to all nations"), and Acts 1:8 ("and in all Judea and Samaria, and to the ends of the earth"). It is the "push-factor" that drove the apostles and other missionaries to preach in new areas where "Christ was not known" (Rom. 15:20). Acts 1:8 represents the programme for – and also the outline of – the book of Acts depicting the history of the mission of the early church as witnesses in the power of the Holy Spirit.

Both "attraction mission" and "sending mission" are therefore a result of the working of the Holy Spirit, as seen for example in Acts 13:2, 4, and here in Acts 2:42-47. They do not stand in opposition to one another, but complement one another. The missionaries and other witnesses who "go out" are at the same time members of and sent out from Spirit-filled congregations (Acts 8:4; 11:19-21; 13:1-4; 1 Thess. 1:6-8).They also establish new congregations everywhere into which people are invited. The attractive Spirit-filled congregations are as important for the mission of the church as the sent Spirit-filled witnesses. The one cannot exist without the other. The church is in its essence a *missional church,* a witness to the world both through what it is and what it does.

In the letter to the Ephesians, Paul explains the connection between charismatic ministries and the growth of the church. Apostles and evangelists normally "go out" in the world as itinerant ministers; while prophets, pastors and teachers normally "stay" and work in a local congregation. Yet, all of them contribute to the growth of the church, spiritually and numerically:

> It was he [Christ] who gave some to be apostles, some to be prophets, some to be evangelists and some to be pastors and teachers, to prepare God's people for the works of service, so that the body of Christ may be built up [...] Speaking the truth in love, we will in all things grow up into him who is the Head, that is, Christ. From him, *the whole body*, joined and held together by every supporting ligament, *grows and builds itself up in love,* as each part does its work (Eph. 4.11-12, 15-16).

On this foundation, we may raise an important question: is growth a necessary characteristic of the Spirit-filled church? We know that the church over 2000 years has grown tremendously from around 3000 people on the day of Pentecost to almost 2.5 billion people today, but we also know that at certain times in history and in some regions of the world the church has diminished, and even some places disappeared completely. Yet, although the church may not always actually grow, the true church it will always *want to grow and intend to grow*, spiritually as well as numerically.[8] But we also want to add another important perspective:

Much of church growth thinking takes its point of departure in a human perspective on the church, where it is the *present, earthly church* and its members that are counted. However, in *God's perspective* his people consist of both those believers who are alive in the world today (often called in Latin: *ecclesia militans* = the struggling church) and those believers who have already died and are awaiting the final resurrection (often called in Latin: *ecclesia triumphans* = the victorious church). The church will grow numerically *on earth* when the number of *new* Christians exceeds the number of those who *die* in the Lord, but it *also grows* in terms of the *total number of those who are saved for eternity* when the number of Christians who die is higher than the number of new Christians added to the earthly church, and the earthly church as a result diminishes! The only situation in which the real church *does not grow* is if there are *no new Christians* added to the church or if the number of *apostate* Christians surpasses that of new Christians. Thanks to God, the latter situation happens very seldom and is always due to some serious defect in the church.

Thus, the normal situation for the church is that it grows in numbers as a result of the working of the Holy Spirit, as depicted in Acts 9:31: "The church was strengthened; and *encouraged by the Holy Spirit, it grew in number,* living in fear of the Lord" (cp. also Acts 11:20-21, 24).

The Relationship between the Individual Believer and the Fellowship

In the last two chapters, we have dealt with the work of the Holy Spirit in the individual believer and in the fellowship of the church. The image of the body of Christ and its members in 1 Cor. 12 illustrates the *interdependence* between the individual Christians and the fellowship of the church. A *communal* understanding of the coming of the Holy Spirit should not be played out against a *personal* one. It is impossible to imagine a coming of the Holy Spirit on a congregation (as is prayed for in the *epiclesis* of the Eucharistic prayer) without the Spirit touching individuals, or a coming of the Holy Spirit on a person (the gift of the Holy Spirit, or a baptism with the Holy Spirit) without a Christian fellowship to which that person belongs and in which they serve. *Both the believer and the church are "the temple of the Spirit"* (1 Cor. 1:16-17; 6:19; 2 Cor. 6:16; Eph. 2:21). The gifts of the Spirit,

---

[8] This is discussed by professor Charles Van Engen at Fuller Seminary, USA, in his book, *The Growth of the True Church: An Analysis of the Ecclesiology of Church Growth Theory* (Amsterdam: Rodopi, 1981).

the charisms, are supposed to function in the church – especially when Christians come together for worship – communally, not independently or individualistically. The Spirit-filled church on the other hand is dependent on Spirit-filled individuals who serve with their gifts and charisms, and it should therefore encourage and give room for their ministries. What this means in practice will be discussed further in Part Five of this book.

Conclusion

The normal – and *normative – life of the Christian church,* which includes witnessing about Christ in the world, regular fellowship meetings with reading, preaching and teaching of the Word, with prayer and praise, with the sacraments of baptism and eucharist, with sacrificial giving, and with compassionate ministry to the needy – *was initiated on the day of Pentecost when the Holy Spirit was poured out on the disciples, and the Christian church was formed.*

This unity of word and work, of proclamation and demonstration, of individual and corporate witness, of going out and gathering in – always in the power of the Spirit of God – determines the missionary efforts of the apostles and the early church. There is no indication in the Scriptures that this way of being church and doing missionary work was to cease with the passing of the apostles. On the contrary, it should accompany Christians everywhere and characterise the church until the end of the age. God's missional purpose for the church and the power to realise it must be seen in connection with the coming of the Holy Spirit and his gifts to the church and to individual Christians. The apostle Paul writes, "To each one the manifestation of the Spirit is given for the common good" (1 Cor. 12:7), and the apostle Peter concurs,

> Each one should use *whatever gift he has received* to serve others, faithfully *administering God's grace* in its various forms. If anyone *speaks*, he should do it as one speaking the very *words of God.* If anyone *serves*, he should do it with the *strength God provides*, so that in all things God may be praised through Jesus Christ. To him be the glory and the power for ever and ever. Amen (1 Pet. 4:10-11).

This book is written with the conviction that the Holy Spirit has a plan for our world in our time, and that he is ready and willing for us to learn about it and become involved in it. It is an attempt to discern as accurately as possible the work of the Spirit, which means that first-hand experiences and practical observations will be tested in the light of Scripture and theological reflection. We have now laid a *biblical basis that is normative* for our evaluation of the Charismatic renewal. Doctrinal implications and practical applications will be further explored in Parts Four and Five. But first we shall look in Part

Three at the relationship of the Charismatic renewal to the Lutheran Confessions and theological tradition of the Lutheran Church.

Part Three

Made Known by the Holy Spirit

A Lutheran Theological and Historical Perspective

He will bring glory to me by taking from what is mine and making it known to you

John 16:14

(20) "Solus Christus" – Christ Alone

The "Exclusive Terms"

A characteristic feature of the Lutheran theological tradition, expressed both by the Lutheran reformers and the Lutheran Confessions, is the emphasis on the so-called "exclusive terms" – that is, terms that exclude some other views or doctrines. These exclusive terms are often formulated with the help of the word "alone" (Latin: *solus* or *sola*). There are primarily four such exclusive terms: Christ Alone (*Solus Christus*), Grace Alone (*Sola gratia*), Faith Alone (*Sola fides*), and Scripture Alone (*Sola scriptura*). In the next chapters, we will tie our discussion of the relationship between the Charismatic renewal and the Lutheran Confessions to these four terms and then add four more "alones".

Christ and Salvation as Criteria for Biblical Interpretation in the Lutheran Tradition

First, however, we want to state some hermeneutical principles. An important contribution that the Lutheran Confessions could make to the development of a charismatic theology is a *hermeneutic* – that is, a *basic approach to biblical interpretation that keeps to the centre of the scriptural revelation.*

The Lutheran Confessions reflect criteria that one can use to test an interpretation of the Bible. The two basic criteria could be shaped into question form as follows:

1. Does this teaching magnify the honour of Christ? Does it present the biblical subject matter in such a way that Christ's honour is in no way diminished, but rather extolled because it prompts people to declare his lordship?

2. Does this teaching have a saving effect on people? Does it present the biblical subject matter in such a way that sinners are not left to despair, but rather find godly comfort as they are liberated from the destructive power of Satan, sin, and death?

A Lutheran hermeneutic would test any doctrine, or theology as a whole, against these two basic and interrelated criteria.[1] They would not be applied

---

[1] These criteria are most programmatically stated in Melanchthon's *Apology of the Augsburg Confession*, article IV (on Justification), but they are repeated and consistently applied throughout *The Book of Concord.* Melanchthon wrote: "In this main controversy the main doctrine of Christianity is involved; when it is properly understood, *it illumines and magnifies the honour of Christ and brings to pious consciences the abundant consolation they need*" (Tappert (ed), *The Book of*

only now and then, but consistently and to the Bible as a whole.[2] The authority of Scripture would not be reduced to these two categories narrowly conceived, yet they would stand as sentinels over the whole enterprise of interpretation. It is in this way that the Lutheran Confessions contend for the apostolicity and the catholicity of its teaching. It is Christ, the author of our salvation, who stands at the centre of all Christian thinking and living. "It is because of him that you are in Christ Jesus, who has become for us wisdom from God – that is, our righteousness, holiness and redemption. Therefore, as it is written: 'Let him who boasts boast in the Lord'" (1 Cor. 1:30).

The Lutheran Confessions and the Charismatic Movement

When Lutheran theology approaches the Charismatic movement, it must evaluate it on the basis of the entirety of the Bible, interpreting the texts according to the principle stated above. It is not sufficient merely to quote a series of "proof texts" that seem to confirm the existence of a "charismatic dimension" in the Bible; nor is it adequate to have a correct principle of interpretation, but fail to apply it to the entirety of the Bible. If a hermeneutical principle has validity, it can be applied to the whole Bible, including, for example, 1 Corinthians 12-14.[3]

Concord, Apol. IV, 2-3, p. 107, see also CA XXIV, 24-25, 30-32, pp. 58-59, italics added).
As indicated before, many Lutheran churches have the whole *Book of Concord* (BC) as their confession, while others have only the *three ecumenical creeds* from the ancient church, *the Augsburg Confession* (AC) and *Luther's Small Catechism* (SC). In this Part Three, we will draw on the whole *Book of Concord* where all Lutheran confessions are included. All page numbers refer therefore to Tappert (ed), *The Book of Concord.*

[2] Just as it is important to note the statement of these criteria in principle and the consistency with which they are repeated in *The Book of Concord,* it is equally important to note *how* they are actually applied. Here, one must acknowledge that they are not used in reductionist fashion that asserts this "hermeneutical principle" at the expense of what might be called the "scriptural substance". From the beginning to the end, the Confessions make clear that normative doctrine is to be drawn from the *fullness of Holy Scripture.* Scripture in turn is to be interpreted in such a way that the hermeneutical criteria stated above are not contradicted but rather promoted (See Apol. IV, 5, p. 108; FC SD, Rule and Norm, pp. 501-508; FC SD III, 6, p. 540; FC SD V, 1, p. 558; CA XXVIII.21-28, pp. 84-85, italics added).

[3] Luther summed it up well in his *Large Catechism* (LC), where, after clarifying the distinction between the function of the Ten Commandments and the function of the Creed, he wrote: "For the present this is enough concerning the Creed to lay a foundation for the common people without overburdening them. After they understand the substance of it, they may *on their own initiative learn more, relating to these teachings of the Catechism all they learn in the Scriptures,* and thus advance and grow richer in understanding. For as long as we live, we shall have

Using this approach, we will consider a variety of subjects to help develop an understanding of the Charismatic renewal that is based on the Bible and reflects the wisdom that the Holy Spirit gave to the church through the Lutheran reformers.

As we have seen, the Lutheran Confessions bring key theological concerns to a focus through a strategic use of the word "alone". They do not, however, use this term in an absolute sense. That would distort its intended meaning. Rather, "alone" is used to qualify a term in a specific sense. Thus, for example, "grace alone" is directed *against any attempt to earn salvation by one's own effort*, but *not against good works, the sacraments or prayer*; "Scripture alone" is directed *against anything that sets another authority above the Bible*, but *not against ecclesiastical authority or tradition as such.* This will be clearly seen in what follows.

Christ Alone and the Trinity

The Charismatic movement places a fresh emphasis on the person and work of the Holy Spirit. This does not lead to a lack of emphasis on the Son and the Father, an "unitarianism of the Spirit," as some critics have argued. On the contrary, a consistent witness to Jesus as our only Saviour and Lord and a high regard for the structures of creation as given and preserved by the "Father almighty, maker of heaven and earth", have been typical of the many Lutherans involved in the Charismatic movement.[4]

When we interpret Scripture to illumine and magnify the honour of Christ, we do not contradict or detract from the honour due to the Trinity. Rather, in doing this, we interpret our trinitarian faith. When Christ is not properly honoured, neither the Father, who "gave his only Son" (Jn 3:16), nor the Spirit, who "will glorify me" (Jn 16:14), are properly honoured.

For example, a charismatic theology of healing, if it is to honour Christ, will be trinitarian. It will respect what Luther recognised as *the Father's provision* for health and healing in creation, as it has been studied by medical science and observed by common sense.[5] It will recognise the significant role

---

enough to preach and learn on the subject of faith" (LC II, 67-70, p. 420, italics added).

Thereupon, Luther proceeded to follow his own advice as he summarised in his catechism what the Scripture teaches on prayer and the sacraments and interpreted this according to the hermeneutical principle that honours Christ by proclaiming salvation to sinners.

[4] Larry Christenson, *The Christian Family* (Minneapolis, MN: Bethany, 1970).

[5] "Although much that is good comes to us from men (Luther leaves open the possibility of God's miraculous intervention), we receive it all from God through his command and ordinance [...] We receive our blessings not from them (that is, God's creatures) but *from God through them.* Creatures are only the hands, channels and means through which God bestows all blessings [...] Therefore, this way of

that healing played in the *ministry of Jesus*, a ministry that also was carried on by his disciples. It will honour the provision for healing that the *Holy Spirit brings through gifts of healing* and by the quickening of faith and prayer among God's people. Luther wrote:

> Since the devil is not only a liar but also a murderer, he incessantly seeks our life and vents his anger by causing accidents and injury to our bodies [...] Thus, you see how God wants us to pray to him for everything that affects our bodily welfare and directs us to seek and expect help from no one but him.[6]

An approach that unites the work of Father, the Son, and the Holy Spirit magnifies the honour of Christ. His compassion and healing grace continue to reach out to touch broken and suffering lives, as during his earthly ministry.

Christ Alone and Human Responsibility

Charismatics express themselves critically against a secular-humanist mentality that puts the autonomous, self-sufficient human being at the centre of all things. On the other hand, they do not want to fall into the trap of overstating the doctrine of God to the point of obliterating human responsibility. They sense the necessity of maintaining an appropriate tension between God's creation of humankind and *the results of the fall* on one hand (Gen. 1:26-28; 2:7,15-17; 3:23), and *the effects of the new creation in Christ* on the other (2 Cor. 5: 17; Col. 3:10; 2 Cor. 3:18).[7]

The *Formula of Concord*, in effect, asserts the impossibility of the secular-humanist position: our free will is limited both by the fall and by the sovereignty of God. However, the Formula also rejects an overstated position that would take away from the *redeemed children of God the responsibility and capacity to cooperate with God that he himself has given them.* The authors of the *Formula of Concord* wrote:

---

receiving goods through God's creatures is not to be disdained nor are we arrogantly to seek other ways and means than God has commanded (for example, through prayer directed to the 'saints'" (LC I, 11-15, p. 366, italics added), "for that would be not receiving our blessings from God but seeking them from ourselves" (LC I, 26-27, p. 368).

[6] LC III, 114-118, pp. 435-436.

[7] The Lutheran Confessions teach as follows concerning free will: We also declare that to a *certain degree* reason has a free will. For, in those matters which can be comprehended by reason, we have a free will [...] Hearts which are *without the Holy Spirit* are without fear of God, without faith, do not trust or believe that God will hear them, that he forgives their sin, or that he will help them in their troubles; therefore they are *without* God" (FC SD II, 31, p. 527; CA XVIII, 1-7, pp. 39-40, italics added).

> As soon as the *Holy Spirit* has initiated his work of regeneration and renewal in us through the Word and the holy sacraments, it is certain that we can and must cooperate by the *power of the Holy Spirit*, even though we still do so in great weakness. Such cooperation does not proceed from our carnal and natural powers, but *from the new powers and gifts which the Holy Spirit has begun in us in conversion* (italics added).[8]

Thus, the Formula of Concord guards, on the one hand, against a self-confident humanism that claims our freedom to will and carve out our own destiny, and, on the other hand, it cautions against an overstated emphasis on what God is doing that denies the power of the Holy Spirit to communicate new life in Christ to human beings.

Both sides of this dialectic are encompassed in the Charismatic renewal's call for radical dependence on the Holy Spirit. On the one hand, it recognises that, in ourselves, we have no ability to live the Christian life. On the other hand, it rejoices in the power of the Holy Spirit to conform believers to the image of Christ.

---

[8] FC SD II, 65, p. 534; CA XX, 27-34, p. 45.

(21) "Sola Gratia" – Grace Alone

The Lutheran Confessions especially want to guard Christ's honour as Saviour and Lord. Salvation is all his work. Wherever people seek to "imitate Christ" in order to please God and thus achieve their own salvation, the Confessions sound the alarm: by grace alone! To speak of grace draws us immediately to the question of a "charismatic" theology, since a charism is, by definition, a manifestation of grace. But to speak of grace as being "alone" has suggested to some that it comes apart from any instrument or means, and to others that it remains without consequences. The Lutheran Confessions disavow both of these possibilities.

Grace Alone and the Means of Grace

The Lutheran Confessions emphatically teach that grace comes by means of the Word of God and according to the Word of God. Grace without the divinely appointed means of its coming robs Christ of his honour by jeopardising the comfort he would bring to sinners. Grace without means also calls into question the authority of Scripture.

Christ communicates himself to us through what Luther calls the "external Word" – an expression which for him covered the Bible, particularly as it is preached, and the sacraments. In the *Smalcald Articles*, it is said:

> In these matters, which concern the external spoken Word, we must hold firmly to the conviction that God gives no one his Spirit or grace except through or with the external Word which comes before.[1]

Melanchthon made a similar point when he maintained that "justification takes place only through the Word," citing Romans 1:16 and 10:17.[2] The *Augsburg Confession* states the same with regard to how people come to faith:

> To obtain such faith, God instituted the office of the ministry; that is provided the *Gospel and the sacraments*. Through these, as through means, he *gives the Holy Spirit*, who works faith, when and where he pleases, in those who hear the Gospel. And the Gospel teaches that we have a *gracious God*, not by our own merits but by the merit of Christ, when we believe this (italics added).[3]

---

[1] SA VIII, 3, p. 312, see also LC IV, 30-31, p. 440.
[2] Apol. IV, 66-68, p. 116.
[3] CA V, 1-4, p. 31.

The *Formula of Concord* repeats this thought in many contexts and with great vigour.[4]

Although the reformers could document their contention simply by appealing to the witness of Holy Scripture, they also made the case by suggesting that any other approach would, in effect, be an expression of a works-righteousness that would dishonour Christ. Melanchthon, for instance, argued:

> It is good to extol the ministry of the Word with every possible kind of praise in opposition to the fanatics who dream that the Holy Spirit does not come through *the Word* but because of *their own preparations*. They sit in a dark corner doing and saying nothing, but only waiting for illumination (italics added).[5]

The expression "their own preparations" is the key. The so-called "enthusiasts" of Luther's day reversed the direction of the means of grace: rather than speaking of the means that *God uses* to communicate his grace to us, they spoke of the means *they had to use* to gain such grace from God.[6]

This is the framework within which charismatics speak about people being filled or baptised with the Holy Spirit. It is not something that happens apart from the promises given in the Bible. Rather, it is clearly stated in the Bible that Jesus promised to baptise his followers with the Holy Spirit. The *word of promise*, responded to in faith, becomes the means or instrument by which this grace is conveyed and received. Charismatic manifestations of the Holy Spirit likewise occur as we rely on God's Word and not because we ourselves have found a teaching or method for getting the Spirit into our possession.

Nevertheless, the *Lutheran Confessions do not impose limitations on God* as to the means he must use in order to communicate his grace to us. God sets the biblically indicated means of grace before us; he does not thereby impose limits on himself:

> It is indeed correct and true what Scripture states, that no one comes to Christ unless the Father draw him. But the Father will not do this without *means*, and he has ordained Word and sacraments as the *ordinary* [the possibility of an *extraordinary* intervention is left open] means or instruments to accomplish this

---

[4] For example: "It is God's will to call men to eternal salvation, to draw them to himself, convert them, beget them anew, and sanctify them through this means and no other way – namely, through his holy Word (when one hears it preached or reads it) and the sacraments (when they are used according to the Word)", FC SD II, 50, p. 531.

[5] Apol. XIII, 13, pp. 212-213; see also FC Epit. VII, 20, p. 484; FC SD VII, 124, p. 591.

[6] It is the difference between what has been called a "theocentric-evangelical" view and one which is basically "anthropocentric-nomistic", see Regin Prenter, *Spiritus Creator,* pp. 252-254.

> end. It is not the will of either the Father or the Son that any one should refuse to hear or should despise the preaching of his Word and should wait for the Father to draw him without Word and sacraments. The Father indeed draws by the power of the Holy Spirit, but according to his *common* [an *unusual* possibility is again left open] ordinance he does this through the hearing of his holy divine Word (italics and parentheses added).[7]

The Charismatic renewal has emphasised that God has a sovereign right to set his own agenda for the church and communicate his Spirit as he wills. At the same time, however – with its strong view of biblical authority, its experience in worship, its efforts in building Christian community, and its emphasis on being filled with the Spirit – the Charismatic renewal has implicitly taught people to expect to encounter God pre-eminently through the same means of grace emphasised by the reformers: Word, sacrament, and Christian fellowship.[8]

Grace Alone and Good Works

The Lutheran reformers took the apostle Paul's own exclusive language seriously. In order to do justice to such terms as "freely", "not of works", and "it is a gift" (cf. Rom. 3:21; Gal. 2:16; Eph. 2:8-9; 2 Tim. 1:8), the reformers spoke of grace alone. Ever since, Lutherans have had to explain that *this does not do away with good works.*

The reformers did not mean to exclude good works, but rather any trust in good works for one's justification. Justification occurs alone "by grace, for Christ's sake, through faith".[9] The reformers did not reject good works as such, as their opponents frequently charged, for the reformers were ready to admit that there is a sense in which faith or grace "is at no time ever alone." The *Formula of Concord* explains this:

> Good works do not precede faith, nor is sanctification prior to justification. *First* the Holy Spirit kindles faith in us in conversion through the hearing of the Gospel. Faith apprehends the grace of God in Christ whereby the person is *justified. After* the person is justified, the *Holy Spirit next renews and sanctifies him*, and from this renewal and sanctification the fruits of *good works will follow.* This not to be understood, however, as though justification and sanctification are separated from each other in such a way as though on occasion true faith could coexist and survive for a while side by side with a wicked intention, but this merely shows *the order* in which one thing precedes or follows the other. For Dr Luther's excellent statement remains true: 'There is a beautiful agreement between faith and good works; nevertheless, *it is faith*

---

[7] FC SD XI, 76, pp. 628-629, also FC SD II, 90, p. 539.
[8] SA III, IV, p. 310.
[9] CA IV, 1, p. 30: Apol. IV, 73-74, p. 117; FC SD III, 36, p. 545.

> *alone which apprehends the blessing without works. And yet faith is at no time ever alone*' (italics added).[10]

The chief concerns that have been expressed by the Charismatic renewal fall into that area of theology that Lutherans have traditionally called the "Third Article" or "sanctification".[11] Two points are emphasised in the Confessions: justification and sanctification are to be neither mingled nor separated. Applying this to a charismatic context, one could say: charis (grace) and charism (manifestation of grace) are to be neither mingled nor separated. Sanctification, including that aspect of it that has been related to the word charismatic, is the natural and expected *consequence* of our justification. Good works, including the manifestation of spiritual gifts, are not optional extras. They are the necessary accompaniment to justification. The *Formula of Concord* says clearly:

> It is, of course self-evident that *in true conversion* there must be a *change*, there must be *new activities and emotions in the intellect, will, and heart*, so that the heart learns to know sin, to fear the wrath of God, to turn from sin, to understand and accept the promise of grace in Christ, to have good spiritual thoughts, Christian intentions, and diligence, and to fight against the flesh, etc. *For if none of these things takes place or exists, there is no true conversion* (italics added).[12]

Grace Alone and the Law of God

The Reformation's discovery of the gospel of "grace alone" brought with it obvious dangers, two of which we have discussed above. A third danger is expressed in the term *Antinomian*, which means "without or against law". An Antinomian is one who questions the usefulness of the "law" for a Christian; an Antinomian relegates the use of the law to the unregenerate. The Lutheran

---

[10] FC SD III, 41, p. 546 (our italics). For the *intimate relationship between grace and faith*, see Apol. IV, 116, p. 123: "Since this faith alone receives the forgiveness of sins, renders us acceptable to God, and brings the Holy Spirit, it should be called 'grace that makes us acceptable to God' rather than love, which is the effect resulting from it".

[11] SC II, 5, p. 345; LC II, 34-37, p. 415.

[12] FC SD II, 70, pp. 534-535. See also Apol. IV, 348-355, pp. 160-161: "Good works are necessary [...] We are justified for this very purpose, that, being righteous, we might begin to do good works and obey the law. *For this purpose, we are reborn and receive the Holy Spirit, that this new life may have new works and new impulses, the fear and love of God, hatred of lust etc.* The faith we speak of has its existence in penitence" (italics added). Good works and prayer are not a "free option", FC SD IV, 20, p. 554: LC III, 8-9, p. 421.

Confessions, however, from *Luther's Catechisms* (1529) to the *Formula of Concord* (1577), maintain that *the law is useful also for the Christian.*[13]

The usefulness of the law of God is not limited merely to its *accusing* function leading to repentance and faith in Christ when the Gospel is preached to people whose consciences are afflicted by the law. Most Lutheran Antinomians would grant that this so-called "second use of the law" (the "first use of the law" being its use as a general moral law for all) also applies to Christians, since the Christian remains what in the Lutheran tradition is called *simul justus et peccator, justified* and therefore righteous *by faith in Christ* at the same time as he still is a *sinner in himself.*[14] The Confessions, however, say that the law also is useful for the Christians as far as its content is revealed in the Bible and in nature. This is often called the "third use" of the law. The commandments and the exhortations of the Bible continue to instruct the Christians as to the will of God and what he expects of his children. Yet this all takes place in the context of "grace alone", for the obedience of Christians is not their own achievement, but is a result of the working of the Holy Spirit.

It is for this reason that charismatics' strong emphasis on *charis* and *charism* can be so closely wedded to what the Confessions call "delight in the law of the Lord". The *Formula of Concord* says about Christians practising the law:

> Although truly believing Christians, having been genuinely converted to God and justified, have been freed and *liberated from the curse of the law, they should daily exercise themselves in the law of the Lord,* as it is written 'Blessed is the man whose delight is in the law of the Lord, and on his law he meditates day and night' (Ps. 1:1, 2; 119:1, 35, 47, 70, 97). For the law is a mirror in which the will of God and what is pleasing to him is correctly portrayed. It is necessary to hold this constantly before believers' eyes and constantly to urge it upon them with diligence.[15]

The experience of grace has been so profound that, for the Christian as a "new creature", the law is no longer a threat of judgement; it is a call to trust the Lord to accomplish in us the "works and fruits of the Spirit."[16] The

---

[13] LC I, 311-312, p. 407; LC II, 1-4, p. 411; 67-69, pp. 419-420; CA VI,1, pp. 31-32: "It is also taught among us that such faith should produce good fruits and good works and that we must do all such good works *as God has commanded*, but we should do them for God's sake and not place our trust in them as if thereby to merit favour before God" (italics added). See also Apol XII, 143-145, pp. 204-205; FC SD VI, 1-25, pp. 563-568.

[14] The second use of the law is based on Galatians 3:24 where Paul says that "the law was put in charge to *lead us to* Christ that we might be justified by faith", cp. Rom. 3:19-20; 7:25.

[15] FC SD VI, 4, p. 564.

[16] LC I, 311-312, p. 407; FC SD VI, 17-19, pp. 566-567.

Charismatic renewal has done as much as any contemporary movement to encourage the recovery of the Lutheran Reformation's dynamic dialectic of law and gospel.

(22) "Sola Fides" – Faith Alone

More than any other expression, "faith alone" pinpoints what the Reformation was all about. Its proper interpretation is dependent on all the other "alones" discussed here, but the reformers saw faith as the pivotal word in their theology. Without it, Christ could not be honoured and could not comfort the needy sinner. The opponents of the Reformation could speak of Christ, grace, Scripture, and many other things belonging to the Christian tradition, but without faith, the reformers said, "our opponents bury Christ".[1] The *Apology of the Augsburg Confession* says what faith is and what it achieves:

> This faith brings to God a trust not in our own merits, but only *in the promise of mercy in Christ.* Therefore, when a man believes that his sins are forgiven because of Christ and that *God is reconciled and favourably disposed to him* because of Christ, *this personal faith obtains the forgiveness of sins and justifies us.* In penitence and the terrors of conscience, it consoles and encourages our hearts. Thus, *it regenerates us and brings us the Holy Spirit*, so that we can finally obey God's law, love him, truly fear him, be sure that he hears us, and obey him in all afflictions. It mortifies our lust. By freely accepting the forgiveness of sins, faith sets against God's wrath, not our own merits of love, but *Christ the mediator and propitiator.* This faith is the *true knowledge of Christ*, it uses his blessings, it regenerates our hearts, it precedes our keeping of the law" (italics added).[2]

From the outset, the word *faith* has had central significance in the Charismatic renewal. One of the early Lutheran writings to gain wide circulation in the renewal pointed out that faith was the common denominator in most personal testimonies:

> I have spoken and corresponded with a number of people [who have come into the New Testament experience of speaking in tongues]. They describe the results of their experience in a variety of ways: one testifies to a new joy in his Christian faith; another witnesses to a deeper or more constant awareness of the Spirit's indwelling presence; some have found a new freedom to witness to others of what Jesus means to them; another says that he has a far keener sense of the Spirit's guidance than he did before; many testify to an awakened interest, indeed a deep hunger, to study the Bible; a keener awareness of one's own sins and shortcomings is frequently mentioned. The common denominator in all of these seems to be this: it has intensified the sense of the presence of

---

[1] Apol. IV, 18, p. 109.
[2] Apol. IV, 45-46, p. 113.

God – the word of God has become more contemporary, believable – Christ the Lord has become more real; in a word, *faith has been strengthened*.[3]

Faith Alone and the Means of Grace

Faith, like the grace on which it depends, is *mediated*; it does not come without means. The means that God ordinarily uses to communicate his grace to us are the same means by which we come to faith, namely the Word of God and the sacraments. The *Formula of Concord* says:

> We shall now set forth from the Word of God how man is converted to God, how and by what *means* (namely the *oral Word* and the *holy sacraments*) *the Holy Spirit* wills to be efficacious in us by *giving and working true repentance, faith, and new spiritual power* and ability for good in our hearts, and how we are to relate ourselves to and use these means (italics added).[4]
>
> If a person will not hear preaching or read the Word of God, but despises the Word and the community of God, dies in this condition, and perishes in his sins, he can neither comfort himself with God's eternal election nor obtain his mercy. For Christ, in whom we are elected, offers his grace to all men *in the Word and the holy sacraments*, earnestly wills that we hear it, and has promised that, where two or three are gathered together in his name and occupy themselves with his holy Word, he *is in the midst of them* (italics added).[5]

It is not the Word as a sort of magical formula that brings grace and faith, but *Christ himself and his Spirit* who are present when we "occupy ourselves" with his Word. Such an understanding of faith honours Christ and affords peace to struggling sinners. It relieves people of the notion that they must create faith within themselves. It invites them instead to receive faith as a gift that the Spirit brings them through the gospel.

Faith Alone and Human Decision

Among some Lutheran scholars, there has been a strong bias against understanding faith as decision in a psychological sense.[6] This concern is appropriate insofar as it is directed against a mere act of the will, an independent human decision to believe in God. The human will is involved, of course, but the power behind it is not human autonomy; it is rather the Holy Spirit.

---

[3] Larry Christenson, *The Gift of Tongues* (Minneapolis, MN: Bethany, 1963), p. 9.
[4] FC SD II, 48, p. 530.
[5] FC SD II, 57, p. 532.
[6] See for example Edmund Schlink, *Theology of the Lutheran Confessions*, translated by Paul F. Koehneke and Herbert J. A. Bouman (Philadelphia, PA: Fortress Press, 1961), pp. 96-98, 108.

> In conversion through the *drawing of the Holy Spirit*, God makes *willing people* out of resisting and unwilling people and, after such conversion, man's *reborn will* is not idle in the daily exercise of repentance but *cooperates* in all the works that *the Holy Spirit does through us* (italics added).[7]

Although there is co-operation between the Holy Spirit and the reborn human will, this co-operation does not occur "the way two horses draw a wagon together".[8] They are not equal partners who are co-operating; the source and origin of faith's dynamic is always found in God alone. Thus, even after rebirth, our response takes place by the gracious working of God.

This being said, it must still be maintained that decision is an important element of what is meant by "faith alone". Faith needs to be understood both *psychologically and theologically.* Faith as a *conscious experience, psychologically,* in the lives of Christians contains three fundamental elements:

The first is *trust* or confidence (Latin: *fiducia*) which is directed toward God in Christ expressing the conviction that the work of salvation is *for me* or *for us* personally (Latin: *pro me* or *pro nobis*). "This faith brings to God a *trust* not in our own merits, but only in the promise of mercy in Christ."[9]

Secondly, this trust does not only mean *that* one believes, the *act of faith* (Latin: *fides qua*), but it includes also *what* one believes or trusts, the *knowledge* (Latin: *notitia*) of the *content of faith* (Latin: *fides quae*). Faith, therefore, includes historical knowledge of Christ's work of redemption. This historical knowledge is, however, not enough for salvation.[10]

Thus, faith has, thirdly, also an aspect of *acceptance* or *decision* (Latin: *assensus*): "To avoid the impression that it [faith] is merely knowledge, we add that to have faith means to *want and to accept* the promised offer of forgiveness of sins and justification".[11]

In *theological* terms, faith is the *reception* of salvation: "Faith is that worship which receives God's offered blessings [...] It is by faith God wants to be worshipped, namely that we *receive from him what he promises and offers*."[12]

Some recent descriptions of faith utilising the developmental terms of modern psychology have proven helpful.[13] It is possible to compare the

---

[7] FC SD II, 88, p. 538.
[8] FC SD II, 66, p. 534.
[9] Apol. IV, 44, p. 113.
[10] Apol. IV, 48, 50, p. 114.
[11] Apol. IV, 48, 50, p. 114.
[12] Apol. IV, 49, p. 114.
[13] Holsten Fagerberg, *A New Look at the Lutheran Confessions (1529-1537)*, translated by Gene J. Lund (St. Louis, MO: Concordia, 1972), pp. 155-161. See also Thomas A. Droege, *Self-Realization and Faith* (Chicago, IL: Lutheran Education Association, 1978), pp. 35-49.

variety of meanings given to faith in the Lutheran Confessions with the following developmental model (Latin terms corresponding to the Lutheran Confessions in parenthesis and italics):

What Occurs	What It Affects	Type of Description
reception (*accipere*)	Spirit/spirit	theological
trust (*fiducia*)	emotion	psychological
knowledge (*notitia*)	intellect	psychological
decision (*assensus*)	will	psychological

The above model fits the situation of a person baptised in infancy. God's action (theological) permeates the entire subsequent development. Through the word and baptism as means of grace, God includes the infant in his salvific kingdom (Mt. 19:14, see also other texts about baptism). The infant receives God's grace in a passive way.

At the infant stage of development, "decision" is not an appropriate term. An infant does not "decide" to trust its mother or father. *Trust* is created as the child receives its parents' love. Likewise, God's grace and love, communicated through Word and in other ways, create trust in the infant as the infant grows.

Christian parents may bring a child to the Lord in baptism. As it matures in this Christian environment, its *trust* is linked more and more explicitly with *knowledge*. It hears stories about Jesus, and is drawn to express itself to God in prayer and confessions of love, faithfulness, and commitment.

The child comes to the point where it consciously and personally *decides* to heed Jesus' call to discipleship, which it may remember as a milestone along its pathway. As one aspect of its growing experience in Christ, it hears about the need to be *filled with the Holy Spirit (*Acts 1:8; 2:4; Eph. 5: 18), and decides to pray for this (Lk. 11:9-13). It comes into an experience of being filled with the Spirit, accompanied by a manifestation of spiritual gifts, and this also becomes part of its Christian experience and testimony (Acts 8:14-19). Its life in Christ continues to grow and develop towards maturity (Eph. 3:14-19).

What this says is simply that Lutheran theology should not overreact against "decision theology". There is a wrong sense in which this kind of language could be used – that is, if it implies that human decision is the actual power that changes things. But that is not the kind of emphasis you encounter in the Charismatic renewal. On the contrary, testimonies tilt heavily toward the side of telling what *God has done*. Decision as an expression of faith is simply a *response* to what God says or does. *It adds nothing to the salvation or the gifts that God gives: it only reaches out to receive them.* Christ is not honoured, nor is the whole person properly involved in God's work in us, if the element of personal response is downgraded or set aside.

Faith Alone and Experience

As we have already seen in Part Two, the Bible indicates that the experience of the Holy Spirit and his gifts and fruit serve to confirm, seal, and guarantee the reality of our life in Christ which, before our final resurrection, is possessed by *faith alone* (Eph. 1:13-14; see also Acts 11:17; 15:8-9; Rom. 5:1-5; 8:9-11; 1 Cor. 1:4-9; 2 Cor. 1:20-22; Gal. 3:2, 5; Heb. 2:3-4;).

In this *confirming sense*, the Lutheran Confessions make room for *sight and experience*. The *Formula of Concord* says:

> Since the *Holy Spirit dwells in the elect* who have come to faith as he dwells in his temple, and *is not idle in them* but urges them to obey the commandments of God, believers likewise should not be idle, still less oppose the urgings of the Spirit of God, but should exercise themselves in all Christian virtues, in all godliness, modesty, temperance, patience, and brotherly love, and should diligently seek to 'confirm their call and election' so that *the more they experience the power and might of the Spirit within themselves, the less they will doubt their election* (italics added).[14]

The Confessions hasten to add, however, that such experience may in times of temptation grow weak and that then the promises of God are nevertheless to be trusted:

> And if perhaps they should fall into such grave temptation that they feel that they are *no longer experiencing any power whatever of the indwelling Spirit of God* and say with David, 'I had said in my alarm, I am driven far away from thy sight' (Ps. 31:22), then, *regardless of what they experience within themselves*, they should nevertheless join David in the next words, 'But *thou didst hear my supplications when I cried to thee for help*' (Ps. 31:23).[15]

Luther, in his commentary on John 14:21, spoke confidently about *faith being confirmed by experience:*

> Thus, this is a sermon not only of words but of *experience* as well. To be sure, Christ begins with the Word, when he lets us hear the gospel and receive baptism and the sacrament. But the devil comes on the heels of this; he assails and hinders us on all sides, in an attempt to check and obstruct the Word. At this point, *experience must enter in* and enable a Christian to say: 'Hitherto I have heard that Christ is my Saviour, who conquered sin and death; and I believed this. *Now my experience bears this out.* For I was often in the agony of death and in the bonds of the devil, but he rescued me and *manifested himself.*

[14] FC SD XI, 73, p. 628.
[15] FC SD XI, 74, p. 628.

> Now I *see and know that he loves me and that what I believe is true*' (italics added).[16]

In his commentary on Zechariah 4:1-3, Luther makes the same point with reference to visible manifestations:

> For as I have often said, the signs and visions that God gives in addition to the Word are needed to strengthen all the more the faith of weak or saddened souls who cannot cling to the mere Word as well as to a picture or sign. For it is a great thing to believe that God is gracious and favourable to us but a difficult thing for human hearts to achieve. The frivolous fanatics, however, come rushing and roaring along and at once can praise the Spirit so confidently that they tolerate neither picture nor sign but in one moment are able to believe everything without a sign – even the bare word. But though Joshua and Zerubbabel are great men in the eyes of God and indeed have a strong faith, conditions are still so bad that God must use visions and interpretations to nurse them along in the faith as though they were young children (italics added).[17]

In reporting on the closing session of a conference of church leaders in Tanzania in 1985, which had followed five days of intense Bible study, preaching, prayer, worship, and a eucharistic service, and in which there had been noticeable manifestations of the Spirit – visions, prophecies, speaking in tongues, healings – W. Dennis Pederson wrote:

> It was obvious to the people present that the Lord had 'plans' for Tanzania, and all became aware of it as we joined in praise and songs of thanksgiving for the 'filling and empowering of the Spirit of the Lord'. But in our minds the subtle thought intrudes, 'Was it real? Will these days together really mean a change from traditional business-as-usual church practices? Will Holy Spirit revival come to Tanzanian churches?' Only the Lord knows for sure, but he did confirm our ministry through reports received before we left [...] Thanks be to God, he doesn't leave our faith unconfirmed. He finds a way to say, in spite of our ordinariness, weaknesses, and failings, his affirming word, 'Well done, good and faithful servants'.
>
> There were young Catholic nuns attending the school who served us unselfishly as kitchen and dining room helpers. One especially was noticeable to me because she was the first Christian Masai tribal woman I'd seen. In broken English, she told that they had seen for a long while a light 'brighter than the sun' above the roof of the auditorium meeting place. Her report was confirmed by an Anglican Church Army captain who was a member of our team. He had heard a similar report while preparing to witness to a group of 150 college students the night following our conference. (These were students enrolled at the teachers' college where the conference was held, but they themselves were not participants in the conference.) He asked the whole group if the report of

---

[16] AE 24, p. 151.

[17] AE 20, pp. 222-223.

> the light over the assembly hall at midday had been seen by others. About 30 students raised their hands, and reported the light was 'brighter than day light' and remained above the building for quite a while, long enough to gather groups of friends to witness the phenomenon.
>
> We all concluded with agreement that our faith can accept these reports because of the scriptural promise that 'signs and wonders will follow those who believe.' We can't make them happen, we concurred, but at times those evidences do follow Spirit-led and Spirit-dependent ministry."[18]

Such an understanding of faith is a precious heritage that both grounds and interprets charismatic experience. "No one," said Luther, "can correctly understand God or his Word unless he has received such understanding immediately from the Holy Spirit. But no one can receive it from the Holy Spirit without experiencing, proving, and feeling it."[19] Far from undermining true faith, this kind of emphasis is "directed against a faith that is solely a concern of the mind. We learn to know God through the Holy Spirit, but the Holy Spirit uses experience as his school."[20] Such an understanding of faith honours Christ by giving to sight and experience the role assigned to it both by Scripture and the Lutheran Confessions: it *follows faith* as its expected fruit and confirmation granted by the Holy Spirit, rather than preceding faith as its necessary foundation.[21]

---

[18] W. Dennis Pederson, *A Letter Home for Family and Friends from an Itinerant Renewal Teacher and Evangelist,* unpublished report (Minneapolis, MN: International Lutheran Renewal Center, 1985), pp. 16-17. Pederson was a prominent leader in the Lutheran Charismatic renewal in the USA, see Appendix.

[19] AE 21, p. 299; WA 4, p. 546.

[20] AE 13, pp. 110-112; WA 4, p. 149; WA 40/3, pp. 542-545.

[21] For further documentation of this position in *The Book of Concord,* see Apol. IV, 275-276, p. 148; LC III, 93-98, p. 433; LC IV, 21, p. 439; FC SD VIII, 27, p. 596.

(23) "Sola Scriptura" – Scripture Alone

Next to "faith alone" as the pivotal truth of biblical revelation, the reformers insisted on "Scripture alone" as the proper source and norm for all Christian teaching. As the *Formula of Concord* says at the beginning:

> We pledge ourselves to the prophetic and apostolic writings of the Old and New Testaments as the pure and clear fountain of Israel, which is the *only true norm* according to which all teachers and teachings are to be judged and evaluated (italics added).[1]

The authority of Scripture as given by God is contrasted to human doctrines or opinions. The biblical passage most frequently cited in the *Book of Concord* is Matthew 15:9, "They worship me in vain; their teachings are but rules taught by men".[2] The position taken by Melanchthon in the *Augsburg Confession* on "matters in dispute", and his commentary on these in his *Apology of the Augsburg Confession*, make it particularly clear that Lutheranism is committed to the principle of *sola scriptura.* This principle is often called the *formal principle* of the Lutheran Church, explaining the *authority* for Christian teaching, while the other "alones" are called the *material principles*, explaining the *content* of that teaching.

What are the implications of this principle for the understanding of the role of tradition, on the one hand, and the possibility of further divine guidance, on the other?

Scripture Alone and Tradition

The reformers recognised that although they maintained "Scripture alone", Scripture, like faith, "is at no time ever alone".[3] Scripture must be interpreted. A false application can dishonour Christ. Thus, while Scripture stands unrivalled in authority, we are concerned for its proper interpretation.

The process by which the canon of Scripture was formed is not free from tradition. The Lutheran reformers from the start recognised the three ecumenical creeds from the ancient church as traditions conveying an authoritative interpretation of Holy Scripture. They also honoured liturgical

---

[1] FC SD, Rule and Norm, 3, pp. 503-504.

[2] *The Book of Concord*, Index of Biblical References, p. 641.

[3] FC SD III, 41, p. 546.

traditions and maintained them, except when they were convinced that they dishonoured Christ.[4]

The Charismatic renewal has given a high place to the authority of Scripture. At the same time, it has been able to appreciate and affirm good traditions that do not contradict the gospel or require what Scripture does not require. The Charismatic renewal has found expression in a variety of denominational settings, and it has been notable for honouring those respective heritages and traditions. Such traditions, according to the Lutheran Confessions, can help promote tranquillity, good order, discipline, and harmony.[5] We should not scorn such traditions, although we should oppose their misuse.

We should also be free to create new forms and practices that correspond with practices in the Scriptures, or are recommended or admitted by the Scriptures. Christians may also create or employ different forms and practices that are relevant in their various cultural contexts, as long as these are not contrary to Christian teaching but serve the life and mission of the church.

Scripture Alone and Guidance

Scripture is recognised by virtually all Christians as the normative expression of divine revelation.[6] The question raised by the Charismatic renewal, however, is whether the text of Scripture itself is the only channel by which

---

[4] Melanchthon could write about the most important confession of the Lutheran church, the *Augsburg Confession*: "Since this teaching is grounded clearly on the Holy Scriptures and is not contrary or opposed to that of the universal Christian church, or even to the Roman church (in so far as the latter's teaching is reflected in the Fathers), we think that our opponents cannot disagree with us in the articles set forth above." CA Summary after Art. XXI, p. 47; see also CA Conclusion, 5, p. 95. He wrote: "With regard to church usages that have been established by men, it is taught among us that those usages are to be observed which may be observed without sin and which contribute to peace and good order in the church, among them being certain holy days, festivals, and the like. Yet we accompany these observances with instruction so that *consciences may not be burdened by the notion that such things are necessary for salvation.*" AC XV, 1-4, pp. 36-37.

[5] Apol. XV, pp. 215-222.

[6] The basis paragraph of the World Council of Churches which all member churches must subscribe to, contains a confession of the Triune God, the divinity and salvific work of Jesus Christ and *the authority of the Scriptures*: "The World Council of Churches is a fellowship of churches which confess the Lord Jesus Christ as God and Saviour according to the Scriptures, and therefore seek to fulfill together their common calling to the glory of the one God: Father, Son and Holy Spirit." Cf. WCC website. However, Orthodox member churches of the WCC (and the Roman Catholic Church which is not a member) may put *church tradition on a par with the Bible as authority in the church.*

God speaks to people, or whether people can expect to experience divine guidance through believing the promises that Scripture makes in regard to such things as answers to prayer, counsel with fellow believers, or charismatic gifts such as the word of wisdom, word knowledge, prophecy, speaking in tongues, interpretation of tongues, and discernment of spirits.

People involved in Charismatic renewal maintain that such revelatory gifts belong to the promise of Pentecost and that the promise of Pentecost belongs to the entire era of the church, not merely to its formative years. Does the standard of "Scripture alone" allow room for this kind of experience of divine guidance?[7]

Some important distinctions must be made. The Lutheran Confessions call Scripture the only source and norm "according to which as the only touchstone all doctrines should and must be understood and judged as good or evil, right or wrong."[8] Lutherans have traditionally distinguished between what Scripture as a whole *prescribes* and what it merely *describes.* What it prescribes as normative doctrine cannot be essentially modified or augmented, but only applied – in all times and places. However, what it describes may or may not find parallels in contemporary experience; if parallels do occur, they need to be judged by what Scripture does in fact prescribe.

For instance, both in the Old and New Testaments, the Lord guides his people by means of charismatic revelations. In special situations, he speaks through prophets, visions, and dreams in order to encourage, console, warn, and help them. The kind of thing we find in Scripture might in fact also happen in church history and today: visions (Acts 10:19; 11:6), divine calling (Acts 13:1-4), discernment of secret thoughts (Acts 13:9-10; 5:3-9), divine guidance of the work of missionaries (Acts 8:29; 11:12-17; 16:6-10), and direct insight into God's will and purpose (Acts 10:19). But we are always obliged to test such experiences by Scripture (Acts 17:11).

The point of this essential distinction is that Christ's atoning work for us is finished, and therefore the revelation about it is also finished; but *that which the risen Christ accomplishes through his Spirit in the church still goes on.* We cannot modify or augment that which has been finished by Christ, but we must allow his finished work to bear its promised fruit in our lives. To have visions or revelations similar to those reported in Scripture need not compromise the finished work of Christ. Indeed, Scripture itself encourages believers to expect this kind of gifts in their lives.

Essentially that is what Luther was saying in the oft-quoted, but seldom understood, passage taken from the *Smalcald Articles*, in which he insisted

---

[7] To this question, see also Excursus 2 below.

[8] FC Epit., Rule and Norm, 7, p. 465.

that the Spirit and the "external Word" always go together.[9] He was not trying to drive a separating wedge between revelations in Scripture and contemporary revelations. He simply insisted that all revelation must be rooted not in mere subjective experience but in the external Word – an expression that Luther equated with "the Scriptures", especially as proclaimed, and with "the sacraments."[10] Luther's concern was to preserve the honour of Christ by carefully maintaining the distinction between the finished work of Christ and the work which he is still seeking to accomplish in us and through us.

Luther's insistence on the essential priority of the external Word helps set charismatic experience in the right context. Because we believe this Word, there is no reason to doubt that the Holy Spirit can be stirred by faith and prayer (2 Tim. 1:6-7) to move us to prophesy and to manifest his revelatory gifts (1 Cor. 12:7-11, 31; 14:1, 26-33). Scripture itself gives us this expectation, and nothing in the Lutheran Confessions contradicts that expectation, as long as the finished work of Christ for our salvation is in no way compromised.

Scripture Alone and the Holy Spirit

In spite of the reformers' insistence on the sole authority of Scripture as source and norm for all doctrine, they did not think of Scripture as something that could be divorced from God's sovereign Spirit, something we could take into our own hands and manipulate for our own purposes. Any attempt to wrest the authority of Scripture from the sovereign God, whose Spirit resists domestication, was abhorrent to them. Even while contending against the "enthusiasts'" attempt to divorce Word and Spirit, Luther rigorously insisted on the sovereignty of the Spirit – the Holy Spirit's resistance to manipulation and domestication.[11]

How did Luther resolve the tension between Scripture as bearer of the Spirit and the Spirit as sovereign Lord distinct from Scripture? Rather than resolve the tension, he creatively maintained it in his understanding of the dynamic role of prayer and its relationship to the means of grace.[12]

---

[9] SA III, VIII, 3-13, pp. 312-313. Also AE 4, pp. 125-127; AE 24, pp. 365-367; AE 43, pp. 198; 201-202.

[10] "The Lutheran Church and the Charismatic Movement: Guidelines for Congregations and Pastors" (A Report of the Commission on Theology and Church Relations of the Lutheran Church-Missouri Synod, April 1977) in McDonnell (ed), *Presence, Power, Praise – Documents on the Charismatic Renewal*, Vol. 2, pp. 311-314.

[11] Prenter, *Spiritus Creator*, pp. 101-107, 168.

[12] Prenter, *Spiritus Creator*, pp. 107-108, 124-127, 171, 294. See also chapter 24 of this text where the important role of prayer in a Lutheran theology of the Holy Spirit is dealt with.

(24) "Sola Oratio" – Prayer Alone

Most summaries of Lutheran doctrine confine themselves to the four "alones" discussed in the preceding chapters. However, the Lutheran Confessions draw from Scripture four additional "alones" that are relevant to a charismatic theology: prayer alone, the church alone, baptism alone, and the Holy Spirit alone.

In his *Large Catechism*, Luther spent more time discussing prayer than any other subject, except the Ten Commandments.[1] His treatment was calculated to stimulate the reader to fervent and joyful prayer, but not by arguing that it is necessary in order to achieve grace; rather, it is necessary because one already has been "graced".

Prayer Alone and Grace

Having already been made God's children through faith and baptism, we are both obligated and privileged by God the Father's command and promise to approach him in expectant prayer. Luther wrote:

> This we must know, that all our safety and protection consist in *prayer alone*. We are far too weak to cope with the devil and all his might and his forces arrayed against us, trying to trample us under foot. Therefore, we must carefully select the weapons with which Christians ought to arm themselves in order to stand against the devil. [...] But by *prayer alone* we shall be a match both for them [the human enemies] and for the devil, if we only persevere diligently and do not become slack. For whenever a good Christian prays, 'Dear Father, thy will be done,' God replies from on high, 'Yes, dear child, it shall indeed be done in spite of the devil and all the world' (italics added).[2]

Contemporary Lutherans have not yet learned to appreciate Luther's own pious and audacious prayer life.[3] Although he was sharply critical of the prayers of "monks and priests, who howl and growl frightfully day and night," his criticism was based on the following generalisation:

> None of them has ever undertaken to pray out of obedience to God and faith in his promise, or out of consideration for his own needs. They only thought, at

---

[1] LC III, pp. 420-436.

[2] LC III, 30-32, p.424.

[3] See Luther's emphasis on "earnest prayer" in connection with baptism in AE 53, pp. 102-103, and also Martin E. Lehmann, *Luther and Prayer* (Milwaukee, WI: Northwestern, 1985).

> best, of doing a good work as a payment to God, not willing to receive anything from him, but only to give him something.[4]

For Luther, "prayer alone" was no contradiction of "grace alone", but an inevitable expression of it.

Prayer Alone and the Means of Grace

There is a nervousness in some parts of Lutheranism that, by urging the importance of prayer, we will diminish appreciation for the "means of grace," the Word and sacraments. One Lutheran study commission expressed the concern this way:

> Only Baptism, the Lord's Supper, and the use of God's Word are external means. By these alone the Holy Spirit has chosen to work among us in grace. Prayer, for example, is not a means of grace but a proper response to God's grace as offered in the sacrament of Baptism.[5]

The theological concern behind such a statement is understandable: it is a concern for "grace alone." But its practical impact can lead to the worst kind of imbalance, producing *passive Christians who don't expect any experience of the Holy Spirit outside the doors of the church. It also expresses a too narrow understanding of how God's grace is given to us.* Melanchthon writes in the Apology about the *sacramental quality of prayer*:

> Ultimately, we should list as sacraments all the things that have God's command and a promise added to them, then why not *prayer*, which can most truly be called a sacrament? It has both the command of God and many promises. If it were placed among the sacraments and thus given, so to speak, a more exalted position, this would move men to pray. Alms could be listed here, as well as afflictions, which in themselves are signs to which God has added promises. No intelligent person will quibble about the number of sacraments or the terminology, so long as *those things are kept which have God's command and promises* (italics added).[6]

Neither does this scepticism about prayer reflect Luther's own vigorous concern for prayer. It tends to make prayer an optional extra by speaking of it merely as "a proper response", rather than as "a necessary response". Luther wrote:

---

[4] LC III, 25, p. 423.
[5] *The Lutheran Church and the Charismatic Movement: Guidelines for Congregations and Pastors* (A Report of the Commission on Theology and Church Relations of the Lutheran Church-Missouri Synod, April 1977), in McDonnell (ed), *Presence, Power and Praise*, p. 312.
[6] Apol. XIII, 16-17, p. 213.

> To pray, as the Second Commandment teaches, is to call on God in every need. This God *requires* of us; he has not left it to our *choice*. It is our *duty* and *obligation* to pray if we want to be Christians (italics added).[7]

Again:

> And I suspect that people turn out so badly after Baptism because our concern for them has been so cold and careless; we, at their Baptism, *interceded* for them without zeal. [...] See to it, therefore, that you are present in true faith, listen to God's Word, and *earnestly join in prayer* [...] For as I said, the human additions do not matter very much, as long as Baptism itself is administered with God's Word, true faith, and *serious prayer* (italics added).[8]

And again: God wants us to acknowledge faith as his gift. He wants it recognised as a proffered gift *for which we must ask him.*[9]

A theological distinction relative to the expression "means of grace" could prove helpful at this point. The *Book of Concord* distinguishes between the following:

- means of communicating God's grace = Word and sacraments[10]
- means of receiving God's grace = faith[11]
- means of asking for God's grace = prayer[12]

These three distinguishable aspects of the term "means of grace" should neither be lumped all together nor disengaged from each other. God has joined Word and sacraments, faith, and prayer together. They cannot accomplish his purpose if we separate them.

A matter of practical application in charismatic theology at this point would be giving prayer (Acts 1:4, 12-14) its necessary role in relation to Jesus' promise to baptise with the Holy Spirit (Acts 1:5; 2:32-33). If "Scripture alone" is our source and norm, then Word and sacraments, faith, and prayer for the Holy Spirit will be found in a close relationship, which, if not heeded, will frustrate the grace of God, dishonour Christ, and rob believers of their full inheritance (Acts 20:27; Rom. 15:19, 29). *Specific prayer for the Holy Spirit* (Lk. 11:9-13) *and his "good things" (Mt. 7:7-11) is not optional,* either for Scripture or the Lutheran Confessions. It is by *calling upon God that we are saved*, through *faith,* after having *heard the Word* (Rom. 10:13-14). *It is also in prayer as a result of faith that we appropriate all the good gifts that God has in store for us* (Mt. 6:3; 7:7-11).

---

[7] LC III, 8-9, p. 421.
[8] AE 53, pp. 102-103; AE 24, pp. 382-384.
[9] AE 23, p. 183.
[10] FC SD II, 50-54, pp. 530-531.
[11] Apol. IV, 116, p. 123; FC SD III, 10, p. 541; III, 43, p. 547.
[12] LC III, 49-54, pp. 426-427.

(25) "Sola Ecclesia" – The Church Alone

Bishop Cyprian of Carthage (died in 254 A.D.) insisted together with many other church fathers that "outside the church, there is no salvation"; and again, "he cannot have God as a Father who has not the church as his mother." Provided that the church is understood as created by the Gospel and the Holy Spirit, and not merely as a hierarchical institution, Luther would agree. He wrote:

> [The church] is the mother that begets and bears every Christian through the Word of God [...] Where Christ is not preached, there is no Holy Spirit to create, call, and gather the Christian church, and outside of it no one can come to the Lord Jesus Christ [...] Outside of the Christian church (that is, where the Gospel is not) there is no forgiveness, and hence no holiness. Therefore, all who seek to merit holiness through their works rather than through the Gospel and the forgiveness of sin have expelled and departed themselves from the church (italics added).[1]

The Lutheran Confessions manifest a deep appreciation for the church, because the church also honours Christ. Christ wills and creates his church (Mt. 16:18). The church consoles and equips struggling sinners through its gospel ministry, which includes "the mutual conversation and consolation of brethren."[2]

The Church Alone and Unity in Christ

At the heart of any understanding and expression of the church is the early confession, "Jesus is Lord!"[3] Historically, renewal movements have often led to division and the forming of new religious groups or denominations. The extent to which the Charismatic renewal has remained within the churches is closely related to its strong emphasis on the lordship of Christ. Although many charismatics have left or been put out of their churches, many more have remained because they believed it to be the Lord's will. They have generally been supportive of the church.[4]

---

[1] LC II, 42, 45, pp. 416, 418; cf. Apol. IX, 2, p. 178.

[2] SA III, IV, p. 310.

[3] Cf. the confession of Peter in Matthew 16:16 and Acts 2:36, cp. 1 Corinthians 12:3: Philippians 2:11.

[4] Richard Quebedeaux, *The New Charismatics* (New York, NY: Doubleday, 1976), p. 189.

Luther emphatically rejected the Pope's claim that Christians "must be obedient to him in order to be saved", and by that making himself "equal to and above Christ". He was even willing to die for his opposition to this claim.[5]

Yet, on the other hand, Melanchthon could write:

> Concerning the Pope, I hold that, if he *would allow the Gospel*, we, too, may concede to him that superiority over the bishops which he possesses by *human right*, making this concession for the sake of peace and general unity among the Christians who are now under him and who may be in the future (italics added).[6]

Thus, on the one hand, we need to be extremely wary of absolutising church structures that usurp Christ's authority as head of the church. On the other hand, we should take pains to avoid a privatising and individualising interpretation of "faith alone" that succeeds only in breaking up what should be the unified body of Christ, "a holy community."[7] Unity among Christians is surely one of the key priorities of the Holy Spirit – a priority that has received strong emphasis in the Charismatic renewal. Working for the unity of churches who are "creatures of the gospel", *to the full extent that truth allows*, has been one of the most noticeable marks of the renewal.

It should be almost unnecessary to state that this Christian unity today also includes believing Catholics. Although Lutheran charismatics would disagree with some Catholic doctrines concerning the papacy, the view of the papacy that Luther opposed is not still held by the Roman Catholic Church, and therefore also Luther's harsh judgement of it no longer applies.

The Church Alone and Its Mission to the World

That the church is "*in* the world but not *of* the world" does not imply that the church lives a ghetto-like existence in the world, finding its end in its own existence. Rather, it is *sent into the world*, consecrated to extend the kingdom of Christ, not by using the world's sword but by using the sword of the Spirit. Accordingly, Luther wrote these important words about *mission* in the *Large Catechism,* explaining the second petition of the Lord's prayer, "Thy kingdom come":

> God's kingdom comes to us in two ways: first, it comes here *in time*, through the Word and faith, and secondly, in *eternity*, it comes through the final revelation. Now, we pray for both of these, that it may *come to those who are not yet in it*, and that it may come by *daily growth here* and *in eternal life*

---

[5] SA II,!V, 12-13, p. 300.
[6] SA III, Signatories, p. 316.
[7] LC II, 49, p. 417.

> *hereafter to us who have attained it*. All this is simply to say: 'Dear Father, we pray Thee, give us thy Word, that *the Gospel may be sincerely preached throughout the world* and *that it may be received by faith* and *may work and live in us*. So we pray that thy *Kingdom may prevail among us through the Word and the power of the Holy Spirit*, that the devil's kingdom may be overthrown and he may have no right or power over us, until finally the devil's kingdom shall be utterly destroyed and sin, death, and hell exterminated, and that we may live forever in perfect righteousness and blessedness' (italics added).[8]

This quote from the Large Catechism is one of the clearest and most important Lutheran statements of what the kingdom of God is and of the need for world mission in the power of the Spirit.

Immediately preceding this quoted text on mission, Luther defines the *kingdom of God*, which we pray for the coming of:

> What is the kingdom of God? Simply what we have learned in the Creed, namely that God has sent his Son, Christ our Lord, into the world to redeem and deliver us from the power of the devil and to bring us to himself and rule us as a king of righteousness, life, and salvation against sin, death, and an evil conscience. *To this end, he also gave his Holy Spirit to teach us this through his holy Word and to enlighten and strengthen us in faith by his power* [...] We pray that, led by the Holy Spirit, many may come into the kingdom of grace and become partakers of salvation, so we may all remain together eternally in this kingdom which has now made its appearance among us (italics added).[9]

Charismatic experience must be understood in the context of the Holy Spirit's work of equipping the church for world mission and evangelisation, thereby honouring the risen Christ, who breathed his Spirit on his apostles and said: "As the Father has sent me, I am sending you" (Jn 20:21-23; cp. Lk. 24:44-49; Acts 1:4-5, 8).

The combined ecumenical and missional thrust of the Charismatic renewal has been closely related to the perception that, without unity, the church lacks both the resources and the credibility needed for the task of world evangelisation (Jn 17:15-21).

The Church Alone and the Ministry with Word and Sacraments

The Lutheran Confessions do not pit the "priesthood of all believers" (1 Pet. 2:5, 9) and the "pastoral office" against one another. The distinction is not one of quality or character, but one of *call and function*, providing a way for the variety of gifts and callings in the body of Christ to come to expression.

---

[8] LC III, 53-54, p. 427.

[9] LC III, 51, 52, pp. 426-427. Note how close this understanding of the kingdom of God and mission is to the biblical exposition in Part Two of this book.

Those who are ordained to the pastoral ministry (1 Tim. 4:11-16; 2 Tim. 1:6-7; Tit. 1:5-9) have a shepherding role, and as such exercise an oversight function (Acts 20:28; 1 Pet. 5:1-4). A primary function of their oversight is to raise up, encourage, order, and release other ministries in the body of Christ. The Lutheran Confessions value the pastoral ministry not as an end in itself but because it is a necessary function in the church's proclamation of the Gospel and administration of the sacraments. The Augsburg Confession says:

> To obtain such faith [that is, justifying faith; cf. Art. IV], God instituted the office of the *ministry, that is, provided the Gospel and the sacraments. Through these*, as through means, *he gives the Holy Spirit, who works faith*, when and where he pleases, in those who hear the Gospel (CA, Art. V, italics added).
>
> It is also taught among us that one holy Christian church will be and remain forever. This is the assembly of all believers among whom the Gospel is preached in its purity and the holy sacraments are administered according to the gospel. For it is sufficient for the true unity of the Christian church that the Gospel be preached in conformity with a pure understanding of it and that the sacraments be administered in accordance with the divine Word (CA, Art. VII).[10]

The office of the ministry serves to build up the entire church, and it is therefore the right of the church to elect, call and ordain ministers. Thus, Melanchthon wrote:

> It is necessary for the church to retain the right of calling, electing, and ordaining ministers. This right is a gift given exclusively to the church, and no human authority can take it away from the church. It is as Paul testifies to the Ephesians when he says, 'When he ascended on high, he gave gifts to men' (Eph. 4:8, 11, 12). He enumerates *pastors and teachers* among the gifts belonging exclusively to the church, and he adds that they are given for the work of ministry and for building up the body of Christ. Where the true church is, therefore, the right of electing and ordaining ministers must of necessity also be (italics added).[11]

Curiously, Melanchthon cited Ephesians 4 and specifically mentioned "pastors and teachers," but he entirely omitted discussion or even mention of "apostles, prophets, and evangelists." This has prompted one commentator to ask:

> Is the doctrine of the one church office of preaching the Word and administering the sacraments perhaps a human arrangement that overlooks the

---

[10] CA V, 1-2: VII, 1-2. pp. 31-32.
[11] Treatise 67, p. 331.

> wealth of spiritual gifts? Or, was the wealth of spiritual gifts intended only for the time of the founding of the church?[12]

Therefore, those involved in Charismatic renewal can affirm the pastoral ministry as a God-given office in the church, exercising oversight particularly for the indispensable ministry of Word and sacraments. *These ministers* should be called by the church as a matter of order:

> It is taught among us that nobody should publicly teach or preach or administer the sacraments in the church without a regular call.[13]

How this "regular call" may be practiced can vary under different circumstances, but it should be emphasised that it is the *church, the believing community*, who has the right to call people to this ministry with Word and sacraments.

At the same time, we should leave room for the Spirit to raise up the entire variety of ministries promised in Scripture. All the charisms should be allowed to function in the church.

We must confess that, historically speaking, Lutheran churches have been clergy-dominated. Far from raising up and releasing the various ministries of the people in the church, the pastoral office has all too often simply taken over: pastor and minister have become synonymous terms, applied exclusively to the ordained ministry. In the New Testament, *every believer was a "minister", that is, serving in some capacity*. The terms laity and clergy are not found in the Bible, and the distinction between them has therefore no biblical warrant. The ordained ministry is but one among many ministries or charisms.

One of the concerns being expressed by the Charismatic renewal is that the *priesthood of all believers*, one of the great Reformation insights, should come to practical expression, not only in one's personal relationship with God but also in one's calling and ministry in the body of Christ. This would magnify the honour of Christ as the full range of gifts and ministries are used to build up the fellowship and carry out the evangelistic commission.

The Church Alone and the Denominations

Jesus prayed for the unity of his disciples (Jn 17:21). Paul testified to the reality of one body and one church. Anything else would dishonour Christ and put salvation in jeopardy (Eph. 2:11-22; 4:3-6; 1 Cor. 3:3-7; 12:12-13. How does this square with a global church divided into a multitude of denominations?

---

[12] Schlink, *Theology of the Lutheran Confessions,* p. 308.

[13] CA XIV, p. 36.

Melanchthon distinguished between defining the church "properly speaking," namely, as "God's true people, reborn by the Holy Spirit",[14] and the church "according to the outward associations of the church's marks".[15] He said, in effect, that "properly speaking," the church is one, although this essential unity is still "hidden under the cross."[16] The *Augsburg Confession* says that unity can be exercised where there is agreement in the teaching of the gospel and in the administration of the sacraments – otherwise not.[17]

This parallels the thought of the apostle Paul, who seemed to distinguish between differences that are foundational, that is, at the very heart of the gospel and therefore divisive (Gal. 1:6-9), and those that do not break the unity of the Spirit but need to be worked at until a unity of the faith is attained (Eph. 4:1-3, 13; cf. 1 Cor. 3:2-7, 21-23). He did not indicate how much the exercise of unity is curtailed in the latter case. He simply exhorted the believers with great passion to work at the problem in the confidence that it can be overcome.

The quest for unity is certainly one of the significant marks of organised Christianity in our time. The Charismatic renewal has had a strong ecumenical thrust from the beginning, which found expression at different levels.

At a personal level, Christians found each other, as fellow believers, across denominational lines. At another level, charismatic ministry in congregations and conferences and publications often came from people of other traditions as well as from one's own. There were few denominational barriers. The ecumenism that occurred at these levels was noteworthy for its spirit of love, mutual respect, and patience.

At another level, charismatic leaders have undertaken to wrestle with some of the tough theological and pastoral questions that historically have divided the church. Here, distinctions must be made between foundational, divisive issues and issues of lesser importance.[18] Given the strong ecumenical thrust of the movement, and recognising this as a genuine work of the Holy Spirit, *charismatic leaders must exercise the spiritual discernment necessary to deal with disunity on the basis of both truth and love.* They must clarify sound *biblical norms for unity, and not advocate the exercise of church unity simply on the basis of agreement in matters of charismatic experience.*

At the same time, they must press forward in a humble and untiring quest for an ever-increasing manifestation of unity in the body of Christ. Disunity

---

[14] Apol. VII-VIII, 14, 22, 29, pp. 170, 172-173.

[15] Apol. VII-VIII, 3, p. 169.

[16] Apol. VII-VIII, 18, p. 171.

[17] CA VII, 2, p.32; see also CA XXI, 1-2, pp. 47-48.

[18] Treatise 38, pp. 326-327; FC SD , Rule and Norm, 15, pp. 506-507; FC SD, III, 6, p. 540.

with other believers can never be taken lightly. It, too, is an evidence of sin and hinders the work of the Spirit. It militates against spiritual growth.

The path towards greater Christian unity may involve several steps and take time. It should include a willingness on the part of individual Christians and the denominations to admit that we all "*know in part*" (1 Cor. 13:9, 12), to *correct mistakes, misunderstandings* and *errors* of the past, to *repent* lack of love and understanding of others, to *appreciate the value of the theological and spiritual contributions of others*, to come together to *study the Bible together* with regard to issues of contention, to *pray and praise together*, to *work together in mission, evangelisation and diakonia,* and to *practice visible unity* in various creative ways, such as common services, conferences and ecumenical organisations, even without full unity. All Christians in the "one, holy, Catholic, and apostolic church"[19] should be able to live together and practice "unity in reconciled diversity" despite the continuing existence of different denominations.

[19] The Nicene Creed, 19.

(26) "Solum Baptisma" – Baptism Alone?

Closely related to the issue of whether one dares to speak of the "church alone" as the "mother that begets and bears every Christian" is the question regarding the role of the sacrament of baptism. Is "baptism alone" the seed by which the "mother church" legitimately conceives? If so, do Word and faith and charisms become optional extras?

The earliest Lutheran reformers *did not* speak of "baptism alone" as explicitly as they spoke of the other "alones" discussed above. Yet, they did stress the *necessity of baptism for salvation.* The *Augsburg Confession* says,

> This inborn sickness and hereditary sin [original sin] is truly sin and condemns to the eternal wrath of God all those who are not born again *through Baptism and the Holy Spirit* (italics added).[1]
>
> It is taught among us that baptism *is necessary and that grace is offered through it.* Children, too, should be baptised, for in baptism they are committed to God and become acceptable to him (italics added).[2]

Luther, however, said only that Christ binds *us* to baptism, *not that Christ has limited himself to it.* It is the wilful rejection of baptism which jeopardises one's salvation.[3]

The Lutheran reformers' sharp disagreement with the Anabaptist reformers slowly pushed their successors to formulate their teaching in such a way that one could speak meaningfully also of "baptism alone". They criticised the teachings of the Anabaptists – in ways that we today may deem too harsh – because of their view,

> [...] that the children of Christians, because they are born of Christian and believing parents, are holy and children of God even without and prior to Baptism. Therefore, they do not esteem infant Baptism very highly and do not advocate it, contrary to the express words of the promise which extends only to those who keep the covenant and do not despise it (Gen. 17:4-8, 19-21).[4]

The passages from Scripture cited to establish the point are taken from the Old Testament, even though the particular issue of baptism is a New Testament one. That does not invalidate the point if its presupposition is valid, namely, that *baptism is God's fundamental means of establishing a*

---

[1] CA II, 2, p. 29.
[2] CA IX, 1-2, p. 33; see Apol. IX, 1-3, p. 178; LC IV, 6, p. 437.
[3] LC IV, 31, p. 440.
[4] FC SD III, 4, p. 634.

covenant relationship with his people in the New Testament.[5] Paul did operate with this conviction in Colossians 2:9-15,[6] but it is a conviction that requires qualification as we shall see.

Baptism and the Word of God

Jesus' words according to John 3:5, "No-one can enter the kingdom of God unless he is born of water and the Spirit", would seem to call for a "baptism alone" interpretation, although the verses immediately following make it clear that the connection between water and the Spirit is not one that robs the Spirit of his sovereignty. And the "born anew" passage in 1 Peter 1:23-25, found in a letter considered by many commentators to be at least in part a baptismal homily, lets the reader know what Luther later also emphasised in the *Small Catechism*:

> It is not the water that produces these effects, but the *Word of God connected with the water*, and *our faith which relies on the Word of God connected with the water*. For without the Word of God, the water is merely water and no Baptism. But when connected with the Word of God, it is a Baptism, that is, a gracious water of life and a *washing of regeneration in the Holy Spirit*, as St Paul wrote to Titus (3:5-8) [...] (italics added).[7]

The connection between water and Spirit was, for Luther, not such that the effect of Baptism is achieved merely through the application of water. Rather, *the effect is always dependent on the Word (God's promise and institution) and the work of the Holy Spirit.* And this in turn leads to another qualification of the meaning of "baptism alone".

Baptism and Faith

With remarkable frequency and consistency, the New Testament connects baptism with faith. *Only faith is able to receive and manifest the salvific effects of baptism.*[8] Peter said, "*Repent* (which includes *faith*) and *be baptised*, every one of you in the name of Jesus Christ for the *forgiveness of*

---

[5] A covenant between God and human beings has a quality that distinguishes it from covenants between mere human beings. In a covenant with God, God remains sovereign and remains Saviour. Humans are never an equal party with God in the covenant, but can only be "graced" by God through the covenant, even though it calls for a human response of faith and obedience.

[6] See also Rom. 4:9-12; Eph. 2:12; 1 Cor. 11:25; Mt. 26:28.

[7] SC IV, 10, p. 349.

[8] See, for example, Mark 16:15-16; Mt. 28:18-20; John 3:5, 16-18; Acts 2:37-42; 8:12; 9:10-19; 10:44-48; 16:25-34; 18:8; 19:1-7; 22:12-16; Gal. 3:23-29; Eph. 2:8-9; 5:25-27; Col. 2:8-15; 1 Pet. 1:3-2:3; 3:21.

your sins" (Acts 2:38). In other passages where faith is not mentioned explicitly, it is implied.[9]

The Lutheran Confessions recognise this relationship between faith and baptism and direct it with great vigour against any notion that baptism saves automatically or magically, that is, simply by virtue of its performance. The fact that the heart of baptism is *the objective Word of promise*, signalled to the reformers the *necessity of faith*, since, as they repeated over and over again, *only faith can receive such a promise.*

> Thus, we teach that in using the sacraments there must be a faith that believes these promises and accepts that which is promised and offered in the sacrament. The reason for this is well-founded. A promise is useless unless faith accepts it. The sacraments are signs of the promises (italics added).[10]

On this question, Luther steered a course between two extremes. On the one hand, some *Catholic* scholars had said *too little* about faith. Baptism became a near-magical rite that guaranteed salvation. Luther, however, said in the *Large Catechism*:

> Since these blessings are offered and promised in the words which accompany the water, they cannot be received unless we believe them whole-heartedly. Without faith, Baptism is of no use, although in itself it is an infinite, divine treasure [...] We insist on faith alone as so necessary that without it nothing can be received or enjoyed [...] Where faith is lacking, [baptism] remains a mere unfruitful sign.[11]

The Radical Reformation, which included the Anabaptists, on the other hand, had said *too much* about faith: baptism was not valid unless faith was present. Luther wrote about this:

> When the Word accompanies the water *Baptism is valid*, even though faith be lacking. For *my faith does not constitute Baptism but receives it*. Baptism does not become invalid even if it is wrongly received or used, for it is bound not to our faith but to the Word (italics added).[12]

For Luther, it was important to distinguish between the *validity and the effects* of baptism. *Without faith, there are no salvific effects*, such as forgiveness of sins and a new birth. Yet *baptism is still valid*, just as the gospel is valid regardless of our faith in it. Therefore, those who had no faith at the time of their baptism or fell from faith after baptism, did not need to be

---

[9] Acts 8:35-38; Rom. 6:3-19; Titus 3:4-8.
[10] Apol. XIII, 19-20, p. 213.
[11] LC IV, 33-34, 37, 73, pp. 440, 441, 445.
[12] LC IV, 53, 86, p. 443.

baptised again but might return to their baptism in faith and *then* enjoy its salvific effects.[13]

The promises relating to baptism hold "baptism alone" and "faith alone" in tension: each one expresses an aspect of the truth that honours Christ and saves sinners. Neither is complete by itself. It would be contrary to the Confessions to set a rigid standard of belief and life as a precondition for receiving baptism; it is, after all, the beginning point of the Christian life, not an achievement along the way. Yet, it is contrary to the intention of the Confessions when pastors in state or folk church situations are required to administer baptism to every child, even when those who bring the child to baptism and promise to raise it in the faith have no sincere intention of doing so, do not participate in the life and worship of the congregation and are ignorant of basic Christian beliefs.

Baptism and the Christian Life in the Spirit

As fundamental as baptism is in Lutheran confessional theology, it is not reduced to a mere past historical event. It is expected to produce positive results in one's life as the Christian in faith lays continual claim to the benefits promised in baptism. Thus, we read in Luther's *Large Catechism:*

> A *Christian life* is nothing else than a *daily baptism*, once begun and ever continued [...] Repentance, therefore, is nothing else than a return and approach to baptism, to resume and practice what had earlier been begun but abandoned (italics added).[14]

Baptism must be seen not only in terms of what it *initiates,* but also in terms of what it *continues* to produce in the life of a Christian.

The strong emphasis on justification in baptism has sometimes led Lutheranism to a reduced emphasis on sanctification, in terms of both the fruit of the Spirit (for example, Gal. 5:22-23) and the gifts of the Spirit (for example, 1 Cor. 12:4-11). However, the Lutheran Confessions themselves never understood justification in such a limited way. Their teaching on baptism, linked as it was to justifying faith, clearly set forth baptism's all-inclusive, sanctifying consequences.[15] In the *Small Catechism*, Luther emphasises these consequences of baptism for the Christian life:

---

[13] LC IV, 77, 86, p. 446.

[14] LC IV, 65-79, pp. 445-446.

[15] "To put it most simply, the power, effect, benefit, fruit and purpose of Baptism is to save [...]. To be saved, we know, is nothing else than to be delivered from sin, death, and the devil and to enter the kingdom of Christ and live with him forever", LC IV, 24-25, p. 439. See also Luther's important word about good "Easter-preachers" and bad "Pentecost-preachers" in his treatise *On the Councils and the Church* in AE 41, pp. 113-115.

> What does baptising with water signify? Answer: it signifies that the old Adam in us, together with all sins and evil lusts, should be drowned by daily sorrow and repentance and be put to death, and that the *new man should come forth daily*, and rise up, cleansed and righteous, to live forever in God's presence. Where is this written? Answer: in Romans 6:4, St Paul wrote, 'We were buried therefore with him by baptism into death, so that as Christ was raised from the dead by the glory of the Father, we too might *walk in newness of life*' (italics added).[16]

Luther actually used an argument from the *experience of the Holy Spirit* in his defence of infant baptism:

> That Baptism of infants is pleasing to Christ is sufficiently proved from his own work. God has sanctified many who have been thus baptised (as infants) and has given them the Holy Spirit. Even today there are not a few whose *doctrine and life attest that they have the Holy Spirit.* Now if God did not accept the Baptism of infants, he would not have given any of them the Holy Spirit nor any part of him [...] God has *confirmed Baptism through the gift of the Holy Spirit* (italics added).[17]

It is as if Luther uses Peter's argument when he baptised Cornelius and his house according to Acts 10:44-48 in the opposite order. While Peter concluded from the *demonstrable reception of the gift of Holy Spirit* that they *should be baptised*; Luther concluded from the *demonstrable reception of the gift of the Holy Spirit* that *infant baptism which had already taken place was approved by God.*

Later, Lutheranism was tempted to understand faith in a merely passive sense, as that which "receives" the fullness of salvation, without recognising sufficiently how this faith then grows and develops and actively proceeds to acknowledge, to trust, and to assent to everything that the lordship of Jesus implies. This faith goes on to pray that what has been objectively received in baptism will be increasingly expressed in daily life.

> In order that we may see it through and abide and persevere in it, we should *implore* God to give us his grace, of which he has assured us in *holy Baptism*, and not doubt that according to his promise he will give it to us. We have his Word, [...] 'how much more will the heavenly Father give the Holy Spirit to those who ask him?' (Luke 11:11-13) (italics added).[18]

Thus, "baptism alone" is not to be understood in a way that unbiblically limits the scope of God's gift. The continued working of the Holy Spirit, including his charismatic manifestations, is an expected accompaniment to

---

[16] SC IV, 12-13, p. 349.
[17] LC IV, 49-50, pp. 442-443.
[18] FC SD XI, 72, pp. 627-628.

baptism. The Charismatic renewal recognises this active, daily effect of baptism by emphasising the practical results in the fruit and the gifts that the Holy Spirit accomplishes in the life and ministry of the baptised.

Baptism and Confirmation

The Charismatic renewal agrees with the Nicene Creed that "one baptism for the forgiveness of sins" is sufficient. Luther said that rebaptism could add nothing but the external sign of more water to the "one Baptism" whose effect and signification continue and remain constant. He said simply, "We need not again have the water poured over us".[19] Lutheran charismatics take the same position.

However, the *continuing results of baptism are such that they confirm our baptism.* Church practice has narrowed the concept of "confirmation" down to a once-in-a-lifetime rite. In Scripture, however, confirmation is experienced repeatedly, as faith exercises itself in prayer and obedience.[20]

Confirming signs and wonders were experienced by Jesus at his baptism, his transfiguration, and on many other occasions. His disciples experienced them particularly at Pentecost, but also before and after.

Neither Scripture nor the Lutheran Confessions pit the one baptism against continuing charismatic manifestations of the Holy Spirit. Rather, they confirm the abiding reality of baptism. The issue of rebaptism has no essential connection with charismatic experience as such. The focus is rather on that which continues to express and confirm what God has done in baptism.

The historical background of confirmation as a rite, or sacrament in the Catholic tradition, is the prayer in the early church for the gift of the Holy Spirit and its charismatic manifestations, with anointing and/or laying on of hands in connection with water baptism. It is described from the 3rd century. Since every priest could baptise but only the bishop pray for the Holy Spirit with anointing, the growth in number of churches made it impossible for the bishops of larger dioceses with many congregations to be present at every baptism. Therefore, they would gather those who had been baptised as infants at a later time when they had reached the age of reason for what was to be called "confirmation", where the bishop would pray for them individually with anointing with oil and laying on of hands. The prayer would be for an outpouring of the Holy Spirit with manifestations of the gifts of the Spirit. This separation of baptism in water and prayer for the Holy Spirit into two

---

[19] LC IV, 77-78, p. 446; see also FC SD II, 69, p. 534. Biblical evidence is found in such passages as Romans 11:29; 2 Timothy 2:13; and in the simple but significant fact that there was no "recircumcision" in the Old Testament, but only repentance, conversion, and return to the covenant.

[20] See Jungkuntz, *Confirmation,* p. 7.

separate sacraments – often divided in time by several years – became common in the Roman Catholic Church,[21] while the unity of water baptism and prayer with anointing for the Holy Spirit was kept and is still practiced in the Eastern Orthodox churches.

After the Reformation, the Anglican/Episcopal church kept the rite of confirmation, while the Lutheran church discontinued it. It was, however, reintroduced in the Lutheran church in the 18th century as a programme for Christian education of young people and a ceremony where church members confirmed their Christian faith. As such, it was obligatory. In recent times, confirmation has been made voluntary for church members and requires no confession of faith on the part of the confirmands. It is preceded by a period of Christian instruction and is itself a ceremony where the pastors of the congregation pray for the confirmands individually by laying on of hands.

Confirmation has been emphasised by the Catholic Charismatic renewal as an important instrument for spiritual renewal. One might suggest that confirmation also in the Lutheran church could recover some of its original emphasis as a confirmation of faith and a prayer for the fullness of the Holy Spirit with his fruit and gifts, at least for those church members who would want this kind of confirmation.

Baptism and the Eucharist

"Baptism alone" is directed against the notion that Baptism is not a sacrament, or that it is optional, or that it does not communicate grace in its most fundamental and comprehensive form, as new life. It is not directed against those things that nurture or express the new life.

The expression "baptism alone" thus does not downgrade or eliminate the Eucharist. The Lord's Supper, as a matter of fact, functions in relationship to

---

[21] To the practice of confirmation in the ancient church, see Montague and McDonnell, *Christian Initiation,* pp. 31, 48, 80, 341. Regarding the Roman Catholic Church today, they recommend that "openness to the full meaning of baptism should be sought and developed through prayer and the encouragement of the Christian community. The sacrament of confirmation could be a particularly important occasion for such an awakening or breakthrough, though we should also beware of limiting the work of the Holy Spirt to a sacramental timetable", p. 341. In the Roman Catholic Church, the effects of confirmation are seen among others as: "the special outpouring of the Holy Spirit as once granted to the apostles on the day of Pentecost [...] It increases the gifts of the Holy Spirit in us [...] It gives special strength of the Holy Spirit to spread and defend the faith in word and action as true witnesses to Christ, to confess the name of Christ boldly, and never to be ashamed of the Cross." *Catechism of the Catholic Church,* 1302-1303. For the relationship between baptism and confirmation, see also B. Neunhauser, *Baptism and Confirmation* (New York, NY: Herder & Herder, 1964), especially pp. 47-48.

baptism, nurturing in its God-appointed way the life bestowed through holy baptism.

The Charismatic renewal among Lutherans has given particular recognition and expression to the centrality of the Eucharist in the life of Christians.[22] Lutheran charismatic Christians have echoed the teaching of the apostle Paul that the *spirituality of baptised persons will be expressed in lives that are both sacramental* (1 Cor. 10-11) *and charismatic* (1 Cor. 12-14).

[22] CA XXIV, 1, p. 56; Apol. XXIV, 35, p. 256. There has been a considerable output of worship materials from Lutheran congregations involved in the Charismatic renewal, for example from Resurrection Lutheran Church, Charlotte, North Carolina.

(27) "Solus Spiritus Sanctus" – The Holy Spirit Alone

The first part of Luther's explanation of the Third article of the Apostles' Creed in the *Small Catechism* reads as follows,

> I believe that by my own reason and strength, I cannot believe in Jesus Christ, my Lord, or come to him. But *the Holy Spirit has called me through the Gospel, enlightened me with his gifts, and sanctified me and preserved me in true faith*, just as he calls, gathers, enlightens, and sanctifies the whole Christian church on earth and preserves it in union with Jesus Christ in the one true faith (italics added).[1]

In his explanation to the Third Article of the Creed in his *Large Catechism*, Luther wrote: "But God's Spirit alone is called Holy Spirit, that is, he who has sanctified and still sanctifies us."[2] Then he commented briefly on how the Spirit sanctifies us through "placing us in the bosom of the church" where "he preaches to us and brings us to Christ," where we "daily obtain full forgiveness of sins through the Word and through signs [sacraments]," and where he causes us to "become strong in faith and in the fruits of the Spirit" and to be "illuminated and blessed by the gifts of the Holy Spirit" until our holiness is instantly perfected and eternally preserved through "the resurrection of the body and the life everlasting." Thereupon, he summarised his thought with the assertion: "No human wisdom can comprehend the Creed; *it must be taught by the Holy Spirit alone*" (italics added).[3]

Thus, Luther did not shrink from speaking of the "Holy Spirit alone". Like every other "alone" of which Luther spoke, it must not be absolutised outside of its context, but applied specifically to the falsehood he wished to negate and the truth he wanted to assert.

The church cannot become holy, that is, the unique people of God, by dint of mere human effort, but the *Holy Spirit alone can accomplish God's purpose in God's people.* That is why many in the church today who long for the church's renewal are seeking it there, where Jesus promised we could find it – in the Holy Spirit alone (Jn 16:5-15).

---

[1] SC II, 6, p. 345.

[2] LC II, 36, p. 415.

[3] LC II, 67, p. 420.

Theology of the Cross

Lutheran theology is dialectical theology. It lives in paradox and tension. It recognises that many aspects of biblical truth come to us in the form of contraries-statements that seem logically contradictory, yet each of which expresses an aspect of the truth. Dialectical theology takes hold of both sides of paradoxical truth: the high and the low found in Mary's Magnificat, the weak and the strong in Paul's theology, the law and the gospel in the Bible, the call of all and the election of some, etc. It recognises that the life of a Christian is marked both by the humiliation and suffering of the cross, and by the glory of the resurrection.

Luther scholars have given special attention to what is called Luther's *theologia crucis* –theology of the cross.[4] Appeals to the theology of the cross in relation to the Charismatic renewal have often been truncated. They have simply opposed the theology of the cross to a theology of glory rather than relating the two dialectically.[5] Mary's low can only be understood in relation to the fact that God made her high; Paul's weakness cannot be separated from the fact that God made him strong; the gospel has no meaning apart from the law; and Luther's theology of the cross is bound together in dialectical tension with the glory of the resurrection.

Peter tried to break the dialectic. He wanted Jesus to avoid the cross, but Jesus rejected his objection as Satanic (Mk 8:31-33). Jesus did not reject the glory that the Father had ordained for him. He only insisted that the glory could not be separated from his journey to the cross as the trusting, obedient, and suffering servant of God (Mk 8:27-31; Is. 52:13-53:12).

Charismatic theology does not oppose a theology of the cross, but it testifies that the cross of Jesus Christ is not barren. Like the grain of wheat that falls to the earth and dies (Jn 12:24), it bears much fruit. Charismatic manifestations are "significant" (Jn 20:30-31; 14:12) expressions of the kingdom that springs forth from the cross (Mt. 11:2-6; Lk. 24:25-27; Phil. 3:10). Furthermore, they help equip God's people for taking up their crosses and following Jesus in the task of evangelising the entire world (Lk. 24:44-49; Mk 16:15-18; 28:16-20). They glorify and honour Christ as they help to bring God's great salvation to sinners who are crying out, "Brethren, what shall we do?" (Acts 2:32-42).

---

[4] Althaus, *Theology*, pp. 25-34, 55-63.

[5] See for example the conflicting statements regarding "cross" and "glory" in Frederick D. Bruner and William Hordern, *The Holy Spirit – Shy Member of the Trinity* (Minneapolis, MN: Augsburg, 1984) pp. 51, 57, 66.

(28) The Work of the Holy Spirit in the Theology of Martin Luther

By Tormod Engelsviken

Introduction

So far, we have mostly discussed the relationship between the Charismatic renewal and the Lutheran Confessional writings. These writings reflect the theology of a number of Lutheran reformers in the 16th century, pre-eminently Martin Luther. In this chapter, we want to take a harder look at *Luther's own understanding of the work of the Holy Spirit.*

The Norwegian professor of systematic theology, Leiv Aalen, has correctly pointed out that the struggle of the Reformation concerned itself basically with the *third Article of the Creed, the article on the Holy Spirit.*[1] The peculiar characteristics of the evangelical Lutheran understanding of Christianity are apparent in the doctrine of the *personal appropriation of salvation.*[2] The doctrines with which the Reformation is commonly associated, e.g. sola gratia, sola fide, and sola scriptura can all formally be traced back to medieval Catholicism or medieval opposition to the Roman Catholic Church. What gives these doctrines their essentially *new meaning in the Reformation*, starting with Luther, is the basic insight which has been classically expressed in Luther's *Small Catechism* in the explanation to the *Third Article* of the *Apostles' Creed,* where the *Holy Spirit* is the subject:

> I believe that by my own reason or strength I cannot believe in Jesus Christ, my Lord, or come to him. But the *Holy Spirit* has *called me through the Gospel, enlightened me with his gifts*, and *sanctified* and *preserved me in true faith*, etc. (italics added).[3]

The importance of the doctrine of the Holy Spirit within the framework of Luther's theology cannot be discovered by simply focusing on texts where the Holy Spirit is explicitly mentioned, or where the Holy Spirit is said to have a work distinct from that of Christ. The importance of the Holy Spirit is

---

[1] Leiv Aalen, *Testimonium Spiritus Sancti Internum som teologisk prinsipp* (Testimonium Spiritus Sancti Internum as Theological Principle, Oslo: Lutherstiftelsens forlag, 1938), p. 14.

[2] Aalen, *Testimonium*, p. 14.

[3] Tappert, *The Book of Concord,* p. 345.

only understood if it is seen within the structure of Luther's total understanding of Christianity.

The Pentecostal/Charismatic movement in our time has – as we have seen – raised new questions to the Lutheran understanding of the work of the Holy Spirit. To some of these questions, one may find direct answers in the tradition of Lutheran theology, especially in its struggle with what we today call the *Radical Reformation*, whose representatives were pejoratively called "enthusiasts" (German: *Schwärmer*) by the Lutheran reformers. Other questions may be answered indirectly, in the sense that Lutheran theology may imply certain answers without explicitly dealing with the questions themselves. Finally, there may also be questions to which Lutheran theology does not provide an answer because both biblical exegesis and church experience have moved into areas the fathers of the Reformation could not foresee. In these last cases, the answers given by Lutheran theologians, even if they are not found in the Lutheran tradition, should at least be *compatible with the overall Lutheran understanding of the Holy Spirit's work* and preferably be found *in continuation with insights already present at the time of the Reformation.* This is what we shall attempt to do in this chapter.

Obviously, we are not intending to present a total, systematic description of Luther's thoughts on the Holy Spirit. We want to focus especially on issues which are directly or indirectly relevant for a discussion of the relationship between the theology of Martin Luther and the theology and experience of the Charismatic renewal, and then place both the questions asked and the answers given within the larger framework of Luther's pneumatology.

It has been our intention to take into account all relevant material in Luther's own writings, yet we are aware that the material underlying this study necessarily is limited.[4] In addition to direct references to Luther's own writings, we shall also draw on some important studies of Luther's theology that have relevance for our theme.

The Double Work of the Holy Spirit as Agent and Gift

We want to start by drawing on an important distinction that Luther makes between *two different aspects* of the work of the Holy Spirit in relation to human beings. On one side, the Spirit works *as an agent on people*, and on the other side, the Spirit works *as the indwelling Spirit, as a gift, in Christians*. Although it is the same Spirit working in both ways, it is important for our understanding to distinguish between these two functions.

[4] We shall not try to draw distinctions between the theology of the younger and older Luther, especially since it has been argued convincingly that there are no basic differences as far as the doctrine of the Holy Spirit is concerned, cf. Prenter, *Spiritus Creator,* p. 246.

The distinction is found already in the New Testament, especially regarding the role of the Holy Spirit in baptism: "It is the common conviction of the primitive Christian church that *baptism takes place by the Holy Spirit and that the Holy Spirit is imparted with baptism.*"[5] The German scholar D. Noesgen shows that this also applies to Luther's view:

> He distinguishes from early on between the Holy Spirit as *sender* and the Holy Spirit as *sent* into the heart. This distinction implies that Luther both can call *faith a work of the Holy Spirit communicated through the Word* and also say that *with faith the Holy Spirit is given* so that he immediately resists and reduces sins (our translation from German, italics added).

Luther distinguishes between "the work of the Spirit *on* the hearts", and "the indwelling of the Spirit *in* the hearts".[6] We shall see that this distinction is important both for the view of the work of the *Holy Spirit in creating faith* through the Word of God and the sacraments, and the view of the *indwelling Spirit that is given to faith* and how it relates to the believer's new life of sanctification and ministry.

Luther places the work of the Holy Spirit in the theological field of *soteriology*, the doctrine about how *salvation is appropriated* to people by the Spirit. He is interested primarily in the Spirit's work of *making people Christians*, and secondarily in *making them "good" Christians*, although these two aspects of the Spirit's work cannot be separated, as *justification* and *sanctification* cannot be separated. Luther can describe the work of the Spirit as:

> How to rescue men from sin and death by *making them children of God*, righteous and heirs of eternal life; how to *build the kingdom of God and destroy the kingdom of hell*; how to *fight against the devil* and overcome him; how to *give comfort, strength and support* to a believing conscience (italics added).[7]

If this is the aim of the Holy Spirit's operation, one may go on to ask *how* the Spirit performs this work. Here, the church plays a central role.

---

[5] Edmund Schlink, *The Doctrine of Baptism*, trans. J. A. Bouman (St Louis, MO: Concordia, 1972), p. 58.

[6] D.K.F. Noesgen, *Geschichte der Lehre vom Heiligen Geist* (History of the Doctrine of the Holy Spirit, Gütersloh: Druck und Verlag von C. Bertelsmann, 1899), p. 138.

[7] Martin Luther, *Luther's Works*, Vol. 24, p. 360. *Luther's Works*, edited by Jaroslav Pelikan and Helmut T. Lehman, 55 volumes (St Louis, MO: Concordia; Philadelphia, PA: Fortress Press, 1957, hereafter called *LW*).

The Church

The question of *where one could meet the Spirit* occupied Luther. In the continuation of our quote above from the *Small Catechism,* Luther says,

> [...] he [the Holy Spirit] calls, gathers, enlightens, and sanctifies the whole *Christian church* on earth and preserves it in union with Jesus Christ in the one true faith. *In this Christian church,* he daily and abundantly forgives all my sins, and the sins of all believers [...][8]

The church is where the Spirit works, and his primary work as the *Holy* Spirit is to make people *holy,* to *sanctify* them. This is done according to Luther through "the church, the forgiveness of sins, the resurrection of the body, and the life everlasting [...] He first leads us into his holy community, placing us upon the bosom of the church, where he preaches to us and brings us to Christ".[9]

The church is the community of people of God created by the Spirit, and the Spirit uses the church for his continued creation and preservation of God's people. In this way, the Spirit makes the prerequisite for his own work.[10] The Spirit may operate outside the church in creation and preservation,[11] but *his work of salvation and sanctification is only found in the church.*

The work of the Holy Spirit is personally understood, but not individualistically. It does not belong only to the private or interior sphere of life. The work of the Spirit takes place through *public signs, in the open.* The church is hidden in the sense that it properly speaking consists only of *believers*, and only God knows in whom faith is present,[12] but this does not mean that the *means* of the operation of the Spirit are hidden. In Luther's definitions of the church, there are often references both to the *invisible faith* and the *visible means* which the Spirit uses to create this faith. He says,

> Now the heavenly Jerusalem above is the church, that is, believers scattered throughout the world, who have the same Gospel, the same faith in Christ, the same Holy Spirit, and the same sacraments.[13]

The double understanding of the church as both *personal and functional* is also present in the *Augsburg Confession,* Art. VII, and it is beautifully and simply expressed by Luther in the *Smalcald Articles*:

---

[8] *The Book of Concord,* p. 345.

[9] Explanation to the Third Article of the Creed in the Large Catechism, *The Book of Concord,* p. 415.

[10] Prenter, *Spiritus Creator,* p. 242.

[11] Althaus, *Theology,* p. 440.

[12] Althaus, *Theology,* p. 292.

[13] *LW*, Vol. 26, p. 439.

> Thank God, a seven-year-old child knows what the church is, namely, holy *believers* and sheep who hear the *voice of their Shepherd* (italics added).[14]

One misses the point if one dismisses either the reference to "believers" (personal faith) or the reference to the "voice of the Shepherd" (the Word and the sacraments). In this sense, the relationship to the church precedes any relationship to Christ and his Holy Spirit: "Whoever seeks Christ must first find the church. Now the church is not wood and stone but the group of people who believe in Christ. Whoever seeks the church should join himself to them and observe what they teach, pray and believe. For they certainly have Christ among them."[15]

Why is the church important as the place where one may seek and find Christ? The answer is given in the basic task of the church: to preach the Gospel and administer the sacraments. These are the means of the Holy Spirit.[16] Luther expresses the same thought in his commentary on John 14:25-26:

> Thus you must learn from this text *how and where you are to look for the Holy Spirit* – not up above the clouds but in the place to which Christ directs you [...] *He is down here on earth*, just as Christendom is here on earth [...] Thus we must picture him as being *in close association with the office and order of Christendom, the Word and the sacraments* [...] *The Holy Spirit is present wherever they are present* (italics added).[17]

It is through them the Holy Spirit creates faith and makes people holy. The spirit does this by *giving Christ*, "for it is the Holy Spirit who gives you Christ and his holiness and who works faith in you."[18]

The Word of God as the Primary Means of the Holy Spirit

The primary means of the Holy Spirit is the *Word* of God, in the form of the written Scripture and the spoken word (Latin: *verbum vocale*). Luther simply regards Scripture as a whole as the Word of God given by the Holy Spirit. In innumerable places, he can simply refer to the Holy Spirit as the author of Scripture. However, this does not mean that Scripture automatically is God's word *to me*. Theology is basically the interpretation of Scripture. But this is to Luther not only an intellectual exercise; it is insolubly connected with the question of one's standing in the sight of God. Luther is therefore looking for God's word to *him, personally,* in Scripture.

---

[14] *The Book of Concord*, p. 315.
[15] Reference in Althaus, *Theology*, p. 287.
[16] *The Book of Concord*, p. 31.
[17] *LW*, Vol. 24, p. 171.
[18] *LW*, Vol. 24, p. 172.

In this connection, he early distinguishes between the *Spirit and the letter.*[19] Unless the Holy Spirit speaks to *me* through the Word, Scripture remains only letter. The letter is historical information, a thing of the past, unless the Spirit makes it *present.* The letter is Law, the Spirit is Gospel. The letter, by recounting past events, calls on us to do, to imitate, to understand. The Spirit, however, is hidden in the letter, and uses the letter to address us, to give us life in Christ, who is the centre of the Scripture. The Spirit bridges the gap between the Christ of history and the risen Christ of the present. "The risen Christ lives his risen life in our midst in this message [...] by the Holy Spirit the risen Christ's present life is in our midst by the Gospel."[20]

The Word is an *outward thing*. It comes through Scripture or through preaching, and the Spirit reveals Christ through it. One has to distinguish between the Word as an outward event, and the Spirit's accompanying *inward revelation of Christ*. The doctrine which reveals the Son of God "is revealed by God, *first by the external word and then inwardly through the Spirit* [...]. Therefore, the Gospel is a divine Word that comes down from heaven and is revealed by the Holy Spirit, who was sent for this very purpose."[21]

This means that the Spirit in one sense is *limited to this Word.* It is the corollary of the limitation of God's revelation in Christ. God has revealed himself for salvation *in Christ only.* The outward Word corresponds with the incarnation of Christ. *Just as God comes to us in the incarnate Christ, the Spirit brings us Christ in the Word.*[22] This frees human beings from seeking Christ outside the Word. The fact that the saving work of the Holy Spirit is bound to the Word is therefore nothing else but an expression of the *christocentricity* of the Spirit's work and its *gospel-character.* This connection between the outward Word and the inward work of the Spirit is clearly expressed in the *Smalcald Articles*: "We must hold firmly to the conviction that God gives no one his Spirit or grace except through or with the external Word which comes before."[23]

The Word does not become gospel ("good news") *for us* without the Holy Spirit's inner testimony (Latin: *testimonium Spiritus sancti internum*). The Word is therefore a *necessary vehicle for the Spirit* (because is it the word about Christ), but it is *not sufficient* in the sense that the Word always *automatically* brings the Spirit. The Holy Spirit retains his freedom, his sovereignty. This freedom is emphasised by the fact that the Word "comes before" the Spirit. *The Spirit does not always come with the Word creating*

---

[19] Gerhard Ebeling, *Luther: An Introduction to His Thought*, translated by R. A. Wilson (London: Collins, 1979), p. 99.

[20] Prenter, *Spiritus Creator,* p. 112.

[21] *LW*, Vol. 26, p. 73; *LW*, Vol. 40, p. 146.

[22] Althaus, *Theology*, pp. 36-37.

[23] *The Smalcald Articles,* VIII, 3, *The Book of Concord*, p. 312.

faith in the gospel. Sometimes, the Word remains *without fruit*, and sometimes the Spirit *comes later*. This is the Spirit's hidden decision:

> *Before* all other works and acts *you hear the Word of God*, through which the Spirit convinces the world of its *sin* [through the Law]. Then we acknowledge our sin, we *hear of the grace in Christ* [through the Gospel]. In this Word, the Spirit comes and *gives faith where and to whom he wills* (parentheses and italics added).[24]

If human beings could always bring about the coming of the Holy Spirit for salvation simply by preaching the Word or administering the sacraments, they would control the Spirit and thus make the word into a law. Only if God's sovereignty is emphasised in relation to the Word (and the sacraments as well) so that these become *effective for salvation only when received* in *faith freely given by the Holy Spirit,* is the *Gospel*-character of the Word retained. Then the only proper human attitude to the Word is that of *expectation* and *prayer*.[25] The movement goes *from God to human beings*, not from human beings to God. When the Word becomes a saving word, it is always by the power of the Spirit.

The fact that the Holy Spirit only comes through the Word means that salvation only comes through Christ, who is the content of the Word. The tension between the *necessity* of the Word and the *insufficiency* of the Word for the Holy Spirit's appropriation of salvation to human beings is necessary if the Gospel shall remain truly *gospel: which means the message that salvation is by the grace of God for Christ's sake through faith, and not by works*, not even by works such as listening to or preaching the Word, or by receiving or administering the sacraments as if this was sufficient in itself.[26]

Election

The fact that the *Holy Spirit does not always create faith in those who hear the Word*, raises the difficult question of God's election or predestination. There is a tension between the *universality* of the God's redemption in Christ and the *particularity* of God's election. Luther himself tended toward so-called *double predestination*: that some people were predestined by God for salvation, others for damnation. Most other Lutheran reformers and the Lutheran church as a whole did not follow him in this view. They would agree that the Spirit creates faith in the elect, but that those who do not believe do so as a result of their own choice. The *Augsburg Confession* puts it positively but does not say anything about those who do not believe, when it

---

[24] *LW*, Vol. 40, p. 149. See also Prenter, *Spiritus Creator*, pp. 249-250.
[25] Prenter, *Spiritus Creator*, p. 250.
[26] Prenter, *Spiritus Creator*, pp. 126-127.

says that God "gives the Holy Spirit, who works faith, *when and where he pleases* (Latin: *ubi et quando visum est Deo*) *in those who hear the Gospel*".[27]

With regard to judgement, Article II of the *Augsburg Confession* states that "this inborn sickness and hereditary sin [original sin] is truly sin and condemns to the eternal wrath of God all those who are not born again through Baptism and the Holy Spirit".[28] It does not, however, say that this is God's will or decision. This view of election of the believers may not be logically wholly satisfactory. It does, however, come to grips with the biblical view that God both "wants all men to be saved and come to a knowledge of the truth" (1 Tim. 2:4) and that some are elected (Mt. 22:14; Rom. 8:28-30; 1 Cor. 1:26-29). Peter writes his first epistle "to God's elect, strangers in this world [...] who have been chosen according to the foreknowledge of God the Father, through the sanctifying work of the Holy Spirit, for obedience to Jesus Christ and sprinkling by his blood" (1 Pet. 1:1-2). Prenter argues that this tension between the universality of Christ's redemption and the particularity of those who believe unto salvation, cannot be solved logically, only christologically.[29]

Law and Gospel

It is necessary to look at the *contents* of the Gospel which the Spirit brings home to the hearts. The Gospel in a wider sense includes the Law as it drives us to Christ. The *first* work of the Holy Spirit when the Word is read or preached is to *reveal the Law*. Luther comments on John 16:8: "Through the words of the apostles, the *Holy Spirit* will convince the whole world of sin." This is:

> An office which entails *convincing the world of sin*; that is, attacking all its deeds and conduct, and telling people that by nature they are *guilty and sinners before God*, and that they must *either obey this message about Christ or be eternally damned and lost*"(italics added).[30]

This *experience* of being under the *wrath of God* is brought about as the "alien work" (Latin: *opus alienum*) of the Holy Spirit, and is then followed by his "proper work" (Latin: *opus proprium*), the *Gospel*, the *experience of the grace of God by forgiveness of sins for Christ's sake through faith.* "The Gospel guides us from the tyranny of the law into the freedom of the Gospel."[31]

---

[27] CA, Art. V, 2, *The Book of Concord*, p. 31.
[28] CA, Art. II, 2, *The Book of Concord*, p. 29.
[29] Prenter, *Spiritus Creator*, p. 128.
[30] *LW*, Vol. 24, p. 336.
[31] Prenter, *Spiritus Creator*, p. 208.

What is the Gospel in this narrow sense? Luther says that the Holy Spirit provides through the Gospel of Christ the *defence against the two weapons of the devil*: *sin and the penalty of sin*. Through the Gospel, the Holy Spirit gives a comfort that is stronger than the terror of the devil, saying:

> God *does not want to be angry with you*, nor does He want to reject you; for Christ, *God's Son, died for you*. He *paid for your sins*; and *if you believe in him*, these will *not be imputed to you*, no matter how great they are (italics added).[32]

The gospel thus contains both the *information* that the *law's demands have been met* in Christ and that the *penalty of sin has been paid*, but it also contains – and that is what really makes it gospel, "good news" – *a direct address which includes a promise of forgiveness of sins*. "The Gospel is the preaching of forgiveness of sins through the name of Jesus Christ."[33]

It is the *promise-character* of the Gospel that makes it especially fit for *oral* proclamation. When it is *preached*, the *personal address* is more obvious. *Christ is drawn out from the pages of the Bible and in the Gospel offered by the Holy Spirit to the hearers as a gift.*

Faith and the Presence of Christ in the Believer

The only right response to God's promise in the Gospel is *our faith in it*, the expectation that it will be fulfilled. But this faith is nothing that human beings themselves can produce; it is created by the Holy Spirit. "Faith [...] comes only through God's word or gospel."[34] We have already seen it stated in the *Augsburg Confession*, Art. V:

> To obtain such faith (justifying faith, cp. Art. IV) God instituted the office of the ministry; that is, provided the Gospel and the sacraments. Through these, as through means, he gives the Holy Spirit, who works faith, when and where he pleases, in those who hear the Gospel. And the Gospel teaches that we have a gracious God, not by our own merits but by the merit of Christ, when we believe this.[35]

When the Spirit is said to create faith, this implies that *also Christ himself is given*, for faith is the *reception of Christ* whom the Gospel offers, as Luther says, "For it is the *Holy Spirit who gives you Christ* and His holiness and who *works faith* in you."[36] When faith apprehends Christ, the believer is justified.

---

[32] *LW*, Vol. 24, pp. 291-292.
[33] Althaus, *Theology*, p. 256.
[34] Althaus, *Theology*, p. 47; *LW*, Vol. 35, p. 368.
[35] CA, Art. V, 1-3, *The Book of Concord*, p. 31.
[36] *LW*, Vol. 24, p. 172.

This received righteousness of Christ is the only one that can comfort troubled consciences. It is:

> The righteousness of grace, mercy and forgiveness of sin. In other words, this is the *righteousness of Christ and the Holy Spirit*, which we *do not perform but receive*, which we do not have but accept, when God the Father grants it to us through Jesus Christ (italics added).[37]

The non-imputation of sin is due to a change of place between Christ and the sinner. We have real fellowship with Christ through faith. Therefore, sin is not imputed to us or held against us.[38]

The Spirit never operates as an *agent creating faith* unless he is also *given as a gift to the believer.* This important *sequence of salvation* is clearly expressed by Luther:

> God alone – without any entreaty or desire of man – must *first* (1) come and give him a *promise.* This word of God is the beginning [...] God must anticipate all [of man's works and thoughts], and make a promise clearly expressed in words, which man *then* (2) takes and keeps in good, firm *faith.* Then there *follows* (3) the *Holy Spirit* who is *given to man for the sake of the same faith* (italics and numbers added).[39]

The order is clear: (1) The word of the gospel comes first, then (2) faith is created by the Holy Spirit (as agent) which then is followed by (3) the reception of the Holy Spirit (as gift). *We cannot avoid seeing how this view corresponds with what we have previously seen in several New Testament texts about Christian initiation, such as Acts 2:37-38; 10:43-45; 11:17; 15:7-8; Galatians 3:2.*

Justification and Sanctification

Corresponding to this doubleness in the work of the Holy Spirit as *agent* first creating faith in the Gospel and then being given as a *gift* to those who have faith, there is also a doubleness in *justification.* The relationship between the gift of the Spirit and justification is explained by Luther in his commentary on Galatians 3:2: "Then what does justify? Hearing the voice of the bridegroom, hearing the proclamation of faith – when this is heard, it justifies. Why? Because is brings the Holy Spirit who justifies."[40] Justification has therefore two aspects:

---

[37] *LW*, Vol. 26, p. 6.
[38] Prenter, *Spiritus Creator*, p. 30.
[39] *LW*, Vol. 35, pp. 82-83.
[40] *LW*, Vol. 26, p. 208.

> *First, through the forgiveness of sins and the imputation of righteousness, on account of faith in Christ; secondly, through the gift of the Holy Spirit, who creates a new life and new impulses* in us, so that we keep the Law also in a formal sense (italics added).[41]

The first is the *perfect, imputed righteousness of Christ, God's grace as his favour, his gracious disposition towards us* (Latin: *favor Dei*) received in faith; the second is our *own beginning righteousness* given by the *Holy Spirit*, grace as a *gift in our lives* (Latin: *donum*). Luther says about this in his Preface to Romans:

> Between grace and gift there is this difference: *Grace* actually means *God's favour*, or the good will which he *in himself* bears toward us, by which he is disposed to *give us Christ* and *to pour into us the Holy Spirit with his gifts* [...] The *gifts and the Spirit increase in us* every day, but they are not yet perfect since there remain in us evil desires and sins that war against the Spirit [...] Nevertheless, *grace* (as the favour of God) does so much that we are accounted *completely righteous before God.* For his grace is not *divided or parcelled out, as are the gifts*, but takes us completely into favour for the sake of Christ our Intercessor and Mediator. And *because of this* his *gifts are begun in us* (italics and parenthesis added).[42]

Grace as the *favour of God* is always *complete.* It covers and applies to the whole human being (Latin: *totus homo*). When regarded as a sinner in himself, but under grace as the *favour of God*, the believer is *at the same time* fully justified and a sinner (Latin: *simul justus et peccator*). When regarded as a receiver of the *gift*, however, the believer is *partially* sinful and *partially* just.[43] These two effects of faith: on the one hand, the *total forgiveness of sins*; that is, the imputation *to us* of *Christ's perfect righteousness*, which is Christ's own but alien to us (Latin: *justitia aliena),* and, on the other hand, the *gradual overcoming of sin in us,* are both a result of the work of the Spirit, the first a result of the Spirit's work as an *agent*, *on us,* the second as a result of the Holy Spirit as a *gift, in us.* Luther says:

> Our empty law is ended *by Christ* who fills the vacuum *first by being outside us*, because he himself fulfils the Law *for us*; then he also *fills it with the Holy Spirit* who *begins* this new and eternal obedience *within us*.[44]

These two works cannot be separated, although they must be distinguished. They both represent *the presence of Christ with us in faith.* Yet, the first work has *priority*: "However, the first *foundation* is the stronger

---

[41] *LW*, Vol. 26, p. 260.
[42] *LW*, Vol. 35, pp. 369-370.
[43] *LW*, Vol. 26, p. 376.
[44] Quoted by Althaus, *Theology*, p. 234.

and more important, for although the second amounts to something, it does so only through the power of the first."[45]

This irreversible order of the appropriation of salvation is primarily a *logical* sequence, but some elements may also involve *time intervals*. A long or a short time may elapse between the preaching/hearing of the Gospel and the reception of it in faith, depending on the sovereign work of the Spirit and the human response. However, faith, justification and the gift of the Spirit are always *immediately* connected without any time interval. *One cannot receive justifying faith through the work of the Holy Spirit, without also receiving the gift of the Holy Spirit. Faith and the reception of the Spirit go together.*

On the basis of what we have seen so far, we may conclude that faith always brings with it the gift of the Holy Spirit, because faith apprehends Christ as truly present in the believer's heart in the Holy Spirit. Luther may describe this *faith as an active thing*, because it brings Christ and the Holy Spirit.[46] If it is not active, it is not faith.[47]

Prayer for Salvation and the Holy Spirit

Faith expresses itself in prayer. This prayer is also a result of the work of the Spirit. Commenting on Zechariah 12:10, Luther says:

> Christ says, 'Just as you will have the "Spirit of compassion", through whom you will be taught what the Father's will is and what he has accomplished through me and given to you, so you will have a "Spirit of supplication". Then you will be able to call upon God from the heart in my name'. No one can pray properly unless he prays in the Spirit of grace, who assures the heart that it has a merciful God in Christ and that it can joyfully call him Father.[48]

Prayer is therefore not to be understood as a work preparing the heart for the Holy Spirit, but the only right answer to the promise of the Gospel.

If the saving effects of the Word and the sacraments are seen as taking place automatically, merely by being performed (Latin: *ex opere operato*), there would be no room for prayer and expectation. Then, the Spirit would be guaranteed simply by the outward Word or sacrament. Luther opposed such a concept which was found in the Catholic church, and Prenter says about Luther's view:

> It is such a concept that Luther makes impossible by laying down *an interval of time between the work of the outward word and the coming of the Spirit.* It is in this interval of time that the *prayer for the Spirit* shall live, and the

---

[45] Althaus, *Theology*, p. 236.
[46] Althaus, *Theology*, p. 235.
[47] *LW*, Vol. 24, p. 344.
[48] *LW*, Vol. 24, p. 405.

> expectation of the promise of God, and the motion of faith away from [...] *justitia propria* [one's own righteousness by the law] to *justitia aliena* [the alien righteousness of Christ given to the believer].[49]

The *length* of time is of no concern. "Fulfilment is certain in the very moment that the promise is accepted [...] the *prayer is answered in the very moment the prayer is uttered* – but also not a moment before."[50] We again see the tension between the *Spirit as creator of faith* (faith here expressed in prayer), and *the Spirit as given to faith.* The fact that it is prayer that apprehends the Spirit does not imply any synergism; that is, a kind of co-operation between God and human beings in salvation. *Prayer is simply the expression of faith.* The difference between prayer as a spiritual *method* and prayer as *claiming the promises of God* has been emphasised by the Swedish theologian Gustaf Aulén: "Christian prayer has as any other human function its technique, but it is no method (a method must when it is followed, automatically lead to the desired result); it is a pleading of God's promises in the Word".[51] Luther connects this prayer with the Spirit's own intercession for the believers in his groaning "that words cannot express", Romans 8:23, 26.[52]

The inherent relationship and order between the preaching of the gospel, faith, and calling upon God in prayer leading to salvation is also clearly expressed by Paul in his famous "mission-logical" sequence in Romans 10:13-15.

Baptism and the Holy Spirit

We must also make brief mention of the *two other means of grace*, or means of the Holy Spirit: baptism and the Eucharist. So far, we have mainly concentrated on the Word as the means of grace because we recognise both the sacramental character of the Word and the Gospel-character of the sacraments. Prenter says about Luther, "The Word and the sacraments are in Luther united in one sacramental concept [...] What we said [...] about the Spirit's relation to the Word also applies to the sacrament, because the Word is part of the sacrament, and the sacrament is never without the Word."[53] The sacraments share in the Word's character of being *outward and coming from God to human beings.* The sacraments are, however, different from the Word in one respect: They do not only contain the promise, but also an outward

---

[49] Prenter, *Spiritus Creator*, p. 127.
[50] Prenter, *Spiritus Creator*, p. 127; Althaus, *Theology*, p. 39.
[51] Quoted in Aalen, *Testimonium*, p. 49.
[52] *LW*, Vol. 26, pp. 380-381; Prenter, *Spiritus Creator*, pp. 89-90.
[53] Prenter, *Spiritus Creator*, p. 160.

confirmation of the promise, a *sign*. Through this sign, the sacraments seal the promise for the individual.[54]

Baptism is in a special way related to the gift of the Holy Spirit. In his comment on Galatians 3:27, "For all of you who were baptised into Christ have clothed yourselves with Christ", Luther says:

> To *put on Christ* [clothe oneself with Christ] according to the Gospel is a matter, *not of imitation* but of a *new birth* and a *new creation*, namely that I put on *Christ himself*; that is, his innocence, righteousness, wisdom, power, salvation, life, and *Spirit* [...] This happens by the rebirth and renewal that takes place in *Baptism* [...] For in those who have been baptised a new light and flame arise, *new and devout emotions* come into being, such as *fear and trust in God and hope*; and a *new will* emerges (parenthesis and italics added).[55]

Luther understood baptism as the reception of salvation and *with it* Christ and the Holy Spirit with all their various gifts. It was an experience that *changed* the baptised persons empirically by giving them new emotions and a new will to do what is pleasing to God. Baptism is the work of God and *valid* even if the recipient is an unbeliever. This does not, however, mean that Luther gives up the freedom of the Spirit in baptism, because the same applies to baptism as to the Word: *Only when it is received in faith does it actually benefit the recipient*. Relying on Augustine, Luther says, "Not the sacrament, but the faith that believes the sacrament is what removes sin". And this faith is again created "where and when God pleases" by the Holy Spirit.[56] This means that the order of salvation regarding the interval between the outward sign and the inward reception also applies to baptism, as does the response in faith expressed through prayer, and the expectation of the gift of the Spirit.

This similarity between the Word and the sacrament of baptism should be evident, yet is seems necessary to point it out here because in later Lutheranism the doctrine that saving faith is given "where and when God pleases" has been applied to the *preaching of the Gospel* (the Word) – which of course in the church's experience does not always lead to faith and salvation – but *not to baptism* which often has been understood almost to have an automatic saving effect by merely being performed.

This development has taken place under the pressure of infant baptism in state churches in Europe where *all the people* were baptised. It was a concern for the church to say something about what God was doing with *all* infants in baptism, regardless of the personal faith of the infant, their parents or sponsors.

Regarding infant baptism, the *Augsburg Confession* says:

---

[54] Prenter, *Spiritus Creator*, p. 138.

[55] *LW*, Vol. 26, pp. 352-353.

[56] CA, Art. V, *The Book of Concord*, p. 31.

> Baptism is necessary and [...] grace is offered through it. Children, too, should be baptised, for in Baptism, they are committed to God and become acceptable to him.[57]

The doctrine of baptism cannot, however, fully be built on what takes place in infant baptism. It should be built on what takes place in the baptism of adults. In an adult baptism, personal faith may or may not be present at the time of the actual baptism. If baptism is not received in faith, it does not save, and, consequently, the Holy Spirit is not given. A person may, however, come to faith, be born again, and receive the Holy Spirit with all the gifts of salvation *after* baptism – even several years after as the case may be – but this reception of salvation will always take place *on the basis of the promise of God given in baptism.* Baptism is therefore not completed until faith is added. As said before, however, faith and the gift of the Spirit cannot be separated in time. The Spirit is given as a gift to those who have faith.

The question of whether or how faith is present in infant baptism is not easily solved. There is no biblical and theological warrant for the view that faith is given in baptism, although this has sometimes been maintained by later Lutheran theologians.

The most common and reasonable answer is that the *infants are included in the family* so that it is the *faith of the parents* – or those who bring the infant to baptism – which receives salvation. This faith then must be personally appropriated by the child as it grows up. The liturgy of infant baptism should therefore not contain any statements of what God has done in it – this would violate against the freedom of the Spirit and imply a human "control" of the God's salvific action by simply performing the rite. The liturgy should say *what God* promises *in baptism – forgiveness of sins and the gift of the Holy Spirit – and then leave it to the Holy Spirit to create the faith that receives these promises, whether this is the faith of the parents at the time of baptism or the conscious faith of the child at a later stage.* Yet, we should always remember that Jesus received the little children and said that "the kingdom of heaven belongs to such as these" (Mt. 19:14).

There are cases in the Bible when the Holy Spirit was given before baptism, as in the case of Cornelius (Acts 10), and there are also cases when the Spirit was given after baptism, as in the case of the Samaritans (Acts 8). While baptism is not absolutely necessary for salvation – God has tied us but not himself to it– the *Word is necessary* because it contains the Gospel about Christ that is believed for salvation.[58]

There is also another significant *difference between baptism and the Word*: a proper use of the sacrament of baptism presupposes that it is administered to people who *already confess the faith* or are raised in a

[57] CA, Art. IX, *The Book of Concord*, p. 33.

[58] Althaus, *Theology*, p. 349; *LW*, Vol. 36, p. 67; *LW*, Vol. 32, p. 14.

believing family (as in the case of infants), while the preaching of the Word should be addressed *to all people regardless of faith.*

The Eucharist and the Holy Spirit

The Eucharist or the Lord's Supper can be seen in the same way as baptism. In the discussion with the Swiss reformers, it became clear that Luther did not, like the Swiss, see spirit as the opposite of flesh understood as bodiliness, but as the opposite of flesh understood as sinfulness. Therefore, the material character of the sacrament could be no hindrance for the Holy Spirit. Luther wrote:

> Everything that comes from the Holy Spirit is spirit, spiritual, and an object of the Spirit, in reality and whether it is physical or material, outward or visible: similarly, everything which comes from the natural power of the flesh, without Spirit, is flesh and fleshly no matter how inward and invisible it may be.[59]

Spiritual is not the same as inwardly, and the sacraments may even have a bodily effect![60] This emphasis on the physical and outward elements, the bread and wine, as vehicles of the Holy Spirit is typical of Lutheranism as opposed to a purely spiritual or inward understanding of the Spirit's work in the sacrament.

The same applies to the Eucharist as to baptism: it is not the sign in itself that saves, but the *sign together with the promises of God that accompany the sign.* Forgiveness of sins and union with Christ are given to those who receive the sacrament with faith in the promises of God (cf. 1 Cor. 11:16-22).

The Holy Spirit as Gift

We have already seen that the Holy Spirit is a gift given to faith. Luther paraphrases Galatians 3:2 in his commentary in this way:

> But *after the Gospel* has come, and *before* you had performed any *work or fruit of the Gospel*, you immediately receive the Holy Spirit, *merely by hearing with faith* (italics added).[61]

This means that there are no preparations and no conditions for the reception of the Spirit on the part of human beings within their own power. The necessary conditions are only the *preaching of the Word* and *faith.* The German Lutheran scholar Edmund Schlink says, "The Holy Spirit is active

---

[59] Quoted in Althaus, *Theology*, pp. 395-396; *LW*, Vol. 37, p.99.
[60] Prenter, *Spiritus Creator*, pp. 131, 137, 285-286, cf. 1 Cor. 11:30.
[61] *LW*, Vol. 26,.p. 203.

as the Spirit of the Father and the Son, and *he imparts himself* to the believer by implanting him in Christ and making him a child of God."[62]

It is precisely this indissoluble *unity of Christ and the Spirit which creates the unity of justification and sanctification*, or in other words, the two aspects of justification as we have mentioned earlier. One aspect being justification as a *forensic or legal* act by which the sinner is *declared* righteous by God for the sake of Christ, *outside us* (Latin: *extra nos,* cf. Rom. 3:20-26; 2 Cor. 5:19), and the other aspect being justification as being *in Christ* or Christ *indwelling us*, the righteousness of God *in us* (Latin: *in nobis*) (1 Cor. 1:30; 2 Cor. 5:17). It is, therefore, impossible for Luther to think of the saving presence of Christ apart from the gift of the Holy Spirit, or the gift of the Holy Spirit apart from Christ's gift of salvation. Grace, as God's *favour*, is "the *good will which in himself* he bears toward us, by which he is disposed to *give us Christ* and to *pour into us the Holy Spirit with his gifts*."[63]

The Holy Spirit testifies that we by faith are the children of God. Luther says; "Together with the gift of sonship, moreover, we have also received the Holy Spirit, whom God, through the Word, sends into our hearts, crying: 'Abba! Father!'".[64]

The Role of Experience

Luther placed great emphasis on *experience.* When the Holy Spirit testifies in us, the Word as law and gospel becomes truly *felt*. Distinguishing between law and gospel can only be done by *experience*; that is, it is a matter of the Holy Spirit. As Prenter says, "The real distinction between law and gospel is not made in theology, but in the *experience of the Holy Spirit himself*".[65] The Holy Spirit is active both through the law that causes us to repent of our sins and drives us to Christ, and through the gospel that creates faith, justifies us and gives us Christ and new life. And this is not only a work done by the Spirit in Christian initiation as one comes to faith for the first time, but it is a *continuous* work of the Holy Spirit. Therefore, the Holy Spirit is also *continually* given, as Luther expresses it in his comments on Galatians 3:5:

> It is as though he [Paul] were saying: 'It was not enough that God gave you the Spirit once. But the same God has always abundantly supplied and increased the gifts of the Spirit, so that when you have once received the Holy Spirit, He might always grow and be more efficient in you.'[66]

---

[62] Schlink, *Doctrine of Baptism*, p. 70.
[63] *LW*, Vol. 35, p. 369.
[64] *LW*, Vol. 26, p. 374.
[65] Prenter, *Spiritus Creator*, p. 209; *LW*, Vol. 26, p. 379.
[66] *LW*, Vol. 26, p. 219; Schlink, *Doctrine of Baptism*, p. 63.

The Gifts and Evidence of the Holy Spirit

What are these *gifts of the Holy Spirit* which Luther so often refers to? They are not primarily the charismatic gifts mentioned in 1 Corinthians 12, but rather the *benefits of salvation* that the Spirit brings with him. It is a *new creation*:

> When I am baptised or converted by the Gospel, the Holy Spirit is present. He takes me as clay and makes of me a new creature, which is endowed with a different mind, heart and thoughts; that is, with a true knowledge of God and a sincere trust in his grace.[67]

The Spirit makes human beings able to fulfil the law of God, not "out of fear and compulsion but out of a willing heart".[68] And the law includes both the first and the second table of the Ten Commandments: both the relationship to God and to other people. It is obvious from these references and others that Luther held that *the Holy Spirit causes a real empirical change* or *transformation in the believers affecting all areas of their lives.*

Christians should be concerned about whether or not they have the Holy Spirit. The *assurance of the Holy Spirit's presence is tied to the assurance of being in the grace of God.* Luther states, "Now Christ is completely certain that in His Spirit He is pleasing to God. Since we have the same Spirit of Christ, we, too, should be certain that we are in the state of grace on account of Him who is certain". Then Luther goes on to describe the internal testimony of the Spirit, "by which the heart should believe *with complete certainty* that it is in the *state of grace* and that *it has the Holy Spirit.*"[69]

There are also *signs or evidence* which may tell Christians that they possess the Holy Spirit. These are *drawn from experience* after one has come to faith in Christ, such as some of the following:

> To enjoy hearing about Christ, to teach, give thanks, praise and confess Him, even at the cost of property and life; to do one's duty according to one's calling in a manly way, in faith and joy; not to take delight in sin; not to invade someone else's calling but to serve one's own; to help a needy brother, comfort the sorrowful, etc. By these signs, we are assured and confirmed *a posteriori* that we are in a state of grace.[70]

We notice here the similarity between this saying and the description of the results of being filled with the Holy Spirit as we have seen them both in the New Testament and in the Charismatic renewal. *Zeal for mission* is also seen by Luther as a sign of the indwelling Spirit:

---

[67] *LW*, Vol. 24, p. 226.
[68] *LW*, Vol. 35, p. 367.
[69] *LW*, Vol. 26, p. 379.
[70] *LW*, Vol. 26, p. 379.

> There is nothing I want more than to make His Gospel known to the world and to convert many people. These things certainly testify that the Holy Spirit is present.[71]

The gifts of the Spirit are also described with regard to our *freedom in the Spirit*, "We are speaking about the freedom of the Spirit, where we are dead to the Law, sin, and death, and where we live and reign as free men in grace, the forgiveness of sins, righteousness and eternal life".[72]

The Fruit of the Holy Spirit

Luther does not distinguish in principle between the gifts of the Spirit and the fruit of the Spirit. The fruit is a new ethical life in which one is enabled to keep the commandments of God: "In brief, the fruit of our spirit is the fulfilment of God's Ten Commandments". In fact, Luther may even say, "We know that the Spirit won for us by Christ is given for this purpose alone, that we should fulfil the commandments of God."[73]

This does not mean, however, that the Christian who has received the Spirit has become sinless or perfect. It is true that the Christian *in Christ* has been delivered from the law, from sin, and from death. Therefore, the Spirit of life, not the law, shall reign in the *consciences*, which are where human beings become aware of their standing in the sight of God.[74] But Christians still have the flesh. "It is impossible for human nature to fulfil the Law. In fact, in those who are justified and who have the Holy Spirit, the law in their members is at war with the law of their mind" (Rom. 7:23).[75] The natural vices remain in human beings even after they have accepted faith, but they "are being forced to serve the Spirit who dominates them so that they do not rule; yet this does not happen without a struggle".[76]

This is *the struggle between our sinful nature and the Spirit* which Paul describes in Galatians 5:16-26. In this struggle, the Spirit shall rule in our *conscience*, which means that we as believers with our whole person are *perfectly righteous* in the sight of God on the basis of Christ's alien righteousness and under God's grace understood as His *favour*. At the same time, we have the Spirit as a gift fighting sin and making us *increasingly righteous and holy* in the way we live our lives.

This struggle to *become in experience what we already are by faith in Christ*, is fully dependent on the alien righteousness we receive from Christ: "If we look at the flesh, we are sinners; if we look at the Spirit, we are

---

[71] *LW*, Vol. 26, p. 379.
[72] *LW*, Vol. 26, p. 439.
[73] *LW*, Vol. 26, pp. 40, 56.
[74] *LW*, Vol. 26, p. 139.
[75] *LW*, Vol. 26, p. 148.
[76] *LW*, Vol. 26, p. 189.

righteous. We are partly sinners, and partly righteous." "Yet, our righteousness is more abundant than our sin, because the holiness and the righteousness of Christ, our Propitiator, vastly, surpass the sin of the entire world."[77] This struggle against the sinful nature provides us also with an *outward righteousness.* Luther says,

> To the extent that *by the Spirit we struggle against the flesh,* to that extent we are *outwardly righteous*, even though it is *not this righteousness that makes us acceptable in the sight of God* (italics added).[78]

This outward righteousness may be *ambiguous*. The empirical quality may be a fruit of the Spirit as long as the sinner is under the grace of God, but it may also be a fruit of the sinful nature, the flesh, when human beings seek to do good works out of self-interest or try to be justified before God by them.

Although there are different views held among Luther scholars as to whether Luther meant that there was an *observable growth or progress in sanctification* among Christians, Luther's words that "throughout life He [the Holy Spirit] goes on purging the sin that inheres, not only in the Galatians, but in all men of all nations",[79] seem to indicate a growth and *increase in holiness which is empirical and experiential.* Yet, this growth should never be regarded as a basis for our righteousness before God. The work of the Holy Spirit as a gift, dwelling in us and creating the fruit of love toward God and our neighbours, remains always partial and incomplete in this life, struggling with the continued reality of our sinful nature.

The Holy Spirit and the Conflict with the Devil

We have seen in Parts One and Two that the struggle against the devil and his demonic forces is central both in the New Testament and in the Charismatic renewal. What does the Lutheran reformation, and in particular Martin Luther, have to say on this matter?

To Luther, the devil was the most important of the three demonic forces which were opposing God and his salvation. Human beings in their unredeemed state were held captive to sin by *the world, their own sinful nature (the flesh) and the devil.* Luther had a more severe view of the devil than was common in the Middle Ages, and a much stronger biblical orientation. He did not leave anything to human speculation.[80]

The devil was seen as the "Prince of this world" (Jn 12:31; 14:30); ruling a kingdom that is opposed to God's kingdom (2 Cor. 4:4). He has a real

---

[77] *LW*, Vol. 27, p. 68.
[78] *LW*, Vol. 27, p. 72.
[79] *LW*, Vol. 26, p. 189.
[80] To Luther's view of the devil and his work, see Althaus, *Theology*, pp. 161-169.

spiritual existence of his own and a personal will directed against God and his will. Althaus says that Luther, in addition to the *biblical testimony* about the existence and activity of the devil, also "on the basis of his own experience […] bears witness to the reality and terribleness of the power of the devil".[81] Luther says paradoxically, "By the grace of God, I have learned to know a great deal about Satan."[82] This *experiential* dimension is important since it confirms the biblical message. By basing his view of the devil on the Bible, the doctrine of the ancient church and his own experience, the devil becomes "inseparably connected to the centre of Luther's theology".[83]

Satan or the devil is the great opponent of God, Christ and the Holy Spirit. He is at work in all that is opposed to God's will for his creation and for human beings. Therefore, he may be at work in all suffering, misfortune, sickness, and even in death. He tempts and leads people to sin against God, he persecutes Christ and his church, and he attempts to prevent people from receiving salvation in Christ. Every person is tempted by the devil. Neutrality in the conflict between God and Satan is impossible. One is either in God's kingdom of light or Satan's kingdom of darkness (cf. Jn 1:5; Eph. 2:2; 6;12; Col. 1:13; Acts 26:18; 1 Pet. 2:9).

In salvation, believers are *liberated from the power of Satan.* This is a work of the Holy Spirit. Luther says:

> Whoever has not been *grasped by Christ* and is not under *the power of His Spirit*, is under the power of the devil. And *no other power can take a man away from the power of the devil except the Spirit of God*; this Spirit is the stronger man who according to Jesus' parable (Lk. 11:21-24) overcomes the strong man.[84]

The main weapon of the Holy Spirit in the fight against Satan and his attacks is the Word of God (Eph. 6:17). In spite of his superhuman power, the devil is still subject to the almighty God. *Luther does not simply ascribe the bad things in life to the devil and the good things to God in a dualistic way.* He asserts strongly that *God can use the devil* as his instrument of judgement and wrath, and he may also use him in the lives of Christians to keep them humble and lead them to trust in God alone.

God and the devil, however, have *different intentions.* The intention of the devil is always to lead people away from God and his will and to destroy them, while God's intention is to save people, to set them free, and to drive them to his grace. The same misfortune, for example temptation or sickness, can therefore be seen both as Satan's attack and as the will of God. Althaus

---

[81] Althaus, *Theology*, p. 161.
[82] *LW*, Vol. 37, p. 361.
[83] Althaus, *Theology*, p. 162.
[84] Althaus, *Theology*, p. 164.

explains this seemingly contradictory experience, saying that according to Luther:

> Believing that God is merciful when we experience his blows in time of misfortune, 'is an art' *which only the Holy Spirit gives* [...] It is the task of *faith* to overcome the Satanic purpose in temptation by trusting in the unquestionable mercy of God hidden under the distress of that temptation.[85]

One of the effects of the work of the indwelling Holy Spirit in the believer is fighting Satan and his power. Luther often refers to the struggle against the devil as part of sanctification.

The *basis for the victory of Christ over the devil* and the reason why he frees his faithful from the power of the devil is *his redemptive work* as described in the second article of the Apostles' Creed. In his explanation, Luther says:

> I believe that Jesus Christ [...] is my Lord, who has redeemed me, a lost and condemned creature, *delivered and freed me* from all sins, from death, and *from the power of the devil* [...] *with his holy and precious blood and with his innocent suffering and death* (italics added).[86]

This is in accordance with the New Testament where the apostle Paul writes that Christ on the cross suffered the punishment of sin and triumphed over the demonic powers, thus providing forgiveness of sin and victory over Satan. "He [Christ] *forgave us all our sins*, having cancelled the written code, with its regulations, that was against us and stood opposed to us: he took it away, nailing it to the cross. And having *disarmed the powers and authorities* [the demonic powers], he made a public spectacle of them, *triumphing over them by the cross*" (Col. 2:13-15).

In his explanation of the petition "Deliver Us from Evil" in the Lord's prayer in the *Large Catechism,* Luther makes it clear that this is a prayer "speaking of the devil as the sum of all evil in order that the entire substance of our prayer may be directed against our arch-enemy." Among the evils included are "poverty, shame, death, and, in short, all the tragic misery and heartache of which there is incalculably much on earth." The petition is put last, "for if we are to be protected and delivered from all evil, his name [God's] must first be hallowed in us, his kingdom come among us, and his will be done. Then he will preserve us from sin and shame and from everything else that harms or injures us."[87]

---

[85] *LW,* Vol. 12, p. 374; Althaus, *Theology*, pp. 166-168.

[86] LC II, 4, *The Book of Concord*, p. 345.

[87] LC III, *The Book of Concord*, pp. 435-436. See also Luther's explanation to the petition, "And lead us not into temptation" where the flesh, the world and the devil

Luther also believed in the existence of *demons* or evil spirits associated with the kingdom of Satan. He thought that one could and should drive the evil spirits out of the possessed by prayer. One case of possession from the time of the Reformation is recorded by Luther's associate Johannes Bugenhagen, and Luther accepts this possession as a fact.[88] The Lutheran church after the Reformation held on to this belief and actually made provisions for how pastors should handle cases of possession, although as it was said, "such examples are at the present time [1685] rare in Christendom", yet we should not think "that we now are totally free from these attacks by Satan".[89]

The firm belief in victory over Satan and his demonic forces through Christ and his Spirit is beautifully confessed in Luther's famous hymn, the so-called "Battle Hymn of the Reformation", which is not about a battle with human beings but with the evil spiritual forces opposing God and his people:

> A mighty fortress is our God, A bulwark never failing,
> Our helper, he amid the flood of mortal ills prevailing,
> For still our ancient foe doth seek to work his woe.
> His craft and power are great, And armed with cruel hate,
> on earth is not his equal.
> Did we in our own strength confide, our striving would be losing,
> Were not the right Man on our side, the Man of God's own choosing,
> Doest ask who that may be? Christ Jesus, it is He,
> Lord Sabaoth is his name, From age to age the same,
> *And He must win the battle.*
> And though the world with devils filled, should threaten to undo us.
> We will not fear, for God but willed, His truth to triumph through us.
> The Prince of Darkness grim, we tremble not for him,
> His rage we can endure, For lo! His doom is sure,
> *One little word shall fell him.*
> That word alone all earthly powers – no thanks to them – abideth,
> *The Spirit and his gifts are ours, through him who with us sideth*
> Let goods and kindred go, this mortal life also,
> the body they may kill, God's truth abideth still,
> *His kingdom is forever* (italics added)

---

are mentioned as those who tempt Christians, LC, III, *The Book of Concord*, pp. 433-435.

[88] See John Warwick Montgomery (ed), *Principalities and Powers: A New Look at the World of the Occult* (Minneapolis, MN: Bethany Fellowship, 1973), pp. 196-205.

[89] Oskar Skarsaune and Tormod Engelsviken, "Possession and Exorcism in the History of the Church," in Moreau et al, (eds), *Deliver Us From Evil*, pp. 65-87.

The Holy Spirit and the Charisms

Luther was primarily an exegete and, in his work with the Scriptures, he had to deal with some of the same questions that are being discussed in the present Charismatic renewal, including the understanding and place of the spiritual gifts, the charisms.

As we have seen, Luther was interested in the *evidence* of the possession of the Holy Spirit. He would not have been – as some contemporary Lutherans seem to be – surprised if he had been asked the question that Paul asked in Acts 19:2: "Did you receive the Holy Spirit when you believed?" Luther would have answered with an emphatic "Yes". We have mentioned some of the evidence he points to: he maintains that Paul used the *visibility of the reception and the work of the Spirit* as an argument for the authenticity of the lawless gospel. This is obviously an argument from *experience*, and this experience is, in Luther's understanding, not limited to the "Gentiles' Pentecost" when Cornelius was converted (Acts 10), but was a *general phenomenon also in the Pauline congregations*:

> Therefore, the Holy Spirit gives His approval to the faith of the Gentiles without the law of circumcision [...] He descended in a visible form upon the uncircumcised who heard the Word.[90]

This "form", it is assumed by Luther, is speaking in tongues, and so also in the experience of the Galatians, since he refers to the Cornelius incident in Acts 10:44 in his comment on Galatians 3:2.[91] Luther speaks of "evident experience" which testifies that the Spirit was granted to those without the Law.[92]

There is, however, a *limitation* in Luther's view. To Luther, these manifestations of the Spirit were limited to the New Testament church.[93] He saw the *visible signs and the miracles* that were performed by the hands of the apostles as aiming at establishing the message during the first period of the church's history. Therefore, "miracles are no longer necessary to confirm this doctrine. For the accompanying signs were given principally [...] to substantiate the new message of the apostles." When the doctrine had been established – as Luther thought that it had been – miracles were no longer necessary.[94]

Luther nevertheless admitted that miracles still occurred within the Catholic church. He did not claim that they were all false, but if they were used to further doctrine that contradicted what Jesus taught, they were of the

---

[90] *LW*, Vol. 26, p. 79.
[91] *LW*, Vol. 26, p. 203.
[92] *LW*, Vol. 26, p. 205.
[93] *LW*, Vol. 26, p. 204.
[94] *LW*, Vol. 24, pp. 367-368.

devil. The devil, however, could not do real miracles, only artifices through which he bewitched the senses.

Luther had no illusions as to the attracting power of miracles, especially healing miracles, when he wrote, "If […] the devil began to perform miracles through some pseudo-saint and restored a sick person to health, you would see people streaming to him in droves; and no amount of preaching and warning could stop them". And to those who were looking for miracles and turning away from the sound doctrine of Christ, he said, "If teachings, signs, life, and activity are in opposition to this chief doctrine and article of Christ […] one should ignore and reject them, even if it snows miracles every day."[95]

Miracles were thus for Luther *no sure indicator* of the presence of the Spirit, but they *had to be tested on the doctrine of Christ.* At the same time, however, he claimed that in the early Christian church – even after New Testament times – the miracles served the Christian message by demonstrating the Holy Spirit's supernatural and superhuman power:

> Thus at that time they saw the Spirit's work confirmed by miraculous signs in the apostles and later in the holy martyrs. […] This could not flow from natural or human power or strength.[96]

Luther expressed the difference between the primitive church and the later church as a twofold work of the Spirit:

> The Holy Spirit is sent forth in two ways. In the primitive church, he was sent forth in a manifest and visible form […] This was the first sending forth of the Spirit; it was necessary in the primitive church, which had to be established with visible signs on account of the unbelievers, as Paul testifies, 1 Cor. 14:22: 'Tongues are a sign, not for believers but for unbelievers' […] But later on, when the church had been gathered and confirmed by these signs, it was not necessary for this visible sending forth of the Holy Spirit to continue. The second sending is that by which the Holy Spirit, through the Word, is sent into the hearts of believers […] This happens without a visible form, namely when through the spoken word we receive fire and light, by which we are made new and different […][97]

We have quoted this so extensively because this extract shows that Luther saw the circumstances surrounding the reception of the Spirit in his time as different from those of the primitive church, belonging to two different epochs.

---

[95] *LW*, Vol. 24, pp. 369-371.
[96] LW, Vol. 24, p. 123.
[97] *LW*, Vol. 26, pp. 374-375.

Prophecy

Luther dealt with *prophecy* in several places. In his comment on John 16:13, "He will declare to you the things that are to come", Luther maintained that there are two types of prophecy. The first type is the prophecies found in the Old Testament where the prophets also prophesied about secular things.

> The second type of prophecy, that of which our text speaks, tells us how the kingdom of Christ will fare and about the conditions that are to prevail in his kingdom [...] These are the prophecies of the Holy Spirit; they are revealed only to Christians.

The apostles became these kind of prophets, and the Book of Revelation is one such prophecy. Interestingly, Luther wrote: "To this category also belongs whatever else may have been said about early Christendom by [church-]fathers but was never recorded." Luther does not limit prophecy to the Bible and biblical times, for he continues, "The Spirit of prophecy is still present in Christendom, but not so markedly as in the apostles. We, too, can predict and know such things, but only if we have learned this from the books of the apostles."[98] It is not clear here whether Christian prophecy at the time of Luther was understood simply as saying forth what the Bible already had said, or if it contained a real new prophecy after the pattern of the apostles. The former view is probably the correct one, since Luther insisted that no new revelation is to be expected. In a comment on prophecy as described in 1 Corinthians 12 and 14, he understands it as "prophecy which interprets the writings of prophets". It is simply identified with preaching. Yet we should be careful not draw too simple or general conclusions as to Luther's view since he also acknowledged other kinds of prophecy, not found in Scripture.[99]

The Holy Spirit and the Ministry of the Word

Regarding the *ministry of the Word*, Luther would stress the need for an outer, orderly *call* from a congregation for anyone who would take on the *preaching ministry*. However, he also acknowledged a *charismatic authentication of ministries*. There had been people, like the prophets and the apostle Paul, who had received an inner, direct call from God. This kind of call and ministry had to prove itself by "outward signs and witness". These signs might include the ability to perform miracles. Even a ministry without signs and without an outer calling could be performed by a Christian *among the pagans*, or *in the case of an emergency*. Luther spoke about *his own call* in the following terms:

---

[98] *LW*, Vol. 24, p. 365.

[99] *LW*, Vol. 35, pp. 399-400; cp. also *LW*, Vol. 24, p. 367.

> I cannot establish [my right to preach] by showing that I have been called to the office of the ministry by a vision of God but by the fact that I have been compelled to do this by other people and must do it for the sake of other people. Thus I have *the authorisation of the Spirit of love* which does not seek its own but is diligent in seeking the welfare of others (italics added).[100]

Thus, the possibility of a special prophetic calling was held open by Luther. The revelation of the Holy Spirit gives *enlightenment* (Latin: *illuminatio*) so that one can understand the reading and hearing of the Scriptures. If the Spirit calls anybody to a special prophetic ministry, "it is true that the Holy Spirit does not give this gift without preaching and teaching, unless He wants to perform a special miracle". However, after the time of the apostles and the writing of the Bible, Luther thought – as we have seen – that "no new revelation or miracle is necessary".[101]

The Gift of Miracle-Working Faith

Paul Althaus discusses at length how Luther dealt with the problem of saving faith in relation to the *gift of faith* mentioned in 1 Corinthians 13:2, "If I have the gift of prophecy and can fathom all mysteries and all knowledge, and if I have a faith that can move mountains, but have not love, I am nothing."[102] This text was used against Luther by the Catholics to prove that people were not saved by faith alone. Luther would, as we have seen above, insist that true faith would immediately "become active through love", and that faith and love were inseparable. How then can faith be without love as in this text? Luther asked:

> Wherever there is true faith, the Holy Spirit is also present. And where the Holy Spirit is present, love and everything else must be there. How can he [Paul] then speak as though someone might have faith without love?[103]

Luther went through several stages in his interpretation of this text. One interpretation that he favoured in 1525 is that Paul's examples are examples of things that are *impossible*, such as "speaking with the tongues of angels" (v. 1) or "fathom all mysteries and all knowledge".

In a later interpretation, Luther identified the faith in 1 Corinthians 13:2 with the *gift of faith* in 1 Corinthians 12:9 *which is not the same as justifying faith.* According to 1 Corinthians 12:9, this faith is a gift of the Spirit. Faith that works miracles is indeed true faith; but if the person who has this faith does not produce love, then the person falls away from faith, and this faith in

---

[100] Althaus, *Theology*, pp. 330-331.
[101] *LW*, Vol. 24, p. 367.
[102] Althaus, *Theology*, pp. 429-445.
[103] Quoted in Althaus, *Theology*, p. 429.

fact becomes "nothing".[104] Faith is no longer faith in God, but has become presumption and pride. Luther meant that he could observe this both in the Bible and in his own time when people who first had received the gospel did not endure in true faith but made it a reason for boasting. Biblical examples would be Balaam (Num. 22-24), King Saul in the Old Testament and Ananias and Sapphira in the New Testament (Acts 5:1-11).

Luther argued that, even though a person might lose their living faith, they might still continue to have the gift of performing miracles originally granted to such faith. Saving faith and the gift of faith are distinguished.[105] The gift is always given to *living faith*, but the gift may be retained even after the living faith has been lost and is dead. Thus, Luther opened up for the possibility that the miracles of God could be performed by people without living faith. This fact does not, however, make the miracles any less God's work, although they do not say anything about the spiritual status of the person who performs them. According to Luther, it often happens in the church that evil people do miracles in virtue of their office.[106] These miracles may benefit the people, but not those who perform them.

Luther's Reformation Programme for Charismatic Renewal

We began this chapter with the idea that Luther understood the work of the Holy Spirit as a work in and for the church. The charisms are no reason for boasting and they are no proof of the spiritual status of the charismatic person. Suffering and persecution are used by the Spirit in order to keep his people humble:

> Rejoicing in the Lord, who is our glory, we thus remain in order. In spiritual gifts we far surpass others; but because we acknowledge these as gifts of God, not our own, granted to us for the building up of the body of Christ (Eph. 4:12), we do not become proud on their account.[107]

The basis for the believers' gifts and ministries in the church is their sharing in Christ's priesthood through "baptism, regeneration, and the anointing of the Holy Spirit".[108] "The priesthood [of all believers] means: we stand before God, pray for others, intercede with and sacrifice ourselves to God and proclaim the word to one another".[109] In this understanding of the priesthood of all believers lies a programme for a Lutheran charismatic renewal already established from the time of the Reformation.

---

[104] Althaus, *Theology,* pp. 433-434.
[105] Althaus, *Theology*, p. 434.
[106] Althaus, *Theology*, p. 437.
[107] *LW,* Vol. 27, p. 103.
[108] Althaus, *Theology*, p. 314.
[109] Althaus, *Theology*, p. 314; *LW*, Vol. 40, pp. 21, 32.

Excursus 2: Does God Speak Directly Today? Prophecy, Revelation, Call, and Guidance

By Tormod Engelsviken with reference to Regin Prenter

Some Lutheran critics of the Charismatic renewal, especially in the early stages of the renewal, often appealed to Luther's words in the *Smalcald Articles* (SA):

> In these matters, which concern the external, spoken Word, we must hold firmly to the conviction that God gives no one his Spirit or grace except through and with the external Word which comes before.[1]

This statement has been taken by some to mean that the Holy Spirit is bound to the Word in such a way that he *only works while the Word is actually preached or read or while the sacraments are administered.* This view has been called "actualism" and it is used against all experiences of the Holy Spirit which are not *directly connected* to the Word and the sacraments, such as prophecy, speaking in tongues, revelations, personal calls and guidance. Obviously, this view would negate the validity of much of charismatic experience today. It relegates such experience simply to human or even demonic factors as being contrary both to the Word of God and the Lutheran Confessions. But is this true?

In order to clarify the matter, the foremost authority on Luther and the Holy Spirit, the Danish professor Regin Prenter, was invited to a theological conference in Oslo, Norway, in 1981, where he gave two lectures on the work of the Holy Spirit. The first one had the title "The Work of the Holy Spirit in the Church", and the second "Does God speak directly today? Prophecy – revelation – call – guidance." We shall summarise the main points from Prenter's presentation.[2]

Prenter begins by referring to two statements in the Lutheran Confessions about the work of the Holy Spirit in the church, namely Luther's explanation of the Third Article of the Apostles' Creed in the *Small Catechism* (SC) and

---

[1] *Smalcald Articles*, VIII, 3, *The Book of Concord*, p. 312.

[2] The lectures were held in Danish and are published in Lars Østnor (ed), *Jeg tror på Den hellige ånd. Vår lutherske kirke i møte med den karismatiske utfordring* (English: I Believe in the Holy Spirit: Our Lutheran Church Meeting the Charismatic Challenge), (Oslo: Land og kirke/Gyldendal Norsk Forlag, 1982). Prenter's articles are found on pp. 16-29 and 121-135. Summary, translation and comments are by Tormod Engelsviken.

Art. V in the *Augsburg Confession* (CA). He summarises the SC in this way: "Without the Holy Spirit, the word is without effect", and the CA: "Without the word, the Holy Spirit is absent". The church acknowledges this when it prays: "Come, Holy Spirit and fill the hearts of the believers, and ignite the fire of your love in them."

Prenter further agrees with the statement in SA, and says, "All claims to possess the Holy Spirit before and independently of listening to the Gospel of God in the sermon or sacraments are deceptions. We cannot *possess* the Spirit, who himself is God. But he *possesses us.* The Holy Spirit who is poured out over us in holy baptism, is not given in our power."[3] He goes on to say that, "Our Lutheran Confession asserts inescapably that there exists an indissoluble connection between the Spirit and the word, the word and the Spirit." This connection must be understood on the basis of Jesus' words about the Spirit in his Farewell Discourse to his disciples in John 13-17 where he calls the Holy Spirit "the Spirit of truth", and especially John 14:26: "But he Counsellor, the Holy Spirit, whom the Father will send in my name, will teach you all things and will remind you of everything I have said to you." The task of the Holy Spirit in the church is therefore to *speak.*

According to Prenter, not everything, however, is said by pointing out this connection between the Spirit and the word. He asks two self-critical questions: are those Christians in the history of the church, from the enthusiasts at the time of the Reformation to the Spirit movements in our day (The Pentecostal/Charismatic movements), who speak about the work of the Holy Spirit and the Spirit's creative power through powerful deeds, healings, speaking in tongues, victory over sin and renewal of life, more in line with both the Old Testament and the apostle Paul? Has Lutheran theology wrongly and one-sidedly emphasised John's testimony about the Holy Spirit at the expense of other aspects of the Bible's teaching about the work of the Spirit, for example in Paul?

Prenter intended to answer these questions in his second lecture. In his first, he lays the groundwork by arguing that when the *Augsburg Confession* speaks about the *giving* of the Spirit on the day of Pentecost and later through the means of grace – the word and especially the sacrament of baptism – it *does not exclude that the Holy Spirit also* works *before and after it is given.* The Holy Spirit was also active before Pentecost, as one of the persons of the Trinity, for example by speaking through the prophets in the Old Testament and by the conception of Jesus. The Spirit continues to work both *before and after* he is being poured out also in the centuries after the ascension of Jesus. He works both *inside* and *outside the church* in various ways. "In the church he has through the miracle of Pentecost given himself to us and is (continually) giving himself to us in word and sacraments in order to create in us faith, hope and love, and the eternal life where sin and death are

---

[3] Østnor, *Jeg tror*, pp. 16-19.

conquered. But by giving himself to us the Holy Spirit does not cease to be sovereign God." *When the Holy Spirit is Lord (God), as we confess in the Nicene Creed, we cannot set limits for his work.*[4]

In his second lecture, on the question of whether God speaks directly today, Prenter understands "directly" as meaning *"unmediated"; that is, without the means of grace, the Word and the sacraments.*

Prenter asserts that God spoke directly and unmediated to the *prophets* in the Old and New Testaments, when they, in the moment of *revelation*, received a message from the Holy Spirit which they should convey to the people of God. The Bible also contains stories about how God *called* people whom he had chosen for his service through words addressed *directly* to them, as for example Abraham, Moses, Mary, Peter, and Paul to mention some of the most prominent examples. The Spirit of God also *guided* these people on the way as they followed their individual ministries.

Prenter then goes on to ask whether a corresponding direct, unmediated speech may occur today. His emphatic answer is that there are *no compelling reasons based on the testimony of Scripture and confirmed by the confession of the church to answer the question with a clear and decisive no.*[5] The question is therefore not *whether* God speaks directly today, but rather *how* he does it.

In answering this question, Prenter maintains that, firstly, the message must not contradict what the Holy Spirit has said through the Gospel to the whole people of God, the truth about Jesus Christ, the Son of God. Secondly, it must serve God under the lordship of Jesus Christ, and not one's own happiness and prosperity. Thirdly, there may be false prophecy today that may look like genuine prophecy, as was the case in the Old Testament. Therefore, it is not enough that somebody *claims* to prophesy in the name of God. Prophecy, call and guidance must be tested, as indicated in 1 John 4:1-3 and 1 Thessalonians 5:19-21. It would, however, be a misunderstanding to assume that the church may prevent false prophecy, call and guidance by closing the door to all such practices. For those who belong to the church of God, it is impossible to hinder the free operation of the Spirit of God. Hence Paul, for example, did not forbid speaking in tongues, but demanded that it should serve the building up of the body of Christ.

In his lecture, Prenter is very clear in his criticism of those in the Lutheran church who "do not give space for the free operation of the Spirit besides and outside of his regular operation in the church through the ministry of the word and sacrament."[6] In that case, the Lutherans would misinterpret their own confession. He says:

---

[4] Østnor, *Jeg tror*, pp. 26-28.

[5] Østnor, *Jeg tror*, pp. 121-122.

[6] Østnor, *Jeg tror*, p. 125.

> The fact that the Spirit is not given to people without the mediation of the outer word, *does not mean* that the Spirit does not work in those who receive it at any other time than in the limited moment when baptism is performed, when one listens to the sermon, or partakes of the Lord's supper [...] Such *actualism* [...] is contrary, not only to the whole biblical testimony about the work of the Spirit, but also to the doctrine of the Lutheran confession (italics added).[7]

What then is the reason why the Spirit operates besides and outside the direct mediation through the word and sacraments? In his answer to this question, Prenter refers to the *indwelling of the Spirit* and the "*the free actions of love*" that the Spirit produces. He quotes the *Augsburg Confession*, Art. XX which says, "When through faith the Holy Spirit is given, the heart is moved to do good works. Before that, when it is without the Holy Spirit, the heart is too weak."[8] The Holy Spirit is not only the Spirit of truth, but also the Spirit of love. The *Spirit does not lock himself into the word and sacraments*; on the contrary, the Spirit who is *poured out* with the word and sacraments as his means, is *infused into* the hearts in order to create faith and the fruit that faith produces when it is active in works of love (Rom. 5:5).

This distinction between the *poured out* and the *infused or indwelling Spirit* leads to a distinction between the Spirit himself as person and the gifts of the Spirit in 1 Corinthians 12:4-11.[9] *It is the infused, or indwelling, Spirit who "gives them (the charisms) to each one, just as he determines" (1 Cor. 12:11).* They are manifestations of this Spirit (1 Cor. 12:7). Prenter enumerates in this connection the various gifts of the Spirit, including prophecy, healing, and working of miracles, besides apostles and teachers, with reference to 1 Corinthians 12:28.

In his conclusion concerning the way God speaks directly to people today in prophecy, revelation, call, and guidance, Prenter says:

> The Spirit (1) *first gives faith* when the gospel is heard in preaching and sacrament, and (2) *then renews the hearts* of the believers so that they do works of love, and (3) *finally* [...] the Spirit himself as Lord *gives his various forms of gifts for ministries* that work together in building up the church, the one body of Christ (italics and numbers added).[10]

Preaching and the administration of the sacraments go together with free praise and works of love. *Prophecy* is a work of love in the church, made possible by a special gift of the Holy Spirit. *Call and guidance* are also steps on the long and narrow road of the free service of love. *Love* should be the

---

[7] Østnor, *Jeg tror*, p. 125.
[8] *CA*, XX, 29-31, *The Book of Concord*, p. 45.
[9] This distinction corresponds to the distinction made above between the Holy Spirit as *agent* and as *gift*.
[10] Østnor, *Jeg tror*, p. 129.

guiding principle: "The free action of love is a gift from the Holy Spirit" (1 Cor. 13). And Prenter goes on: "*The Spirit speaks directly to people when he calls them to a special ministry.*" This call of the Spirit may come as a sudden inspiration, but it is more common that it takes place through the guidance of the Spirit through what the believers *experience* in their lives and through what they *learn* by using the means of grace, not least the *word of God and prayer*.[11]

Thus, we may conclude from this brief presentation of Regin Prenter's important lectures that the practice of the gifts of the Spirit *today*, including those gifts that involve a *direct personal word, work, call or guidance from the Spirit*, is in accordance with both *Scripture* and the *Lutheran Confessions.* It is a manifestation of the operation of the *indwelling Holy Spirit* in and through the believer for the upbuilding of the body of Christ.

The fallacy of the "actualist" position held by some Lutherans, can in our opinion also be demonstrated by the fact that this view would imply that Christians who have heard the word of God, have believed in Christ, have been baptised in his name and received the Holy Spirit, would be without the gift of the Spirit and his activity in their lives if such Christians should happen to be in a situation without a Bible or access to any fellow Christians who could preach to them or give them the sacraments. This may be the case when Christians are illiterate, isolated, in prison, or in a totally non-Christian environment. That would be the very opposite of what Christ promised his disciples in Luke 12:12 when he said, "The Holy Spirit will teach you at that time what you should say". It would also be contrary to what persecuted Christians and thousands of others have experienced throughout the history of the church when the Spirit has inspired their words, called and equipped them for various ministries and guided them throughout their lives.

Although we agree with Prenter in his view of the charisms as manifestations of the Holy Spirit through individual Christians in the church, we do not wish to limit the work of the Spirit exclusively to believers who have received the Spirit. In his sovereignty, God may also speak and act *directly* in the lives of people who are *not* Christians or *before* they become Christians. There are several biblical examples of this. Christ revealed himself *directly* to Paul and called him to conversion and apostleship *before* he came to faith and received the Holy Spirit (Acts 9:4-6, 17-18). An angel of God also spoke to Cornelius *before* he became a believer and was filled with the Spirit (Acts 10:3-6, 44-48). Even non-Christians are sometimes forced or led to speak prophetically unwillingly or unknowingly, as in the case of Balaam (Num. 22-24) and the high priest Caiaphas (Jn 11:49-52).

These examples are not unique to the biblical revelation. Reports and testimonies from around the world even today confirm that Christ sometimes reveals himself through visions, dreams and prophecies to people who are

---

[11] Østnor, *Jeg tror*, p. 134.

not Christians and thus draws them to the Bible or the church where they may hear the gospel, come to faith and be saved. *These direct encounters with God and his Spirit do not in themselves save since they do not contain the whole gospel, but they may be important as a preparation for faith.*[12] They are important for the growth of the church in the world today, yet they are exceptional, preliminary, and partial, and can therefore never replace regular Christian mission with word, deeds and signs (Rom. 15:18-20; 10:12-17), which through the work of the Holy Spirit leads people to saving faith and full inclusion in the church.

[12] Among the many books that document these experiences, especially among Muslims, we could mention Seppo Syrjänen, *In Search of Meaning and Identity: Conversion to Christianity in Pakistani Muslim Culture* (Helsinki: Finnish Society for Missiology and Ecumenics, 1984).

(29) Final Evaluation: The Reformation and Charismatic Renewal

by Tormod Engelsviken

In this brief conclusion and evaluation of the Lutheran Reformation view of the Holy Spirit's work, we want, firstly, to point out some important Reformation insights which we believe correspond with the New Testament, and, secondly, to indicate some areas where the Reformation in our opinion did not adequately reflect the biblical understanding of the work of the Holy Spirit.

The Biblical and Reformation View

Firstly, we shall outline *the basic understanding of the Reformation* concerning the role of the Holy Spirit both *in the initial appropriation of salvation* and *in the ongoing Christian life. In our view, it corresponds in a significant way to what we have already seen in the biblical section in Part Two*. We want to summarise it in the form of a simple outline of the process of salvation, along a sequence ("timeline") marked by numbers:

1. *Without Christ, all human beings* are in a lost state of being *guilty* of sin, under the *judgement* (wrath) of God and the *power of the devil.*
2. *The Word* about *Christ's redemptive work* in history, with a *personal promise* of *salvation for those who believe in Christ and his work* (the Gospel), should be communicated in word and deed for all people through the ministry of the church. It is a means of the *convincing and convicting work of the Holy Spirit.* The church *intends to reach all human beings with the gospel* through its missionary work which is not completed until the return of Christ.
3. *Faith* is created by the Holy Spirit in *some* of those who hear the Gospel. This faith is expressed by human beings in *prayer, in a calling upon God,* receiving the promised salvation contained in the Gospel. Some hearers of the Gospel do *not,* however, believe. They reject the offer of salvation, based on their own volition, and therefore lose their salvation. A time interval is possible between 2 and 3, between hearing and believing, since faith may come immediately upon hearing or at a later time.
4. *Those who believe* the *message of the Gospel* and the *personal promise of salvation, receive immediately grace* as the *favour of God,* and are

declared perfectly or totally righteous in the sight of God because of Christ (justification). They are forgiven of their sins, are acquitted in the judgement of God, are reconciled with him and are liberated from bondage to the evil powers. This reception of salvation normally takes place in the sacrament of baptism, but may also happen before or after baptism depending on the time when people come to faith. There is no time interval between 3 and 4, between faith and justification, because justification follows faith *immediately.*

5. Those who are justified before God by faith immediately also receive *the Holy Spirit* as a *gift.* The gift of the Spirit results in the *indwelling of the Spirit* and the *presence of Christ in the believer.* The gift of the Spirit is an *experiential reality* with observable results in the believer's life. The indwelling Spirit renews the believer spiritually and causes a *growth in holiness and in fighting sin (sanctification, fruit).* The indwelling Spirit also grants *gifts* for ministry and building up the church (*charisms*). Both the fruit and the gifts are supposed to continue throughout the believer's life. There is no time interval between 4 and 5, between the initial justification and the sanctification that follows, but there is an important logical order: justification always precedes sanctification as its foundation.
6. *Those who are reconciled to God through a living faith and have received the Holy Spirit as a gift* are raised bodily by the same Spirit to eternal life, either after their physical death or at the return of Christ (*the resurrection of the body*).

Baptism is the initial sign of the new covenant initiating people into the church, granting forgiveness of sins, union with Christ, and the gift of the Holy Spirit to those who believe. It is always *valid* since it contains the promise of God but only *effective for salvation* when received in faith. The sacrament of the *Lord's Supper* also grants forgiveness of sins and union with Christ through participation in Christ's body and blood.

The reception of God's grace and the Holy Spirit through faith does not take place only once at the beginning of the Christian life. It is a lifelong experience. The process outlined above is therefore not to be understood as a static event that takes place once, but as a dynamic process in which the Holy Spirit is actively present, doing his saving, sanctifying, and equipping work in the believers throughout their lives.

While Christians do not "co-operate" with God in the appropriation of salvation through faith in justification (against synergism), they do co-operate with God as "a new creation" in the continued process of sanctification. God and the believers are not, however, "equal partners" in this co-operation; the believers are always *totally dependent upon the new life of Holy Spirit who is working in and through them.*

We can now see how this Reformation understanding of the work of the Holy Spirit in its main features corresponds both with the biblical testimony and with the teaching and experiences of the Lutheran Charismatic renewal, as described in Parts One and Two. This correspondence applies to *all the elements of the appropriation of salvation in Christ,* yet it is particularly obvious in connection with the view of *the Holy Spirit as a gift to believers demonstrated by empirical evidence of the indwelling Spirit and the presence of Christ, and through granting them the gifts and the fruit of the Spirit.*

Some Weaknesses in the Understanding and Practice of the Reformation

Secondly, with regard to the relationship between the Reformation and the Charismatic renewal, the most obvious *fault of the Reformation* in relation to the work of the Holy Spirit was, in our opinion, the view of Luther and other reformers that *the Holy Spirit works in different ways before and after the establishment of the church by the apostles*, and that therefore some of the gifts and workings of the Spirit are not to be expected in later church history, e.g. miracles.

With the exception of the testimony of the *eyewitnesses* to Jesus' life, death and resurrection and the ministry of *the twelve apostles* who received a special commission and authority to speak on behalf of Jesus, and whose ministry is therefore not repeatable, the Charismatic renewal believes that *all other aspects of the Spirit's work as experienced in the early church, including the whole range of spiritual gifts, should continue until the return of Christ. Both the history of the church from the beginning through the centuries and the experience of Christians today give evidence of this*. It is noteworthy that the Luther-scholar professor Regin Prenter, as we have seen, argues that it is not contrary to the Lutheran Confessions to expect a direct, unmediated, work of the Holy Spirit even today as far as, for instance, calling, guidance, prophecy, speaking in tongues are concerned.

While the Reformers formulated the *doctrine* of the priesthood of all believers, a *practical ministry* of the lay people *using their spiritual gifts* in the church and towards the world was not initiated or developed during the time of the Reformation. The Reformers had too little to say about the use of the charisms in the present-day church.

Although Luther would emphasise the *universal scope* of Christ's redemption and the *obligation of Christians to share the Gospel with non-believers both within and outside Christendom*, no systematic or organised mission work was initiated by the Reformers outside the "Christian" areas of Europe, nor was there enough emphasis on *the power of the Holy Spirit for mission.*

Some of these weaknesses and omissions were addressed more than a hundred years after the Reformation by the Lutheran *Pietist movement*, to which we now turn.

(30) Pietism: Between the Reformation and the Charismatic Renewal

by Tormod Engelsviken

The Historical Background

The Reformation in the 16th century was an international movement of reform and renewal in the church that led to the recovery of central features of biblical Christianity. At the same time as it renewed the church and brought salvation and new life to millions of people, it also caused division in the church. In addition to the old division between the Eastern Orthodox churches and the Roman Catholic Church, the Reformation led to new denominations in opposition to the Roman Catholic Church. Some of them were loyal to the Lutheran reformation and called themselves Lutheran, others were influenced by the Swiss reformers Calvin and Zwingli and called themselves Reformed, while others again carried forward the ideals of the Radical Reformation and later formed Anabapist and Baptist churches. The Anglican church in England combined elements from different traditions, yet in general belonged with the other new denominations to what became the *Protestant* wing of Christendom.

The religious peace that was reached in Augsburg, Germany, in 1555 made possible a legal, peaceful coexistence in the same territories between the two opposing confessions and forms of the church, the Protestant and the Catholic. Yet in the following century the tragic "Thirty Years War" (1618–1648), which was partly religious, brought terrible suffering and devastation to the peoples of Europe.

During the approximately 100 years from the end of the Lutheran Reformation with the publication of the *Book of Concord* in 1580, until the beginning of the Pietistic renewal movement in 1675 with the publication of *Pia Desideria* by the German pastor Philipp Jakob Spener (1635–1705), the Lutheran church had been dominated by a theological stream that has been called "Lutheran orthodoxy". One of the aims of this stream was to develop the Lutheran doctrine and to defend it against its opponents in the Catholic Church and in the Reformed churches. The main emphasis was placed on *right doctrine* ("orthodoxy") and less on Christian practice.

We do not wish to denigrate the period of Lutheran Orthodoxy. It brought clarity to many Lutheran doctrines and in that way preserved the doctrinal legacy of the Reformation. It also produced devotional literature of immense lasting influence in the Lutheran church and throughout Christendom, for example, through books like Johann Arndt's famous *True Christianity* (1605–1610). Arndt can be seen as a forerunner of Pietism and was held in high esteem by the Pietists.

The spiritual programme of Pietism was first presented by Spener in a preface to a new edition of a book by Arndt in 1675. In his books, Arndt emphasised the mystical union between Christ and the believer, the life of Christ *in* the believer, over against a one-sided doctrinal emphasis on the forensic side of justification which paid almost exclusive attention to the death of Christ *for* people.

Characteristics of the Pietistic Movement

Like the Reformation movement before it and the Charismatic movement after it, the Pietistic movement was an international and interdenominational movement. It originated in the Lutheran church but influenced and had parallels both in the Reformed churches in the form of *Puritanism* and later *Methodism,* and even in the Roman Catholic Church. It was simultaneously a unifying ecumenical movement and a challenging renewal movement that caused some new lines of division, mostly *within* and not *between* denominations. The so-called "old Pietism" from 1675 and during most of the 18th century was a *revolutionary* movement whose main theological opponent was Lutheran orthodoxy, while the "new Pietism" in the 19th and 20th centuries appeared as a more *conservative* movement opposing the liberal theology that was influencing the Lutheran churches in the aftermath of the Enlightenment in the late 18th century.

In spite of the debt it owed to Lutheran Orthodoxy, and the agreement on the fundamentals of Lutheran theology such as *sola scriptura, sola gratia* and *sola fide,* the Pietists wanted to move the emphasis from correct *theoretical doctrines* in the church to *biblical and personal practice and experience*. The intention was to renew the church by taking it back to the original biblical form of Christianity. The Pietists share this vision with both the earlier Reformers and the later Pentecostal/Charismatic renewal. They did not want to oppose the Reformers but to *complete* their work, especially that of Martin Luther, by taking it a step further and implement some of the great visions that had not yet come to satisfactory fruition in the church or in the lives of the believers. In doing so, they came into conflict with the Orthodox tradition.

The central biblical concept and experience that was brought to the fore by the Pietists was *regeneration* or new birth (cf. Jn 3:5; Tit. 3:5), or becoming a child of God (Jn 1:12-13). They understood it in a comprehensive way as including both justification and the beginning of the new life in Christ. Regeneration presupposed *repentance* or *conversion from sin.* They would refer to Luther's 95 theses from 1517 against the Catholic understanding of indulgences, and especially to his understanding of *repentance* as expressed in the famous first thesis, *"When our Lord and Master Jesus Christ said, 'Repent!' he willed the entire life of believers to be one of repentance"*.

The Pietists would, however, put less emphasis on baptism as the beginning of the Christian life since they lived in a state church situation where practically all people were baptised as infants, yet most people were indifferent or nominal Christians. Although they would not deny that God granted his grace in baptism, they would nevertheless put more emphasis on the *experience of conversion in adults* who through the preaching of the Word came to faith and were born again. Some Pietists would even speak of a *second regeneration mediated by the Word* in those adults who had fallen away from God after their baptism and thereby lost their salvation. Pietism became a *revival movement* where its preachers urgently exhorted baptised Christians to repentance of sin and conversion to Christ to avoid God's righteous judgement, and to receive new life in Christ through the experience of regeneration. This regeneration could be experienced as a process of several steps or as an instantaneous experience that happened at a certain place and time, and hence could be shared with others through personal testimonies.

An authority on Pietism, Martin Schmidt, says that an utterance by Martin Luther was repeatedly referred to by the Pietists and elevated to the *Magna Charta* of the Reformation.[1] It was the following section of Luther's *Preface to Romans* in the translation of 1522, about faith and its fruits:

> *Faith,* however, is a *divine work in us* which changes us and makes us to be *born anew of God* (Jn 1:12-13). It kills the old Adam and *makes us altogether different men,* in heart and spirit and minds and powers; and it *brings with it the Holy Spirit.* O, it is a living, busy, active, mighty thing, this faith. It is impossible for it not to be doing good works incessantly. It does not ask whether good works are to be done, but before the question is asked, it has already done them, and is constantly doing them (italics added).[2]

This is a quote that the Lutheran Charismatic renewal would wholeheartedly agree with. It shows a *remarkable and significant similarity between the concerns of Luther's Reformation, the Pietistic movement and the Charismatic movement.* There are also many other similarities or common concerns between the Pietistic and the Charismatic movements, and we shall briefly mention some of them.

---

[1] Schmidt, *Pietismus*, pp. 17-18.

[2] Luther's "Preface to the Epistle of St. Paul to the Romans" (1522), *LW*, Vol. 35, p. 370.

The Bible

For the Pietists as for the Reformers, *the Bible* was the supreme authority in all matters of Christian doctrine and life but even more than the Reformers they would insist that the Scriptures be preached, read and shared. This increased use of Scripture would take place in private as ordinary Christians became more literate through better education, and increasingly would be able to own their own Bibles. The spiritual ideal of returning to the life and experience of the apostolic church was a motivation for Bible study.

The Pietists' emphasis on Christian sanctification and ministry created a great interest in the person, life and earthly ministry of Jesus as well as in the ethical and spiritual admonitions found in the epistles. The view of the Scriptures as the only authority and source of true Christianity gave the Pietistic movement a certain freedom in relation to the established state and church order, and enabled it to initiate new forms of church life and ministry, often in critical opposition to the traditional forms. Yet, the Pietistic movement stayed within the established Lutheran church, and its leaders, such as Spener and August Hermann Francke (1663–1727) served in leadership positions within that church.

Fellowships and the Priesthood of all Believers

One such new form of church life practiced by Pietism was the *conventicles or smaller fellowship groups* of earnest, born-again Christians coming together outside the ordinary, official worship services of the church. These groups might be led by a Pietistic pastor or even by lay people. Luther had wanted to establish such smaller groups of committed Christians but had not been able to do so. Now, it became a reality in the Pietistic movement.

This meant that the empirical church now consisted of *two concentric circles*, the outer circle where all the baptised were included and the inner circle where the active, confessing, "regenerate" or "born again" Christians organised themselves and did their work relatively independently of the official state church. These inner circles have been called *ecclesiolae in ecclesia* ("small churches within in the church"). They have been a lasting legacy of the Pietistic movement until today, particularly in state and folk churches with large numbers of baptised, nominal Christians.

In these fellowships, Christians could practice the doctrine of the *priesthood of all believers,* a part of the Lutheran Reformation theology, but never fully realised in the church. In the meetings of the fellowships or conventicles, however, which had a more voluntary and informal structure than the church services, Christians who were not ordained ministers, the lay people, could use their gifts. They could preach the gospel, read and interpret the Bible, share testimonies about their conversion and Christian experience, console and encourage each other in mutual counselling, pray with and for one another, and practice different ministries of evangelism, mission, and social service.

The meetings gave opportunities for leadership and ministry to ordinary people who had no opportunity within the official church structure where the pastoral ministry dominated and most often was based on one's inherited place in society and a required theological education. The fellowship meetings were an important arena for evangelising non-believing church members and for recruiting missionaries and other church workers. They also became places where voluntary giving to the work of the Lord took place.

The strong emphasis in Pietism on leading a moral life could sometimes turn into legalism when even the smallest details of life were regulated. This has given Pietism a bad reputation in some Christian circles today. This criticism, however, is in general undeserved because it overlooks the *inner motivation* that inspired the Pietists. The emphasis on the fruit of the Holy Spirit, and particularly on *love for God and neighbour* was characteristic of Pietistic spirituality. And this love was not merely an inner feeling – Pietism is not only about God and the soul in the inner man – but showed itself both in serious attempts at avoiding sins and temptations, and in a holy, God-fearing life with acts of mercy and compassion.

Diakonia and Education

We cannot enumerate all the initiatives that originated with the Pietistic movement in areas such as *diakonia*, involving care for the needy, the orphans and the sick, and *education* with schools on all levels for all people. Many of the diaconal and educational institutions and programmes in today's church and society have their origin in Pietism.

The foremost representative of this concern is the second main leader of the old Pietistic movement, August Hermann Francke (1663–1727), who in Halle, Germany, built large institutions that later inspired similar institutions in many other places. Especially famous and ground-breaking was his *Waisenhaus*, house for orphans, where he cared for children and young people. The modern *welfare state* in Europe and America owes a great debt to the Pietistic movement, although many of its institutions have been secularised in the modern world. The Pietists were people who themselves were transformed by the Gospel and who in turn were instrumental in transforming society.

Mission and Evangelism

The most revolutionary and long-lasting contribution of the Pietistic movement to the church and to the world at large was its recovery of *mission and evangelism* as a permanent obligation of the church.

They opposed the view of Lutheran Orthodoxy that had been dominant in the church since the Reformation – based on Paul's words in Romans 10:18 and Colossians 1:23 – that, firstly, God's word had already reached the whole world, and that the apostles had fulfilled the missionary commission during the first generation of Christians. The commission in Matthew 28:18-20 was therefore not valid in post-apostolic times.

The Orthodox theologians had also argued, secondly, that the commission to preach the gospel in the whole world applied only to the apostles since they alone had the privilege of doctrinal infallibility and miracle-working power to authenticate their message.

They had also maintained, thirdly, that the pagans had themselves to blame for their unbelief because of general revelation (Rom. 1:18-20) and the universal preaching of the apostles. Therefore, they did not need a second chance.

Against this denial of the missionary obligation of all Christians by the leading Orthodox Lutheran theologians in Wittenberg, Germany, the Pietists – together with some Orthodox before them – held that *God's mercy and love for all* demand that the gospel also be preached to the pagans. They referred to many other Old and New Testament texts to show that the gospel must be preached to all people. The missionary obligation rests on the Christian church at all times. But how then should this missionary obligation be carried out in practice?

The Pietists gave several answers to that question and all of them implied *action*. The *first Pietistic mission was a state mission.* The King of Denmark and Norway had been inspired by Pietism and felt a spiritual responsibility for his subjects in the Danish colony of Tranquebar on the south-east coast of India. He therefore sent two German Pietistic pastors from Halle who had experienced a missionary calling, Heinrich Plütschau und Bartholomeus Ziegenbalg, to India in 1705. They became truly pioneer missionaries, and blazed the trail for later missionaries all over the world, both Lutheran and others, by preaching the gospel in the vernacular, translating the Bible, establishing schools, caring for the suffering, and eventually establishing an independent church with a local clergy. This Lutheran Pietistic mission work in India started almost 90 years before the work of the famous Baptist missionary William Carey in Serampore in north-east India.

The most extensive Pietistic mission was carried out by the *Pietistic Moravians* under the inspiration of their founder and leader Count Nikolas Ludwig von Zinzendorf (1700–1760). According to Zinzendorf, mission should have its basis in the "assembly of the children of God", not in colonial powers or state church structures. Zinzendorf also believed that the pagans were under the direct influence of the Holy Spirit prior to the preaching of the Word. The Spirit had therefore prepared the way for the gospel. During the years 1730–1760, the Moravians sent out many lay missionaries to many parts of the world.

In the 19th and 20th centuries, strong new Pietistic and evangelical revivals in Europe and North America led to the formation of *many societies for home and foreign mission*. The mission societies that were established in almost all churches were based on the principle of voluntarism and they mobilised millions of dedicated Christians to sacrificially support the mission work in prayer and with money. Thousands of men and women were sent out as missionaries, often for life-long services as evangelists, pastors, teachers, nurses, doctors and social workers, all of them carrying a message of conversion, regeneration, and a life transformed by the power of God. The importance of this mission movement in the history of the worldwide church can hardly be overestimated.

(31) Lutheran Precursors of the Charismatic Renewal

by Tormod Engelsviken

During the period of revival and renewal in the churches in the 19th and 20th centuries, there were several outstanding laypeople, pastors and missionaries who through their various ministries became precursors and trailblazers for the present Charismatic renewal. They appeared in churches of different denominations in many parts of the world and were used mightily by the Holy Spirit to initiate revivals where large numbers of Christians were renewed and non-Christians converted. When the Charismatic renewal appeared on the world scene in the last part of the 20th century, these pioneers had already given it great credibility. We could mention many examples, such as John Song in China, Sadhu Sundar Singh in India, Festo Kivengere in Africa, Lars Levi Læstadius in Sweden, Thomas Ball Barratt in Norway, William Seymour in USA, and many more. We shall, however, limit ourselves to outlining the work of *four Lutheran pioneers who became precursors of the Charismatic renewal* by *demonstrating the power of the Holy Spirit and the use of his gifts.* They are, in chronological order, the following:[1]

Hans Nielsen Hauge, Norwegian Evangelist and Industrial Entrepreneur

The first one is the Norwegian revival preacher, industrial entrepreneur and social reformer *Hans Nielsen Hauge* (1771–1824). He was a farmer's son from the south-eastern part of Norway who in April of 1796 had a *life-transforming spiritual experience* while ploughing his father's fields. *It happened when he was singing a hymn to himself which contained a prayer expressing a heartfelt longing for union with Jesus and for the power of the Holy Spirit.* The second verse began with the following prayer, "Strengthen me powerfully in my soul, that I might know what the Spirit can do". Hauge writes later in life that while he sang the next phrase of this verse, "Myself

[1] These examples are taken from Norway, Germany, China, and Madagascar. Many others could certainly have been mentioned. Christians from other parts of the world may want to expand the list of examples based on knowledge of their own history.

and all that I have, I will freely surrender if you alone will dwell in my soul",[2] he had an almost ecstatic spiritual experience. In his own words:

> My soul was so uplifted to God that I was unaware of myself, because I was outside myself [...] My soul felt something supernatural, divine and blessed. There was a glory that no tongue can describe. [...] I especially felt a passionate and burning love for God and my neighbour. My mind was renewed. I grieved over all the sins and felt a strong desire that people should get to share the grace with me. I was filled with a passionate desire to read the Bible and Jesus' own teaching.[3]

Hauge's experience was not a conversion experience since he was a baptised and confirmed believer who had previous studied the Bible and devotional literature on a daily basis. It was rather an experience of a deep life-transforming encounter with God in his grace and love granted by the Holy Spirit, an experience that called him to and equipped him for a life-long ministry of evangelism, counselling, writing, and spiritual and practical leadership. His followers later understood his experience as his "Spirit baptism", which they wrote on a plaque placed where he had had his experience near his birth place, which today is a museum.

The result of Hauge's experience was an immediate, burning evangelistic zeal that led him to first share his experience with his own family and later to a ministry as an itinerant evangelist. During the next eight years, he walked or ran (!) 15 000 km through Norway's mountainous countryside, visiting towns and cities, preaching, counselling and establishing fellowships of converted Christians who gathered in their homes for "upbuilding". His serious message of repentance of sin, new birth and the obligation and power to lead a holy life in obedience to Christ caused a strong countrywide revival the like of which Norway has not experienced either before or after Hauge's time.

Hauge's preaching ministry as a layman was, however, in conflict with the Danish-Norwegian *Conventicle Act* of 1741,[4] which prohibited religious meetings or lay preaching without the presence or permission of the local pastor. He made enemies among the clergy whom he criticised for their

---

[2] Our own translation of parts of the hymn, "Jesus, din søte forening å smake", which again is a Norwegian translation of a German hymn from 1712 by the Pietist Johann Ludwig C. Allendorf.

[3] Quoted from Steinar Thorvaldsen, *A Prophet Behind the Plough: Hans Nielsen Hauge and His Ministry* (Tromsø: Tromsø University, Eureka Digital 1-2010), pp. 2-3. The book contains several quotes from Hauge's own writings translated into English.

[4] Norway got a democratic constitution in 1814 when it separated from Denmark and entered into a union with Sweden. The Conventicle Act was abolished in 1842, due in part to the influence of several of Hauge's followers, the "Haugeans", in the Norwegian Parliament.

rationalistic preaching and lax living, and among some local state officials, who feared him as a rebel. He was arrested several times, and was finally put in prison in 1804, where he was incarcerated without sentence for many years. He was finally sentenced to two years imprisonment, and then released in 1811.

Hauge was an avid reader and was influenced by the devotional literature of the Orthodox and Pietistic periods, among them Johan Arndt's *True Christianity*. Although he was formally an uneducated man, he wrote about 40 publications with a circulation of about 150 000 copies in a total Norwegian population of about one million! He was by far the most read author in Norway in his time. He was also an industrial entrepreneur and started factories and businesses around the country together with many of his friends. This happened during a period of extreme poverty with an urgent need for economic and social development in Norway.

During his later years, Hauge's relationship to the official state church improved and in his spiritual testament to his "friends", he recommended them to remain within the Lutheran state church, attend the official worship service and receive the sacraments, while at the same time continuing as an independent revival and renewal movement within the church. His friends followed his advice. The Haugean revival caused a renewal and vitalisation of the Norwegian Lutheran church that had lasting effects. He has been named the most important layman in the history of the Nordic churches. The epitaph on Hans Nielsen Hauge's grave monument in Oslo is the following quote: "I have sworn obedience to the Spirit of God, and he has helped me to be faithful to my intention."[5]

Johann Christoph Blumhardt, German Pastor and Healer

Our second example is the German Lutheran pastor *Johann Christoph Blumhardt* (1805–1880) who was a humble parish pastor in the small town of Möttlingen in Württemberg in southern Germany, the heartland of the Pietistic movement in Germany.[6] He came to prominence after he was challenged by the severe suffering of a young woman by the name Gottliebin

---

[5] Our translation from Norwegian. Hauge is mentioned in Schmidt, *Pietismus*, p. 157. To our knowledge, there is no large, authoritative book on Hauge in the English language. There are, however, many books on Hauge in Norwegian. The most thorough among them is the doctoral dissertation by Bishop Andreas Aarflot, *Tro og lydighet. Hans Nielsen Hauges kristendomsforståelse* ("Faith and Obedience: Hans Nielsen Hauge's Understanding of Christianity", Oslo: Universitetsforlaget, 1969).

[6] Blumhardt is mentioned in Schmidt, *Pietismus*, p. 153. See also Fridrich Zuendel, *Johann Christoph Blumhardt: A Biography* (new edition, Walden, NY: Plough, 2019) and Dieter Ising, *Johann Christoph Blumhardt – Life and Work* (Eugene, OR: Cascade, 2009).

Dittus, who was possessed by several evil spirits that manifested themselves in her person and her home, in 1840. Blumhardt deemed that the only solution was an expulsion of the spirits according to the practice of Jesus in the New Testament. He began what was later called "Blumhardt's battle" which lasted for two years until the demons were finally totally expelled in 1842. Early during the exorcism, Blumhardt prayed, "Lord Jesus, help us. We have seen long enough what the devil can do; now we want to see what the Lord Jesus can do." The last words that were said by the demons before they left were "Christ is Conqueror".

The exorcism of Gottliebin Dittus drew public attention, and people streamed to Möttlingen where a strong revival movement emerged around Blumhardt. People were converted, healed, reconciled, and many lives renewed and transformed. The small town could not accommodate all the people who came to visit Blumhardt, who also carried out an extensive personal counselling ministry. As a consequence, he had to move, and in 1853 he bought a thermic spa in the town of Bad Boll near Stuttgart where he continued his healing and counselling ministry until his death in 1880.

Blumhardt had a strong expectation of a future coming of the kingdom of God and a new large outpouring of the Holy Spirit. He wrote with regard to Jesus' promise of the Holy Spirit:

> A small part of it was already fulfilled in the time of the apostles. Sadly, since then, the endowment with the Spirit has receded into the background, so that it is no longer what it was. Indeed, if it was then given on a limited scale, must it not now be fulfilled on a larger scale [...] Since we need the Spirit again, God will also give it again. We have the promise.

Blumhardt's ministry and fame also spread outside of Germany to the English-speaking world, and his healing ministry had great influence on the leaders of the healing and holiness movements that occurred toward the end of the 19th century, and which eventually merged with the classical Pentecostal movement in the early part of the 20th century.[7]

Marie Monsen, Missionary in China

Our third example is the missionary teacher and nurse, *Marie Monsen* (1878–1962) from Bergen in Norway who in 1901 went as a single missionary for the *Norwegian Lutheran Mission* to China, where she stayed more or less continuously for more than 30 years until her final return to Norway in 1932.

Women have not received the place in church and mission history that they deserve. They were, for cultural and theological reasons, seldom given the opportunities that their divine calling and gifts would warrant. *Single*

---

[7] See Vinson Synan, *The Holiness-Pentecostal Tradition.*

female missionaries were, however, toward the end of the 19th century and onwards given a freedom to minister with both their natural abilities and spiritual gifts in a way that their married sisters in the home countries most often lacked. One such pioneer female missionary was Marie Monsen who in spite of being a lay woman with little theological education became an instrument of a great charismatic revival in China and an activist for the ministry of women in church and mission in Norway.[8]

Marie Monsen had a deep conviction that men and women are on equal terms as instruments of God in the evangelisation of the world,[9] and she showed this throughout her ministry. She had experienced a personal call to mission work and went out to China in 1901 for the newly established *Norwegian Lutheran Mission* (1891). During her first years in China, she worked effectively as an educator, primarily for girls and women, but she also felt that she was inadequate in her ministry.

In 1918, she had a strong experience of renewal in the Holy Spirit, an experience of God, that the historian of religion and an expert on Marie Monsen, Lisbeth Michaelsson, has called somewhat imprecisely "a dramatic rebirth in the Holy Spirit, a 'second blessing' characteristic of the holiness movement".[10] The life and ministry of Marie Monsen from then onwards took on a new supernatural dimension. She would experience concrete divine guidance and protection, supernatural healings through prayer, and exorcism of evil spirits.

In 1925, she renounced her wages from the mission and lived on the basis of the promises of God, according to the faith-mission principles. From that same year, she began her third and last period as a missionary, and it was during this period that her ministry would draw the attention of thousands both in China and other countries. From 1927, she travelled extensively in the north of China as a revival preacher. The revival had been prepared by two decades of prayer both by herself and others. She was described by her missionary colleagues as a "charismatic preacher with great authority" and with a message of repentance of sin, followed by grace of God and the bliss of forgiveness by faith in Jesus.

The revivals usually began with the Christian leaders, then moved to other Christians and finally spread to non-believers who were converted in great numbers. The revival was accompanied by charismatic phenomena such as healing, speaking in tongues and visions. Monsen understood herself as a

---

[8] Daniel E. Bays, "Marie Monsen", in Gerald H. Anderson (ed), *Biographical Dictionary of Christian Mission* (New York: Macmillan Reference, 1998), pp. 468-469.

[9] Lisbeth Michaelsson, "Marie Monsen's Achievement", in Tormod Engelsviken, Notto R. Thelle and Knut Edvard Larsen (eds), *A Passion for China: Norwegian Mission to China until 1949* (Oxford: Regnum, 2015), pp. 89-90.

[10] Michaelsson, "Achievement", p. 96.

messenger of God, a chosen vehicle of the Holy Spirit. She would challenge "intellectual believers" who were spiritually dead. They had to humble themselves, give up confidence in their own positions and abilities, confess all their sins and empty themselves in order to be born again and filled with the Holy Spirit. She shares how she experienced her own ministry:

> I was carrying a larger burden than I realised: the future of our missionary work, but without understanding that the Spirit was working upon me in order to empty me for my confidence in my abilities and education, and if possible to make a missionary who was nothing in her own mind – one of the chosen – who had to learn only to reckon with him, and what he was capable of.[11]

A great revival that occurred in Shandung province from 1927 to 1937 (called the Shantung Revival) had two main human sources: Marie Monsen and indigenous Chinese Christians. It affected several missions and churches, such as American Southern Baptists, Presbyterians and Methodists, and was a momentous event in Chinese church history with influence on Christianity in many parts of China. One stream of the revival developed in a more Pentecostal direction with an exclusively Chinese leadership independent of the missions, and with great emphasis on the gifts of the Holy Spirit.[12]

After Monsen returned to Norway in 1932, she continued her ministry of preaching and counselling and wrote several books about her spiritual experiences in China. These books became missionary bestsellers and had a great impact, both in Norway and America. They created expectations of future revivals among many Christians. Some of the books were translated into English and new editions have been published until recently. The titles of her most well-known books indicate the character of her ministry: *The Awakening: Revival in China, a Work of the Holy Spirit* (1961); *A Present Help: Standing on the Promises of God* (1961), *The Power of Prayer: Does the Bible have a Gospel for the Sick?* (Norwegian, 1962), and *Everything is Possible for God* (Norwegian, 1962).

Professor Michaelsson says about the legacy of Marie Monsen: "More than anything else it is the gifts displayed in her preaching and writing that have secured Marie Monsen a name in posterity". Monsen died in 1962 on the eve of the eruption of the Lutheran Charismatic Renewal which she certainly would have heartily welcomed. Her legacy was carried on by her missionary colleague from China and well-known author, Asbjørn Aavik (1902–1997), who had been deeply influenced by Marie Monsen and became a treasured speaker in the Norwegian Lutheran charismatic renewal in the 1970s and 1980s.

---

[11] Michaelsson, "Achievement", p. 106.
[12] Michaelsson, "Achievement", p. 105.

Nenilava, a Malagasy Prophetess and Revival Leader

Our fourth example of extraordinary servants of God instrumental in renewal and revival is maybe the most remarkable of them all. It is the Malagasy evangelist, revival leader and prophetess, most often called *Nenilava* (1918–1998), a nickname literally meaning "Tall mother", because, at 1.90m, she was taller than most Malagasy women. She grew from humble origins in Manakara in south-east Madagascar to become "the most important tool for revival in the country",[13] highly respected by Christians both in Madagascar and abroad.

Nenilava ministered in the first of four revival movements that have had great impact on Malagasy church life. This movement had its origin within the Lutheran church and is called *Fifohazana.*[14] It began in 1894 with a man of noble birth by the name of *Rainisoalambo* (1844–1904) at a time when he was already fifty years old. He worked as a traditional Malagasy diviner and healer, but while he was seriously ill, he had a vision of a man dressed in white who told him to throw away his charms. Convinced that the man was Jesus, he obeyed the command, was healed from his illness, and became a committed Christian. He shared his experience with family and friends, and a revival soon began. He went from house to house proclaiming the gospel of forgiveness of sins. He would warn his followers against copying the preachers in the churches who preached about the power of Christ but did not dare cast out sickness or demons. In his view, preaching and the signs that followed should never be separated.

In spite of his criticism of some preachers, the revival stayed within the Lutheran Malagasy church, although it remained independent of the formal church structure. The leaders of the revival were called "shepherds". Their ministry consisted of preaching, counselling, exorcism, healing, and strengthening of the believers.[15] On their visits to new places, they usually co-operated with the local pastors and Christian leaders. The revival led to renewal of Christians, increase in church attendance, and establishment of new churches through conversions of non-Christians.

It was within this revival movement that Nenilava carried out her ministry and became its most outstanding leader. Aged ten, she had experienced the call of Jesus through dreams, voices and visions. In 1941, she began her ministry after having been ordered by Jesus to expel demons from a suffering

---

[13] Kjetil Aano, a missionary to Madagascar who later became a prominent mission leader in Norway, in the newspaper *Dagen,* 17th March 2015.

[14] The revival and its two main protagonists Rainisoalambo and Nenilava are described and discussed in the scholarly study by Cynthia Holder Rich (ed), *The Fifohazana: Madagascar's Indigenous Christian Movement* (Amherst, NY: Cambria Press, 2008).

[15] See the doctoral dissertation by Hans Austnaberg, *Shepherds and Demons: A Study of Exorcism as Practised and Understood by Shepherds in the Malagasy Lutheran Church* (New York: Peter Lang, 2008), p. 44.

woman. When the demons left, they are reported to have said, “We leave because the one who is stronger than us has come”. This call took place on 2nd August 1941, and the day is commemorated in the church in Madagascar even today.

Nenilava felt at first very inadequate for a preaching ministry because she was uneducated and ignorant, yet when she was asked to speak, “she was filled with the power of the Holy Spirit, she felt a deep peace, and she spoke with conviction”. The audience was startled because they felt that God was speaking directly to them.[16] The results of her preaching were confession of sins and conversions to Christ.

This was the beginning of her life-long ministry, as Nenilava travelled widely in Madagascar as an evangelist during the period 1941–1975, and later worked mostly from her home in Antananarivo. Her meetings were crowded, and renewal and revival accompanied her ministry everywhere.

There were three main aspects of her ministry: firstly, proclamation of the gospel with a strong emphasis on repentance and forgiveness of sins; secondly, casting out of demons and laying on of hands in the name of Jesus and in the power of the Holy Spirit for liberating people from evil and strengthening their faith; thirdly, spiritual care for individual Christians through personal counselling after preaching and exorcism.[17] In her ministry, she manifested several of the gifts of the Spirit, including healing, speaking in tongues, prophecy and words of knowledge which she used in counselling people. She often knew supernaturally what was in people’s hearts and could give concrete help, for example by using texts from the Bible that spoke directly to their situation. She would also claim that Jesus told her what to say. Her ministry led to conflict with some missionaries and other church leaders, but it was officially recognised by the church in 1953.

The area where she lived during the first period was *Ankaramalaza* in south-east Madagascar. One of the great achievements of Nenilava was the establishment there of a centre, called *toby,* for helping people spiritually, medically and socially. In this centre, lay shepherds, 80% of them being women, would be trained for a period of about two years and then consecrated for the ministry of preaching, healing and exorcism. Similar centres eventually spread all over Madagascar and their number increased to almost 40 during Nenilava’s lifetime. More than 25 000 persons have been consecrated as shepherds, with 500–700 new shepherds being consecrated every year.[18] This has taken place in the Malagasy Lutheran church which,

---

[16] Austnaberg, *Shepherds*, p. 52.

[17] Adrianasolo Jaona and Randrianmanantena Yvonne, “The Prophet Nenilava and the Development of the Ankaramalaza Revival Movement”, in Rich, *Fifohanzana*, pp. 27-46. The chapter is based on eyewitness accounts.

[18] Austnaberg, *Shepherds*, p. 9.

with about four million members, is one of the largest Lutheran churches in the world.

The shepherds are primarily occupied with preaching and expulsion of evil spirits. The services in which this takes place, either in a *toby* or in a parish church, consist of hymn singing, free prayer, bold preaching and then always a session of personal ministry with healing and expulsion of evil spirits. This last session consists of two parts. The first, called "work", begins with the singing of the hymn "Come, O, Holy Spirit" and the reading of four biblical passages (Jn 14:12-17; Mt. 18:18-20; Mk 16:15-20; Jn 20:21-23). Then the shepherds, standing in front of the congregation dressed in ceremonial white attire, command in Jesus' name the demons to leave those who show visible signs of being assaulted by them. The fight against the evil powers may apply to a wide range of demonic assaults, from sinful temptations, demonic influence and oppression, to cases of possession when the demons have taken full control of a person. After the demons are driven out and the afflicted have become quiet and calm, the second part, called "strengthening", is performed by laying on of hands with individual prayer and promise of forgiveness of sins and the reception of the Holy Spirit.

Some have wondered about what really takes place in the exorcisms. The answer to that question is very much dependent on one's worldview and faith. After serious investigation, the researcher Abigail Evans in the *Anglican Church Study Group on Possession and Exorcism* concludes, "After reading the vivid descriptions of the possessed people and the accompanying exorcism, there is no way of confusing them with typical psychotic episodes". Medical doctors and shepherds work together in order to diagnose people correctly. All of the various ministries in the revival are performed "under the guidance of the Holy Spirit".[19]

People with various problems: poor, sick, widows, orphans, handicapped people, and people assaulted by demons come or are brought to the *toby* for help, and they receive it according to their needs through various medical and social services as well as spiritual counselling and exorcism. The ministry in the *toby,* as initiated by Nenilava, represents a holistic, biblical, and spiritual approach to the relief of human suffering. The strength of the revival is explained by Malagasy scholars as due to God's grace, the power of the Holy Spirit, and its relevance for the basic needs of the Malagasy people.[20]

As Nenilava's fame and influence grew, she was recognised more and more as a unique spiritual leader. She also visited abroad, and in 1973 she was in Norway where she had an audience with the King of Norway and received St Olav's Order. She was also later awarded the Malagasy Order of Honour. At her funeral in 1998, representatives of the Malagasy government

[19] Rakotojoelinandrasana Daniel, "Holistic and Integrated Care for Spirit, Mind, and Body as Practiced by the Fifohanzana", in Rich, *Fifohanzana*, pp. 94, 102.
[20] Rakotojoelinandrasana, "Holistic", in Holder Rich, *Fifohanzana*, p. 103.

were present to honour her ministry. Nenilava's life story is a remarkable example of how Jesus through the Holy Spirit may call, equip and use a Malagasy woman of humble background to accomplish a great work leading thousands of people to salvation from sin, liberation from evil powers, and transformation of life.

Conclusion

After having described these four protagonists of what we would call *Lutheran renewal and revival movements with strong emphasis on the work of the Holy Spirit and with many charismatic traits,* we shall sum up this description of the persons who became precursors of Lutheran Charismatic Renewal by pointing out the characteristics they seemed to have in common:

- A personal, conscious relationship to the Holy Spirit
- A palpable experience on the indwelling, or the fullness, of the Holy Spirit and of intimate union with the indwelling Christ
- A concern for restoring the Christian life and practice as modelled by Jesus and the early church as described in the Bible
- A strong and persevering faith in the promises of God and his protection
- A strong personal experience and demonstration of the fruit of the Spirit, such as love, joy and hope
- An extensive practice of the gifts of the Spirit, including such gifts as healing, exorcism, prophecy and supernatural occurrences (not so much the case with Hauge)
- A strong emphasis on the power of prayer and dependence on God's Spirit
- A burning zeal for evangelism and mission, for sharing the gospel with others
- A strong concern for suffering people which leads to the provision of practical help of people in need
- The establishment of and active participation in fellowships of earnest, committed, reborn Christians
- A demonstration of a humble, yet authoritative and powerful preaching
- A faithful ministry over many years, sometimes meeting with criticism and resistance, yet leading to strong revival and renewal movements with conversion of large numbers of people and lasting transformation of individuals and societies.
- An innovative and independent, even revolutionary attitude and practice, yet faithful adherence to the doctrines and ethics of classical, biblical Christianity.

All of these common traits are also, as we have seen in Parts One and Two of this book, found in New Testament Christianity and in the Charismatic renewal. They may serve as a *historical pattern for reform, renewal and revival in the church.* The church is in its essence – as a missional community of believers where Christ and his Spirit are present – *always the same* (Latin: *ecclesia semper eadem*), but it is also a dynamic community where the *Spirit is always working to reform and renew* the church (Latin: *ecclesia semper reformanda*). In the following Parts Four and Five of this book, we shall lay out in greater detail how we believe the Holy Spirit doctrinally and practically reforms and renews the church in our time.

Part Four

Taught by the Holy Spirit

Doctrinal Concerns in the Charismatic Renewal

When he, the Spirit of truth, comes, he will guide you into all truth. He will not speak on his own; he will speak only what he hears, and he will tell you what is yet to come. He will bring glory to me by taking from what is mine and making it known to you. All that belongs to the Father is mine. That is why I said the Spirit will take from what is mine and make it known to you."

John 16:13-15

(32) Faith

The Source of Faith

One of the marks of spiritual renewal is that faith – not mental acceptance of an idea, but true biblical faith – gets rehabilitated. When the Holy Spirit brings renewal, confidence in God displaces doubt. God's presence and purpose become a daily reality in the lives of people touched by the Spirit's renewing work. The doctrines and duties take on new meaning. "It seems as though every gift and every blessing I have already experienced in the Lord is refreshed and revitalised," was the way a 71-year-old Lutheran pastor described his own renewal in the Holy Spirit.[1]

Renewal of this kind cannot be understood simply by reference to psychological, sociological, or other scientific categories. It is, at its most fundamental level, the grace of God seeking us out. It is the Holy Spirit creating true and assured faith. Faith in Christ is not a human achievement. Indeed, it is not a human possibility at all. Only the Holy Spirit can create true faith. "For it is by grace you have been saved, through faith – and it is not from yourselves, it is the gift of God – not by works, so that no-one can boast" (Eph. 2:8-9). A long tradition of evangelical scholarship has held that in this key passage of Scripture, "gift" refers to the entire preceding clause, to "faith" as well as to "grace". Salvation in its entirety, including the faith to receive it, is a gift of God.

As we have already seen, Luther began his explanation to the Third Article of the Apostles' Creed by pointing out this relationship:

> I believe that I cannot by my own understanding or effort believe in Jesus Christ my Lord, or come to him. But the Holy Spirit has called me through the gospel, enlightened me with his gifts, and sanctified and kept me in true faith.[2]

Faith and Justification

It is especially important to see the work of the Holy Spirit at the point where faith begins, that is, when one is justified before God and becomes a Christian. Justifying faith is central to the Christian life. "Man is justified by faith apart from observing the law" (Rom. 3:28) and "Without faith it is impossible to please God" (Heb. 11:6). But if we understand faith as our own achievement, then we have opened the door to futility and despair: faith

---

[1] Christenson, *Gifts of Tongues*, p. 16.

[2] Martin Luther, *The Small Catechism, in Contemporary English* (Minneapolis, MN: Augsburg, 1979), p. 14.

becomes a work that I must perform in order to win God's favour, and if my faith falters, I am condemned. The Lutheran bishop Lowell Erdahl wrote:

> Biblical and theological writing about justification by faith seeks to make a distinction between living by faith versus living by works. Yet when I first heard of justification by faith, I misunderstood it to mean that I was justified (that is, forgiven and saved) on account of and because of my faith. Faith for me became a good work that I had to perform in order to get God to love and save me. When my faith faltered, I was doomed. Years of parish teaching and experience convince me that I am not alone in having experienced this misunderstanding.[3]

True Faith versus "Imitation Faith"

There is something that goes by the name of "faith" that is not biblical faith at all but is merely the mental acceptance of an idea. True faith holds not only the idea of Christ, but Christ himself as a living presence.

The difference between true faith and what Regin Prenter calls "imitation faith" is not easy to put down in words, because, as he points out in his study of Luther's view of the Holy Spirit, virtually the same words are used to describe both true faith and imitation faith.[4] There may be, psychologically speaking, a certain joy and satisfaction that accompanies imitation faith, and we may describe it similarly to the way we describe the joy that accompanies true faith. That which makes the difference, however, is the presence and action of the Holy Spirit, and this is only clear to the experience of faith.

To believe in the intellectual idea of Christ is a distinct and not-too-difficult human possibility, especially if it is a truth generally held in one's culture. It is not, however, the same as experiencing the real Christ. One may hold orthodox views of Christ for a variety of reasons. But the Holy Spirit alone creates true faith, whereby one is actually united with the living Christ as the present and redeeming Lord.

The dividing line between true faith and imitation faith may not be easy to mark, but one sign of spiritual renewal is a recognition that one has been hovering very near that line in everyday experience, as the following testimony illustrates:

> I grew up from childhood believing in God. Like my father before me, I learned the clear difference between right and wrong from my mother and my Sunday school teachers [...] I knew the Lord's Prayer, the Apostles' Creed, and I answered all the questions in the affirmative just before the pastor laid his hands on me when I knelt at the altar in my white robe with pink carnation on my confirmation day, while mother and relatives looked on approvingly. But in my

[3] Lowell Erdahl, "Viewpoint", *The Lutheran Standard*, 18th November 1983.

[4] Prenter, *Spiritus Creator*, pp. 60-61.

> heart, there was an emptiness born of an honest recognition that I was not, and likely never would be, the Christian I was supposed to be. Well, I would try to be one anyway, for a while at least, I concluded that day.
>
> Within a few months I gave up my struggle to live like I had been taught. It was too much for me. I found that I couldn't live the good life of real believers. At church college, I decided to live the life anyway, without the inner assurance. Students and professors alike seemed to be doing it, and perhaps that's all there was to it anyway. I believed in God, I concluded, and was baptised. What more did anyone require of me? Nothing more, it appeared, so why not enrol in theological studies too? Why not be a missionary and go all the way for God? So I prepared for the ministry, was ordained, and became a missionary candidate.
>
> But inside me there was turmoil caused by unresolved conflict between who I should be and who I actually was as a Christian. Eventually the disparity between the "ought" and the "actual" took its toll in my behaviour and in my relationships with those closest to me. I ended up resigning. I turned in my ordination papers and quit the God business.
>
> He did not, however, quit on me. At my worst, he came with grace indescribable. From a Friday to a Monday in Holy Week 1972 he moved. He gave me a great, life-astounding gift. He made me a "true believer". Faith was given to me, somehow, exactly 20 years from the day of my confirmation.
>
> He renewed my mind, primarily. I "saw" for the first time how he was always there from my baptism, but I had not before known him as a living presence. I never "understood" before. He does not require faith: he gives faith as a gift. He himself has done all things necessary for my salvation. He required nothing of me that he himself was not willing to work in and through me.
>
> My evangelical friends tell me that I was "born again" that weekend in 1972. Perhaps I was, but I'd rather say that I was "born again in the Holy Spirit", because since then I have found that along with the gift of true believing faith has come the gift of the Paraclete, ever present in my consciousness.[5]

We do not want to paint an idealised picture of a renewal movement. Renewal movements, by virtue of their very popularity, have their share of the problems that go with life and growth, including the problem of imitation faith. But the Spirit is disturbing the false notion that equates mental acceptance with true faith. He is warning us that we can convert people to a belief system without converting them to Christ. The Spirit is bringing people to a fresh experience of Christ, not as a mere idea, but as Lord. At the centre of the Charismatic renewal is not an idea but Jesus himself, the Living One, present and active among his people by the working of the Holy Spirit.

---

[5] W. Dennis Pederson, personal testimony (see Appendix).

Martin Luther's Understanding of Faith

Luther recognised that true faith is not something that springs up from within ourselves. It is created as a gift of God. Through the working of the Holy Spirit, Christ is received as the living, redeeming Lord. This was a radical break with the common understanding of faith. He writes:

> Faith is not something dreamed, a human illusion, although this is what many people understand by the term. The reason is that, when they hear the gospel, they miss the point; in their own hearts, and out of their own resources, they conjure up an idea which they call "belief", which they treat as genuine faith. *Faith, however, is something that God effects in us* (italics added).[6]

How do people today understand and use the word faith? According to common usage, faith refers to an innate ability, that is, *something that comes from within myself*: I am the subject, the one who has faith; I place this faith of mine in God, who is the object of my faith. Luther, however, understood faith as going beyond a strict subject-object relationship to a point of dynamic identification of subject and object. In one of his writings, we virtually see this development taking place:

> Faith, if it be true faith, is a *sure trust and confidence of the heart*, and a firm consent *whereby Christ is apprehended*: so that Christ is the object of faith, Yea *rather he is not the object, but, as it were, in the faith itself Christ is present* (italics added).[7]

The gift of faith is inseparable from the gift of Christ himself. Apart from the reception of Christ as the living Lord, mediated by the Holy Spirit, all talk of faith is imitation. No-one can recognise, believe in or confess Christ except by the power of the Holy Spirit. "No-one can say Jesus is Lord", except by the Holy Spirit" (1 Cor. 12:3). Luther stated emphatically:

---

[6] *Reformation Writings of Luther*, Vol. 2, translated by Bertram Lee Wolff (New York: Philosophical Library, 1956), p. 288.

[7] Martin Luther, *Commentary on Galatians*, edited by Philip Watson (Westwood, NJ: Fleming H. Revell, n.d.), p. 343. The Finnish theologian Markku Antola has written a doctoral dissertation where he has studied exactly the emphasis which is expressed here, see Markku Antola, *The Experience of Christ's Real Presence in Faith: an Analysis of the Christ-Presence-Motif in the Lutheran Charismatic Renewal* (Helsinki: Luther Agricola seura, 1998). It corresponds also with an emphasis in Finnish theology on union with Christ, as represented by the so-called Finnish school of interpreting Luther.

> True faith cannot be manufactured by our own thoughts, for it is solely the work of God in us, without any assistance on our part. As Paul says in Romans, it is God's gift and grace, obtained by one man, Christ.[8]

Faith is thus the personal reception or appropriation, by grace alone, of the person and work of Jesus Christ, brought about by the Holy Spirit.

Repentance and Faith

The faith which the Holy Spirit works in a believer brings about a fundamental reorientation that is described by the biblical words *repent and believe*: one turns away from a self-directed life (repentance) and embraces a life that confidently trusts and obeys Christ (belief). In evangelical circles, this truth has been prominently taught with regard to the initial step of faith – that is, describing how one *comes to Christ*. It needs to be extended to describe also how one *lives in Christ* (Col. 2:6-7). A Spirit-filled and Spirit-directed life is nothing other than a life that day by day turns away from reliance on self to trust Christ in everything.

The church, as God's pilgrim people on earth (1 Pet. 2:11), is constantly in need of renewal. Around the year 140 A.D., Hermas, one of the apostolic fathers, had visions that showed the development of the church as a process of rejuvenation. He saw the church in the form of an old woman who had lost her former beauty as the bride of Christ. A voice told Hermas that, through heartfelt repentance and God's renewing grace, the church's former beauty could be regained.[9] Hermas thus established a major theme in the history of the church: the church's need for continuing renewal through repentance. Spiritual awakenings, not forged by human hands, yet intimately connected to sincere repentance, are signs that the Holy Spirit is doing his renewing work.

Until the final resurrection, Christians will have to contend with the painful reality of sin. Denying it only thickens the cataracts of self-deception, and calls God a liar (1 Jn 1:8-10). But the awareness of sin that leads to repentance comes only through the Holy Spirit. Without him, we remain blind to sin and blind to Jesus (Jn 9:35-41; 15:22-27).

When people are reluctant to recognise and repent of sin, it is a sign that the Holy Spirit is being resisted. Individual believers commit sins: sins against righteousness, love, and humility. Congregations come under the bondage of sin: pride, neglect, party spirit. The whole church may become

---

[8] *The Precious and Sacred Writings of Martin Luther*, edited by John Nicholas Lenker, vol. 4 (Minneapolis, MN: Lutheran in All Lands Company, 1904), reprinted under the title "Justification by Faith", in *The Protestant Pulpit* (Nashville, TN: Abingdon-Cokesbury, 1974), p. 15.

[9] "Pastor Hermas, Visiones 1-4", *Die Vision: Erfahrungsformen und Bilderwelt*, edited by Ernst Benz (Stuttgart: Ernst Klett, 1969), p. 213.

corrupted by sin: presumption, faithlessness, worldliness, heresy, self-seeking. All sins need to be acknowledged, repented of, and washed away in the forgiveness that flows from the cross and resurrection of Christ. The Spirit alone creates such repentance (Ps. 51:7-12).

Where the people of God are eager to recognise and repent of sin, it is a sign that the Holy Spirit is at work and is being received. Most revivals in church history have begun after people have been convicted of sin in their conscience and confessed them to God and to one another. It is the devil's ploy to coax God's people away from repentance, as though repentance were an admission that one was not living in victory and the Holy Spirit's presence had been lost, or that God is satisfied with people regardless of their sin. The latter would be "cheap grace" as opposed to "costly" grace. Sin cost Christ his life. Repentance is God's confirmation that the Holy Spirit is truly present, for the Spirit alone creates true repentance. Luther argued, as we have seen, in the first of his famous 95 Theses that the entire life of a Christian should be characterised by repentance.

Is the Holy Spirit present in the Charismatic renewal, as it seeks to live out its calling in the church? One place to test this question is at the doorway of repentance, for repentance is always a key indicator of the Holy Spirit's presence.

Charismatics have too often held up their spiritual gifts and their ministries of the Spirit as a rebuke to the church's deadness, while forgetting the words of Jesus: "Blessed are the poor in spirit, for theirs is the kingdom of heaven" (Mt. 5:3). The Holy Spirit would call attention not only to our spiritual riches but also to our human poverty and weakness, and not least to our lack of the unity for which Christ prayed (Jn 17:21). The Holy Spirit can accomplish more with an ounce of repentance than with a ton of self-confident gifts and ministries! Only as we as charismatic Christians ourselves live in true repentance, can we by the power of the Spirit lead other Christians and the church to repentance.

Where the Holy Spirit leads us to repentance, there follows the evidence of the Spirit's presence in the unity and harmony that he alone is able to create. At a Pan-African Spiritual Leaders' Conference in Nairobi in 1983, Koline Mbona, Anglican bishop from Zaire, spoke with compressed simplicity and candour to his fellow church leaders:

> There is one sickness in all the world, and in Zaire: sin. There is one need in all the world, and in Zaire: a Saviour. There is one answer in all the world, and in Zaire: the Holy Spirit. There is one problem in all the world, and in Zaire: church leaders. Brethren, we are the stumbling block of the Holy Spirit.[10]

---

[10] Larry Christenson, "God is Speaking – Are you Listening?" *International Lutheran Renewal*, no. 49 (December 1983), p. 2.

The most outstanding feature of this particular conference was the love and approbation expressed between church leaders and renewal leaders. A genuine appreciation for the church and for past workings of the Holy Spirit blended with an excitement and anticipation concerning his workings in the present renewal. This is not the ordinary experience when church leaders and renewal leaders get together. What made it possible? It was the kind of artless courage and honesty to which the bishop gave voice, in a word: repentance.

Certainty of Faith

The word of Jesus was without apology. It moved his contemporary hearers to wonder, even alarm. They sensed his power and authority. The certainty with which Jesus spoke was characteristic of all his utterances.[11] The early Christian proclamation carried the same *certainty* as the words of Jesus. The missionary message (Greek: *kerygma*) was a bold declaration that salvation was to be found only in the name of Jesus (Acts 4:12). His atoning death and bodily resurrection were convincingly testified to as historical events (1 Cor. 15:3-11; Lk. 24:34). The faith of early Christianity bears the stamp of deep, joyful certainty.

Believers have peace with God through Jesus Christ; they stand in grace (Rom. 5:1-5). They experience forgiveness of sin as a present reality (Eph. 1:7; Col. 1:14; 1 Jn 2:12). Hebrews speaks of the unshakable *certainty and boldness* (Greek: *parresia*) of a Christian's direct access to God (Heb. 10:19), and urges believers to approach God in this way (Heb. 4:16). The first epistle of John also speaks of the gift of *parresia* toward God, with special reference to the coming judgement (4:17): believers have nothing to fear in the judgement because of the *certainty* of God's forgiving love. Paul was *certain* that God, who began a good work in the Philippians, would bring it to completion until the day of Christ Jesus (Phil. 1:6). With great *certainty*, Paul testified that nothing can separate us from the love of God (Rom. 8:38-39). Clearly, the New Testament is out of step with modern notions that exalt doubt as a desirable virtue. The main emphasis in the New Testament is on *assurance of salvation*.

As certain as the declarations of Scripture are, however, they bring no assurance apart from the working of the Holy Spirit. Therefore, the Spirit is

---

[11] Jesus began many of his utterances with the Aramaic word *Amen*, usually translated "verily" or "truly". It could be translated: "It is certain, it stands fast, it is so!" The church has used it universally as a conclusion to a prayer or as a liturgical response. Jesus used it to introduce and intensify his own words (cf. Mk 11:23; 10:15; Lk. 18:17; Mt. 5:26; 13:17; 18:3, 13, 18). Jesus' use of the *Amen* formula is "the only objective parallel to the prophetic formula 'Thus says the Lord'. It gives expression to his authority and power". Joachim Jeremias, *Neutestamentliche Theologie, Die Verkündigung Jesu* (Gütersloh: Gütersloher Verlagshaus Gerd Mohn, 1971), p. 45.

called the first fruit (Rom. 8:23); and the guarantee, deposit and seal of our future salvation (2 Cor. 1:22, 5:5; Eph. 1:13-14; 4:30). It is the Holy Spirit who testifies with our spirit that we are the children of God (Rom. 8:15-16).

The Charismatic renewal has sometimes been labelled "anti-intellectual" because of the way that it approaches Scripture. We examined this question to some extent in Chapter 7. Here, we simply draw attention to the fact that the use of Scripture can never be divorced from the faith-risking life of prayer and conscious dependence on the Holy Spirit.

Also, regarding the proclamation of the Word, there should be a conscious dependence on the Spirit. We can be content neither with correct doctrine nor with soul-stirring preaching. There should be the evidence of the Spirit: a Spirit-filled instrument, a Spirit-anointed Word, with Spirit-given signs following. Like Paul, we cannot be satisfied with plausible words of human wisdom; there needs to be the demonstration of the Spirit and power (1 Cor. 2:4).

Where certainty of faith is absent, one must pray that the Holy Spirit will make the Word certain, for faith is meant to be certain. It was fundamental to Martin Luther's theology that faith is unconditional certainty. Thus, he replied firmly to the humanist Erasmus of Rotterdam:

> *The Holy Spirit is no sceptic.* He has written neither doubt nor mere opinion into our hearts, but rather solid assurances, which are more sure and solid than all experience and even life itself (italics added).[12]

The church today languishes under the legacy of humanism. According to post-modern humanism, certainty in spiritual matters – as in all matters – is written off as pride, narrowness of mind, or sheer ignorance. Humanism would agree with the German poet Goethe, that to search is more noble than to have found. Doubt is widely regarded as a virtue. Yet all the while human beings long for that sense of unconditional truth that will put strength and fibre into their lives.

It is well to be on guard against triumphalism, which confuses certainty with a fleshly confidence that faith always results in victory in the arena of this world. But we must also guard against the opposite tendency: the danger of slapping that same label of triumphalism on what really is Spirit-given certainty. In the midst of a doubt-filled generation, the Spirit of God is at work today, as in every age, leading people to certainty of faith. Wherever we make room for him, scepticism must back off. And what the Spirit makes certain to us we can share with others, knowing that through the certain testimony of witnesses the Holy Spirit also brings certainty to others.

---

[12] In *De servo arbitrio* (1525), WA 18, p. 605; AE 33, p. 24.

Faith and Experience

The first powerful impression of both participants and observers of the Charismatic renewal is the central role that personal experience plays in the renewal. The hearts of those in historical renewal movements, from Luther through Spener and Francke, Zinzendorf and Wesley, Hauge and Blumhardt, Monsen and Nenilava down to the present day, are at least "strangely warmed" (as John Wesley said) if not set ablaze by vivid spiritual experience. The Swedish New Testament scholar and bishop Krister Stendahl, who himself was neither a charismatic nor an evangelical Christian, has termed this "high-voltage religion":

> Opening up the full spectrum of religious experience and expression is badly needed in those churches that have suppressed the charismatic dimension. Flashlight-battery-voltage Christianity is certainly not strong enough for fighting the drug habit. And no religious tradition can renew itself without the infusion of raw and fresh primary religious experience. It could well be that the charismatic movement is given to the churches as one such infusion. We non-charismatics need not become charismatics – glossolalia is a gift, not a goal or an ideal – but we need to have charismatics among us in the church if the church is to receive and express the fullness of the Christian life. Thus, we need them.[13]

The need for "raw and fresh primary religious experience" is set against the backdrop of modern secular consciousness, which either denies or suppresses religious experience. The rationalism of secular culture has made wide inroads into the church, with corrosive effects on the expression of a truly biblical faith. The Charismatic renewal is a needed reminder of the church's origins: the early church not only thought and talked about God in a reasoned manner; it also experienced his presence in demonstrable ways. Its faith "did not rest in the wisdom of men but in the power of God" (1 Cor. 2:5).

Biblical faith is union with Jesus Christ, characterised and confirmed by the intervention of the Holy Spirit. It is a faith inseparably linked with experience. Not only does the Charismatic renewal challenge people to experience the reality of God in their lives, it says that apart from the real experience of God, there is no such thing as biblical faith.

Faith is often contrasted with unbelief, or, in other contexts, with good works. In a more fundamental way, however, the real opposite of faith is fear: the essence of faith is personal relationship with God, and it is often fear which blocks it. *When Jesus reveals himself, his glory and power to his disciples he or an angel tells them not to fear* (Lk. 1:30; Mt. 14:26-33; 17:7; 28:5; Lk. 12:32). Jesus said, "Don't be afraid; just believe, and she will be healed" (Lk. 8:50). And Paul wrote, "For you did not receive a spirit that

---

[13] Krister Stendahl, "The New Testament Evidence", in Michael P. Hamilton (ed), *The Charismatic Movement* (Grand Rapids, MI: Eerdmans, 1975), p. 56.

makes you a slave again to fear. But you received the Spirit of sonship" (Rom. 8:15). The promise that believers do not have any reason for fear can have particular application in the areas of the world where the fear of evil powers is widespread and keeps people in spiritual bondage. The Charismatic renewal proclaims freedom from this fear through the lordship of Christ and the power of the Holy Spirit (Heb. 2:14-15; Lk. 1:74-75; 1 Jn 4:18; 2 Cor. 3:17-18).

The Lutheran pastor David Dorpat has pointed out a certain fear of the charismatic experience among some people:

> Many [...] Christians feel threatened by the Pentecostal experience. This is true even though in the New Testament this experience and the experiential manifestations of the Spirit were, apparently, a normal part of daily Christian experience [...] The fear that someone or something might take over one's life is not altogether bad. There are powers that would take over a person's life and use that person, not for God's purposes, but for man's or Satan's. But the Scriptures tell us to present our bodies as a living sacrifice: to present ourselves, body and soul, to God and to let him control us. Every call to discipleship is a call away from self, a call that creates a battle in the will. It's the will of man in conflict that says: "I want to control my own life. There are certain things that I have planned that I want to do, and therefore I hesitate to ask God to fill me with his Spirit, because I know that if I really do surrender to him, maybe he will take over and I won't be able to do the things I want to do [...] The fear of losing control is a real issue with many.[14]

Millions of people around the world today are experiencing the surprise of God's nearness and power. The work of the Holy Spirit is finding expression in their lives, giving them assurance, salvation and freedom from fear. The Holy Spirit is confirming the experience of faith.

[14] David Dorpat, "Hindrances to Faith", *International Lutheran Renewal*, no. 57 (August 1984), pp. 1-2.

(33) The Importance of the Biblical Worldview

Faith and Reason

Faith and reason are sometimes contrasted, as though a person with faith must of necessity lay reason aside, and vice versa. It would be more accurate to contrast faith and unbelief, and then note how each utilises reason. The Holy Spirit does not tell us to abandon reason when he leads us into truth. What he does is reveal to us truths which we must include in our reasoning process.

Unbelievers do not include the truths of faith in their reasoning process. The truths of faith are non-existent or irrelevant to their considerations. "The fool says in his heart, 'There is no God'" (Ps. 14:1). Some unbelieving persons may reason superbly, but their conclusions will be skewed because they proceed from the premise that God does not exist. Believers, however, relate their reasoning process to the revelation of God. "We have the mind of Christ [...] We do speak a message of wisdom among the mature, but not the wisdom of this age or of the rulers of this age, who are coming to nothing" (1 Cor. 2:16, 6). *The truth of Christ is the beginning point or premise from which spiritual reasoning proceeds.*

The Disturbing Challenge of the Charismatic Renewal

A pastor in a Lutheran congregation, which had begun to experience some charismatic phenomena, announced an information meeting for members who had expressed misgivings about these things. The pastor presented a brief Bible study showing that such things as healing, speaking in tongues, and prophecy were common to the experience of the early church. Some members who had recently come into charismatic experiences shared their testimonies.

As the questioning and discussion got under way, one of the members who had been upset by these goings-on said, "Pastor, it's supernatural, and that's what scares us!" It would be hard to overestimate the significance of this simple statement from a disturbed church member. In a few words, she put her finger on perhaps the most disturbing aspect of the Charismatic renewal: it challenges the anti-supernatural worldview of modern culture, especially in the Western world. Despite certain changes that have taken place in recent years, of which we shall take note, the worldview of this culture is still largely dominated by naturalism.[1]

---

[1] This chapter 33 should be read together with chapters 2 and 7 which provide a deeper understanding of the importance of worldview. The main focus in this chapter is the challenge of the Charismatic renewal to the worldview of naturalism,

The Secular Worldview of Modern Culture

Naturalism, according to definition, is "the philosophical doctrine denying that anything in reality has a supernatural significance; specifically, the doctrine that scientific laws account for all phenomena, and that teleological conceptions of nature are invalid; loosely, materialism and positivism. In theology, it is the denial of the miraculous and supernatural in religion, and the rejection of revelation as a means of attaining truth." Closely akin to naturalism in terms of practical outcome is *rationalism*, defined as "reliance on reason as the basis for establishment of religious truth; a view that reason and experience rather than the non-rational are the fundamental criteria in the solution of problems."[2]

The influence of naturalism and rationalism is so widespread in modern culture that it scarcely requires documentation. Its effect on the church has been enormous. Rudolf Bultmann, probably the most influential Lutheran theologian of his generation, wrote, "The forces and laws of nature have been discovered, and therefore we can't believe in 'spirits' [...] whether good or evil."[3] He saw with great clarity that the issue at stake was that of our worldview. The Bible, he said, must be "demythologised", because:

> Modern man acknowledges as reality only such phenomena or events as are comprehensible within the framework of the rational order of the universe. He does not acknowledge miracles because they do not fit into this lawful order. When a strange or marvellous accident occurs, he does not rest until he has found a rational cause.
>
> The contrast between the ancient world view of the Bible and the modern world view is the contrast between two ways of thinking, the mythological and the scientific [...] the world view of the Scripture is mythological and is therefore unacceptable to modern man whose thinking has been shaped by science and is therefore no longer mythological. Modern man always makes use of technical means which are the result of science. In case of illness, modern man has recourse to physicians, to medical science. In case of economic or political affairs, he makes use of the results of psychological, social, economic, and

---

especially in the Western world. The Charismatic renewal in non-Western churches must deal with other non-Christian religious worldviews that are predominant in their own contexts, such as the Chinese worldview in China, the Hindu worldview in India, the Buddhist worldview in South-East Asia, the Islamic worldview in Asia and Africa, and the worldview of traditional religions in Africa and among tribal people in many parts of the world. To deal with the relationship of the Charismatic renewal to each worldview falls outside the scope of this book, but is an important task for the development of contextual theologies in different regions.

[2] Both definitions are from *Webster's New Collegiate Dictionary* (Springfield, MA: Merriam, 1949), pp. 560, 977.

[3] Hans Werner Bartsch (ed), *Kerygma and Myth* (London: SPCK, 1953), p. 69.

> political sciences, and so on. *Nobody reckons with the direct intervention by transcendent powers* (italics added).[4]

Like any widely held system of presuppositions, there is some unevenness in the way that this anti-supernatural worldview expresses itself throughout a pluralistic culture. There are large pockets of resistance to its pervasive influence in society, and there have been evident strains since the middle of the 20th century as it has been challenged by increasingly assertive non-Western cultures.

Church members who have never heard of Rudolf Bultmann, and who would in fact be scandalised by his denial of the miracles of Scripture, nevertheless come down to pretty much the same in their everyday life: they disregard the supernatural.

Bultmann's influence in the theological community has waned in recent years. But when it comes down to practical ministry, as distinct from theoretical or doctrinal discussion, much seminary training still reflects a world view that is indifferent to the supernatural. This world view places heavy reliance on reason and on the social and psychological sciences, while paying scant attention to such things as prayer, spiritual gifts, deliverance from demonic power, or healing. And where God's Word is used, it is frequently a Word stripped of much of its power by the tendency to conform to the prevailing world view. Rationalism still provides the essential substructure for thought and practical decisions in modern culture, and its influence is also strongly felt in the mainline Western churches.

Two World Views in Conflict

In the pages of the Bible, as biblical scholar Ben Johnson has ably shown, we encounter quite a different world view. He says about the biblical world view:

> That world view holds that the universe has been created by God by an act of will, that Jesus Christ is his pre-existent Son, that the universe consists of both visible and invisible creatures, among them angels, demons, principalities, and powers. It believes that God is present in his creation in a variety of ways, among them through his holy angels, through his Spirit by which he inspires people to prophesy, that he reveals himself to people in dreams and visions, as well as through natural means (clouds, fire, etc.). It believes that he acts through signs and wonders, that he intends the perfection of the world and his people, and that he will finally come again in power to set things right. Specifically concerning his Son, Jesus Christ, it believes that he was born of a virgin, taught

---

[4] Rudolf Bultmann, *Jesus Christ and Mythology* (New York: Charles Scribner's Sons, 1958), pp. 37-38, 36.

with authority, did miracles and exorcisms, raised the dead, walked on water, and was himself raised from the dead after an atoning death.[5]

No one can set this summary of the biblical world view alongside a definition of naturalism without seeing at once an irreconcilable conflict. To accept the presuppositions of naturalism is to deny the presuppositions of the Bible, and vice versa. Any talk of biblical authority must begin here: "The issue is the adequacy of the biblical world view".[6]

Many people, and not a few theologians, have shied away from the starkness of this confrontation. Some Christians have dealt with the conflict by surrendering the question of world view to naturalism without a struggle and reducing the sphere of biblical authority simply to "religious questions". This avoids a head-on collision with the secular world view by abandoning most of the field of human knowledge and experience to the authority of naturalism and rationalism. The result has been a trivialising of the gospel. Religious belief has been consigned to a corner, marked "private opinion", without any claims to represent objective truth. It has been effectively domesticated by the secular world view: realities that shaped the life and experience of the early church – answered prayer, divine guidance, miracles, encounter with demonic powers, reproach and suffering, the Holy Spirit, healing, angelic visitations – are either dismissed outright, rationalised or spiritualised. Divine intervention is excluded from the list of expectations.

One certain way to make faith irrelevant is to fence it off from the arena where people make most of their practical decisions. That is what we do when we say that the biblical worldview has relevance only as regards "religious questions". The gospel presupposes the doctrine of God as an active participating agent in the world. It presupposes the death of his Son as an expiation for sin. It presupposes, at its very heart, the historical truth of the resurrection. All of this flies in the face of naturalistic presuppositions. The gospel is pre-eminently history – the record of what God has done and is doing in the world and among the people whom he has created. And, therefore, it is impossible to speak meaningfully about the gospel without becoming involved in questions of world view. The New Testament has 7957 verses, of which 3874 (49%) are related to happenings that do not fit into naturalism's world view![7]

What kind of a world is it in which we live out our lives, in which Jesus Christ carried out his mission, and in which we are called to be his witnesses? Did God create the entire universe and all life including human beings? Did God intervene in various ways in the history of the Jewish people? Was Jesus

---

[5] Ben Johnson, "The Authority of the Bible: Its World View", *Trinity Seminary Review*, 2(2), pp. 6-8.

[6] Johnson, "World View", p. 2.

[7] Bultmann, *Jesus Christ and Mythology*, p. 15.

the incarnate Son of God born by a virgin? Did he rise bodily from the dead never to die again? Is it possible that dead believers can be resurrected and live forever? Are there such things as invisible spirits without bodies, who are opposed to God and serve a master called Satan, who seek to influence people and do them harm, but who can be driven away through encounter with someone of greater spiritual power and authority? Can physical sicknesses be healed through prayer and the laying on of hands? Is it possible to come into possession of valid knowledge through such things as dreams, visions, and prophecies? Can spiritual authority directly alter the normal course of events in the world of nature? Does God answer prayers? Does he call people and guide them through their lives?

Some conservative Christians might be tempted to brush such questions aside with a confident, "Of course, I believe such things! I believe everything that's in the Bible." But think about it for a moment: how do you think you would feel if you were asked to give a report on some things that had been going on in your house, asked by people to whom you were responsible and who gave every evidence of being upset by some stories that had come to their ears? You begin by reporting that an angel appeared to you during your prayer time one morning, telling you to send some men to a nearby town to fetch a person whom you did not know, and that this person, in response to a vision he had seen as well as to your invitation, came and talked to a group of people whom you had invited for the occasion, and that while he did so the Holy Spirit fell on the whole group and they broke forth in exalted speech – prophecy and unknown tongues. This incident, that actually took place in Cornelius' house, is recorded in Acts 10. When two world views that are opposed to one another come into conflict, something has to give. Which should we choose?

Epistemology

The issue we must come to grips with is that of epistemology. Epistemology has to do with acquiring and validating *knowledge.* In other words, "How do I come into possession of valid knowledge?" More simply, "How do I know what I know?"

Naturalism is still far and away the dominant world view in modern culture. It is the way the average person thinks about reality. Yet, there are sober and thoughtful people who are calling it into question. They are not simply correcting this or that aspect of naturalism's world view: they are challenging its basic presuppositions. A rigid naturalism is being called into question by some well-credentialed scientists and philosophers. Their point of view, of course, is not primarily spiritual or religious but philosophical. What is of particular interest for our purposes is their epistemology.

Werner Heisenberg, the nuclear physicist, in his Gifford Lectures said:

> "The general trend in the 19th century had been toward an increasing confidence in the scientific method and in precise rational explanations [...] modern physics has turned against an over-confidence in scientific explanations; they cover only a very limited part of reality, and the other part, for instance that covered by religion, is infinite.[8]

At this point, a comment by the psychologist Carl Jung is appropriate:

> It is a rational presupposition [of modern people] that everything has a natural and perceptible cause. We are convinced of this. Causality, so understood, is one of our most sacred dogmas. There is no legitimate place in our world for invisible, arbitrary and so-called supernatural forces [...] We distinctly resent the idea of invisible and arbitrary forces.[9]

The struggle between two opposing ways of thinking is nothing new. What we see taking place in much of today's culture is in some ways like a replay in reverse of the struggle between the epistemology of the Greek philosopher Aristotle and that of his teacher, Plato. Plato saw reality consisting of two realms, and he had a theory of knowledge to back it up. He recognised that we gain knowledge of the physical world through sense experience and reason, but he also believed that we have direct experience of a nonphysical realm of reality. In the *Phaedrus*, he spoke of four ways that one may have meaningful contact with the non-physical realm of reality: prophecy, healing, artistic inspiration, and love.

In the West, the thinking of Plato predominated until the 13th century, when it was largely replaced by the naturalism of Aristotle. The critical difference between these two men, for our purposes, was their epistemology: whereas Plato said that we gain knowledge through sense experience, reason, and direct contact with the non-physical realm, Aristotle allowed only the first two, with reason in the driver's seat directing the operation. Plato's sophisticated understanding of the human connection with another world was so completely abandoned that, even today, Platonism carries a popular meaning of devaluing the immediate world.[10] The value of Plato's thinking for our purposes is primarily negative: it does not limit knowledge to what we learn through sense experience and reason. It does not establish the biblical world view, yet it is not hostile to the biblical category of revelation.

---

[8] Quoted in Morton Kelsey, *Encounter with God* (Minneapolis, MN: Bethany, 1972), pp. 96-96.

[9] C.G. Jung, *Modern Man in Search of a Soul* (New York: Harcourt Brace, 1933), p. 130.

[10] Kelsey, *Encounter*, pp. 127-128. It should be noted that while Plato's epistemology has a structural similarity to that of the Bible, in that it allows for the category of revelation, the *source* of revelation is altogether different from that in the Bible, where revelation is by the *Word of the Lord*. Further, the early church, in its battle with Gnosticism, took issue with the cosmology of Neoplatonism.

We encounter a common thread in much modern or post-modern philosophy and theory of science that seriously challenges the underpinnings of naturalism: there are objective dimensions of reality that we do not come to know about simply by means of sense experience and reason.

Challenges from the Theological Community

In his famous book, *The Misunderstanding of the Church*, the Swiss theologian Emil Brunner recognised that we cannot rightly understand the church of the New Testament unless we break out of the straitjacket of naturalism and take seriously the dynamic manifestations of the Holy Spirit. He says that:

> Present day evangelists and missionaries usually realise this fact far better than we theologians who not only undervalue the dynamic power of the Holy Ghost, but often know simply nothing of it [...] The not unreasonable fear of an excess of enthusiasm, of the para-logical, has certainly had the effect of causing the apostle's injunction, 'Quench not the Spirit' (1 Thess. 5:19) to be disregarded and of confining attention to his warnings against the overvaluation of the para-logical, dynamic element.[11]

The Charismatic renewal, with its renewed interest in the work of the Holy Spirit, raises at a practical level the very questions that Brunner posed in a theoretical way to an earlier generation of theologians. To what degree has the epistemology of naturalism become a rule of thumb for our practical ministry – even in circles where the miraculous events in Scripture are staunchly upheld?

The Lutheran theologian Bengt Hoffman has pointed out that banishing the word "supernatural" from the theological vocabulary carries with it some epistemological liabilities:

> We 'moderns' have been tutored by scientific materialism to classify as 'superstition' all claims of visionary information or dreams and poetic or prophetic inspiration. Since such phenomena are beyond measurement in the conventional sense, they have been rejected as sources of 'knowledge'. The result is that all manifestations of supernatural life in Luther's (and our) thought have been ignored as time-bound superstition.
>
> Whatever drawbacks there are to the use of the adjective 'supernatural', it does convey transcendental overtones without which the interpretation of faith becomes locked up in scientific materialism [...] We shall have to restore the

[11] Emil Brunner, *The Misunderstanding of the Church* (London: Lutterworth, 1952), pp. 49-53.

> word 'supernatural' to theological legitimacy. It does betoken the fact that biblical revelation is in part an invasion from the (realm of the) para-normal.[12]

In his book, *Encounter with God*, Morton Kelsey develops a philosophical model that takes the non-physical dimension of reality seriously. At the level of practical experience, however, he recognises that Christians must exercise *discernment.* Although there are similarities between, say, the psychic phenomenon of ESP and biblical prophecy, the two are not identical. In the Charismatic renewal, people must be taught to distinguish between what is good and what is not good. When we begin to take the spiritual realm seriously, we soon discover the presence of the demonic as well as the angelic.[13] Not everything supernatural is good. Charismatics may cheer when they see the myth of naturalism exploded. Yet they need to exercise discernment regarding what is offered in its place.

Challenges from Non-Christian Religious Sources

Since the 1960s, naturalism has come in for attack from quite another direction: from non-Christian religions and the realm of the occult. Such diverse interests as Transcendental Meditation, Eastern religions, Scientology, Spiritualism, Satanism and Shamanism have emerged as a "viable contender to secular humanism on the one hand, and the Judeo-Christian tradition on the other."[14] Before 1960, these interests had been restricted to small pockets on the fringe of Western culture. Since then, they have moved into the mainstream, where they have become popularly known as the New Age movement.

Robert L. Burrows' thoughtful analysis of this multi-faceted, multi-focused movement stresses the question of world view:

> Because of the variety of New Age programmes, it is impossible to list criteria that would serve as a basis for recognising the unbiblical world view that undergirds them all. World view is, however, the key ingredient.
>
> The New Age Movement is not tied to any particular organisation, has no overarching hierarchical structure, is diverse in both practice and belief, and although it has prominent spokesmen, has no official leadership. What unites it and links it to the traditions that preceded it is a set *of common assumptions about God or ultimate reality, humanity, and the nature of the human predicament.*

---

[12] Bengt Hoffman, *Luther and the Mystics* (Minneapolis, MN: Augsburg, 1976), p. 221.

[13] Kelsey, *Encounter*, pp. 156-161.

[14] Robert J.L. Burrows, "Americans get religion in the New Age", *Christianity Today*, 18th May 1986, p. 17.

> In spite of the teeming diversity of the cosmos, *ultimate reality or god is pure energy, consciousness, or life force.* Humanity, like the rest of creation, is an extension of god; *divine essence is humanity's true, higher, or real self.* Alienation caused by sinful rebellion is not humanity's problem. *Metaphysical ignorance* is the root of all humanity's woes; it is dispelled by knowledge that is brought about by psycho-spiritual techniques that rid consciousness of the fragmenting effects of reason and the predefining limitations of belief. That is the path to *godhood, self-realisation, cosmic consciousness, enlightenment, and in our day, New Age transformation* (italics added).[15]

The New Age movement registers as another critique of naturalism, indicating how widespread the attack on the secular world view has become. It poses, however, two dangers.

On the one hand, there is the danger of ignorance about the real nature of the New Age movement. Christians can get caught up in some teaching or practice of the New Age movement on the naive assumption that anything opposed to naturalism must be a Christian's ally. Or, one may attempt to "take what is good" from some New Age practice and end up getting more than was bargained for. The New Age movement is not merely a mushrooming of new ideas. It is a revival of ancient religions.[16] Some of its expressions are clearly laden with occult power. Generally speaking, the Charismatic renewal has been alert to this kind of danger. Accurate *discernment of spirits* is one of the marks of a charismatically endowed body of believers.

On the other hand, there is the opposite danger of overreacting to the New Age phenomenon, a rejection of anything that New Age adherents support:

> New Age advocates are typically for ecology, against nuclear weapons, and for grassroots democracy. Being typically New Age, however, does not imply that all those who take similar positions are aligned with the New Age Movement. Those positions can be arrived at through ideologies diametrically opposed. Marx and Jesus were both concerned with the poor. That does not make Marx a Christian, or Jesus a Communist. A concern for ecology, similarly, does not of itself indicate either a commitment to a deified creation or the Deity of creation. Nor are issues rendered illegitimate simply because New Age enthusiasts typically address them (italics added).[17]

The church today may find that some concepts and terms being used in non-Christian settings can be helpful in the church, if we give them a specifically Christian application. But this needs to be done with great care, recognising the kind of "freight" that a concept may bring along with it.

---

[15] Burrows, "Americans Get Religion in the New Age", pp. 18, 23.

[16] Donald G. Bloesch, *The Battle for the Trinity: The Debate over Inclusive God-Language* (Ann Arbor, MI: Servant, 1985), p. 12.

[17] Burrows, "Americans Get Religion in the New Age", p. 23.

An example of this would be the practice of "visualisation". In New Age circles, visualisation is used as a psychic or occult technique: the creative imagination is used to focus mental or occult powers. This does not mean that Christians must avoid using creative imagination in their prayers. The Bible is full of images and metaphors that stimulate the imagination: "A farmer went forth to sow seed [...] a woman lost a coin, and swept the house until she found it [...] the prophet saw a basket of summer figs." Using the creative imagination can help make our prayers more vivid.

For instance, you might meditate on a scene from the Bible, visualising it in your mind's eye. Take the baptism of Jesus, for example: you "see" it in your imagination; you "listen" to the conversation between Jesus and John the Baptist; you "watch" the waters of baptism come over Jesus; you "see" the Holy Spirit descend on him in the form of a dove as he comes up out of the water; you "hear" the voice from heaven, "This is my Son, whom I love; with him I am well pleased" (Mt. 3:17). Using the creative imagination can add to our appreciation of scriptural revelation; it often helps make the truth more vivid and personal.

Instead of simply stating a promise of Scripture, it may help to visualise the promise being fulfilled in your mind's eye. In praying for healing, it is often helpful to "see" the person healed or getting better. This can help activate faith by bringing the truth of Scripture to bear on those parts of our mind that respond more to pictures and action than to logical statements. In other words, the fact that visualisation and meditation is used in the New Age movement doesn't put it off-limits for Christians. The creative imagination is a God-given gift. But, like all gifts, it can be misused. Our use of it must be governed by Scripture.

Naturalism is a philosophy of unbelief, clearly at odds with Scripture. We can thank God that in charismatic Christianity he has raised up a challenge to naturalism. But as certainly as God raises up a standard of truth, Satan will be on hand with his counterfeit. The supernaturalism of the New Age movement is laced with spiritual poison. We need not fear it; we need only be aware of it and on guard against it. "The one who is in you is greater than the one who is in the world" (1 Jn 4:4).

The Biblical Worldview and the Proclamation of the Gospel

Some might object, "Why so much emphasis on the supernatural, on divine intervention, on spiritual experiences such as healing, visions, prophecies, casting out demons, and so on? What about the experience of salvation, the experience of personal faith? Isn't that the most important intervention of all?"

It is. Jesus once said to his disciples, who had just returned from a successful mission, rejoicing that even the demons were subject to them:

> I have given you authority to trample on snakes and scorpions and to overcome all the power of the enemy; nothing will harm you. However, do not rejoice that the spirits submit to you, but *rejoice that your names are written in heaven* (Lk. 10:19-20).

This central experience of faith – the assurance that our names are written in heaven – can be undermined, however, if we cave in to the naturalistic worldview. If we unconsciously accept it, then the very experience of salvation – which is a divine intervention – can get watered down to the level of a psychological event. We end up relating to an idea about God rather than to the Lord himself.

A man who was crippled was once brought to Jesus for healing (Mk 2:5-12). Jesus began by telling him that his sins were forgiven. When some of his critics took exception to this, Jesus said, "Which is easier: to say to the paralytic, 'Your sins are forgiven,' or to say, 'Get up, take your mat and walk?'" Jesus then proceeded to heal the man, to demonstrate that he had *authority over sin as surely as he had authority over sickness – both of which involved divine, supernatural intervention.* Most Christians facing that question today would probably confess that it is easier to say, "Your sins are forgiven" than to say, "Get up and walk." We are used to dealing with matters of faith that take place in the invisible human soul or the invisible relation to God. That, after all, is the sphere of activity and authority that the church has marked off for itself. It can be a fairly comfortable arena in which to operate, because if the words are false or meaningless it could never be proved. Any kind of linkage between the invisible realm of faith and a command to visibly "rise and walk," such as we observe with Jesus, could be a scary thing. It would reveal if you have a biblical world view and believe in a kingdom of God which is a kingdom of power with the demonstration of the Holy Spirit (Mt. 12:28-29; 1 Cor. 2:4-5; 4:20; 12:7-11; Rom. 15:18-19).

Donald McGavran, a missionary to India and later a professor at Fuller Theological Seminary, USA, was a well-known figure in the evangelical community through his lectures and books on church growth. He was asked about the reaction of his colleagues when he began to suggest that healing might be for today:

> Partly by a *theological position* and partly by *observation of evidence* (primarily in Third World countries) I came to the conclusion that missionaries – as well as pastors and serious laymen and women – ought to regard healing much more open-mindedly than they have. They must not narrowly shut themselves off in a corner and say, "That's not reputable," or, "We would endanger our reputations." That's a bit cowardly. We need to be braver than

> that. We need simply to face the fact that *healing does occur, and that God uses healing to bring men and women to Christ* (italics added).[18]

The growth of Christianity in the Majority World is bringing increasing pressure against the rationalism that has been exported from Europe and North America. The American missionary to Nigeria, anthropologist and also professor at Fuller Seminary, Charles H. Kraft, observes:

> To an African, a Christian theology that can offer no more than an impersonal Western medical approach to disease is not only culturally unacceptable but scripturally inaccurate [...] The African expects that anyone speaking for God will automatically be concerned with healing and exorcism. If, then, the person of God attempting to communicate Christ in traditional Africa will not or cannot address the illness problem effectively, the person can expect to make little if any real impact.[19]

This is not to upstage the church's call to preach and pronounce forgiveness of sin, reconciliation with God and renewed life in Christ. It simply points out a potential danger. If we find that we are comfortable *only* with those experiences that happen *invisibly* within one's heart, faith can too easily get watered down to an idea in the mind. In a culture dominated by naturalism, the miraculous aspects of the biblical revelation remind us that God is a living, intervening God

Faith involves being joined with Christ through the working of the Holy Spirit. The present-day Charismatic renewal is precisely a renewal of faith in the God who intervenes in our everyday life. Ben Johnson points out that the weight of history is on the side of the biblical world view:

> The experience of the church through the ages affirms the biblical world view as the way things are, or the way they can be. For neither has the world changed nor has God's way of working with the world changed [...] The clear and simple issue is whether God acted in the ways described in Old and New Testaments, whether he inspired prophets to mantic utterance, whether he sent his Son into the world, whether Jesus cast out demons, healed, died for our sins, was raised for our justification, will return to judge the living and the dead. The issue is really a judgement about God, the nature of the world, and God's interaction with it. If one does not believe he acted in the ways described in the Bible, one has effectively cut oneself adrift from the dynamics of the Judeo-Christian faith. And to affirm that God has indeed acted as described in the

---

[18] Donald McGavran, "The Total Picture", *Christian Life*, October 1982, p. 40.

[19] Donald McGavran, "The Total Picture". The statement by Kraft is inserted by the editor as a boxed item in the article by McGavran.

> Bible and still does, in a cosmic arena which is as it is described in the Bible, is not primitivism.[20]

The Charismatic renewal is challenging the church to proclaim to this generation a Lord who is the same yesterday and today and forever (Heb. 13:8). He is not a God of caprice who changes his world or his way of working in it to conform to the latest philosophical or theological trend. He is the God who has revealed himself in Scripture, the God who intervenes and encounters people in the real and everyday world, in ways and by means that he himself determines, and to which Scripture and church history bear faithful and accurate testimony.

[20] Johnson, "The Authority of the Bible: Its World View", pp. 6-8.

(34) The Relationship between Charismatic Renewal and Theological Tradition

The Charismatic renewal has focused on some aspects of the message of Scripture that have been little-known, or in any case treated as less integral, by large segments of the church. The rediscovery of these aspects of the biblical message has led to a new theological understanding and a new practice in many areas of church life.

A rediscovery of neglected truth often produces its own kind of problem: people experience the truth so strongly that they lose a sense of proportion with regard to other truths, and perhaps more importantly, aspects of the faith; they may even end up in an unbalanced position in which their approach becomes unsound and biblically false.

The Lutheran Charismatic renewal seeks to be a challenge and corrective in two directions: (1) to a church that has ignored important aspects of the biblical message that are decisive for its life and ministry; (2) to groups that have specialised in some of these neglected aspects of truth in an unhealthy way. *In what follows, we want to draw attention to certain areas of truth that have been brought into focus by the Charismatic renewal, areas where the Holy Spirit would inspire sound doctrine as a balance between neglect and unhealthy overemphasis.*

Aspects of Lutheran Tradition that Encourage Renewal[1]

Over the centuries, the Lutheran church has, as we have seen in Part Three, experienced a variety of renewals, revivals, and spiritual awakenings. Charismatics in the Lutheran church generally view Lutheran teaching and tradition in a positive way, as a help and encouragement for renewal, although they recognise that some elements in the Lutheran theological tradition have not always helped the church to live in the power of the Holy Spirit.

At the centre of the Lutheran understanding of the Christian faith stands the cross – the sign of humanity's total dependence on the forgiving grace of God. Life in the Holy Spirit begins at the cross: forgiveness and cleansing by the blood of Jesus is the basic precondition for the indwelling of the Holy Spirit.

---

[1] See also the more comprehensive discussion of the relationship of the Charismatic renewal to the Lutheran theological heritage in Part Three.

Martin Luther deserves our lasting gratitude for setting aside works-righteousness, the notion that we can earn or contribute to our own salvation. He turned the eyes of all Christendom to the righteousness that God freely gives through faith in Christ. He helped re-establish the biblical foundation that must undergird Christian life from beginning to end. In his explanation to the Third Article of the Apostles' Creed, which we have quoted repeatedly, he set before us a succinct and positive expectation for a working of the Holy Spirit that reaches out from the cross to embrace the whole of Christian life and experience:

> I believe that I cannot by my own understanding or effort believe in Jesus Christ my Lord, or come to him. But the Holy Spirit has called me through the gospel, enlightened me with his gifts, and sanctified and kept me in true faith. In the same way he calls, gathers, enlightens, and sanctifies the whole Christian church on earth, and keeps it united with Jesus Christ in the one true faith. In this Christian church, day after day, he fully forgives my sin and the sins of all believers. On the last day he will raise me and all the dead and give me and all believers in Christ eternal life. This is most certainly true.[2]

Here is the Lutheran *Magna Charta* for calling believers in the Lord Jesus Christ to radical dependence on the Holy Spirit. It is a charter for the renewal of the church in every generation.

Aspects of Lutheran Tradition that Have Not Encouraged Renewal

Lutheran teaching and tradition, especially when approached dogmatically rather than historically, have not always encouraged spiritual renewal. A mere glance at the history of the Lutheran church confirms this. Some elements of Lutheran tradition have been used, or misused, in a way that hinders spiritual awakening.

Luther's reaction to what we today call the *Radical Reformation*, what Luther called *Schwärmer* (enthusiasts), has had, over the centuries, a traumatic effect on Lutheranism. To this day, it conjures up fears that we may get too much of the Holy Spirit. The *sola scriptura* (Scripture alone) of the Reformation brought with it a wholesome regard for the authority of the Bible. What we have so often seen in practice, however, is that expectations get narrowed down to the single issue of salvation, which in popular understanding sometimes amounts to "getting my sins forgiven so I can go to heaven when I die." People are not encouraged to expect – and in many cases are discouraged from expecting – many other things that the Word also

[2] Luther, *The Small Catechism in Contemporary English*, pp. 14-15.

speaks about. This became evident when the charismatic gifts first began to be experienced in Lutheran congregations in the early 1960s.[3]

Since the 17th century, scriptural interpretation has been dominated by an intellectual and academic approach. Interpretation anchored in life and spiritual experience has been dismally absent. The bright exception in Lutheranism has been the much-maligned Pietism.[4]

The effect of this intellectual approach has been a highly articulated theology alongside a spiritual life that has often been immature. The gap between clergy and laity is one evidence of this. Misapplied emphasis on the office of the ordained ministry has throttled a healthy development of the priesthood of all believers, for which Luther strove. Despite lip service to the doctrine of the universal priesthood, the Lutheran church has not generally found a way to truly release its member into vital, Spirit-filled, Spirit-gifted ministry. We have generally been a clergy-dominated church.

Another evidence is the generally low level of spirituality among baptised believers. The Lutheran church has continued to practice infant baptism. It has, however, too often failed in bringing the baptised to spiritual maturity. It has not consistently taught them how to live out of the riches of their baptism.

Lutheran theology makes rightly much of the means of grace – the Word and the sacraments. The practical effect of a *too narrow understanding* of this term has, however, often been to limit our field of vision. We don't really look for the Holy Spirit to work except in immediate connection with hearing the Word and receiving the sacraments. Spiritual life becomes the servant of a too narrow theology that disdains experience and in practice *limits* the work of the Holy Spirit to Word and sacrament. But what is *authentic spiritual experience* – such as the fullness of the Spirit, Spirit-empowered mission and service with signs and wonders following, the fruit and gifts of the Spirit, divine guidance, healing, answered prayer, miracles – but *the outworking of the divine Word and the Holy Spirit*?

The Need for Theological Renewal

Many Lutheran charismatics believe that the pastoral seminaries of the church give their students too little practical training in Christian living. Many graduates come into the parish ill-equipped to help people enter into lives of holiness and Spirit-empowered ministry. These pastors have learned

---

[3] McDonnell (ed), *Presence, Power, Praise*, vol. 1. See, for example, "A Report on Glossolalia," pp. 58, 62; "A Statement with Regard to Speaking in Tongues," p. 111. Note, however, a measured encouragement to seek spiritual gifts in "Mühlheim Theses on Community and Charism", pp. 104, 107.

[4] For a more detailed account of the views and practices in Lutheran Pietism, see chapters 30 and 31.

something about the historical-critical study of the Bible, but devote little time to personal Bible study. They have psychological skills but frequently cannot minister God's power to the soul needs of their people. They may have studied the disciplines of Practical Theology, but by the admission of many, they know little about how to pray. Charismatic Lutheran pastors see professionalism too often displacing spiritual formation in the preparation of the clergy. Some ministers view their calling as a *job they do* rather than being *servants of God,* which is what they really are.

This downplaying of practical piety or spirituality is sometimes presented as an expression of Luther's dictum, *simul justus et peccator* – we are at the same moment justified and sinners. This is, to be sure, one of Luther's most penetrating insights, but, to be true to Luther, it must be understood dialectically. It does not mean that everything one does is hopeless, that there is no growth in holiness, and that we can give up the fight against sin. It rather means that in every moment of time, looked at from one side, I am a sinner – "I know that nothing good lives in me, that is, in my sinful nature" (Rom. 7:18) – while looked at from another side, I am fully justified, that is, united to Christ by faith – "Since we have been justified through faith we have peace with God through our Lord Jesus Christ" (Rom. 5:1). The battle between our old sinful nature and the new nature in Christ dominated by the indwelling Spirit of God goes on through all Christian life until the end. "Live by the Spirit, and you will not gratify the desires of the sinful nature. For the sinful nature desires what is contrary to the Spirit, and the Spirit what is contrary to the sinful nature. They are in conflict with each other" (Gal. 5:16-17).

The cleft that some pastors and theologians experience between academic theology and the knowledge of God that they gain in personal devotions and in the practical care of a congregation is echoed in the lives of the people. It is a painful dichotomy that cuts through the lives of many Christians who want to be open both to the world of knowledge that God reveals to us through the careful application of human reason, including the scholarly study of Scripture, and the truth that God makes known to us through prayer, meditation, listening to the promptings of the Spirit within, and exercising the gifts of the Holy Spirit.

The Charismatic renewal has begun to explore ways of healing the split between reason and experience. It sees that the church needs a theology that results from a reasoned thinking through of the biblical faith. But it also sees that this kind of theology must be done in the right context: the communal life of the living church. The believing fellowship offers certain correctives to the autocratic rule of reason: believing prayer, the exercise of spiritual gifts, true worship, and the testing of interpretations and proposals in the experience of the body of Christ.

Where Lutheran theology thwarts spiritual renewal, where the practice of theology has become too much a captive of the academic community, the *Charismatic renewal calls for the theological enterprise to forge closer links with the practicing, ministering fellowship of the church.* This means more than expecting theological professors to be members of some local congregation or sending candidates into congregations for some months of practical training. It means a closer partnership between seminaries and congregations. It means a greater recognition of the gifts and ministries that the Holy Spirit distributes in the body of believers. It may call for a careful and critical look at the practical consequences of the unbiblical distinction between "clergy" and "laity" that is routinely deplored but seldom dealt with.

The living body of Christ, where the Spirit reigns in power, is the crucible in which sound theology must be formed. In this wholesome context, the theologian must actively seek the spiritual support of the congregation and expect the Spirit's guidance and wisdom.

Doctrinal Concerns in the Charismatic Renewal

The Charismatic renewal has not addressed itself to doctrinal formulations in a comprehensive or systematic way. Rather, in keeping with its nature as a movement, it has so far stressed certain truths that appear to have been neglected in the church, or developed in a one-sided way.

It would be misleading to say that its experience has determined its theology; its commitment to the authority of Scripture is well-established. However, a variety of experiences and happenings have to some extent determined which doctrines charismatics have concentrated on. The questions addressed in the next chapters reflect some of the most prominent issues that have arisen in the context of the Charismatic renewal.

(35) The Nature of God and the Nature of Human Beings

The Nature of God

The Charismatic renewal emphasises the indivisible unity of the triune God. It opposes any trichotomy that would divide the Godhead in such a way that one of the persons is related to apart from the others.

It is true, of course, that sound doctrine makes a clear distinction between the Father, the Son, and the Holy Spirit. Yet the Spirit's essential unity with the Father and the Son makes it impossible for us to have a proper relationship with him, or to experience him, without at the same time having Christ as our Redeemer and Lord, and God as our Creator and Father.

It is likewise impossible to have Christ without having the Holy Spirit, who makes him really present and brings to reality his redemptive kingdom on earth. The Charismatic renewal puts particular emphasis on the Holy Spirit, not to neglect the Son and the Father, but rather to point out the fact that it is the Spirit alone who through the gospel brings people into a reconciled relationship with God, a relationship in which an awareness of each person of the Godhead goes hand in hand with a distinct emphasis on the oneness of God.

The Holy Spirit brings an understanding of God in which both his *transcendence* and his *immanence* are emphasised. The holiness of God means that he expresses himself in wrath against all sin and uncleanness. He stands in judgement against all who oppose him. At the same time, because of his eternal love, he extends unlimited and unconditional mercy in his Son, Jesus Christ, to all who come to him in repentance and faith (cf. Eph. 2:1-5, 8).

A doctrinally sound church avoids a notion of God that sees him only as the stern judge who in his majesty distributes impersonal justice. On the other hand, it eschews the caricature of a God who, in the name of love, and without regard to his holy will, treats all people, believers and unbelievers, completely alike. God is not a mere fulfiller of human desires. He is the holy one, drawing us to himself and causing us to bow to his will as the sovereign Lord of all. He will not be trapped in words, but he will unfailingly keep his promises in his own way and his own time.

The Holy Spirit alone can build a people who honour God as God, who respond to him in holy fear and loving faith, and who carry out his will for the church and the world in mission and diaconal service until the return of Christ in power.

The Charismatic renewal has helped restore a balance to the doctrine of God. An emphasis on the Third Article, the doctrine of the Holy Spirit, does not detract from, but rather complements, the attention that should be been given to the other two articles.

The Nature of Human Beings and the New Creation

Sound doctrine will avoid a one-sided or distorted view of human beings. The Charismatic renewal has helped remind the church that humans, created in the image of God, are whole, living beings, a unity of body, soul, and spirit. This speaks, on the one hand, against a "spiritual" view of humans that focuses narrowly on the need of their "souls"" for salvation, and, on the other hand, against an unduly materialistic view that gives primary emphasis to meeting their physical and social needs.

A person stands before God as a whole living being (Latin: *totus homo*), both in the fallen state under the judgement of God and apart from Christ (Eph. 2:1-3), and as a raised and renewed person under the grace of God in Christ (Eph. 2:4-10). The Holy Spirit shows that God's care and concern extend to the whole person.

The Holy Spirit reaches out to embrace the total person with God's grace and power. It will affect life in its totality – the physical, emotional, intellectual, spiritual, and social – all that the Spirit means to bring under the lordship of Christ. At any given time, the Spirit's work will focus on one or another aspect of life. That is the nature of his sanctifying work: it is progressive. But his long-range plan encompasses the whole of life. It is *holistic*.

When one experiences the reality of the Holy Spirit as the personal God, it puts a new perspective on such fundamental concepts as sin and grace. They are understood as *relational* terms. They indicate one's position in relation to God. They are more a description of "where we stand" than of "what we are". They describe how we are relating to God, as enemies under the power of unconfessed and unforgiven sin, or as reconciled children under God's forgiveness and grace. The idea that we have, or can have, an existence apart from God is the devil's illusion. By the act of creation, we are inexorably related to God – either under his judgement or in reconciled communion.

The primary problem of human beings is that they are *alienated from God.* They are without fear, love, or faith in relation to God. Disturbances or conflicts in one's relation to other human beings, in one's relation to the world, or to concrete situations in one's life, are *derivative* problems. Only as the Holy Spirit brings human beings into relationship with the *redeeming presence of Christ* will the power of God be able to effect fundamental changes in their lives, their relationships, and their circumstances.

The Holy Spirit does this in his own way, according to his own timetable, working out the implications of his own wisdom. It is possible, for instance, to be right with God, to be saved, and therefore to be blessed, yet at the same time to be sick in the body or poor in terms of material resources. However, as God's purpose of salvation overshadows the whole of one's life, the Spirit can create strong faith for healing from sickness. Paradoxically, the Spirit can also create in the heart the conviction that the believer will be raised whole and perfect in the final resurrection of the body, whether or not they are healed in this life.

Paul's dramatic announcement of a *new humanity*: "If anyone is in Christ, he is a new creation!" (2 Cor. 5:17) is so radical that we can hardly grasp it. We still often hang on to the familiar, old anthropology and try to use it to explain the new creation. We may conceive of the new creation as merely a *change* in our human nature. Words like commitment, discipleship, and lordship do not in themselves make a new creation, not even if we back them up with exemplary action. Let us overstate the matter to bring out its radical nature: the new creation does not change us one bit. We, that are our human sinful natures, remain as we were. *Our life is joined to another, and therein lies the newness. The new creation happens when we are joined to Christ in his death and resurrection.* The key word is *joined or united.* The new creation happens when "we are in Christ" or "Christ in us".

Of course, there is real change, but it comes about because we are joined to Christ. What makes the new creation new is the fact that we can never again think of ourselves simply as ourselves. In the old anthropology, there is a limited focus: life is defined in terms of the self-sufficient individual. In the new creation, there is an expanded focus: life consists in two lives being united. We are new creatures not because of anything we are or have in ourselves but because our life is united to Christ's life. The new anthropology gets us to asking *what the Lord will do*; in the world, in the church, in us, and through us.

(36) Justification and Sanctification

One of the theological issues that has been brought to the fore by the Charismatic renewal is the relationship between justification and sanctification. This has been a particular concern among Lutherans, because of the central role that justification plays in Lutheran theology.

Both justification and sanctification describe the believer's relationship with God, each from a particular perspective. Justification tells us what the relationship is grounded on: the grace of God freely given in the cross of Christ. Sanctification tells us what happens in the relationship: by God's grace and power, his will is accomplished in us. Both of these are continuing, operative realities in the life of a believer. Although they cannot be separated from one another, we understand that justification is primary and foundational; sanctification is secondary and derivative. All that we are and all that we do as Christians is built on the foundation of being justified freely by God's grace in Christ. Only as we trust in the grace of God freely given in Christ will our lives be sanctified; that is, be set apart, shaped, directed, and empowered to do God's will by the Holy Spirit.

Martin Luther grounded his whole understanding of sanctification in justification: he announced how the Holy Spirit makes the crucified and risen Christ truly present as a redeeming reality; this presence calls forth constant prayer to Christ and the constant work of love for the neighbour.[1] The Holy Spirit does not give me some kind of impersonal "power" by which I can successfully imitate Christ; he gives me Christ himself, so that "I have been crucified with Christ and I no longer live, but Christ lives in me" (Gal. 2:20). Luther's focus was on a person's relationship with the living Christ, made effectual by the Spirit. The implications for pastoral care, for shepherding a person's growth in sanctification, are important.

Luther's concern to preserve the significance of justification as primary can wonderfully vitalise our understanding and experience of sanctification. Sanctification that focuses on the believer's union with the living Christ can help reinforce the sense of total dependence on Christ's redemption, not only in reference to the past and one's need for forgiveness, but also in reference to the present and the call to step forward into good works: "For we are God's workmanship, *created in Christ Jesus to do good works*, which God prepared for us in advance to do" (Eph. 2:10).

Charismatics have a concern for concrete, "incarnational" results. Justification should produce fruit. Of course, this was a concern of Luther as

---

[1] Prenter, *Spiritus Creator*, p. 95.

well.[2] The keynote message at a Lutheran charismatic conference in California set this out with unmistakable clarity:

> Justification has to do with our citizenship in God's kingdom. How do we qualify? The royal edict on kingdom citizenship is this: it shall be a free gift. It includes a number of things. It includes sonship, forgiveness, righteousness, eternal life. And it is given freely – not a word in the Bible about earning or deserving it.
>
> Right here *Pretender to the throne, the flesh* [our sinful nature] turns up and mounts his little eight-word assault, '*Let me tell you what I can do.* It's nice to receive grace, but I can add something to that. I can contribute something of my own to this business of salvation.'
>
> This is a Pretender that God dealt with through the Reformers. They stood against this particular attempt of the Pretender to push Christ off the throne. They said, 'We are not going to take part in this rebellion.' In their documents, they take an *uncompromising stand against any pretender who would seek to add anything to Christ's work of redemption*:
>
>> It is taught among us that we cannot obtain forgiveness of sin and righteousness before God by our own merits, works, or satisfactions, but that we receive forgiveness of sin and become righteous before God by grace, for Christ's sake, through faith, when we believe that Christ suffered for us and that for his sake our sin is forgiven and righteousness and eternal life are given to us (*The Augsburg Confession*, Art, IV).
>
> When the issue is our *justification*, we have to quit telling God what we think we can do and listen when he tells us what he is ready to do. And what he is ready to do is justify us freely, for Christ's sake.[3]

A study conducted by Philip Gehlhar, a pastor of the Lutheran Church – Missouri Synod in the United States, indicates that Lutheran charismatics may be clearer on the issue of justification than the typical cross-section of Lutheran church members. The study indicated that charismatic Lutherans hold a sharper distinction between law and gospel, and a stronger belief in salvation by grace, than other Lutherans. The extent of the difference ranged as high as 40%.[4]

---

[2] Martin Luther, *Preface* to *Romans*, 1522 (AE 35, 370-371; WADB 7, 9ff.). See Karlfried Froelich, "Charismatic Manifestations and the Lutheran Incarnational Stance", in Paul Opsahl (ed), *The Holy Spirit in the Life of the Church* (Minneapolis, MN: Augsburg), pp. 136-157.

[3] Larry Christenson, *Back to Square One* (Minneapolis, MN: Bethany, 1979), pp. 88-89.

[4] Philip Gehlhar, "Are Charismatic Lutherans Confused in Their Understanding of Salvation by Grace through Faith? Summary of a Survey of Lutheran Congregations with Charismatic Pastors" (Westminster, CA: St. Luke's Lutheran Church, 1979). The report states in part: "Charismatic Lutherans are more conservative in their approach to the Scripture and Christian doctrine than their non- or anti-charismatic

The problem comes when one stops with justification, when accepting the doctrine of justification in effect becomes the total description of Christian experience. Common sense alone tells us that *describing Christianity solely in terms of becoming a Christian, or one's standing as a Christian is inadequate.* There is also the question of *living as a Christian*, of walking as a Christian. "Since we live by the Spirit, let us keep in step with the Spirit" (Gal. 5:25). But now comes the crucial transition: how are we then to live this new life?

Here, the same dynamics that we encounter in justification come into play, but in a reverse order. In justification, the *flesh seeks to add* something to the work of Christ: salvation by grace *plus* good works, or experience, or right doctrine, or whatever. In sanctification, the *flesh seeks to subtract* something from the work of Christ: the holiness of Christ *minus* my weakness, or sin, or bad habits, or failures, or whatever.

It is the same basic issue viewed from two perspectives, and the answer is the same in both regards: Christ is sufficient. He is all-sufficient for my justification. He is all-sufficient for my sanctification.

Charismatics find no fault with Luther's doctrine of justification. But they are not satisfied with the inadequate treatment of sanctification that developed in the later Lutheran tradition. With Luther, they insist that the dynamic of justification be extended into sanctification. The keynote address referred to above pointed out the parallel:

> Sanctification has to do with how we live our life, how we behave as citizens of God's kingdom. This gets right down to the daily business of how we treat members of our family, how we manage our finances, how we drive on the freeway, how we pray, how we help those in need.
>
> The royal edict on kingdom living is, "Be perfect, as your heavenly Father is perfect" (Mt. 5:48).
>
> That life which is planted in us as a free gift has a way of expressing itself. It expresses itself in obedience. Paul said that he was given his apostleship to bring about "the obedience that comes from faith" (Rom. 1:5; 16:26).
>
> How are we able to do this? In the gift of eternal life, we receive the Holy Spirit as our enabler, giving us the power to live the life that he calls us to live. "God has done what the law, weakened by the flesh, could not do: sending his own Son in the likeness of sinful flesh and for sin, he condemned sin in the flesh, in order that the just requirement of the Jaw might be fulfilled in us, who walk not

---

counterparts. Charismatic Lutherans hold a sharper distinction between law and gospel, and a stronger belief in salvation by grace than other Lutherans. The extent of this difference is especially noteworthy (between 30 and 40 percent difference). The results of this survey should lay to rest the concerns of Lutheran leaders that a participation in the charismatic movement would lead to a loss of the pure gospel of salvation by grace. Rather it clarifies the believer's understanding of salvation and strengthens his [*sic*] faith".

according to the flesh [not in the tracks of the Pretender], but according to the Spirit [subjects of the Rightful King]" (Rom. 8:3-4).

Here again, the Pretender mounts his little eight-word assault, "*Let me tell you what I can do.* You can't expect me to be perfect, but I'll do my best." This is the Pretender that God has had to deal with down through the history of the church. The apostle Paul speaks to the people who are thinking about these things. "Since we are saved by grace, shall we sin the more that grace may abound?" (Rom. 6:1).

This old Pretender is a sly fox. He will actually make his bid for the throne disguised as an ally of the Rightful King. You will hear him say things like this: "If you stress obedience and righteousness too much it undercuts grace, and we want to live by grace." That is a phony claim. Because the God who offers free, unmerited grace is the same God who calls for unconditional obedience. *It's the Pretender* (our sinful, old nature) *who tries to water down grace in justification, and obedience in sanctification.*

When the issue is our sanctification, we have to quit telling God what we can or cannot do in our own strength and let him tell us what he can do; and that is to call us and empower us to live lives of righteousness and holy obedience.[5]

Justified Christians are totally holy and righteous in the sight of God because of the redemptive work of Christ. They are reconciled with God and therefore in a *perfectly* right relationship to God as his children.[6] However, since the justified Christians as new creations in Christ still have to battle the temptations of the old sinful nature and the attacks of Satan, *their sanctification is not perfect or total, but partial, growing and increasing by the power of the Holy Spirit who co-operates with the new creation. Empirical or experiential holiness* in the lives of Christians, although a result of the work of the Holy Spirit, is therefore *never perfect*, since Christians are still sinners (1 Jn 1:8-10). Yet, the ideal or *goal* given by the law of God, as for instance expressed in Jesus' Sermon on the Mount (Mt. 5-7), towards which the new creation strives in its fight with sin and the devil, *is perfection, that is, perfect love for God and other human beings* (1 Jn 1:5-6; Rom. 13:8, 10; Mt. 5:43-48). This was, as we have already seen, also the view of Luther and the Lutheran reformers.

It is a mistaken critique to charge charismatics generally with giving the doctrine of justification short shrift.[7] The problem, rather, is a distorted

---

[5] Christenson, *Square One*, pp. 89-91.

[6] For reconciliation with God as a result of justification, and the implications of this for the church's ministry of reconciliation, see Tormod Engelsviken, "Reconciliation and Mission", *International Review of Mission*, 109(2), (Nov. 2020), pp. 163-179.

[7] See for example the tendency to see Pentecostal/Charismatic teaching on the infilling of the Holy Spirit as compromising Christ's sufficiency in regard to justification/ regeneration/ conversion in such writers as Frederick D. Bruner, *A*

perception that crops up again and again in some forms of traditional Lutheranism: the emphasis on justification becomes so dominant that a shadow of works-righteousness is cast over the whole area of sanctification. The practical result is that the work of Christ gets narrowed down to forgiveness and nothing more: "If God will just forgive my sin and take me to heaven, I can expect nothing more."[8]

Charismatics take issue with such a view – not by detracting from the doctrine of justification, but by calling attention to a deficient doctrine of the Holy Spirit as it relates to sanctification. One Lutheran charismatic leader said, "There is nothing more in salvation than Jesus, but there is more in Jesus than salvation."[9]

Justification and sanctification participate in the same reality, which is Christ himself. In justification and sanctification, the Holy Spirit unites our life with Christ's life, ending once and for all our self-sufficient existence – the self-sufficient life that rebels against God, or the self-sufficient life that attempts to serve God in its own strength.

It is from this standpoint that the practical teaching on *guidance* which we find in the Charismatic renewal takes on added significance. How a work is *initiated* becomes crucially important. If the Spirit is able to guide us to the work that *God has prepared beforehand for us to walk in*, then we can step out in obedience and in faith, trusting God for the results.

The Problem of Antinomianism

The justified sinner who is forgiven and declared righteous for Christ's sake receives a new life. By the imputation of an "alien righteousness", the righteousness of Christ, not their own, the believers become righteous before God through the working of the Holy Spirit. Living in union with Christ, they

---

Theology of the Holy Spirit (Grand Rapids, MI: Eerdmans, 1971), pp. 261-284; James D. Dunn, *Baptism in the Holy Spirit* (Philadelphia, PA: Westminster, 1970), p. 95; Richard A. Jensen, *Touched by the Spirit* (Minneapolis, MN: Augsburg, 1975), pp. 61-62; Lindberg, *The Third Reformation?* pp. 260-263. Lindberg asserts that there is no discussion of justification in Larry Christenson's major writings, but he ignores books by Christenson where the theme of justification is dealt with several times: *The Renewed Mind* (Minneapolis, MN: Bethany, 1974) and *Back to Square One* (Minneapolis, MN: Bethany, 1979).

[8] Statement of an official of a major Lutheran denomination in the USA to Larry Christenson.

[9] Delbert Rossin, in a message given at the Southern Lutheran Conference on the Holy Spirit, 1980. Here Rossin uses salvation according to its commonly understood meaning of obtaining forgiveness which is narrower of course than we often find in the New Testament and in Luther. For example, see Luther's *Small Catechism* VI, 6, p. 352. There is much that God has given in Christ (1 Cor. 3:21-23) that believers do not regularly appropriate.

are brought into a new life of holiness. Christ, who lives within them by the Spirit, day by day conforms the believers to his own image (2 Cor. 3:17-18).

Apart from this relationship by faith with Christ, we have no righteousness, no new life, no strength, and no hope. We do not receive "righteousness" or "new life" as something that we then control and operate. We receive Christ by faith, and he is our wisdom, righteousness, holiness, and redemption (1 Cor. 1:30). "Therefore, as it is written, 'Let him who boasts, boast in the Lord'" (1 Cor. 1:31).

While Luther sought to preserve the biblical understanding of justification, in his treatise *On the Councils and the Church*, he spoke out strongly *against those who separate justification from sanctification and denied the importance of the latter:*

> That is what my antinomians,[10] too, are doing today, who are preaching beautifully (as I cannot but think) with real sincerity about Christ's grace, about the forgiveness of sin and whatever else can be said about the doctrine of redemption. But they flee as if it were the very devil the consequence that they should tell the people about the third article, of sanctification, that is, of the new life in Christ.
>
> They think one should not frighten or trouble the people, but rather always preach comfortingly about grace and forgiveness of sins in Christ, and under no circumstances use these or similar words, 'Listen! You want to be a Christian and at the same time remain an adulterer, a whoremonger, a drunken swine, arrogant, covetous, a usurer, envious, vindictive, malicious, etc.!'
>
> Instead, they say, 'Listen! Though you are an adulterer, a whoremonger, a miser, or other kind of sinner, if you but believe, you are saved, and you need not fear the law. Christ has fulfilled it all!'
>
> Tell me, my dear man, is that not granting the premise [Easter] and denying the conclusion [Pentecost]? It is, indeed [...] taking away Christ and bringing him to nothing at the same time as he is most beautifully proclaimed! And it is saying yes and no to the same thing. [...] *They may be fine Easter preachers, but they are very poor Pentecost preachers, for they do not preach about the sanctification of the Holy Spirit but solely about the redemption of Jesus Christ, although Christ* [...] *did not earn only grace for us, but also the gift of the Holy Spirit, so that we might have not only forgiveness of, but also cessation of sin.*
>
> Now he who does not abstain from sin, but persists in his evil life, must have a different Christ, that of the Antinomians; the real Christ is not there, even if all the angels would cry, 'Christ! Christ!' [...] *But our Antinomians fail to see that they are preaching Christ without and against the Holy Spirit because they propose to let the people continue in their old ways and still pronounce them*

---

[10] Antinomianism comes from the Greek words *anti* = against and *nomos* = law, and is the view that Christians who are justified by grace are not obligated to keep the law of God, or that the law should not be preached to Christians.

> *saved. And yet logic, too, implies that a Christian should either have the Holy Spirit and lead a new life, or know that he has no Christ*" (italics added).[11]

This famous statement of Luther met with a chorus of assent when it was quoted at a session of an International Lutheran Charismatic Leaders' Meeting in Finland in the summer of 1981.[12] There was a general perception that this depicted a situation present in the many churches today, and that any presentation of the work of the Holy Spirit must speak in a responsible way to this issue.

An emphasis on the lordship of Christ, with a clear call to obedience, has been a hallmark of the Charismatic renewal. It is not understood within the renewal, however, as jettisoning justification, but rather as a question of emphasis and balance, as one young charismatic Lutheran pastor stated in a pastoral letter to his congregation:

> An imbalance has come into Lutheran theology. The imbalance is in the understanding of grace. A doctrine that sees little room for human response to divine initiative must settle for a grace that can forgive but cannot enable. God comes off looking like a coach whose team keeps losing. But that's all right – he's a forgiving coach. He talks little about discipline, about giving it all you've got, about the possibility of having a winning season. He doesn't lay anything heavy on his players. His training standards are low. His redeeming quality as a coach is that he's nice. When his players consistently lose, he isn't hard on them [...].
>
> Contrast this with the New Testament concept of grace [...] God does not change his absolute standards – but he supplies the power by which those standards can be met. New Testament grace goes beyond forgiveness into enablement. God is interested in doing much more than merely forgiving his people – he wants to change them. He wants to enable them to reach their destiny in Christ. Grace is what makes that possible.[13]

Luther says in the *Large Catechism* about the relationship between God's law contained in Ten Commandments and the gospel of grace contained in the Creed:

---

[11] AE 41, 113-115.

[12] An International Lutheran Charismatic Leaders' Conference was held near Helsinki, Finland, in the summer of 1981 (see the Introduction to this book). The Lutheran archbishop of Finland, Mikko Juva, together with Carl Mau, executive secretary of the Lutheran World Federation, visited the conference one evening. The need for a responsible theological and pastoral perspective on charismatic renewal in the Lutheran church was discussed at some length. Out of this conference, a planning committee was formed to put together the International Lutheran Charismatic Theological Consultation which was responsible for the first edition of this book.

[13] Paul Anderson, "The Nature of Grace," *Loaves and Fishes*, no. 153 (San Pedro, CA: Trinity Lutheran Church, April/May 1982), p. 3.

> Therefore the Ten Commandments do not by themselves make us Christians, for God's wrath and displeasure still remain on us because we cannot fulfil his demands. But the Creed brings pure grace and makes us upright and pleasing to God. Through this knowledge we come to love and delight in all the commandments of God because we see that God gives himself completely to us, with all his gifts and power, *to help us keep the Ten Commandment: The father gives us all creation, Christ all his works, the Holy Spirit all his gifts* (italics added).[14]

The Holy Spirit teaches the church that justification promises more than a forensic (legal) act accomplished before God in heaven. It also promises a real beginning of renewal of our relation to God here on earth, whereby through faith we come to share Christ's own life. Nor is justification related merely to the past, a once-for-all event. The righteousness of Christ is *continuously* imputed to the believer. It is the ever-present, ever-effectual ground of our right standing with God. It is the ground of our every action. A Christian's whole life and ministry is rooted in justification by grace through faith alone; and sanctification is a consequence and manifestation of that reality in our day-by-day life by the working of the Holy Spirit. A doctrinally sound church is taught by the Spirit to see both justification and sanctification as gifts of God to be received by faith.

---

[14] *LC*, On the Third Article, 68-69, p. 420.

(37) Theology of the Cross

The new life in Jesus must be sought and continually refreshed. To experience the essence of forgiveness is not to feel mere psychological relief from guilt but to cling to the cross of Jesus even though all feelings and evidence at the moment be contrary. Likewise, to experience the essence of holiness is not merely to experience virtue or victory, but to cling to the risen Christ even though all immediate appearances be to the contrary – bad habits slow to change, prayers going unanswered, ministry bogged down and going nowhere.

Charismatics have been faulted for having a theology of glory rather than a theology of the cross. In fact, the Charismatic renewal has thrown fresh light on the theology of the cross by insisting that spiritual experience must be understood in relation to the real and objective working of the Holy Spirit, and not simply in terms of certain outward acts or inner responses. As Walther von Loewenich wrote, "Wherever in theology the Holy Spirit is taken seriously into account, we are not dealing with the theology of glory but with the theology of the cross."[1]

The heart of a theology of the cross was stated by Luther in the explanation to Thesis 21 of the Heidelberg Disputation:

> He who does not know Christ does not know God hidden in suffering. Therefore, he prefers works to suffering, glory to the cross, strength to weakness, wisdom to folly, and, in general, good to evil. There are people whom the apostle calls 'enemies of the cross of Christ' (Phil. 3:18), for they hate the cross and suffering and love works and the glory of works [...] It is impossible for a person not to be puffed up by his good works unless he has first been deflated and destroyed by suffering and evil until he knows that he is worthless and that his works are not his but God's.[2]

A Theology of Glory Glories in What We Do.
The Theology of the Cross Glories in What Christ Does.

What we do is open to inspection and understanding. There is nothing mysterious about it. Think for a moment of self-sufficient religious people. They act with wisdom or virtue; they do well; they love and serve with distinction. A theology of glory steps in and says that such behaviour figures large in God's kingdom. That is its error. The flaw in a theology of glory is that it believes flesh and blood can inherit the kingdom (cf. Jn 3:3; 1 Cor.

---

[1] Prenter, *Spiritus Creator*, 111.

[2] AE 31, 53

15:50). The theology of glory does not see how radically human presumption and boasting have been dealt with in the cross.

A theology of the cross begins and ends with Christ. What Christ has done has kingdom validity. What happens in Christ and through Christ has kingdom meaning and kingdom force. At this point, someone might object, "Then why not call it a theology of *Christ*?" This is where Luther's insight comes into sharpest focus. It *is* a theology of Christ. But how do we *know* Christ, how do we *experience* Christ, how do we *serve* Christ? It is in the shadow of the cross that we meet Christ, and it is through the cross that we minister in his name. This is experience, profound experience, and one enters into it only and always by the working of the Holy Spirit.

It is a paradox. As mere human beings, we are helpless and weak; worse, we are spiritually dead. We need new life from God. But we do not find it by vaulting out of our human predicament, thereby coming into blessed and unbroken communion with God, experiencing his new life as strength and power in everything we do. No, paradoxically, we experience the new life as we are led by the Spirit yet further into weakness and helplessness by being joined to Christ in his humiliation and shame on the cross, and only then being raised with him (Phil. 3:8-11).

Those who fault the Charismatic renewal for spreading a theology of glory may not realise how deeply charismatic experience is rooted in weakness and helplessness. A group of lay people in a Lutheran congregation, who had a ministry of counselling and prayer, summarised their experience in this way:

> A person comes to you with a problem. You sense in yourself an emptiness. You realise that you have nothing to give this person. You are helpless. In your helplessness you cry out (inwardly) to God. Like the 'friend at midnight', you ask for something to give to this one in need. God imparts through you a word of wisdom – maybe a vision or picture or inward impression – which helps that person. Maybe you realise at the time what the Lord is doing, but maybe not. You may have to live with the thought that you blew it, and only find out months later that the person was actually helped. (And then, sometimes, you actually do blow it!) When the next person comes, you are right back to the point of emptiness and helplessness and crying out to the Lord again.[3]

A theology of the cross despairs of every situation *apart from the Lord.* One is like the psalmist, who sees himself surrounded by enemies:

> In thee, O Lord, do I seek refuge;
> let me never be put to shame;
> in thy righteousness deliver me!

---

[3] Discussion at a meeting involved in a monthly prayer ministry service at Trinity Lutheran Church, San Pedro, California, in the late 1970s. Reported by Larry Christenson.

> Incline thy ear to me, rescue me speedily!
> Be thou a rock of refuge for me, a strong fortress to save me!
> Yea, thou art my rock and my fortress;
> for thy name's sake lead me and guide me,
> take me out of the net which is hidden for me,
> for thou art my refuge.
> *Into thy hand I commit my spirit*;
> thou hast redeemed me, O Lord, faithful God (Ps. 31:1-5).

The psalmist recognised that personally he was no match for his adversaries. It was not by his own might or power, but by the intervention of God, that he would prevail. To be in such a position is the essence of the cross: Jesus spoke words from this psalm as he hung on the cross.

To be always at the mercy of strong enemies, except for the Lord, is to despair of anything I might do, and reckon only on what the Lord will do. "I am weak, but thou art mighty, hold me with thy powerful hand!" The theology of the cross results in strength out of weakness; a theology of glory results in weakness out of (presumed) strength.

Some theologians tend to link a theology of glory primarily with such things as healings, miracles, and answered prayer, and at this point many fault the Charismatic renewal: its emphasis on power and victory over difficulties, they say, is evidence that the renewal does not have a theology of the cross.[4] In actual practice, this criticism has some validity. The strong emphasis on answered prayer and miracles has led to a certain amount of self-centeredness in the Charismatic renewal, a preoccupation with miracles and material prosperity. A number of charismatic leaders have therefore spoken out against a shallow, "bless me" mentality that one frequently encounters in the renewal. This is a danger that one should always be aware of in a movement that expects the intervention of God in daily life.

To identify either the theology of the cross or a theology of glory simply with outward or inward circumstances, however, is to miss the point. It is a question rather of whether one's life and ministry centre and rest in Jesus or in oneself. If a woman prays for a member of her prayer group and the person is healed and there is great rejoicing, that fact alone does not tell us that the woman is living by a theology of glory. If she has prayed in obedience to the Spirit, recognises the healing as Christ's gracious intervention, and continues to look only to him, she will remain under the cross because she recognises that it was his work, not hers. In the face of the next sickness that she encounters in her ministry of healing, she will be as helpless and dependent on God as ever, looking to Christ alone.

It may be somewhat more natural to look to Christ and cry out to him in a circumstance of deep distress. On the other hand, it may be easy when things

---

[4] Bruner and Hordern, *The Holy Spirit – Shy Member of the Trinity*, pp. 66-70.

go well and prayers are answered, to presume that we ourselves have things well in hand. But this, according to Scripture, is a delusion:

> When I felt secure, I said,
> "I shall never be shaken."
> O, Lord, when you favoured me,
> You made my mountain stand firm;
> But when you hid your face,
> I was dismayed (Ps. 30:6-7).

God has only to hide his face, and the delusion of a theology of glory is exposed. The cross is a way of life that transcends circumstances, good or bad; it is a place of total and continual dependence on Christ *in any and all circumstances*. Except for him, we are lost, helpless, and utterly at the mercy of our enemies – not only in regard to our own salvation, but also in regard to our daily life and ministry.

The cross is the sign *par excellence* of our Christian life, for it shows our utter helplessness, the imminent triumph of our foes except for the intervention of God. If a "victory" takes us away from the cross, it is only because the eyes of the flesh have taken over and we do not see the true shape of our existence, which is still ringed about with enemies, still needing to cry out to the Lord.

In some ways it might actually be easier, from a human point of view, to live a theology of the cross in times of adversity, because our sense experience corresponds to or reinforces our state of dependence on the Lord. When outward circumstances seem to be going well, our sense experience can more easily deceive us as to our real condition, which is still one of total dependence on Christ, still at the mercy of enemies, except for him.

You never outgrow the weakness. In the scheme of this world, success breeds confidence, and confidence produces more success. It's an upward journey. But in the kingdom, the cross remains at the centre. God may have manifested wisdom, healing, and miracles through you for 30 years, but today you find yourself back at square one again, weak and helpless, clinging to Christ with empty hands. Luther's last written words were, "We are beggars; this is true."[5]

A gentle warning is in order at this point. There can be a subtle concession to the human sinful nature (the flesh) in the theology of the cross if the negative personal or subjective dynamics are *overstressed* – the lack of an experience of God, our failure, weakness, helplessness, suffering, and doubt. Luther's own presentation runs the danger of being misunderstood as a subtle form of *imitatio* piety: inner struggle and suffering become the way that the flesh chooses to imitate Christ in order to obtain the favour of God. A true

---

[5] AE 54, 476.

theology of the cross accepts adversity when God gives it as his appointed means to reveal his presence, grace and love in the midst of suffering, but it does not pander to our sinful nature's desire to make public or even boast of our struggles. Bob Mumford put it well: "When you go through a storm, it's important not to spend the rest of your life talking about it." Such ego-gratifying talk can undergird a theology of glory.

Compared to the reality of Christ, our struggles are little. The cross itself was "little" to Christ, compared to that which it brought forth. Consider Jesus, "who for the joy set before him endured the cross, scorning its shame, and sat down at the right hand of the throne of God" (Heb. 12:2; see also Rom. 8:18).

From the cross flows the whole life and victory of Christ, and that – not our subjective struggles – should chiefly occupy our attention.

(38) The Kingdom of God and the Church

The Kingdom of God[1]

Charismatic experience results in a new awareness of the kingdom of God as a *living, present reality*. In its most primary sense, Christian experience is also a foretaste of the *coming kingdom*.

The importance of the kingdom of God in the message of Jesus according to the Synoptic gospels is well-established, but its significance for the church today is an area still calling for theological work. The concepts "church" and "kingdom" are frequently used today more or less synonymously, even though the New Testament does not equate them. But then, what is the relationship between the kingdom of God and the church? What is the meaning of Jesus' message about the "the coming of the kingdom of God" and what are its practical implications for the church and its ministry today?

Strangely enough, the kingdom of God – in spite of its centrality in the message of Jesus – has not been the subject of thorough theological exploration or significant doctrinal discussion until quite recently. It is especially in the field of mission, in *missiology*, that the kingdom of God has been a central concern during the last fifty years or so. In our presentation here, there is not a great abundance of historical or traditional theology to refer to. We shall therefore primarily look at the biblical testimony and apply this to church and mission in our time.

After Jesus had been baptised by John the Baptist, he stood forth publicly with his own message: "The time has come. *The kingdom of God is near.* Repent and believe the good news [the gospel]" (Mk 1:15). The preaching of Jesus about the kingdom of God is "gospel" or "good news" (Greek: *euangelion*) about *salvation* (cf. Is. 52:7; Rom. 10:15). The preaching of the gospel, *evangelisation, is the major task of the disciples of Jesus at all times and among all people* (Mt. 24:14; Mk 13:10; 16:15-16; Acts 8:12; Rom. 1:16; 15:19-20).

While the actual *coming of the kingdom of God* was a *new thing* on the scene of history, connected to the coming of Jesus, the *promise of the kingdom* goes back to the Old Testament. In the Psalms, God is repeatedly portrayed as the everlasting king: "The Lord is king for ever and ever" (Ps. 10:16; 29:10). As the supreme king, he reigns over all the earth and over all the nations:

---

[1] This section on the kingdom of God is a new text written by Tormod Engelsviken. The first edition of this book contained only a very short section about the kingdom of God.

> How awesome is the Lord Most High, the great King over all the earth! [...]
> For God is the king of all the earth; sing to him a psalm of praise.
> God reigns over the nations; God is seated on his holy throne (Ps. 47:2, 7-8)

God is the king of the world and has always been so, but in a vision by the prophet Daniel, God, "the Ancient of Days", who sits on his throne, is seen as handing over the kingdom to a "Son of man":

> In my vision at night I looked, and there before me was *one like a son of man*, coming with the clouds of heaven. He approached the Ancient of Days and was led into his presence. *He was given authority, glory and sovereign power; all peoples, nations and men of every language worshipped him.* His dominion is an everlasting dominion that will not pass away, and *his kingdom is one that will never be destroyed* (Dan. 7:13-14).

In the interpretation of Daniel's vision also "the saints, the people of the Most High" will share in this kingdom (Dan. 7:27). In Jesus, who in the gospels is called the Son of Man, and through God's people, this prophecy and its promise are fulfilled.

Jesus' proclamation of the kingdom of God contained an urgent call to *conversion* or *repentance* (Greek: *metanoia* = change of mind) *and faith.* Conversion implies on the one hand *confessing one's sins* and *turning away from them,* and on the other hand *turning to God believing* that he by his grace will forgive them. It then leads to *new life* in communion with God. The preaching of repentance and forgiveness of sins in the name of Christ is also a standing commission for the Christian church (Lk. 24:47; Acts 2:38). This call for conversion and faith was originally directed by Jesus to unrepentant sinners among the people of Israel, but was later expanded to include *all people, Jews and Gentiles.* Today, the call for conversion is extended to people of different nations and people groups, to people of different religions and people with no religion, to secularised people and nominal Christians.[2]

The gospel that Jesus proclaimed was the gospel of the *coming of the kingdom of God.* The kingdom of God is a translation of the Greek expression *basileia tou theou* (from Greek: *basileus* = king, and the genitive of *theos* = God). It can be translated either as "God's rule/reign as king" or as "God's kingdom", his "royal realm".

In the first case, the emphasis is on God exercising his royal power, often with an *ethical* emphasis: his just and good reign. In modern mission

---

[2] The relationship between conversion and Christian mission, as reflected in the work of an international Lausanne *Consultation on Conversion* held in Hong Kong in 1988, is dealt with in David Wells, *Turning to God: Biblical Conversion in the Modern World* (Exeter: The Paternoster Press, 1989).

theology, this understanding has often been related to God's universal work to create a better and more just society in the *world.*

In the second case, the emphasis has been on the "area" or "place" where God's *salvation* is present and available. It has a more *soteriological* meaning and is closer related to God's salvation-historical work in and through the *church.* "Area" should not, of course, be understood in a geographical sense, but rather as the "place" where Christ is believed in and salvation is received.

While the first interpretation, "rule" or "reign", is most common among theologians today, there are good reasons to assert that the second interpretation, "kingdom" or "realm" is the more adequate rendering. Yet, they may be seen as complementary rather than contradictory.[3]

Some Norwegian New Testament scholars have argued – in our view convincingly –that the term "kingdom of God" corresponds better to the *content* of Jesus' proclamation of the kingdom as the gift, time and place of salvation.[4]

The "nearness" of the kingdom places it in an *eschatological context.* The time of salvation is coming and is in fact already present. God's plan of salvation is being realised in history. Still, it is *not yet* fully realised. That will happen when Christ returns in power and establishes his eternal, perfect kingdom (Mk 9:1). Yet, many of the gifts of salvation that fully belong to the future kingdom are granted *already in this life on earth.* This "not yet – already" distinction is basic to the understanding of the kingdom of God.

The "not yet" new creation of heaven and earth, the "not yet" bodily resurrection of all believers, and the "not yet" eternal life in the presence of God belong to the future, perfect kingdom. In the story of the Rich Ruler (Lk. 18:18-30), eternal life (v. 18), entry into the kingdom of God (v. 24), and salvation (v. 26) are tied so closely together as to be virtually identified with each other.

The salvation that is given *already* on this side of death and resurrection consists first and foremost of a *new and reconciled relationship to God.* As a result of conversion and faith, all sins are *forgiven* (Mt. 9:2, 6); those who humble themselves before God and confess their sins are *justified* (Lk. 18:13-14); people are taken into close *communion with God* (Mt. 5:3-10), and receive *eternal life* (Mt. 25:34, 46), a life that begins already in the present (Jn 5:24). Through faith in Christ, they become *children of God* (Jn 1:12; 3:3)

---

[3] The missiologist Michael W. Goheen includes both aspects in his definition: "The kingdom can be characterised as the inbreaking of God's *dynamic power* to defeat all that stands against his rule, and as the arrival of the *comprehensive salvation* of the world" (italics added). See Michael W. Goheen, *Introducing Christian Mission Today: Scripture, History and Issues* (Downers Grove, IL: IVP Academic, 2014), p. 55.

[4] See Hans Kvalbein, *Fortolkning til Matteusevangeliet*, Vol. 1, 2nd edition (Oslo: Luther, 2009), pp. 48-59, 117-118; and "The kingdom of God in the Ethics of Jesus", *Studia Theologica,* 51(1), 1997, pp. 60-84.

by baptism and the Holy Spirit (Jn 3:5). Paul – who does not use the term kingdom of God often – summarises the content of the present kingdom in this way: "For the kingdom of God is not a matter of eating and drinking, but of *righteousness, peace and joy in the Holy Spirit*" (Rom. 14:17). All these three terms may also be used to denote the content of salvation. They reflect the teaching of Jesus about the kingdom as seen in the gospels.

Salvation in the kingdom of God here and now involves more than just a right relationship to God. There are also *other gifts* that are granted to the citizens of the kingdom of God: the sick are healed, the demon possessed are delivered, the hungry are satisfied, people in danger are rescued, sinners have their lives renewed, the marginalised and outcasts are included in the community, the worth of humans is upheld, prayers are answered etc. These gifts may be given differently to various individuals depending on their needs and situations. They are not perfect since the citizens of the kingdom of God are still sinners who live in a sinful world marked by the consequences of the fall; for example, the healed may be sick again, and those who are raised from the dead will later die. Some of these gifts are miraculous acts of Jesus or supernatural interventions of God, others are natural – yet God-given – and experienced as part of people's daily life in the kingdom. For those who experience these gifts in their own lives they become part of the *kingdom blessings* they receive here and now, yet at the same time they are also *signs of the future*, a *partial anticipation of the future consummated kingdom.*

One of the most explicit texts connecting Jesus' divine power, his liberation of those who were oppressed by Satan, and the work of the Holy Spirit with the coming of the kingdom of God is Matthew 12:28-29, where Jesus says:

> But if I drive out demons by the Spirit of God, then the kingdom of God has come upon you. Or again, how can anyone enter a strong man's house and carry off his possessions unless he first ties up the strong man. Then he can rob his house.

According to Jesus' programmatic speech in the synagogue in Nazareth at the beginning of his ministry, as recorded in Luke 4:18-19, his proclamation of the kingdom of God was done in the power of the Spirit and included these basic gifts of salvation: good news to the poor, liberation for prisoners, sight for the blind, release of the oppressed, and God's grace. These words of Jesus are primarily to be understood *religiously* or *metaphorically* about the fundamental change in people's relationship to God and the overcoming of forces that hinder this relationship, yet they also have tangible consequences in such areas as economy, health, society and politics.

It has been facetiously said that "Jesus preached the kingdom, but what came, was the church", as if the kingdom and the church were something completely different. While they are not identical, they are nevertheless inextricably related. Any kingdom has a people, and the people of the kingdom of God are those who receive the kingdom or enter the kingdom and thereby constitute the fellowship of *disciples of Jesus* (Mt. 5:5, 10;[5] Lk. 12:31-32; 22:29-30). This fellowship is the precursor of the church that came into existence on the day of Pentecost, and where the confession to Jesus as the Son of God is the foundation (Mt. 16:16-18), and Jesus himself is present when the believers gather in his name (Mt. 18:20). The kingdom of God is not a universal kingdom or rule in the sense that the whole world and all human beings will enter into it or receive it; it is limited to those who repent (Mk 1:15), who receive the kingdom in childlike faith (Mt. 19:14) and who in their spiritual poverty and need come to God and are received by him (Mt. 5:3).

Jesus' *Sermon on the mountain* contains a radical *ethics* for the people of the kingdom about radical and sacrificial love and good works (Mt. 5:16, 38-48; 7:12). But it also contains *promises* of the gifts of the kingdom to the disciples that they, in spite of suffering and persecution, may live without worry in the fatherly care of God (Mt. 5:3-12; 6:25-34). They have God as their father and can come to him with the expectation that he will answer their prayers (Mt. 6:6-13; 7:7-11; Mt. 18:19-20).

In many of the *parables* of Jesus about the kingdom of God, the *growth* or *expansion* of the kingdom is a central feature. This growth is a result of the preaching of the Word of God (Mt. 13:18-23). The seed sown by Jesus himself, which is "the sons of the kingdom", will grow in the world together with the "sons of the evil one", sown by the devil, and not be separated until the end of the age (Mt. 13:24-30, 36-43). *What is growing* when the kingdom of God grows, is not the rule of God, because he is already in power, but the *number and influence of his children in the world as a result of evangelism and mission.*

Signs of the presence of the kingdom are *the miracles of Jesus*, *the preaching of the gospel and the confession of faith in Jesus.* Jesus said in his answer to John the Baptist who wondered whether he was the coming Messiah:

> Go back and report to John what you hear and see: The *blind receive sight*, the lame walk, those who have leprosy are cured, the deaf hear, the dead are raised, and the *good news is preached to the poor. Blessed is the man who does not fall away* on account of me [or "who does not lose faith in me", *Jerusalem Bible*] (Mt. 11:2-6, 11-12).

The disciples were sent out by Jesus to preach the kingdom of God, to heal the sick, and to drive out demons (Lk. 9:1-2, 6; 10:9; Mt. 10:1, 7-8). The

[5] Note that in the gospel of Matthew the common expression is "kingdom of heaven" where "heaven" simply is another word for God, not a place above the earth.

response of their listeners decided their relationship to *Jesus* but also their relationship to *God*: "He who listens to you listens to me; he who rejects you rejects me; but he who rejects me rejects him who sent me" (Lk. 10:16).

The most important thing for the disciples in their ministry was, however, not their power over the evil spirits, but their relationship to God, their own salvation:

> Do not rejoice that the spirits submit to you, but *rejoice that your names are written in heaven.* At that time Jesus, *full of joy through the Holy Spirit*, said, "I praise you, Father, Lord of heaven and earth, because you have hidden these things from the wise and learned, and revealed them to little children. Yes, Father, this was your good pleasure (Lk. 10:20-21).

Which group do we belong to; the "wise and learned" or "the little children" to whom God has revealed the things of the kingdom of God?

In addition to the word of God – or rather inextricably linked to it – are the *good works* of the disciples drawing people to God: "You are the light of the world [...] let your light shine before men, that they may see your good deeds, and praise your Father in heaven" (Mt. 5:14-16). The same can be said about the supernatural signs and miracles that are an integral part of the coming of the kingdom (Mt. 11:2-6, 11-12; 12:28). The preaching of the word of the gospel (Greek: *kerygma, logos*), the good works, service (Greek: *ergon, diakonia*) and the signs and wonders (Greek: *semeia kai terata*) were all taking place by the *power of the Holy Spirit.* They were characteristic both of the kingdom ministry of Jesus during his earthly life and the life and mission of the early church. They were not, however, limited to Jesus or the disciples in the apostolic age. They are also for us and for the world today (Jn 14:12-14; Acts 1:6-8; 8:5-6, 12; Rom. 15:18-20; 1 Cor. 2:4-5; Gal. 3:3-5; 1 Thess. 1:5; Heb. 6:4-6; Mk 16:15-18). "The kingdom of God is not a matter of talk but of power" (1 Cor. 4:20).

Jesus came to save the world (Jn 12:47) and his death on the cross and his resurrection were sufficient for the reconciliation of the whole world to God (Jn 1:29; 2 Cor. 5:19-20; Col. 1:19-20). Salvation is therefore for all. It is *universally available.* It is, however, *not universally received*, neither at the time of Jesus, today, nor in the future. The very concept of entry into the kingdom presupposes the possibility of being outside the kingdom, outside the realm of salvation in Christ. Hence, Jesus' message of the kingdom describes with great seriousness the two possible final outcomes: at the last judgement all people will be gathered before Jesus, the king, and be separated into two groups; those who will inherit the kingdom, and those who will be lost forever (Mt. 25:32, 34, 41). The urgent call to enter the kingdom and the warning against the danger of being left outside is a recurring theme in Jesus' proclamation of the kingdom (see for example Mt. 7:13-14; 13:36-43, 47-50; 21:41-44).

Finally, we want to address the question of *how people may enter the kingdom* of God, the realm of God's salvation. The answer seems to be very simple, and yet so difficult: one enters the kingdom by coming to Jesus (or being brought to him!) and receiving it as a child does, given freely without any effort or merit on the receiver's part (Lk. 18:17); or by heeding the call of Jesus, becoming his disciple and following him as Master (Mt. 4:18-22). When Jesus called Matthew, the sinful tax collector, and he followed him, Jesus said, "I have not come to call the righteous, but sinners" (Mt. 9:9-13). Zaccheus, another tax collector, was saved by receiving Jesus in his home and repenting of his sins (in that order!) (Lk. 19:1-10). It is by *hearing the word of God, the message of Jesus, and believing it, that one is saved into the kingdom of God.* Jesus said:

> This is the meaning of the parable (the Parable of the Sower): the seed is the *word of God.* Those along the path are *the ones who hear*, and then the devil comes and takes away the word from their hearts, so that they may not *believe* and be *saved* [...] But the seed on the good soil stands for those with a noble and good heart, who hear the word, retain it, and by persevering produce a crop (Lk. 8:12, cp. Mk 4:20).

Jesus also said that the entry into the kingdom of God requires a new birth (Jn 3:3). This birth that makes us children of God comes about by water (baptism) and the Spirit (Jn 3:5). In the context of the gospel of John, this implies receiving Jesus in faith:

> To all who *received* him, to those who *believed in his name*, he gave the right to become the *children of God* – children born not of natural descent, nor of human decision or a husband's will, but *born of God.* (Jn 1:12-13; cp. Jn 3:16).

There are many examples in the gospels that the *gifts of salvation in the kingdom of God are received by faith in Jesus*, for example forgiveness of sins (Lk. 5:20; 7:48-50), eternal life (Jn 3:16) and healing (Mt. 8:10, 13; 9:22). The confessing of Jesus is decisive for salvation (Mt. 10:32; 11:6, cp. Rom. 10:8-10). By believing that Jesus is the Christ, the Son of God, we have life in his name (Jn 20:31).

The Holy Spirit points us to the glorious and perfect *fulfilment of the kingdom at the second coming of Christ* (Rom. 8:18-25). The kingdom will only be fully realised on the last day, at the resurrection of the body and the renewal of the whole creation.

> Now have come the salvation and the power and the kingdom of our God, and the authority of his Christ (Rev. 12:10; cf. 21:1-5; 22:17).

The consummation of the kingdom of God is therefore the content of the Christian's sure *hope granted by the power of the Holy Spirit* (Rom. 15:13, cf. 1 Pet. 1:3-5).

In the Lord's prayer, the church and individuals believers are taught to *pray for the coming of the kingdom of God*, and the church has added the confession, "For yours is the kingdom, the power and the glory for ever. Amen" (Mt. 6:10, 13).

The Sending of the Church

The nature and mission of the church are of great importance since the church is comprised of the people who belong to the kingdom of God, and who are entrusted by their Lord with the great commission:

> And this gospel of the kingdom will be preached in the whole world as a testimony to all nations, and then the end will come (Mt. 24:14).

The preaching the gospel of the kingdom is thus set in a universal and eschatological perspective (cp. Mt. 28:19-20). According to God's great plan of salvation, he has *sent* his *Son*, his *Spirit* – and his *people*! This is often called *the mission of God* (Latin: *missio Dei*).[6] God's mission is about realising and expanding the kingdom of God, and God's main instrument for this is his people, the church. One could say it succinctly: *The mission of God has a church and the church has a mission from God.*

The founding and *sending of the church* coincide in time and place with the *sending of the Holy Spirit* on the day of Pentecost, and these two sendings are theologically closely and indissolubly connected: the Holy Spirit creates the church and empowers it for its mission. The empowered church with its spiritual gifts serves God's salvific purposes under the guidance of the Holy Spirit. It is in and through the church that the Holy Spirit makes the redemptive work of Christ a living reality in the lives of people.

The two most central biblical texts connecting the sending of the Holy Spirit and the sending of the church are Jesus' own words:

> As the Father has sent me, *I am sending you*. And with that he breathed on them and said, '*Receive the Holy Spirit*. If you forgive anyone his sins, they are forgiven; if you do not forgive them, they are not forgiven' (Jn 20:21-23).

---

[6] A more detailed discussion of the concept of "missio Dei", is for instance found in Tormod Engelsviken, "Missio Dei: The Understanding and Misunderstanding of a Theological Concept in European Churches and Missiology", *International Review of Mission*, 92(367), (2003), pp. 481-497.

> But you will *receive power when the Holy Spirit comes on you*; and you will be *my witnesses* in Jerusalem, and in all Judea and Samaria, and *to the ends of the earth* (Acts 1:8).

This sent church – the *missional church* – is therefore a church baptised (Acts 1:5) and empowered (Acts 1:8) by the Holy Spirit. *The Charismatic renewal is about a renewal of this missional church in all areas of its life and work.*

Characteristics of a Renewed Church

In the final report of an ecumenical conference in Geneva in 1980 on questions concerning Charismatic renewal, these things were named as elements of a renewed and unified church:

- New openness toward the lordship of Jesus;
- Renewal of the spiritual life of the church in its local congregations;
- Spontaneity, openness, freedom, and joy in praise and worship;
- New interest in the Bible as God's living Word;
- Deeper experience of the reality, holiness, and transcendence of God;
- Deeper interest and new openness in regard to the essential doctrines of the Trinity, the divinity of Christ, his death and resurrection, confirmed in experience;
- Renewal of the service of healing for the sick;
- Lay leadership;
- New incentives for evangelisation, missions, and witness in the power of the Spirit.[7]

These are characteristics of the church in the New Testament, as we have already seen in the biblical section of this book. The dynamic of the church, as it confronts us from the perspective of the New Testament, is challenging, even disconcerting. It presents itself to us as a spiritual measuring stick. Because God remains true to himself, the goal of renewing contemporary Christianity will be nothing short of its participation in the spiritual reality from which the New Testament church draws its life. But what does that mean?

When reflecting on the New Testament church, we should, first of all, be aware of three possible dangers:

1. *The danger of idealisation.* From the Gospel of Matthew to the Revelation of John, the church of Jesus Christ is admonished, warned, and

---

[7] Arnold Bittlinger, *Erneuerung in Kirche und Gesellschaft* (Renewal in Church and Society), 7, (1980), p. 25. This excerpt is translated by William Sims. See also Arnold Bittlinger, *Charismatic Renewal: An Opportunity for the Church?* (Geneva: World Council of Churches, 1979), and Arnold Bittlinger (ed), *The Church is Charismatic: The World Council of Churches and the Charismatic Movement* (Geneva: World Council of Churches, 1981).

criticised. Specific misdeeds and sins within the church are named. It is obvious to every reader of the New Testament that the congregations of that time were not perfect congregations. We should not idealise them.

2. *The danger of harmonisation.* Biblical research has brought to light a great variety of approaches to congregational life and theology. The church at Jerusalem differed from the church at Corinth, and both of these were in many respects unlike the congregations addressed in the Pastoral Epistles or in Revelation. Some biblical scholarship may overemphasise these differences to the point that any sense of unity nearly disappears; yet one thing is clear: one pattern for the New Testament church has never existed. Variety can add great richness to the church. It would impoverish the church to set forth one expression of early Christian church life as normative for all expressions. The message, life and form of the church need to be contextualised in various cultures and situations, as happens in the New Testament.

3. *The danger of ecclesiological fundamentalism.* The danger inherent in every form of fundamentalism lies in the failure to take historical distance seriously. It seeks to recapture the truth in the same form in which it was cast by the biblical texts. Ecclesiological fundamentalists leap over 2000 years of church history in an attempt to refashion the church today after "the model of the primitive church." In effect, they discount the work of the Holy Spirit during the whole history of the church.

The Holy Spirit is concerned to point out to us not simply the form or forms of the church that we see in the New Testament but also the essence of the church. Certainly, what God did at the beginning has a unique place in our understanding of the church, and it is often the task of a renewal movement to remind the church of its origins, as the Old Testament prophets reminded Israel of the exodus from Egypt and covenant at Sinai. The origins of the church, as recorded in Scripture, provide valuable insight into God's purpose and plan for the church. Most especially, they remind us of God's faithfulness and provision, and call forth a response of faith. But God wants to lead the church not simply back to its beginnings but forward to its fulfilment. In this, there can and should be a thoughtful appreciation for the ways in which the Holy Spirit has enriched the church through the centuries, and an openness to what he wants to do today.

Names for the church in the New Testament take various forms. Some terms relate particularly to Christ: "body of Christ" or "bride"; some to the Spirit: "temple of the Holy Spirit"; some to the Father: "people of God", "household of God", and "church of God". A biblical understanding of the church will be clearly *trinitarian.*

It is no accident, however, that the ancient creeds mention the church in the Third Article, in direct connection with the Holy Spirit. This reflects the church's awareness that only by the working of the Holy Spirit can the church accomplish its task under the lordship of Christ to the glory of God the Father.

The Third Article of the Nicene Creed, a confession shared by almost all Christian churches today, deals with the Holy Spirit and the church:

> *I believe in the Holy Spirit*, the lord and giver of life, who proceeds from the Father and the Son; who together with the Father and the Son is worshipped and glorified; who spoke by the prophets.
>
> *And I believe one holy, catholic, and apostolic church.* I acknowledge one Baptism for the remission of sins, and I look for the resurrection of the dead and the life of the age to come" (italics added).[8]

In the Nicene Creed, we confess *four marks of the church* (Latin: *notae ecclesiae*): unity, holiness, catholicity, and apostolicity.[9]

Unity

Firstly, the *unity* of the church is grounded in the oneness of the Triune God, the one faith, one body (the church), one baptism and one hope of the church. It is created and upheld by the Holy Spirit, and may therefore be called "the unity of the Spirit" (Eph. 4:3-6). This unity is a given fact embracing all God's children on earth, and yet the church is admonished to keep it and practice it in a visible way: "Make every *effort to keep the unity of the Spirit* through the bond of peace" (Eph. 4:3). The unity is a testimony to the world and therefore has great missional significance (Jn 17:21). There is no place for division or separation in the church. The church has to reject all forms of racism, casteism, tribalism, nationalism, sexism etc. that view and treat human beings as having different worth or standing before God or in society (Gal. 3:28). One of the great testimonies of the early Pentecostal revival in Azusa Street in USA in 1906 was that it overcame the racial barriers that divided God's people. In today's world, the overcoming of these and other barriers is an expression of the unity in Christ and a sign of the work of the Spirit: "For through him we both (Jews and Gentiles) have access to the Father by one Spirit" (Eph. 2:14-18).

The unity of the Spirit is also an inspiration for the *ecumenical movements,* such as the World Council of Churches, World Evangelical Alliance and the Lausanne movement for world evangelisation, that strive to overcome the divisions caused by different doctrines, traditions, practices and cultures in

---

[8] *The Book of Concord*, p. 19.

[9] This section on the marks of the church is written by Tormod Engelsviken, cp. also Tormod Engelsviken, "Church/ecclesiology", in John Corrie (ed), *Dictionary of Mission Theology. Evangelical Foundations* (Downers Grove, IL: InterVarsity Press, 2007), pp. 51-55. The dictionary article also contains a short overview of different historical views of the church. See also Charles van Engen, "Church", in A. Scott Moreau (ed), *Evangelical Dictionary of World Missions* (Grand Rapids, MI: Baker Books, 2000), pp. 192-195.

the church. While there is not one form of the church that is normative for all times, and *diversity is a value in a body of Christ* as exemplified by the variety of charisms, *deep doctrinal divides should be overcome* and "unity in reconciled diversity" should be a goal. The Charismatic renewal has from the beginning been a sort of ecumenical movement without a central organisation, yet uniting Christians of various traditions and doctrinal persuasions without forcing them to give up their own deep convictions and confessional identities.

Holiness

Secondly, the *holiness* of the church is also *given in Christ* and therefore all believers are perfectly holy *in Christ.* "It is because of him that you are in Christ Jesus, who has become for us wisdom from God – that is our righteousness, *holiness* and redemption" (1 Cor. 1:30). Therefore, Paul can address *all* Christians – even those who are morally imperfect – as "sanctified in Christ Jesus and called to be holy" (1 Cor. 1:2). According to the Apostles' Creed, the church is the "communion of saints" (Latin: *communio sanctorum*), and the *Augsburg Confession* says that the "church is the assembly of saints and true believers".[10]

The church that already is perfectly holy in Christ must *strive to grow* in practical, experiential holiness. This takes place both in the lives of *individual* believers as they, by the power of the Spirit, try to become what they already are in Christ, pursuing a life of faith and love that is pleasing to God and reflecting the image of the Lord (1 Jn 3:21-23; 2 Cor. 3:17-18; Col. 3:9-10), and in the life of the church as the body of Christ, the *community* of believers (Eph. 4:15-16).

Although the church as holy is *different from the world* in the sense of *not being of the world,* it is *not separated from the world,* because it is called to be *in the world.* As being in the world, both individual Christians and the church will influence, penetrate, and sometimes even transform society through holy living and loving service. As ambassadors of grace, goodness, justice, holiness and reconciliation, they serve as light and salt in the world (Mt. 5:13-16). The kingdom of God will grow like a mustard seed or penetrate the world like yeast (Mt. 13:31-33). The holiness of the church should not exclude other people, but attract sinners to Jesus as the church is an *open fellowship* that will include all who repent and believe.

Those who are sanctified by the word of God are sent out in the world by Jesus, as he prayed for his disciples before his death and resurrection:

> My prayer is not that you take them out of the world, but that you protect them from the evil one. They are not of the world, even as I am not of it. *Sanctify*

---

[10] CA, Art. VIII (What the church is), 1, *The Book of Concord,* p. 33.

> *them by the truth, your word is truth.* As you sent me into the world, I have sent them into the world. For them I sanctify myself, that they too may be truly sanctified (Jn 17:15-19).

Protection from the power of Satan, proclamation of the Word of God, mission to the world, and the sanctification of people of God are all a *fulfilment of Jesus' own prayers.*

Catholicity

Thirdly, the *catholicity* of the church means that the church is *universal,* drawing its members from the whole world, from "every nation, tribe, people and language" (Rev. 7:9). Through most of its history, the church has been universal in *intention.* Jesus commanded his followers "to make disciples of all nations" (Mt. 28:19), a staggering commission for a small group of eleven fearful apostles. The church has obeyed this commission – admittedly to various degrees and in various ways down through its history – but today we can ascertain that the church is universal not only in intention but also in *reality.* More than 2.2 billion people in all continents and almost all countries belong to a Christian church, and a high proportion of them are committed Christians who, by the Holy Spirit, confess Jesus Christ as God and Saviour to the glory of God.

This remarkable historical fact is actually one of *the most convincing arguments for the truth of Christianity and the power of the Holy Spirit.* No human being could have envisaged this growth of the kingdom of God and his church, and it is a privilege for us who live today to be part of this worldwide harvest taking place before the return of the Lord in glory. However, the missional task is not yet completed as there are still people who have not heard or responded to the gospel. Therefore, the words of Jesus are still relevant:

> I tell you, open your eyes and look at the fields! They are ripe for harvest. … Ask the Lord of the harvest, therefore, to send out workers into his harvest field (Mt. 9:37; Jn 4:35; cp.1 Cor. 3:6-9).

The slogan of the Lausanne Movement, "The whole church taking the whole gospel to the whole world" is an appropriate expression of this universal mission of the church.[11]

---

[11] *The Lausanne Covenant*, paragraph 6. To the missional nature of the church and the role of the Holy Spirit in the mission of the church, see also Chapter 55 and Excursus 5.

Apostolicity

Fourthly, the *apostolicity* of the church primarily means that the church goes back to the apostles and is *built on the faith and words* of the apostles as expressed in the New Testament (Mt. 16:16-18; Eph. 2:19-22). While some churches, such as the Roman Catholic, Orthodox and Anglican, have emphasised the ecclesiastical office of the bishop as necessary for apostolicity through an unbroken "apostolic succession" from the first apostles (especially the apostle Peter) by laying on of hands, most Protestant churches, including the Lutheran Church, have maintained that all churches that share the faith of the apostles are apostolic.

It is a priority task for Christians at all times "to devote themselves to the apostles' teaching" (Acts 2:42). Paul admonishes the Thessalonians to "stand firm and hold to the teachings we passed on to you, whether by word of mouth or by letter" (2 Thess. 2:15) Preserving the apostolic doctrine through being a teacher is a *gift of the Holy Spirit* (1 Tim. 4:13-16). All Christians – and charismatics in particular – should be concerned about apostolic doctrine since it is necessary for salvation (2 Tim. 4:16). Doctrinal ignorance or indifference is not a Christian virtue. There has always been and always will be a fight in the church both *for true* doctrine and *against false* doctrine (Acts 20:29-31; 2 Pet. 2:1-3).

In another sense, the church is also apostolic because it is *sent* in mission and evangelism. The word "apostle" (Greek: *apostolos*, from *apostellein* = send) means a "sent one", a messenger. A church without mission cannot claim to be an apostolic church in this sense. This apostolic ministry extends to more people than the original twelve apostles, as both Paul and Barnabas who were "sent on their way by the Holy Spirit" (Acts 13:2) can be called apostles (Acts 14:14). Both the ministries of the twelve apostles and that of other messengers with the gospel, missionaries, can be called *gifts of the Spirit* together with prophets, evangelists, teachers, and pastors (Eph. 4:4). There is, however, no evidence in the New Testament that these other missionaries/apostles should have a superior position of authority in the church. As far as the term "apostle" is used in the later history of the church or even today it may be used to denote pioneer missionaries to a certain people or country, or simply missionaries who are sent out from their churches.

Dependence on Jesus and the Holy Spirit

The Charismatic renewal has given expression in highly practical ways to the fact that the church is the *body of Christ* consisting of *various members* who represent different spiritual gifts or charisms (1 Cor. 12-14; Rom. 12:3-8; 1 Pet. 4:10: Eph. 4:4). Making room in liturgical and other services for *free charismatic expressions* – prophecy, speaking in tongues, testimony, and prayer for the sick with the laying on of hands – is one example of this. Another is the attention given to *divine guidance* in and for a congregation. One of the workshops at the Fifteenth International Lutheran Conference on the Holy Spirit in Minneapolis, Minnesota, in 1986, for instance, carried this title and description:

> Discerning God's Will in the Church Council [...] All too often Church Councils can get bogged down in just the 'machinery' of church life. We need to give top priority to discovering and responding to God's will, if we are to lead a congregation into real spiritual renewal. This workshop will focus on practical helps for structuring the prayer, relationships, meetings, and work of the Church Council in ways that will make 'Thy Will Be Done' a dynamic reality in the congregation.

This kind of *practical dependence on the Holy Spirit* does not deny, but rather illustrates, the fact that everything that the Spirit does in and through the church is based on the saving act of Jesus Christ. The Holy Spirit can only reveal what God has already done in Jesus Christ; he can only develop what is already given in Jesus Christ. The Spirit stands in the service of Christ and the eschatological reality brought through him and present in him.

The New Testament often describes the relationship between Jesus Christ and his church in terms of contrast: shepherd/flock, bridegroom/bride, master/disciples, Lord/servants. Other statements describe the relationship in terms of organic unity: vine/branches, head/body.

Both of these emphases are important. On the one hand, the church must see itself *as over against Christ*, responsible to him, submitted to his lordship. The frequent reference to the lordship of Christ in the Charismatic renewal answers to this reality. On the other hand, the church must see itself *as one with Christ*: it has no life of its own apart from the life that Jesus Christ himself possesses. The church possesses nothing that does not belong to Jesus Christ, who came in the flesh, was crucified, and rose from the dead, and is seated by the right hand of God in power, and also is present in his body, the church. The very being of the church consists in being in Christ, but this becomes reality only as the church lives in dependence on the Holy Spirit.

Just as God expects nothing from individual believers other than that which they are already in Christ, so he expects nothing from the church as a whole other than that which it already is in Christ. In Jesus Christ, the life of the kingdom of God has already begun. Individual believers are drawn into this reality by the Holy Spirit through faith and baptism. The Holy Spirit labours so that Jesus Christ may be fully formed in the church (Gal. 4:19).

It is all too easy to borrow an ideal for the church from some element in the surrounding culture; in times past: the Roman province, the feudal fief, the royal state, or the village meeting; in our time: the voluntary organisation, the successful corporation, the accepting fellowship, the counselling clinic, or the service agency. Any ideal for the church is irrelevant unless it clearly has its roots in the new life in Jesus Christ. Whatever is given by God in Jesus Christ ought to come to visible manifestation in the church, even if such manifestations have been absent for centuries.

(39) Baptism

A vivid experience of the Holy Spirit can be like a new beginning of the Christian life. When Luther described his own famous "tower experience", he said that he felt as if his soul were born anew.[1] The natural result of such an experience is the impulse toward commitment, a desire to make a radical break with the past and live for God in a new way.

What is at work here is the reality of one's baptism: one's death and resurrection with Christ is taking place at the level of more conscious experience. The Holy Spirit is bringing the reality of one's baptism into focus, whether one was baptised as an infant or later. An experience of the Holy Spirit is not a call to be re-baptised but to live in the reality of one's baptism.

The Holy Spirit leads us to think soundly. He grafts believers into the body of Christ in baptism (1 Cor. 12:13). He does not repeat this work every time a believer has a vivid experience of the Spirit's life and power. The church correctly interpreted the sense of Scripture when it confessed in the Nicene Creed, "I believe in one baptism for the remission of sins."

A man who was planning to join a charismatic Lutheran church in the United States told the pastor that he had been baptised four times, and wondered whether this presented any problem. He had been baptised as an infant in the Roman Catholic Church, baptised as a teenager in a nondenominational church, baptised in the armed services after a conversion experience, and baptised in an ecumenical prayer group after experiencing the baptism with the Holy Spirit. The pastor did not make a big issue of it. "The way I see it," he said, "you had one baptism and three baths." Behind that seemingly offhand response, however, lay some intense prayer and study as to the purpose and effect of Baptism. What began as an inquiry into the early church's practice of baptism led to the realisation that the overriding reality is simply the fact that *God acts in Baptism*.[2] Once that is established, a sound practice of baptism can follow.

Infant Baptism

With our emphasis on faith in connection with baptism and receiving the gift of the Holy Spirit, the question of infant baptism naturally arises. Should

---

[1] AE 34, 337.

[2] Christenson, *Charismatic Renewal*, p. 57.

infant baptism be practiced? Does God grant the Holy Spirit in infant baptism?[3]

As is well known, the question of adult or infant baptism is not explicitly dealt with in Scripture. The baptisms described in the New Testament were primarily baptisms of believing adults, although there is a possibility that sometimes children may also have been included (Acts 11:14; 16:33). The same thing is true today where the church is in a first-generation missionary situation: the most frequent form of baptism is adult baptism, even in churches that practice infant baptism. One does not normally baptise children of non-Christian parents. The basic framework for New Testament teaching on baptism, therefore, is the practice of adult baptism in a predominantly pagan culture. However, if infant baptism has been practiced from the earliest times, and even by the apostles, the church must have had good reasons to do so.

There seem to be two basic reasons for infant baptism. Firstly, God has sovereignly made baptism an integral part of Christian initiation. The Spirit is active in baptism. In and by the Spirit, forgiveness of sin, new life and the gift of the Spirit are united to baptism (cf. Acts 2:38; 22:16; Eph. 5:26; 1 Cor. 6:11; Gal. 3:27; Col. 2:11-14; Tit. 3:5-7; 1 Pet. 3:21). Through the new birth in baptism, a person enters the kingdom of God (Jn 3:3, 5).

Secondly, even small children have the need and the right to enter the kingdom of God. Jesus' words speak of the necessity for children to be born into the kingdom: "Let the little children come to me, and do not hinder them, for the kingdom of heaven belongs to such as these" (Mt. 19:14). Jesus did not say that the children automatically belong to the kingdom or that they are born into the kingdom by natural birth. He said that the kingdom belongs to such; that is, the *kingdom is meant for children also. They are brought into the kingdom by being brought to Jesus.* If Scripture points to baptism as the objective point of entry into the kingdom, then it seems unnatural to withhold it from children who are being raised in a Christian home. Children have, as we know, been baptised in the Christian community from the earliest times.

Even if children do not have a conscious, articulate faith such as adults have, this is not a hindrance to their being accepted into the kingdom; that is, being saved. Where he does not encounter resistance, the Holy Spirit is well able to unite a person to Christ, whether adult or child. It is not the innocence of the children but their helplessness and dependence on God for their salvation that make them fit for the kingdom. In their dependency, they receive the kingdom when they are brought to Jesus by believing family members and received by him.

---

[3] To the theology of baptism and infant baptism in the Lutheran tradition, see also Chapter 26: "Solum Baptisma" – Baptism Alone, in Part Three.

As they grow up, their unconscious dependence on Jesus grows into a conscious dependence. Like physical life, spiritual life must grow and mature. What begins in baptism must come to open, conscious expression.

Baptism regularly includes prayers for the Holy Spirit and his gifts, and that needs to be taken seriously.[4] As we have seen above, prayer for the Spirit with an expectation of a tangible demonstration of spiritual gifts was part of the Christian initiation in the ancient church.[5]

People can deliberately leave God or fall away from him after baptism. They must be then brought back to repentance and faith. They do not need to be re-baptised, for God's promises at their baptism are still valid. Through faith, they can re-enter the kingdom and receive the gifts of the kingdom once again. In this sense, there is certainly a place for preaching conversion to baptised Christians who have fallen away after baptism.

Infant Baptism and the Gift of the Holy Spirit

Scripture speaks of even very small children believing, being filled with and manifesting the Spirit (Lk. 1:15; cf. Ps. 8:2; 22:9-10). While this does happen from time to time in charismatic circles, it is not the common experience in connection with infant baptism. So do children receive the gift of the Holy Spirit when they are baptised?

As we have seen, the primary focus in Acts is on the conscious experience and manifest demonstration of the Spirit in an adult believer's life. The natural development from childhood to adulthood has also its parallel in spiritual life. Accordingly, just as a little girl baptised in infancy later should be encouraged to take the conscious step of faith whereby she personally appropriates and confesses her calling as a child of God, she also should be encouraged to pray that Jesus would confirm her calling by filling her with the Holy Spirit so that she can be an effective witness.

This, in effect, has been the historic focus of the practice of confirmation, where the following blessing has been said in the Lutheran church:

> The Father in Heaven, for Jesus' sake, renew and increase in thee the gift of the Holy Ghost, to thy strengthening in faith, to thy growth in grace, to thy patience in suffering, and to the blessed hope of everlasting life.[6]

---

[4] In the order of the worship service for the Church of Sweden (Lutheran) it is suggested that the pastor, and, if possible, relatives and assistants, lay their hands on the child's head and pray silently, after which the pastor says, "God of life, fill [name of the child] with your Spirit", cf. *Gudstjänstordning för Svenska Kyrkan* (1982), p. 12.

[5] See Montague and McDonnell, *Baptism in the Spirit.*

[6] "Order of Confirmation", *Service Book and Hymnal* (Minneapolis, MN: Augsburg, 1958), p. 246. See also Theordore Jungkuntz, *Confirmation and the Charismata.*

Similar blessings or prayers may also be said, with or without laying on of hands, outside the formal setting of a confirmation liturgy. In the Charismatic renewal, this has been a common practice. Our life in Christ is dependent on the Holy Spirit from beginning to end, and his working is appropriate at every stage of our life and walk.

(40) God's Fatherly Provision

Closely connected with the Charismatic renewal's emphasis on the present kingdom of God and his plan of salvation is a revitalised faith in such things as God's guidance and direction, his healing power, and his fatherly willingness to provide for our material needs. Blessing is not only "spiritual". God touches and blesses every aspect of our lives. When Jesus had spoken of God's provision for food and clothes, he closed by saying, "But seek first his kingdom and his righteousness, and all these things will be given to you as well" (Mt. 6:33). The Holy Spirit is also renewing the classical faith in the *providence of God.*

Guidance

A Lutheran lay leader in Germany said that the most important aspect of charismatic renewal for him was the experience of *divine guidance.* He was a man with wide-ranging family, church, and business responsibilities. He had experienced a marked conversion through the ministry of the so-called *Marburger Kreis*, so he was no stranger to daily Bible reading and prayer, meaningful fellowship, and active participation in the life of the church. Yet, in common with many Christians, he had not seriously reckoned with *the possibility of actually knowing the will of God in regard to the basic life decisions that one must make.* This became a reality after his experience of being filled with the Holy Spirit. It did not make decisions easier – if anything, they became more difficult. But the way of approaching them was different: discerning the will of God became the first consideration rather than a prayer tacked on at the end of the process.[1]

Tormod Engelsviken has shared an experience of what he holds to be the Holy Spirit's guidance in theological matters. During a consultation arranged by the *Theological Working Group of the Lausanne Movement* in Oslo, Norway, in 1985, on the topic "the Holy Spirit and Mission", the participants reached a deadlock as charismatics and non-charismatics in the consultation could not reach agreement as to the place of "signs and wonders" in the church. Then some participants suggested that the theological debate be put on hold while each participant in prayer sought guidance from the Lord on the matter. All agreed to this and, after a break of about two hours, they came together again in a new spirit of openness and fellowship. Now they were able – almost "miraculously" – to reach a general agreement although there may still have been some differences of emphasis. The outcome of the

---

[1] Albrecht Fürstl Castell, in private conversation with Larry Christenson.

consultation was later presented in the book *God the Evangelist: How the Holy Spirit Works to Bring Men and Women to Faith.*[2] This practice of seeking first the Lord's will in prayer should more often be used in church meetings and theological debates. In this way, many unnecessary conflicts could be avoided and the church could move forward in unity.

This kind of testimony has been widely repeated throughout the Charismatic renewal. *One of the fundamental convictions of the movement is that God still speaks to people today as he did in Bible times.* Such gifts as prophecy, word of wisdom, and a word of knowledge often come to practical application at the point of guidance. Many also experience an inner voice or nudging, or feel that some verse or portion of Scripture speak to their needs for guidance in a personal way, maybe even apart from their historical context and meaning.

In the Charismatic renewal, teaching on divine guidance is usually rich in anecdotes, based on paradigms or analogies drawn from Scripture. Witness predominates. Whereas other aspects of the Charismatic renewal, such as baptism with the Holy Spirit or spiritual gifts, are often the subject for careful argument and persuasion, with guidance, it is more likely to be a lively report of what happened last week!

Two principles are almost universally stressed: the *authority of Scripture* and the *need for confirmation.* Both speak to the need of testing guidance against objective standards. Aside from this, however, teaching on guidance is generally unsystematised. The sovereign freedom of the Holy Spirit has probably been experienced here more than in any other area of Charismatic life and ministry. The Spirit does not always work according to neatly predictable rules. He will catch us by surprise, confront us with the unexpected, and only afterward will we see how appropriate and wise his dealings with us were. To be led by the Spirit means that we remain open and flexible, so that he can do in us and through us what his wisdom determines is necessary and good.

Providential Care

In this area, and especially in regard to healing, there is considerable theological diversity across the spectrum of the Charismatic renewal. Lutheran Charismatics have not generally drawn up a rigid doctrine about healing that sooner or later comes into conflict with reality. While Lutherans, along with Charismatics generally, have had a strong emphasis on healing, they have recognised that there is mystery here with which we must learn to live. Even the most committed and faith-filled Christian may be caught in the

---

[2] David F. Wells, *God the Evangelist: How the Holy Spirit Works to Bring Men and Women to Faith* (Grand Rapids, MI: Eerdmans, 1987).

grip of sickness. Until Christ comes again, death comes to us all, and most often through sickness.

A positive attitude toward prayer and a conviction that God will provide for us does not commit a person to a "theology of success or prosperity", although this charge is often levelled at Charismatics. To become successful in the eyes of the world is not the same as receiving God's promise that he will supply us with the things necessary for life (Mt. 6:19-33). God measures his blessings according to a kingdom standard that we may not always understand. He causes us to abound and to be abased (Phil. 4:11-13). He may shower us with unexpected abundance; then he may bring us into lean times. You don't have to talk with many Charismatics before you discover how real this is. God does not provide for everyone in the same way or at the same time. Faith in his provision is one side of the matter, but divine sovereignty is the other. Lack of faith is not the only or even main reason why people may not be healed or experience material blessing.

To recognise the ambiguities that we encounter regarding divine providence, however, is not the same as being resigned to them. It is at this point that the Charismatic renewal challenges the church. When our teaching about divine providence leads to resignation or indifference, something is wrong. The problem in the church today is not that people believe too much about God's providential care, but that they believe too little or too seldom. While many church members acknowledge that God can heal or intervene with special blessings, they do not generally expect it to happen in their case. At the level of practical experience, God's fatherly care is often little more than a theological phrase. It does not shape our day-to-day expectations.

The Lord wants that to change. Human logic may tote up a list of unanswered prayers and conclude that belief in divine providence is simplistic. The Holy Spirit, however, is the master of paradox. In one situation, he can speak his quiet word of comfort when we sit in darkness with unanswered questions; then at another times, he can quicken in us the faith that God will indeed intervene. The Lutheran church has generally emphasised the side of darkness and ambiguity. Overzealous Charismatics have emphasised the side of God's intervention. Both sides of the paradox are true, but only the Holy Spirit can lead us to apply the right truth at the right time.

Faith

One could almost reduce the Charismatic renewal to this: it is a *revitalisation of faith*. God's love and power are even more overwhelming than we thought or taught. There is a passive side to faith that quietly takes God at his Word. In a sense, this kind of faith is a foundation on which all else is built. But there is also an active side to faith that is greatly encouraged by concrete answers to prayer. Jesus does rebuke "little faith" (Lk. 8:25; 24:25) and praises "great faith" (Mt. 8:10; 15:28); but even "little faith" can accomplish great things (Lk. 17:5-6).

The Charismatic renewal's teaching on faith must be seen as parallel to its theme of dependence on the Holy Spirit. As we have seen in earlier chapters, faith is not a human achievement. It is a precious gift of God given to us through the Holy Spirit. Great faith, therefore, comes through a humble willingness to be totally dependent on what God gives. It is not the product of a legalistic pressure on a person to "have faith". It comes rather from trust and openness to the Spirit, as we feed on God's promises and our experiences as his beloved children.

Spoken Confession

Today, the Holy Spirit is stressing the importance not only of believing, but of *giving voice to what one believes*. Luther advised people in his day to recite the Creed aloud, for God and for the powers of darkness. His letter to pastor Severin Schulze in Belgern in 1545 applied this truth in a practical situation:

> Venerable Sir and Pastor!
>
> The tax collector in Torgau and the counsellor in Belgern have written and asked, on behalf of Mrs John Komer, that I give some good advice and comfort in order that her husband might be helped. I know of no worldly help to give. If the physicians are at a loss to find a remedy you may be sure that it is not a case of ordinary melancholy. It must be rather an affliction that comes from the devil, and this must be counteracted by the power of Christ and with the prayer of faith.
>
> This is what we do and what we have been accustomed to do, for a cabinetmaker here was similarly afflicted with madness and we cured him by prayer in Christ's name.
>
> Accordingly, you should proceed as follows: go to him with the deacon and two or three good men, confident that you as pastor of the place are clothed with the authority of the ministerial office. Lay your hands on him and say: 'Peace be with you, dear brother, from God the Father and from our Lord Jesus Christ.' Thereupon repeat the creed and the Lord's Prayer over him in a clear voice, and close with these words:
>
>> O God, almighty Father who have told us through your Son, "Verily, verily I say unto you, whatsoever you shall ask the Father in my name, he will give it to you," who has commanded and encouraged us to pray in his name, "Ask and you shall receive," and in like manner said, "Call on me in the day of trouble and I will deliver you and you shall glorify me," we unworthy sinners, relying on these words and commands, pray for your mercy with such faith as we can muster. Graciously deign to free this man from all evil and put to naught the work that Satan has done to him, to the honour of your name and the strengthening of the faith of

> believers, through the same Jesus Christ your Son our Lord, who lives and reigns with you, world without end. Amen.
>
> Then when you depart, lay your hands on the man again and say: 'These signs shall follow them that believe: they shall lay their hands on the sick and they shall recover.' Do this three times, once on each of three successive days. Meanwhile, let prayers be said from the chancel of the church publicly until God hears them [...] other counsel than this we have not.[3]

Charismatics know from experience the usefulness of this and similar practices. Yet the Holy Spirit also works discernment. One cannot make magic out of spoken confession. In other words, one cannot simply confess what one wants to happen, assuming that God will bring it to pass as long as it is taken from Scripture. Romans 10:9 says that "if you confess with your mouth, 'Jesus is Lord', and believe in your heart that God raised him from the dead, you will be saved." This promise cannot, however, be indiscriminately applied to everything one may choose to confess out loud. The word of faith must be quickened or energised by the Spirit. Otherwise, we are dealing not with faith but with presumption.

The Experiential Side of the Christian Life

Whatever else people may know about the Charismatic renewal, they know that *it has brought the experiential side of the Christian faith to the fore again.* Luther's sharp criticism against dead orthodoxy sounds like an echo of present-day conversations in the Charismatic renewal. If God is a real God and Jesus is a real Lord, he will not leave people unaffected in their emotions, thinking, and will – they will experience the reality of an encounter with him.

Lutheran Pietism echoed the same kind of concerns about Lutheran Orthodoxy that one might hear today from Charismatic Lutheran pastors: a stress on faith as an intellectual body of doctrine and a mechanical view of the means of grace and worship as if they had salvific effect merely by being performed, and suspicion of anything resembling a different or personal kind of piety. From this perspective, Pietist leaders such as Spener and Francke helped to expose the poverty of much current Lutheran theological practice in their day. They highlighted the need to return to an authentic Reformation view of faith that historian Williston Walker has called, "that vital relationship between the believer and God which Luther had taught [and for which] had been substituted very largely a faith which consisted in the acceptance of a dogmatic whole."[4]

---

[3] WABr 11, no. 4120, pp. 111-112.

[4] Williston Walker, *A History of the Christian Church* (New York: Scribner's, 1959), p. 445. See also the chapter on Pietism in this book.

The experiential dimension of the faith, however, must also be looked at from another perspective: the Holy Spirit does not renew the faith of some of God's people in order to exalt them above other Christians. During a meeting of Anglican, Lutheran, and Roman Catholic renewal leaders in England in 1985, this word of prophecy came during one of the worship sessions: "I am not calling you to tell the church that it is wrong, but to show the world that I am alive."[5]

If anything, a renewal of faith is a renewal of servanthood. The Holy Spirit wants to break down false barriers between charismatics and non-charismatics. It is certainly proper, indeed necessary, to make distinctions between Christians in terms of their function or calling in the body of Christ. Sometimes Scripture also makes distinctions between Christians in terms of the quality of their Christian life or commitment (for example, 1 Cor. 15:10; Phil. 2:21-22), but this is a dangerous game and generally to be avoided (2 Cor. 10:12). Historically, it has had a poor track record.

One historical example would be the Cathari. The Cathari, whose greatest activity was in southern France and northern Italy during the 12th century, laid particular emphasis on faith tested by suffering and life in the power of the Holy Spirit. One of their number, Alacaicus, wrote enthusiastically, "The Cathari are holy people. For the sake of Christ, they suffer great persecution, while the Catholics enjoy richly all the pleasures of the world."[6] Within their ranks, the Cathari differentiated between the "perfect" and the merely "believing." The latter were lacking in fundamental spiritual experience. Acceptance in the body of the "perfect" was gained through the impartation of the Paraclete, that is, the gift of the Holy Spirit. Their rigorous ethic went hand in hand with a perfectionistic understanding of the church. Their emphasis on experience gave vitality to their movement, but their lack of concern for biblical teaching made them highly susceptible to syncretism in many forms. Their strength became a weakness because they used it as a basis for making unwise distinctions among Christians. Charismatics would well be warned by such an example.

A case in point would be the loose way that Charismatics sometimes throw around terms like "Spirit-filled" as a designation for Charismatics. People who have been filled with the Spirit will surely need to be encouraged to be filled again, or filled continually (Eph. 5:18). In that sense, Charismatics will be as much in need of "filling" as some non-charismatics. Some non-charismatics may be powerfully filled with the Spirit, even though they have not shared some of the experiences associated with the Charismatic renewal.

---

[5] Reported by Larry Christenson in a letter to the constituency of the International Lutheran Renewal Center, 27th November 1985.

[6] Peter Meinhold, *Geschichte der kirchlichen Historiographie*, vol. 1 (Freiburg/Munich: Karl Alber, 1967), p. 212.

All Christians have the Holy Spirit (Rom. 8:9; 1 Cor. 12:13). When personal experience is preached in a manner that exalts one group of Christians over another rather than exalting Christ, Luther's battle with the enthusiasts of his day becomes relevant once again, with his emphasis on the "external Word" in Scripture, preaching, baptism, and the Lord's Supper. Experience can serve to strengthen and confirm faith; it should not be a source of division among the faithful.

(41) Truth and Authority

Christ as the Truth

Pentecost was a demonstration that Jesus was Lord and Messiah (Acts 2:36). It transformed the lives and ministries of the disciples: they were supernaturally empowered to be *witnesses of the truth concerning Jesus*.

On the day of Pentecost, Peter boldly proclaimed the *truth of the resurrection* facing those who had rejected Jesus as Messiah. But truth was not only what was proclaimed. The *outpouring of the Spirit was truth as event*, truth confirmed by wind and fire and tongues, truth embodied in a band of disciples who had been weak and fearful but who now were bold in the Spirit. It was truth that reverberated with authority, calling people to repent and turn to *him who is the Truth*.

The issue of truth and authority is at the heart of the Charismatic renewal. It calls us to live under the lordship of Christ, to bring every thought captive to him who is the Truth (2 Cor. 10:5) and who has all authority in heaven and on earth (Mt. 28:18). This is not a simple human possibility, a matter merely of subscribing to the right theory. The ministry of the gospel, the apostle Paul reminds us, is a gift of God's grace given "through the working of his [God's] power" (Eph. 3:7). Only the dynamic of the Holy Spirit can establish truth and authority in the church.

Alan G. Padgett who is a professor of Systematic Theology at Luther Seminary in Saint Paul, USA, understands "truth as the *mediated disclosure of being* (or reality)". He argues that this concept of truth has its roots in Scripture, and that "the value of this proposed understanding of truth is its flexibility. It allows us to find truth in art and poetry, *in spiritual experience and religious worship*, as well as in logic and science" (italics added).[1] Thus truth claims may have different forms, yet they are true as long as they disclose reality.

Truth and Life

An aspect of the Charismatic renewal that deserves more attention is its concern for truth. Discussion of the movement often centres on the question of experience, but that is part of a much larger question, the question of truth. When the Holy Spirit leads, he leads into truth (Jn 16:13). *Charismatic*

---

[1] John G. Padgett, "'I Am the Truth': An understanding of Truth from Christology for Scripture", in Alan G. Padgett & Patrick R. Keifert (eds), *But Is It All True? The Bible and the Question of Truth* (Grand Rapids, MI: Eerdmans, 2006), pp. 106-107.

experience is important because it is an aspect of truth into which the Spirit wants to lead the church.

The Spirit teaches us to consider truth in a new way. Truth cannot be adequately expressed *merely* in terms of scholarly opinions, theological perspectives, or even true doctrine. These things can exist quite apart from spiritual life. Truth is related to life. It is the reality of the kingdom of God that has come in Jesus Christ. This truth is experienced wherever the Holy Spirit makes salvation in Christ a reality in the lives of believers. Jesus said,

> I am the way and the truth and the life (Jn 14:6).
>
> Yet a time is coming and has now come when the true worshippers will worship the Father in spirit and truth, for they are the kind of worshippers the Father seeks (Jn 4:23).

Truth is like the promised land: it is given to God's covenant people. It is given through the word of promise in order that we shall walk into it under the guidance of the Holy Spirit. Truth is not something we merely think about. It is something we experience – in reading and hearing the Word of God, in the sacraments, in praise and worship, in spiritual warfare, in exercising the gifts of the Spirit, in service, and in suffering. As we live in the truth, we experience the grace and truth that came and still are coming through Christ (Jn 1:17).

> To the Jews who had believed in him, Jesus said, 'If you hold to my teaching, you are really my disciples. Then you will know the truth, and the truth will set you free' (Jn 8:32).

We learn what it means that "every place that the sole of your foot will tread on I have given to you, as I promised to Moses" (Josh. 1:3).

Scripture and Experience

Truth related to experience and truth related to Scripture has sometimes been set in opposition to one another. In the Charismatic renewal, however, it has generally been the case that experience is measured by the standard of Scripture. Charismatics, both Lutheran and non-Lutheran, underscore Luther's insistence that the Word is primary and that experience must be weighed against that standard.

In the Charismatic renewal, the Holy Spirit has created a profound respect for the written Scripture as the true and powerful Word of God for people today. The Spirit creates an expectancy of encounter with the triune God through personal reading and study of the Bible. Without the Holy Spirit, the study of Scripture would be another weary effort of the flesh. Scripture would be dead letter, not life-giving truth. The focus of expectation must be not simply on the Bible, but on the Holy Spirit and his use of Scripture to accomplish God's will with us.

The Holy Spirit creates a church that desires to be guided into the full truth of Scripture, into fresh insights and new understanding. He shows the church where it needs to be reformed, corrected, and renewed in order to be faithful and obedient to the never-changing Word. He shows where the church must stand fast in the truth without compromise. A Spirit-led church is a teachable church, willing to subject all areas of its life and doctrine to the scrutiny of Scripture, under the guidance of the Holy Spirit.

When the Spirit brings renewal, the Bible comes alive as God's personal letter to us in our present, concrete existence. The Holy Spirit inspires believers to become a Bible-believing, Bible-studying, Bible-formed, Bible-living people.

The Authority of the Bible

One of the *characteristics of renewal movements in general is a heightened sense of the authority of Scripture.*

This was clearly the case, for example, in Pietism. Spener and Francke advocated widespread use of the Scriptures in the life of the church and of each individual Christian. They taught the depravity of humanity and the need for regeneration and sanctification through the biblical message. Spener emphasised that lay people should read the Bible extensively, that they should study entire books consecutively, and that they should gather for house meetings to discuss the Scriptures in "an apostolic kind of church meeting."[2]

When Francke began his theological professorship at Halle, Germany, he replaced the study of philosophy with biblical exegesis, exchanged polemics for active Christian service, and replaced scholastic commentaries with his own Bible lectures, thus reforming theological education.[3] In general, he followed Luther's distaste for too much philosophy in theological education and moved at every hand to establish the pre-eminence of Scripture for Christian life and ministry, propounding 2 Timothy 3:16-17:

> All Scripture is God-breathed and is useful for teaching, rebuking, correcting and training in righteousness, so that the man of God may be thoroughly equipped for every good work.

---

[2] Philipp Jakob Spener, *Pia desideria*, edited by Theodore G. Tappert (Philadelphia, PA: Fortress, 1964), p. 87. See also the chapter on Pietism in this book.

[3] Marie E. Richard, *Philipp Jakob Spener and His Work. Augustus Hermann Francke and his Work* (Philadelphia, PA: Lutheran Publication Society, 1897), pp. 108-109.

Within the Charismatic movement, the authority of Scripture has been assumed from the outset. At a Charismatic conference in 1975, Lutheran pastor Larry Christenson made this remark:

> One of the issues that has given real strength to the Charismatic renewal is the fact that it has accepted the basic ground rules [of scriptural authority] without debate. I can't recall ever participating in a charismatic teaching session or prayer group where there was a basic argument about any of the cardinal doctrines of the Christian faith, such as justification by faith, the virgin birth, the atonement, the divinity of Christ, the validity of the moral law. All of these things are accepted without question.[4]

The Conference of Bishops of the United Evangelical Lutheran Church in Germany issued a document on the Charismatic renewal in 1976 in which they said, "We note with gratitude that these [charismatic] communities, as arms of the Lutheran church, take their stand on Holy Scripture."[5]

Roman Catholic participants in the Charismatic renewal, from a slightly different perspective, likewise hold to a high view of scriptural authority:

> Strong and increasing pressures on God's people are trying to choke out the Word of God. Within the church, these pressures are manifested in a subtle but powerful spirit of criticism, scepticism, and uncertainty. Once these seeds of doubt are sown, the protection that the certainty and clarity of God's Word was intended to provide for his people is removed, and it is easy to be seduced into many different things. The Catholic church teaches that once you have formed your conscience on the objective Word of God and the teaching of the church, then your conscience is in a position to tell you the right thing to do. But today many people are saying, 'I'm going to read everything, experience everything, and see what I feel is right to me.' This is an incredible attack on the Word of God and on the authority of God.[6]

The Danish pastor and renewal leader, Ole Skjerbæk Madsen's statement on biblical authority illustrates the high regard for Scripture that one typically finds among Lutheran Charismatics:

> If the church wants to be the church, and to know God, it must continue steadfastly in the apostles' teaching. With the Confessions of our church, we declare that the Word of God, as it is found in the prophetic and apostolic writings – the whole Bible – is the authority in the church. A church that does

---

[4] Christenson, *Back to Square One*, p. 73.

[5] McDonnell, ed., *Presence, Power, Praise*, Vol. 2, p. 269.

[6] The Catholic charismatic leader Ralph Martin in a speech given at the 1980 Notre Dame National Charismatic Conference.

> not honour the whole Bible as God's Word and authority in the church, by the same token does not know Christ Jesus as Lord – he who is the Word of God.[7]

Critics who contend that Charismatics "set experience above Scripture" are hard put to come up with the evidence. In response to a critic who maintained that Lutheran charismatic leader Larry Christenson "had often indicated that the Christian faith is based on experience and that theology is only an explanation of that experience", Christenson replied in a letter that represents the position of the Lutheran Charismatic renewal:

> Nothing could be further from the truth [...] I am quite sure that I have never done so, for it is absolutely contrary to my personal conviction [...] I accept the Bible as the inspired Word of God and as the only infallible rule of faith and life. I would insist that the Scriptures define, explain, interpret, and take precedence over the experience, not the reverse.
>
> I *have* said that Scripture itself is the record of what the men of God who wrote the Scripture *experienced.* In other words, they did not arrive at their writings by mere speculation or imagining, as is true of many humanly wrought philosophies. The Christian faith is the *empirical* faith, par excellence (cf. 2 Pet. 1:16-19; 1 Jn 1:1-4). Men encountered the living God in outward events, and inwardly, as they were given to understand the meaning that God wanted them to see in those events [...].
>
> Of course, in one sense the Bible does not need any corroboration; it is a faithful testimony whether received or not. Yet it is the nature of our evangelistic enterprise to bear personal witness that what the Bible says has also proven true in one's own experience. It is in this sense that I recognise and appreciate "experience", namely as that which bears witness to the truth revealed in Scripture. Whether this is a testimony to forgiven sin, answered prayer, healing, or growth in understanding [...] is a secondary matter. The primary thing is that it accords with Scripture, not be in contradiction to Scripture.[8]

Through the experience of the Holy Spirit, the Bible ceases to be merely a formal authority. It becomes a practical authority for everyday Christian believing and living. The gap of 2000 years is bridged. The Spirit makes the words of the prophets and apostles relevant for people today.

Bertil Gärtner, Lutheran bishop of the Gothenburg diocese in Sweden and an acknowledged New Testament scholar, challenged his audience with this thought in a workshop at a European charismatic conference in 1986: "There will never be renewal if the Bible is not at the centre. It must be the book above all others that we study. It must be our authority." He went on to say, however, that if we accept the Bible as our authority, we will walk contrary

[7] Ole Skjerbæk Madsen, "The Authority of Scripture", *Ånd og Liv* (December 1982), pp. 5-6.

[8] Larry Christenson, personal correspondence with John MacArthur, 15th November 1979, in regard to MacArthur's article in *Moody Monthly* (November 1979), p. 38.

to many theologians and leaders in the church today. He quoted a Harvard theologian who described the Bible as "a great but archaic monument in Western culture."[9]

Charismatics would respond that, although the languages of the Bible are those of different old human cultures and the biblical revelation took place in distant history, the Bible remains in every generation the Holy Spirit's primary instrument for conveying God's wisdom and will to those who will receive it. The Bible brings us the narrative of God's saving acts in history and the Spirit's authentic interpretation of those acts. This is not a demonstrable fact, but a statement of faith. Only the Holy Spirit can establish this authority of Scripture in the believer.

The Place Accorded to Tradition

In the Roman Catholic and Orthodox churches, the authority of *sacred tradition* is placed alongside the authority of Scripture, and Charismatics from these churches generally hold to this understanding.[10] Also among some Protestant Charismatics there seems to be an increased appreciation of the place and value of tradition.

Tradition is operative among any group of Christians. The written creeds and confessions are indicative of that. The three ancient creeds, especially the *Nicene Creed,* are acknowledged by most churches. In addition, Anglicans have their *Thirty-Nine Articles* and *The Book of Common Prayer*; the Reformed, their *Westminster* and *Heidelberg Catechisms*, the Methodists, their *Twenty-five Articles*, the Lutherans, their *Augsburg Confession, Luther's Small Catechism* and, for some Lutherans, the whole *Book of Concord.* In our time, the *Lausanne Covenant* (1974) serves as an ecumenical, evangelical confession. *These confessional writings have authority in the churches in so far as they reflect the teaching of the Bible.* They may be viewed as theological norms that are themselves "normed" by the Scriptures (Latin: *norma normata*).[11] All these churches, and also in more informal ways, Baptists, Congregationalists, Pentecostals, and independents of every stripe, not to mention local congregations and fellowships, have their distinctive traditions in theology, worship, and practice that can, on occasion, carry the weight of considerable authority.

---

[9] Bertil Gärtner in a workshop of Acts 86, an all-European ecumenical charismatic conference held in Birmingham, England, 23th-27th July, 1986.

[10] Kevin Ranaghan, then chairman of the Catholic Charismatic Renewal in the United States, speaking to an annual seminar of charismatic leaders in St Louis, Missouri, in May 1982, pointed out that Catholic teaching on the place of tradition is accepted as normative by Catholic charismatics.

[11] To the relation between the Scriptures and the Confessions in the Lutheran Church, see also the chapter "'Sola Scriptura' – Scripture Alone" in Part Three of this book.

One of the characteristics of the Charismatic renewal has been a heightened appreciation of the *corporate* aspect of the Christian faith, and this has resulted in a practical, if not a formal, emphasis on the value of tradition. The movement has tended to play down the Protestant myth of an authoritative Scripture that is unaffected by human interpretation and tradition.

What good is Scripture in the hands of people operating independently of the Holy Spirit? As the Scripture itself is the work of the Spirit, so also must be our understanding and interpretation of it. One of the ways that he instructs us is through the wisdom and understanding that he has already given to the church in times past.

(42) Confirming the Word

The disciples of Jesus were sent by him to represent him and speak in his name; that is, on his behalf and with his authority. It was actually Jesus himself who worked through them. Paul says:

> I glory in Christ Jesus in my service to God. I will not venture to speak of anything except *what Christ has accomplished through me* in leading the Gentiles to obey God by what I have said and done (Rom. 15:17-18).

Jesus appointed and sent out his apostles and other disciples already during his earthly ministry (Lk. 9:1-2; 10:1-3). They were to do the same work that Jesus did: preach the kingdom of God, heal the sick and drive out all demons (Luke 9:1-2). For this, they were given "authority" (Greek: *exousia*) and "power" (Greek: *dunamis*).

The consequence of this sending with authority and power from Jesus was that *their words were as the words of Jesus himself*: "He who listens to you listens to me; and he who rejects you rejects me; but he who rejects me rejects him who sent me" (Lk. 10:16; cp. Mt. 10:40; Jn 13:20).

The witnesses of Jesus speak on his behalf: "We are therefore Christ's ambassadors, as though God was making his appeal through us. We implore you on Christ's behalf: Be reconciled to God" (2 Cor. 5:20). This authority to speak and act on Christ's behalf does not include all thoughts and experiences that the minister might have – fruitful and inspiring as they may be – but is dependent on the minister's *faithfulness to the Word of God in the Bible*. This applies to the use of all spiritual gifts that express themselves through words:

> Each one should use whatever gift he has received to serve others, faithfully administering God's grace in its various forms. *If anyone speaks, he should do it as one speaking the very words of God.* If anyone serves, he should do it with the strength God provides, so that in all things God may be praised through Jesus Christ (1 Pet. 4:10-11).

To speak God's word on behalf of Christ is a great privilege given to humans but it is also a great responsibility for which they will be held accountable.

This authority is not, however, an authority that works automatically apart from the Holy Spirit. With the authority of the witnesses as representatives of Christ comes the endowment with the power of the Holy Spirit. Without the empowering of the Holy Spirit, any "truth" that we proclaim will be without authority. Truth without spiritual authority will be without effect in spiritual matters. "For the kingdom of God is not a matter of talk but of power" (1 Cor. 4:20). Jesus, filled with the Spirit, taught with authority, differently from the Jewish teachers of the law (Mt. 7:28-29; Lk. 4:14-15, 18-19, cp. Mic. 3:8).

Spiritual authority does not depend on acceptance by a secular or ecclesiastical system. These systems may accept or resist spiritual authority, but they cannot control it. An ecclesiastical system may provide the framework in which spiritual authority is exercised but, without the dynamic of the Spirit, there will be no functioning of real authority. Spiritual authority is an authentication given by the Spirit when he leads us into the truth. It is God's confirmation of the Word of God.

This understanding of spiritual authority has a long and honourable tradition in the church. Ignatius, the martyr-bishop of Antioch (ca 115 A.D.), was the forerunner of an "Asia Minor theology," and he is numbered among those theologians who, along with the gospel of John, gave the Eastern Church its unique character. He is described as a "charismatic" bishop.[1] He is generally recognised as the first "monarchical bishop", yet he did not see his authority as deriving from an ecclesiastical office. He usually began his letters with the words, "Ignatius, the God-bearer" (Greek: *theophoros*). He based his spiritual authority on the knowledge that Christ lived in him. The expressions "indwelling" (Greek: *enoikesis*) and "union" (Greek: *henosis*) with Christ make clear the nature of his own spiritual experience and pneumatology. For Ignatius, as in the New Testament, the experience of Jesus Christ and of the Holy Spirit were clearly and inseparably linked.

Ignatius sealed his testimony with his blood. Like Stephen, he saw heaven opened (Acts 7:55).[2] Before his martyrdom, Ignatius wrote to the church at Rome: "Let me be given to the wild beasts, for by their means I can attain to God. I am God's wheat, and I am being ground by the teeth of beasts, so that the pure bread of Christ may be made of me."[3] Ignatius did not speak as a hero, brave unto death. Rather, Christ, the one who is present in his church and who brings the dead to life, spoke in him. Therein lay Ignatius' authority.

In charismatic leadership conferences, one frequently hears charismatic authority defined as "the authority of influence rather than of office". It is interesting that one so strongly associated with the ecclesiastical office of bishop as Ignatius should speak so "charismatically" on the question of authority. To some extent, it reflects the observation of Lutheran theologian

---

[1] Peter Meinhold, *Studien zu Ignatius von Antiochien* (Wiesbaden: Franz Steiner, 1979), p. 9. See the letters of Ignatius of Antioch: Polycarp 2, 2; Philadelphians 7, 1; Trallians 4, 1; Ephesians 20, 1.

[2] Ernst Benz (ed), *Die Vision. Erfahrungsformen und Bilderwelt* (Stuttgart: Ernst Klett, 1969), p. 420, n. 8.

[3] Ignatius, *Letter to the Romans* 4, 1.

Hans von Campenhausen that in the second century ecclesiastical authority and charismatic authority still had a good working relationship.[4]

Although in the later history of the church authority has most often been combined with or based on ecclesiastical office and/or theological education, the history of revival and renewal, however, shows that lay and unlearned people are often the instruments of the Holy Spirit. All of the leaders mentioned above in connection with the Pietistic movements, both ordained and unordained, educated and uneducated, old and young, men and women exuded spiritual authority and served in ministries granted them by the Holy Spirit. This is also the case in the present Charismatic renewal.

Confirmation of Truth through Signs and Wonders

The truth and authority of Jesus' ministry were confirmed by the signs he performed,[5] and Jesus promised the same kind of confirmation to his disciples: "I tell you the truth, anyone who has faith in me will do what I have been doing. He will do even greater things than these because I am going to the Father" (Jn 14:12).

The Charismatic renewal has been sounding this theme in most of the established churches of Western culture. But the note is being heard even more clearly from some of the churches and movements in the Majority World, almost all of which are charismatic, although many have had little or no historical connection with the Charismatic movement as such.[6] These churches are concerned about truth, but by that they do not mean simply a more carefully worded statement of church doctrine. Behind their phenomenal growth is the biblical understanding of truth as something that must not only be taught but also done in the power of the Spirit. They are

---

[4] Hans von Campenhausen, *Ecclesiastical Authority and Spiritual Power in the Church of the First Three Centuries*, translated by J.A. Baker (Stanford, CA: Stanford University Press, 1969), p. 178.

[5] See also the section on "signs and wonders" in Part Two of this book.

[6] An example of this may be the *Ethiopian Evangelical Church Mekane Yesus*, which in 2021 is the largest Lutheran church in the world with more than 10 million members. It is a strongly charismatic church which experienced and practiced healing and expulsion of evil spirits long before the arrival of the Charismatic renewal in Ethiopia, see Tormod Engelsviken, "Exorcism and Healing in the Evangelical Churches in Ethiopia", *Journal of Mission Theology* 1(1), (1991), pp. 80-92. A Danish version of the article is "Åndeuddrivelse og helbredelse i de evangelikale kirker i Etiopien," *Mission – Nordisk missionstidsskrift* 105(1), (1994), pp. 19-24. Similar experiences are found in Madagascar, China, Germany and many other countries around the world (see for example the chapter on Lutheran precursors of the Charismatic renewal in this book).

churches that expect the proclamation of truth to be accompanied by signs and wonders.[7]

What they are saying to some of the established churches is something like this: "If you talk about salvation and sing about God's marvellous deeds but do not pray for the sick, do not deal with demonic bondage, leave no room for God's miraculous intervention and confirmation, your 'truth' is too theoretical. If you declare that the Holy Spirit brings us to faith, but do not demonstrate his presence in your ministry, your 'truth' is deficient."

In 1960, representatives from American, German, and Scandinavian missions met together with African synods to discuss the formation of one united Lutheran church in southern Africa. Many voices were raised against coming together into one united church. Just before the vote was taken, a loud thunderclap was heard. The people were stunned because it was the dry season and there were no clouds in the sky. The Africans spontaneously cried: "The Lord has spoken!" The vote to form the united church was unanimous.[8] This kind of experience is not easily accepted in churches in which ecclesiastical machinery is expected to operate in a predictable way. Some charismatic groups would have trouble with it as well. The uncomfortable fact for us to ponder, however, is that it is not foreign to Scripture!

Demonstration of Truth in Life

As a spiritual awakening initiated by the Holy Spirit, the Charismatic renewal is called to help the church not only to articulate truth, but to *demonstrate* it. As a movement, it is spreading and having effect worldwide – in deeply traditional churches, in congregations, in groups, in the lives of individual Christians. In the setting of Lutheran folk churches, the movement is sometimes referred to simply as "spiritual congregational renewal". That says several things: renewal is genuinely taking place; the Holy Spirit is the one behind it; it comes to a focus in the congregation. It also says that the experience of truth is a reality that must be continually renewed in the life of God's people.

If the Charismatic renewal is to be an advocate of the truth, it must itself be as open to the judgement of Scripture as it calls the church to be. Is the fruit of the Spirit (Gal. 5:22-23) evident in the lives of charismatic leaders?

---

[7] See for example the whole issue of the journal *Christian Life*, October 1982, which covers in depth the course "Signs and Wonders and Church Growth" at *Fuller Theological Seminary* in California, USA, from a biblical, historical, theological, and practical perspective. See also Keener, *Miracles,* where he documents that miracles are experienced by millions of people all over the world today and are crucial for the growth of the church.

[8] The Swede Helge Fosseus has supplied this information from his experience as a missionary bishop in southern Africa (See Appendix).

Does the ministry taking place in the context of the renewal measure up to biblical standards? This kind of evaluation, of course, is somewhat subjective. But charismatics should welcome it. They should invite church leadership and membership to test the renewal on the basis of biblical criteria. Charismatic leaders should also encourage participants in the movement to place their beliefs and practices under the scrutiny of Scripture.

At the same time, charismatics challenge church leaders, and all segments of the church, to examine their positions and practices in the light of the Word of God. Testing is vital in order to avoid deception, on the one hand, or rejection of truth, on the other. The institutional church needs to examine itself as diligently as it scrutinises renewal movements. Frequently, the rise of renewal groups is an evidence of an institution's failure to hear and adjust to the purposes of the Spirit.

Charismatics have not always given sufficient attention to the manner in which they challenge the church. The renewal cannot force its message on the church. It can only declare it and live it in the power of the Spirit, openly inviting the church to test the message against the Word, leaving the results to God. The truth and authority radiating from revivals depend on their willingness to have no official power and influence, to serve the cause of truth from a position of weakness and humility.

Charismatics often experience a *loss of prestige* as a gateway into new freedom and new authority in their ministries. A fresh experience of the Spirit may put them at odds with institutional goals and leadership and bring them to that old doorway into the kingdom of God: death to self, resurrection with Christ, fellowship in his sufferings, and freedom to proclaim and do the truth, which is the ground of true authority. Unashamed commitment to biblical truth will inevitably bring church leaders into conflict with standards of truth and behaviour that prevail in secular society and in secularised segments of the church, a reality that church leaders are not always eager to embrace. Leaders who are bound by the settled conformity of colleagues and tradition may have too much to lose – too much status, too much acceptance, too much influence, too much approval, too much prestige. The presence of a widespread renewal movement challenges church leaders to weigh their commitment to institution and tradition and human opinions against their commitment to biblical truth and authority.

Charismatics are not what Luther called *Schwärmer* – spiritual enthusiasts who reject biblical authority, institution and organisation, order and tradition.[9] Their experience helps them recognise a neglected biblical perspective: truth is something we enter in led by the Spirit. Only as we *do* the truth can we come to *know* the truth. "Jesus answered, 'My teaching is

[9] Karlfried Froelich, "Charismatic Manifestations and the Lutheran Incarnational Stance", in Paul Opsahl (ed), *The Holy Spirit in the Life of the Church* (Minneapolis, MN: Augsburg, 1978), pp. 141, 149-150.

not my own. It comes from him who sent me. *If anyone chooses to do God's will, he will find out whether my teaching comes from God or whether I speak on my own*'" (Jn 7:16-17).

Not One Way among Many

The Charismatic renewal does not represent simply one among several possible ways of building or renewing the life of individuals and congregations. Its central emphasis is not something that could just as well be replaced by another renewal emphasis. Rather, it focuses on the truth by which the church and every other movement in the church must live, which is total *reliance on the Holy Spirit*. This is *not an optional way*, but is the *only way* in which the Lord continually refreshes and renews his church.

As in other areas, so also in questions of truth, charismatics call for a radical dependence on the Holy Spirit. This is not a stance or a blessing for the few. It is a challenge to the whole church to be led by the Spirit into the truth.

What effect this approach to truth will have on one's standing in the established church or in the secular community is hard to tell. For some, surely, it will mean a loss of prestige or position. For some, even persecution. Others will find an eager response to their words and ministry. All of that is, in a sense, incidental. It is the province of the Spirit. Our part is to do the truth. The Lord tells us plainly how that will happen: "When he, the Spirit of truth, comes, he will guide you into all truth" (Jn 16:13).

Part Five

Led by the Holy Spirit

Practical Concerns in the Charismatic Renewal

Therefore, brothers, we have an obligation – but it is not to the sinful nature, to live according to it. For if you live according to the sinful nature, you will die; but if by the Spirit you put to death the misdeeds of the body, you will live, because those who are led by the Spirit of God are sons of God.

Romans 8:12-14

(43) The Power of the Indwelling Christ and the Fullness of the Holy Spirit

In this final part of the book, we shall look more in detail at the practical concerns of the Charismatic renewal. It is, however, mandatory *not to separate* the biblical understanding (Part Two), the historical Lutheran perspectives (Part Three), the doctrinal concerns (Part Four) and the practical concerns in this Part Five, because they all overlap to a large extent and because one part may inform the other and vice versa. As we now turn to the final part dealing primarily with practical concerns, let us have this important interdependence between doctrine and practice in mind.

Union with Christ

Charismatics talk freely about Jesus' presence and activity in their daily lives. In the Charismatic renewal, it is common and acceptable to share personal religious experience. This readiness to talk about Jesus points to a widely shared reality in the Charismatic renewal: a heightened awareness of Jesus' presence, not only in regard to salvation, but in one's daily life. Jesus pictured our inner life as a well that receives from him a spring of living water that never runs dry (Jn 4:14). He said that when people come to him and drink, the Holy Spirit flows out of them like a river (Jn 7:37-39). Charismatics see words in the Scriptures like these as both the source and confirmation of a relationship with Christ that is all-consuming.

Our relationship with Christ is not a matter of co-operation between two independent partners, not even if we allow the Lord the greater share of the credit and take the smaller part for ourselves. It is not a matter of asking him to help us, as though we were essentially self-sufficient creatures but could make a better performance if we had a little help. It is rather that we have no life, no possibilities except as the Holy Spirit joins Christ's life to our life. Christ communicates his life to us, and we respond in faith to this impartation of life.

Our response is critical, of course, because God will not do anything in us against our own will, without the "yes" of faith. But this is something quite different from striving in our own strength to grow spiritually – clenching our teeth, screwing up our willpower, targeting our resolve – and then calling for an assist from "grace" when we come up short. The way of growth is, rather, along the lines of faith, recognising the mighty presence of the Holy Spirit, yielding to him as he communicates Christ's life to us, surrendering to him and allowing him to direct and control us in such a way that Christ's life can be released.

Why is this life foreign to so many? Maybe it is because we simply have not in faith welcomed the Holy Spirit into our lives. We have not prayed expectantly, with the church through the centuries, "Come, Holy Spirit." For it is the powerful working of the Spirit that creates, sustains, and makes fruitful our life in Christ.

The Fullness of the Holy Spirit

How one *grows as a Christian* has been a more widespread emphasis in the Charismatic renewal than how one becomes a Christian in the first place. Its teaching has been experience-oriented: it has sought the *practical application* of spiritual truth in people's lives. Central to this quest has been teaching on the fullness of the Holy Spirit as the dynamic power of God that makes true growth possible.

A new dimension of growth and Spirit-anointed ministry can open up when one prays to receive the fullness of the Holy Spirit. When the Lord fills us with the Holy Spirit, he often effects immediate and even surprising changes in our life and behaviour. It is as if, at the outset, he wants to imprint on our consciousness the reality of the Spirit's presence and power, perhaps with a view to sustain us in the times of struggle that lie ahead. An experience of being filled with the Spirit can be tremendously important in releasing the dynamic of Christ's life in us and through us.

The Theology of Being Filled with the Holy Spirit

As we have suggested earlier, the manner in which one experiences being filled with the Spirit can vary considerably, but the reality of it is necessary. Perhaps the greatest single theological contribution of classical Pentecostalism has been its insistence that effective ministry and mission require the infilling of the Holy Spirit. Theologians in mainline churches have tended to dismiss the so-called "second blessing" theology of the Holiness and Pentecostal movements, which holds to a distinct work of the Holy Spirit subsequent to salvation. What they cannot dismiss, however, is the essential truth that is imbedded there. The idea of a distinction between the work of the Holy Spirit by which we receive new life and a work by which we are empowered for ministry was not introduced by Pentecostalism. As we have already showed, a "charismatic work of the Spirit" can be traced from the pages of the New Testament, through the church fathers, into every century of the church's history.[1]

---

[1] See also Harold D. Hunter, *Spirit Baptism: A Pentecostal Alternative* (Lanham, MD: University Press of America, 1983), pp. 29, 193.

Pentecostal theology has had an undeniable influence on the Charismatic renewal, especially in the early years of the movement. *Charismatic theologians, however, have also sought to bridge the gap between the Pentecostal way of describing the Spirit's work and the traditional Protestant and Catholic ways of doing it.*[2] Bridging this gap is also one of the purposes of this book. The task is twofold: on the one hand, to affirm the essential truth of a charismatic work of the Spirit; on the other hand, to bring an added historical perspective to the way that truth is presented theologically. Lutherans, for instance, will bring to the inquiry their particular understanding of the Reformation and Pietism, Catholics and Anglicans their understanding of confirmation, Methodists their emphasis on sanctification.[3]

---

[2] See for instance "The Holy Spirit in the Charismatic Life and Renewal of the Church Today", in J.D. Douglas (ed), *Let the Earth Hear His Voice: International Congress of World Evangelization at Lausanne.* Official Reference Volume (Minneapolis, MN: World Wide Publications, 1975), pp. 1150-1153, cf. also the doctoral dissertation of Tormod Engelsviken, *The Gift of the Spirit;* Kilian McDonnell (ed), "Theological and Pastoral Orientations on the Catholic Charismatic Renewal: Malines Document I", in *Presence, Power Praise*, pp. 13-69; Christenson, *Charismatic Renewal Among Lutherans.*

[3] We refer to the presentation of Pietism in a previous chapter, but would like to add the following here: Philip Jacob Spener and August Hermann Francke, who became the chief spokesmen for Pietism, created a tidal wave of influence in their day – a tidal wave which is still being felt in the Lutheran church. They both desired to be orthodox Lutherans who, however, placed strong emphasis on the doctrine of sanctification. One prominent Lutheran historian believes that they were the inspiration for John Wesley's major emphasis on sanctification, which would put them in the line of influence that helped shape the Pentecostal and Charismatic movements, cf. Tappert (ed), *Pia Desideria,* p. 24. In *Pia Desideria,* Spener stressed that pastors, first of all, must experience spiritual renewal. Francke maintained that all seminarians should be professionally guided into the devotional life "because theology is a practical discipline and does not consist only of knowledge and study", A.H. Francke, *Of Useful Preaching: A Guide to the reading and Study of the Holy Scriptures* (Philadelphia, PA: David Hogan, 1923), p. 112ff. The leader of the Moravian Pietistic missionary movement, Count von Zinzendorf, and the Moravians had a profound influence on John and Charles Wesley. The Methodist revival, and the Holiness movement in America that grew out of it, were the precursors of the modern-day Pentecostal and Charismatic movements (Synan, *The Holiness-Pentecostal Movement in the United States*, 1971, pp. 217-223). In this entire line of development, the issue of personal religious experience and spiritual growth is written large. John Wesley's heart was "strangely warmed" as Luther's *Preface to Romans* was being read at a meeting in Aldersgate in 1738. Wesley proclaimed and longed for the fullness of Christian experience, of entire sanctification and the indwelling of the Holy Spirit. For Wesley, Christian perfection is directly linked to Pentecostal reality. While Lutherans may not agree with Wesley's doctrine on the "second blessing", his concern for sanctification and the experience of the Holy Spirit is shared by Lutheran charismatics.

With the experience of the Charismatic renewal, the Holy Spirit has thrust us beyond the point of simply theorising. Around the world and across the whole spectrum of the body of Christ, people are experiencing the reality of being filled with the Spirit.

The Need for the Fullness of the Holy Spirit

What the Charismatic renewal sees as often missing in the life of the church is the appropriation of the power to lead a new life. It is not enough to include the Holy Spirit and his gifts in our theology: he must come to expression in our lives. It is with regard to the broad question of sanctification – the exercise of spiritual gifts being a part of this – that Lutheran charismatics have placed their understanding of the indwelling of the Spirit.

As part of a larger discussion of baptism, Larry Christenson has presented two basic aspects of the ways being filled with the Holy Spirit may be experienced:

> In any relationship there will be times of *quiet growth* and moments of more *dramatic breakthrough.* The balance between two modes of development will vary from individual to individual [...] For a time, to begin with, a *breakthrough-experience* may separate a person from his or her roots. That person is all caught up in the exploration of a new dimension of life [...] But if a breakthrough experience is to contribute something of value to life, it must establish itself in relation to the basic foundations of the life from which it sprang [...] Those who have experienced the blessing of a baptism or renewal in the Holy Spirit will find that blessing deepened and enhanced as they come to see it as a means of continuing and multiplying that life into which one has been initiated by water and the Word (abbreviated, italics added).[4]

Without the Holy Spirit, the most precious truths can become a snare. Renewal movements have warned that the Lutheran emphasis on unconditional forgiveness and expressions such as "simultaneously saint and sinner" can lead to a gospel of "cheap grace". The antidote to this is not a vigorous restatement of our theology but the working of the Holy Spirit. He alone can make costly redemption and costly discipleship realities in our lives. We do not hold title to the spiritual treasures that we recognise and appreciate in our own tradition. They belong to the treasure store of the Spirit. At most, we hold them in trust for the body of Christ. But even then, they remain only a remembrance – until the Spirit fills us and makes them live again. The Charismatic renewal, with its emphasis on being filled with the

---

[4] Larry Christenson, *What About Baptism*? (Minneapolis, MN: Augsburg, 1986), pp. 19-20.

Spirit, is not the enemy of our traditions: it points to the only way that traditions remain alive.[5]

[5] Note the famous theologian Jaroslav Pelikan's maxim as quoted by Richard John Neuhaus in *The Religion and Society Report* 3(4), (April 1986), p. 1: "Tradition is the living faith of the dead, traditionalism is the dead faith of the living."

(44) Obedience to Christ as Lord

It was the day of a national election, and a men's morning Bible study group was holding its regular weekly meeting. They were reading Matthew 28:18, "All authority in heaven and on earth has been given to me." One of the men commented, "Won't it be great to know that, finally, the right man will be in charge?" It was an understandable slip, putting this little election-day thought on the authority of Christ into the future tense. It is the way we often talk about the lordship of Christ: something that happens somewhere out there in the future, or somewhere up there at a higher stage of the Christian life that we may aspire to, although we fall short of it in experience.

The Holy Spirit glorifies Christ by revealing who he is. He does this not only with words, but also by example (2 Cor. 3:2-3). He reveals Christ as Lord by actually establishing his lordship in the lives of believers.

The Lordship of Christ: A Foundational Truth

The Holy Spirit is very present-tense about Christ's lordship. The Holy Spirit comes with the gospel of the kingdom of God, the good news that "he [God] has rescued us from the dominion of darkness and brought us into the kingdom of the Son he loves, in whom we have redemption, the forgiveness of sins" (Col. 1:13-14). As surely as Christ rescues us, just as certainly he brings us into his kingdom. The Holy Spirit gathers the redeemed people of God under the lordship of Christ – not sometime in the future, not at some higher stage of the Christian life, but here and now, present tense, active.

The Holy Spirit is letting it be known that a gospel without lordship is no gospel. The Spirit does not come with the good news of salvation and then add on the lordship of Christ. The lordship of Jesus Christ is integral to the good news. All authority has been given to him. On that fundamental truth, Scripture is unmistakably clear. "But in your hearts acknowledge Christ as the holy Lord" (1 Pet. 3:15). This verse says literally according to the Greek text: "But sanctify Christ the Lord in your hearts", and can only mean that we should confess, honour, and glorify Christ as what he really is, namely Lord.[1]

The apostle Peter ended the first evangelistic sermon (preached after the disciples had received the gift of the Spirit on the day of Pentecost) with the following words, "Therefore let all Israel be assured of this: God has made

---

[1] Cf. Fritz Rienecker, *Sprachlicher Schlüssel zum Griechischen Neuen Testament* ("Linguistic Key to the Greek New Testament", Giessen: Brunnen Verlag, 1963), p. 580.

this Jesus, whom you crucified, both *Lord and Christ*" (Acts 2:36, cp. Acts 10:42-43). *Forgiveness of sins and salvation is dependent on faith in Christ as Lord.* There is no Christian mission that does not include the proclamation of Jesus as Lord:

> "he word is near you; it is in your mouth and in your heart, that is the *word of faith* we are proclaiming: That if you confess with your mouth: *'Christ is Lord,'* and believe in your heart that God raised him from the dead, *you will be saved* [...] Everyone who calls on the name of the Lord will be saved (Rom. 10:8-9, 13).

Obedience to the Lord: A Work of the Holy Spirit

But the Spirit does not leave it there – or, more properly, he does not leave *us* there. That would consign us, at best, to a valiant striving in our own strength to demonstrate our gratitude for the gift of salvation by honouring Christ as Lord in our lives. The result of that is a burdensome life under law and obligation. Our sinful human nature cannot live under the lordship of Christ – not with the best of will and good intention. It cannot live in obedience to this King.

The Lord calls us to radical dependence on the ongoing work of the Holy Spirit within and among us. The Spirit alone can produce obedience to the lordship of Christ.

The Charismatic renewal has laid particular stress on the issue of Christ's lordship. The Holy Spirit comes to make that lordship real. Through the Holy Spirit Jesus, takes authority. He works his will in us in new ways. Spirit-inspired obedience glorifies Christ, for it testifies to his lordship. A sign that one has truly received the outpoured Spirit is that the authority of Christ becomes more operative in one's everyday life (Acts 5:32).

The theme of obedience is frequently applied to the monastic tradition, most often in a negative sense. Protestants are prone to dismiss monasticism as a legalistic system. Yet if one goes back to the root, one often discovers a distinct emphasis on divine initiative; obedience is willed and wrought by the Holy Spirit.

Although having its roots in the East, monasticism took on a decidedly Western form through Benedict of Nursia, founder of the monastery at Monte Cassino in Italy. Until the 12th century, the monastic Rule of St. Benedict held sway in the Western church. In a vision, Benedict had seen the whole world before his eyes, as if purged and purified in a single sunbeam.[2] He saw the fallen world in divine light, as the new earth to be created by the God who makes all things new (Rev. 21:5). For the world illumined by the light of

---

[2] Gregory the Great (504–604), Dialog 2, c. 5. See Benz (ed), *Die Vision*, p. 504, n. 1.

God, no effort is too great, no prayer in vain, and no time wasted by honest toil. The rigid, tightly organised Benedictine Order was a church-renewal movement for the sake of the world, which Benedict had seen restored – transfigured – in heavenly light.

True enough, spiritual disciplines can degenerate into a legalistic system. But the other side must be held in perspective too: many of the men and women who founded renewal movements and religious orders, calling people to lives of obedience, were acting in response to a revelation of the Holy Spirit.[3]

Obedience is a fundamental mark of a Spirit-filled believer. Scripture uses the plainest imagery to bring home this truth. The apostle Paul introduced himself to the Christians in Rome quite matter-of-factly as "Jesus Christ's slave" (Rom. 1:1, Living Bible). He thanked God for their life in Christ (Rom. 1:8), in turn characterising them as "slaves to obedience which leads to righteousness" and "slaves to God" (Rom. 6:18, 22). He both introduced and concluded his letter by stating that the God-given goal of his ministry was "to call people from among all the Gentiles to the obedience that comes from faith" (Rom. 1:5; 15:18; 16:26).

It is not enough merely to hold this as a doctrine. It must be a reality that the Holy Spirit works out in our lives. Day by day, we live out of the scriptural expectation that the Holy Spirit is applying the Lord's will in our lives, working in us a glad and grateful obedience.

He does this in many ways. Willingly and patiently, he teaches us to recognise and respond to his ways. It is a privilege and a joy to have Christ as our Lord. We should always remember the saying: "If Christ is not Lord *of all*, he is not Lord *at all*". There is no area of life that is exempt from the lordship of Christ. What that means in practice has to be worked out in different situations: in society, in the church and in our daily living as Christians. Even when our human sinful nature, the flesh, rises up in rebellion, the deeper reality of his indwelling presence teaches us to obey and to rejoice in obedience – because "the right man really is in charge."

---

[3] Note, for example, the inscription on the tombstone of the Norwegian revival leader Hans Nielsen Hauge, quoting one of his last statements: "I have sworn obedience to the Spirit of God, and he has helped me to be faithful to my intention", see Chapter 31.

(45) Holiness

The Call to Holiness

To become holy is God's urgent call to his people. Today, as always, God calls his people to be holy because God himself is a holy God (1 Pet. 1:15-16; Rom. 1:7; 1 Cor. 1:2; Eph. 1:4). Christ died in order to *sanctify the church*, which is his bride and body, so that he might present the church to himself as "holy and blameless" (Eph. 5:25-27). In the Lord's Prayer, Jesus taught his disciples to pray that the hallowing of the name of God would occupy first place in their prayers (Mt. 6:9). Jesus himself prayed, "Holy Father, protect them by the power of your name [...] so that they may be one as we are one [...] For them I sanctify myself, that they too may be truly sanctified" (Jn 17:11, 21). The life of God's people and the credibility of their witness to the world depend on holiness.

To be holy means quite simply that it becomes visible in our lives that we – as individuals and as church – belong to God; that we are indeed the body of Christ. It means to be transformed into the image of Christ.

> And we, who with unveiled faces all reflect the Lord's glory, are being *transformed into his likeness* with ever-increasing glory, which *comes from the Lord, who is the Spirit* (2 Cor. 3:18; cf. Rom 8:27; 2 Cor. 4:4)

The best description of holiness is the character of Christ. To be holy is to bring forth the fruit of conversion: to forgive as Christ forgives, to love as Christ loves, to be compassionate as he is compassionate, to be righteous as he is righteous, to be honest, selfless, and pure as he is honest, selfless, and pure.

The call to be holy is a command. Yet beneath the command lies the promise: God gives what he demands. It is this perception, perhaps more than anything else, that is a bulwark against legalism in a sound Charismatic renewal. The emphasis is not on a self-produced but a Spirit-wrought holiness. *It is God's Holy Spirit who transforms us into the image of Christ. He alone can do it.*

The Ways of the Holy Spirit

Although they sometimes surprise us, the ways of the Spirit are not arbitrary or whimsical. As God, he is a God of order and peace (1 Cor. 14:33, 40). It can be helpful to recognise in a general way how he works, so long as we do not seek to turn this knowledge into abstract principles and begin to govern our life by them. The Spirit may direct us to apply particular biblical principles. That is something quite different from using principles as a basis for acting independently of the Spirit. That would thrust aside the sovereignty of the Spirit and bring us back under the bondage of the law.

Scripture and prayer are two of the principal tools that the Spirit uses to shape our lives. He uses them in known and dependable ways.

Through the *words of Scripture*, the Holy Spirit teaches us basic truths and principles of the holy life. When spiritually renewed people begin to talk about biblical standards of holiness, the cry of "legalism!" is not far behind. But this is often a superficial judgement. One must come closer and discern the root of this quest for holiness. It may be truly given by the Spirit: a humble recognition that we really are fallen creatures. No part of us has escaped the ravages of the fall, including our faculties of moral judgement. It is not only our *will and ability* that are defective; our *understanding* of what constitutes true holiness is also flawed. Biblical standards of holiness are the gift of a gracious God to those who have been called to live holy lives and recognise that they do not know where to begin.

Christian growth begins with the humble recognition that we are strangers to the ways of God. We must be instructed in the ways of holiness. Through the words of Scripture, the Spirit must show us that which we cannot know by natural reason alone, namely, the kind of life that is pleasing to God.

In the *school of prayer,* the Holy Spirit makes the truth of Scripture real and personal to us. He enlightens our understanding. He guides us to its proper application. It is no accident that spiritual renewal and prayer are inevitably linked together.

Through both Scripture and prayer, the Holy Spirit reveals to us our own heart. This is critical to the life of holiness. One often struggles with the same faults and weaknesses, commits the same sins again and again. The way out of this is not to pull oneself together by one's own efforts. At best that may produce a temporary result, and then one is overtaken again. The way out is to turn to the Lord in prayer and ask for the Holy Spirit to reveal the nature of the difficulty. Perhaps its hidden roots lie buried in our unconscious and must be revealed through the operation of a spiritual gift. It may be festering away in a forgotten memory about a situation in which we sinned and did not receive forgiveness or were hurt and did not forgive. A major part of our "old nature" is made up of memories in which forgiveness did not take place. As long as these remain buried in our hearts, they can exercise control over us, and we are quite helpless to prevent it. Jesus spoke with great concern about what we carry in our hearts. In writing about the holy life, many of the church fathers stressed the importance of the self-knowledge given us by the Holy Spirit. When the Spirit reveals an area that needs to be dealt with, we may also trust him to quicken the faith by which we can forgive and receive forgiveness.

The Norwegian revival leader Hans Nielsen Hauge shares what he did during the half year before his life-transforming spiritual experience in 1796:

> When I was alone, I fell on my knees and prayed that he would reveal in me his Son's love, give me his Holy Spirit, and teach me to know my corruption to do evil and my lack of power to do good.[1]

It takes time to come to a place of inner silence in our prayer life so that we can truly begin to listen. By nature, without the leading of the Spirit, we do not permit God to speak out his mind: we do not hear and thus cannot obey. One does not simply think about God, one must hear and hearken to his voice.

Martin Luther was fond of the words of the mystic Tauler's words: "If God would speak, you must be still." It takes patience and endurance to come to the place where prayer really does become a two-way conversation. But without a prayer life that includes real listening, no deep and lasting growth can take place. A decade before meditation became one of the cult expressions of counterculture in the West, the Charismatic movement had been quietly cultivating the practice of Christian meditation as one aspect of its concern for renewal.

What happens in the heart must be worked out in terms of practical faith and obedience. One cannot simply "wait for something to happen." Often, we do not experience that the Holy Spirit has dealt with an area of our heart until it is tested in practice. We must step out in the freedom Christ has given us, yielding ourselves in obedience, living the life of holiness and obedience that is ours in him.

Two Dangers

While clearly rooted in Scripture, *Luther's teaching on justification was also an expression of his own experience of justification.* It stressed the new attitude of the pardoned sinner before God. Luther himself sometimes included in his explanation of justification not only the legal sense of absolution or forgiveness of sins (forensic justification) but also the sense of sanctification by unity with Christ (sanative justification). "God, in Christ, conquers and heals the nature of man as that of a sinner, hostile to God."[2] Christ's substitutionary, atoning death and his powerful resurrection constitute the basis for a new relationship with God (Rom. 4:25). God himself works the wonder: out of his enemy, he makes a friend. We are reconciled with God in Christ in order to live a new life (Rom. 5:10; 6:4, 11-12).

In applying this to daily life, two ditches must be avoided. On one side is the soft shoulder of passivity: "If the Holy Spirit alone can make me holy,

---

[1] From Hans Nielsen Hauge's *Beskrivelse over det åndelige livs løp og strid,* 1804.

[2] Cf. Luther's sermon on John 9 from 1518, WA 1, 267-273. See also Ernst-Wilhelm Kohls, *Luther oder Erasmus* (Basel: Friedrich Reichardt, 1972), p. 88.

then I have no responsibility." On the other side is the gully of willpower and self-determination: "I must accomplish my own sanctification."

A person driving into the first ditch careens headlong toward moral breakup and a spiritual standstill. In the second ditch, we may plow on a way, striving with our own power to steer a holy course, but then we stall out. Despite the best of intentions, the life of holiness gets mired down. So we thumb through the New Testament and determine, perhaps, that travelling this highway is, after all, an impossible ideal. Or we begin to compare ourselves with others along the wayside and happily conclude that we are just as good, or better, than our neighbour, and this is the beginning of spiritual pride. On both sides, the problem is the same: we do not reckon realistically with the persistent purpose and dependable power of the Holy Spirit to bring us to holiness.

Paul's words in Philippians 2:12-13 is a critical passage for a right understanding of Christian growth. "Continue to work out your salvation with fear and trembling, for it is God who works in you to will and to act according to his good purpose." Here, Paul uses the term salvation to cover the whole process of redemption, which Christ works out in us through the Holy Spirit. The Holy Spirit creates in us the will to be holy, and he gives us the power to live a sanctified life.

Paul knew from experience that this is no life of passivity. It is work, effort, struggling, striving (1 Cor. 9:24-25; Col. 1:28-29; Phil. 1:27; 2 Tim. 4:7). Yet it is crucial, in the very moment of striving, to depend on Christ and the Holy Spirit, who are giving both the will and the power to live a holy life. Paul wrote:

> But by the grace of God I am what I am, and his grace to me was not without effect. No, I worked harder than all of them – yet *not I, but the grace of God that was with me* (1 Cor. 15:10).

(46) Discipleship and Stewardship

Discipling and Pastoral Care

Jesus commissioned his disciples *to make disciples* (Mt. 28:19), not merely believers in an intellectual sense, Christians in a nominal sense, or converts in a statistical sense. People do not necessarily grow in discipleship by being baptised, by making a decision for Christ, by believing a doctrine, by going to church, or by attending a class. While these and other things may be appropriate steps along the way and may help people become more knowledgeable, they do not necessarily make people more faithful.

Disciples are made not simply by teaching but by *training. Maturity comes not only by obtaining information from the Word of God, but by having spiritual formation in the Word of God.* Spiritual formation involves more than preaching and teaching: it requires pastoral care that helps people to live in the Word of God. In the Charismatic renewal, the idea of teaching is being broadened to include practical training in discipleship, in which believers are encouraged and supported in Christian growth not only by teaching in an academic sense, but by the personal association and example of a spiritual mentor.

"Feed my sheep" is still Christ's commission to the shepherds of his church, and it requires many more shepherds than are presently available. The task of effectively applying the Word to individual lives is too large for the ordained clergy alone. One of the concerns that the Charismatic renewal has addressed is the need to equip shepherds, lay as well as clergy, to nurture Christ's flock.

The Small Group

The initial rapid spread of the Charismatic renewal came primarily through *prayer groups* and *house meetings* that were spontaneous and largely unstructured. As the movement developed, the small group continued to play a decisive role as the place of pastoral care and directed spiritual growth. Small-group experience from other movements, especially the church-growth movement, was freely adopted by charismatics. People who made some initial steps of faith and experienced a measure of spiritual renewal were encouraged to commit themselves to meet with others on a regular basis for prayer and directed spiritual growth. The renewing, nurturing, evangelising ministry of the small group rose up between the renewal of the individual and the renewal of an entire congregation

The precise format of small groups varies greatly throughout the renewal, but certain elements tend to predominate:

- biblical teaching that is simple and practical;
- prayer, intercession, and the practice of spiritual gifts;
- stress on committed, loving relationships;
- personal testimonies and ministry, primarily through prayer, in which the Word is applied to people's practical needs.[1]

Through intercession and training, small groups can serve as cells of spiritual renewal, sending fresh impulses of life into congregations. They help extend the shepherding ministry among the laity. They become a training ground for leadership in the congregation, "schools of discipleship" that both directly and indirectly affect the spiritual life of the entire congregation.

Giving

A mark of the Spirit-led believer and Spirit-led church is a *giving attitude*, reflective of God's nature. It is a basic principle of life; it is a practice into which the Holy Spirit leads us. It begins with the conviction that everything belongs to the Lord and is at his disposal. It touches every area of life – time, abilities, gifts, money, and property. It is the invitation of a gracious God to share in and give expression to his life. It is grace, not law or legalism.

Lutheran state and folk churches in Europe have traditionally been supported by a government- or church-taxing system, while voluntary mission work and social work within these churches have been supported by the members. In other countries, the churches are generally supported by free-will contributions. Even critics of the Charismatic renewal admit that giving patterns among charismatics are above average. Charismatic Lutheran pastors consistently report that the renewal results in less need to talk about stewardship, yet increased giving.

Generous giving is certainly not unique to the Charismatic renewal. The fact that it often occurs more or less spontaneously, however, indicates that it is linked to an understanding of faith that moves quickly toward practical expression. Generous givers frequently testify that scriptural promises of blessing in connection with tithing, such as Malachi 3:10, prove true in their own experience, although this is not a primary issue. *The motive for giving is not to receive reward.* Generosity is its own reward. It is a way of life. Jesus said: "It is more blessed to give than to receive" (Acts 20:35).

The central truth of stewardship is that God is the source of material possessions. This fits well with the dynamic understanding of faith that is threaded through the Charismatic renewal, the expectation that God intervenes in everyday life. The believer places faith not in possessions but in God, trusting God for all one's needs (Mt. 5:25-34; Phil. 4:19). The focus

---

[1] See also the Excursus 5 in Chapter 55 on the characteristics of charismatic churches where small groups have been important.

of expectation is on God's fatherly care, not on one's visible income or resources. We are able to give generously because we are children of a generous Father.

It is not a question of our giving something to God and his kingdom either out of duty or gratitude. If that is the motivation, we are back under the law; giving quickly becomes either a burden or a source of pride. Rather, as in every other area of life, we depend on the working of the Holy Spirit: we can give generously because the giving, serving, sacrificing presence of Christ is alive within us by the Holy Spirit.

This understanding is essential. If stewardship becomes an inflexible obligation, it loses its spiritual dynamic. The Spirit must remain in control, which also means that there will be some understandable variety in stewardship practices. The giving patterns in countries where there is a folk church, well-supported by taxation, may differ from what happens in countries where church support is voluntary. In the former case, spiritually renewed believers may direct more of their giving to voluntary associations such as mission societies or evangelistic works, while in the latter, one's primary giving may be through the local congregation. In a family where not everyone is Christian, the income may have to be considered differently than if everyone were Christian. What is essential is that the way we handle material possessions comes fully under the lordship of Christ.

The temptation to have a materialistic outlook, finding our essential comfort and security in material things rather than in the Lord, is always close at hand. It is no accident that Jesus frequently warned against serving the god of money (Mt. 6:24; Lk. 16:13-15, 19-31; 18:18-30). Covetousness and greed appear prominently in various catalogues of sins in the New Testament (Rom. 1:29; Eph. 5:5; Col. 3:5). "The love of money is a root of all kinds of evil. Some people, eager for money, have wandered from the faith and pierced themselves with many griefs" (1 Tim. 6:10).

The emphasis on stewardship that has been prominent in the Charismatic renewal has not been used primarily as a money-raising technique. That could become a matter simply of transferring a materialistic outlook from the personal to the congregational level. Rather, it is a recognition that stewardship represents a need for the believer. *Cheerful and generous giving is the Lord's antidote to the love of money.* Personal stewardship would be a necessary emphasis even if a congregation had a huge endowment and needed no offerings to carry on its ministry.

Generous givers say that they cannot out-give God. One man, who had the true spiritual gift of generosity (Rom. 12:8), put it this way: "I shovel it out the front door, and God shovels it in the back door, and he's got a bigger shovel than I do." Those who have taken this step of faith share with enthusiasm the blessings of giving. They have discovered the pure joy of it.

Charismatic churches challenge believers in all areas of activity, including the church's financial needs. This does not mean, however, that they continually dun the people for money. The direction of the challenge is more toward God than toward the people, a matter of prayer more than of promotion. There may actually be very little said about money in the open gatherings or services of the congregation. The emphasis is on the working of the Spirit, trusting God for the church's finances. In one charismatic Lutheran congregation, the stewardship programme one year consisted solely in a group of men who gathered every Tuesday morning at 6:00 a.m. to pray for the financial needs of the congregation. The congregation's income increased dramatically.

In 1973, after years of financial struggle, North Heights Lutheran Church in Saint Paul, Minnesota, decided to shift from the traditional "promotional" approach in stewardship to trusting God and his Word in regard to finances. Individually and as families, the members sought to step out in faith in order to implement what they sensed to be God's will. They looked to God as their source of income. Groups of spiritually renewed members met weekly to pray for the finances that would enable the congregation to carry out the ministry God had entrusted to it. In the ensuing ten years, the church's income rose from 30% to 50% annually.

If we focus our expectations only on observable human resources, we will always look to the rich as the givers, the poor as the receivers. Although there is a certain logic, and also biblical support, for this approach, it may be less than the whole answer. In Ethiopia, research has shown that both in terms of percentage of income and in overall amount, poorer Christians out-give their more prosperous neighbours. These and other illustrations suggest that we need to look beyond our traditional approach to stewardship. Sacrificial giving can be practiced by believers without particular regard to income. We may remember the words of Jesus about the poor widow who gave two coins of very little worth:

> I tell you the truth, this poor widow has put more into the treasury than all the others. They all gave out of their wealth; but she, out of her poverty, put in everything – all she had to live on"(Mk 12:43-44).

This kind of giving also took place in the New Testament churches in Macedonia:

> And now, brothers, we want you to know about the *grace* that God has given the Macedonian churches. Out of the most severe *trial*, their overflowing *joy* and their extreme *poverty*, welled up in rich *generosity*. For I testify that they gave as much as they were able, and even beyond their ability (2 Cor. 8:1-3).

Generosity that flows from the heart does not come naturally to us. The believer must ask the Holy Spirit to bestow and release the gift of generous giving. When it happens, it is by God's grace and for his glory.

A Lifelong Process

Christian discipleship is a lifelong process in which the Holy Spirit conforms us to the image of Christ so that our lives reflect his glory. It will not be completed in this life (Phil. 1:6). Yet Christ clearly expects that when our lives are joined to him, we will be "fruitful" (Jn 15:5; Phil. 1:11). When the Holy Spirit has control of us, he produces observable results (Gal. 5:22-25). For he works according to the Father's will, and that will is for us to become holy and to bear fruit. It is not an option, it is a demand. But it is a demand that God himself makes possible through the indwelling of Christ by the Holy Spirit.

(47) Manifesting Spiritual Gifts

The early church manifested an astonishing abundance of spiritual gifts. It proclaimed the gospel not only in truth but with power. God underscored the spoken message with the signs and gifts that followed (Mk 16:20; Acts 4:30; 14:3; 1 Cor. 1:4-8; Gal.3:5; Heb. 2:3b-4).

Some of these signs and spiritual gifts have, however, been assumed to not have present-day relevance. Any serious talk of manifesting spiritual gifts must therefore begin by considering what the Bible says about their use.

The apostle Paul introduced the concept of *charism* (Greek: *charisma*) into the vocabulary of the New Testament. The term is related to the Greek word for grace (*charis*), and should be understood as an outworking of God's grace, a gift freely given. It may refer to the gift of salvation (Rom. 6:23; Rom. 5:15-17). It may also refer to other gifts granted by God, the content of the gift being determined by the context (Rom. 1:11; 11:29; 1 Cor. 7:7).

In the Charismatic renewal, charisms have been used primarily in the specialised sense that one finds in Romans 12, 1 Corinthians 12, Hebrews, and in the Pastoral Epistles (see especially 1 Pet. 4:10), where it means *specific gifts granted by the Holy Spirit to individual members of the congregation. Charisms are spiritual endowments that the Holy Spirit gives to believers in order to equip them for powerful and effective ministry. Sometimes the term also describes the ministries themselves.*

Unity and Diversity of Spiritual Gifts

By comparing the various lists of charisms in the New Testament, it becomes evident that they embrace great diversity. There are references to events and to persons, to spontaneous acts of supernatural power and to permanent, unspectacular ministries, to directly inspired speech and to premeditated instruction, to the breaking in of the transcendent God, and to patient and humble service.

Distinctions between charismatic and natural gifts are not always clear-cut. There may be a connection between natural talent and charismatic ministry, although this is not necessarily so. Sometimes the Spirit grants gifts that seem contrary to a person's natural endowment. He reserves the right to do the unexpected (see 1 Cor. 1:26-31). When – and only when – a natural talent is placed at the disposal of the Spirit does it become a spiritual gift, a charism.

The characteristic thought of Paul, which all ages find difficult to grasp, was the enormous freedom of the Spirit and the diversity of the Spirit's gifts on the one hand (2 Cor. 3:17; 1 Cor. 12:14-30), and the common foundation and common goal of the gifts on the other (1 Cor. 12:4-7, 11; Eph. 4:11-16). The diversity of gifts is grounded in a strong unity. Scripture clarifies this distinction in two particular ways.

Firstly, the variety of gifts have their *origin in the one, triune God.* In 1 Corinthians 12:4-6, Paul says:

> There are different kinds of gifts (Greek: *charismata*), but the same *Spirit.* There are different kinds of service (Greek: *diakoniai*), but the same *Lord.* There are different kinds of working (Greek: *energemata*), but the same *God* works all of them in all men.

The charisms are given by the Spirit, but at the same time they express the servant nature of Christ and the fatherly provision of God. The doctrine of the charisms is a part of the New Testament doctrine of the Spirit, but set in a trinitarian context.

Secondly, the *church is the body of Christ* in a real sense (1 Cor. 12:12). Different members with differing gifts all belong to the one body. The place and function of each member is determined by the gift that one exercises (1 Cor. 12:14-16; Rom. 12:4-8). The gifts are a manifestation of the Holy Spirit (1 Cor. 12:7, 11). They should come to expression in every aspect of a congregation's life and ministry (1 Cor. 14:26; Eph. 5:18-20; Acts 2:42-47). There should be a profound, *Spirit-directed interplay of the various gifts in the ministry of a congregation. No member is without a gift, and no member has all the gifts* (1 Cor. 12:7, 11, 27, 29-30).

In seeking to explain or encourage the use of spiritual gifts, charismatics sometimes take an overly individualistic approach. They underscore – and sometimes misuse or misunderstand – texts such as, "You can *all* prophesy [...]" and "I would like *every one* of you to speak in tongues" (1 Cor. 14:31, 5). This can come across to non-charismatics as pressure or manipulation – or even false doctrine. It does not mean that all Christians necessarily should have these two gifts, but that all Christians should be encouraged to seek them and allowed to exercise them if and when they receive them (1 Cor. 12:29-31; 14:1).

Certainly, there is a time and place for individuals to be confronted with their own need to be empowered by the Holy Spirit, and this may include the manifestation of specific gifts. But the full spectrum of spiritual gifts needs particularly to be urged *in relation to the congregation.* The congregation is a microcosm of the body of Christ. Our goal for the congregation should be nothing less than the full spectrum of spiritual gifts in full and effective operation. If that goal is declared in power, we can trust the Holy Spirit himself to address specific members in regard to specific gifts.

Receiving and Evaluating Spiritual Gifts

Charisms can and should be *sought*: "Eagerly desire the greater gifts [...] Follow the way of love and eagerly desire spiritual gifts, especially the gift of prophecy" (1 Cor. 12:31; 14:1). The gifts of the Spirit are sought primarily through *prayer* (1 Cor. 14:13). They may be given by intercession and laying on of hands by leaders in the church (Acts 13:3-4; 14:23; Rom. 1:11; 1 Tim. 4:14; 2 Tim. 1:6-7).

Some of the criteria for evaluating spiritual gifts are:

Firstly, spiritual gifts manifest the early *confession* of the church, "Jesus is Lord" (1 Cor. 12:3; cf. 1 Jn 4:2).

Secondly, they express the *unity* of the one body, one Spirit, one hope, one faith, one baptism, and one God and Father (Eph. 4:4-6; cf. 1 Cor. 12:12, 20; Rom. 12:4-5).

Thirdly, they are for the *common good* and *build up the church* (1 Cor. 12:7; Eph. 4:11-16). All charisms should contribute in some way toward these goals.

Fourthly, they are *governed by love* (1 Cor. 13; 14:1; Rom. 12:9; Eph. 4:15-16). Those who manifest gifts without love are counted as nothing (1 Cor. 13:1-3).

The Dispensational Question

Does the Holy Spirit distribute spiritual gifts today, or was that a special consideration given only at the beginning, to "get the church established"? This is a familiar argument, which usually goes by the name of "dispensationalism" or "cessationism". The idea is that history is divided up into different epochs or dispensations. God's purpose, and therefore his action, varies according to the dispensation; for example, God dealt differently with people before the Flood than he did after the Flood, differently before the giving of the law at Sinai than afterward.

According to some dispensationalists, the early church lived in a different dispensation than the church today. When the New Testament was completed, God inaugurated a new dispensation in which the gifts of the Spirit were no longer necessary. Today we have the Scripture. All we have to do is proclaim the Word and invite people to accept it "by faith."

While this theology is primarily taught among certain groups in the Anabaptist tradition, it has also found its way into some circles of Lutherans.[1]

[1] "The Charismatic Movement and Lutheran Theology" (A Report of the Commission on Theology and Church Relations of the Lutheran Church-Missouri Synod, January 1972), in McDonnell (ed), *Presence, Power, Praise*. Vol. 1, pp. 345-347.

Hints of it can be found in both Luther and Calvin, although it is not a developed or consistent position.[2]

The implication in dispensationalism is that signs and wonders were a necessary scaffolding for establishing the authority of the Word in the early church. Once the Word was enshrined in an authoritative Scripture, these means could be dispensed with. According to this understanding, many spiritual gifts belong to the infant stage of faith; the church today walks in faith along a higher plane. It offers, however, only a superficial explanation for the allegedly absence of gifts and miracles in the church today. In comparing the situation of the early church with the situation today, it misconstrues the issue to set faith and signs in opposition to one another.

The Spirit-inspired proclamation of the gospel in the early church was in *word and in deed.* Those addressed by this audible-visible gospel responded to it in faith, or rejected it in unbelief. In regard to faith, the situation of the early church was no different from ours: it came as a gift through the working of the Holy Spirit.

The dispensationalist explanation separates what God has joined together: the Word and signs that follow are two sides of the same coin. The real issue is this: Has the Holy Spirit, in our day, chosen to work in a different way than he did in the early church? Neither Scripture itself, nor church history, nor present common Christian experience supports such a contention. On the contrary, even today the Holy Spirit desires to manifest the sovereign power of Christ's victory over the devil, sin and death in an incarnational way through specific and varied gifts given to members of Christ's body, as he did at the beginning. It may be that the miraculous gifts are more frequent at certain times in history and in certain contexts, such as missionary situations, yet they do occur always and everywhere.[3]

Spiritual gifts flow from Christ himself. The fullness of the kingdom is seen in Christ and his ministry, both his earthly ministry where words and miraculous deeds were integral parts, and his death and resurrection where atonement for sin, victory over the devil, and resurrection from the dead were achieved once for all. Through the Holy Spirit, we have access to the rich store of Christ's gifts. In a sense, spiritual gifts represent a continuation of

---

[2] See the discussion of Luther's views in Part Three. Luther believed that some gifts belonged to the apostolic age and were not necessary any longer, but he cannot be described as a dispensationalist. The same was the case with Calvin, see John Calvin, *Commentary on the Epistle of Paul the Apostle to the Romans*, translated and edited by John Owen (Grand Rapids, MI: Eerdmans, 1955), p. 460. Calvin made a distinction between "the miraculous graces by which Christ *at first* rendered illustrious his gospel" and "the ordinary gifts, such as were to *continue perpetually in the Church*" (italics added).

[3] See, for example, Keener, *Miracles,* for abundant evidence of miracles occurring in the whole world today.

Christ's incarnational ministry (Jn 14:12). Through them, the Holy Spirit continues to minister Christ's love in a demonstrative way.

Encouraging and Desiring Spiritual Gifts

All spiritual gifts are an exercise of the power and authority of Christ. Within the body of Christ, however, the gifts interrelate in a particular way.

Some gifts involve the exercise of a Spirit-given *ministry*. Here, the gift is a Spirit-anointed *person* who manifests a particular ministry of Christ within the body of believers: for example apostle, prophet, evangelist, shepherd, teacher, elder and overseer (Eph. 4:11; 1 Cor. 12:28; Acts 20:28-29).

Other gifts involve the exercise of a Spirit-given *ability or power*. Here the gifts are specific *demonstrations of the Spirit*, manifested through believers, enabling them to minister to other members or to non-believers with resources beyond their own natural abilities (1 Cor. 12:4-11; Rom. 12:6-8; Heb. 2:4; 1 Pet. 4:10).

It is important that these types of charismatic gifts be recognised and properly related in the daily life of a body of believers. Some have responsibility *in relation to the other gifts* as part of their ministries, for example shepherds (pastors), elders, and overseers (Eph. 4:11; Acts 20:17, 28; 1 Tim. 3:1-7; 4:13-14; 2 Tim. 1:6-7; 2:2, 24). They may be compared to a captain or a coach: they teach, encourage, develop, enable, and order the functioning of the charismatic gifts. One of the tasks of these ministry gifts is to equip the saints. They may teach and inspire faith in a way that encourages and releases charismatic gifts. They help brothers and sisters recognise and use their gifts for the good of all. Their charisms have as a purpose to prepare God's people for works of service, so that the body of Christ may be built up (Eph. 4:12). They are also charged with the task of opposing false teaching and keeping order (Acts 20:29-30; 1 Cor. 14:33, 40; 1 Tim. 1:3; 2 Tim. 2:15).

To speak of order, however, without active *encouragement* of spiritual gifts is more or less pointless: there will be nothing to order. Scripture tells us that we should "eagerly *desire* spiritual gifts" (1 Cor. 14:1), and for a very good reason. Without desire, there will be no quickening of faith and expectation. In discussions about spiritual gifts, you often run into the contention, "Oh, I am open to any spiritual gift that the Lord wants to give me." The scriptural word, however, is much stronger than "being open". The Greek word *zeloein* (1 Cor. 12:31; 14:1) means to "strive", "desire", "exert oneself earnestly". "Being open" is essentially a passive attitude. It does not yield the same practical result as "striving after" or "eagerly desire". Charismatic spirituality includes encouraging people to eagerly desire the spiritual gifts. It is a responsibility of those who lead God's people to encourage an active faith and expectancy for all of the spiritual gifts. Scripture leaves no doubt that spiritual gifts are to be recognised, sought after, and used. Christ does not only *commission* disciples, that is, give them a task or calling; he also *empowers* them through the Holy Spirt with spiritual gifts so that they can carry out that calling.

Where gifts are absent from the life of the church, the primary responsibility must rest with the leaders. They must, first of all, proclaim the availability and desirability of spiritual gifts, as did the apostles. Faith is kindled by the Word. Then they must provide a climate that actively welcomes the gifts, gives them a place to grow and develop, and disciplines and orders them in the Lord's service. A truly Spirit-filled church helps its people enter into the Spirit-filled life, informs them about spiritual gifts, helps them to discover their gifts, encourages them to seek gifts, aids them in releasing their gifts, instructs them in the proper use of gifts, and provides the setting for corporate use of gifts.

Spiritual Gifts in the Early History of the Church

The exercise of spiritual gifts, as described by Paul in Romans 12 and 1 Corinthians 12, into the second and third centuries, is well-documented. Justin Martyr (beheaded in Rome in 165 A.D.) examined the charismata in his discussion with the educated Jew, Tryphon. In his *Dialog with Tryphon* (ca. 160 A.D.), Justin wrote: "Among us one can see men and women who have received gifts from the Spirit of God."[4]

Irenaeus, famous bishop of Lyon after 177 A.D., also spoke of spiritual gifts: "Yet we hear in the church of many brothers who have prophetic gifts, who speak through the Holy Spirit in tongues, who bring to light the hidden things of men, for their salvation, and explain the mysteries of God."[5]

Origen from Alexandria, a great scholar in the ancient church, who died 253/54 A.D. at the age of 70, as a result of torture during the persecution under emperor Decius, referred expressly to the gifts of the Spirit in a letter to his opponent Celsus: "Christians cast out demons, accomplish many healings and, according to God's will, see into the future."[6]

The ancient church bore witness not only to the exercise of spiritual gifts, but also, in accord with the apostle Paul, to the fact that use and misuse of such gifts are often quite close to one another. The institutional church came to suspect Spirit-gifted laity. The movement called *Montanism* arose during the second century. In 156-157 A.D., Montanus and two women, Prisca and Maximilla, appeared as prophets in Phrygia (Asia Minor). They strove against what they saw as the increasing worldliness of the church. Maximilla declared: "The Lord has sent me. Whether I want to or not, I must proclaim

---

[4] Justin Martyr, *Dialogus cum Tryphone Judaeo*, c. 88 (Migne SG 6, 685).

[5] Irenaeus, *Adversus Haereses* V, 6, 1 (Migne SG 7, 1137).

[6] Origen, *Contra Celsum* I, 46; VII, 8 (Migne SG 11, 745; 1432).

his will."[7] It seems that the form of prophecy in Montanism was more of a problem than the content. The Montanists were accused of speaking in a trancelike state, which was considered a sign of a false prophet. They often spoke in the first person, for example: "I am the Paraclete [...] I am the word and the Spirit and the Power." Their opponents apparently chose to take such expressions in a literal sense, contending that Montanus claimed to be the incarnation of the Holy Spirit.

The historical questions in relation to Montanism are difficult to answer because the only references to Montanism that we have, aside from brief comments by the church father Tertullian, occur in writings by its opponents. Montanus expected the imminent return of the Lord, and the outpouring of spiritual gifts in his movement was seen as inaugurating the final stage of history in which the Holy Spirit would be operative in a special way. This claim – and the ecstatic form of the prophecy – seem to be the only fair arguments against Montanism that can be historically substantiated. There was no major doctrinal error. The main burden of Montanus and his followers was ethical, and it was their ethical rigour that attracted men like the church father Tertullian to the movement.

If the Montanist controversy did not immediately lead to a common scepticism towards all prophecy in the church, this was nevertheless the ultimate outcome. The unhappy result of the movement was that, in later periods of church history, some of the charismata were met with scepticism; lay people with extraordinary spiritual gifts were often judged to be heretics or sectarians. The judgement of the Catholic scholar Kilian McDonnell, that "the church never really recovered its balance after it rejected Montanism" is a fairly accurate assessment of how the church came to regard some of the charismata.[8]

In the hermit monks influenced by Antonius the Great, there was a rebirth of charismatic piety, reflected, for example, in the sayings of the desert fathers. Their spiritual life had its source in the contrite heart, the fruit of which was humility. Through the ascetic life, the hermits fought desire and temptation; fasting and silence were central to their way of life. Out of the silence the charismata grew, especially the word of knowledge, wisdom, and prophecy. Gifts of healing and power over evil spirits were also known among the desert fathers.[9] In principle, the ancient church clung to the

---

[7] Epiphanius, *Haereses* 48, 13, 1.

[8] McDonnell, *The Baptism with the Holy Spirit as an Ecumenical Problem*, p. 44. See also McDonnell and Montague, *Christian Initiation and Baptism in the Holy Spirit*, for evidence of the expectation and practice of charismatic gifts in connection with baptism in the church during its first several centuries.

[9] One of the desert fathers, Apa Matthew, healed a girl by commanding an evil spirit to leave her. The spirit complained because it was tormented by the command. Apa Matthew's healing power was widely known. Cf. W.C. Till, *Koptische Heiligen und Märtyrerlegenden* II (Rome: Orientalia Christiana Analecta, 1935-1936), pp. 13-14.

recognition of the charismata, even though, with the passage of time, the practical reality diminished.

Spiritual Gifts: Their Use in the Church Today

The Holy Spirit is no different today than he was in the days of the early church. The Spirit still has this unimaginable store of spiritual gifts for building up the body of Christ and bringing its witness to the world. The "priesthood of all believers" (1 Pet. 2:9-10) becomes functional as people begin to discover and use their spiritual gifts.

The Charismatic renewal is sounding this word of hope and faith in the church today: "*Spiritual gifts – all of them – are part of God's provision for the church. Let us use them!*" The word *us* is important, for the exhortation is addressed to the renewal itself as much as to the church. The Charismatic renewal is not in a position to lecture the church on its neglect of spiritual gifts, although we have done this time and time again, and need to ask forgiveness. The renewal itself has just begun to make room for receiving and developing spiritual gifts. We have seen in Scripture far more than we have experienced, and it is this – the promise of Scripture – that we hold up in the midst of the church: "Come, as brothers and sisters of the Lord who went about doing good, healing all who were oppressed, let us together seek the gifts promised in his Word. Let us spread his gospel in demonstration of the Spirit and of power!"

Even though imperfectly understood and used, spiritual gifts are a practical part of the gospel ministry. They help build the congregation and the individual believer; they glorify Jesus; they put the love of God into action (1 Cor. 12:3, 7; 13:9; 14:1, 3-5, 12, 24-26; Gal. 3:5).

Discernment

The congregation needs to *test* spiritual gifts for authenticity. Precisely because spiritual experience is so important, life in the Holy Spirit must be subject to the closest scrutiny. The history of the early church reminds us how important is the ministry of testing or "distinguishing between spirits" (1 Cor. 12:10; 1 Jn 4:1-3). What spirit is at work in a given situation – God's Holy Spirit, the human spirit, a demonic power, or a mixture of influences? Special watchfulness must be exercised in regard to the use of some spiritual gifts, for instance, prophecies that are directed to specific individuals or are about the future.

To the practice of exorcism in the ancient church, see also Skarsaune and Engelsviken, "Possession and Exorcism in the History of the Church", in Moreau (ed), *Deliver Us From Evil*, 2002, pp. 65-82.

Theological perspective is indispensable. Otherwise, the work of God can be damaged by false teaching, misunderstanding, spiritual pride, unwillingness to be taught, and sectarian isolation. The special gift of "distinguishing between spirits" should be exercised with humility in the fellowship of the Christian community, and under the leadership of people with recognised ministries, such as pastors and teachers.

The dangers that are connected with the exercise of the spiritual gifts dare not, however, lead to such an overcritical stance that every spiritual outbreak gets squashed almost before it gets started. We must live with a measure of risk if we want to experience life in the Holy Spirit. *Possible misuse should not prevent proper use*, as the apostle Paul demonstrates by his instructions to the Corinthian church in 1 Corinthians 12-14.

An Examination of Three Gifts

We must allow room for continuous teaching and learning to take place, as Paul said, "Now about spiritual gifts, brothers, I do not want you to be ignorant" (1 Cor. 12:1). While the Charismatic renewal has called the church to be open to the full range of spiritual gifts, some gifts have been more prominently associated with the movement than others. It would go beyond our purpose to discuss in detail all the different charisms, but it is worth taking further note, in the following three chapters, of three gifts that are particularly associated with the movement and which play an important role in charismatic spirituality: prophecy, speaking in tongues, and healing. They are also somewhat controversial in the church at large, and a clarification of their meaning and practice can be helpful.

(48) The Gift of Prophecy

Introductory Explanation

The basic meaning of the word prophecy (Greek: *propheteia*) is the proclamation of a divinely inspired message. It denotes *a special charism in the New Testament church* (Rom. 12:6; 1 Cor. 12:10, 29; 13:2; 14:1, 22). It was a widespread phenomenon in the early church until about 300 A.D.

Christians who speak prophetically in public proclaim a message from God by the inspiration of the Holy Spirit. Peculiar to prophetic speech as distinct from ordinary speech is the element of revelation (Greek: *apokalypsis,* 1 Cor. 14:26, 30). What is revealed is not necessarily the future; more often, prophecy deals with the present situation, especially deeper and hidden truths about the situation of individuals and the church (1 Cor. 14:24-25; Rev. 2-3). Prophecy leads to a keen awareness of God's presence. Prophecy may evoke confession of sin and acknowledgment of the presence of God.

Congregational prophets are not in a state of ecstasy. There is no irresistible constraint to deliver the message. They may begin or stop speaking at will (1 Cor. 14:29-33). True prophets cannot, however, speak prophetically on demand or by their own will or initiative, only if a message has been received from God.

The function and purpose of the gift of prophecy is to bring the word and will of God to bear on a particular situation. This may take place through the convicting and judging of sin, and through pointing to God's promises, as we see in the prophetic words to the churches in Revelation 2-3. Prophecy is primarily directed toward the church and Christians.

Although prophecy is a charism by which the Spirit conveys his message in a spontaneous, unpremeditated way through believers to believers, prophets speak within the framework of the apostolic tradition contained in the New Testament. Prophets may play a role in the development of doctrine, but they cannot go beyond or against the message delivered to the church by the apostles. The theological criterion applicable to prophetic utterance is similar to all other proclamations in the church: its content must agree with the confession of faith (Rom. 12:6; 1 Cor. 12:3; 1 Pet. 4:10-11; 1 Jn 4:1-3). Scripture is therefore the norm for testing all prophecy.

The words of prophets should be tested because there is always a danger of false prophets and prophecies (Mt. 7:15-23; 24:24; 1 Cor. 12:3; 1 Thess. 5:19-21; 1 Jn 4:1-2). This testing should be done by the leaders of the church, by other believers with gifts of prophecy (1 Cor. 14:29) or the gift of distinguishing between spirits (1 Cor. 12:10). Basically, all Christians are encouraged to test messages on the basis of the revealed Word of God (Acts 17:11; 1 Thess. 5:20-21).

Timothy, for example, received a spiritual gift through a prophetic message when he was prayed for, but his gift had to be used according to the "pattern of sound teaching". The Holy Spirit himself would help preserve this sound teaching based on Scripture and the words of Paul himself:

> Until I come, devote yourself to the *public reading of Scripture*, to preaching and to teaching. *Do not neglect your gift*, which was given to you *through a prophetic message* when the body of elders laid their hand on you (1 Tim. 4:13-14).
>
> What you heard from me, keep as *pattern of sound teaching*, with faith and love in Christ Jesus. Guard the good deposit that was entrusted to you – guard it with the *help of the Holy Spirit* who lives in us (2 Tim. 1:13-14; cf. 2:15).

Although the prophetic message must be confirmed in a responsible way and must be conform with sound teaching, yet it is not simply a theological statement or ordinary preaching and teaching of the Word of God; it is a revelation given by God in a specific situation to specific people (Acts 13:1-3; 21:9-11; 1 Tim. 4:14; Rev. 2-3).

Prophecy is a particularly valuable gift for edifying or building up the church (1 Cor. 14:3, 12, 26, 31). It should therefore be sought by Christians (1 Cor. 12:31; 14:1). It can bring the truths of Scripture to bear in particular situations with great force.

After this introduction to the gift of prophecy in the New Testament churches, we want to delve deeper into the *practice of the gift of prophecy in the church today* and suggest that it ought to be considered in the light of some basic questions.

What is Prophecy?

The background of biblical prophecy is found in the Old Testament. The Hebrew idea of a prophet (Hebrew: *nabi*) carried with it the understanding that the prophet spoke words that had been divinely revealed, as a messenger of God, and the declarer of God's will.[1] Prophecy might include an element of prediction, but not necessarily so. The central meaning of the verb "to prophesy", both in Hebrew and Greek, is to speak forth, to proclaim on behalf of someone else.

This basic meaning of the word sheds light on the function of *New Testament prophets*. The word describes someone who makes something known or public, especially one who speaks for God. God's prophets receive

---

[1] Gesenius, *Hebrew and Chaldee Lexicon of the Old Testament Scriptures*, translated by Samuel P. Tregelles (Grand Rapids, MI: Eerdmans, 1954), p. 528.

inspiration to speak a divinely given message. The message can come in a variety of ways: through words, as pictures or inner impressions, through dreams or visions, or through inspired application of a particular text in Scripture.[2]

Prophecy, as distinguished from the gift of teaching or counselling, is not arrived at by a process of study or reasoning. It has a certain quality of spontaneity. It has more the immediate sense of being *received* than of being arrived at by a logical process. Prophecy is also different from the prophet's own general wisdom, biblical insight, or recognition of needs among those that are being addressed. A prophecy does not start in the prophet's brain, but in God himself. When God sees the need for prophetic revelation and finds someone who is ready and able to speak for him, then he will impress his message on the prophet by the Holy Spirit. Therefore, although it may exercise the prophet's thought and concern even over a considerable period of time, the message that the prophet brings is essentially not his own or premeditated.

The biblical meaning of prophecy is not identified with every inspired utterance. There can be testimonies, teaching, and preaching that are certainly inspired by God. The difference between these and what the Bible means by prophecy is not the content of the message but the way in which the message is given. In the case of teaching, the message depends partly on a person's personality, knowledge, training, and insight, whereas prophecy has its origin in God. Prophecy does not depend on a man's or woman's natural talents or intellectual powers, though these do to some degree influence both the content of the prophecy and the way in which it is conveyed.

What is the Biblical Role of Prophecy?

In the Old Testament, God revealed his message through his prophets, a term widely used. Besides those usually named as prophets, the term was applied to people like Abraham, Aaron, Miriam, and Moses. There is a promise in the Old Testament of a future prophet:

> The Lord said to me [Moses]: 'What they say is good. I will raise up for them a prophet like you from among their brothers; I will put words in his mouth, and he will tell them everything I command him. If anyone does not listen to my words that the prophet speaks in my name, I myself will call him to account'. (Dt. 18:17-19)

Above all, God has revealed himself through his Son (Heb. 1:1-4; Jn 1:17-18), who is *the* prophet. Although Jesus outwardly bore certain similarities to the scribes, he lacked the prerequisites for rabbinical service in the usual

---

[2] Christenson, *Charismatic Renewal*, pp. 107-111.

sense. He was not viewed as a professional theologian, but rather as a charismatic figure (Mk 1:22), and the unanimous opinion was: "He is a prophet." This was continually expressed among the people (Mk 6:15; Mt. 21:11-46; Lk. 7:16; Jn 4:19; 6:14; 7:40-52; 9:17) and even among the Pharisees, although with a touch of scepticism (Mk 8:11; Lk. 7:39). The religious leaders demanded a sign from Jesus precisely because he was viewed as a prophet; the sign was a means by which he could legitimise the claim. According to Luke 24:19, Jesus' disciples also saw him as a prophet. Jesus was finally arrested and accused as a false prophet. Jesus himself did not reject the opinion that he was a prophet. Although he was certainly *more than a prophet*, he did see himself in the ranks of the prophets (Lk. 13:33; Mk 6:4; Lk. 4:24; Jn 4:44). As the true bearer and giver of all spiritual gifts, Jesus continues his prophetic ministry as the exalted Lord, through his body, the church.

The Pentecost message proclaimed that the age had now come when prophecy should be frequent among God's people (Acts 2:17; cf. Joel 2:28). The importance of the prophetic ministry in the early church is indisputable. It is immediately evident in the growth of the church: in Judea (Acts 21:10); in Jerusalem (Acts 11:27-30; 15:32), in Caesarea (Acts 21:9), and in Antioch (Acts 13:1). The presence of prophets in Thessalonica (1 Thess. 5:20), in Ephesus (Acts 19:6; Eph. 4:11), and in Rome (Rom. 12:6) may be assumed as well. The significance of prophecy in the early church is further evidenced by the fact that specific individuals are named as prophets.

The high regard for prophecy in the church at Corinth is well known. Paul reckoned the ministry of the prophet among the charismata given to the body of Christ (Rom. 12:6; 1 Cor. 12:10, 28). He urged the Corinthians to seek this gift eagerly (1 Cor. 14:1, 39). Prophetic speech was esteemed as a gift of the Holy Spirit, more valuable, for instance, than speaking in tongues, unless the tongue was interpreted. The importance of this spiritual gift was underscored when Paul stated that God had "appointed" the ministry of prophets, second to the apostles (1 Cor. 12:28, cp. Eph. 4:11). Paul himself possessed the gift of prophecy and employed it in his letters (Rom. 11:25-27; 1 Cor. 14:6; 15:51-58). In Ephesians, he stresses the fundamental significance of the post-resurrection prophetic ministry for the entire church (Eph. 2:20; 3:5; 4:11).

New Testament prophecy often operates in the *direction of spiritual or pastoral care*: "Everyone who prophesies speaks to men for their strengthening, encouragement and comfort" (1 Cor. 14:3). The extent to which one, through prophetic utterance, may come face to face with God is made abundantly clear from 1 Corinthians 14:24-25:

> But if an unbeliever or someone who does not understand comes in while everybody is prophesying, he will be convinced by all that he is a sinner and will be judged by all, and the secrets of his heart will be laid bare. So he will fall down and worship God, exclaiming, 'God is really among you.'

And finally, the book of Revelation, taken as a whole, is an outstanding testimony to the place of prophecy among the early Christians. The seven letters to the churches in Asia Minor are presented as direct, prophetically received words from the risen Lord. The ministry of prophets receives prominent mention throughout the book (Rev. 11:18; 16:6; 18:20-24; 22:9). The reader is urgently warned against undervaluing the claims of this prophetic writing (Rev. 22:6-7, 18-19).

What is the Role of Prophecy in the History of the Church?

It would be incorrect to state that the church has known no prophecy at all in the post-New Testament era. There is evidence of prophetic activity down through the history of the church, especially during the first three centuries.[3]

Lutheran Pietism, for instance, experienced a renewal of prophetic gifts. On the basis of Scripture, they also rejected arguments suggesting that spiritual gifts ended with the apostles.[4]

Prophecy has been a common occurrence in the mission of the church in the last hundred years, as seen for instance in Africa. It has not been Western missionaries who have brought the gift of prophecy to Africa, but African Christians themselves.

The African prophet William Wade Harris (ca. 1865–1929) from Liberia in West Africa received his calling to be a prophet through a vision of an angel while he was in prison in 1910. As an itinerant prophet and evangelist, he was God's instrument in the conversion of about 100 000 people during a short ministry period, mostly in Ivory Coast and Ghana. His ministry was the origin of the large Harris revival movement.[5]

Likewise, Simon Kimbangu (1889–1951) in Congo gave origin to the largest African instituted church with several million members through a five-month ministry as a "healing prophet" in 1921 before he was arrested and kept in prison for the rest of his life. He also had the gift of tongues.[6] There were also prophets in the African Instituted Churches in Southern Africa.[7]

During the persecution of the Pentecostal *Mullu Wongel Church* (Full Gospel Church) in Ethiopia in 1973, in which the top leadership of the dominant *Ethiopian Orthodox Tewahedo Church* was heavily involved, an Orthodox monk from a monastery far from Addis Ababa came into one of

---

[3] See the discussion in the previous chapter.

[4] Brown, *Understanding Pietism*, p. 106.

[5] See Bengt Sundkler and Christopher Steed, *A History of the Church in Africa* (Cambridge: Cambridge University Press, 2000), pp. 197-201.

[6] Sundkler and Steed, *History,* pp. 780-781.

[7] Bengt Sundkler, *Bantu Prophets in South Africa* (2nd edition, London: Routledge, 1961).

the orthodox churches in the capital and denounced the persecution claiming that the Pentecostals were Christian brothers. This message had been given to him in an unexpected prophecy.[8]

In the chapter on Lutheran people who have prepared for the Charismatic renewal, we have mentioned the female prophet Nenilava in Madagascar who led a large revival movement.

We must admit, however, that there also is a large problem of false prophets in Africa that should alert us to the need of testing all prophetic claims.[9]

Taken as a whole, however, in spite of the many examples of prophetic ministries in the church, prophetic utterance is a slender thread in the tapestry of church history. Bruce Yokum is correct when he writes, "It is clear that since the third century prophecy has been neither continuously manifest in the church nor common to the whole church at any one time."[10] In the Pentecostal/Charismatic movements the gift of prophecy has come to the fore perhaps more widely than at any time since the second century.

Prophecy Today?

As it is used in the global church today, the word "prophetic" often means social criticism. It is most often used about the church's stand in the world with regard to social, economic and political questions and with particular emphasis on its struggle for liberation, justice, and the integrity of creation. Those are good and necessary causes, inspired by the prophets of the Old Testament and their harsh criticism of the oppression of the poor and marginalised and their fight against injustice. This ministry of the church has sometimes been called "prophetic diakonia".

When we speak of prophecy in the Charismatic renewal, however, we usually have in mind spontaneous utterances inspired by the Holy Spirit. Most Christians have no sense of the lack of this kind of prophecy in the church. They do not generally expect that God will speak prophetically to us today. Prophecy has not found a place in everyday church life. Yet the Holy Spirit is working toward the day when the churches will again expect and take to heart his prophetic word.

Thoughtful participants in the Charismatic renewal recognise that prophetic revelation in the renewal has often been elementary. Most of the

---

[8] Reported by Tormod Engelsviken who was a missionary in Ethiopia at the time and in close contact with the Mullu Wongel Church. Tormod Engelsviken, *Mulu Wongel: A Documentary Report on the Life and History of the Independent Pentecostal Movement in Ethiopia 1960-1975* (Oslo: The Free Faculty of Theology, today: MF Norwegian School of Theology, 1975, unpublished).

[9] See for example the article by Moses Owojaiye, "The Problem of False Prophets in Africa", *Lausanne Global Analysis*, 20th November 2019, Vol. 8, Issue 6.

[10] Bruce Yokum, *Prophecy* (Ann Arbor, MI: Servant, 1976), p. 22.

prophecies are rather generalised words of encouragement and exhortation. This is not to say that they have not been genuine or important (perhaps we need more encouragement than we realise), but it probably also illustrates the fact that "we prophesy in part" – imperfectly (1 Cor. 13:9-10). We have been schooled in the ways of reason, but not in the more spontaneous modes of revelation. We should expect to grow and develop in the exercise of spiritual gifts. It is worth the time and effort, for it will make the church more responsive to the leading of the Spirit.

On occasion, the Spirit wants to break through with prophetic revelation. When the prophetic word is again spoken and received, the church will have taken one more believing step toward biblical normalcy.

How Does Present-Day Prophecy Relate to Biblical Authority?

Jesus confirmed the Old Testament as the word of God. By word and deed, he realised God's redemptive plan when he was on earth, always consistent with the written revelation in the Old Testament. Jesus said, "Do not think that I have come to abolish the Law and the Prophets; I have not come to abolish them but to fulfil them" (Mt. 5:17-18, see, for example, also Jn 10:34-35; Lk. 24:27, 45-47). The gospels, and particularly the gospel of Matthew, emphasise again and again how *Jesus fulfilled Old Testament prophecies* (see, for example Mt. 1:22-23; 2:5-6, 4:14-16; 8:17; Lk. 4:21; 24:46-47). These prophecies about Christ and salvation had been inspired by the Holy Spirit, as the apostle Peter explains:

> Concerning this salvation, *the prophets*, who spoke of the grace that was to come to you, searched intently and with the greatest care, trying to find out the time and circumstances to which the *Spirit of Christ in them* was pointing when *he predicted* the sufferings of Christ and the glories that would follow. It was *revealed to them* that they were not serving themselves but you, when they spoke of the things that have now been told you by those who have *preached the gospel to you by the Holy Spirit* sent from heaven (1 Pet. 1:10-12, cf. Rom. 1:2; 16:25-26).
>
> Above all, you must understand that no prophecy of Scripture came about by the prophet's own interpretation. For prophecy never had its origin in the will of man, but *men spoke from God as they were carried along by the Holy Spirit* (2 Pet. 1:20-21).

Not only the prophetic parts of Old Testament, but also the *New Testament has come into being through the work of the Holy Spirit.* Jesus entrusted his mission to the apostles and equipped them with the Holy Spirit to be witnesses who remembered and interpreted what he had said and done (Jn 14:26; 16:14; 20:21-22; Acts 1:8). He wrapped the teaching of the apostles in the mantle of his own authority (see, for example, Mt. 10:40-41; Lk. 10:16; Acts 15:7; 1 Cor. 14:37).

In their ministry the *apostles received revelation from the Holy Spirit*, as Paul says:

> As it is written, 'No eye has seen, no ear has heard, no mind has conceived what God has prepared for those who love him', but God has *revealed it to us by his Spirit* [...] We have not received the spirit of the world but the *Spirit who is from God*, that we may understand what God has freely given us. This is what we speak, not in words taught us by human wisdom but in *words taught us by the Spirit*, expressing spiritual truth in spiritual words (1 Cor. 2:10-13).

Thus, the authority of the written Scriptures of both the Old and the New Testament rests ultimately on the authority of Jesus Christ and the Holy Spirit. Our confidence that the written Scriptures are the Word of God is rooted in our trust in Christ and the Spirit.

This belief in the authority of the Bible does not, however, imply that the whole Bible has come into being as if the authors were under the control of the Holy Spirit and only wrote what the Spirit dictated them. As can be observed by both plain reading and scholarly exegesis the Bible contains *many types of texts*: historical narratives, laws, poetry, prayers, wisdom sayings, visions, prophecies, biographies (the gospels), sermons, parables, letters, apocalyptic texts etc. The authors – and they were many – used their faculties, their knowledge, their reason, as well as their own experience when they wrote. They would base their writings on passed-on tradition, on their own personal experience, on the eyewitness accounts of others, on direct revelation, etc. They would express their own response to the word of God in praise and thanksgiving, lamentation and confession. Sometimes they would write alone, but often together with or on behalf of others. They would report what other people had said and done as well as express their own views and opinions. In all they did and said they were children of the periods in history in which they lived and the cultures to which they belonged.

Different texts could also have different weight or degrees of authority. The apostle Paul, for example, would as a general rule speak in the name of the Lord (1 Cor. 1:10) and thus with his authority, but at times he would also say, "I have no command from the Lord, but I give a judgement as one who by God's mercy is trustworthy" (1 Cor. 7:25), "in my judgement" (1 Cor. 7:40), or "I am not talking as the Lord would, but as a fool" (2 Cor. 11:17), thereby indicating that he was expressing his own opinion therefore one not binding for everybody.

We also have to take into account the *progressive nature* of God's revelation as he reveals more and more of himself and his plan of salvation until it is fully accomplished (Mt. 11:25-27; Jn 1:17-18; Rom. 11:25; 16:25-26; 1 Cor. 15:51; Col, 1:26; Heb. 1:1-2; Rev. 10:17). The *difference between the two covenants*, the Old and the New Testament, must also be taken seriously. It means that much of the Old Testament – particularly the ceremonial and penal laws and some of the promises – is meant for people of Israel alone at certain points in their history as God's elect people, and therefore does not apply in general or to the church today.

This immense *diversity of the biblical revelation* is a great challenge for the interpretation and application of the Scriptures. Yet, on the basis of the Bible itself, we do believe that this diversity was willed by God and worked out under the guidance of the Holy Spirit. There are many reasons why we can claim that the Bible is God's authoritative Word. Let us sum up the most important:

1. The words of Jesus and the apostles about the authority and inspiration of the Scriptures.
2. The historical fulfilment of the Old Testament prophecies in the life of Jesus and the church.[11]
3. Eyewitness accounts as the historical basis of the gospels and Acts (Lk. 1:2; Acts 1:1, 21-22; 2 Pet. 1:16-18).[12]
4. The authority granted to the apostles to speak on behalf of Christ, as seen in the gospels, Acts and the Epistles.
5. The guidance and inspiration by Holy Spirit of the apostles and their disciples in the writing of the New Testament.

Since it is the same Holy Spirit who speaks through the Scriptures and in today's congregational prophecies, the Spirit will never inspire a prophecy that contradicts his own word. All present-day prophecy must therefore be submitted to and tested by the Bible.

Prophecies are not meant to bring fundamentally new doctrinal material to the church. Rather, a prophetic message applies or expands on biblical truth, emblazoning certain passages or truths on the hearts of individuals, groups, congregations, or even the church as a whole.

It is possible, of course, that God through prophetic revelation could give providential direction on issues not directly dealt with in Scripture. Scripture itself does not prescribe precise limits for prophetic revelation. This lies

---

[11] Both in the New Testament as well as in the ancient church the fulfilment of the Old Testament prophecies was seen as proof of the truth of the gospel and was a main argument in the mission of the church. See for example Oskar Skarsaune's study of the writings of the 2nd century church father Justin Martyr: *Proof from Prophecy* (Leiden: Brill, 1987). The ancient creeds do not state anything about the Bible, but the Third article of the *Nicene Creed* says about the Holy Spirit: "[...] who spoke by the prophets", *The Book of Concord*, p. 19, thereby signifying the importance of the inspired prophetic writings.

[12] For convincing arguments for the historical reliability of the gospels based on eyewitness accounts within living memory of the events, see the thorough study by the New Testament scholar Craig S. Keener, *Christobiography. Memory, History, and the Reliability of the Gospels* (Grand Rapids, MI: Eerdmans, 2019).

within the sovereignty of God. In the meantime, we can receive with thanksgiving the gift of prophetic revelation, faithfully submitting it to the authority of Scripture.

Do We Need Prophecy Today?

Prophecy brings home with added force the fact that God really does speak to us. It highlights his nearness and concern. Prophecy can increase our trust in the living and caring God, in his willingness to guide us even in the most ordinary situations. It confesses Jesus as the only Lord and Saviour. We need this in secularised cultures, in which God, if he is believed in at all, is kept at a distance and has no real influence on everyday life and decisions. And we need this in non-Christian religious cultures, where it is important to distinguish between the deception by false gods and evil spirits on the one hand, and the direction of the true God, the Lord Jesus Christ and his Holy Spirit on the other.

> For even if there are so-called gods, whether in heaven or on earth (as indeed there are many "gods" and many "lords"), yet for us there is but one God, the Father, from whom all things came and for whom we live; and there is but one Lord, Jesus Christ, through whom all things came and through whom we live (1 Cor. 8:5-6).
>
> No-one can say 'Jesus is Lord' except by the Holy Spirit (1 Cor. 12:3).
>
> Dear friends, do not believe every spirit, but test the spirits to see whether they are from God, because many false prophets have gone out into the world. This is how you can recognise the Spirit of God: Every spirit that acknowledges that Jesus Christ has come in the flesh is from God, but every spirit that does not acknowledge Jesus is not from God (1 Jn 4:1-3).

The gift of prophecy can help restore a lively trust in the Lord who leads in his unfailing love the people he has redeemed (cf. Ex. 15:13), helping us to walk in faith step by step. Prophecy serves especially to strengthen, encourage, and comfort the people of God (1 Cor. 14:3).

A good illustration of that is the seven prophetic letters to the churches in Asia Minor (Rev. 2-3). Some of these churches were drifting away from their devotion to the Lord; some were falling victim to dangerous heresies; some were headed into hard times. They needed a clear word that would rebuild their relationship with the Lord and prepare them for what lay ahead. It is easy for us to drift off centre in our Christian calling, to lose sight of that which concerns the Lord, to lose our first love for Christ, to disobey him and compromise with the world, to be led astray by false teaching or false prophecy. Through properly using the prophetic gift, our real needs can be addressed, and God can rebuke, correct, encourage, and console his people.

Prophecy makes the Word of God more personally relevant because it pinpoints the word that God has for a particular person or situation. We live in cultures that are often oblivious to the biblical concept of sin and guilt, and in some regard lean toward an almost hedonistic understanding of Christianity, merely as a way to an abundant and happy life. It is the ministry of the Spirit to convict of sin and create faith in Christ, and he knows what Christians need to hear individually in order to see their sin and their need for salvation. The gift of prophecy can also make our evangelistic outreach more effective by pinpointing the word that the Spirit wants to bring in a given situation (2 Sam. 12:7; Jn 4:17-19; 1 Cor. 14:24-25; Acts 8:30-35).

In the New Testament, prophecies normally dealt with the current time and situation, showing hidden things that needed to be uncovered, applying biblical truths to a present need. On occasion, however, prophecy can throw light on future events, in order to prepare Christians for what is to come. In the Old Testament, but also in the gospels, in Acts, in the epistles and in Revelation, there are numerous examples of revelations and prophecies that *predict future events* (see, for example, Jesus, Mt. 24-25; 26:31-35; Ananias, Acts 9:10-12; 22:15; Cornelius, Acts 10:5-6; Agabus, Acts 11:28; 21:10-11; Paul, Acts 20:22-23, 29-30; 22:10; 26:17; 27:34; Rom. 11:25-26; 1 Cor. 15:22-25, 51-52; 1 Thess. 4:16-17; John, Rev. 1:3, 19; 2:10; 3:10 etc.). These predictive prophesies may enable the church to prepare for what lies ahead. A word from the risen Lord, who through his suffering, death, and resurrection has defeated Satan – what a preparation for those headed into a time of persecution! The church that is prophetic today will be stronger tomorrow.

Distinguishing Between Prophets

With regard to *predictive prophecy*, there is, however, a special need to issue a warning. There are false predictive prophecies both in the history of the Old Testament and today. We may learn from the Old Testament to distinguish between true and false prophecy.

It was *characteristic of the false prophets* that they prophesied for money or favours by predicting victory, peace, and prosperity (1 Kings 22:6, 13-14, 23, 28; Jer. 5:12-13; 6:13; 23:9-40; Mic. 3:11). "They lead my people astray, saying 'Peace', when there is no peace" (Ez. 13:10). They were not sent by the Lord and were prophesying "delusions of their mind" (Jer. 14:14-15; cp. Jer. 27:14-15; Zach. 13:2-4). Therefore, *the true prophets sent by God had to fight against the false prophets* and condemn them in the name of the Lord:

> The word of the Lord came to me: 'Son of man, *prophesy against the prophets of Israel* who are now prophesying. Say to those who prophesy out of their own imagination: "Hear the word of the Lord! This is what the sovereign Lord says: "Woe to the foolish prophets who follow their own spirit and have seen

nothing… Their visions are false and their divinations a lie.'" They say: 'The Lord declares', when the Lord has not sent them; yet they expect their words to be fulfilled' (Ez. 13:1-3, 6, cp. Jer. 5:30-31; Is. 9:14-16).

There are at least three biblical criteria for the evaluation of prophets and predictive prophecies:

The first criterion is that God-inspired predictive prophecy will be *fulfilled and come true.* "You may say to yourselves, 'How can we know when a message has not been spoken by the Lord?' If what a prophet proclaims in the name of the Lord *does not take place or come true*, that is a message that the Lord has not spoken. That prophet has spoken presumptuously. Do not be afraid of him" (Dt. 18:21-22). "But the prophet who prophesies peace will be recognised as one truly sent by the Lord *only* if his prediction comes true" (Jer. 28:9).

The second criterion is that even if what has been predicted in a prophecy does take place, the prophet is *not to be accepted* if they *lead God's people astray* by false teaching: "If a prophet, or one who foretells by dreams, appears among you and announces to you a miraculous sign or wonder, and if the sign or wonder of which he has spoken takes place, and he says, 'Let us follow other gods and let us worship them', you must not listen to the words of that prophet or dreamer" (Dt. 13:1-3, 18:20; cf. Mt. 7:22; 24:24).

The third criterion is that a true prophet cannot have a lifestyle that is contrary to God's will and commandments. "And among the prophets of Jerusalem I have seen something horrible: they commit adultery and live a lie. They strengthen the hands of evildoers, so that no-one turns from his wickedness […] from the prophets of Jerusalem ungodliness has spread throughout the land" (Jer. 23:14-15, cf. Mt. 7:15-21).

These criteria may also be applied to present-day prophecy. It means that, before recognising a prophetic message or ministry, the church should know whether or not both the teaching and the personal lifestyle of the prophet are in accord with biblical norms. In addition – as in the case of predictive prophecy – one may wait and see whether the prophecy is fulfilled before accepting it as being from the Lord or acting upon it.

There have unfortunately been some examples of highly publicised false predictive prophecies among people associated with extreme forms of the Charismatic movement, for example, when some self-appointed "prophets" predicted political outcomes of elections in the United States in 2020, which did not come true. Leaders of the Charismatic renewal must take the very heavy and ungrateful responsibility – as did the true prophets in the Old Testament – of disclosing and condemning false prophecy in order to protect the church against error and deception.

Prophecy in the Public Arena

In the Old Testament, God's prophets attacked social injustice and the oppression of the poor. Even though this was in the context of theocratic Israel, it has relevance for today. Lutheran doctrine speaks about the "first use of the law," *usus politicus*, that is, the application of God's law in social, cultural, economic, and political affairs. God's desire for social justice and his concern for those who suffer has not changed. Prophetic messages, directed first of all to the church, can help Christians see God's agenda for freedom, equality and justice in society at large.

Both in church history and in the present time, bold Christians have spoken out prophetically against widespread social evils, such as slavery, the oppression and exploitation of indigenous people and other minorities, anti-Semitism, racism, apartheid, the caste system, abortion, economic inequality, religious persecution, violation of human rights, the oppression of the poor and the destruction of creation. The list could obviously be made longer. However, it must also be admitted that many Christians have consciously or unconsciously been guilty of these same evils and need to repent of them.

Anyone who has listened to debates in the public arena knows that the theme of human rights and social justice evokes a clash of wildly divergent opinions. There is disagreement not only as to how to achieve justice in society but also as to what constitutes justice. Although the church in its stand against social evils has depended mostly on the Bible and not on new prophetic revelation, there is also the possibility that we through the prophetic gift today can discern God's will and his plans better and therefore serve him more effectively in the public arena.

Prophecy in the Church

God's prophets in the Old Testament attacked false spiritual security, superficial worship, and empty religious traditions. Christians can fall victim to the same ills. A Lutheran congregation that was quite content with its religious routine, suddenly found itself with a new pastor who preached faith, surrender, and commitment to Christ as though it really ought to matter. After about a year had gone by, a small group began to agitate for his removal. They arranged a congregational meeting to force his resignation. At the meeting, they rehearsed a litany of grievances with considerable acrimony and at some length. Finally, the chairman asked if there was any further discussion. A teenage girl who had sat silently throughout the meeting stood up and quietly said, "Let him who is without sin cast the first stone." The meeting was thunderstruck. Someone said, "I move that we table this matter indefinitely." It was tabled without even the agitators raising a dissenting voice. A prophetic word can jar people out of complacency because it is pointed and direct, alerting them to the fact that God himself is concerned about them and dealing with them.

The nature of the prophetic gift answers to its function in the church. The church is the body of Christ (Rom. 12:5; 1 Cor. 12:27). Christ is the head (Eph. 1:22-23). Prophets are a communication link between the head and the members: they transmit the mind and will of the head to the members. As the members in a physical body pay heed to the impulses that come from the nerve centre of the brain, so members in the body of Christ need to listen to what their spiritual head wants to say to them through his prophets. In this way, the prophetic gift becomes a strategic part of Christ's work for bringing the church on earth to maturity.

The whole of Scripture testifies to the fact that prophecy is a key element in God's dealings with his people. The strong evangelistic outreach of the early church was closely linked to the ministry of prophets (see for example, Acts 13:1, 3). This was a logical consequence of the Old Testament promises that, in the age to come, there would be an outpouring of the Spirit on all believers.

God himself has appointed some to prophetic ministry in the church (1 Cor. 12:28; Eph. 4:11). The order in which the gifts and ministries are listed is worth noting. Prophets are consistently listed as number two, right after apostles (see also Eph. 2:20; 3:5). The prophetic ministry has particular significance for the well-being and up-building of the church. There is no suggestion in Scripture that God intends this ministry to be superseded or dispensed with prior to the second coming of Christ. He wants prophets in the church today, and that is a call to obedience: we should seek in every way to encourage a responsible exercise of the prophetic gift. God is looking for more than a passive, theoretical acceptance of spiritual gifts in the church. A passive acquiescence to "whatever gifts he wants to give me" can be the cover for resistance to any actual manifestation of spiritual gifts.

The early church had a deeper dependence on receiving prophetic direction from the Lord than does the church today. When they faced important choices, they sought the Lord's guidance through prophets. When a congregation today has important choices to make – setting right priorities, recognising the gifts and ministries of the different members, coming up with a strategy for evangelism or a building programme – we might well take a cue from the early church (see Acts 10, 13 and 15). So too for individuals and groups that seek guidance from the Lord: we should ask those whom God has gifted prophetically to help us discern the Lord's will.

Spiritual gifts, pre-eminently prophecy, must be actively encouraged among us. In public worship, prayer meetings, and private gatherings, we need to cultivate an expectant faith in the God who speaks through his prophets. We need to create an atmosphere in which the prophetic gift can be freely expressed, grow, and mature. Then the Lord can more perfectly strengthen, encourage, and comfort his church. Then the church can minister not simply in the power of human understanding, but in the power of divine knowledge and wisdom.

How Does the Prophetic Ministry Function?

Prophecy has nothing to do with uncontrollable ecstasy. The prophet who receives a message from God is not compelled to speak it out immediately (1 Cor. 14:32). In a worship service, prophecy should be offered in an orderly way, at a time provided for it.

Not everyone will prophesy, even though prophecy seems to be one of the more widely distributed spiritual gifts. Some believers may never receive a prophecy; others, only a few times in their lives. Some may prophesy rather freely, but the prophecies remain quite general or superficial, or of a mixed spirit; leaders in the congregation may need to impose some restraints. But others prophesy regularly under a clear anointing of the Spirit; the gift is manifested with increasing maturity and authority. The congregation comes to see that they have among them one with the "ministry" of a prophet.

A prophet is under a holy call from God to convey the revealed message. The form in which this is done may vary. Since the message of prophets in the Old Testament was God-given, it was often introduced with the phrase, "Thus says the Lord." In the New Testament, we see the phrase, "the Holy Spirit says" (Acts 21:11). At other times, however, a prophecy is given with no distinctive introduction (Acts 13:2). The form "Thus says the Lord" could be so unfamiliar in some churches that it would actually hinder the acceptance of the prophetic word. A lower-key introduction, such as, "I sense that the Lord wants to tell us…" might be a more helpful way of preparing people to receive a prophetic word. Prophets should seek to be sensitive not only to the content of the message but also to the most appropriate way to convey it, for that, too, is part of the wisdom of God.

A special ministry is when the gift of prophecy is used in situations of personal counselling and intercession for individual Christians. In these cases, the words are most often words of "strengthening, encouragement and comfort", but sometimes there are also directions and advice given. The question is then how the person who receives the message can ascertain whether it is from God and know how to respond.

The leadership group of the charismatic *Oasis movement* in the Lutheran Church of Norway has formulated the following guidelines for what could be called "personal prophetic ministry". These could also be useful elsewhere:

> Personal prophetic ministry" is common in many charismatic circles. An example could be that people with a prophetic gift offer a ministry of "prophetic intercession" for individuals, or are willing to "listen to God for people". This

practice is not described in the Bible and must therefore be subordinated to what the Bible says about prophecy and gifts of revelation in general.

Human beings cannot decide if and when God will reveal himself. Spontaneous revelations are not something that can simply be ordered from God – they are always something that God may give in his sovereignty. Hence, there should always be openness to the possibility that God does not speak, neither *when* expected nor *as* expected. Neither can we ignore the human factors in such ministry situations. The situation in itself creates an expectation both in the person who shares, and the person who receives. This is, nevertheless, not different in principle from other prophecies and revelations that are shared. They must always be tested on the Word of God, and we have to acknowledge that there is a human factor in all revelations. The congregation should therefore make a careful choice of those who are assigned such a ministry and put emphasis on their experience and maturity.

These reservations with regard to "personal prophetic ministry" are mostly concerned with its form and organising, and with the expectations that are communicated. The fact that an intercessor listens to God in order to hear if God has something to say to the person who seeks intercessory prayer, is not contrary to what the Bible says about the prophetic gift. It is rather a response to the words of the Bible about seeking and using the gifts.

Among those who have received prophecy as their spiritual gift and ministry, there are many who experience that God gives revelations to those who seek such "ministry". They may pray for several people in succession, and God may give something that may be communicated to practically all of those who are prayed for. Many who have sought intercessory prayer testify to the fact that they have received life-transforming messages from God in such situations.

The practice of "prophetic intercession" may be a challenge to the leadership of a congregation or a meeting. It creates a need for co-operation between the different ministries and gifts. Gifts of "distinguishing between spirits" and spiritual counselling ought to be used by the ministries that surround those who receive prophetic intercession. When handled properly, this practice does not challenge what the Bible says about gifts of prophecy and revelation.

We have however, to be particularly cautious with personal prophecies that predict future events in the lives of people ("predictive prophecy") or give guidance to people as to how they should act in certain situations. Both the history of the church and much experience have shown that such concrete prophecies, when false, can cause great damage, both in the lives of individuals and congregations.[13]

We might add that in situations when people receive "predictive" or "directive" prophecy, the prophecy should be subjected to testing by others

---

[13] These guidelines have been translated from Norwegian in a slightly edited form. They are printed in Larry Christenson, Asbjørn Simonnes and Tormod Engelsviken (eds), *Velkommen, Hellige Ånd – karismatisk fornyelse i kirken* (Ottestad: Proklamedia, 2018), p. 278.

in the Christian fellowship. It should also be acted upon only if it is a *confirmation* of what oneself understands to be the will of God. There is no doubt that the Holy Spirit guides Christians corporately as well as individually through spiritual gifts exercised by other Christians, but no one is under obligation to act on predictions or follow directions given by others.

The apostle Paul himself did not respond to Agabus' personal prophecy about his imprisonment, although the prophecy was genuine. He did not even follow the well-intended advice of his followers, but held on to his own conviction. Even so, the conclusion was: "The Lord's will be done" (Acts 21:10-14). Words and prophecies from people – as true or well-intended as they may be – can never replace our own responsibility for following our own convictions and make our own decisions in obedience to God.

The church today needs bold and humble prophets who faithfully both *listen to and speak the word given to them by God.* The counterpart to this is a people who *listen to that word with reverence, with discernment, and with a predisposition to obey the Lord.*

(49) The Gift of Speaking in Tongues

The gift most prominently associated with the Charismatic renewal in the popular mind is speaking in tongues. It has played a major role in the spread both of the Pentecostal and the Charismatic movements.[1] In the last 120 years, it has become more widely experienced than at any time since the days of the early church.

Those who have experienced speaking in tongues testify to the blessings that the gift has brought into their lives, especially their personal prayer lives.[2] Critics say that it occasions spiritual pride, causes division among Christians, or at least is overemphasised in charismatic circles. This raises questions that call for serious and balanced consideration.

What Is the Basic Meaning of the Term "Speaking in Tongues"?

The gift of tongues is sometimes called *glossolalia,* a transliteration of the Greek terms *glossa* (tongue) and *lalein* (to speak). The basic meaning of the word tongue in classical Greek is the physical organ in the mouth. But it is also used metaphorically, and then it can mean a *language* or dialect. In English, as in other languages, the corresponding word to *glossa* in Greek can also be used metaphorically to mean language or a manner of speaking, as in the English expression "one's mother tongue". It should be noted that in the New Testament "to speak in other tongues" (Greek: *lalein heterais glossais,* Acts 2:4) is an expression that has *nothing to do with the physical organ*, but refers *to a special kind of religious or spiritual speaking.*[3]

Speaking in tongues is speech inspired by the Holy Spirit (Acts 2:4), and is one of the gifts, the *charismata,* of the Spirit (1 Cor. 12:10, 28; 14:2, 4-6, 13-19, 26-28). Its meaning is not understood by the speaker and usually not by anybody else (1 Cor. 14:2; Acts 2:6). It is not framed by the speaker in the

---

[1] Luther P. Gerlach and Virginia H. Hine, *People, Power, Change – Movements of Social Transformation* (Indianapolis, IN: Bobbs-Merrill, 1970), pp. 120, 125, 188.

[2] Christenson, *Charismatic Renewal*, pp. 17-31. See also Christenson, *Speaking in Tongues*, pp. 13-14, 27-28, 76-79 and Erwin Prange, *The Gift Is Already Yours* (Plainfield, NJ: Logos, 1973), p. 53.

[3] Gerhard Kittel (ed), *Theological Dictionary of the New Testament*, Vol. 1 (Grand Rapids, MI: Eerdmans, 1964), pp. 719ff. Also William F. Arndt and Wilbur Gingrich, *A Greek-English Lexicon of the New Testament and Other Early Christian Literature* (Chicago, IL: University of Chicago Press, 1957), p. 161. The literal translation of "speaking in tongues", for example in the German *Zungenreden* or in the Scandinavian *tungetale* may unfortunately carry with it strongly negative connotations and could be replaced by *Sprachenreden* or *språktale* respectively.

way of a learned language. It is a spontaneous linguistic expression. The speaker does not consciously determine what they are going to say. The speech does not proceed from the conscious reasoning process (1 Cor. 14:14). It is para-rational speech prompted by the Spirit.

This does not mean that speaking in tongues is necessarily ecstatic or strongly emotional, or that it is uncontrolled. The gift itself has no particular emotional aspect; there can be as little or as much emotion as with any other speaking, depending on the emotional state of the person who is speaking. It is subject to the speaker's conscious control; they can start or stop it at will, speak louder or softer, slower or faster, and so forth, even though the actual procession of words or sounds is not consciously determined.

What is the Purpose of Speaking in Tongues?

It is mentioned in three writings in the New Testament: Acts, 1 Corinthians, and the secondary ending of the gospel of Mark. In Mark, it serves primarily as a sign that one is a believer (Mk 16:17), and in Acts that one has been filled with the Spirit (Acts 2:4; 10:46; 19:6). In 1 Corinthians, it is described as a form of *private prayer* for personal edification (1 Cor. 14:2, 4, 16, 28). When used with the sister gift of interpretation of tongues, it can also be a communication to the church, similar to prophecy (1 Cor. 14:5, 13, 27).

Like the other charisms, the purpose of speaking in tongues is to edify or build up the church. Unlike other gifts, however, it most commonly does this *indirectly*: it *builds up the individual believer*, who then is able to contribute more effectively to building up the church. In 1 Corinthians 14:18-19, the private edification through speaking in tongues is related to the public edification of the church through prophecy. The gift of tongues is uniquely suited to private devotions, and this has been its primary application in the Charismatic renewal. Many charismatics, who have seldom if ever spoken publicly in tongues, do so regularly in their private prayer times, and testify to its value.

The common occurrence of "singing in the Spirit" in charismatic worship takes place when everybody begins singing in tongues, each one using their own "tongue" and improvised melody. Sometimes it blends into a rich harmony. Although 1 Corinthians 14:15 suggests that "singing with the spirit" is different from "singing with the mind", the practice of common singing in tongues is not attested to in Scripture, although one finds something like it in the history of Christian worship in the practice known as "jubilation."[4] It is not a single voice speaking out to be heard by the

---

[4] Eddie Ensley, *Sounds of Wonder* (New York: Paulist Press, 1977). The author makes a case for a connection between glossolalia and jubilation, even though it is not specifically stated in the church fathers. The church father Augustine of Hippo says: "Where speech does not suffice [...] they break into singing on vowel sounds,

congregation, which would call for interpretation. It is a chorus of praise directed toward God, and therefore no interpretation is required. Although it may not benefit the minds of those present, it can still build up their spirits in the same way that speaking in tongues does in private. Moreover, the corporate dimension can help prepare the congregation for the exercise of other spiritual gifts in the worship service.

Speaking in tongues, because of its unusualness, can serve in a special way to alert us to the reality of God.[5] The wife of a Lutheran pastor described it as "a daily reminder of the Spirit's presence." On occasion, it may serve as a sign to sceptics or unbelievers (Acts 2:4; 1 Cor. 14:22).

Tongues may also serve as a *sign* to other Christians that the gift of the Spirit has been received (Acts 10:45-46; 19:6). However, other signs are also mentioned in connection with receiving the Spirit – prophecy (Acts 19:6), extolling God (Acts 10:46), and miracles (Acts 9:18). There is no biblical basis for the claim that speaking in tongues is the *only* initial evidence of having received the Spirit. There is also no indication that there are two different kinds of tongues: one a sign of receiving the Spirit, the other a spiritual gift. The same term is used throughout the New Testament without significant variation. It is a case, rather, of the same basic gift being used by the Spirit in different ways, to accomplish different purposes.

The occurrence of speaking in tongues on the day of Pentecost was unusual because *it was understood* by those who stood by and listened (Acts 2:6, 8). Occurrences of this kind of so-called *xenoglossia* (speaking by the Spirit in a *known foreign language* which the speaker has never learned) have

---

that though this means the feeling of the soul may be expressed, words failing to explain the heart's conceptions" (*Sounds of Wonder*, p. 8). John Chrysostom says: "Though men and women, young and old, are different, when they sing hymns, their voices are influenced by the Holy Spirit in such a way that the melody sounds as if sung by one voice [...] for when we sing the angels blend their voices with ours and we blend our voices with theirs" (*Sounds of Wonder*, p. 13).

[5] There was an occurrence of speaking in tongues in a Presbyterian congregation in London already in the 1830s under its pastor Edward Irving. He said about tongues: "The unknown utterance [in tongues] is for us a prevenient sign that the words addressed to our understanding are a message from God, a prophecy in the power of the Spirit, an utterance impelled by the Holy Ghost, and not the utterance of an enlightened and pious human intellect". Quoted in Ernst Adolph Rossteuscher, *Der Aufbau der Kirche Christi auf den urspünglichen Grundlagen: Eine geschichtliche Darstellung seiner Anfänge* (Siegen: Hermann Neier Nachf, 1871, reprinted 1969), p. 258. See also Larry Christenson, "Pentecostalism's Forgotten Forerunner", in *Aspects of Pentecostal-Charismatic Origins*, edited by Vinson Synan (Plainfield, NJ: Logos, 1975), pp. 15-37, and *A Message to the Charismatic Movement* (Minneapolis, MN: Bethany, 1972). Christenson draws significant parallels between the history and spirituality of the Catholic Apostolic Church, sometimes wrongly called Irvingianism, and the present-day Pentecostal/Charismatic movement, which is all the more remarkable in that there was no historical link between the two.

also been reported in present times. Risto Santala, a Finnish missionary in Israel, analysed a tape of glossolalia utterances that a research team of the American Lutheran Church had obtained during a visit to Trinity Lutheran Church in San Pedro, California, and determined that it was a clearly spoken mixture of Hebrew and Aramaic, a hymn of praise cast in Old Testament bridal imagery.[6] There are no theological or other reasons for excluding the possibility of such an occurrence today.

What is the Value of Speaking in Tongues?

For many people, speaking in tongues is a strong experience of *God's presence*. The comprehensive study of Charismatic renewal made by the Lutheran church in the German Democratic Republic (DDR, the former communist East-Germany) characterised speaking in tongues as "a praying in the Holy Spirit remarkable for its clarity and simplicity, bypassing critical intellectual reflection, a standing in the presence of Christ that comes ever and again as a surprise, each time it is experienced. Speaking in tongues ushers the worshiper into the presence of God."[7]

Speaking in tongues is not against reason, but its utterances are *not determined by reason.* It is not a question of downgrading the intellect, but of recognising its limits, and restoring a measure of balance. In the life of faith, a restrictive rule of reason can close us off from those workings of the Spirit that come along other lines, and without which faith can degenerate into an intellectual belief system.

A teacher of a high-school Bible class came into the experience of speaking in tongues, and several months later one of his students remarked, "You know, he's changed; he believes it more now than he used to." This is not the kind of change that one learns out of a book. It springs from deep personal experience of the Holy Spirit's work in one's life. The teacher did not make extravagant claims in regard to his own experience. "I realise," he said, "that many people have come into blessings similar to mine without speaking in tongues. But this is the way that God chose to lead me into a deeper walk with him, and I thank him for it."

When many people witness to an experience that has deepened and strengthened their Christian faith, the church should not whisk it away without a hearing, calling it "emotionalism." Especially so, since we are not dealing simply with a new church programme or approach or technique, but

---

[6] Risto Santala, *Armolahjoista armon tasolta* (Helsinki: Karas-Sana Oy, 1978), pp. 80-89. The details of Santala's very interesting report in English translation can be found in Larry Christenson (ed), *Welcome, Holy Spirit* (Minneapolis, MN: Augsburg ,1987), pp. 409-411.

[7] Hubert Kirchner et al. (eds), *Charismatische Erneuerung und Kirche* (Berlin: Evangelische Verlagsanstalt, 1983), p. 58. Translated by Larry Christenson.

with a manifestation of the Holy Spirit that is clearly spoken about in the Bible. The testimonies of people who speak in tongues often illustrate what the Bible says about the gift, even though the person may not consciously plan it that way:

- "It is a form of prayer." "Anyone who speaks in a tongue does not speak to men but to God" (1 Cor. 14:2).
- "We don't understand what we are saying, but we know that we are communing with God." "He utters mysteries by the Spirit" (1 Cor. 14:2).
- "Sometimes, however, we do get a sense of what we are praying about. It may be a rather *general sense* that the prayer is a confession or a petition or an intercession, but then it may also be a very *specific sense* of exactly what is being prayed." "Anyone who speaks in a tongue should pray that he may interpret what he says" (1 Cor. 14:13).
- "One of the most beautiful aspects of the gift is singing in tongues, where words and melody flow spontaneously together. It helps overcome our stiffness and formality – a new dimension of freedom in praise and worship." "I will sing with my spirit" (1 Cor. 14:15).
- "We are spiritually strengthened and built up through the use of this gift." "He who speaks in a tongue edifies himself" (1 Cor. 14:4).
- "It is praise and worship. That is what we sense most often." "You are praising God with your spirit [...] you may be giving thanks well enough" (1 Cor. 14:16-17).
- "Occasionally we use the gift in a public meeting – a prayer group, church service, or charismatic conference – with interpretation following." "If anyone speaks in a tongue, two – or at most three – should speak, one at a time, and someone must interpret" (1 Cor. 14:27).
- "Most often, however, we use it in private devotions. Far and away, this is the greatest blessing of speaking in tongues. It enriches the personal prayer life." He speaks "to himself and to God" (1 Cor. 14:28).
- "Sometimes we don't know how to pray, or what to pray for. Then we can pray in tongues, trusting the Spirit to give the prayer that is needed in that situation." "The Spirit helps us in our weakness. We do not know what we ought to pray for, but the Spirit himself intercedes for us with groans that words cannot express" (Rom. 8:26).[8]
- "We had been pretty vague on the Holy Spirit. We 'believed' but it was more a theological than a personal conviction. The experience of speaking in tongues has helped make the Holy Spirit a fresh and

[8] In Krister Stendahl, "Glossolalia – the New Testament Evidence," in *Paul Among Jews and Gentiles, and Other Essays* (Philadelphia, PA: Fortress, 1976), p. 111, Stendahl, who is not himself a charismatic, cites his own and other scholarly opinion that interprets Romans 8:26 as a reference to glossolalia.

> personal reality in our lives." "All of them were filled with the Holy Spirit and began to speak in other tongues as the Spirit enabled them [...] The Holy Spirit came on them; and they spoke in tongues (Acts 2:4; 19:6).

This amazing correspondence between the spontaneous testimonies to the experience of speaking in tongues today and the biblical description of it is a strong argument for the authenticity and usefulness of this gift.

How Should the Church Practically Handle the Gift of Speaking in Tongues?

Speaking in tongues can be overemphasised or abused. The apostle Paul addressed that kind of a situation in the church at Corinth, and what he wrote is part of Holy Scripture. Nothing that he wrote can support an argument against tongues, only against its abuse. Once this basic truth is grasped, our consideration of tongues can be cast in the positive framework that Paul himself reflected when he said, "I thank God that I speak in tongues more than all of you" (1 Cor. 14:18). The cure for abuse is not disuse, but proper use.

Churches have generally handled or responded to speaking in tongues in one of three ways. We will look briefly at each of these ways, then suggest a fourth way that we believe is more suitable both to the teaching of Scripture and in the context of the Lutheran church.

One common response to speaking in tongues has been simply to banish or disallow it. Sometimes, this is backed up with a theological rationale such as dispensationalism – "tongues were intended only for the apostolic age". We have dealt with the question of dispensationalism earlier: there is nothing in Scripture that allows us to limit certain spiritual gifts to the apostolic age.[9] Scripture does not draw that kind of distinction between the gifts – assigning some to the apostolic age, while others continue. To be consistent, dispensationalism would have to consign all of the charismata to the apostolic age, something that not even the most thoroughgoing dispensationalist has ever suggested. Dispensationalism is not a scriptural way of addressing the question, but is an attempt by Bible-believing Christians to reconcile the miracles of Scripture with the absence or decline of miracles in the church later on, and/or the rationalism of Western culture.

Churches may disallow tongues with less elaborate theological rationale. In the early days of the Charismatic movement, Episcopalian bishop James Pike branded speaking in tongues as "heresy in embryo," and banned its

---

[9] The only exception is the ministry of the twelve apostles since their witness presupposed a personal knowledge of Jesus' work from his baptism to his ascension (Acts 1:21-22).

public use in the parishes of his diocese.[10] Churches, or influential individuals, can effectively discourage speaking in tongues on other grounds, or in less formal ways, as well: for instance, tongue speaking will be explained in terms of psychological aberration or emotional instability;[11] the occurrence of tongue speaking in non-Christian settings will be cited to cast a shadow of suspicion on the practice as such;[12] tongues will be charged with causing controversy and division; it will be dismissed as contrary to a church's tradition.[13]

No argument or oblique tactic that seeks to banish speaking in tongues from the church can take its stand on Scripture. "Do not forbid speaking in tongues" (1 Cor. 14:39) stands like a sentinel, guarding the place of even this so-called least of the gifts. This includes its occasional use in public. While the gift of tongues is used primarily in one's private devotions, the fact that the Spirit gives the companion gift of interpretation indicates that tongues can also play a role in public worship. To allow it in private but prohibit it in public is a mediating position that does not rest on solid scriptural ground. Paul's discussion of the question, and his final admonition to "forbid not," deals primarily with how the *use of the gift is to be ordered in public worship.*

Some biblical scholars argue that these words of Paul are directed to a particular congregation a long ago time, and are not necessarily authoritative

---

[10] McDonnell, *Presence, Power, Praise*, p. 100.

[11] Paul Qualben, a psychiatrist who participated in a field study of glossolalia for the American Lutheran Church in 1963, said in a lecture at Wartburg Theological Seminary, Dubuque, Iowa, in April 1972, that initially they expected to encounter people who were emotionally unbalanced, but that in fact this did not prove to be true. The people who spoke in tongues that they interviewed and tested were a cross section of ordinary Lutheran congregations. (Reported by Larry Christenson.) The theory of psychological aberration among tongue speakers has now been generally abandoned by psychologists and psychiatrists as based on unfounded prejudice.

[12] Arthur Lovekin, *Glossolalia: Behavioral Science Perspectives on Speaking in Tongues* (New York: Oxford University Press, 1985), p. 40. The occurrence of speaking in tongues in non- or pre-Christian settings is frequently alluded to as accepted wisdom. Lovekin, however, does a thorough study of the sources and concludes that, "there is no well-documented instance of phenomena similar to apostolic glossolalia in either the preceding or contemporary pagan, or Jewish religion [...] The ecstatic prophet (in non-Christian religions) has to lose consciousness; and this is nowhere to be found in apostolic glossolalia. In no case of ecstatic prophecy is the prophet ever portrayed as being able to interpret his own unintelligible speech. The apostolic experience of glossolalia must be interpreted as something new." See also Morton Kelsey, *Tongue Speaking* (New York: Crossroad, 1964, rev. ed. 1981), pp. 138-145, who also relying on first hand study of sources, comes to the same conclusion as Lovekin.

[13] McDonnell, *Presence, Power, Praise*, p. 58. A study commission of the American Lutheran Church observed that "speaking in tongues is not Lutheran" appeared to be a commonly voiced attitude among Lutherans, but one that, in the view of the commission, was not helpful.

for the church today.[14] According to this view, Paul's words are "descriptive, not prescriptive." Without addressing the larger question of scriptural authority which this raises (we have dealt with that in earlier chapters), one might ask quite pragmatically: who is better able to offer good counsel on speaking in tongues than the apostle Paul? We are not looking here at a situation or question unique to the first century. When we consider how spiritual gifts should contribute to orderly and edifying worship, we have to deal with essentially the same kind of questions that the congregation in Corinth dealt with. There is more of the universal than the particular in Paul's advice.

Even if 1 Corinthians as a text was not considered binding on the church in this regard, the apostle Paul's credentials for offering sound counsel on speaking in tongues would still put any present-day theologian in the shade. Paul spoke in tongues himself. He knew what the gift was about from personal experience. He had first-hand experience and a Spirit-given understanding of a whole range of spiritual gifts that most theologians have only read about. He was not angered, nor was he intimidated, by speaking in tongues. He was not hostile to the gift, nor did he overvalue it. He dealt with the abuses without defensiveness, in a pastoral way that works well today, if one takes the time and trouble to put it into practice.

Whom could we turn to in the church today who could counsel us on speaking in tongues with the measure of understanding, wisdom, and balance that the apostle Paul brought to this question? We would like to quote the judgement of Lutheran New Testament scholar Christer Stendahl, who does not identify himself with the Charismatic renewal:

> It is not a question whether glossolalia is a theologically proper phenomenon – of course it is. It is rather a question how this phenomenon can be a force to the benefit of the whole church. It is in that sense that Paul's vision and perspective strike me as unsurpassed both in wisdom and vitality.[15]

A *second response* to speaking in tongues has been to tolerate it; to allow its presence in the church, but to discourage its "promotion". If this were understood as a counsel of balance, spoken into a situation badly out of balance, it would be consistent with Scripture. In practice, however, church officials have said this in situations where speaking in tongues has barely made an appearance, where the mere presence of the gift, not its abuse, has raised questions. To forestall potential problems, without openly repudiating scriptural authority, they tell those who have the gift that they may use it, but they should not promote it in any way. The other side of that coin is that one

---

[14] McDonnell, *Presence, Power, Praise*, p. 61.
[15] Stendahl, "Glossolalia", p. 124.

should not seek the gift.[16] This approach sees speaking in tongues essentially as a problem to be contained.

Scripture takes a decidedly different approach: "Eagerly desire spiritual gifts" (1 Cor. 14:1). Paul openly promoted spiritual gifts, including tongues: "I would like every one of you to speak in tongues" (1 Cor. 14:5). His concern was not that too many people might speak in tongues, but that tongue speakers might neglect to seek and value other gifts as well (1 Cor. 12:14-31).

The counsel against promoting tongues appears benign, even pastoral. But what does this counsel actually say?

To begin with, it faults God: he has given the church a gift that is insignificant, causes problems, and which we could just as well do without. Our attitude toward spiritual gifts touches on our attitude toward God himself. If we demean a gift, do we not denigrate the one who gives it? In providing for the church, God does not do foolish or inconsequential things. Here, we must guard against the tendency of the flesh to judge and control even the things of God. Paul's warning not to despise prophesying (1 Thess. 5:20) could be applied to any of the spiritual gifts, including tongues.

From another point of view, the counsel that allows speaking in tongues but discourages its promotion is simply unnatural. On the one hand, it seeks to affirm the gift as a good thing for those who have it, but, on the other hand, to discourage sharing this good thing with others. In what other area of church life would we take such a line? Here is a Lutheran congregation with a remarkable evangelism outreach in its community – they have more adult baptisms than infant baptisms. Or, here is a person who studies the book of Ephesians in her personal devotions and comes to some tremendous insights. We would hardly say, "These things are all fine, just don't promote them. The Spirit may have given you something good in evangelism or Bible study, but don't share it with others." It's in the nature of human relationships, not to mention Christian fellowship, to share your good experience with others. If speaking in tongues is a good gift of God that comes back into the church after a long period of disuse, some healthy promotion of the gift is both inevitable and desirable.

A *third response* to speaking in tongues is one which, in a sense, underlies the other two: the position of classical Pentecostalism that speaking in tongues is "the initial physical evidence of baptism with the Holy Spirit." Mainline churches generally, and evangelical Protestants in particular, have opposed this theological formulation. Attempts to banish or merely tolerate tongues can be traced in part to a reaction against the doctrine of "initial evidence." The implication of this Pentecostal teaching, of course, is obvious: if you haven't spoken in tongues, you haven't been baptised with the Holy Spirit.

---

[16] McDonnell, *Presence, Power, Praise*, pp. 102, 111, 63.

Lutheran charismatics have generally steered clear of this Pentecostal position.[17] They recognise that tongues was a widespread experience in the early church and that many people are experiencing it today in connection with being filled with the Spirit, although it may be less widespread among Pentecostals and charismatics than has been supposed.[18] Lutheran charismatics would recognise it as *a piece of* evidence of being filled with the Spirit, but stop short of calling it *the* evidence.

How then should we handle speaking in tongues – if the gift should not be disallowed, nor merely tolerated, and if it should not be touted as the evidence of being baptised with the Spirit? A practical outline takes shape if we look at the positive alternative imbedded in each of the three positions that we have described:

- Speaking in tongues should be recognised and permitted in the church. It is a gift of the Holy Spirit. Let us quote Stendahl again:

> As I read Paul it seems to me crystal clear that if the Presbyterians and Episcopalians and Lutherans, and all 'proper' Christians, including the Catholics, did not consciously or unconsciously suppress such phenomenon as glossolalia, and if other denominations did not especially encourage them, then the gifts of the Spirit – including glossolalia – would belong to *the common register of Christian experience.*[19]

The first major Lutheran treatment of speaking in tongues to come out of the Charismatic renewal set the context for a sane valuation of the gift:

> God does all things well. What he has appointed for his Church has behind it wise purpose and meaning, for the mere reason that he is the one who has appointed it. His wisdom, though often beyond the clumsy reach of human reason, is perfect. Our task is neither to defend nor downgrade a gift of the Holy Spirit, but rather to discover the purpose and meaning that God had in mind when he appointed the gift for his church (1 Cor. 12:28).[20]

- The gift of speaking in tongues should not only be permitted in the church, it should be welcomed and encouraged, along with the other

---

[17] Christenson, *Speaking in Tongues*, p. 54. This is generally true in other mainline churches as well.

[18] Kenneth S. Kantzer, "The Charismatics Among Us", *Christianity Today*, 22nd February 1980, pp. 25-27. David Barrett, one of the authors of World Christian Encyclopedia, in a lecture to a group of charismatic leaders at Glencoe, Missouri, 7th May 1986, said that out of 44 million people in the United States who designated themselves as "charismatic" "only" six million (about 14%) spoke in tongues. This number is, of course, very uncertain and can vary significantly among different groups of Pentecostals and Charismatics.

[19] Stendahl, "Glossolalia", p. 121.

[20] Christenson, *Speaking in Tongues*, p. 7.

gifts of the Spirit. Hand in hand with encouragement must go sound teaching on the proper use of the gift. Scripture holds these two elements continually in balance.

- Speaking in tongues should be kept in an appropriate theological context. It goes beyond the clear implication of Scripture to tie the Holy Spirit exclusively to this one gift, as the initial evidence of his coming. This in no way detracts from the unique blessing that speaking in tongues is meant to bring in the life of the believer.

Pastoral Guidelines

What this comes down to is not so much a doctrine as an attitude that leads to *wise pastoral care.* The American Lutheran Church published a series of essays on the Charismatic renewal that included the following set of *guidelines for pastors.* They were formulated by a charismatic pastor concerning the renewal as a whole, but with particular reference to speaking in tongues as a focal point of the movement. This is a revised summary of the guidelines:

1. *Become informed.* Seek to obtain an accurate and balanced view of what is happening in the Charismatic movement and what it stands for. Discuss the matter with other Christians who have first-hand experience.

2. *Offer guidance.* People who have had charismatic experiences need to realise their need for spiritual authority. An experience may awaken a person to new potential in the Christian life, but it may not be a mature one. Maturity comes through patient discipleship. The pastor must be ready to accept the responsibility of guiding members who have had charismatic experiences.

When a congregation has a fair number of charismatics, a prayer group could be started within the congregation itself. This should be set under the leadership of a responsible person who would keep in regular touch with the pastor and leaders of the congregation. If the prayer group is publicly announced and open to all who wish to attend, there need be no divisiveness. Indeed, its ministry of prayer and intercession can become a great blessing to the entire congregation.

3. *Accept.* People who have had charismatic experiences need to feel that they and their experiences are accepted by their pastor. Rejection or mere tolerance closes the door to effective pastoral ministry.

4. *Evaluate.* To accept a person and that person's experience does not mean that the pastor must accept the person's own theological explanation of that experience. Lutheran charismatics have sometimes described their experience in terms which are foreign to our heritage, for example, in the categories of classical Pentecostalism. The very name by which the renewal has come to be known, that is, *the Charismatic movement*, suggests that its uniqueness is primarily historical, not theological. To accept the Charismatic movement, therefore, does not mean that one accepts some set of doctrines.

Rather, one accepts a particular work of the Holy Spirit which is taking place among us, seeking to understand it and relate to it in a positive way. It can be understood and experienced within the framework of our Lutheran heritage and tradition.

5. *Establish Order*. In the manifestation of the charismatic gifts in the congregation, two extremes should be avoided: (1) undue emphasis on any one gift; (2) suppression of any one gift. No gift of the Holy Spirit is without its special value, or God would not have set it in the church. When manifested in an orderly way, according to scriptural guidelines, each gift can bring its distinctive blessing to the body of Christ. The pastor must offer guidance and direction so that order and balance are maintained.

In the early years of the Charismatic renewal, Lutheran theologian George Aus offered this advice in regard to the gift of speaking in tongues:

A. To those *who have experienced the gift*: (1) Be sure that the purpose for which you use it is positive, that is, for edification – whether private or corporate. (2) Let the Spirit sift your motives in the public use of the gift. (3) Be in prayer that if the gift becomes divisive it be not due to you or to your use of the gift, for example, when it is used to exalt self in the display of spiritual excellence. (4) Beware of spiritual pride.

B. To those *who have not experienced the gift*: (1) If the exercise of the gift by others edifies you, thank God. (2) Do not be disturbed by the fact that it has not been given to you. This fact does not mean that something is wrong with you or that you are an inferior or carnal Christian. (3) Your function in the edification of the congregation may call for other gifts.

6. *Counsel patience*. Where differences or disagreements crop up in a congregation, precipitous action should be avoided. Both sides should be counselled to prayer and patience with the expectation that the Holy Spirit will bring unity. This will not necessarily mean uniformity, but more likely, a deepened respect for one another and for the God-given variety of our experiences. Both those involved in the Charismatic renewal and those not involved need to learn to appreciate the gifts that the others have. And both need teaching in order to understand more fully how the Charismatic renewal can serve in helping to build up the life of the church.

7. *Take a positive attitude*. Essentially, the Charismatic movement is made of people. There is no need for any of them to be lost to the Lutheran church. As we relate to them in a positive, pastoral way, the majority will respond with gratitude. Deep down, sheep know that they need a shepherd.[21]

---

[21] See Larry Christenson, "The Pastoral Ministry in Relation to the Charismatic Movement", in Walter Wietzke and Jack Hustad (eds), *Towards a Mutual Understanding of Neo-Pentecostalism* (Minneapolis, MN: Augsburg, 1973), pp. 31-34.

Conclusion

In light both of the biblical testimony and of practical experience, *speaking in tongues should be regarded as a valuable spiritual gift to be sought and practiced in the church.* It can contribute to spiritual renewal in one's personal devotional life, open up new levels of prayer and praise both for the individual believer and for the congregation and thus contribute to building up the church.

(50) The Gifts of Healings

When charismatics talk about *miracles*, their most common illustration is likely to be healing. When they talk about proclaiming the gospel with "signs following," the sign that is uppermost in their mind is almost certain to be healing. To some extent, this is a reflection of their experience, but more importantly it reflects the proportions of Scripture. In the New Testament, healings outnumber all other miracles combined.

Although speaking in tongues, interpretation of tongues and prophecy have had only limited expression outside the Pentecostal and Charismatic movements, the ministry of healing has been more widely accepted. Healing has been part of the ministry of the Christian Church from the beginning. The church historian Amanda Porterfield writes in her authoritative study of healing in the history of the church:

> [Christian] healing has persisted over time and across cultural spaces as a defining element of Christianity and a major contributor to Christianity's endurance, expansion and success.[1]

Among Lutherans, while healing through prayer has never been a major emphasis,[2] it did find expression in the ministry of Luther himself, and, closer to our own time, in the influential ministry of Johann Christoph Blumhardt in Germany.[3] Parts of the Lutheran church have been hospitable to the healing practice.[4]

In the Anglican Communion, there was a renewal of the healing ministry several decades before the Charismatic movement arrived on the scene. In 1932, Episcopalian clergyman John Gaynor Banks began to publish the magazine *Sharing* to encourage the ministry of healing in the historic churches. This led in 1948 to his founding of the *Order of St. Luke*, which included members from all the mainline Protestant churches, both clergy and laity, with significant participation also by members of the medical

---

[1] Amanda Porterfield, *Healing in the History of Christianity* (Oxford: Oxford University Press, 2005), p. 19. See also Andrew Daunton-Fear, *Ministry of Healing and Exorcism from the First to the Fifth Century* (Milton Keynes: Paternoster, 2009).

[2] Martin E. Marty, *Health and Medicine in the Lutheran Tradition* (New York: Crossroad, 1983), pp. 86-88.

[3] See also references in the chapter on Pietism and the Lutheran precursors to the Charismatic movement in Part Three.

[4] See, for example, the book by the Norwegian Peder Olsen, *Healing Through Prayer*, translated by John Jensen (Minneapolis, MN: Augsburg, 1962).

community. Divine healing has been reported from all continents – often in connection with mission and revival – long before the beginning of the Charismatic renewal in 1960s.[5]

The Charismatic renewal has drawn on these sources and added its voice to a rising chorus of prayer for God to "stretch out his hand to heal" (Acts 4:30). Physical or psychological healing, whether as an instantaneous event or a gradual process, is recognised as God's personal intervention to bring a person from sickness to health, as an expression of his will and power to alleviate suffering and make people whole.

A Biblical Perspective on Healing

In circles that do not feel comfortable with talk of miracles, serious discussion of biblical healing is sometimes deflected by citing medical science as God's gift of healing for today. A favourite sermon illustration is the story of the doctor who puts a cast on a boy's broken leg and tells him, "God heals your leg. We just hold it in place for him." Of course, it is true that all healing comes from God. When a broken leg mends, it is because God has built into the body the power to mend. When antibiotics fight infection in our bodies, it is because medical science has discovered certain things about the created order and put them to use. But the Bible, in speaking about healing, usually has reference to an intervention of God that brings about healing by other than natural or medical means.

In situations where people become narrowly preoccupied with the miraculous, it may be necessary to broaden their vision by calling attention to the blessing of God through natural and medical healing. But this is not usually the case. In Western culture, one has gone to the opposite extreme by narrowing healing down to medical science alone. We need the biblical perspective to restore balance.

Actually, by focusing on the intervention of God, the Bible immeasurably broadens our perspective on healing. Healings were an integral part of the ministry of Jesus. His motive for healing was love and mercy toward human beings who were suffering – suffering not only the immediate pain of physical sickness, but also the oppression of Satan (Lk. 13:16). When Jesus healed the sick, he illustrated the essence of his entire mission, which was to make well what had become sick; his healings were an expression of the salvation that came with the kingdom of God. Biblical healing is a divine intervention, an incursion of the kingdom of God into the kingdom of Satan,

---

[5] No book contains so many documented cases of healing as the 1000 page study by Keener, *Miracles*. He documents that millions of Christians have testified to the experience of healing and that it has been very important for the growth of the church in missionary situations. See also Engelsviken, "Exorcism and Healing", 1991, and Engelsviken. "Deliver Us From Evil", 2018.

a foretaste of the age to come in which an all-embracing healing will extend even to the whole creation (Rom. 8:21).

When Peter preached to the household of Cornelius (Acts 10:34-43), he set Jesus' miracles of healing and deliverance from demonic power (v. 38), his death and resurrection from the dead (v. 39-40), and forgiveness of sins by faith in him (v. 43), in one unified context: wherever sin and sickness have entered the creation, Jesus does his saving and healing work.

The root sickness is our broken relationship with God (Is. 53:4-6; 59:2; Mic. 6:13). Christ's work of atonement brings the deep healing of forgiveness, reconciliation, victory and deliverance (Hos. 6:1; Mal. 4:2; Col. 2:13-15; 1 Pet. 2:24). He heals our faithless backsliding (Jer. 3:22). He conquers the last enemy, death (1 Cor. 15:26).

His healing also extends to our relationships with other people. The individualistic view of human life that is typical of Western culture has hidden the extent of our sickness. The Bible does not see us as well apart from wholesome relationships in family, community, and society (Is. 3:4-7; Rev. 22:2). The ability to live together as God intends us to do – to love one another, forgive one another, pray even for enemies – is impossible until the Holy Spirit brings the healing presence of Christ into our lives.

Jesus heals a sick and fallen world. Poverty, famine, and calamity are evidences of a sick and fallen creation. His feeding of the hungry and his stilling of the storm are signs that he comes to heal the whole creation.

The Bible's perspective on healing goes far beyond the meaning that we normally attach to the word. Healing – like salvation or redemption – takes in all of life. This perspective can open the way to a Spirit-empowered ministry of healing, but it poses a particular danger: the very breadth of the vision can tempt us to neglect the Bible's more frequent and specific meaning, which is healing people's physical and psychological sicknesses. The danger of an enlarged perspective on healing is that we could satisfy ourselves with a new definition of healing while our ministry remained unchanged. Everything we do can be understood in some sense as "healing," so we content ourselves that we really are a healing church, even though actual healings, in the traditional sense, are not part of the picture.

The biblical perspective should be the basis for an altogether different result: not a complacent neglect of physical and psychological healing, but increased confidence that this, too, can be part of our experience. We should lay hands on the sick and pray for them to be healed at the same time as we proclaim the forgiveness of sins, following the example of Jesus when he healed a paralytic man:

> Which is easier: to say to the paralytic, 'Your sins are forgiven,' or to say, 'Get up, take your mat and walk'? But that you may know that the Son of Man has authority on earth to forgive sins […] He said to the paralytic, 'I tell you, get up, take your mat and go home.' He got up, took his mat and walked out in full

> view of them all. This amazed everyone and they praised God saying, 'We have never seen anything like this!' (Mk 2:9-12)

Lutheran pastor William Vaswig has reported widely how his son was healed of incurable schizophrenia through prayer.[6] The well-documented healing was not only a blessing to the young man and his family, but became an arresting testimony of faith. Actual physical and psychological healings are signs that tell a sceptical world that our gospel has real effects in the real world, and does not only consist of words (cf. Rom. 15:18-19; 1 Cor. 2:4-5).

Establishing a Ministry of Healing in the Local Congregation

Healing presents a different set of dynamics than some of the other spiritual gifts, such as speaking in tongues or distinguishing between spirits. A church where people speak in tongues or cast out demons may be dismissed as fanatic or quaint. The general response to a church that heals is likely to be more positive, for it touches people at a point of great need. In the face of the pervasive and painful reality of sickness, theory tends to become more pliable. In many otherwise traditional congregations, introducing a ministry of healing is likely to meet with a favourable response.[7]

One thing, more than any other, keeps pastors and leaders from introducing a ministry of healing into their congregations: *fear of failure.* This is often camouflaged by theological objections to charismatic healing, but the real issue is a fear that nothing will happen. At this point, ironically, it is not charismatics, but their critics, who place experience above the Word: from the church's non-experience of healing, they proceed to build a theology that dismisses spiritual healing as a present-day reality. If a theologian were to lay hands on half a dozen sick people and see them dramatically healed before their eyes, theological objections would melt away.

Charismatics, however, do not rest their case for healing on their successful experience. John Wimber, whose ministry included a strong accent on healing, said, "We fail more often than we succeed."[8] The motivation for entering into a healing ministry is not experience, but the commandments and the promises in the Word. Charismatics are not seeking

---

[6] William Vaswig, *I Prayed. He Answered* (Minneapolis, MN: Augsburg, 1977), pp. 28-38.

[7] John Wimber, "Zip to 3000 in 5 Years", *Christian Life*, October 1882, pp. 18-23. See also the book in which the Vineyard leader and healer reflects on the significance of the healing ministry, John Wimber, *Power Healing* (San Francisco, CA: Harper, 1991). Another useful introduction to the healing ministry is Francis MacNutt, *Healing* (Notre Dame, IN: Ave Maria Press, 1991/2001).

[8] John Wimber, in a message at Acts 86, an all-European ecumenical charismatic conference, on 24th July 1986, said that "failures" outnumber healings in his ministry.

to rally the church around the banner of their own experience; even when they testify to some miracles of healing, they know that they have only scratched the surface of what is promised in Scripture.

A.O. Aasen, a pioneer Lutheran pastor in Canada and the United States, who quietly practiced a ministry of healing for more than 60 years, and was himself dramatically healed of cancer at the age of 80, said to a young seminary student who had an interest in healing:

> Don't be discouraged if things don't happen overnight. We are surrounded by a world of unbelief – some of it is in the church – and even Jesus could do no mighty works in Nazareth, because of their unbelief. But it's in the Word. If it wasn't in the Word, we'd have no business talking about it. Because it is in the Word, we have no business neglecting it.[9]

Charismatics are saying to the church, "Come, let us together seek the Lord. Let us take him at his Word. Let a ministry of healing be restored to God's people."

A healthy ministry of healing must include sensitive pastoral care to help people deal with unanswered prayers. A simplistic approach, that explains every failure as a lack of faith on the part of the sick person, has wrought untold and unnecessary harm and grief to people living under a burden of sickness; it is true neither to Scripture nor to experience. The issue is more complex. There is much we have yet to learn about healing. But that should not detain us from praying for it. When the central focus of our prayers is on Christ the Healer, and not simply on healing as such, we can enter with confidence into a ministry of healing. He will work healing among us. And, by the Holy Spirit, he will remain with us in times when prayers go unanswered.

Scripture suggests a variety of ways in which a ministry of healing may come to expression. *Healings may take place as members of the body of Christ simply pray for one another.* If prayer really is our access to the healing power of God, what is more natural than believers praying for one another; not only in their private intercessions, or only in cases of desperate extremity, but personally and directly in our everyday encounters with sickness? A healing ministry begins with the simple conviction that God really does answer prayer. Any believer can be part of the congregation's ministry of healing.

Healings may come through the exercise of charismatic gifts of healings. Scripture uses a double plural in reference to charismatic healing: "gifts of healings" (1 Cor. 12:9, New American Standard Bible). This suggests some variety. Some people have a general gift to pray for the sick. Others seem to have a gift to pray for certain kinds of illnesses. Sometimes, healing comes

---

[9] In private conversation with Larry Christenson, 1959.

after long periods of intercession, sometimes at a single word of command. Sometimes, people are healed through their own prayers, sometimes, through the prayers of others. One thing is certain: there is no one formula for spiritual healing. Healing is a sovereign intervention of the Holy Spirit. He himself will frustrate any attempt to reduce the ministry of healing to a method.

Healing may be linked to the exercise of other charismatic gifts. For instance, a word of knowledge given by the Spirit may show people how to pray more accurately and effectively with regard to a particular sickness. Robert Whitaker, a Presbyterian minister, told how their adopted son was healed after an elderly couple received a word of knowledge that his epileptic seizures were related to a trauma the boy had experienced before he was adopted.[10]

Healing, especially emotional healing, can come through *private confession and absolution.*[11] Scripture links together confession and healing: "Confess your sins to each other and pray for each other so that you may be healed" (James 5:16). Both Scripture and medical science alert us to the close link that can exist between guilt and sickness. Private confession appears to be especially necessary and helpful in dealing with certain categories of sin and guilt: bad relationships with parents, sexual misconduct, and traffic in the occult.

Evangelistic preaching should ideally be linked with a strong ministry of healing. It was this way in the ministry of Jesus, and it was carried on by his disciples. The early believers prayed:

> Enable your servants to speak your word with great boldness. Stretch out your hand to heal and perform miraculous signs and wonders through the name of your holy servant Jesus (Acts 4:29-30).

The linking together of *faith and miracle* is not something peculiar to the mind-set or culture of the first century. It is a demonstration of the Spirit that is effective in every age and culture.

In 1979, James Roberson, pastor of Our Saviour's Lutheran Church in Albany, New York, was a guest speaker in a small congregation in Japan. His proclamation of the gospel included the scriptural promise, "These signs will accompany those who believe: [...] they will place their hands on sick people, and they will get well" (Mk 16:17-18). At the end of the service, a man in the front row stood up and came forward to grasp Pastor Roberson's hand – and suddenly the whole congregation began to praise God. Not knowing the language, Pastor Roberson did not understand at first what was happening. Later, his translator told him that the man who came forward was

---

[10] Roger Whitaker. Personal testimony shared on several occasions.

[11] Agnes Sanford, *The Healing Light* (Saint Paul, MN: Macalaster Park, 1947), pp. 120-129.

well-known in the congregation, and for years had been crippled on his right side from a paralytic stroke.

In the Bible, healing is frequently associated with the ministry of spiritual leaders: in the Old Testament Moses and the prophets healed (Num. 12:13; 1 Kings 17:21-22; 2 Kings 5:10-14); in the New Testament, the apostles and other leaders carried on Jesus' healing ministry (Jn 14:12; Acts 3:7; 6:8; 8:7; 9:34; 19:11; 28:8-9). The elders of a congregation are given special responsibility and authority to pray for the sick. As it is written:

> Is any one of you sick? He should call the elders of the church to pray over him and anoint him with oil in the name of the Lord. And the prayer offered in faith will make the sick person well; the Lord will raise him up. If he has sinned, he will be forgiven. Therefore, confess your sins to each other and pray for each other so that you may be healed. The prayer of a righteous man is powerful and effective (James 5:14-16).

It is important to note that while healing may be linked to the faith of the sick person, this is not necessarily always the case. Here, healing is attributed to *the faith of the elders.* There are times when it is appropriate to challenge the sick person to have faith for healing, other times when it is not. In Scripture, we find times when healing is attributed to the faith of the afflicted person (Mt. 9:22; Mk 10:52; Acts 14:9). In Mark 2:5, however Jesus responded to the faith of the friends of the sick person. It is an unbiblical, unwise and dangerous practice indiscriminately to lay responsibility for healing faith on the sick person. In some cases, sick persons are too weary and discouraged to exercise faith. The Holy Spirit must guide us in the way that we minister healing in individual cases.

Inner Healing

An aspect of healing that has gained particular prominence in the Charismatic renewal goes by the name of "inner healing." The concept seems to have originated with Agnes Sanford, who called it "healing of the memories." The idea is that Jesus can heal the psychological, emotional, and spiritual wounds that fester in the memory. She focused on two basic factors that must be taken into account in this kind of healing, which she illustrated in her *Schools of Pastoral Care* with a verse from a familiar hymn: "There is a balm in Gilead to *make the wounded whole*; There is a balm in Gilead to *heal a sin sick soul*".

The concept of healing the memories can bring fresh meaning and reality to a foundational truth of Scripture: it can be a helpful restatement of the doctrine of forgiveness and reconciliation. Its particular value lies in the emphasis that it places on the actual appropriation of forgiveness and the willingness to forgive others, and healing from the effects of sin, through the ministry of prayer. Care needs to be exercised that the emphasis on healing does not bypass the reality of guilt and the need for repentance.

Healing the memories can deal not only with the wrongs that we have done, but also with the wrongs that have been done against us. One reason for the strong response to the ministry of inner healing is the fact that the need is so widespread. Our common life structures – family, friends, church, school, workplace, community – can deal harsh blows to the individual, especially the young and defenceless. Who pauses even to note, much less deal with, the wounds inflicted by rejection, neglect, fear, unkindness, bullying, teasing, shame, and failure? Many unhealed hurts lie buried or undealt with in our memories. It is true that anyone who is in Christ is a new creation; the old has gone, and the new has come (2 Cor. 5:17). But for many there is a gap, sometimes a gigantic gap, between the promises of redemption and the actual experience of it. Healing of memories, again, emphasises *appropriation.* God is with the lowly: "I live in a high and holy place, but also with him who is contrite and lowly in spirit, to revive the spirit of the lowly and to revive the heart of the contrite" (Is. 57:15: cp. Sal. 34:18.). Jesus invited those who carried burdens: "Come to me, all you who are weary and burdened, and I will give you rest. Take my yoke upon you and learn from me, for I am gentle and humble in heart, and you will find rest for your souls." (Mt. 11:28-29). This can become an experienced reality through prayer for inner healing.[12]

Healing and the Atonement

Jesus' own ministry of healing was seen as a fulfilment of the prophecy of Isaiah that "he took up our infirmities and carried our diseases" (Mt. 8:17; cp. Is. 53:4). In its context of the prophecy of the salvific effects of the death of the Servant of the Lord (Is. 52:13-53:12), this is one of the clearest Old Testament references to the atonement. In a comprehensive sense, therefore, we can say that on the cross Jesus dealt with the full effects of sin, including sickness (1 Pet. 2:24).

This does not mean, however, that the Holy Spirit will invariably bring healing by faith. We cannot draw a straight line between forgiveness and healing, saying, "As certainly as he carried my sins and therefore forgives

[12] The ministry of inner healing may be closely associated with the ministry of reconciliation, both "vertical" reconciliation with God (2 Cor. 5:20) and "horizontal" reconciliation between human beings (Eph. 2:14-18). The Catholic scholar Robert Schreiter has developed this ministry of reconciliation in greater details, see the two chapters: Robert Schreiter, "The Emergence of Reconciliation as a Paradigm of Mission: Dimensions, Levels and Characteristics" and Knud Jørgensen, "Hope in a Fragile World: The Reconciling Mission of the Church", in Robert Schreiter and Knud Jørgensen (eds), *Mission as Ministry of Reconciliation* (Oxford: Regnum, 2013), pp. 9-29 and 321-330.

me, just as certainly will he heal this sickness." Forgiveness deals with the *guilt* caused by sin. It *does not remove sin itself* as a reality in the lives of Christians. While *guilt* is *always* removed by faith in Christ when a person is *justified*, sin itself is not (cp. the Lutheran expression that a Christian is *simul justus et peccator*: at the same time righteous and sinner). Sickness, however, differently from sin, does not imply any guilt. It is a condition of all human beings until the final resurrection of the dead. Sin, the results of sin and sickness will continue to exist in this life until "the creation itself will be liberated from its bondage to decay and brought into the glorious freedom of the children of God […] We ourselves, who have the first fruits of the Spirit, groan inwardly as we wait eagerly for our adoption as sons, the redemption of our bodies. For in this hope, we were saved" (Rom. 8:21, 23).

Perfect, lasting healing is therefore never a reality in this life, where sin and the results of sin have permeated the whole cosmos. However, healing is a foretaste of the coming world, a sign of the kingdom. Although the "mystery of evil" will not be fully solved in this world, and suffering will persist until the end, Christians may glory in the fact that on the cross Christ has conquered sin, death, and the devil and has therefore also broken the power of sickness. In reference to the Lord's Supper, the church fathers set healing in the broadest possible context, calling it the "medicine of immortality."[13] In a special way, both healing and the Lord's Supper point us to the ultimate healing and salvation that will occur when Christ returns and establishes his eternal kingdom on the new earth (Lk. 22:18).

In conclusion, we say that the Lord sometimes, but not always, yet maybe more often than we expect, may heal sickness as a foretaste of the complete healing that will take place in the consummated kingdom of God. In John's mighty vision in Revelation of the New Jerusalem, he sees that the leaves of the "tree of life […] are for the healing of the nations" (Rev. 22:2). In this sense, healing and all other gifts of salvation are included in Christ's sacrificial work as the Lamb of God on the cross and in the resurrection (Rev. 7:14-17; 22:3-5).

This is a great encouragement for Christians to pray for the sick with the expectation that God may heal them, and at the same time it is also a great comfort for those who are not healed here on earth, that God will be with them in their suffering and ultimately heal them completely in their bodily resurrection from the dead.

---

[13] Ignatius of Antioch, Epistle to the Ephesians 20. 2.

(51) The Church: Workshop of the Holy Spirit

At a charismatic conference on church renewal, one of the speakers began his address by stating, "I want you to know that I have discovered the New Testament pattern for the church – 37 different times!" He wanted at the beginning to dissuade people from the idea that church renewal is a matter of finding and following a simple biblical formula. Renewal of congregational life is a renewal of life in Christ in and with his body. It stems from a fresh release of the Holy Spirit among the people of God. It is not simply a set of principles that we discover and put into practice; it is firstly something that we receive. Charismatics focus on some practical ways that the lordship of Christ and the power of the Holy Spirit can become greater realities in present-day church life.

Jesus, the Source and Model for the Church's Ministries

Jesus himself was, in all the fullness of his ministry, the model and source of what the various ministries in the church would become:

- Jesus was an *apostle*, truly commissioned and sent by God (Heb. 3:1; Mk 9:37; Jn 3:17; 5:36-38; 6:29, 57; 11:42; 17:18, 25; 20:21; Acts 3:20, 26).
- Jesus was the *prophet* "like Moses" (Dt. 18:15; Mt. 13:57; Mk 6:4; Lk. 7:16; 13:33; 24:19; Jn 6:14; Acts 3:22).
- Jesus was an itinerant *evangelist*, who went about proclaiming the promised good news, the *euangelion* (Mk 1:15; Is. 61:1; Lk. 4:18-19, 43-44; 8:1).
- Jesus was a *teacher*, who spoke and explained the words of God (Mt. 5:2; 13:54; Mk 4:2; 6:6; Jn 17:8). It is, however, important to note the difference between Jesus and the Jewish scribes. Jesus was a unique teacher who taught with authority (Mt. 7:28-29).
- Jesus was a *healer*, who healed the sick and suffering and bore our diseases (Mt. 4:23; 8:16-17; 19:2; Mk 6:56; Acts 10:38; 1 Pet. 2:24).
- Jesus was a good *shepherd* (*pastor*), who cared for his sheep (Heb.13:20; Jn 10:1-18; 21:15-17; 1 Pet. 2:25; Mt. 26:31).
- Jesus was a powerful *exorcist*, who defeated Satan and drove out evil spirits (Mk 2:21-28; Mt. 8:16; 12:28-29; Acts 10:38)
- Jesus was a caring *servant* (*diakonos,* deacon), who came to earth not to be served but to serve (Lk. 22:27; Mk 10:45; Rom. 15:8; Jn 13:1-17).

- Jesus is the *high priest*, who sacrificed his own life for us and always lives to make intercession for us (Heb. 2:17; 3:1: 4:14-15; 7:25; 9:11-13).

The church as a continuation of the ministry of the incarnate Son of God on earth is a frequently echoed idea in the Charismatic renewal; Jesus' earthly ministry is carried on through the church. "'As the Father has sent me, I am sending you.' And with that he breathed on them and said, 'Receive the holy Spirit'" (John 20:21-22). "Your attitude should be the same as that of Jesus Christ" (Phil. 2:5). Jesus, who fully revealed who God is and wants, is a source and model for all ministers and every believer in the church:

> And *do not grieve the Holy Spirit of God,* with whom you were sealed for the day of redemption [...] *Be imitators of God,* therefore, as dearly loved children and *live a life of love, just as Christ loved us and gave himself up for us* as a fragrant offering and sacrifice to God (Eph. 4:30; 5:1-2).

The Church as the Body of Christ

In the theology of the New Testament, the concept of the church as the body of Christ is most fully represented by Paul. This does not mean that the Pauline churches were the only variety of the New Testament church. Perhaps the Pauline churches even differed among themselves, depending on local circumstances. Other models are also present in the New Testament: the Jerusalem congregation, led by a council of elders, a form taken over from the synagogue, and congregations with the structures described in the Pastoral Epistles, which may be evidence of a development within the New Testament itself. However, "Paul is the first and, within the New Testament, the only one who has developed a genuine, explicit, and hence for us, comprehensible, doctrine of church."[1]

This doctrine is found – with certain differences – in Romans, 1 Corinthians, Ephesians, and Colossians. It is the doctrine of the "body of Christ", to which every believer belongs, and in which every believer is blessed with spiritual gifts and ministries. According to this doctrine, every believer is meant to function as a charismatic, one who has received one or more spiritual gifts, charisms (1 Cor. 12:7, 11, 27-30).

The relationship between the spiritually gifted members of the body and Christ, as head, is critical to the understanding of this image of the church, as the German theologian Edmund Schlink has pointed out:

> Through the rich variety of spiritual gifts Christ in his fullness comes to present-day manifestation – in the congregation first of all, then through the

---

[1] Emil Brunner, *Dogmatik III: Die christliche Lehre von der Kirche, vom Glauben und von der Vollendung* (Zürich: Theologischer Verlag Zürich, 1960), pp. 57ff.

> congregation to the world. The variety of spiritual gifts can appear in different congregations at different times and in differing forms. But the variety is always in essence a manifestation of the one gift, Jesus Christ. As head of the body, he is the source and bearer of all spiritual gifts. They function at his behest. They manifest the power of his name, each gift bearing its appropriate witness.
>
> Fellowship among the spiritually gifted people exists because of their common possession of the one gift, Jesus Christ. Christ himself is the one who really 'has' the spiritual gifts. He is the one apostle, the one teacher, the one evangelist, the one shepherd, the one deacon of the new covenant. He is the head of his body, the leader of his church. He makes known divine power, and is the author of all powers, signs, and wonders in Christendom. It is thus in sharing together the one gift, Jesus Christ, that the church becomes 'the fellowship of spiritual gifts.'[2]

The understanding of the congregation as the body of Christ had particular application to *worship*. Worship was not only a celebration *for* the congregation, but was also in large measure a celebration *by* the congregation, each member actively participating. Paul taught that when the body comes together for worship, every member should have something to contribute (1 Cor. 14:26). Of course, this admonition assumed that spiritual gifts were widely distributed in the body.

As early as the post-apostolic era, the practical implications of this teaching began to be lost. Especially in the area of worship, the idea of a spiritually gifted fellowship was replaced with a model in which the gifts of the Spirit were centralised in one person, or at most a few persons.

In the second century, the *monarchical episcopate* arose, which elevated the idea of "office" and further removed the gifts from the people. The overseer or bishop (Greek: *episkopos,* Acts 20:38, cp. 1 Tim. 3:1) became the overarching leader of the congregation (later of many congregations). The Lutheran Reformation developed a modified interpretation of the "office" or "ministry" of the local pastor consciously oriented toward justification by faith.[3] The "office" was understood as a service, a ministry, appointed by God to kindle faith by proclaiming the Word and administering the sacraments. This provided a more *functional* understanding of the pastoral office. The officeholder is first of all a Christian among Christians, standing *in* the congregation. There was no *qualitative* difference between him and the rest of the congregation. The biblical idea of *oversight*, however, was also maintained: the pastors as shepherds of the flock stand *over against* the

---

[2] Edmund Schlink, *Der kommende Christus und die kirchlichen Traditionen: Beiträge zum Gespräch zwischen den getrennten Kirchen* (Göttingen: Vandenhoeck & Ruprecht, 1961), p. 164. (Excerpt translated by William Sims.)

[3] Note the relationship between Articles IV, V and XIV in CA, *The Book of Concord*, pp. 30-31, and the discussion in Part Three of this book.

congregation with divinely appointed authority and responsibility (cp. Acts 20:28).

The "priesthood of all believers" was a central teaching of the Reformation, but its scope was limited to the area of personal access to God: one did not need to go through a priest to obtain forgiveness. The wider implication of the teaching – that every believer participates in the gifts and calling of the priesthood to "declare the praises" or "declare the wonderful deeds" of God (1 Pet. 2:9, NIV and RSV) – was not developed. The traditional distinction between clergy and laity was in practice, although not in principle, maintained. The early church's understanding of a fellowship of spiritually gifted and ministering people was not fully recovered. The Lutheran church, as a whole, remained a church dominated by clergy. Although great steps towards a more biblical understanding and practice of the priesthood of all believers took place in Lutheran Pietism, the doctrine still awaits full practical realisation. If we believe alongside Paul that the church is a fellowship of spiritually gifted people, then we must take practical steps – not least in the church's worship life – for these gifts to come into service.

If a person has, for example, the gift of prophecy, how do we make room in our worship services for this gift to be manifested? Paul said that, in a time of worship, two or three may speak in tongues, with interpretation following (1 Cor. 14:27). What might the Holy Spirit wish to do with that gift today? We do not suggest that worship should be given over to prophesying and speaking in tongues. Even in outspokenly charismatic worship services, these particular gifts are not given undue weight. But because these gifts have not been commonly manifested in our churches, they help bring the *basic issue into focus: how ready are we to let the Holy Spirit bring a fully gifted body into operation?* By giving attention to spiritual gifts, the Charismatic renewal has brought this question to the fore.

The Church as a Ministering Fellowship

The Holy Spirit is working to recover the early church's practice of allowing many Spirit-gifted ministries to function in the congregation. This is not something that can be consigned simply to the infancy of the church. It belongs to the nature of the church. Edmund Schlink is again helpful:

> Paul taught the variety of spiritual gifts so fundamentally that his statements can in no way be limited to the congregations in Corinth or Rome, or even to the Pauline congregations of the church's formative period. Rather, according to Paul's declarations, the rich variety of the Spirit's gifts belongs to the essence of the church in all places and at all times. The church, as the Body of Christ, is an organism having many gifts and many ministries. Paul formulated his teaching so generally and so basically that it cannot be relegated to one

> historical period. On the contrary, these statements must be included in the doctrines of church and office, even if they are not reflected in most of the other New Testament Scriptures.[4]

This emphasis is finding practical expression in the Charismatic renewal against the background of differing ecclesiastical traditions. The Lutheran doctrine of ministry, the Roman Catholic doctrine of consecrated priesthood, Presbyterian polity – these views remain essentially unchanged. What is changing in many places today is the role of the laity.

In charismatic churches and groups, Spirit-gifted lay Christians are increasingly ministering with evident and acknowledged spiritual authority. They function in leadership; they give spiritual care; they preach and teach; they speak prophetically; they intercede in prayer; they pronounce blessing; they serve the needy. In many areas, they minister alongside trained theologians and ordained clergy. In 1985, Fred Hall, a charismatic Lutheran layman from the United States, was invited to give a series of Bible studies at an annual conference of pastors and deacons in Tanzania. At the end of the conference, Lutheran bishop Erasto Kweka said, "It has been unusual to have a layman teach the Bible to pastors, but we see how the Holy Spirit has used him, and we are thankful."

Increased participation in ministry has been vigorously championed in charismatically renewed Lutheran congregations. In worship services, they are moving beyond traditional support roles, such as ushering and baby-sitting, into leading worship, teaching, preaching, and public prayer. Some Lutheran congregations find it useful to have lay members wear a robe or an alb when they minister before the congregation in public services. It helps break down the artificial and unbiblical distinction between clergy and laity, and at the same time conveys the sense of special calling that is symbolised by a distinctive dress.

In other areas of church life, outside the worship service, ordinary Christians are doing more of the ministry that people have traditionally expected from the clergy: visitation of the sick, spiritual counselling, doctrinal instruction. That which is distinctive in the Charismatic renewal is not simply that all Christians are urged and recruited to become more active, but that there is a more conscious recognition of the sovereignty of the Holy Spirit to call and anoint people for ministry.

This is not something that happens suddenly. It is a deepening conviction that must imbue both those who minister and those who receive ministry: they must see that the essential factor in all ministry, whether by clergy or laity, is the working of the Holy Spirit. The problem of a clergy-dominated church is not something that has been one-sidedly imposed on the laity by

---

[4] Schlink, *Der kommende Christus und die kirchlichen Traditionen*, pp. 161-162.

the clergy. Dwarfed expectations on the part of the laity regarding their own ministry are at least half of the problem.

On the one hand, many lay members have a self-imposed spiritual inferiority complex. They entertain no realistic expectation that they could receive gifts and anointing to minister in the power of the Holy Spirit.

An insurance executive who belonged to a charismatic Lutheran congregation was asked by his pastor to become part of a group of Christians who conducted a special prayer service in the congregation each month. They were stationed in teams at the altar of the church, and people desiring personal ministry would come to them for prayer. A variety of spiritual gifts would be manifested – prophecy, word of wisdom, word of knowledge, healing. At first, the man declined. He had experienced the power of this ministry first-hand, when he himself received it from his fellow members, but he could not imagine something "as far out as prophecy coming through me." When the pastor persisted, he agreed to "stand up there and pray silently while the others do the ministry." It was not long, however, before he began to receive prophetic revelation himself. He became a permanent member of the prayer-ministry team. The first barrier to be overcome is within the lay ministers themselves.

On the other hand, many lay people are not prepared to accept the ministry of other laity as fully authentic. They have a professionalised view of the ministry: a pastor is an educated, trained official; ministry by a non-ordained person is a well-intentioned effort by a spiritual amateur. The surest way to overcome this mindset is for a person to actually experience Spirit-empowered ministry at the hands of a fellow lay member. One of the pastor's important tasks is to present and commend the ministry of those whom the Spirit has gifted, so that other members will be encouraged to avail themselves of a ministry that the Holy Spirit has raised up.

The increased attention that the Charismatic renewal has given to spiritual gifts is helping make the doctrine of the priesthood of all believers more than a doctrine. This is an appropriate way for the formal structure of the church to be augmented, or even corrected, by a substructure. We may never arrive at the place where there are a specific number of gifts and ministries, bearing the same name, in every congregation. But when the grand total of Spirit-anointed ministries in the congregation and in the church as a whole increases, then the church will manifest more and more of the fullness of Christ. The body of Christ will be strengthened, to the glory of God.

The Church as Community

One of the unique features of the Charismatic renewal has been the formation of *ecumenical communities*. They have grown up principally in metropolitan areas and provide a corporate expression of charismatic renewal. They often begin as a prayer fellowship and grow to include such features as extended households, regular meetings, disciplined teaching, pastoral care, private schools, and community-service projects. Some Lutherans belong to these communities, but the majority of members are Roman Catholic.

According to the Catholic charismatic scholar Kilian McDonnell, the recognition of *church as community* (Greek: *koinonia*) is a distinctive emphasis that the Charismatic renewal contributes to the renewal of the whole person and of congregations. True Christian community embraces both Jesus' intimate concern for the welfare of the individual members of his body, and his desire for each member to lose their life in fruitful service for the kingdom of God. McDonnell claims that the churches have:

> Only sporadically grasped the importance of community in the Charismatic renewal. Unless the role of community is grasped, one has failed to understand what the renewal is saying. It seems to me that the primary consequence of the resurrection and of Pentecost is not the exercise of gifts but community formation.[5]

Among Lutherans, the experience of community has most commonly been an extension of congregational life. A Lutheran congregation moving strongly in charismatic renewal often has many things in common with ecumenical charismatic communities. Lutheran charismatics generally understand community in the practical sense that a person in one charismatic Lutheran congregation described it: "*submission to the lordship of Christ, and a high level of personal commitment of the members to one another.*"

A church in renewal will gather together frequently for Bible study, worship, preaching, teaching, sacraments, testimonies, prayer, practice of spiritual gifts, fellowship, offering and sharing of material means, mission, and service to other Christians and the world. The distinctive experience of community, however, requires also *smaller groupings* within the congregation. The importance of cell groups for healthy body life is being increasingly recognised. This is where the members' personal commitment to one another can be most readily expressed. They provide pastoral care, personal nurture, and also evangelistic outreach. Both the larger gatherings of the congregation and cell groups are necessary ingredients for building Christian community. All of these elements were present in the earliest days of the church (Acts 2:42-47; 4:32-35; 5:42).[6]

---

[5] Kilian McDonnell, "Towards a Critique of the Churches and the Charismatic Renewal", *One in Christ*, vol. 16, no. 4, p. 331.

[6] See also the more detailed description of the essential characteristics of the Spirit-filled church in Acts 2:42-47 in chapter 38.

(52) The Church: Institution and Free Movements

When charismatics talk about the church, they often fall into "us/them" patterns of speech. Traditional church members do the same thing in talking about charismatics. Properly understood, "us/them" talk may not be all bad. It expresses something that is essential to an understanding of church renewal, namely, how free movements relate to the institutional church.

Two Structures within the Church: Institution and Movement

Throughout the history of the church, there have been two structures in which Christians have gathered together: institution and movement. A biblical example often referred to is the congregation in Antioch – the "institution" – from which the relatively independent mission of Paul and Barnabas and their missionary bands – the "movement" – emerged (Acts 13:1-4).[1]

In our day, "institution" is represented by denominational structures, from national and regional offices down to local congregations. "Movement" is represented by groups that operate beyond normal parish structures, such as mission societies, diaconal organisations, religious orders, charismatic communities, Bible-study fellowships, and prayer groups.

Most of the *Christian congregations* that were established in the New Testament era were structurally patterned on the model of the Jewish synagogue. This structure embraced the community of the faithful in any given place. The defining characteristic of this structure is that it included the full age-sex spectrum of the entire community.

Paul's *missionary band* was represented by persons who committed themselves to a complementary mission endeavour in addition to the evangelism of the local church. The defining characteristic of this structure is that it did not include the entire community but was selective and had a particular aim and purpose. The congregation was, however, in some sense more basic than the movement. The missionary movement emerged from the congregation (Acts 13:1-3), the missionaries reported back to the congregation (Acts 14:26-28), and they established congregations as a result of their missionary work.

Thus, on the one hand, the structure that we call the New Testament church is a prototype of all subsequent Christian fellowships, where old and

---

[1] This structure is discussed in Ralph D. Winter and P. Beaver, *The Warp and Woof: Organizing Christian Mission* (Pasadena, CA: William Carey Library, 1970), and Ralph D. Winter, "The Two Structures of God's Redemptive Mission", *Missiology: An International Review*, January 1974, p. 124.

young, male and female are gathered together as normal biological families in aggregate. On the other hand, Paul's missionary band can be considered a prototype of all subsequent missionary endeavours represented by committed, experienced workers who affiliate themselves as members to a second additional structure.

The Historical Development of Institutional Authority

From the outset, the institutional aspect of the church faced the problem of maintaining order and orthodoxy in the face of a variety of influences and movements. This is one of the main tasks of the institutional aspect of the church, and it almost invariably sets it in tension with all movements, whether good or bad. While institution and movement serve complementary functions, they are not always complimentary toward one another.

In 96 A.D., Bishop Clement of Rome wrote his letter to the Corinthians. His shrill admonition was directed against elements threatening the unity and order of the congregation: "Submit yourselves to the priests, accept chastisement unto repentance, bend the knee of your hearts."[2] Disharmony in the Corinthian church was evident even in Paul's time, when the charismatics were unwilling to maintain order. Thus, the command: "Learn obedience!"

The church at Rome had its roots in the church at Jerusalem, with its strong emphasis on the church's institutional elements. Even in early Christendom, the Roman church had taken on the task of defence against heresy. When the church father Irenaeus spoke of "the greatest and oldest church, a church known to all men, which was founded and established at Rome by the most renowned Apostles Peter and Paul," he wished to establish its claim to institutional leadership.[3]

The *major doctrinal and spiritual threat* to the young church was posed by *Gnosticism*. Gnostic heresy refused to take the incarnation seriously; neither did it take in earnest the attendant problem of sin. The stumbling block for the gnostic was Jesus' shameful death on the cross. The foundation of Christian faith, as expressed in John 1:14, "the Word became flesh," was inconceivable. The Holy Spirit was understood by many Gnostics as a sort of heavenly light ray which is imprisoned in the bodies of mortal humans.

Gnosis ("knowledge") also had its practical side. Gnostics claimed to know the escape route from the labyrinth of existence. They knew how their souls could return to the realm of light. Because of their knowledge, they felt themselves superior to mere believing church Christians. Here was a movement that perverted the gospel and threatened to corrupt the church. How did the church deal with this kind of challenge? The development of

---

[2] *1 Clement* 57.

[3] Irenaeus, *Adversus Haereses* III, 3, 1-2.

firm, hierarchical authority was greatly accelerated. Rigid order was raised up as a bastion against the assault of Gnosticism.

The book *Didache* ("The Teaching of the Twelve Apostles") is thought by many scholars to have originated in Syria in the first half of the second century.[4] It puts us in touch with earlier practice in the church, when the charismatic dimension was still generally accepted, and when the responsibility of the institutional structure to provide discipline and order was also recognised.

Like Paul, the *Didache* referred to the gift of prophecy. True prophets would speak in the Holy Spirit and differentiate themselves from false prophets primarily by their lifestyle. The life of real prophets would resemble the Lord's.[5] Their words would include concrete instructions for the congregation. The *Didache* permitted prophets to "give thanks as much as they desire" in the course of a liturgical service of the Eucharist. While the prophets were speaking in the Spirit, their words became liturgical language. Their utterances were worship and praise for the gift of the Eucharist.[6] *Their prayers were the wellspring of liturgy in the early church.* On the other hand, according to the *Didache*, false prophets gave themselves away in that their instructions were not bound up with continuous praise of God. Pseudo-prophets sought honour for themselves and made a business of their prophetic abilities. The *Didache* warns emphatically: "Whoever speaks in the Spirit saying, 'Give me money' or some such thing should have no hearing [...] but whoever enjoins giving for those who suffer want should be judged by no one."[7]

This healthy interplay later gave way to an increasing distance between institutional and charismatic authority. Generally speaking, by about 150 A.D., a *monarchical episcopate* had developed out of the ranks of the clergy. One office bearer in a given congregation bore the sole, final authority as leader. The institutional aspect of the early Catholic church was clearly moving into ascendancy over free charismatic influences. The early Catholic church did practice the gift of spiritual discernment, as apocryphal gospels (special favourites with the Gnostics) were rejected and the New Testament Scriptures were given canonical status and became the basis of a binding Rule of Faith.[8]

The negative side of this development was that the sphere of ministry for spiritually gifted church members was greatly reduced. In the battle against heresy, spiritual gifts freely operating among the Christians became suspect.

---

[4] Berthold Altaner, *Patrologie* (Freiburg in Breslau: Herder, 1955), pp. 37-40.
[5] *Didache* xi, 8
[6] *Didache* x, 7.
[7] *Didache* xi,12.
[8] Altaner, *Patrologie*, p. 235.

As time passed, it became ever more difficult to distinguish their proper use from their misuse.

The Tension between the Institutional Church and the Renewal Movements

During *the Middle Ages,* institutional authority greatly expanded its sway in the church. The Roman Catholic Church stood under the standard of the papacy's universal rule. The pope enjoyed the highest respect as the possessor of supreme authority. Considered to be the successor of the apostle Peter, he established infallible, unalterable rules of faith. Because of the might of his hierarchical office, to him was attributed the "charism of power." The *Book of Canon Law* was regarded as divine law. At the new universities in Europe from the 12th century, *Scholasticism* was flourishing. According to the scholastics, the fundamental spiritual gifts were science, law, art, and the priesthood.[9] The gift of understanding, it was taught, was expressed in theology and science; the administrative gifts in law and hierarchy; the prophetic gifts could be seen in those artists whose work was dedicated to the church. Charisms were eclipsed by Canon Law.

When the persecuted minority church became a majority state church in the Roman Empire from the late fourth century its institutional form – the *congregational pattern of the ancient church became pervasively replaced by a geographical pattern* adapted from the Roman government. This new pattern, the Christian *parish church,* still preserved the basic constituency of the early church, namely, the combination of young and old, male and female. This pattern of geographical parishes has been retained in state and folk churches in Europe through the Middle Ages and the Reformation until our time, but it has not held sway in free churches and younger churches elsewhere in the world after the Reformation in the 16th century.

In spite of the church hierarchy and rigid legal structures, the Middle Ages were rich in renewal movements and spiritual awakenings. Several religious orders became fountainheads of spiritual and missionary activity, as for instance the Franciscans and the Dominicans.

The *monastic tradition thus developed a second structure.* This new widely proliferating structure undoubtedly had no connection with the missionary band in which Paul was involved, but, by the fourth century, there were already two very different kinds of structures in the church – the diocese with its bishop and the monastery with its abbot – both of them significant in the transmission and expansion of Christianity. The diocese and the

---

[9] Franz Anton Staudenmaier, *Der Pragmatismus der Geistesgaben oder das Wirken des göttlichen Geistes im Menschen und in der Menschheit* (Tübingen: Heinrich Laupp, 1835), p. 23.

monastery are historically unrelated to the two structures in New Testament times – yet they are functionally similar.[10]

It is not possible here to discuss in detail the rich charismatic traditions to be found in the history of monasticism, but out of the many examples in various times and places, four individuals, two men and two women, can be cited whose spiritual activity bore fruits of revival and brought blessing to the universal church: Benedict of Nursia (d. 550), Hildegard of Bingen (d. 1179), Francis of Assisi (d. 1226), and Birgitta of Sweden (d. 1373). Their movements, although at first resisted by ecclesiastical officials, were finally accepted and helped strengthen the tradition of charismatic authority in the church.

Other spiritual movements such as the Cathari, Waldenses, Joachimites, and Hussites, however, did not find a home within the established church, to the detriment of the church and the movements themselves. As the Roman Catholic Church became more worldly, spiritual awakenings were increasingly perceived as threats to the established order. The history of the church in the Middle Ages proves that the church as the body of Christ suffers when office and charismata stand opposed to one another.

Two Structures in the Protestant Churches and How They Relate to Each Other

Although the Reformation itself began as a movement within the church, the Protestant reformers made no provision in their churches for anything akin to free movements. The Protestant Reformation started out by actually attempting to do without any kind of structure comparable to the religious orders for monks and nuns in the Roman Catholic Church. Luther and the other Protestant reformers attempted to renew the life of the church through the congregational structure. The renewal was attempted at the general level of church life. Even though Luther had been an Augustinian monk and had found faith in that order, neither he nor any other Protestant reformers adopted any of these patterns. Lutheranism produced a *diocesan structure* that was similar the Roman Catholic diocesan tradition, but without the orders.

Professor of church history, Trygve Skarsten, perceives the lack of Protestant movement structures as a far-reaching weakness in the resulting tradition:

> Protestantism, and to be more specific, Lutheranism, resembled an unwieldy torso with its arms and legs severed and with little possibility of movement and mission. Not until new structures were devised could the Lutheran churches reach out effectively at home and abroad. An attempt to devise new

[10] Winter, "Two Structures of God's Redemptive Mission", pp. 126-127.

> [movement] structures occurred in the early eighteenth century [...] but it was not until the evangelical awakening of the early nineteenth century had unleashed the pent-up spiritual energy of Christendom on both sides of the Atlantic that the new structure known as the 'voluntary society' came into its own.[11]

History has demonstrated time and again that the church needs both the structures of institution and movement to renew itself and reach out effectively in mission and service.

Both structures contribute to the life and health of the church. Institutional structure provides for stability and permanence. Movements provide for spontaneity and change. The place of the church's institutional structures is generally understood. The role of movements, however, is less clearly understood and accepted. Especially in their early stages, movements are often resisted by the institution. What is needed is a new perception of the interdependence of these two basic structures within the church.

Movements and their organisations can often be seen as a protest or criticism of the society or institution in relation to which they exist. This is, however, usually not their primary focus. In most instances, the primary focus is a positive one – mission at home and abroad, numerical and spiritual growth, compassionate caring for people in need. But if, on the one hand, it is assumed that the institutional church is the only legitimate form in which the church exists, it is highly unlikely that movement structures will be seen in a positive light. Rather, movement organisations will be often be seen as illegitimate, competitive, and destructive. This puts the institutional church in a defensive posture. It is apt to reject the reform and renewal brought to bear by movement organisations. When this happens, movement organisations tend to be cut off or cut themselves off from the institutional church. They are apt to become suspicious of it and may even in some cases become divisive, and even sectarian.

If, on the other hand, it is assumed that *the church truly exists in both institutional and movement structures,* movement organisations may be perceived in an altogether different perspective: as complementary, constructive, as "glad responses to the Spirit of God." This does not necessarily diminish the challenge a movement organisation brings to bear on the institutional church – but it is now perceived to be born out of a caring spirit rather than a negative reaction. This perspective views movement

---

[11] Quoted in *Institutions and Movements: Two Structures within One Church*, edited by Larry Johnson (unpublished paper prepared on behalf of the *Affiliation of Lutheran Movements* for discussion with members of the Commission for a New Lutheran Church, p. 4. The discussion was held 5th April 1984, at Luther Northwestern Theological Seminary, St. Paul, Minnesota. Some of the following paragraphs are indebted to Johnson's paper.

organisations and institutional structures in such a way that mutual correction and growth are encouraged.

This is a framework of understanding within which the Charismatic renewal makes its appeal to the church. It has been called into life to meet a special need: to remind the church that God calls it to radical dependence on the Holy Spirit in every area of its faith and life. The church cannot lift its voice in worship, nor go out in mission, nor stretch out its hands in service except by the initiative and power of the Holy Spirit. This is no new teaching, but a fundamental of the faith that needs to be recovered in thought and experienced in life.

Renewal movements need the institutional church with its regular worship, preaching and teaching of the Word of God, administration of the sacraments, and Christian fellowship, and the *institutional church needs the inspiration, new life, mission and service offered by movements*. Every individual and institution needs continuous renewal in order to remain vigorous. The church needs always to be reformed (Latin: *ecclesia semper reformanda*). Renewal movements can be vital correctives. However, renewal efforts are often rejected or, at best, tolerated by the establishment. At the same time, many renewal groups may take a judgemental position in relation to the institutional church. They desire radical, immediate change. But seldom does correction come rapidly. Change is usually a slow process. Both institution and movement need to give serious thought to how they relate to one another.

Institution facing Movement

It is proper for the church to test the Charismatic renewal to evaluate whether it is from God, human beings, or even Satan. Indeed, all church teachings and practices should be re-examined continuously to guard against creeping error. The primary test is the biblical one: is it true to the whole and the heart of Scripture?

Lutheran charismatics believe that this renewal is truly biblical, that it represents an initiative of the Holy Spirit to bring neglected aspects of biblical faith back into the active life of the church. It is not an innovation, but a renewal of basic elements of the Christian faith as attested to in Scripture. *But charismatics not only call attention to neglected truth, they also strongly reaffirm the foundations of the faith.* They are trinitarian both in emphasis and practice. The authority of the Bible as God's Word is strongly stressed. The distinction between law and gospel is maintained. Appropriation and assurance of salvation by grace through faith in Jesus Christ in its full sense are emphasised and experienced. Christian living and sanctification based on the guidance of the Scriptures are strongly underscored. The call to Christian witness, mission, and service is sounded clearly and frequently.

Every society has its ideal and norm, with its ideal always being higher than what is the normal performance. Several options are available to deal with this performance gap. One remedy is to scold society for its low performance level, then apply the law more strictly. Eventually, this approach produces negative and rebellious reaction. A second method is to lower the ideal in order to bring it more in line with what is normal. Instead of narrowing the gap, however, lowering the ideal results in lowering what is normal also, because the two follow parallel lines. A third option is to defend what is common and normal and neglect the ideal, thus in effect resisting and restricting change. This often tends to be the approach of the established churches. *A fourth approach is to focus on the ideal and thus raise what is normal. The approach of the Charismatic renewal is to stress the biblical model and ideal and trust the Holy Spirit to raise performance.*

Every society has individuals who are deviants from what is normal or common. On the one hand, *deviants who insist on the ideal* are often ostracised from the mainstream and sometimes even persecuted. The next generation may honour them as prophets ahead of their time and may erect monuments in their memory. On the other hand, *deviants who are below the norm* may be placed under discipline, unless they become too numerous and powerful, in which case they may drag down the norms of the whole society. In time, this may generate a counterrevolution from the idealists.

As a social order, the church responds in similar fashion. Renewal, revival and prophetic movements have often been rejected throughout biblical and church history, not just by society at large but by the ecclesiastical hierarchy, which has seen no need for renewal and does not recognise renewal when it comes.

Three basic choices face institutional church leaders in relation to the Charismatic renewal: reject it, ignore it, or recognise it.

The church may choose to *reject the renewal* in a deliberate manner for doctrinal, political, pastoral, psychological, or sociological reasons. This may be done with or without a hearing. Church officials may define the Charismatic renewal as being in biblical or theological error. Or they may decide that the renewal threatens the church's unity and peace. Or they may declare that the movement has been found wanting on the basis of some bad examples and unfortunate experiences. Or they may describe the movement sociologically as foreign to the church's traditional pattern of behaviour, and thus unacceptable.

In the 1960s, many mainline Protestant churches tended to reject the Charismatic renewal one way or another.[12] When charismatics talked about being persecuted and suffering, most often it was in reference to the institutional church. Such suffering has been widespread among charismatics

---

[12] See McDonnell, *Presence, Power, Praise,* Vol. 1, 1980. The documents in this volume cover the period 1960-1974. In considerable degree, the documents produced by Protestants churches during this period attempt to respond to a new phenomenon that is perceived as a threat to peace and order.

who have remained loyal to their churches. It tells us something about the way church authorities often have related to the movement.

By the early 1970s, it became apparent that the movement was not going to go away, and since then the response has often been to *ignore* it in the sense of not taking the challenge it represented to the church seriously. The practical effect of this is that the renewal is rejected.

Church officials may, however, choose – and have also at times chosen – a third option, which is to *recognise the renewal*, so that it can positively influence the life of the church. Both church officials and charismatics must see clearly what this option entails. It does not mean that the church adopts or takes over the renewal in an official or semi-official way. Lutheran charismatics have sometimes so yearned to be accepted by the church that they have not seen this clearly. They unconsciously model their idea of acceptance after official programmes or institutions of the church. This kind of acceptance, however, could be disastrous. One of the fundamental dangers faced by any renewal movement is that of being domesticated. A thoroughly domesticated renewal can easily lose its prophetic edge, and therefore its calling. This does not call for an adversary relationship between a renewal movement and the church. A healthy tension is necessary, but this can be in a spirit of love and communication.

Recognising the Charismatic renewal is something different from adopting or endorsing it. It is more subtle. It is less official, yet at the same time more effective. Recognition may occur when an official states his or her agreement with a charismatic. It may be an occasion when charismatics present a position that is seriously heard and considered. It has to do with the way that church officials and charismatic leaders speak about each other and relate to each other. It is more a matter of tone than of official policy. It is a concrete and consistent demonstration of regard that can be expressed in a variety of ways. For instance, theological seminaries or church conventions may invite a charismatic to be the speaker for a lecture series. Bishops may risk their popularity by taking a stand against those in a congregation who want to dismiss a pastor simply on the ground of the pastor being charismatic. A church commission may seek counsel from charismatic congregations that have demonstrated effective ministry in a particular area. Church officials may bring greetings, preach, or celebrate the Eucharist, at a charismatic convention.

These kinds of actions do not involve official endorsement of a movement. What they do, is recognise the presence of a renewal movement in the church and encourage its healthy expression. More importantly, they say convincingly that people involved in the renewal are fellow members, whose calling and gifts are appreciated in the church.

In giving this kind of recognition to the Charismatic renewal, the church does not and should not lay aside its responsibility to continue to evaluate and, where necessary, to correct the renewal. Theologians, officials, pastors, and parishioners need to examine the renewal in the light of Scripture. Church leaders owe it to their constituency to make such an evaluation. If the Charismatic renewal is truly from God, it will stand up under scrutiny.

Movement facing Institution

The Charismatic renewal is also faced with *three major options*: isolation, institutionalisation, or witness.

Large numbers of charismatics have felt frustrated with or rejected by their church. Some have chosen to leave their congregation or denomination and join more active churches. In the absence of a lively alternative church, some have established home meetings as a substitute. Although these kinds of actions may have been beneficial for the people concerned, it also means that valuable members have become lost for churches or *individual charismatics have become isolated from the larger Christian fellowship*.

Lutheran charismatic leaders have generally counselled charismatics to have prayerful patience with the church and not to reject it. They have challenged charismatics to love the church, to pray for it, and to serve it, just as Jesus does (Eph. 5:25-27). Leaving the institutional church or one's spiritual home congregation is always a last resort.

A renewal movement may become *institutionalised* either by becoming a parachurch organisation within the denomination or by leaving its historical setting and forming a new church or denomination. Church history records numerous examples of renewal movements moving in these directions. Many have organised themselves as a mission society, a diaconal organisation, an evangelistic association, a spiritual-life federation, or religious order.

There are both advantages and disadvantages connected with institutionalisation. *Some degree of institutionalisation may be necessary* in order to realise the objectives of the movement, to keep its identity, and to carry it forward to new generations. The disadvantages can be that spiritual movements within the larger church run the danger of being relegated to the periphery of church life, exerting only a limited influence on the larger church. When the renewal becomes a new church or denomination, formed around newly discovered experience and teaching, the life span of the movement may be greater, but its influence is restricted to its own membership, and it runs increased risk of falling victim to imbalance.

A third alternative is that the renewal becomes a *witness* in and to the church. On the one hand, this means being a bold, *prophetic* voice, recalling the church to its high calling. On the other hand, it also means being a *servant* – repenting of sin, allowing the Holy Spirit to do his cleansing and painful work – first of all in the renewal – giving and serving in humble ways, interceding for the people of God as Moses interceded for Israel (Ex. 32:7-14, 30-32), praying with persistence for the church's renewal.

Being a witness means seeking out ways to express love and regard for the church. Charismatics need to model this in their relationships with both church officials and church members. Again, it is not a matter of setting up official structures, but of finding natural ways to recognise and honour Christian brothers and sisters. A church leader may be invited to speak or conduct a workshop at a charismatic conference. Charismatic leaders and church officials may meet informally from time to time to discuss questions or problems of common interest, to pray with one another, or simply to socialise.

When relationships of mutual trust and regard are built between charismatics and Christians who do not identify with the Charismatic movement, each respecting the integrity of the other, the *"us/them" dichotomy* can be lived out under an *overarching we*. The church in both its expressions – institution and movement – will be a more credible witness to the lordship of Jesus Christ over all things in the church.

The Burden of the Charismatic Renewal for the Church

The institutional church is in serious need of renewal. The Lutheran church in some parts of the world, particularly in Europe and North America, is experiencing a measurable decrease in membership, as well as a perceived decline in influence. Its evangelistic zeal has been waning and its missionary force declining. Church attendance and programme participation involve only a small fraction of the total baptised membership. Responsible polls indicate that many Lutherans lack assurance of personal salvation or proper understanding of justification by faith.[13] That alone constitutes a crying need for renewal in the Lutheran church.

In other parts of the world, the challenges may be different: in growing Lutheran churches, there are needs for more workers in the church, better Christian education of the church members, care for the poor and sick in the church and in society, the need to face the onslaught of Satan and religious persecution, and speak out against injustice and corruption.

Scripture gives prophetic images of a comprehensive salvation and renewal that come to the people of God through the Holy Spirit: Ezekiel's vision of the Spirit giving life to the dry bones in the valley (Ez. 37:1-14), Joel's prophecy of an end-time outpouring of the Spirit (Joel 2:28-29), the Servant of the Lord being filled with the Spirit bringing justice to the nations (Is. 42:1-4), Jesus Christ anointed by the Spirit preaching good news to the poor and proclaiming "the year of the Lord's favour" (Is. 61:1-2; Lk. 4:18-19).

The shape of a renewed church may be quite different from its present form, yet the essentials of our life in Christ will be abundantly evident. The

[13] Strommen, *A Study of Generations*, p. 150.

Holy Spirit will be recognisably present in the church's life and ministry. There will be a strong biblical orientation in preaching, teaching, and daily life. The gifts of the Spirit will be in operation in the public life of the church and the private life of church members. Jesus will be acknowledged as head of the church and his will sought for all things. The rule of God will be established in the belief system, structural order, worship, and ministry of the church. The church will be increasingly ecumenical. The growing unity of the body of Christ will be demonstrated to the world as a positive witness to the gospel. The church in renewal will seek to fulfil the Great Commission through evangelisation at home and transcultural mission to the ends of the earth. It will be both an example and an advocate of justice, peace and reconciliation in the world.

One of the unique and encouraging features of the Charismatic movement as a whole has been its determined insistence to remain within the church. By and large, it is a movement within rather than outside of the institutional church. Richard Hutcheson, a Presbyterian church official, points this out:

> Unlike many previous spirit-centred movements, the charismatic movement is not essentially anti-institutional, but is rather making a conscious and generally successful effort to remain within the existing churches. A remarkably high percentage of individual charismatics and charismatic groups are making a determined effort to support, remain loyal to, and work within the existing structures of their own congregations. They are often the most loyal, most enthusiastic, and most active workers and supporters. A great many non-charismatic ministers would be startled to learn how many of those they regard as pillars of the establishment speak in tongues in their private and small group devotions.[14]

Present-day charismatics are not more holy than participants in earlier renewal movements. They have certainly done their share of complaining about the institutional church. They have not always borne rejection and criticism with grace. And yet it is true, as Hutcheson points out, that the movement has so far tended to remain within the church more than many previous movements. This must be seen as a special grace of God, both for the church and for the Charismatic renewal. The Spirit is holding both institution and renewal in his embrace, softening fleshly dogmatism, quieting the voices of strident intransigence, giving our generation the chance to grasp and experience more deeply the true nature of the church.

The church has its institutional side, which embraces all believers and all areas of being church; providing structure, stability and continuity; and it has its movement side, which the Spirit calls into being to meet special needs, correcting end empowering the church's life and ministry. Can these two, in

---

[14] Richard G. Hutcheson Jr., *Mainline Churches and the Evangelicals* (Atlanta, GA: John Knox, 1981), pp. 105-106.

our day, so submit to the Holy Spirit's authority that the church will recover what has been lost – a mutual regard that bequeaths to the people of God both the strength of institution and the innovation of movement?

(53) Young People in the Ministry of the Church

by Tormod Engelsviken[1]

The family model of church order and the term "elder" (Greek: *presbyteros*) as a designation may, when understood superficially, give the impression that older people should lead the church and that there is no significant place for youth in church ministry. Nothing can be farther from the truth. In the Bible – and most of the writings of the Bible belong in a cultural context which was patriarchal and where older men were dominant – the important role of the ministry of young people is emphasised again and again, often contrary both to the people's and their own expectations.

When the man of God, Samuel, was sent by God to Bethlehem to anoint a *king* for Israel, "the elders of the town trembled when they met him". God's chosen king was David, a shepherd boy who was the youngest among his brothers. He was God's choice of a leader for Israel because "the Lord looks at the heart". The Spirit of the Lord came upon the young David in power from the day of his anointing by Samuel (1 Sam. 16:1-13, see v. 4, 7, 11-13). On the background of this event, God says in Psalm 89:19:

> I have bestowed *strength on a warrior*; I have *exalted a young man* from among the people. I have found David my servant; with my sacred oil I have anointed him. My hand will sustain him; surely *my arm will strengthen him.*

Furthermore, one of the most important *prophets* in the Old Testament, Jeremiah, was young when he was called to become a prophet. Again, God says:

> Before I formed you in the womb I knew you, before you were born I set you apart; *I appointed you a prophet to the nations.* "Ah, Sovereign Lord," I said, "I do not know how to speak; I am only a child." But the Lord said to me, *"Do not say, 'I am only a child (or young).'* You must go to everyone I send you to and say whatever I command you. *Do not be afraid of them*, for *I am with you and* will *rescue you* (Jer. 1:4-8).

These two Old Testament texts are ample evidence of how God chooses to use young people for his service, and should give confidence and boldness to young people who experience the calling and empowering of God.

In the New Testament, many of the most outstanding servants of God and leaders of the church were young. Jesus himself was only 30 years old when

[1] This chapter is contributed by Tormod Engelsviken.

he began his public ministry after his baptism, full of the Holy Spirit (Lk. 3:21-23; 4:1, 14, 18.). John the Baptist, who was filled with the Holy Spirit from birth (Lk. 1:15; 41, 44) was half a year older than Jesus, and probably began his prophetic ministry before he was 30 years old. Most of the apostles would be younger than Jesus. In the early church, the apostle Paul was a young man when he was converted, received his call as an apostle to the Gentiles and was filled with the Holy Spirit (Acts 7:58; 8:1; 9:1, 15-18; 26:15-18).

This should come as no surprise since the prophet Joel had received the word of the Lord which was fulfilled on the day of Pentecost, and quoted by Peter in his sermon:

> 'In the last days,' God says, 'I will pour out my Spirit on *all* people. *Your sons and daughters will prophesy*, your *young men will see visions,* your *old men will dream dreams*. Even on my servants, both *men and women,* I will pour out my Spirit in those days, and they will prophesy' (Acts 2:17; Joel 1:1, 2:28-29).

These were remarkable and quite revolutionary words if we take into account the culture of the time and its view of young people and of women. The point is that the Spirit will be poured out on *all,* without difference between age or gender groups, and we might also add: ethnic and social backgrounds. This is what happened on the day of Pentecost (Acts 1:14: 2:4, 17), and it continued to happen as ever new people came to faith, were baptised, received the Holy Spirit, and were included in the church (1 Cor. 12:13).

> You are *all* sons of God through faith in Jesus Christ. For *all* of you who have been baptised into Christ, have clothed yourselves with Christ. There is neither Jew nor Greek, slave nor free, male nor female, for you are *all* one in Christ (Gal. 3:26; Col. 3:11).

This also means that all these human differences are abolished as far as the reception of gifts, the *charismata,* of the Spirit are concerned. In his sovereignty, the Holy Spirit gives them "to each one, just as he determines" (1 Cor. 12:11).

A relevant case is the *young man* Timothy who had received a gift which was given him "through a prophetic message when the body of elders laid their hands" on him. His gift(s) was "the public reading of Scripture, preaching and teaching", tasks that obviously were such that some people in the church could think that he was too young to carry them out with any authority. Therefore, his mentor Paul says to him,

> Don't let anyone look down on you because you are young, but set an example for the believers in speech, in life, in love, in faith and in purity [...] Watch

> your life and doctrine closely. Persevere in them because if you do, you will save both yourself and your hearers (1 Tim. 4:12-16).

Young people have certain advantages that God may use, not least their strength and their willingness and ability to fight for the Lord. "Your troops will be willing on the day of battle. Arrayed in holy majesty, from the womb of dawn *your young men* will come to you like the dew" (Ps. 110:3). "I write to you, young men, because you are *strong*, and the *word of God lives in you*, and you have *overcome the evil one*" (1 Jn 2:14).

If we look at the *history of the church*, we may observe that God continues to use young people, particularly in movements of revival, renewal and reform. A few examples will bear this out: Martin Luther (born 1483) was only 34 years old when he published his 95 theses in 1517 and became the undisputed leader of the Reformation. August Hermann Francke (born 1663) was 24 years old when he was converted and became the leader of the Pietist movement. Count Nikolaus von Zinzendorf (born 1700) was in his twenties when he initiated the Moravian Pietistic fellowship. William Carey (born 1761), the "father" of the modern Protestant mission movement was about 31 years old when he wrote his famous book on mission, *Enquiry*, founded the Baptist Missionary Society, and became a missionary to India in 1792. Hans Nielsen Hauge (born 1771) was 25 years old when he had his life-transforming experience of the Holy Spirit in 1796 followed by only eight years as an itinerant evangelist and revival leader until he was imprisoned in 1804. His ministry changed and renewed church life in Norway for decades. The prophetess and revival leader Nenilava in Madagascar was called to her ministry during her teens.[2] Larry Christenson (born 1928) was 33 years old when he got involved with the Lutheran Charismatic renewal in the United States in 1961 and became its informal inspirational and theological leader for decades.[3]

One of the most remarkable examples of how God uses young people in our time, is the largest mission organisation in the world today, the Pentecostal/Charismatic *Youth With A Mission* (YWAM) with more than 10 000 cross-cultural missionaries all over the world. It was born out of a vision by its founder, Loren Cunningham, who when he was only 20 years old saw waves of youth covering continent after continent. The Norwegian branch of YWAM grew out of the Charismatic renewal in Norway and celebrated its 50th anniversary in 2022. During these years, it has grown to be the largest

---

[2] See the brief descriptions of some of these reform, renewal, revival and mission leaders in Part Three of this book.

[3] Comment by Tormod Engelsviken. Larry Christenson died in 2017.

mission organisation in Norway in terms of sending out cross-cultural missionaries, mostly young people.[4]

The reason while the Holy Spirit so often elects young people to do his work of renewal and mission in the church, may be exactly the characteristics of youth described in the Bible as being strong, having a deep commitment to the Word of God, being willing to fight against Satan's opposition and following the vision that God has given them. The fact that God is calling young people to ministry and endowing them with spiritual gifts should give the young people courage to serve in positions often reserved for older people, and the older people the courage to recognise the gifts of the young and give them both opportunity and responsibility to use their gifts freely for the benefit of the whole church and its mission.

Young leaders, of both genders, may need mentoring by older leaders, just as Paul studied under Gamaliel (Acts 22:3), and mentored the young Timothy, who also in turn was charged with teaching others. This is the essence of the right Christian *tradition*:

> You then, my son, *be strong* in the grace that is in Christ Jesus. And the things that *you have heard me say* in the presence of many witnesses, entrust to reliable men who will also be qualified to teach others. (2 Tim. 2:2, cp. 1 Cor. 15:1, 3).
>
> You know all about my teaching, my way of life, my purpose, faith, patience. Love endurance, persecutions, sufferings [...] But as for you, *continue in what you have learned* and have become convinced of, because you know *those from whom you have learned it*, and how from infancy you have *known the holy Scriptures* (1 Tim. 3:10-15).

This training of young leaders may take place in the family (1 Tim. 1:5), in the church, through Bible study (2 Tim. 3:15-16), and – today – also in Bible schools and theological seminaries that are faithful to the Scriptures.

---

[4] The remarkable history of YWAM, Norway, is told in Tonje Haugeto Stang, *Ringer i vann. Historien om Ungdom i Oppdrag gjennom 50 år* ("Rings in Water. The History of Youth With A Mission through 50 Years", Ottestad: Proklamedia, 2022).

(54) The Church: An Ordered Body

Charismatics have addressed themselves to questions of order regarding the two primary areas in which the renewal has functioned: the movement itself, and the local congregation. It has had little or nothing to say about larger church structures, although its experience both within the movement and in local fellowships is not without implications for the church at large.

Order in the Charismatic Renewal

To speak about "order" in the same breath with "charismatic renewal" may seem to fulfil the classic definition of humour: the juxtaposition of the incongruous. Certainly, the renewal has nothing comparable to the defined structure and established procedures of a denomination. If one looks at the worldwide phenomenon of the renewal in terms of structure, then one must say that innovation and variety are the rule; uniformity, the exception. In this sense, there is no standard or well-defined "order" in the Charismatic renewal. Yet a crucial component of order is exercised in and by the renewal, and that is *spiritual authority*.

Catholic scholar Kilian McDonnell once asked David du Plessis, widely recognised as an ambassador of classical Pentecostalism to the historic denominations, to speak to a group of bishops, and commented, "We want someone who can speak from a position of authority." Du Plessis, who held no office, represented no organisation, demurred: "I have no authority." "Indeed you do," countered McDonnell. "It carries no title, is subject to no election, has no jurisdictional boundaries, is recorded in no minutes; it is non-official, non-legal, nonbinding. But it is authority!"

It is characteristic of renewal movements that they give rise to another stream of authority in the church, alongside that of the official institution. As McDonnell rightly observed, it is a different kind of authority: not the authority of office, but the authority of influence. Yet its effect in the church can be considerable, and may even go beyond that of official institutional authority. Where charismatic or spiritual authority is recognised and received, it can significantly shape individual lives and the life of the church as a whole.

The Charismatic renewal has raised up a considerable cadre of leaders who, to varying degrees, make up part of this second stream of authority in the church. Many renewal movements have come to a focus in the person of a single "charismatic" leader who, at the least, symbolised the movement. Names like Francis of Assisi, Ignatius of Loyola, Martin Luther, John Calvin, Philipp Jakob Spener, August Hermann Francke, Nikolaus von Zinzendorf,

John Wesley, William Carey, Hans Nielsen Hauge, Carl Olof Rosenius, and William Booth spring to mind. No such single figure has arisen in the Charismatic renewal. Because the movement is so widespread – on every continent and in every denomination – its leadership is also widespread. What one sees is not a single leader who leads or represents the movement, but rather a network of relationships among many leaders.

Order is related to goal or purpose. A single family, a business enterprise, a church, or an entire nation establishes an order that it believes will help it accomplish certain goals. The goal of the Charismatic renewal is neither to take over nor to replace the institutional church. Individual charismatics may have positions in the structure of their denomination (charismatic parish pastors would be the prime example), but the purpose of the Charismatic renewal, as a movement within the church, is to speak to the church, be a presence in the church, encourage the church, serve the church, and bear witness to the church.

The kind of order that will accomplish that goal in all the different nations and cultures of the world, and in every denomination throughout the entire body of Christ, calls for incredible diversity and a great deal of grass-roots initiative. The order that has grown up in the Charismatic renewal is appropriate to its purpose: not a centralised or highly co-ordinated organisation but a relatively loose and fluid set of relationships among charismatic leaders. These relationships form a communication link that encompasses the globe and reaches into virtually every denomination in Christendom. Charismatic leaders know each other, correspond with each other, meet in a variety of situations and configurations, consult with one another, and undertake common projects that serve or give expression to the renewal. All of this takes place with a very minimum of structure and organisation. Charismatic leaders have not sought to organise much of anything beyond the level of denominational renewal committees and ad-hoc committees that convene meetings and conferences or initiate special projects. The order that they give to the Charismatic renewal is a sense of solidarity in the common purpose of calling the church to a renewed dependence on the Holy Spirit. This solidarity is expressed in their relationships with one another.

More significant than anything that charismatic leaders do or organise is just the way that they move about in the body of Christ with evident love and regard for one another, recognising, honouring, and drawing on one another's ministries. While there have been some breaks in relationships between some charismatic leaders, on the whole, these relationships have served to give an order to the movement that is commensurate with its purpose.

When Philip Potter, general secretary of the World Council of Churches, asked David du Plessis whether the Charismatic movement was the "real ecumenical movement today," du Plessis is reported to have said, "My dear

Philip, we are so far ahead of you we can't even see if you're still coming."[1] In an open seminar at the World Council of Churches Assembly in Nairobi in 1975, Kilian McDonnell, himself a professional ecumenist for the Vatican, said that "the most significant thing happening ecumenically today is in the charismatic renewal."[2] It is a different kind of ecumenism, unofficial and relatively un-programmed. Yet, through an infrastructure of relationships among its leaders, the Charismatic movement is sending strong impulses for reconciliation, unity, and renewal throughout the global body of Christ.

Order in Congregational Life

The second area in which the Charismatic renewal has addressed itself to the question of order is in regard to congregational or parish renewal. The reason for this is that the place where the renewal has had the greatest freedom to reshape structure is at the level of the local church. A charismatic Lutheran pastor who has the support of the lay leadership can exercise considerable freedom in bringing changes to a local congregation. This is the level at which the Charismatic renewal has had its greatest impact in the Lutheran church. Concern for congregational order in the Charismatic renewal has been an extension of its emphasis on the lordship of Christ. If Christ is truly Lord of the church, then its structure and operation cannot be a matter of indifference or mere preference, but should be reflective of his will in the matter.

In this, as in most other matters, charismatics have taken *Scripture* as their point of departure. Lutheran charismatics have generally steered a middle course between claims of having discovered the scriptural pattern for *the* "New Testament church" and the liberal notion that Scripture has nothing whatever to say on the subject. There is a readiness in the Charismatic renewal to evaluate some present-day church practices in the light of scriptural patterns and precedents.

On the one hand, as we have noted earlier, it seems clear that the New Testament does not present a single, universally normative structure for a Christian congregation. On the other hand, Scripture is certainly not silent regarding questions of order, structure, and authority in the church. What the Holy Spirit led the church to do in its formative years with regard to order is part of the apostolic witness, part of canonical Scripture. We may assume that the Spirit will apply the same wisdom to our situations.

It is true that "the situation is different today" but repeating that slogan should not be our point of departure in establishing the order of a congregation. For it is also true that *the Holy Spirit is able to apply the same*

---

[1] Hutcheson, *Mainline Churches and the Evangelicals*, p. 174.

[2] Kilian McDonnell in an open forum at the 1975 Assembly of the World Council of Churches in Nairobi, Kenya. Reported by Larry Christenson.

basic truth in a great variety of situations. The Spirit may indeed set aside some patterns from the past and utilise present-day practices in ordering the life of a congregation, but he is not bound to do so, nor are we free to do so if he wills something else.

Alternative Concepts for Ordering Congregational Life

If one were to look for a touchstone of the teaching of the Charismatic movement with regard to congregational order it would probably be focused in words like *elder or church council.* This stems first of all from the study of Scripture. The role of elders figures prominently in governing structures both in the Old and New Testaments. The other side of this is the fact that charismatics have recognised some of the weaknesses inherent in a congregation that simply structures itself after the model of a democratic society. This change in concept is sometimes described as a transition from democracy to kingdom. In explaining this transition to a group of pastors, Herbert Mirly, pastor of Resurrection Lutheran Church in Charlotte, North Carolina, USA, said:

> We did not need to change the constitution of our congregation as this transition got under way. It was a matter of how we understood and used the existing structure. For instance, we used to come to a congregational meeting with the idea that we must 'make certain decisions.' When we began to see the congregation as an expression of 'kingdom,' we approached the whole thing differently. God makes decisions. Our business is to discern as accurately as we can what he has decided and then proceed to obey him. The so-called 'voters meeting' became a prayer meeting or a 'discernment session.' We still discuss the issues, but the attitude and approach is altogether different: instead of choosing up sides and seeing who can muster 51% of the vote, we are all standing on the same side of the line participating in the process of listening to the Lord and seeking his will in the matter.[3]

A related concept for understanding congregational order has been that of *family.* The model of family tends to produce in a congregation an ordered set of relationships rather than simply a procedure for handling issues. At first glance, this seems to lead to a more centralised, authoritarian structure, but the opposite is more usually the case. Loving and sensitive parents and grandparents probably listen more sympathetically to their children than elected officials listen to their constituency. They listen because they love and seek the best for the family. Charismatic congregations who have developed the family concept might well decide to wait if as few as 10% of

---

[3] Herbert Mirly, talk given at Lutheran Charismatic Regional Leaders' Meeting, Inamia, Minnesota, USA, March 1983. (See Appendix.)

the members feel uneasy about a particular action; in a family, maintaining unity is normally more important than pushing through a particular decision.

Excursus 3:
A Family Model of Church Government

A charismatic Lutheran congregation who had experimented with a family model of church government for about ten years included the following statement in its annual report:[1]

> What we see emerging in our midst is a particular understanding of church order and leadership that is significantly different from that which many people have grown up with and have come to take for granted. It has several interrelated features.
>
> 1. *Leadership is a particular gift and calling.* The old idea was to give almost everyone who was willing to serve a turn on the church council.[2] If we saw those whom we would like to see develop further, we would grab them for the council. 'That way we will get them involved,' so we thought. The council was looked on as a place to develop leaders.
>
> What we have come to see is that leadership is a particular gift and calling in the Body of Christ. While there will inevitably be some real development in any person who serves on the council, the council is essentially a ministry for those who have already demonstrated the gift and calling for leadership. Our concern in nominating people for the council is not to 'get them involved,' or to 'give them a chance to grow,' but rather to discern the ones whom the Lord has given the calling of leadership in the congregation.
>
> We must set aside the worldly notion that leadership is a place of higher status, while those members who are not part of the leadership occupy a lower status. The call of a council member is in essence no different than the calling of a Sunday school teacher, a pastor, a custodian, an usher, or a nursery attendant. The calling of each and every one is *to serve.* Leadership is simply a necessary function in the Body of Christ to which some members are called, because God has gifted and equipped them for serving in this particular way.
>
> When we understand leadership in this way, then it becomes evident that not everyone is called to serve on the council. Just as not everyone has a calling to teach, or play the organ, or manage finances, or do marriage counselling. Some members will never be called to serve on the council. Not because they are less important or respected in the congregation, but simply because that is not their calling under God.

---

[1] "1975 Annual Report", *Trinity Lutheran Church*, San Pedro, California, pp. 16-18.
[2] The "church council" may have different names in different church structures, like "parish board", "council of elders" etc. The point is that it is a group or fellowship of leaders with both spiritual and practical responsibilities.

Indeed, it has been our experience that the very nature of congregational life is such that a relatively small number of people have the calling to serve on the church council. Council members rotate off the council at least every three years, but after a year's 'sabbatical' have frequently been called back into active service. What we have had in effect is a small pool of leaders from which we each year select a council. New members may be drawn into this 'pool of leadership' as their gifts and calling for leadership become evident.

If one looked at this practice from a human point of view, it could be dubbed a clique. But what is it from God's point of view? Does God call people to the important ministry of leadership for three years, and then set them aside so as to 'give somebody else a chance'? This is a human way of reckoning, which attaches some special status to the ministry of leadership. We repeat: no member of the Body of Christ is more honoured or significant than any other. Each simply has a different function. Those who have had the calling to serve on the church council, in a congregation our size, consist of a pool of probably no more than twenty people. With the simple passage of time, some people will be added to this pool, while others will move away, be called to another ministry, become less active, or be promoted to the heavenly councils!

We do not see the evolving of a small cadre of leaders in our congregation as a sign that we are in a rut, or having the same old people run everything. Rather, we believe this is the result of a definite leading of the Spirit. It has resulted from his work among us, to strengthen and build up the Body of Christ.

2. *From political assembly to family.* As we enter into a deeper apprehension of the church order and leadership which the Spirit is working among us, we have to unlearn some of our traditional ways of thinking about church order. As Americans we have experienced great blessings from the political system of representative democracy. But the foundational concept of democracy is alien to the church. Under democracy, the leaders are ultimately responsible to the people who elect them. In the church, leaders are ultimately responsible to God.

A political system is a poor model for church order. Far better is the model of a family, 'the household of God' (1 Tim. 3:15).[3] The nature of a Christian congregation is much more akin to a family than to a democratic government. According to the family model, the leaders of the congregation fulfil the role of parents. They are responsible for the leadership and the direction of the family.

Parents' ultimate accountability for their family is to God. They are responsive to their children, but they are responsible to God. Likewise, the leaders of a congregation must be responsive to each and every member. Leaders are expected to have wisdom, and one of the qualities of the 'wisdom that is from above' is that it is easily 'entreated' (James 3:17), which means that a church council member is someone you can feel free to come and talk to, someone

---

[3] To the church as a new family in the New Testament and the early church, see Karl Olav Sandnes, *New Family: Conversion and Ecclesiology in the Early Church with Cross-Cultural Comparisons* (Pieterlen, Switzerland: Peter Lang, 1994).

with whom you can share your problems and concerns. God may use something that you share to help formulate a decision or direction taken by the council.

While leaders must be responsive to the people, they cannot ask simply, 'What does the congregation want?' If they take that line, they would be like parents who make decisions simply on the basis of 'what the children want.' Those called by God to leadership responsibility will have to press on to ask, 'What does God want?' Leaders who end up being simply an echo of the people have abandoned their God-appointed calling to lead.

The family is an appropriate model for the church because it embraces people at all different levels of (spiritual) development: tiny babes (a 40-year-old man can be a babe in Christ), children, young men and women, mothers, and fathers. It is the calling of the spiritual parents to give leadership to the family. They are the ones that God has equipped for the task. Blessed is the congregation where such 'parents' have been raised up by God, have entered into their calling, and have been gratefully received by the people.

Where the responsibility and authority of leadership rests in a council of spiritual elders, the congregation is spared the mistakes and immaturities of purely democratic decisions. (Even in the secular sphere, especially given the enormously increased power of the mass media, we are beginning to see how subject the decisions of the people are to whim and passing fad.) Moreover, the fact that leadership rests in a council, and not in a single individual, protects the congregation from the dangers of a spiritual dictator. Council members serve as a healthy check and balance on each other. Indeed, as we look at the leadership God has given us, the diversity of gifts, talents, and personalities he has put in the same 'pool' is truly amazing.

3. *Esteem them highly.* Those who are called to the ministry of leadership bear a heavy responsibility. They need your prayers, your support, your counsel and conversation, your heartfelt co-operation. They are not in a position of leadership because they are perfect but simply because the call of God is on their life for this particular service. By God's grace, their service will bless and upbuild the congregation.

The Goal of Good Order

Order is not an end in itself, but a means for achieving a right balance between freedom and unity. When the church is well-ordered, individual members will experience freedom, yet the body as a whole will be able to live and act in unity. It is not something achieved at a single stroke. Bodies of believers grow into it as they allow themselves to be led by the Holy Spirit. If the Charismatic renewal has a contribution to make in this area, it will not be a successful formula for ordering congregational life, but a demonstrated willingness to hear and follow the leading of the Spirit. The *goal of the various ministries* in the church (Eph. 4:11) is expressed in the following way in Ephesians 4:12-16 (cp. also Eph. 4:3-4),

> […] to prepare God's people for *works of service*, so that the body of Christ may be *built up* until *we all reach unity* in the faith and in the knowledge of the Son of God and become *mature*, attaining to the whole measure of *fullness in Christ*. Then we will no longer be infants, tossed back and forth by the waves, and blown here and there by every wind of teaching and by the cunning and craftiness of men in their deceitful scheming. Instead, speaking the *truth in love*, we will *in all things grow up* into him who is the *Head, that is, Christ. From him* the whole body, joined and held together by every supporting ligament, grows and builds itself up in love, as *each part does its work.*

(55) The Church:
A Worshipping and Praying Community

During his life on earth, Jesus spoke of a time when true worshippers would worship the Father in spirit and truth (Jn 4:23). When the disciples on the day of Pentecost were filled with the Holy Spirit, the first thing they did was break forth into exalted praise and worship of God. The 3000 who came to faith that day entered into a community that centred its life in worship and prayer (Acts 2:42, 46-47). In equipping the church for mission, the Holy Spirit brings people into a new dimension of worship.

A pastor in a Lutheran congregation which had been deeply affected by the Charismatic renewal routinely asked people in his adult membership class, "Why do you want to be a member here?" The most common response was, "Because of the love that I have felt in the worship." When a study of the Charismatic renewal was made in the German Democratic Republic, one of its chief marks visibly was the central place given to praise and adoration in renewal gatherings. For many people, charismatic renewal has brought a *heightened sense of God's presence in worship*, and this has led to a greater degree of personal involvement. *Spectators at worship have been converted into participants.*

Even to outside observers, an accent on worship has been one of the most noticeable characteristics of the Charismatic renewal. News items on charismatic conferences typically carry a picture of a crowd of people with *hands upraised in worship*. This is an interesting phenomenon: even secular editors, who may see nothing more than an interesting departure from staid decorum, nevertheless recognise that worship is somehow central to this movement.

But it is of course more than a matter of upraised hands. That is just one of the ways in which the Holy Spirit may choose to help people respond to a sovereign God. Perhaps our response to God has been so controlled and intellectual that we need to do something like raise our hands to enhance the sense of abandonment. But we would miss the point if we became preoccupied simply with outward gestures. The Holy Spirit wants to lead us in exactly the opposite direction: away from reliance on our own efforts or forms of worship into a dependence on him to orchestrate our meeting with the Lord. At the heart of charismatic worship is a radical willingness to obey the Lord, which is as much a challenge to the Charismatic renewal as it is to the church at large.

David Preus, speaking as presiding bishop of the American Lutheran Church, once complained that in many of the Lutheran churches he visited, the worship was just plain dull. The same kind of complaint can be heard about some charismatic prayer groups, after they have been going for a while. To begin with, people often find charismatic worship a refreshing experience. Some of this can be due simply to novelty: new songs, new expressions, new style – a welcome break from liturgical routine. But if it does not get beyond mere novelty, the work of the Spirit is wasted. When the newness wears off, charismatics can find themselves back in essentially the same place that Bishop Preus described. The liturgical procedures have been shuffled around, but the same old problem is there again: dull worship.

Worship in spirit and truth is simply not a human possibility. Only the Holy Spirit can bring it about. It cannot be reduced to set forms, although it may find expression in a structured service. It cannot be equated with any particular mood or feeling or style. It is what happens when the Holy Spirit fills us, making our bodies his temple (1 Cor. 6:19), and prompts us to respond to God our Father, and Jesus our Lord and Saviour (Eph. 5:18-20). The Holy Spirit may lead us to express this in a variety of ways, but the worship never becomes our possession, in an absolute sense. It is God's work through us. The essence of charismatic worship is not found in particular forms, but in the awareness that every occasion of worship calls for a fresh dependence on the Holy Spirit.

Through the ministry of the Holy Spirit, the Lord himself is present in worship. Divine worship is a festival of his presence. It is a *foretaste of the new creation,* where eternal life centres around the worship of God (Rev. 7:11-15).

The Charismatic renewal has had two principal gathering points: the local prayer group or home fellowship who meet on a regular basis, and regional or national charismatic conferences that people attend once or twice a year. In these settings, the worship elements that have been most prominently emphasised in the renewal are praise, ministry of the Word, personal testimonies, and prayer.

Praise

One of the popular choruses of the Charismatic renewal has been from Psalm 92:1:

> It is a good thing to give thanks unto the Lord. It is a good thing to give thanks unto the Lord And to sing praises unto thy name, O Most High (KJV).

An upsurge of praise has been one of the marks of the renewal. Praise as an intellectual concept or a liturgical expression may have been familiar, but for many people, spontaneous and heartfelt expressions of praise have come as a new and refreshing experience. It is worth noting that one of the distinctive features of the Charismatic renewal, speaking in tongues, is chiefly a vehicle for praise (see Acts 2:4; 10:46; 1 Cor. 14:16).

Praise cannot be reduced to a formula, yet, as Lutheran pastor Paul Anderson has pointed out, Scripture portrays praise in more vigorous terms than we would normally use to describe a Sunday morning Lutheran church service:

> The Hebrew word *halal,* from which the word *hallelujah* comes, means 'to make a noise.' Praise enlists the vocal cords. We did not learn silent meditation from the Hebrews; they were an expressive bunch. The Hebrew word *zamar* [praise] includes the playing of musical instruments, and the verb for thanking includes the motion of holding out the hands. Clearly, praise is meant to engage the voice and body. Those who only worship God in silence miss the joy of exuberance. They would do well to read Psalm 47 and obey the commands: 'Clap your hands, all peoples! Shout to God with loud songs of joy! God has gone up with a shout, the Lord with the sound of a trumpet. Sing praises to God, sing praises! Sing praises to our King, sing praises.' Those whose devotional life includes only quiet meditation may have precious moments with the Lord, but the *hallelujah* is missing.[1]

Praise honours and gives glory to God for who he *is*. When the Holy Spirit reveals God to us, praise is the appropriate response. In essence, praise expresses our love to God. One of the things that continues to attract people to the Charismatic renewal is *a sincere and unashamed love and admiration for God that expresses itself in praise.*

Spontaneity and Tradition

The Charismatic renewal has sometimes tended to equate unstructured spontaneity with the Holy Spirit. Its most common form of worship has been the "prayer and praise service" with spirited singing, free prayer, exercise of spiritual gifts, personal testimonies, and biblical teaching – all of this with a bare minimum of structure. This has helped open up the worship experience to greater participation by the people, and it has produced a significant new body of worship songs. But it has also had the tendency to separate the renewal from the church's heritage of formal worship.

In some places, there has been a conscious effort to blend together charismatic worship and liturgical worship. This does not happen spontaneously. It requires thought, planning, and a sustained effort by both leaders and people to enter more deeply and fully into the reality of worship, but it has produced the renewal's finest contribution to the worship life of the

---

[1] Paul Anderson, "Finding the Balance in Worship," *Loaves and Fishes*, no. 183 (Trinity Lutheran Church, San Pedro, California: May/June, 1986), pp. 6-7.

church. Through the Holy Spirit, liturgical worship, which may have become lifeless, can be filled with joy, love, warmth, and a sense of God's presence.

This may require a decisive step by the leaders of a congregation to *open up the liturgical order and allow for charismatic expression* – free prayer, prophecy, tongues and interpretation, and testimony. Lutheran liturgies can be readily adapted to this kind of free expression without losing their traditional character. Early Christian liturgies made room for free expressions following the reading of Scripture and during the distribution of Holy Communion. In larger congregations, or in services that draw people from a wider circle than the local parish, new charismatic liturgies and worship styles may also be introduced.

Luther once expressed the desire for services that would be oriented toward ministering to people's personal needs, but said that he did not have the people for it.[2] Today, the people are there, in growing numbers: the Spirit is distributing the gifts by which we can minister to one another's needs. When we encounter the living God in worship, we often find that he himself turns our attention to some of the practical needs of those around us and opens up the service to a time of personal ministry.

Neither liturgical form nor non-liturgical expression will in itself produce vibrant worship. Liturgy is an outline for worship. It can help release the corporate and individual adoration of God in an orderly, yet free expression. But the Holy Spirit is the initiator and inspirer of true worship. When he directs our worship, questions of spontaneity and structure are caught up into the greater awareness that we are encountering the living God, and that he is in control.

Ministry of the Word and Sacraments

Wherever the Holy Spirit is welcomed and honoured, the proclaimed Word will be experienced. What God says, God does. We should expect the Word to be at work in many ways and at many levels during worship services.

Charismatic worship has also helped to intensify the sense of encounter that is inherent in the sacraments. In *baptism*, God initiates us into a covenant relationship with himself. Our sins are forgiven and we are born again and become children of God. We become part of the body of Christ and receive the Holy Spirit (Jn 3:3-5; Acts 2:42; 22:16; 1 Cor. 12:13; Eph. 5:26; Tit. 3:5; 1 Pet. 3:21).The experience of death and resurrection with Christ in baptism can become a reality not only for the person being baptised, but also for those remembering their own baptism during the liturgy (Rom. 6:1-4).

During general and individual *confession and absolution*, people can be forgiven and set free from bondages just as certainly as through a pointed ministry of deliverance (Jn 20:22-23; 1 Jn 1:9).

---

[2] Martin Luther, *Deutsche Messe*, 1526 (AE 53, 64; WA 19, 75).

Jesus Christ, *truly present in the Eucharist*, is the Lord who forgave sin, healed the sick, died and rose again and is seated at the right hand of the Father. When we celebrate his precious presence and receive his body and blood in bread and wine, we are proclaiming the reality of his death until he comes again; we appropriate the benefits of his death and we manifest our unity in him (1 Cor. 11:23-32; 10:16-17). Burdens of sin, sickness, and alienation are lifted at the Lord's table.

Through the *proclaimed Word*, both the judgements of the law and the promises of the gospel come into the midst of a worshipping people – not merely as ideas, but as realities (Is. 55:11; Eph. 5:17: Heb. 4:12-13). "The Spirit gives life; the flesh counts for nothing. The words I have spoken to you are Spirit and they are life" (Jn 6:63). The Charismatic renewal represents a reaction against preaching and teaching that contents itself simply to articulate Christian doctrine or interesting human thoughts. *The Word should be preached with authority in all its fullness, with a personal address and a challenge to the listeners to respond in repentance and faith.* The product of the proclaimed Word is not only a body of knowledge, but a demonstration of the Holy Spirit in changed lives and situations.

The most widespread ministry in the Charismatic renewal has been that of *teaching*, but it has been *life and action-oriented* teaching (2 Tim. 3:16). This partly explains the hostility that has sometimes been directed against the movement. The opposition that a renewal movement encounters stems more often from what is done than from what is taught.[3] When the Holy Spirit stands at the centre of the teaching, the "doing" is what God accomplishes. This is obvious when the Word is confirmed by miraculous signs and wonders. But it is equally true, although less obviously so, in manifestations of faith, love and holiness; it is his gracious doing, not ours.

Prayer

Is it really necessary to make a case for prayer? Of course, prayer belongs to the life of the church! But what is the actual shape of the church's prayer life? Here, we must consider not only the setting of people gathered for worship, but the whole life of God's people. Worship as event is part of a larger tapestry: worship is a way of life, and prayer is one of its principal expressions.

The Charismatic renewal came on the scene calling for a renewal of spiritual gifts in the ministry of the church. This occurred in a particular setting. *The principal locus of the renewal, particularly in its early stages,*

[3] Ern Baxter, a popular charismatic Bible teacher, made the observation that we are not hated for our ideas, but for putting our ideas into practice. Ern Baxter, "The Power of a Superior Passion", *New Wine Tape of the Month*, WT 104 (Mobile, AL: Integrity Communications, 1986).

the instrument through which it was spread, was the prayer group. Many people who had grown up in churches in which prayer found little expression outside of formal liturgies began to meet in homes and hotels and church basements to pray. People's involvement in the renewal could be fairly accurately gauged by their participation in a prayer group. *The emphasis on charismata occurred in the larger context of a renewed emphasis on prayer.* For those within the renewal, such charismatic distinctive qualities as being filled with the Holy Spirit and experiencing spiritual gifts had the character of a *personal response to the Word of God, kindled by prayer.*

Renewal movements always bring with them *an element of rebuke.* The Charismatic renewal is a rebuke to a church whose prayer life has drifted into formalism or disuse. How often do long hours of discussing and planning church business end with the half-guilty reminder that we should ask God's blessing on our efforts? Activities, discussions, seminars, papers – how efficient are they? Do they achieve God's purpose? Have we not abandoned the greatest privilege and the most revolutionary power available to us as Christians? The Holy Spirit does not flow through mere methods and institutions. He needs people who pray.

Through the ministry of the Holy Spirit, we experience *the power of God in our prayers*. Together with our prayers, offered in the name of Jesus, the exalted Lord and the Holy Spirit intercede for us according to God's will (Heb. 7:25; Rom. 8:26-27). Prayer in the power of the Holy Spirit is God's instrument for bringing his kingdom to reality among us (Zach. 12:10; Eph. 6:18; Jude 20; Rev. 5:8-10). We start the prayer that the Lord taught us by praying for the hallowing of God's name and the coming of his kingdom (Mt. 6:10).

The New Testament shows us that Jesus was much given to prayer (Mk 6:46; 14:23; 14:32-39; Mt. 14:23). *He is the model of a person who lived out of conversation with God.* Prayer was a central factor in key events of his life: his baptism and transfiguration (Lk. 3:21; 9:28-29), the choosing of the Twelve (Lk. 6:12-13), and being recognised as Christ (Lk. 9:18-20). Jesus withdrew himself from the crush of those seeking healing in order to pray (Mk 1:35; Lk. 5:16). Jesus frequently prayed in solitude, on a mountain-side, for instance (Mk 6:46; Mt. 14:23; Lk. 6:12). In each case, Jesus was a person bound to the Father through prayer. In the garden of Gethsemane, he showed by example the foundation on which all true prayer is built: subordinating one's own will to that of the heavenly Father.

Just as *Jesus is himself the pray-er pre-eminent*, so he is also the *master teacher* of prayer. The disciples asked Jesus for instruction in prayer (Lk. 11:1); they observed that his ministry and prayer were closely linked together. He directed those who pray to go to a secret place (Mt. 6:6). He also made a special promise to those who pray together (Mt. 18:19). He encouraged prayers of faith (Mk 11:24). He consistently affirmed that such prayers will always be heard (Mt. 7:7-11; Lk. 11:9-13). Above all, he gave to his disciples the name of God that is particularly appropriate to prayer: *Abba, Father.* Above all, he left his disciples a prayer that stands out uniquely in both content and form. It is learned, memorised, and prayed daily by millions of Christians all over the world, commonly called the *Lord's prayer* or *Our Father* (Mt. 6:9-13).

The Acts of the Apostles shows clearly that prayer held great significance for the early Christians (1:14; 2:42; 6:4; 9:11; 10:9; 12:5, 12; 13:3; 16:25; 20:36; 21:5). The working of the Holy Spirit is experienced through prayer and, conversely, always leads one back to prayer (Acts 2:1-4; 4:24-31). In the Epistles, as well, one sees that prayer was a decisive component of congregational life. The admonitions to unceasing prayer confirm this (Rom. 12:12; Col. 4:2; 1 Thess. 5:17; Eph. 6:18; Jude 20; 1 Pet. 4:7; Phil. 4:6). At meetings of early Christians, it is clear that everyone, men and women alike, had the opportunity to speak aloud in prayer (1 Cor. 11:4-16).

Prayer played an essential role in the expansion of the Christian church (Acts 4:29; 13:1-4; 2 Cor. 1:11; Col. 4:2-4; 2 Thess. 3:1). The apostle Paul made it clear how dependent he was on the prayers of the church and the Holy Spirit (Rom. 15:30-32; 2 Cor. 1:11; Phil. 1:19; 1 Thess. 5:25). On the other hand, the apostle prayed constantly for his churches (Eph. 1:16-23; Phil. 1:9-11; Col. 1:3, 9-13; 2 Thess. 1:11-12). Intercession extended beyond the bounds of the Christian community, with special concern for secular rulers (1 Tim. 2:2-4; Rom. 13:3).

Given all of the above, it is striking that nowhere is mention made of any prayer technique. Questions about prayer mostly concern *content*: why we should pray and what we should pray for. Most decisive is the fact that all prayer proceeds from faith. We cannot pray aright by virtue of any inherent power. The ability to pray must be given, just as the ability to believe. Thus, we remain, at all times, dependent on the Spirit of God in our seasons of prayer.

Jesus told his disciples that they could not do anything apart from him (Jn 15:5). This is a difficult word. Something in us must die if we are to say, "I can't do anything apart from Jesus." No, not even pray. Like the disciples, we need to come to the master Teacher, and say, "Lord, teach us to pray." Jesus responded to the disciples' request with the words of the Lord's Prayer (Mt. 6:9-13; Lk. 11:2-4). His High Priestly prayer underscores the theme of intimate communion with the Father: "Father, just as you are in me and I am in you. May they also be in us" (Jn 17:21). After Christ's ascension, the disciples joined together in prayer and waited for the coming of the Holy Spirit (Lk. 24:52-53; Acts 1:14). On the day of Pentecost, the Lord ushered them into a new dimension of fellowship with God. Immediately, this found expression in exalted prayer, and nowhere was their relationship with God more evident in the time that followed than in their prayers.

What Practical Steps Does God Set before Us?

When we want to apply in practice the rich message of prayer in the Bible without emphasising one particular prayer technique, we may emphasise the following attitudes and actions:

Humility. We should humble ourselves before God and confess our complacent contentment with lives so meagre in prayer. We enter into the riches of prayer first of all by recognising our poverty. The Norwegian Lutheran theologian Ole Hallesby who has written one of the world's most influential books on prayer[4] says that "To pray is to open your door to Jesus and admit him into your need".

Commitment. God's presence should become the centre of our lives; daily we should seek his face. In personal audience, we should ascribe glory to him, the holy and almighty God. This means a significant commitment of time. Luther's scribe and companion, Veit Dietrich, said of him, "No day passes that he does not give three hours to prayer, and those the fittest for study."[5] Luther wrote to his co-worker Philip Melanchthon:

> Whatever aspect matters may assume, we can achieve all through prayer. This alone is the almighty queen of human destiny. Therewith we can accomplish everything, and thus maintain what already exists, amend what is defective, patiently put up with what is inevitable, overcome what is evil, and preserve all that is good.[6]

For Luther, prayer was no mere matter of the intellect or of memorised sentences. It was the heart in conversation with God. We see what is before our eyes, but God looks on the heart. The more naturally and truly the heart opens up to God in prayer, the more certainly and freely the time of prayer will have its effect in one's daily life.

Prayer does not always have to be expressed in words, as Hallesby says,

> There come times when I have nothing more to tell God. If I were to continue to pray in words, I would have to repeat what I have already said. At such times it is wonderful to say to God, "May I be in your presence, Lord? I have nothing more to say to you, but I love to be in your presence."

Of course, regular study of the Bible will comprise a part of the prayer time. This is necessary for one to learn to distinguish between the voice of God and other voices, including one's own thoughts. The Holy Spirit stands by, the teacher who helps us recognise the thoughts and guidance of God and

---

[4] Ole Hallesby, *Prayer* (Minneapolis, MN: Augsburg Publishing House, 1994). First published in Norwegian with the title *Fra bønnens verden* in 1927.

[5] Martin E. Lehmann, *Luther and Prayer* (Milwaukee, WI: Northwestern, 1985), p. 133.

[6] Lehmann, *Luther and Prayer*, p. 143.

apply them to our lives. "Watch and pray so that you will not fall into temptation" (Mk 14:38; Lk. 4:5-7).

Praying together. Closely linked with prayer is the ministry of spiritual counsel and direction, which can take place in a natural way within the intimate and accepting atmosphere of a prayer group. This is an important step in the renewal of prayer.

Nothing so undermines fellowship as scheming and contention, and nothing so works against this as a fellowship of prayer in which together we come into the presence of God. Fellowship in prayer calls us out of isolation and loneliness. It calls us to listen to one another and bring one another's needs before God. It can foster a childlike trust that the Father will influence and change things now happening in one another's lives.

To begin with, prayer groups are often surprised by specific answers to prayer, even though Scripture is full of such promises. Fear and timidity about praying for one another ebbs away where people are bound together in the love of God. Simply and directly, they can lay their common concerns before God. The Holy Spirit is their Paraclete, their Counsellor before the throne. He directs their thoughts, helping them recognise the Lord's will in specific circumstances. When they pray *in the name of Jesus,* they know that their prayers are heard and will be answered according to God's will (see Mt. 18:19-20; Jn 14:13-14; 1 Jn 5:14-15).

Prayer for the sick with the laying on of hands and/or anointing with oil carries with it a particular promise of God (Mk 16:18; James 5:13-16).

Representative prayer. In worship services, the pastor or leader may bring the concerns of the entire congregation before God. The pastor should depend on the Holy Spirit's guidance in preparing this kind of prayer. This may come as members of the congregation bring word of particular needs in some area of their common life. The members stand behind the pastor in prayer. They silently identify with what is spoken, which is an indispensable part of the prayer. They understand that the pastor gives voice to their own prayers. While one voice speaks, many hearts are joined together in prayer.[7]

Special prayer burdens. The Holy Spirit may entrust some people with prayer responsibilities for particular needs of the time. Some members of the congregation may sense an urging to form a prayer fellowship that will meet

---

[7] Ole Skjerbæk Madsen (see Appendix) observed that the general prayer in the communion service of their congregation (Betlehemskirken, Copenhagen, Denmark) took on added vitality when specific intercessions for members of the congregation were incorporated. They usually have 20-25 such petitions, which have been brought to the attention of the pastors or the deacons the previous week. Answers to prayer are reported to the congregation. This is an example of a widely used liturgical form that is readily adaptable to free expression and that could also include charismatic gifts such as prophecy, speaking in tongues, word of knowledge, and discernment of spirits.

together regularly to seek the Lord's face, or a handful of people will receive a burden to intercede for the sick.

What a divine mystery, that God, who knows all things and has all power, nevertheless waits for our prayers! What changes have been wrought in community, church, and nation through persistent and prevailing prayer! The above actions are not meant to present a comprehensive program for prayer renewal, but are simply illustrative of the immense variety of practical steps that the Holy Spirit may prompt us to inaugurate.

Prayer and Power

The emphasis of the Charismatic renewal on power – on signs and wonders – is not born of human bravado but of the humbling recognition that in ourselves we have nothing to give to desperate people; we can only minister when Christ by his Holy Spirit ministers through us, as also the apostle Paul experienced:

> I will not venture to speak of anything except what Christ has accomplished through me in leading the Gentiles to obey God by what I have said and done – by the power of signs and miracles, through the power of the Spirit (Rom. 15:18-19).

We have come into a dead end and need to repent. In the Lord's Prayer, we are taught to begin prayer by recognising the holiness of God. In the Bible, God's holiness refers not only to his purity but also to his power to judge, deliver and save. Only the heavenly Father is holy. There is no holy father on earth. Martin Luther's hymn verse is the testimony of the Charismatic renewal: "Did we in our own strength confide, Our striving would be losing."

Through the Spirit, God makes the impossible possible, and for this we should pray with expectation. Out of many churches and denominations, God is summoning a company of praying people who fully expect him to bring renewal through the Holy Spirit.

The Priority of Prayer

In a renewed church, prayer has an essential priority: prayers of thanksgiving, praise, and worship; urgent intercession; assured claiming of divine promises; and ever-fresh prayers of repentance. Prayer rests on the simple conviction that all good things in the church are worked by God. Again: "Apart from me you can do nothing" (Jn 15:5). At its heart, prayer is a confession of faith, an agreement with the Word and will of the mighty triune God, Father, Son, and Holy Spirit. Let us quote Hallesby again, "Prayer is the breath of the soul, the organ by which we receive Christ into our parched and withered hearts", and, "Helplessness united with faith produces prayer, for without faith there can be no prayer".

When we say that the Holy Spirit makes us a worshipping people, it is another way of saying that he leads us into the experience of God. Worship is the experience of God. In worship, the Holy Spirit causes us to experience the presence of God in praise, the grace of God in Word and sacrament, and the power of God through prayer. For people who experience this kind of reality, worship becomes a way of life.

Jesus said, "Where two or three come together in my name, there am I with them" (Mt. 18:20). Paul said that together we are the temple of the Holy Spirit (1 Cor. 3:16). In a distinctive – perhaps we could say in an intensified – way, the Lord is present when Christians come together for common worship and celebration of the Lord's Supper. In the gathered community of believers, we should expect to experience the manifest presence of God. As the church learns to pray and praise in the Holy Spirit's power, it will experience an increasing measure of new life and vitality. God seeks a praying church.

Prayer Groups and Personal Ministry

Spiritual renewal of congregations often begins in small prayer and Bible study groups. Here, people experience the presence of Jesus in an intense way, learn to live from the Word of God, and experience the Holy Spirit and his gifts. Retreats, conferences, and visits to renewal centres serve a similar function: they help people respond to the reality of God in a new way.

Spiritual counselling also plays a leading role in renewal. Here, people experience, some for the first time, the reality of repentance, forgiveness, and absolution. Frequently, this is the setting for a ministry of deliverance from bondages, through prayer and blessing, command, and the word of power. Prayer in tongues can be a special help in the ministry of counselling. As a counsellor exercises this gift, usually in silent petition, the Lord will often give a vision or revelation that pinpoints a need in the person's life.

In the Pietistic renewal, Christians were urged to come together to study the Scriptures, pray for each other, sing, and give testimonies. In these informal settings, ministry was dependent on lay people who led in exposition of Scripture, in testimony, and in prayer ministry. Home fellowships, prayer meetings, and cell groups are also commonplace in the Charismatic renewal. This is the setting in which lay leadership and ministry are most often identified and developed. The experience in small groups becomes a foundation for the Holy Spirit to work in the entire congregation, so that the healing power of the gospel streams forth from a healing fellowship. Small groups that meet under the leading of the Holy Spirit are often dynamic and unconventional. Their form will vary and change. One thing, however, remains constant: worship and adoration occupy the foreground.

Although the Charismatic renewal has emphasised the need for anointed leadership in worship, it recognises at the same time that it is the Holy Spirit, not the pastor or worship leader, who gives life to the worship. It is the Spirit who makes us aware of Jesus and causes us to experience his presence.

The Holy Spirit longs to work through a many-membered body. Paul said that the agenda of worship should allow for anyone to bring a hymn, a word of instruction, a revelation, a tongue, or an interpretation (I Cor. 14:26). Where we do not restrict the Holy Spirit, he will inspire gifts and ministries in the whole body of believers. Our worship will rise to the Father as a symphony, manifesting the presence of Jesus and releasing his abundant blessing (Mt. 18:19).

(56) The Church: A Missional Community

The Church as Sent and as Sender

The church is sent by Jesus to the world. "As the Father has sent me, I am sending you. And with that he breathed on then and said, 'Receive the Holy Spirit'" (Jn 20:21). This sending (Greek: *apostole*; Latin: *missio*) of the Son by the Father and the sending of the church and the Holy Spirit by Jesus is called the *mission of God* (Latin: *missio Dei*). It means that a basic characteristic of the church is that it is "sent" by God. This is the meaning of the word "missional" when it is used about the church. The extension of the church's life and ministry outward toward the world is often called the church's *missionary work* because the church is the subject, the "sender". But this sending by the church is derived from and dependent on the very *nature* of the church itself as sent, as missional. The Spirit-renewed church *does missionary work*, because it is *missional in its very being and nature.* These two aspects of mission: the church itself as sent by God (missional) and the church as sender to the world (missionary) are very important in contemporary missiology.

What Is Mission?

There have been many attempts at defining mission. The famous missiologist David Bosch refuses to formulate one definition, but in what he calls an "interim definition", he mentions altogether 13 different points![1] In a new Norwegian textbook on missiology, Tormod Engelsviken has proposed the following definition, fully aware that much more could be included:

> *Christian mission is God's sending of the church to the world.* This sending has its origin in the Triune God, Father, Son and Holy Spirit. It implies the commission to proclaim the gospel of the kingdom of God in word and deed with the intention that all people everywhere come to faith in Jesus Christ as God and Saviour, be baptised into the Christian church, live together as Jesus' disciples in the world and receive salvation in the kingdom of God both here on earth and eternally in the new creation.
>
> Mission crosses borders because it aims at reaching people who have not yet heard or received the gospel in faith. These borders may be geographical, cultural, religious and generational.

---

[1] See David Bosch, *Transforming Mission. Paradigm Shifts in Theology of Mission* (Maryknoll, NY: Orbis, 1991), pp. 8-11.

> Diakonia (social service) towards both individual people and society is part of the comprehensive and holistic nature of mission. It is a testimony to the love and care of Jesus Christ even if it does not have conversion as its intention.[2]

We notice in this definition that salvation in the kingdom of God is the overarching goal of mission, and that mission has a Trinitarian basis, where the Father is the source, the Holy Spirit the motivator and the power, and faith in Christ the intended outcome.

Mission is also always on the *move across different kinds of borders*. The borders may be geographical ("in Jerusalem, and in all Judea and Samaria, and to the ends of the earth", Acts 1:8), cultural or national ("go make disciples of all nations", Mt. 28:19), religious ("Therefore since we are God's offspring, we should not think that the divine being is like gold or silver or stone – an image made by man's design and skill. In the past, God overlooked such ignorance, but now he commands all people everywhere to repent", Acts 17:29-30), and generational ("The promise is for you and your children and for all who are far off", Acts 2:39).

The primary target of mission is *people who have not yet heard the gospel*. Paul wrote, "It has always been my ambition to preach the gospel where Christ was not known" (Rom. 15:20). But also *those who may have heard but not yet come to faith in Christ* should be reached with the gospel anew. This applies for instance to the Jewish people, as Paul writes, "My heart's desire and prayer to God for the Israelites is that they may be saved" (Rom. 10:1), and to people in nations that have been evangelised earlier but where many have not responded to the gospel or have fallen away from faith, as is the case for instance in Europe and America, but also elsewhere in the world.

The proclamation of the gospel takes place in *words*, orally, and also in *deed*, in practice, "by the power of sign and wonders, through the power of the Spirit" (Rom. 15:19). Just as in the mission of Jesus, proclamation and miracles go together, where miracles confirm the message of grace (Acts 14:3; Jn 20:30-31), so also the church in its mission should proclaim the gospel with the prayer and expectation that it may be accompanied by supernatural evidence (Acts 4:29-30). The "deeds", however, should also include "non-miraculous" (although Spirit-empowered!) ministry to people in need, so-called *diakonia*. This ministry may not have conversion to Christ as its intended aim but simply aim at alleviating human suffering. Yet, when done in the name of Jesus, it is a testimony to his love for the suffering and the lost and to the Holy Spirit's power to give to Christians the same love (Rom. 5:5; Gal. 5:22; 1 Jn 4:19-21). Even where diakonia does not have a missionary *intention*, it still has a missionary *dimension*.

---

[2] Tormod Engelsviken, "Misjonsteologi og misjonal teologi", i: Jeppe Bach Nikolajsen et al (eds.), *Missiologi. En innføring* (Oslo: Cappelen-Damm, 2022). Translated and slightly edited by Tormod Engelsviken.

Mission should be understood as being *comprehensive and holistic* with a primary focus on people's reconciliation with God. But it should also include God's concern for healing of the body, for alleviating human poverty and suffering, for establishing reconciled and healthy social relationships, for just societies and for the preservation of God's wonderful creation.

The Holy Spirit Empowers a Witnessing Church

All the missionary commands of Jesus to the disciples (the church) after his resurrection contain an *explicit reference to the Holy Spirit*, either with emphasis on repentance and forgiveness of sins (Jn 20:21-23: Lk. 24:47), or on discipling, baptism and teaching (Mt. 28:19) or on power for witness (Lk. 24:48-49; Acts 1:8). In addition, the ending of Mark refers to the signs that will follow the believers which include gifts of the Holy Spirit such as expulsion of evil spirits, speaking in tongues, and healing (Mk 16:15-16).

It is therefore no accidental coincidence that the Son (and the Father) sends the Holy Spirit *and* establishes the church *at the same time*, and through the same momentous salvation-historical event: *the experience of the reception of the Holy Spirit by the disciples on the day of Pentecost* (Acts 2:1-4).

Jesus declared the *power* and *extent* of the church's missionary task when he told his disciples, "You will receive power when the Holy Spirit comes on you; and you will be my witnesses in Jerusalem, and in all Judea and Samaria, and to the ends of the earth" (Acts 1:8). This is the primary purpose of the church and the privilege and obligation of every believer (Acts 8:4; 1 Pet. 2:9). It is the purpose for which the Spirit's *power* is given. And the missionary task *extends* to all nations and persons in the whole world (Mt. 28:19, 1 Tim. 2:4), to the "ends of the earth" – geographically – and to "the end of the age" – temporally (Mt. 28:20).

Despite these clear words about the necessity of the Holy Spirit for mission, there has in the past been a widespread neglect of the Holy Spirit's power in many parts of the church. This has hampered Christian witness. In practice, church leaders have often failed to recognise that lay people filled with the Holy Spirit are the primary witnesses to spread the gospel, and have therefore often depended on human methods and strategies. Some churches have become very programme- and activity-centred. Yet only as we receive the power of the Spirit can we be effective witnesses and useful instruments for him.

The Holy Spirit does not make us witnesses automatically. We may have clear teaching about the Holy Spirit in our theology. We may have come to faith in Christ through the working of the Holy Spirit. Yet the Lord says that we need to be empowered by the Holy Spirit if we are to become his witnesses.

The early church consisted of a small group of people who not only believed in Christ for their own salvation, but who also received the charismatic anointing of the Holy Spirit to become powerful witnesses. A fundamental perception of the Charismatic movement, which it holds in common with earlier renewal movements, considers that the Spirit can repeat everything he has done in the past, and that nothing less is adequate to the church's evangelistic task.

In general, the Lutheran church has been more interested in being evangelical than being evangelising. Orthodox theology has not necessarily led to active evangelism; this emphasis has come through various revival movements. We need to ask ourselves why it is that, in some Lutheran churches, it is common for people to become Christians without at the same time becoming active witnesses or engaged in mission.

The Holy Spirit is urging on the church the realisation that Jesus' statement, "You will be my witnesses," was an all-inclusive designation. In Christ's body, every member is important and needed. Not every Christian may be called to be an evangelist, yet all Christians are called to be witnesses. A witness in court is called to tell what they have seen or heard. The Holy Spirit is opening the ears of many to heed the call to become witnesses to what they have seen and heard, and to ask for the empowering of the Spirit to do exactly that.

Evangelism may take place spontaneously or in a planned way. Charismatics have laid special stress on spontaneous witnessing. Even without an organised evangelism programme in the church, growth may come as people are filled with the Spirit and become witnesses at home, work, and school in spontaneous ways. Many opportunities to be a witness arise in the normal course of everyday life when there is no opportunity for a planned approach or response. The Holy Spirit works changes in our lives that become like walking sermons to other people. They evoke curiosity and interest, and often the question, "What is it that you've got?"

Evangelism can also involve thorough training, in which people receive knowledge, tools, and help from other people. Evangelicals have led this kind of evangelism. In some places, charismatics have taken the lead in utilising evangelistic programmes. Wherever and however evangelism takes place, the power of the Spirit is indispensable.

A charismatic approach to evangelism has certain emphases that may differ in basis and method from some traditional approaches to evangelism. One charismatic Lutheran pastor pinpointed *hearing from God* as the first key to what he termed "radical evangelism." The second key was *obeying God.*[3] Evangelism in charismatic circles tends toward more conscious dependence on the Holy Spirit, greater emphasis on participation of all

[3] Jim Roberson, "Radical Evangelism! What Is It?" *International Lutheran Renewal*, 85, (Dec. 1986), p. 1.

members, emphasis both on proclamation and on miraculous signs following, and witness both by individuals and through the life of a body of believers.[4]

A primary fruit of congregational renewal, through the working of the Holy Spirit, is that new witnesses are produced. They are able to share with others what they themselves have experienced – the Lord who saves them, grants them new birth, equips them with his Spirit, and opens to them the secret of his joy. The missionary power of the Holy Spirit works through individual witnesses.

Yet, the Holy Spirit also works through Spirit-filled congregations in assembly. A pastor of a fast-growing Lutheran church in Phoenix, Arizona, USA, said that their primary tool for evangelism was Sunday morning worship. There is no more convincing evidence of the reality of God than a truly Spirit-filled assembly of believers. In such assemblies, God is a flaming reality and a living presence. And he enkindles in his people a love and service that reaches out to those in need – those in sickness, sorrow, bondage, and despair.

Without the Spirit, witness and mission can become a legalistic duty. In the first years of the Charismatic renewal, priority was given to personal spiritual renewal. By the mid-1980s, however, the theme of world evangelisation had clearly gained the high ground. The strongest witness of the Charismatic renewal, the standard by which history will judge it, will be its contribution to the spread of the gospel into all the world.

Mission and the Jewish People

It is significant that the Christian church that was established on the Day of Pentecost, after the outpouring of the Holy Spirit, was mainly a *Jewish church.* The coming of the Spirit happened on the *Jewish* Feast of Weeks (Nu 28:26) and was the fulfillment of the prophetic promises to Israel in Ez. 36:25-27: "I will sprinkle clean water on you and you will be clean; I will cleanse you from all your impurities and all your idols. I will give you a new heart and put a new spirit in you; I will remove from you your heart of stone and give you a heart of flesh. And I will put my Spirit in you and move you to follow my decrees and be careful to keep my laws. You will live in the land I gave your forefathers; you will be my people, and will be your God",

[4] A very useful book on evangelism in the power of the Holy Spirit is John Wimber and Kevin Springer, *Power Evangelism, Revised and Updated Edition* (Grand Rapids, MI: Baker, 2009). An important Pentecostal and charismatic perspective on mission is Younghoon Lee and Wonsuk Ma (eds), *Pentecostal Mission and Global Christianity* (Oxford: Regnum, 2018) that contains important articles by a number of authors, most of them from the Global South. See also Wells, *God the Evangelist,* reflecting a Lausanne-consultation on mission and the Holy Spirit held in 1985.

see also Ez. 11:19 and Jer. 32:19. These promises were important to several Jews during the Feast of Weeks.

When Gentiles were included in the church due to Christian mission, and the majority of its members after some years were Gentiles, this did not mean that the Gentile church replaced the Jewish people as God's covenant people. Israel was still God's people. Paul describes the privileges of the Jews in Rom. 9:3-5, among them the divine glory, the law, the temple worship and the promises. And last but not least: the patriarchs belong to the Jews, and "from them is traced the human ancestry of Christ".

God has not rejected Israel (Rom. 11:2). There is a remnant chosen by grace (Rom. 11:5), for "God's gifts (Greek: charismata!) and his call are irrevocable" (Rom. 11,29). The Gentile Christians are drafted into the olive tree, which is Israel, and share in the nourishing sap from the olive root together with its natural branches, the Jewish believers (Rom. 11:16-18).

Although the majority of Jews have not yet accepted Jesus as their Messiah, it may not be accidental that the growth of Jesus-believing "Messianic Jews" in Israel and elsewhere over the last fifty years has taken place at the same time as the Charismatic renewal has emerged. Although many Messianic Jews have been critical of the historical churches, one of the surprising ways of the Spirit is the establishment of cooperation between Messianic Jews and Catholic charismatic congregations.

Witness to the people of Israel should always be a priority in the mission of the Christian church of Jesus-believing Jews and Gentiles. The gospel is "the power of God for the salvation of everyone who believes; *first for the Jew, then for the Gentile*" (Rom 1:16).

The Missionary Challenge before the Church Today

Experts estimate that the world's population at the time of Jesus was around 170 million people. Today a population explosion has swelled the earth's population to more than 7.8 billion people. Jesus spoke of discipling the nations. The Holy Spirit can direct missionaries into more than 200 nations and many more people groups. Today, an unprecedented number of people have not yet been evangelised, although the percentage of Christians of the world population has remained constant at about 30% (a little less than one-third) over the last 100 years. The relative reduction both of the general population and number of Christians in Europe, North America and Oceania compared to Asia, Africa and South America has been more than compensated for by the enormous growth of the church in the latter part of world where the majority of the world's population lives. Christian churches today list a combined membership of more than 2.5 billion. Yet more than one-fourth of the earth's population have still not heard that a man called

Jesus lived on earth, died on a cross, rose from the dead, and sent forth disciples with the message of salvation.[5]

The magnitude of the missionary task facing us staggers our imagination, to say nothing of our faith. Yet, compared to the task facing only 12 apostles 2000 years ago, mission today by no means is "mission impossible". Reaching all the nations and people on earth can be done, and the church should never give up that vision.

Christians are a minority in the world today. Yet, this has always been the situation, and there have never in history been more Christians than today, both in terms of actual numbers and in terms of percentage of the world's population. Only 33% of all Christians live in Europe and North America today, where the number of nominal, non-practising Christians is also high. 67% of all Christians – the majority – live in the majority world in Africa, Asia and Latin-America where the proportion of nominal Christians is much lower than in the West and therefore the proportion of active, believing, witnessing Christians much higher. This augurs well for the future growth of the church in majority world.

The Holy Spirit is calling *all* believing Christians to do battle in the face of *mounting opposition and persecution.* More Christians live under governments hostile to the Christian faith than live in free societies that permit them to work and worship unhindered.[6] More Christians have been martyred since 1900 than in the first three centuries of the Christian era. Islam is the next largest religion in the world today and is growing. Ancient religions, such as Hinduism and Buddhism, which in the past have lost members to Christianity, have adopted aggressive methods to keep and regain members. Anti-Christian secular ideologies dominate in China and in the West challenging the church and its mission in new ways. Systems of unbelief – Communism, secular humanism, scientific materialism, hedonism, naturalism, and rationalism – have led millions to deny the truth of Christianity, or in any case to live as practising atheists. A frightful array of addictions holds millions in physical, emotional, and spiritual bondage. Lack of political freedom, economic injustice, abject poverty, starvation, oppression of minorities, discrimination, violation of human rights, wars, diseases, pandemics, and the destruction of the environment continue to hunt and hurt a large proportion of the world's population. The Holy Spirit is sending us into a world of unprecedented needs and challenges.

---

[5] The best statistics are found in Gina A. Zurlo and Todd M. Johnson (eds), *World Christian Encyclopedia*, 3rd edition (Edinburgh: Edinburgh University Press, 2019).

[6] An excellent source of information on mission, religious freedom, and persecution in today's world is Hans Aage Gravaas, Christof Sauer, Tormod Engelsviken, Maqsood Kamil and Knud Jørgensen (eds), *Freedom of Belief and Christian Mission* (Oxford: Regnum, 2015).

Direction and Power for Mission: the Holy Spirit

God's mission for the church requires the guidance of the Holy Spirit at every stage. The Scripture asks, "Who has understood the Spirit of the Lord, or instructed him as his counsellor?" (Is. 40:13), and the answer is that no one gives counsel to the Spirit of God. He is the Counsellor. If we do not give the Holy Spirit priority in our planning and in our activities, we cannot possibly achieve the real purposes of God. The word of God is always the same, "'Not by might nor by power, but by my Spirit,' says the Lord Almighty" (Zech. 4:6). Mission history knows failures. But it has also succeeded when it has followed the lead of the Spirit and been faithful to the Lord's guidance. Without the power and gifts of the Holy Spirit, God's church is helpless to reach the nations (Lk. 24:49). Jesus' great post-resurrection commissions present the task of a world-embracing mission but the motivation, guidance, and power for the task did not come until the day of Pentecost.

The Acts of the Apostles shows how God called and guided the church in its mission. He called and sent the missionaries by revelation (Acts 9:3-5; 26:14-19) and through words from the Spirit (Acts 10:19-20; 13:1-4). The Spirit guided them by both preventing them from going some places (Acts 16:7) and by telling them through angels and visions to go to other places (Acts 8:26; 16:9-10). Paul, for example, would also follow a planned mission strategy that took him to the most important cities and centres, to the Jewish synagogues first and then to the Gentiles (Acts 9:20; 13:5; 17:18), but he also used every opportunity for unplanned witness and proclamation under various circumstances (Acts 16:13, 31).

In the mission of the church today, and particularly in the Pentecostal and Charismatic movements, there are many examples of missionaries being supernaturally called to mission and later guided in their work by the Holy Spirit, even to new and unknown peoples and places. We should pray for this kind of divine guidance in all mission work while at the same time not neglecting the obligation to use our knowledge and reason to strategise and make priorities in mission as best as we can. The one does not exclude the other.

Especially in one area, the Pentecostal and Charismatic movement has contributed significantly to our understanding and practice of mission, and that is the area of the supernatural, including the role played by such phenomena as healing, exorcism, power encounters, dreams, visions, etc.

Observations of this aspect of mission work played a large part in initiating the experimental course entitled "Signs, Wonders, and Church Growth" at Fuller Seminary in Pasadena, California, in the early 1980s, according to the in-depth report of *Christian Life* magazine. We quote from its interesting report:

> The seminary catalogue described the course as focusing 'on understanding the effects of supernatural signs and wonders on the growth of the church. It is

approached from biblical, theological, historical and contemporary perspectives. Special attention is given to the ministry of healing. Field experience is an important dimension of the course.'

Early Christians shared their faith in Jesus Christ with the confidence that God also would confirm their witness 'by signs, wonders and various miracles and by gifts of the Holy Spirit' (Heb. 2:4). After a long period of decline, a renewal of these signs and wonders is appearing in both Protestant and Catholic church circles.

For the most part, this emergence of spiritual life has stemmed from the grass-roots, not from ecclesiastical or theological sources. Groups of believers – sometimes led by a single courageous pastor, sometimes not – have provided the launching pad from which the Holy Spirit has moved. The renaissance first began in the 20th century. But not until the early 1950s did it surface in the historic Protestant denominations; in the early 1960s in the Roman Catholic Church.

Now, for the first time, it is being given serious consideration by theologians and scholars. According to Peter Wagner [one of the professors who team-taught the experimental course at Fuller], it came out of the reaction of Third World students to the various courses on church growth developed by Fuller's famous professor, Dr Donald A. McGavran, recognised worldwide as the dean of the theory of church growth. These Third World students said, 'We appreciate the great help Fuller's courses have been to us. But something else is happening in our countries that Western theologians and missiologists are ignoring. The result is enormous church growth of a first century type.' McGavran, who has repeatedly visited Asia and Africa, reported it true: in many cases native evangelists prayed for the sick, they were healed and an astonishing number of conversions resulted.

Other professors contributed similar reports of signs and wonders resulting in massive church growth in other parts of the Third World they had visited. Later, when the faculty of the School of World Mission huddled to consider the phenomena, they came up with the recommendation that an experimental course on the subject of signs, wonders and church growth be offered.

For Dean Gilliland, professor of Contextualization of Theology at Fuller Seminary, the experimental course came as no surprise. 'What we saw as a faculty, in the beginning,' Gilliland said, 'was that we should offer this as a course because we ought to be open to the Holy Spirit. If there is something that the Spirit should be teaching the churches today, we here at the School of World Mission don't want to resist.'[7]

---

[7] *Christian Life*, 44(6), (October 1982), pp. 10, 18, 64. Tormod Engelsviken, as a visiting scholar at Fuller Seminary at the time, participated in one of these courses and can confirm the positive impact it had on a large number of students. The course was, however, discontinued after some time due to a controversy at Fuller Seminary, primarily with regard to its practical dimension and its academic status.

This linking together in world mission of proclamation of the Gospel and supernatural signs challenges the Charismatic renewal as much as it does the institutional churches. While the renewal has had an emphasis on spiritual gifts, a strong emphasis on world mission was largely absent during the first two decades of the movement. Its energies were taken up with establishing an experiential and theological base for charismatic phenomena in a deeply secularised Western culture. Now there is a fresh initiative of the Spirit to bring these two things together by letting the gospel spread according to the New Testament pattern, by proclamation, service, and "the power of signs and miracles, through the power of the Spirit" (Rom. 15:19).

Mission in the power of the Holy Spirit is not only a biblical promise, nor merely a theoretical theological thesis; *it is documented empirically through a study of recent mission history.* Who could in their wildest imagination have foreseen that this revival, which by God's grace was set in motion by an Afro-American evangelist in Azusa Street in Los Angeles in 1906, the sermon of an Episcopalian priest in 1960 and the experience of a group of Catholic academics in 1967, would grow to the largest renewal and mission movement in the history of the church? From almost nothing in 1900, the Pentecostal/Charismatic Movement has grown to ca. 635 million in 2020.[8] 86% of it is found in the Global South. Never in history – whether in world history or church history – has a religious movement grown so fast and so persistently, both inside the church and in the world at large, as the Pentecostal/Charismatic movement over the last 120 years. It continues to grow. "I will make you a light for the Gentiles, that you may bring my salvation to the ends of the earth" (Is. 49:6). It is happening in our time! What a great God we have!

[8] Documentation: *World Christian Encyclopedia,* 2019.

Excursus 4: Characteristics of the Spirit-filled Missional Church?[1]

The Missional Church – Its Nature and Task

The concept of "missional church" which has come to prominence in missiology since the 1990s has challenged the Western understanding and practice of mission, yet it is not less relevant for the mission of the church in the majority world in the South.[2] In this excursus, we shall, firstly, look at missional ecclesiology and its biblical basis, and then, secondly, present an empirical study of the characteristic traits of some missional churches in Malaysia in South-East Asia – all with a view to *the role of the Holy Spirit in the church and mission.*

The difference between the terms missionary and missional when used about the church, is – as we have seen already – that "missionary" often indicates an *activity* that is carried out by the church – something that the church *does* – primarily the sending out of missionaries, while the term "missional" indicates the *essence* or *nature* of the church – what the church *is – that it itself is sent by Christ.* The church does missionary work and sends out missionaries to the world (Latin: *missiones ecclesiae*) because it is itself sent by God to the world (Latin: *missio Dei*).

It is God, not the church, who is the real initiator and subject of mission. It was the Son of God, Jesus Christ, who himself was sent by the Father, who sent – and still sends – the Holy Spirit and the church (Jn 20:21-22; Lk. 24:48-49). This means that *each Christian, each local church and the whole universal church* are sent to the world with the message of salvation. The church does not *become* missional by sending out missionaries but it sends out missionaries because it *is* missional.

The purpose of mission is to proclaim *the kingdom of God*, to bring salvation with all its dimensions and gifts to the world by expanding the kingdom and making disciples. It has been said that the church is the only

---

[1] This excursus is written by Tormod Engelsviken and is based on his chapter "Missional Church: Theory and Practice, and a Malaysian Case Study", in Gillian Mary Bediako, Benhardt Y. Quarshie, and J. Kwabena Asamoah-Gyadu (eds), *Seeing New Facets of the Diamond. Christianity as a Universal Faith. Essays in Honour of Kwame Bediako* (Oxford: Regnum Africa, 2014), pp. 144-161.

[2] The concept has become well-known through several publications of the network "The Gospel and Our Culture" in USA, for example Darrell Guder (ed), *Missional Church – A Vision for the Sending of the Church in North America* (Grand Rapids, MI: Eerdmans, 1998) and Darrell Guder, *Called to Witness: Doing Missional Theology* (Grand Rapids, MI: Eerdmans, 2015).

organisation that exists for those who do not belong to it, namely the world, but this is a truth that needs some modifications. Since the church is the people of the kingdom of God and these people must grow if the kingdom is to grow, one of the main purposes of mission is the *growth of the church*. The church is therefore both an *instrument* and a *goal* of mission. The call to discipleship and the call to mission belong intrinsically together, as Jesus' call of his first disciples shows us, "Come, follow me, and I will make you fishers of men" (Mt. 4:19, cp. also Acts 9:15; 26:16). Those who *receive* the gospel by the Holy Spirit are also supposed to *spread* the message to others, as the Christians in Thessalonica did:

> You *welcomed the message* with the *joy given by the Holy Spirit* and so you became a model to all the believers in Macedonia and Achaia. The Lord's *message rang out from you* not only to Macedonia and Achaia – your faith in God has become known everywhere (1 Thess. 1:6-8).

It is simply not possible to be a disciple of Jesus and filled with the Spirit without being engaged in spreading the gospel to non-believers. In this sense, we may speak of the "mission of all believers" as part of the "priesthood of all believers". We are all as "a chosen people, a royal priesthood, a holy nation, a people belonging to God" called to "declare the praises" (or "the wonderful deeds", RSV) of Christ (1 Pet. 2:9).

The *necessity of mission* in God's plan of salvation is laid out by Paul with convincing sequential logic: *Sending* (mission) leads to *preaching* which leads to *hearing* which leads to *believing* which leads to *calling on the name of the Lord* which leads to *salvation.* This necessary sequence can also be turned the other way around: *the intended end result – salvation – presupposes and requires the beginning – sending, mission* (Rom. 10:13-15).

The Holy Spirit Creates Motivation for Mission

This doctrine of the necessity of mission is accepted in theory by most evangelical Christians today, but it is a long stretch from holding to the idea of mission to actually getting involved in the *practice* of mission. We may ask: what *motivates and enables* Christians to move from theory to practice, from doctrine to a lifelong personal commitment to sharing the gospel with others and doing mission to the ends of the earth in order to make disciples of all nations?

Christians have historically had *many different motives* for mission, some pure and some impure. The Dutch missiologist Johannes Verkuyl enumerates the following *pure motives*: obedience to the Great Commission, love, mercy and pity for the suffering world, the honour of God, salvation of the lost, the motive of haste or urgency, and the personal motive of a calling, all of which have been important in the history of mission and can also be found in the Bible.[3]

There are obviously also combinations of these motives. For example, the missionary *par excellence,* the apostle Paul, speaks about his *obedience* to the heavenly *vision and call* (Acts 26:19-20), of being under the *obligation* to preach the gospel to Jews and pagans (Rom. 1:14-15). He is compelled both by the positive *fear of God* (2 Cor. 5:11) and by the *love of Christ* because Christ died for all (2 Cor. 5:14), a love that has been poured into his and other Christians' hearts by the Holy Spirit (Rom. 5:5; Gal. 5:22).

But how are these biblical motives experienced and internalised in such a way that they become a strong, binding and lasting *personal motivation for missionary action in the individual believers and in the church*? The main biblical answer to this question is that this happens *through the work of the Holy Spirit*. The Great Commission was given by the risen Christ prior to the day of Pentecost, but it was not until the Spirit was poured out on the disciples on that day that their mission work began and the church began to grow. The reason was that although the redemptive work of Christ was already finished, the disciples had to wait for the power of the Holy Spirit before they could start their mission work as witnesses:

> Repentance and forgiveness of sins will be preached in his name to all nations, beginning at Jerusalem. You are witnesses of these things, I am going to send you what my Father has promised; but stay in the city until you have been clothed with power from on high (Lk. 24:47-49; Acts 1:8).

How did the Spirit give power and create motivation for mission in the believers in the early church, and how does he do it today? The answer is manifold but crucial: He does it by inspiring the believers to lead lives as disciples of Jesus, to follow him on a daily basis, to listen to his words and obey them, to observe his works (Mt. 4:19). He does it by convicting the believers of their sins and showing them God's love and grace displayed in Christ's vicarious atoning death for sins and victorious resurrection as Lord (Jn 16:8-11; 2 Cor. 5:14; Acts 2:36). He does it in response to expectant and persistent prayer (Acts 1:14; 4:31). He does it through the disciples' experience of receiving the fullness of the Spirit and his gifts (Acts 2:1-4; 4:33), with power and boldness as witnesses (Acts 4:13, 31), giving them a deep personal conviction (1 Thess. 1:5), fellowship with other disciples in the common task (Acts 2:44) and both fear and love of God (2 Cor. 5:11, 14).

Mission motivation becomes a *holy compulsion*, as Paul expresses his own missionary obligation in the strongest possible words:

---

[3] Johannes Verkuyl, *Contemporary Missiology: An Introduction* (Grand Rapids, MI: Eerdmans, 1978), pp. 163-175.

> When I preach the gospel, I cannot boast, for I am *compelled* to preach. *Woe to me* if I do not preach the gospel. If I preach voluntarily, I have a reward, if not voluntarily, I am simply discharging the trust committed to me (1 Cor. 9:16-17).

Missionaries in the History of the Church

This missionary obligation, even compulsion, can be *empirically or experientially* documented in churches, renewal movements and individuals throughout church history. A study of the *common characteristics* of well-known missionaries in history from a variety of Christian traditions has resulted in the following general conclusions.[4]

The missionaries have had a strong spiritual conviction, a consciousness of having been called and sent by God, and courage and perseverance that have all carried them through opposition, persecution, disease, death of family members, and many other difficult circumstances. Some have made the ultimate sacrifice and voluntarily laid down their lives for Christ.

Interestingly, most of these missionaries have also most often belonged to movements of renewal and revival within the churches. They have wanted to represent "genuine Christianity", sometimes over against indifferent or "nominal" Christianity. They have not been satisfied with the church as it is, but have worked for renewal and change, expansion and growth.

Not all Christians have the gift and calling to become cross-cultural missionaries, but all Christians are called to be witnesses and can learn from the lives and ministries of the missionaries. The missionaries have been a great inspiration for many Christians to be witnesses in their own context and to support the missionary outreach of their churches or mission organisations through concrete prayer and sacrificial giving.

Characteristics of Some Missional Churches Today

It has been a sad fact that the missionary zeal that has been found in revival and renewal movements *within the church* has not as a rule penetrated or set its mark on *the whole church.* Is it possible that whole congregations and churches can become "missional", not only in theory but in actual practice? In order to find out, I turned my eyes away from the large state and folk churches in Europe and America, towards the younger churches in the majority world in the Global South.

Many church leaders in the West expected the growth of these churches to decrease when the period of colonialism was over in the 1960s, and most

---

[4] See Tormod Engelsviken, "Who has taken care of the missionary task of the church through the ages?" *Swedish Missiological Themes*, 91(4), (2003), pp. 481-504.

colonies became independent nations. Many churches also became independent of foreign churches and missions, either because the missionaries were forced out, as in China and India, or the missionaries left voluntarily. However, these expectations proved wrong. After political independence from the colonial powers in the West, there has been an unprecedented growth of the churches in the majority world so that the point of gravity of Christianity has moved from the Global North to the Global South. The face of Christianity as a world religion has changed dramatically.[5] Would it be possible, in light of this change, to find independent churches in the South where mission in the power of the Holy Spirit penetrated the whole church?

I chose to carry out an *empirical study* of eight churches/congregations in Malaysia in South-East Asia. The churches were of different denominational backgrounds: Anglican, Lutheran, Methodist, Free Evangelical, Brethren, Pentecostal and Independent. They numbered from 100 to 2000 members each. I chose them because they were active in mission and evangelism and (with one exception) had a charismatic emphasis. The study was carried out during a period of some weeks in Autumn 2002.[6]

These churches are not necessarily typical of all churches in Malaysia, but I think they ideally represent growing, missional, charismatic churches in Malaysia, and also in the Global South generally. I will not here describe the general situation of the Christian church in Malaysia or its history,[7] except for one important fact: the church in Malaysia lives and serves in a country dominated by a Muslim majority represented by the ethnic Malay people. This implies severe restrictions on the church as to its visibility in society and its possibility to evangelise publicly. It is illegal to convert ethnic Muslim Malays to Christianity. The majority of Malaysian Christians have either a Chinese or Indian background, or belong to the indigenous population, who live mostly in Malaysian Borneo.[8] This was also typical of the local churches that I studied.

---

[5] This change is amply documented, see for example the 3rd edition of the *World Christian Encyclopedia* (2020), Philip Jenkins, *The Next Christendom: The Coming of Global Christianity* (Oxford: Oxford University Press, 2002), and Sebastian Kim and Kirsteen Kim, *Christianity as a World Religion* (London: Continuum, 2008).

[6] As an empirical study, it was a qualitative one, where I used qualitative in-depth interviews with leaders and church members, participatory observation at worship services and group meetings, and read whatever I could find of material about the churches.

[7] To the history of the church in Malaysia, see Robert Hunt, Lee Kam Hing and John Roxburgh (eds), *Christianity in Malaysia: A Denominational History* (Petaling Jaya: Pelanduk Publications, 1992).

[8] About 28% of Malaysia's population of 33 million are of Chinese descent and 9% are of Indian descent. Christians represent about 10% of the total population.

Some of the questions that I asked were: What is it that motivates people and churches for mission? In what ways are theology, spirituality, church structures and practical church work influenced or determined by the missional perspective? What are the marks of the church that demonstrate its missional nature? How do the churches relate to the social, cultural and religious context in Malaysia? I had been inspired by the work of the Malaysian Methodist professor and bishop Hwa Yung in my search for a contextual, yet biblically and theologically sound Asian theology of mission.[9]

The result of my research may be summarised briefly in nine characteristic marks that all these churches had in common to a larger or lesser degree:[10]

1. Although the churches represented different historical traditions from Anglican to Pentecostal, they all shared a *basic common theology* that may be called *evangelical*. By that I mean a theological conviction that emphasises the authority of the Bible as the Word of God, the eternal lostness of human beings without Christ, Jesus Christ as the only Saviour and Lord through his substitutionary atoning death on the cross and his bodily resurrection, justification by faith alone and the necessity of conversion and personal faith for salvation. This evangelical theology was integrated with spirituality and missionary practice in such a way that it was not only a theoretical or dogmatic position, but became fundamental and operational in the missional practice of the churches and their members.
2. The *Bible* was not only seen as the authoritative word of God, but was also commonly *used and studied* in the church services, in smaller groups and in private devotion. It became a source and inspiration for spirituality, mission and service. In light of the fact that many members were first generation Christians, their familiarity with the content of the Bible was amazing. The believers felt obliged by the words of the Bible, both in terms of faith and lifestyle.
3. Jesus was seen as the *only Saviour*.
   a. Not one of my interviewees was in doubt that *Jesus was the only Saviour* from an eternity without God, although the human predicament could be described with different contextual terms, as for example the absence of certainty of salvation (former Muslims), or as bad karma as a result of evil deeds (former Hindus). Many also mentioned liberation from the power and fear of evil powers. Jesus as the one who conquers and frees people from evil spirits was to some as important as Jesus who forgives sins, although he does both.

---

[9] See Hwa Yung, *Mangoes or Bananas? The Quest for an Authentic Asian Christian Theology* (Oxford: Regnum, 1997).

[10] More characteristics could undoubtedly have been found if I had asked more and better questions. This is therefore not an exhaustive list.

   b. We shall quote one of Hwa Yung's conclusions: "If Asian theology is to be truly contextual, it must first be able to empower the church in its evangelistic task of bringing people to repentance and faith in Christ [...] Secondly, it must be able to facilitate the pastoral ministry of the church including church planting and growth, and the nurture and teaching of disciples to maturity in faith. Thirdly, a contextual theology will be such that it will be able to do the above tasks in a manner which *takes Asian cultures and worldviews seriously.* This would necessarily involve the practice of *"power encounters" in the healing and exorcism ministries*, and serious attention given to inculturation. Finally, as a logical concomitant of the above, it must be able *to* empower the Asian church in apostolic cross-cultural missions to other people" (italics added).[11] The churches that I studied did fulfil the requirements suggested by Hwa Yung to a large degree.

4. The emphasis on Jesus Christ did not eclipse an emphasis on the *Holy Spirit and his work.* Seven of the eight churches I studied may be characterised as Pentecostal or charismatic, and most of them had experienced a charismatic renewal in the 1970s or 1980s that led to growth in the congregation and to missionary outreach. The charismatic impulse had first and foremost led to a renewal of individual believers through a personal experience of the Holy Spirit. Simultaneously, whole congregations had also been influenced by the renewal of their members and leaders. Church services and other church gatherings gave room for the exercise of the gifts of the Spirit, and, typically, a formal Anglican liturgy might be followed by a time for personal ministry and healing through the use of the gifts of the Spirit and intercession. Characteristic of the services was also the large place given to worship and praise.
5. It may be a bold assertion to say that *mission permeated everything* that the majority of these churches did, but it seems to hold true that mission was not only one of many good causes, but the main one. Especially impressive was the Anglican church in Tawau in Malaysian Borneo with its pastor (later bishop) Albert Von. The church was named "A Prayer House for All Nations", and its main sanctuary was decorated with the flags of all the nations of the world. When I visited the church, I was met by its mission statement: "Christ's last commission is our first commandment". This church did mission work in its own town of Tawau, among the neighbouring indigenous population along the rivers of Borneo and in other countries in South-East Asia, without making a sharp division between home and foreign mission. In the churches that I studied, mission preaching, mission information, mission giving, and

[11] Hwa Yung, *Mangoes or Bananas*? pp. 75-76.

care and prayer for missionaries seemed to belong to their everyday life, and not only to special mission events. Although most cross-cultural missionaries sent out from these churches worked in neighbouring countries in South-East Asia such as Myanmar, Thailand and Cambodia, there were also missionaries sent to the pagans of Europe and North-America!

6. There were great variations in the churches as far as *leadership structures* were concerned. Although most had a rather hierarchical structure, either formally as in the Anglican church with its episcopal system or informally as in the Brethren and Pentecostal churches, my impression was that great emphasis was placed on giving all or as many as possible a ministry in the church, from bishops, priests and elders to parking guides and elevator assistants! The exercise of gifts of the Spirit, *charisms*, such as speaking in tongues, prophecy, healing, and ministry to those afflicted with evil spirits, took mostly place in smaller cell groups led by lay people, but also in some cases in special ministry sessions in the larger worship services. *Prayer and praise* with concrete prayer asking for God's intervention in difficult or challenging circumstances as well as intercession for people in need were common, as well as praying for the power and guidance of the Holy Spirit. Preaching was biblical, powerful and direct, encouraging people to conversion, mission and holy living.
7. Although these churches were remarkably well and thoroughly organised from top to bottom (reflecting Chinese culture?), I learned from the interviews with ordinary church members that most of them were also engaged in *unorganised, informal, personal witness* that did not happen under the auspices of the church. The churches did not have the freedom to have a high public profile but had to depend for their growth on their members' natural contacts with people in everyday life – family members, colleagues, fellow students in schools and universities, and so on. These people were most often religious people coming from Muslim, Buddhist, Hindu or traditional religious backgrounds. Few were atheists or secularists. People's interest in Christianity was often aroused through informal contact with Christians who shared their faith, not by conspicuous church buildings, public advertising, presence in the mass media, or through cultural and religious traditions. This spread of Christianity by witness to the gospel in word and life by ordinary Christians characterises the periods in history when the church has grown most rapidly and when movements of renewal, revival and mission have given individual Christians the love, power and courage to share their faith with others.
8. Somewhat surprisingly, I found that the communication of the Christian message in words and the emphasis on mission were coupled with a *strong social concern*. This was surprising to me since the

churches had no opportunity to run large medical and educational institutions, yet they ministered to the poor, the sick, the drug addicts, the prisoners, the elderly and the lonely in very creative ways. Especially impressive was the ministry to the often marginalised original population, the *orang asli.* This should not have been surprising to me because historically most of the social service of the church, the *diakonia*, grew out of the same renewals and revivals as mission did. It also corresponds with the practice of the New Testament church and the ancient church. Significant amounts of money were given to the church, and *tithing* was frequent. Some of the Christians, especially among the ethnic Chinese, were quite well off financially, and the churches were able to fund their ministries and missions in such a way that the churches in Malaysia in general were independent of foreign assistance. They were instead contributors to international mission. This may be due both to sacrificial giving by their members and sacrificial living by their low-salaried staffs and ministers.

9. The churches in Malaysia cannot depend on a general knowledge of Christianity in the society or religious education in the schools. On the contrary, the public image of Christianity is in general negative and being a confessing Christian may be a social liability for many. Christian education was therefore the sole responsibility of Christian families and the churches. This responsibility was taken very seriously as the churches offered Christian education and training on all levels from kindergarten to theological seminaries. One church even had its own library with Christian books available for its members. I had the privilege of teaching an extension course in missiology at one of the Malaysian theological seminaries. Most of the students were people in various secular professions seeking knowledge and qualifications for ministry in the churches. It is likely that the important task of transmitting the Christian faith to the next generation will be met in a more effective way in a Malaysian cultural context where family loyalty is stronger than in the West. This was done through Christian education on all levels, regular church attendance, and private devotions in the families with Bible reading, prayer and song.

I do not want to paint an idealised picture of these churches because they also had their flaws and weaknesses which will not be discussed here. There were probably also problems and challenges in the churches that I was not told about and therefore was not aware of.

In general, however, it is my deep conviction that these charismatic churches were doctrinally healthy, imbued with spiritual life, and actively missional. The study of these churches did not provide any revolutionary new insights, nor did it come up with a simple recipe for spiritual renewal or church growth.

It nevertheless confirmed what we have seen in the church in the New Testament about healthy local churches; that they were strongly committed fellowships, proclaimed the gospel in word and deed, experienced the power of the Holy Spirit, and grew in numbers and strength. It showed that it is in fact possible even in today's world to foster missional spirituality, motivation, and ministry through preaching and testimonies, prayer and intercession, social service and personal care, sacrificial giving and living, and the ministries of the gifts of the Holy Spirit. What I learned from these Malaysian churches has relevance for churches worldwide as an expression of the positive results of Charismatic renewal.

(57) The Church: A Servant Community

Service as a Gift Motivated by Divine Love

Jesus came into the world to serve (Mk 10:45). Following their Master, all believers are called to serve. Christians serve each other; they also serve those who are not believers.

Serving may not come naturally to human beings, yet it underlies all Christian life and activity. This is a profound truth, but one easily corrupted by legalistic posturing. A recital of human needs, calculated to induce a guilt reaction, does not produce a servant church. Serving is a gift of the Holy Spirit (Rom. 12:7; 1 Cor. 12:5). Jesus' serving, motivated by his love, is incarnated in those who live near him in his church, responsive to his Lordship, built up by his forgiveness, by his Word, and by his body and blood. Serving comes by the working of the Spirit, not humanistic imperatives.

Serving is a gift as truly as are prophecy, speaking in tongues, healings, and revelations. The more spectacular gifts are not higher nor more valuable than the humbler gifts of helping and serving. Both are gifts, which mean that they are not produced by human talent or in response to legalistic demands, but are the result of the Holy Spirit's gracious visitation and empowering.

> Each one should use whatever gift he has received *to serve others*, faithfully administering God's grace in its various forms. If anyone speaks, he should do it as one speaking the very words of God. *If anyone serves, he should do it with the strength God provides,* so that in all things God may be praised through Jesus Christ (1 Pet. 4:10-11).

Serving flows from the love that has been poured out in our hearts by the Holy Spirit (Rom. 5:5) and is a fruit of the Spirit (Gal. 5:22). "Love does no harm to its neighbour" (Rom. 13:10, cp. Gal. 5:13-14).). Professor Hallesby wrote in a commentary on 1 Corinthians 13:13:

> Love wants to be there for others [...] [Human beings] believe by instinct that the meaning of life is to live for oneself, for one's own happiness, enjoyment, advantage and comfort. It is only by a miracle, the miracle of new birth, that it dawns on us that the meaning of life is to live for others.[1]

---

[1] Ole Hallesby, *Daglig fornyelse* (Oslo: Luther forlag, 1979), p. 54. This devotional book, "Daily Renewal", was first published in 1932 and has been reprinted 10 times.

The commandment to love one's neighbour as oneself is fulfilled by actively serving others. Jesus illustrates this with the Parable of the Good Samaritan who served a stranger in need (Lk. 10:27-37).

A charismatic Lutheran pastor in Sweden reported the following:

> We have seen more or less dead Christians and congregations come alive in serving as an answer to their prayers for the Holy Spirit. Rich people say: 'My money isn't mine. It is God's. I am only a steward.' They are happy to give to the poor people, to evangelistic and missionary work. They not only share their money, but their homes and tables too.
>
> But not only rich Christians share – also people in ordinary circumstances. The Holy Spirit lays other people's needs on their hearts. They help each other in practical ways, taking care of each other when anyone is sick, looking after each other's children, comforting each other when someone is in sorrow, and so on. Some have given of their time to known and unknown prisoners, alcoholics, and drug addicts.
>
> Eyes have been opened to see others. Feet have become willing to go to others. Hands have been lifted to serve others. Why do people do this? Why do they bother about each other in this unselfish way? The answer is: the Holy Spirit has worked it in them. He has given them new hearts. He has given them the gift of serving – not as something they must do to qualify as 'good Christians', but as the living presence and power of Christ in their hearts.[2]

Jesus, the Servant

Jesus is the very picture of a servant. He characterised himself as such: "But I am among you as one who serves" (Lk. 22:27). The word that he used for "serve" (Greek: *diakonein*) has the primary meaning of a person who serves at the table (Mk 1:13, 31; 15:41), but it can be used about *any form of service*. At issue is a life given to meet the needs of others.

Everything Jesus said and did demonstrated his attitude of service. His life in its totality was service. Paul expressed this comprehensively in his hymn about Christ in Philippians:

> *Your attitude should be the same as that of Christ Jesus*: Who, being in very nature God, did not consider equality something to be grasped, but made himself nothing, *taking the very nature of a servant*, being made in human likeness. And being found in appearance as a man, he humbled himself and became obedient to death – even death on a cross! (Phil. 2:5-8).

The cross was the final and ultimate expression of service, as Jesus himself described it: "The Son of man did not come to be served, but *to serve, and to give his life as a ransom for many*" (Mk 10:45).

---

[2] This example is provided by Per-Olaf Söderpalm (see Appendix).

Through *word and example*, Jesus set before his followers the *model of service*. He declared service to be the basis for interpersonal relationships, especially within the church (Mk 10:43-44). Servants do not make their way in the fellowship by means of power and force of law, but rather by serving the needs of others (Lk. 22:24-26).

A powerful demonstration by Jesus of his servanthood was his washing of the disciples' feet the last night he was with them (Jn 13:1-17). *As disciples of Jesus, we need to be served by him, and then to serve one another*. Jesus said to his disciples after he had washed their feet:

> Unless I wash you, you have no part with me [...] Now that I, your Lord and Teacher, have washed your feet, you also should wash one another's feet. I have set you an *example* that *you should do as I have done for you* (John 13:8, 14-15).

This attitude of servanthood was continually emphasised in early Christian teaching (Rom. 15:25-27; Gal. 5:13; Eph. 6:7-9; Heb. 6:10; 1 Pet. 4:10-11).

The Servant Church

The church early recognised that service lies at the heart of Christian life and mission. This came to practical expression in the wide-ranging use of the noun *deacon* (Greek: *diakonos* = one who serves) or the verb *serve as a designation for every form of ministry*, from apostle to those who wait on tables (see Acts 6:1-4). Paul understood and taught that spiritual gifts, which are given to every believer (1 Cor. 12:7), are instruments of service (1 Cor. 12:5). This is a theological insight of far-reaching significance. It describes *the basic attitude that motivates the use of all spiritual gifts.*

The servant mentality runs contrary to human nature. When the flesh reasserts control, the desire to have power and dominate others crops up in every area of the church's life – in the relationships between individual believers, in groups of Christians, within the local church, and beyond. Pastors try to lord it over their congregations, congregations over pastors, older people over younger, younger over older, men over women, women over men. Sometimes, spiritual gifts are misused as instruments of domination. Especially dangerous have been attempts by the church to exercise power in the world and over society, instead of serving.

In all ages and everywhere, the Holy Spirit works to conform us to the image of Jesus Christ, the servant. Through baptism and faith, we have a share in Christ's life and his serving love. The more we become servants, the more God is able to entrust to our care.

The needs facing us are beyond counting, and the willing servants so few. Where does the servant church begin? How can the church determine its servant role? It cannot serve everyone everywhere at once; it must be selective. The Spirit-led church looks to the Holy Spirit for guidance. The question then is this: where and how does the Holy Spirit want us to serve? Through thoughtful deliberation, using human knowledge and reason, and all the spiritual gifts, including gifts of revelation, the church may be guided and confirmed in its choice of place and method of service.

The gifts of the Spirit are valuable spiritual tools both in discerning the Lord's will for the servant church and in carrying it out. Spirit-led service is not simply a human or humanitarian ministry. It is a divine work, accomplished through human instruments in spiritual power.

(58) The Church: A Suffering yet Victorious People

Suffering has not been a prominent theme in the Charismatic renewal. Serious critics within the movement cite this as one of the renewal's major weaknesses. Teaching on spiritual power and faith has not been balanced with a biblical perspective on suffering. This is remarkable, inasmuch as some of the greatest sufferings and persecutions of Christians in our day have afflicted those who share a charismatic spirituality and perspective – in Communist countries such as the Soviet Union, China, and North Korea, in many Muslim countries, in India, Nigeria and several other countries.[1] It seems that the courage to confess and share the Christian faith through active evangelism and mission to non-believers in a special way challenges both secular and religious authorities and non-Christian opponents and makes Pentecostals and Charismatics especially prone to persecution. Their plight, however, did not begin to receive major attention in the Charismatic renewal until the 1970s. In the beginning, the formative influences of the movement came more from the United States and Western Europe, where suffering was not as strongly felt as in many other places.

Suffering is not something alien to the life of Christians. It is one of the ways in which we share the life and death of Christ.

> I want to know Christ and the power of his resurrection and the fellowship of sharing in his sufferings, becoming like him in his death, and so, somehow, to attain to the resurrection of the dead (Phil. 3:10-11).

This is not a call to human heroism but to humble dependence on the Spirit, who enables us to walk in the suffering that belongs to our calling.

Suffering needs to be distinguished from punishment. God does occasionally discipline and punish his people for their good, and those who are punished suffer pain (Heb. 12:5-11). This is not identical, however, with the suffering that we encounter because of our witness for Christ. Punishment and suffering can produce similar results: purifying of motives, cleansing of attitudes, strengthening of character, and change in behaviour. They serve, however, somewhat different purposes. Punishment comes because of

---

[1] For more detailed information on the status of freedom of religion and the persecution of the church, see Gravaas (ed), *Freedom of Belief and Christian Mission*. See also the regular reports of *Open Doors* and *World Watch List* on the Internet.

disobedience, has to do with the crucifixion of the flesh and leads to righteousness and peace (Heb. 12:11).

Suffering for Christ's sake is not linked to disobedience, but to being his witnesses, and to living the Christian life. "Everyone who wants to live a godly life in Christ Jesus will be persecuted" (2 Tim. 3:12). Christians may be publicly exposed to insult and persecution or stand in solidarity with those who are treated unjustly or are imprisoned. They may accept loss of property, because they know that they have "better and lasting possessions" (Heb. 10:32-34).

Paradoxically, suffering is twin to *hope*. As happened in the life of Paul, the believer's hope emerges in the midst of suffering – hope both for this life and for the age to come.

> We rejoice in *the hope of the glory of God.* Not only so. But we also *rejoice in our sufferings*, because we know that suffering produces *perseverance*; perseverance *character*; and character, *hope*. And hope does not disappoint us, because God has poured out his love into our hearts by the Holy Spirit, whom he has given us (Rom. 5:2-5, 17; cp. Phil. 3:10-11).

Suffering helps prepare us to *share in the reign of Christ*. Paul endured his suffering "even to the point of being chained like a criminal" for the sake of the elect and their salvation, in accordance with the trustworthy saying, "If we died with him, we will also live with him: if we endure, we will also reign with him" (2 Tim. 2:8-12).

Jesus, the Suffering Servant

The Gospels provide us with a picture of Jesus as one who suffers. Jesus knew beforehand that he was going to suffer and die. His words to his disciples that "the Son of Man must suffer many things [...] and he must be killed and after three days rise again" (Mk 8:31), could serve as a superscript over his whole life.

This saying is in accord with the prophecies about the "Servant of the Lord" in Isaiah 52:13-53:12. The "servant" is described as "despised and rejected by men, a man of sorrows, and familiar with suffering" (Is. 53:3), but by his suffering "he took up our infirmities and carried our sorrows" (v. 4). Jesus as the Suffering Servant suffered and died vicariously for our sins, "he was pierced for our transgressions, he was crushed for out iniquities; the punishment that brought us peace was on him, and by his wounds we are healed" (vv. 5, 8).

This is the great and wonderful mystery of the gospel, a mystery that no human being has thought out: the suffering and death of the Servant of God, who is also the Son of God, was necessary for the fulfilment of God's eternal plan of salvation. The servant would by being punished by God, bear the sins of the world, justify many and thus be "satisfied":

> It was the Lord's will to crush him and cause him to suffer, and though the Lord makes his life a guilt offering, he will see offspring and prolong his days, and the will of the Lord will prosper in his hand. After the suffering of his soul, he will see the light of life and be satisfied; by his knowledge my righteous servant will justify many, and he will bear their iniquities (Is. 53:10-11).

Serving, suffering and saving are indissolubly connected in the ministry of Jesus. He is serving us by giving his life in death as a ransom for sin (Mk 10:45).

The Suffering Church

Jesus prepared his disciples for the path of suffering. He actually called those who suffer and are persecuted "blessed", and promised them the kingdom of God:

> *Blessed* are those who are *persecuted because of righteousness*, for theirs is the *kingdom of heaven.* Blessed are you when people insult you, persecute you and falsely say all kinds of evil against you because of me. Rejoice and be glad, because great is your *reward in heaven*, for in the same way they persecuted the prophets who were before you (Mt. 5:10-12).

This was especially true of those whom Jesus sent out as his messengers. The German New Testament scholar Joachim Jeremias wrote, "Suffering for the sake of Christ is inseparable from service as his messenger. All primary sources are in agreement that Jesus emphasised this continually."[2] Jesus sent his messengers out as sheep among wolves (Mt. 10:16; Lk. 10:3).

The *Acts of the Apostles* portrays the path of the first Christians as a path of suffering. It describes the injunctions against their preaching (4:17-18), their physical punishment (5:40; 16:23), the imprisonment of the apostles (4:3; 5:18; 16:23-24), and the martyrdom of believers (7:57-60; 12:2).

The *apostle Paul* was arrested several times and spent long periods of time in jail as a prisoner (21:33-36; 22:24; 24:27; 27:1). Some of his letters were written from prison (Phil. 1:12-14; Col. 4:10). His letters reflect the role that suffering and persecution had in his ministry. In addition to what we have already noted above, he said that he suffered for the benefit of the church, for which he had become a servant by the commission of God (Col. 1:24-25, cp. Eph. 3:13). Paul's suffering showed that he was only a "jar of clay" that held the treasure of the gospel to show that "the all-surpassing power is from God

---

[2] Joachim Jeremias, *Neutestamentliche Theologie: Part 1: Die Verkündigung Jesu* (Gütersloh: Gütersloher Velagshaus Gerd Mohn, 1973), p. 229.

and not from us." In a series of contrasting words that shows Paul's ability to persevere through the life of Christ in him, Paul spells out the significance of his suffering:

> We are hard pressed on every side, but not crushed; perplexed, but not in despair; *persecuted, but not abandoned*; struck down, but not destroyed. We always *carry around in our body the death of Jesus,* so that *the life of Jesus may also be revealed in our body* (2 Cor. 3:5-10).

In a similar vein, Paul writes movingly in graphic detail to the Corinthian church about his own sufferings as a servant of God, and how he and other Christians are to respond:

> As servants of God we recommend ourselves in every way; in great endurance; in troubles, hardships and distresses; in beatings, imprisonments and riots; in hard work, sleepless nights and hunger; in purity, understanding, patience and kindness; *in the Holy Spirit and in sincere love; in truthful speech and in the power of God; with weapons of righteousness in the right hand and in the left;* through glory and dishonour, bad report and good report; genuine, yet regarded as impostors; dying, and yet we live on; beaten, but not yet killed; sorrowful, yet always rejoicing; poor, yet making many rich; having nothing, and yet possessing everything (2 Cor. 6:4-10).

Although Christians may be persecuted and suffer, *they experience the love of Christ and win the ultimate victory through him*:

> Who shall separate us from the love of Christ? Shall trouble or hardship or persecution or famine or nakedness or danger or sword? As it is written, 'For your sake we face death all day long; we are considered as sheep to be slaughtered.' No, in all these things *we are more than conquerors through him who loved us* (Rom. 8:35-37).

These examples from Paul's writings express a "theology of the cross". What seems like defeat is in reality victory; our way to glory goes through suffering, just as Jesus' way to the resurrection and the ascension went through the cross.

No book in the New Testament depicts the persecution of Christians more vividly and dramatically and with such strong symbolic images as the book of *Revelation*, preparing the Christians for the hard times to come (Rev. 13:5-10, cp. Mk 13:11-12). Yet no other book also describes more clearly and beautifully the final triumph and victory of God and his people than the same book, with its description of the new heaven and earth and the eternal resurrection life (Rev. 20-22). It gives the suffering church strength to endure hardship with a certain hope of future victory and salvation.

> Now have come the salvation and the power and the kingdom of our God, and the authority of his Christ. For the accuser of our brothers, who accuses them before our God day and night, has been hurled down. They overcame him by the blood of the Lamb and by the word of their testimony; they did not love their lives so much as to shrink from death. Therefore rejoice you heavens and you who dwell in them! (Rev. 12:10-12).

Persecution of Christians in the History of the Church and Today

Persecution has been a constant part of the history of the church. Well-known are the terrible persecutions under some of the emperors of the Roman Empire during the first three hundred years, when Christians were martyred by being burned at the stake, crucified, or thrown to the lions as entertainment for the people.[3]

The persecutions have taken different forms; from persecutions of individuals who have converted to Christianity against the will of their families and communities, to genocide of whole Christian populations, as for example the persecution of the Armenian Christians by the Turkish Ottoman Empire in 1915-1916 that cost more than one million Christians their lives.[4] We cannot trace this long and sad history in detail, but only point out that the 20th and early 21st centuries have seen more Christians persecuted than all previous centuries combined. In 2014, 43% of the countries and 76% of the population in the world experienced high or very high restrictions on religious freedom.[5]

According to the *World Watch List,* which is a tool for tracking and measuring the extent of persecutions of Christians in the world today, the most important "*persecution engines*" driving persecution are Islamic extremism, dictatorial paranoia, organised corruption, religious nationalism, tribal antagonism, Communist oppression, denominational protectionism, and secular intolerance. The Christians who are most exposed to persecution are *converts* who have left a former religious and ideological background to become Christians, and those who are called *"missionary-active Christians"*

---

[3] For documentation, see James S. Stamoolis, "Mission, Persecution and Martyrdom in the Early Church", in Gravaas (ed), *Freedom of Belief & Christian Mission*, pp. 67-78. The book also contains significant case studies, for example from China, India, Central Asia, the Middle East, Ethiopia, and the Soviet Union/Russia.
[4] Documented in Raymond Kevorkian, *The Armenian Genocide: A Complete History* (London: I.B. Tauris, 2011).
[5] Brian Grim, "Global Challenges and Opportunities in Religious Liberty", in Gravaas, *Freedom of Belief & Christian Mission*, p. 31.

who are active in the public domain by evangelism, or by social or political activities as Christians.[6]

Pentecostals and Charismatics will often be in both of those groups and be among those who most often suffer persecution. Three examples may suffice:

At the conclusion of an all-Africa charismatic leaders' conference in 1983, participants from one of the countries said their farewells with tears: "We may not see you again in this life," their spokesman said. "Some of our brethren have already been imprisoned. We do not know what will happen to us in the days ahead. Pray for us. Our trust is in the Lord."

At a conference in Kenya of Christian leaders from Muslim countries in the fall of 1993, the Pentecostal bishop and general secretary of the *Assemblies of God Churches* in Iran, Hajk Hovsepian Mehr, told the participants that he expected to be killed by the authorities when he went back to Iran. That came true. He was assassinated in Teheran on 20th January 1994, by unknown killers. The day before his abduction and killing, he had written a letter saying, "I am ready to die for the cause of the Church, so that others may be able to worship their God peacefully and without so much fear". The highly respected church leader is one of many martyrs of our time.[7]

Ethiopia may be a special case worth mentioning since the persecutions there had different "driving engines". When a strong Pentecostal/Charismatic revival broke out among young people in the 1960s and eventually led to the establishment of a rapidly growing, independent Pentecostal Church, called *Mulu Wongel* ("Full Gospel"), the Ethiopian police in association with the leadership of the *Ethiopian Orthodox Church* initiated a brutal persecution that led to the imprisonment of hundreds of young Pentecostals in the fall of 1972. The Pentecostals tried in vain to appeal to the Christian Ethiopian Emperor, Haile Selassie I. The persecution was interrupted by the revolution in Ethiopia in 1974 when the communists came into power. The situation went from bad to worse, since the ideology of the new authorities was opposed to all religion. The emperor was killed in 1974, the Patriarch of the *Ethiopian Orthodox Church*, Abuna Tewoflos, was brutally executed in 1979, and the general secretary of the Lutheran *Ethiopian Evangelical Church Mekane Yesus*, Gudina Tumsa, who was the most outstanding leader among the Evangelical Christians, was abducted and killed in June 1979. Many others, especially among the *Mulu Wongel* members, were persecuted

---

[6] Frans Veerman, "Religious Persecution and Violence in the 21st Century: A Global Survey Based on the World Watch List", in Gravaas (ed), *Freedom of Belief & Christian Mission*, pp. 127-148.

[7] Tormod Engelsviken met Hajk Hovsepian Mehr in Kenya in 1993 and heard his words. Details of his martyrdom can also be found on the website of *Abdorrahman Boroumand Center for Human Rights in Iran*, 2021. *Christian Solidarity Worldwide* and other organisations have also documented the widespread persecution of Christians in Iran.

and imprisoned during the communist regime of terror in Ethiopia 1974–1991.[8]

The cases mentioned here are but a few examples of the widespread and serious persecution of Christians that has taken place in the 20th century by religious and ideological regimes and individuals opposed to Christianity.

Christian Response to Persecution

The *first response* to persecution should be *continued bold testimony*. The apostles were not intimidated but went on preaching the gospel in spite of opposition and persecution. *They placed their obedience to God higher than their obedience to human authorities*. Peter and John replied when they were commanded not to speak and teach at all in the name of Jesus:

> Judge for yourselves whether it is right in God's sight to obey you rather than God. For we cannot help speaking about what we have seen and heard (Acts 4:18-20).

This basic principle for Christians is expressed succinctly by Peter and the other apostles in a similar situation: "We must obey God rather than men" (Acts 5:29). This choice between obedience to God and obedience to human authorities applies, however, only to certain situations:

> The Christian is called to submit to the state, unless the state commands what God forbids, or prohibits what God commands. If the state thus forces us to choose between loyalty to itself and our higher loyalty to God, we must say 'No' to the state because we have said 'Yes' to Jesus Christ as Lord.[9]

Submission to the state where it is not a matter of conscience is confirmed by Jesus' word, "Then give to Caesar what is Caesar's, and to God what is God's" (Lk. 20:25), and by Paul's instruction in Romans 13:1-7 and Peter's in 1 Peter 2:13-17.

The *second response* to persecution is *prayer*. The boldness to face persecution and the power to continue the ministry are gifts of the Spirit that should be prayed for. The early church did: "Now, Lord, consider their

---

[8] The persecution of the *Mulu Wongel* church is documented in Tormod Engelsviken, *Mulu Wongel: A Documentary History of the independent Ethiopian Pentecostal Movement 1960-1975* (Unpublished, Oslo: The Free Faculty of Theology, 1975), Tormod Engelsviken, "Mission. Pentecostalism and Ethiopian Identity: The Beginnings of the Mulu Wongel Believers' Church", *Norwegian Journal of Missiology* 68(4), (2014), pp. 195-215, and the persecution under the Marxist regime in Tibebe Eshete, "Marxism and Church Growth: The Paradox of Church Growth in Ethiopia 1974-1991, in Gravaas (ed), *Freedom of Belief & Christian Mission*, pp. 242-258.

[9] *The Cape Town Commitment*, 2C6 (The Lausanne Movement, 2011), p. 51.

threats and enable your servants to speak your word with great boldness" (Acts 4:29). They also prayed for Peter when he was in prison for the sake of the gospel (Acts 12:5, 12). Paul asked the churches to pray for him when he was in chains (Col. 4:39) or persecuted (2 Thess. 3:1-2). Intercession for imprisoned and persecuted Christians is an important ministry in the church today.

In addition to prayer for their persecuted fellow Christians, Christians are also called to pray for the *perpetrators* of persecution. Jesus said, "But I tell you: Love your enemies and *pray for those who persecute you* that you may be sons of your Father in heaven" (Mt. 5:44-45). Jesus himself did what he had told his disciples to do; he prayed for those who crucified him, "Father forgive them, for they do not know what they are doing" (Lk. 23:34). In the same way, the first martyr, Stephen, filled with the Holy Spirit prayed for his persecutors before he died, "While they were stoning him, Stephen prayed. 'Lord Jesus, receive my spirit.' Then he fell on his knees and cried out, 'Lord, do not hold this sin against them.' When he had said this, he fell asleep" (Acts 7:55, 59-60).

As a *third response*, Christians are called to actively *love and do good* to those who persecute them. "Love your enemies," Jesus says (Mt. 5:44), and Paul concurs,

> Bless those who persecute you, bless and do not curse [...] If your enemy is hungry, feed him; if he is thirsty, give him something to drink. In doing this, you will heap burning coals on his head. Do not be overcome by evil, but *overcome evil with good* (Rom. 12:14, 20-21).

This may seem like an impossible demand but it can be granted as a gift by the Holy Spirit in situations of persecution, as has often been the case in the history of the church. The forgiveness and love of enemies are among the strongest testimonies to the world about the truth and goodness of the Christian faith. When, for example, Christians in Egypt forgave the Muslim extremists (ISIL) who kidnapped and killed 20 Coptic Christians on a beach in Libya in 2015, it amazed the whole country, even the Muslims, and it was given ample space in national and international media.

Fourthly, the command to love and pray for the persecutors does not mean that Christians should passively acquiesce to injustice, violence and persecution towards Christians or other people. Christians are supposed to *defend themselves* against unjust accusations, threats and persecutions. On the personal level, the advice of the apostle Peter is the following:

> But even if you should *suffer for what is right*, you are blessed [...] But in your hearts set apart Christ as Lord. Always be prepared *to give an answer* to everyone who asks you to give the reason for the hope that you have. But do this with *gentleness and respect*, keeping a clear conscience, so that those who

> speak maliciously against your good behaviour in Christ may be ashamed of their slander (1 Pet. 3:14-16).

When Christians are persecuted or discriminated by religious extremists or by religious or political authorities, they may use the *court system* of their country or *international courts of human rights* to defend their case. This is seen repeatedly in the history of the early church in Acts: when Paul demanded a public apology for unlawful arrest in Philippi (Acts 16:35-39), spoke both publicly and in courts in his own defence (Acts 22:1-21; 26:1-32), and even as a Roman citizen appealed to the Emperor and was taken to Rome (Acts 25:11; 26:32).

Jesus promised his disciples *help from the Holy Spirit* when defending themselves:

> On my account you will be brought before governors and kings as witnesses to them and to the Gentiles. But when they arrest you, *do not worry* about what to say or how to say it. At that time you will be given what to say, for it will not be you speaking, but the *Spirit of your Father speaking through you* (Mt. 10:19-20).

In today's world, the church should also use all possible means to defend itself and its members when persecuted. This may be done by different forms of *advocacy* such as spreading information about persecution in the public domain, by assisting Christians in the courts, by working through political and diplomatic channels, by economic assistance to the families of prisoners, etc. In a globalised world, the global church should show solidarity[10] with persecuted churches and individual Christians. "If one part [of the body of Christ] suffers, every part suffers with it" (1 Cor. 12:26, cp. Rom. 12:15).

Fifthly, if persecution persists in spite of all efforts to halt it, Christians are called to either *endure or flee.* There is suffering that can and should be endured.

> If you are insulted because of the name of Christ, you are blessed, for *the Spirit of glory and of God rests on you* […] If you suffer as a Christian, do not be ashamed, but praise God that you bear his name. Those who suffer according to God's will should commit themselves to their faithful Creator and continue to do good (1 Pet. 4:12-19).

Jesus predicted persecutions but promised that "he who stands firm to the end will be saved" (Mt. 24:13, cp. 2 Thess. 1:4; 2 Tim. 2:12).

---

[10] See also Christof Sauer, "Christian Solidarity in the Face of Discrimination and Persecution", in Gravaas (ed), *Freedom of Belief & Christian Mission*, pp. 452-464, where Christian advocacy is discussed also under the perspective of religious freedom as a generally accepted *human right*.

When faced with the prospect of death or imprisonment, however, Christians are allowed – sometimes even encouraged – to *flee to safer places*. Mary and Joseph fled to Egypt to avoid Jesus being killed by King Herod (Mt. 2:13-15). The disciples were told by Jesus, "When you are persecuted in one place, flee to another" (Mt. 10:23; cp. 24:16). This was also what the early Christians in Jerusalem did when persecuted (Acts 8:1, 4). Paul escaped death by fleeing from Damascus in a dramatic way (Acts 9:23-25). Today, this means that Christians under persecution may have to flee from their countries. There is therefore an obligation for Christians in safe areas of the world to respect such decisions and welcome and include religious refugees and immigrants in their societies and churches.

There is a last and ultimate *sixth response* to persecution. When Christians are violently assaulted by mobs or extremists, they are permitted to defend themselves and their communities by *force*. This is a last resort for Christians in danger of losing their lives. There are examples of this just response in Nigeria when Christian churches and villages were attacked by the Islamistic *Boko Haram* movement and the Christians had to fight for their own lives and that of their families and neighbours. These are the exceptions; the rule is that the Christians' defence against persecution should be peaceful and non-violent.

A Final Eschatological Perspective

According to New Testament prophecy, believers will come into times of unparalleled suffering as the end approaches (Mt. 24:9-14). Suffering may come in a variety of ways. In countries that claim freedom of religion Christians may still be discriminated against, laughed at, and mocked. Good friends may be lost or an unbelieving family alienated. One's education, job security or professional advancement may be threatened because of one's active Christian witness. In other countries without this freedom, an open witness for Christ might not be tolerated and result in discrimination, social ostracism, imprisonment or even death. Whoever walks the pathway of discipleship will experience suffering.

The more Christians are filled with the Holy Spirit, the more powerfully they bear witness, the more heartily they live the Christian life, the more consistently they follow Jesus, the more suffering will come their way. A movement that urges people to be filled with the Spirit cannot avoid the consequences: it must help prepare them for suffering.

This does not mean training people in survival techniques. It means extending the central theme of the Charismatic renewal into this area of life; we enter times of suffering, like everything else in the Christian life, totally dependent on the Holy Spirit. We do not shrink from suffering. We recognise it as an integral aspect of Christian experience. In the power of the Spirit, we resist the temptation to avoid or ease the suffering by accommodating ourselves to the world. We trust the Spirit to maintain our fellowship with the serving, suffering Christ and lead us to the final victory:

> The Spirit himself testifies with our spirit that we are God's children. Now if we are children. Then we are heirs – heirs of God and co-heirs with Christ, if indeed *we share in his sufferings in order that we may also share in his glory* (Rom. 8:16-17, cp. Acts 14:22; 1 Pet. 4:13).
>
> He who *overcomes* will inherit all this, and *I will be his God and he will be my son* (Rev. 21:7).

(59) The Church: A Community Engaged in Spiritual Struggle

God calls his church into spiritual struggle. We are involved in a struggle against "the spiritual forces of evil" (Eph. 6:12; Mt. 10:34; 1 Jn 3:8). Spiritual awakening and renewal mean that we will be engaged in heightened spiritual conflict. Over every day of a believer's life stands the banner: "Fight the good fight of the faith" (1 Tim. 6:12).

This presupposes the kind of worldview that has emerged in the Charismatic renewal, and which corresponds with the biblical worldview. It reckons realistically with an invisible, non-physical, spiritual dimension of reality, and with the battle that rages there. The church appropriates and applies Christ's victory over Satan, even as we await and hasten the day of final triumph. The necessary weapons in this spiritual conflict are not human, but divine, and include the gifts of the Spirit. "The weapons we fight with are not the weapons of the world. On the contrary, they have *divine power* to demolish strongholds" (2 Cor. 10:4). "Be strong in the Lord and *his mighty power*" (Eph. 6:10, 14-18).

The lordship of Jesus needs to be established firstly in the lives of believers and the life of the church, with Scripture as the standard of life in the kingdom of God. First priority for every decision must be the will of God. Jesus is head over the church in all things (Eph. 1:22-23). This involves not only bringing people into the obedience of faith (Rom. 1:5; 16:26), but also doing battle with demonic forces. Resisting the attacks of Satan and casting out his demons, deliverance, is a necessary ministry if Christ's rule is to become reality (Mt. 12:28-29; James 4:7; Eph. 6:11, 13).

Spiritual Struggle and Prayer

The church needs to engage in spiritual conflict against demonic forces, not only on the individual level, but also on the corporate level, battling the influence of Satan in religions, ideologies, unjust policies and economic relationships both nationally and internationally. Sin and demonic influence are found in the structures that control various sectors of society.[1]

---

[1] To this aspect of spiritual conflict, see especially the chapter by Knud Jørgensen, "Spiritual conflict in socio-political context", in Moreau (ed), *Deliver Us From Evil*, pp. 213-230, where he among others refers to Walter Wink, *Engaging the Powers: Discernment and Resistance in a World of Dominion* (Philadelphia, PA: Fortress Press, 1992).

The foundation for this ministry is *intercessory prayer.* In bringing the witness of Christ to society at large, we particularly need to be reminded that we are not contending against people, "flesh and blood" (Eph. 6:12). We are engaged in a life-and-death struggle with supernatural evil powers that control much of this world. Before we speak or act prophetically in society, we have to deal with the powers of darkness through intercessory prayer in the power of the Holy Spirit (Eph. 6:18). The prophet Jeremiah called on the Israelites to pray for the pagan and ungodly city where they were exiled:

> '*Seek the peace and prosperity of the city* to which I have carried you into exile. *Pray to the Lord for it,* because if it prospers, you too will prosper [...] I know the plans I have for you,' declares the Lord, 'plans to prosper you and not to harm you, plans to give you hope and a future' (Jer. 29:7, 11; cp. Ps. 122:6-9).

Paul writes to Timothy about the priority of prayer for all, including the authorities:

> I urge, then, first all, that requests, prayer, intercession and thanksgiving be made for everyone – for kings and *all those in authority,* that we may live peaceful and quiet lives in all godliness and holiness (1 Tim. 2:1-2).

The rule of Christ includes both what he wills and works *in the church,* but also *in society at large.* In the Lord's prayer, we are taught to *pray*: "Your kingdom come, your will be done on earth as it is in heaven" (Mt. 6:10). In facing issues of justice and morality, society is encountering Christ the Lord, even though it does not yet recognise him as such. When the Holy Spirit involves Christians in these issues, he brings into the battle the power of discernment, prayer and dependence upon him. Much of this may be a secret work, never mentioned in the public arena. But we dare not forget or neglect it. By God's grace, we participate in the struggles of society with more responsibility and power than meets the eye.

The Church in Spiritual Struggle under the Lordship of Christ

As Christians, we are involved in spiritual struggle under the lordship of Christ.

> For though we live in the world, we do not wage war as the world does. The weapons we fight with are not the weapons of the world. On the contrary, they have divine power to demolish strongholds. We demolish arguments and every pretension that sets itself up against the knowledge of God, and we take captive every thought to make it obedient to Christ (2 Cor. 10:3-5).
>
> Our struggle is not against flesh and blood, but against the rulers, against the authorities, against the powers of this dark world and against the spiritual forces of evil in the heavenly realm (Eph. 6:12).

The church is empowered and equipped for battle with weapons supplied by the Spirit (Eph. 6:10-18). The gifts of the Spirit (1 Cor. 12:4-11) are tools of the Spirit for doing spiritual work and fighting spiritual battles.

The world was created by God to be under his sovereign rule. Man and woman were to be God's delegated authority to govern the world. Through their fall into sin, the devil became "the prince of this world" (Jn 12:31; 16:11). However, the fact remains: "God who made the world and everything in it is the Lord of heaven and earth" (Acts 17:24). God has not abdicated as king of his creation. The risen and exalted Christ is Lord *of all* – or he is not Lord *at all*, as has been said (cp. Mt. 28:18; Rom. 14:9).

Jesus Christ came to earth to defeat the devil (1 Jn 3:8; Mt. 12:29; Col. 2:15) and to inaugurate a time of healing and salvation in the kingdom of God (Acts 10:37). Ultimately "the end will come, when he [Christ] hands over the kingdom to the Father after he has destroyed all dominion, authority and power. For he must reign until he has put all his enemies under his feet" (1 Cor. 15:24-28). Jesus is the incarnate Son of God who conquered the devil and his kingdom through his death on cross and resurrection from the dead (Jn 12:31-33; Col. 2:15; Heb. 2:14-15; 1 Jn 3:8). Jesus is now seated at the right hand of God the Father, from where he reigns over all things, even the evil powers that oppose him and his rule (Eph. 1:20-23; Heb. 2:5-9). Yet we do not fully see it (Heb. 2:8).

The redeemed company of believers is transferred from Satan's kingdom to Christ's kingdom, from darkness to light (Col. 1:13-14; Acts 26:18). They share the reign with Christ (Eph. 2:6; Rom. 5:17), although the form of his rule in this age is not always evident to the eyes; it is most often hidden under the veil of weakness, suffering, and servanthood.

Jesus the Deliverer – Practice and Teaching

There is, however, a *visible, experiential demonstration* of the rule and power of Jesus over Satan and his demons, and that is the expulsion of evil spirits from people who are possessed or attacked by them. This ministry is often called the *ministry of deliverance.*

Jesus proclaimed and demonstrated the advent of the kingdom of God (Mk 1:15). One of the ways he *demonstrated the kingdom and brought it to visibility was by casting out demons.* Deliverance or exorcism played a noticeably large role in his earthly ministry. It was one of its main features. Jesus was widely known a powerful exorcist, and people marvelled at his authority. They recognised what was taking place: a change of rule.

This ministry of Jesus has raised questions in our time: was Jesus simply a child of his age in this regard, a prisoner of superstition; did he simply adapt to the common views of his fellow Jews; or were his exorcisms real expulsions of real evil spirits?

Jesus did recognise that some things were the product of a particular time or culture, for example, some of the traditions of the scribes and Pharisees. He rejected the common popular understanding that diseases or disasters were God's punishment for special sins (Jn 9:1-3; Lk. 13:4). He challenged common ideas of piety and propriety (Lk. 18:9-14; 14:1-14; 21:1-4). He turned values upside down by putting the last and the least first (Lk. 9:46-48; 18:15-17; Mt. 19:29-30). Women were honoured against the expectations of society (Mt.15:28; Lk. 7:36-50) and became the first witnesses to his resurrection (Lk. 24:1-10). Children were placed above adults in the kingdom of God (Mt. 18:1-5; 19:13-15). It is characteristic of the ministry of Jesus that *he did not simply accept or adapt to common views and practices in his own time and culture: he was not afraid to challenge and change them. That among other things is what made his ministry unique.*

When we look at his exorcisms, however, we see that he never dealt with demonic oppression as a wrong teaching or superstition that one must simply set aside. In his battle with demons, he was dealing with something other than merely cultural or religious heritage. Wherever God's power broke forth in Jesus, Satanic forces mounted opposition. Wherever the Holy Spirit involved himself in Jesus' ministry, unholy spirits were stirred into action. Whenever God's triumph is near, Satan fears for his own survival. The German New Testament scholar Leonhardt Goppelt says:

> In opposition to the divine authority manifest in Jesus' ministry, all darkness draws itself together into one demonic kingdom under Satan. In other words, evil is not only recognised as an all-encompassing, super-human power, but it is also a power that comes into action.[2]

Especially in Mark's gospel, Jesus' casting out of demons is portrayed as a *combat* (see, for example, Mk 1:23-28). Jesus understood these battles as the seizing of plunder after binding the strong man, that is, Satan (Mk 3:27; Lk. 11:21-23). The exorcisms showed the power of Jesus over Satan and all his demons for all to see, even his non-believing opponents and the Gentiles (Mt. 12:22-24; 8:28-34).

The exorcisms also brought *freedom and healing* to the possessed and led them back into society. According to Mark's detailed story of the deliverance of a demon-possessed man, Jesus told the man who had been tormented by many demons and isolated from other people: "Go home to your family and tell them how much the Lord has done for you, and how he has had mercy on you. So the man went away and began to tell in Decapolis how much Jesus had done for him. And all the people were amazed" (Mk 5:1-20).

---

[2] Leonhardt Goppelt, *Theologie des Neuen Testaments: Part 1: Jesu Wirken in seiner theologischen Bedeutung*, edited by Jürgen Roloff (Göttingen: Vandenhoeck & Ruprecht, 1975) p. 126.

But Jesus did not only drive out evil spirits, he also *taught what his exorcisms meant.* This teaching is the decisive New Testament evidence that Jesus' exorcisms were not simply an adaptation to the culture or – even worse theologically – that Jesus was ignorant of the real cause of the possession phenomenon. Jesus taught that his exorcisms were (1) *real evidence of his power over Satan*, that (2) *the Holy Spirit was involved in them* and (3) that they were *proof of the coming of the kingdom of God*: "If I drive out the demons by the Spirit of God, then the kingdom of God has come upon you" (Mt. 12:28, cp. Lk. 7:21-23). Joachim Jeremias writes: "Every time Jesus drives out an evil spirit it is an anticipation of the hour when Satan will be *visibly stripped of his power.* Victories over his functionaries are *an anticipation of the eschaton.*"[3]

Cases of *demon-possession have to be distinguished from cases of disease* in the ministry of Jesus. In Jesus' healing of people who are ill, he deals with and speaks to the persons who are ill and treats them as people in need of healing. In cases of demon possession, the people concerned are described as "demonised" (Greek: *daimonidsomenoi*) or as having an evil spirit (Greek: *echein pneuma*), and Jesus *deals with and speaks to the spirit*, not the possessed person. The evil spirits are personal beings with a separate identity from the possessed. They are able to speak, they have their own evil intentions, they have supernatural knowledge of who Jesus is before he says anything, they know his power, and their own future punishment. They submit to Jesus, even kneel before him (Mk 5:6), not in faith, but in fear and defeat. The most characteristic trait of the demons is exactly their *enmity to Christ and his work.* "What do you want with us, Jesus of Nazareth? Have you come to destroy us? I know who you are – the Holy One of God!" (Mk 1:24; cp. Lk. 8:26, 31). They are also powerful, unclean, evil and anti-social (Lk. 8:27-29).[4]

Jesus pronounces judgement on the demons and drives them out and away with a word (Lk. 8:31-33; 4:35; 9:42). They obey his commands to leave, sometimes grudgingly and violently, yet having to acknowledge his superior power and authority. *Only then does Jesus speak words of comfort and encouragement to the persons who have been delivered and returns them to their families.*

---

[3] Jeremias, *Neutestamentliche Theologie*, p. 98.

[4] To a more detailed discussion of spiritual conflict, see Moreau (ed), *Deliver Us from Evil* and Engelsviken, *Spiritual Conflict.* Possession and expulsion of evil spirits is a religious phenomenon, not a medical or psychological one, although in some cases there may be a combination. On the relationship between possession and psychology, see e.g. Jerry Mungadze, "Spiritual conflict in light of psychology and medicine", in Moreau (ed), *Deliver Us From Evil*, pp. 203-212.

Jesus Commissioned His Disciples to Cast out Demons

Jesus empowered his disciples to cast out demons *in his name*. He sent them out to proclaim the kingdom of God and gave them authority over the forces of evil (Mk 3:14-15). Authority over spirits is a recurring theme in Jesus' words of commissioning, and indeed becomes a mark of these words (Mk 6:7, 13; Mt. 10:1, 8; Lk. 9:1; 10:17-20). The twelve apostles and the larger group of 72 disciples received the authority to drive out demons (Lk. 10:1, 17).

Thus, Jesus' victory over the powers of darkness and his liberation of those who were under the control of the devil were central both to his own ministry and to the ministry that he gave to his disciples. An important difference is, however, that while Jesus drove out the demons *on his own authority* with a word of command, his disciples did not act on their own authority but applied the authority of Jesus, as indicated by the invocation of the *name of Jesus.* The name of Jesus is no magical formula but gives expression to the fact that it is Jesus himself who throws out the demons through the ministry of the disciples (Lk. 10:17-20).

The early church believed and confessed that, through his death and resurrection, Jesus had conquered all the evil powers that were subordinate to Satan and hostile to God. He "disarmed" them – that is, took away their weapons (Col. 2:15; Eph. 1:20-23; Heb. 2:14). In faith, Christians have already overcome Satan (1 Jn 2:13b-14). Yet they are called to battle, and to spiritual watchfulness, since the devil still tries to instil fear: "Your enemy the devil prowls around like a roaring lion looking for someone to devour. Resist him, standing firm in faith" (1 Pet. 5:8-9, cp. Heb. 2:15). But the devil may also disguise himself as an angel of light to deceive Christians through falsehood (2 Cor. 10:14).

The names of the devil are a clue to his treachery. He is called the "evil one" (Eph. 6:16; 1 Jn 5:18-19), the "enemy" (Lk. 10:19; Mt. 13:25), the "prince/ruler of this world" (Jn 12:31; 14:30); the "dragon" (Rev. 12; 13; 16:13; 20:2), or the "serpent" (Gen. 3:1; Rev. 12:9; 20:2). There is no doubt as to his ultimate destruction (Mt. 25:41; Rev. 20:10).

A *word of warning* may also be necessary: Although the Bible is very realistic regarding the existence, character, work, defeat and ultimate punishment of the devil and his demons, there is *no detailed doctrine of the demonic, a demonology*, in the Bible. We know that the devil and the demons are created, fallen, spiritual beings, but the Bible tells us nothing about their origin, types, numbers, hierarchies, etc. It also does not tell us the reasons why some people are possessed by evil spirits. The text in Isaiah 14:12-15, which often has been understood as a description of the ambition and fall of Satan, is not about him, but about the king of Babylon (Is. 14:4). We also know very little from the Bible about so-called "territorial spirits" (cf. Dan.

10:13).[5] We should not be too occupied with speculations and theories about evil powers. The Bible shows no interest in such things. Satan and all his works should be *renounced, and only when necessary in order to expose and defeat him, announced.*

The ancient world was full of fear of demons and their influence and this fear shows in its literature. It is therefore a remarkable fact that the New Testament shows *no such fear*. The Christians are sure of their victory in Christ and have no fear of the devil and his demons, because they know that "the one who is in you is greater than the one who is in the world" (1 Jn 4:4). There is triumph over evil and the evil one.

If we look at the *early church* after Jesus' ascension to the Father and the outpouring of the Holy Spirit on the day of Pentecost, it is clear that the victorious struggle with the Satanic forces continued unabated. The book of Acts reckons with the demonic oppression of people. In various ways, it attests to the liberation from such oppression through the ministry of the church (Acts 5:16; 8:6-8; 19:12).

A particular case of possession is described in an eyewitness account by Luke (Acts 16:16-18) that both confirms the stories of the gospel and adds some new details. The context of this case is Hellenistic pagan culture and the use of a spirit of prediction for profit. When confronted with the apostles and their message, the spirit showed supernatural knowledge of who they were, the God they served, and the gospel they preached. Yet, Paul did not want the testimony of the spirit and commanded it in the name of Jesus to leave the slave girl, which it did immediately.

The connection between the occult and evil spirits is also seen in the burning of the sorcery scrolls in Ephesus (Acts 18:17-20). The immediate cause of the burning was an incident where seven sons of a Jewish chief priest by the name of Sceva tried to use the name of Jesus in a magical way to expel a demon. The spirit exposed them as non-Christians without spiritual authority, and then overpowered and hurt all of them (Acts 18:13-16). The story is also a testimony to the fact that the name of Jesus was widely known to have power over evil spirits.

Another example with connection to the occult deals with the apostle Paul's reaction to a sorcerer who was not possessed by a spirit but according to Paul was "a child of the devil and an enemy of all that is right". Paul, filled with the Holy Spirit, rebuked the sorcerer's attempt to oppose him and turn a possible convert away from the faith, by proclaiming God's judgement upon him, a judgement which made him blind for a while (Acts 13:6-12, cp. Acts 5:3).

---

[5] See A. Scott Moreau, "Gaining perspective on territorial spirits", in Moreau (ed), *Deliver Us From Evil*, pp. 259-275.

Weapons of Defence and Attack

How the battle against Satan is to be fought in its particulars is expressed metaphorically in Ephesians 6:10-17, where believers are instructed to "put on the whole armour of God so you can take your stand against the devil's schemes". Important parts of this armour are truth, righteousness, the gospel of peace, faith, and salvation, which are not our own efforts but God's gracious gifts to be appropriated and used by the believers.

All of these parts of the armour are for defensive purposes, but the believers are also told to use weapons of attack: "Take [...] the *sword of the Spirit,* which is the word of God" (v. 17). *The word of God* was also what Jesus himself used when he was tempted by the devil (Mt. 4:1-11). Luther expressed this in his famous hymn, *A Mighty Fortress*: "A word can bind him".

In addition to the word of God, *prayer* is a weapon in the struggle against evil forces. "And *pray in the Spirit* on all occasions with all kinds of prayers and requests. With this in mind, be alert and always keep on praying for all the saints" (Eph. 6:18). Both the use of the *word of God* and of *prayer* should be done "*in the Spirit*". The importance of prayer in order not to succumb to temptation is seen in Jesus' words to the disciples in Gethsemane (Mt. 26:41), and not least in the Lord's prayer where the disciples are taught to pray: "*And lead us not into temptation, but deliver us from the evil one*" (Mt. 6:13).

Submitting to God and resisting the devil carry with it the promise that the devil will flee (James 4:7; cp. 1 Cor. 10:12-13; Heb. 2:18).

Spiritual Struggle in the Church's Mission Today

The post-apostolic church continued the ministry of the apostles and their struggle with the forces of evil, as we already have seen in Parts Two and Three of this book.[6] This history needs therefore not be repeated here. In recent history and in our time, however, there has been heavy opposition to this dimension of the church's mission both from within the church and from the world. This has to do with modern attitudes to the devil, demons and deliverance.

Charismatic experience makes a person more aware both of the good God and of the evil forces around us. Western culture, however, has made an abstraction of evil: it is merely the absence of good, or it is a natural aspect of the human person leading to evil attitudes and actions. It may be embedded in social evils, political ideologies and anti-Christian religiosity, such as injustice, poverty, violence, trafficking, wars, fascism, communism, nationalism, racism, anti-Semitism, extremism, occultism, and prejudices of

---

[6] See Excursus 1 in Part Two and the chapter on Pietism in Part Three. Both Blumhardt and Nenilava were representatives of early Charismatic renewal and they had exorcism as a part of their ministries.

different kinds. It is, however, always seen as a result of impersonal, natural factors such as inherited personal traits and/or influence from an unhealthy environment.

The Bible, however, speaks about *radical evil as having its origin in the devil and his dominion.* It speaks about the devil and the demonic forces in *personal terms*: they are invisible spiritual entities with will, purpose, and supernatural power. Christians who have a biblical worldview regarding evil do not ignore the evil that has its root in human attitudes and actions, as well as in systems and ideologies, but they do not see that as the end of the inquiry. What power is at work behind these manifestations of evil? And how do we deal with it? For Charismatics, the biblical view is more adequate than the secular and naturalistic view of Western culture that denies all spiritual reality, both the existence of God and the devil. It also accords more with actual experience of the radical and irrational character of the evil that we see in the world today, and the experience of the effects of the church's ministry by proclamation of the Word of God, intercessory prayer and deliverance from demonic power. Unfortunately, many confessing Christians today who believe in God do not believe in a personal devil. In their understanding of evil, they have succumbed to the heavy influence of modern non-Christian attitudes. It is therefore even more important for the Charismatic movement to recover the biblical teaching and practice also in this area.

This concern is, however, not only a Charismatic one. It is shared by most Evangelical Christians worldwide, Charismatics and non-Charismatics alike. All the major congresses of the evangelical Lausanne Movement have in fact made important statements in this regard. We quote the following:

> We believe that we are engaged in constant spiritual warfare with the principalities and powers of evil, who are seeking to overthrow the church and frustrate its task of world evangelisation (*The Lausanne Covenant*, 1974).
>
> We affirm that spiritual warfare demands spiritual weapons, and that we must both preach the Word in the power of the Spirit and pray constantly that we may enter into Christ's victory over the principalities and powers of evil (*The Manila Manifesto*, 1989).
>
> We agreed that evangelisation is to bring people from darkness to light and from the power of Satan to God (Acts 26:18). This involves an inescapable element of spiritual warfare (*Lausanne Statement on Spiritual Warfare*, 1993).
>
> In the same great saving act [Christ's death on the cross], completed, vindicated and declared through the resurrection, God won the decisive victory over Satan, death and all evil powers, liberated us from their power and fear, and ensured their eventual destruction (*The Cape Town Commitment*, 2010).

As we have already noticed, an important consultation was held in Nairobi, Kenya, in 2000 with the title "Deliver Us From Evil", convened by the Lausanne Movement and the Association of Evangelicals in Africa. It resulted in an important *Consultation Statement*, and later in two books.[7] We quote with approval from the Consultation Statement:

> Calling people to faith in Christ, inviting them to be delivered from the domain of darkness into the kingdom of God, is the missionary mandate for all Christians [...] The Holy Spirit empowers us for world evangelisation through the interrelated ministries of word (proclamation), deed (social service and action), and sign (miracles, power encounters), all of which take place in the context of spiritual conflict.
>
> Satan is a real, personal, spiritual and created being [...] Satan continues to actively oppose God's mission and the work of God's church.
>
> The powers and principalities are ontologically real beings. They cannot be reduced to mere social and psychological structures.[8]

Among the means that the "powers of this dark world" use, are, "tempting to sin, afflicting the body, emotions, mind and will, taking control of a person [...] distorting the roles of social, economic and political structures, the realm of the occult, false religions, and all forms of opposition to God's work of salvation and the mission of the church".[9] For our purposes in this book, it is significant that the Statement also points to the role of the Spirit:

> *The person and work of the Holy Spirit are central in spiritual conflict*: A) The empowering of the Holy Spirit, the exercise of spiritual gifts and prayer are prerequisites for engaging in spiritual conflict. B) The exercise of spiritual gifts must be accompanied by the fruit of the Spirit. C) The work of the Spirit and the Word must be held together (italics added).[10]

Discerning the Causes of Evil: Physical Evil

The Charismatic renewal has brought the issue of spiritual struggle to the fore. Where this message receives a hearing, the opposite problem sometimes surfaces and must also be dealt with: people begin to see demons behind every bad thing that happens and as the cause of every problem. It is therefore important and necessary to make some distinctions.

We have to distinguish first of all between *physical and moral evils.* Physical evils on the *large scale* include disasters and calamities such as earthquakes, volcanic eruptions, tsunamis, floods, drought, pandemics etc.

---

[7] The books are Moreau (ed), *Deliver Us From Evil* which contains all the papers from the consultation as well as the Consultation Statement, and Engelsviken, *Spiritual Conflict in Today's Mission* which is a *Lausanne Occasional Paper* and a shorter summary of the consultation.

[8] Moreau, *Deliver Us From Evil*, p. xix

[9] Moreau, *Deliver Us From Evil*, p. xx.

[10] Moreau, *Deliver Us From Evil,* p. xxi.

These evils belong to nature and have taken place throughout history, although in today's world some of them may be increased or even caused by climate change due to human ignorance, exploitation and greed, and therefore also have a moral aspect. Yet, these calamities that affect millions of people and cause great harm and suffering cannot be ascribed either to God or the devil. They belong to the "mystery" of evil that has *no explanation revealed by God* (Dt. 29:29). Christians are also suffering under these natural conditions of the created world. They experience that God does not always protect them *from* suffering, but that he always is with them *in* their suffering, sustaining them and giving them the strength to persevere *through* their affliction.

On the *small scale* of individuals and families, physical evil is experienced in disease and misfortunes of different kinds. We have written about healing as a ministry of the church, yet disease is common among all people, even Christians, and, while some experience supernatural healing through prayer, this is still the exception, not the rule.

The Pentecostal New Testament scholar John C. Thomas has made a thorough study of the causes of illness and affliction in the New Testament.[11] His findings may be surprising to many. There is not one, but *three major causes* of illness in the New Testament: God, the devil, and natural, neutral causes.

God is sometimes seen as the source of infirmity or even death. Different from much modern thought, the New Testament authors do not shrink from "assigning to God an active role in the affliction of individuals with disease and/or death". The purpose of God may be *pedagogical.* He wants to teach his people about the seriousness of sin in order to call them to repentance and obedience (Zechariah, Luke 1:18-20; Paul, Acts 9:9, 17; Christians, 1 Cor. 11:29-30; Heb. 12:5-11; Rev. 3:19), or God may also demonstrate his *judgement on evil* and opposition to the gospel (Ananias and Sapphira, Acts 5:1-11; Herod, Acts 12:19b-23; Elymas, Acts 13:10-11; the Israelites, 1 Cor. 10:5-10). There are, however, very few cases in the New Testament where infirmity or illness is ascribed to God, and Christians should not in general be told to look for God's "will" and "meaning" in their suffering. This may only serve to put an extra burden on afflicted people.

A special case is Paul's "thorn in the flesh", which most probably was a physical ailment (2 Cor. 12:7-10). It is described as a "messenger of Satan" who tormented him but, despite prayers to God for its removal, it stayed with him. God's purpose in not answering Paul's prayers – at least in the way Paul

[11] J.C. Thomas, "The Devil, Disease and Deliverance: Origins of Illness in New Testament Thought", *Journal of Pentecostal Theology Supplement Series 13* (Sheffield: Sheffield Academic Press, 1998), pp. 296-319. See also by the same author "Spiritual conflict in illness and affliction", in Moreau (ed), *Deliver Us From Evil*, pp. 37-60.

wanted them answered – was that God had a different plan: He did not want Paul to be conceited by his great revelations. God's answer was therefore: "My grace is sufficient for you, for my power is made perfect in weakness" (v. 9). Paul accepted God's word obediently. It led him to a new view of weakness and affliction, expressed in his paradoxical confession, "When I am weak, then I am strong" (v. 10). Many Christians have found a similar purpose in situations of lasting disease or infirmity, not as a command to be obeyed by their own power, but by God's grace and the power of the Spirit.

Maybe surprisingly, there are fewer cases than one might expect in the New Testament *where disease or infirmity are ascribed to the devil.* We have already looked at the important cases of demonic possession which obviously are caused by the devil and his evil spirits. But, as we have seen, there is a clear distinction between demon possession and illness.[12] *The demonic causation of possession can therefore not simply be equated with the causation of disease.*

There are, however, a few cases where disease or infirmity is attributed to demonic activity. The cases are Simon's mother-in-law who suffered from fever (Lk. 4:38-39) and the woman with a spirit of infirmity (Lk. 13:10-16). In the first case, Jesus *rebuked the fever* which left her. It is not said directly that the fever was due to demonic activity, and Jesus did not engage in conversation with any spiritual entity. The woman who was crippled by a spirit of infirmity was healed by a word of Jesus spoken *to the woman* and with laying on of hands. Jesus did not engage in any conversation with the spirit. Thomas concludes from these cases that, "it appears that the New Testament knows a category of demonic activity separate from demon possession in which individuals who appear to be in a positive relationship with God suffer infirmity".[13] We cannot, however, from these examples, or from Acts 10:38, maintain that all diseases or infirmities are caused by the devil or evil spirits.

In the *vast majority of cases*, nothing is said about the origin of the disease or infirmity. The possible causes appear to be *religiously neutral or even natural.* One could attribute disease to the devil or to the results of sin in the world in general or in individual people in particular, but Thomas shows that "the texts themselves do not explicitly offer support for such a view".[14] On the contrary, in one case Jesus says explicitly that *sin is not the cause* of a particular infirmity (Jn 9:1-3), and he also denies that suffering and disasters are caused by people being especially guilty of sin (Lk. 13:1-5). The New Testament acknowledges that illness that occurs among the people of God can be quite natural, not suggesting that it has any evil origin (Phil. 2:25-30; 1 Tim. 5:23; 2 Tim. 4:20).

---

[12] Thomas supports this view, see "Spiritual conflict in illness and affliction", p. 42.
[13] Thomas, "Spiritual conflict in illness and affliction", p. 44.
[14] Thomas, "Spiritual conflict in illness and affliction", p. 44.

In addition to this biblical evidence, we might add an argument based on the order of creation. Modern biological and medical science – that also is God's gift to Christians when not being contrary to the Word of God – have shown that suffering, disease and death are *part of God's creative order as we know it.* The death of old life is always a condition for new life. Animals that eat animals are dependent upon the death of animals. Humans are also allowed to kill and eat animals. All death involves some suffering. The human body itself is also subject to eventual death, and its death will also most often be preceded by suffering and illness. God has given our body (and the body of animals) the remarkable ability to heal itself and to resist many diseases through the immune system, which is all part of God's good creation. These facts suggest that most *physical evils,* such as natural disasters and pandemics on the *large scale,* and suffering, disease and infirmity *on the small scale,* are *natural* and *neutral* events and therefore should not be directly attributed to God or to the devil. Yet, Christians may still expect and hope for a day of resurrection when in a new and transforming way "creation itself will be liberated from its bondage to decay and brought into the glorious freedom of the children of God" (Rom. 8:21).

An important corollary of the fact that disease or calamity cannot simply be ascribed to the devil or evil spirits, is *the rejection by the church of witchcraft or sorcery as a cause of illness and misfortune.* In some societies, this misunderstanding has led to accusations of witchcraft against innocent persons that have caused social ostracism, immense suffering and even death. The historical witch-hunts where the church was a willing accomplice are tragic examples of a misdirected, unbiblical form of spiritual conflict and must not be repeated today. It is the witch-hunt, *not* the alleged "witches", that is inspired by the devil.

Discerning the Causes of Evil: Moral Evil

When dealing with *moral evils* such as breaking the law of God as it is expressed in the double commandment of love (Lk. 10:27), the "golden rule" (Mt. 7:12) and the ten commandments with their prohibition against idolatry and sins against our fellow human beings (Ex. 20:1-17), the activity of the devil is more pronounced, especially in his role as tempter and opponent of God and his salvation. Yet, even here we cannot simply view the devil as the direct cause of all sin and evil.

There are some cases in the New Testament where the devil *is* the direct cause of temptation or sin. Jesus, having no sinful nature in himself, was tempted directly by the devil (Mt. 4:1-11). Peter was an instrument of the devil when trying to avert the death of Jesus (Mt. 16:22-23). Judas was prompted by the devil to betray Jesus (Jn 13:2, 27, cp. also Ananias in Acts 5:3 and Elymas in Acts 13:10).

In a *fundamental way*, Satan may be said to be behind all temptation and sin (Gen. 3:1-5; Jn 8:44; 1 Cor. 7:5; 1 Jn 3:8-10), yet nobody can excuse their sins and blame the devil for them, saying, "The devil made me do it", as if they were without responsibility themselves. Salvation does not only take place by deliverance from Satan's power but also by repentance, faith and forgiveness of sins. Human beings are not only captive to evil forces, they are also responsible for and guilty of their own sins. Human nature was corrupted by the original fall in sin, and from then onwards one main cause of sin and opposition to God is the *sinful human nature*, the "flesh" as Paul calls it. Opposed to the "fruit of the Spirit" in Galatians 5:22-23 are the "acts of the sinful nature" in Galatians 5:19-21.

The *struggle of the Spirit against the flesh or the sinful* nature is central to the new life in Christ. "For the sinful nature desires what is contrary to the Spirit, and the Spirit what is contrary to the sinful nature. They are in conflict with each other so you do not do what you want" (Gal. 5:17, see also Gal. 5:24-25; Rom. 7:5; 8;3, 6-8, 12-14; James 1:13-14; 1 Jn 2:16). We *cannot be delivered from our sinful nature*! It will not be eradicated. It stays with us and has to be fought in a daily battle in the power of the Spirit until the end.

In addition to sinful human nature, the *world that is opposed* to God is also a cause of temptation and sin. Jesus said, "Woe to the world because of the things that cause people to sin" (Mt. 18:7, cp. Mt. 13:22). This evil world may hate Christ and the Christians, but it stands under judgement (Jn 7:7; 12:31; 15:18). We are called not to conform to the world but be "transformed by the renewing of the mind" (Rom. 12:2; cp.; James 4:4; 2 Pet. 1:4; 1 Jn 2:15-17). There is both a struggle and a triumph in what John writes:

> Everyone born of God overcomes the world. This is the victory that has overcome the world, even our faith. Who is it that overcomes the world? Only he who believes that Jesus is the Son of God (1 Jn 5:4-5; cp. Gal. 6:14).
>
> The world and its desires pass away, but the man who does the will of God lives forever (1 Jn 2:15-17).

In their spiritual struggle, Christians are therefore faced with *three major enemies: the devil, their sinful nature and the world.* The Consultation Statement says, "Spiritual conflict involves more than one enemy; it must engage the flesh, the devil and the world".[15]

Hence not all sins or problems are immediately devil-related. Some of those with considerable experience in the ministry of deliverance have a good rule of thumb: "If everything else fails – counselling, confession, absolution, reconciliation, admonition, discipline – then begin to look for demonic factors."

---

[15] Moreau (ed), *Deliver Us From Evil*, p. xxiv.

It has been jokingly said that when penicillin was first discovered, doctors routinely gave it to every patient. If patients didn't improve in five days, they tried to find out what was wrong with them. That is an illustration that cuts both ways: the church has sometimes routinely administered the wisdom of psychology, psychiatry and sociology to the hurts of its people, and some charismatics have routinely tried to cast the devil out of anyone who came up with something less than a victory testimony. To take the reality of demons seriously is simply to ask the church – the whole church – to be as accurate as possible in the way that it deals with evil. If demonic activity is the problem, or a significant part of the problem, then that must be dealt with. If the problem is bad habits, ingrained wrong attitudes, unconfessed sin, neglected relationships, etc – then those are the things that must be dealt with in the wisdom and power of the Spirit.

A Danish pastor told how his pastoral care of one particular individual had to take several factors into account:

> Claus came to me after he had left a psychiatric hospital. Both he and his mother felt that he had received no help there. He said that he could not speak with doctors about his real problems. About three years earlier, he had entered an occult healing order through what he described as a 'mild Satanist initiation.' He was given a 'small helper', an accompanying spirit. Gradually he began to be assailed by thoughts of murder and suicide, and some months later ended up in the psychiatric hospital. I proclaimed the gospel to him, and made a special point of the victory of Christ over the devil on the cross. Claus found his way back into the faith of the church. The first time I just prayed a general blessing on him, the Spirit of God gave him tears. I shared this word with him: 'Jesus is crying tears of joy because you have turned to him.' In subsequent meetings we dealt with the demonic aspect of his problem. I spoke to the evil spirit and commanded it to leave, in Jesus' name. This broke the occult bondage, with strong physical and psychological reactions. Over the course of half a year, Claus began behaving normally within the fellowship of the congregation. Later he received the gift of tongues, and that was another step forward. He remained under my pastoral care for some time. He experienced some reverses when he became too deeply immersed in books on exorcism, which apparently can be misused in an occult way. This experience impressed on me the fact that effective pastoral care requires accurate discernment.[16]

The Church's Ministry of Deliverance

A church engaged in spiritual conflict assumes the reality of an invisible, non-material realm of existence. It recognises the existence of spiritual beings and the interrelatedness of the physical and non-physical realms.

---

[16] Ole Skjerbæk Madsen (see Appendix) supplied this example from his pastoral ministry.

For Luther, as we have seen, Satanic powers were an earnest reality. He testified to the reality and awfulness of the devil's power, based on his own experience. Paul Althaus wrote:

> It is not possible to try to understand [Luther's] theology on this point as a relic of the Middle Ages, however much he is in agreement with the traditional belief in devils and demons. He took the devil far more seriously than did the Middle Ages [...] that is, without question, because Luther recognised the nature of the lordship of God and Christ with a new clarity, and, as a further result, had a keen eye for the enemy and the depth and difficulty of the all-out war between God and opposing powers. Luther also returned to the viewpoint held by Jesus and by the early church. Luther's statements concerning the devil are closely and inseparably linked to the very core of his theology.[17]

The church of Luther's time reckoned with God's antagonist and the power of his demons. Sometimes, the church lost sight of the victory already won over the powers of darkness by Jesus. Nonetheless, the church was aware that these powers should be taken seriously.

In modem times, this has changed substantially. Among most of the educated today, it is considered unsophisticated, a mark of ignorance, to reckon seriously with Satan and his demons. This has led to enormous superficiality of belief. Because one no longer recognises the extent of demonic power and the danger it poses, one is also no longer able to recognise the full dimension of the salvation that Christ gained for us. One sees no need for spiritual warfare in the sense of Ephesians 6:10-17. When it comes to fighting, one ignores the warning of Ephesians 6:12: one contends with flesh and blood; fights other *people* instead of the powers of evil. Meanwhile, the powers of evil brazenly expand their sphere of influence.

It is ironic that Western culture, which has prided itself on being rid of primitive belief in evil spirits, should witness an unprecedented explosion of occult practices. At the same time as the official elite denies the existence of evil powers, the entertainment industry revels in frightening speculations about supernatural evil in books, films and TV programmes.

In Scripture, God has paved the way for a change that is now taking place. Increasing numbers of believers are recognising that it is not naïve to reckon with the devil and his powers. It is naïve to deny them. We are beginning to sense that we will be able to win the spiritual battle of this age only when we recognise our real opponent. The church has a tremendous stake in the victory of Jesus over Satan and his demons. The Holy Spirit is waiting to bring Jesus' victory to practical reality in our lives.

Spiritual struggle includes the ministry of deliverance from demonic oppression. We do not need a detailed doctrine of demons, an "ontology of the demonic", as it were. Undue fascination with the world of dark spirits is

---

[17] Althaus, *The Theology of Martin Luther*, p. 161.

not wise. It is enough to know that demonic power is real and that it can be overcome in the name of Jesus.

Our missionary task is hindered when we do not deal decisively with powers that hold people in bondage. Accompanying the ministry of deliverance is the gift of discernment of spirits (1 Cor. 12:10). Through the exercise of this gift, the Holy Spirit will often reveal the nature or source of a problem. People may have become demonised through involvement in the occult, pagan religious rites, spiritualism, immorality, or mind-altering drugs.

Since different cultures and societies in the world have different views of the spiritual world and the demonic, the ministry of deliverance has to be contextualised. It may look different in an African or Indian context than in a Western context. *The Consultation Statement* says:

> Because spiritual conflict is expressed in different ways in different societies, we strongly caution against taking ideas, methods or strategies developed in one society and using them uncritically in another.[18]

In Western society, for example, demon possession seems to occur much more seldom than in some other societies. Moreover, when possession and exorcism take place, the person who receives exorcism is often portrayed in Western media as a victim, not of Satan, but of the exorcist, who is seen as a perpetrator of evil. The possession itself is seen as a psychiatric problem. Therefore, it is important to be very cautious and ensure that there is a real case of demonic possession before attempting exorcism. In this process, the church should use experienced counsellors or exorcists[19] as well as psychological and psychiatric expertise to avoid demonic activity being misdiagnosed as mental illness or mental illness as demon possession. The *Consultation Statement* says in this regard:

> The emerging understanding of the complexity of the human person needs significant exploration and examination. Specifically, we call for: A) A sustained dialogue between those engaged in deliverance ministries and those in the medical and psychological professions. B) Urgent sharing worldwide with deliverance practitioners of the current state of knowledge of Dissociative Identity Disorder (DID, formerly called Multiple Personality Disorder). C. A diagnostic approach that allows practitioners to discern the difference between DID "personalities" and spiritual entities, and D) A dialogue between theologians and the medical and psychological professions that develops a

[18] Moreau (ed), *Deliver Us From Evil*, p. xxv.
[19] The Roman Catholic Church has a priest with the office of an exorcist in each diocese.

holistic understanding of the human person, inseparably relating body, mind, emotions and spirit as they function individually and relationally.[20]

In some cultures, especially in the West, being possessed or exposed to exorcism can lead to a significant social stigma that can cause great trauma for the person in question, while in other cultures possession is widely known and culturally and religiously accepted. The deliverance ministry may then be seen only in positive terms as setting people from demonic bondage to a new life in spiritual freedom. The latter is more often the case in the Global South. These differences are important with regard to how the ministry of deliverance is performed, for example whether it is done openly or confidentially.[21]

When it is ascertained that the problem is evil spirits, the first need is deliverance. Demons may be dealt with in a variety of ways: for example, casting them out in the name of Jesus; overcoming them through declaring the power of Jesus' blood and cross; praying for inner healing or cleansing; participating in the sacraments; hearing God's Word; receiving the ministry of a loving and healing community; participating in praise and worship. Deliverance needs to be followed up with teaching and personal pastoral care.

One charismatic Lutheran congregation that takes this ministry seriously has a pastor on staff who has a ministry of deliverance, and along with it a complementary ministry of counselling and pastoral care. As a result, many who are oppressed by demons, or wonder whether they are the target of demonic assault, seek and receive ministry. Several gifts of the Spirit may function in this kind of ministry: discernment of spirits, prophecy, word of knowledge, word of wisdom, healings, speaking in tongues, interpretation of tongues as well as gifts of deliverance.

Scripture warns us that the devil will attack us. We are told to *resist him* firm in faith (1 Pet. 5:8-9; James 4:7), to do battle with him (Eph. 4:27; 6:10-18), to *overcome him* by the blood of the Lamb and the word of our testimony, unmoved even by the threat of death (Rev. 12:10-11). Jesus

---

[20] Moreau (ed), *Deliver Us From Evil*, p. xxvii. The Afro-American psychiatrist Jerry Mungadze, who also has a deliverance ministry, emphasised in his paper at the consultation the importance of distinguishing between mental illness, especially DID which is commonly mistaken for possession, and real spirit possession. This requires knowledge of psychiatry as well as the characteristic marks of demonic possession. He says that the "sagest approach is first to rule out mental illness or psychological problems before assuming that there is a spiritual conflict." Jerry Mungadze, "Spiritual conflict in light of psychology and medicine", in Moreau (ed), *Deliver Us from Evil*, p. 205.

[21] Mungadze says wisely, "A comprehensive understanding of people and the cultures they live in can only enhance whatever type of ministry or secular work one does. The church should be no exception. It needs to develop an awareness of people and their different worlds, "Spiritual conflict in light of psychology and medicine", in Moreau (ed), *Deliver Us From Evil*, p. 210.

promised us that the Spirit that dwells in us is stronger than the spirit that is loose in the world (1 Jn 4:4). That should give us courage and hope.

(60) The Church: A Fellowship of Hope

In one of the oldest artistic representations of Jesus Christ, in the mausoleum of *Galla Placidia in Ravenna*, Christ is portrayed as a Roman general. His symbol of victory is the cross.

The Holy Spirit's revelation of Christ is a revelation of victory, of triumph over the powers of darkness and the kingdom of this world. It is based on the concrete fact of Christ's victory over Satan in the atonement. It is being worked out in the world today through the Holy Spirit, moving toward the final triumph at Christ's second coming.

The church under the cross is a victorious church. It has a Lord who is crucified and risen. As we are committed to following after the cross, we are also committed to follow after the resurrection. The two are inextricably linked. The mystery of this linking is not a contrivance of theology, but a reality of discipleship.

In many quarters of the church, the message of hope is missing. The world over, many pastors and leaders communicate a message not of hope, but of discouragement and resignation. This is not New Testament faith. The church under Christ is not to give way to despair. It is called by the Spirit to a life of victorious hope, undeterred by present circumstances.

In the midst of an anxiety-ridden world, the Holy Spirit is today calling men and women to a living hope:

> In his great mercy, he [God the Father] has given us a new birth into a *living hope* through the resurrection of Jesus Christ from the dead, and into an *inheritance* that can never perish, spoil or fade – kept in heaven for you, who through faith are *shielded by God's power* until the coming of the *salvation* that is ready to be revealed in the last time (1 Pet. 1:3-5).

People who have been mired down in discouragement are giving testimony to this hope. Believers who have fallen into the habit of seeing themselves as losers, are, in the power of the Holy Spirit, laying hold on the promises of the overcomer (1 Jn 5:4). Negative attitudes are giving place to positive faith, insecurity to confidence, and a defensive mentality to the assertion of Christ's victory, even in the midst of sorrow and seeming defeat.

Earl Kuester, a Baptist pastor in Gardena, California, USA, began a healing ministry in his congregation, together with his wife. It brought great blessing to the congregation and to the surrounding community, but when his wife died of cancer, people feared that it would be the end of the healing ministry. The next Sunday night, however, he was at the altar of his church, praying for the sick. "My hope is in Christ," he said simply. This is hope that goes far beyond a new set of mental attitudes or a series of experiences. It is the fruit of faithful discipleship to the crucified and risen Lord, lived out in the power of the Holy Spirit.

The New Testament Concept of Hope

In the New Testament, hope is a term for Christians' ultimate expectation. Few things were as characteristic of the early church as its dynamic anticipation of the world to come. In the centre of Jesus' preaching was the kingdom of God, the fulfillment of which is still being awaited, but which was already beginning to break through in Jesus' words and deeds. Jesus spoke about the kingdom of God in the Beatitudes (Mt. 5:3-12) and in the Lord's prayer (Mt. 6:9-13). The German New Testament scholar Leonhard Goppelt wrote:

> The kingdom of God brings the comfort that eases all suffering, and the satisfaction that eases all hunger. […] Consequently, the kingdom of God includes physical and spiritual healing; in the end, a new world, without want and suffering, a world of peace and justice […].
>
> How does this new thing come about? The kingdom comes through a work of God in humanity […] Consequently, the coming of the kingdom centres in God, and his personal intervention to establish the kingdom […].
>
> The first three petitions [of the Lord's Prayer] are interdependent: God's kingdom will come when God is recognised as God and his gracious will is done. Again, the focus is on God, the orientation strongly theocentric.[1]

The early church awaited the eventual coming of God's kingdom, when Jesus would come again in glory as the Son of man. His second coming (Greek: *parousia)* does not mean his mere return, but rather his coming in majesty and power. The Aramaic-speaking early church prayed for the coming of Jesus as the final fulfilment of God's plan of salvation: "Marana tha – our Lord, come!" (1 Cor. 16:22). This expectation finds expression even in the latest of the New Testament writings:

> Behold, I am coming soon! My reward is with me, and I will give to everyone according to what he has done. I am the Alpha and the Omega, the First and the Last, the Beginning and the End. Blessed are those who wash their robes, that they may have the right to the tree of life and may go through the gates into the city (Rev. 22:12-14, cp. Rev. 7:13-17; 21:1-7; 22:20).

---

[1] Goppelt, *Theologie des Neuen Testaments*, p. 119. (Excerpt translated by William Sims.)

A Hope that Must Be Kept Alive

The church did not always preserve this hope. This failure is often explained by saying that the urgent expectation of Christ's return was a part of the old, apocalyptic worldview, which was refuted by a more sober historical awareness. But in times of spiritual renewal in the church, the expectation of the coming of Jesus springs alive again. The Holy Spirit inflames us with Jesus' own eagerness for the kingdom of God. This desire, that God will reveal himself as God of all (cf. 1 Cor. 15:28; Phil. 2:9-11) is not limited to an apocalyptic worldview.

The Charismatic renewal as a whole has not lined up behind any particular eschatological view in regard to Christ's second coming. The focus is on the kingdom as such, not the events that may attend its coming. You frequently hear the assertion that we are living in the last days, but this is a call to discipleship, not a preamble to a Bible study on prophecy. Christian hope looks beyond the birth pangs of the kingdom to its glory, righteousness, and final victory.

The church is called to proclaim this joyful and glorious hope (Heb. 10:23; 1 Pet. 3:15). All Christians are called to keep this hope in view so that they will not forget what they are called to be, and do, and become. The history of the church confirms the truth spoken by the Lord in Matthew 24:48-51, that if the church forgets its hope, then it also neglects its holiness and its service. And Scripture warns us that in so doing, we not only forget our inheritance, we stand in danger of losing it.

Hope and Holiness

Hope reminds the church of holiness. We belong to the Lord and not to ourselves (Rom. 14:7-8). We are not in this world for our own sake, but for the Lord's sake. We are a holy priesthood, elected and dedicated to serve God and declare his mighty works of salvation to the world (1 Pet. 2:9). It is this hope that helps Christians to live and serve in holiness *in this world without becoming like this world*, as Jesus prayed for them:

> My prayer is not that you take them out of the world but that you protect them from the evil one. They are not of the world, even as I am not of it. Sanctify them by the truth; your word is truth. As you sent me into the world, I have sent them into the world. For them I sanctify myself, that they too may be truly sanctified (Jn 17:15-19).

Christians are called to be conformed to Christ (2 Cor. 3:18) and live lives in fellowship with his death and resurrection looking forward to their own resurrection from the dead (Phil. 3:10). The expectation of the *parousia* is a strong impulse toward holy living. "We know that when he appears we shall be like him, for we shall see him as he is. Everyone who has this hope purifies himself, just as he is pure" (1 Jn 3:2-3, cp. 2 Cor. 7:1).

Hope, Mission and Service

Hope reminds the church of its mission and service. It is sent by Christ as a people who are instruments of God's love, salvation and care for the world (Jn 3:16; 20:21). The hope of the return of Christ at the end of the age is a strong motivation for mission:

> He who stands firm to the end will be saved. And the gospel of the kingdom will be preached in the whole world as a testimony to all nations, and *then the end will come* (Mt. 24:14).
>
> All authority in heaven and on earth has been given me. Therefore go and *make disciples of all nations*, baptising them in the name of the Father and the Son and the Holy Spirit, and teaching them to obey everything I have commanded you. And surely, *I am with you always, to the very end of the age* (Mt. 28:18-20; cp. Mk 16:15).

Although neglect of the hope of Christ's return has been a common flaw in the history of the church, speculations as to the exact time of his return – often caused by false prophecies – have also been frequent. When the disciples asked Jesus about the time of the coming of the kingdom, his answer is important for the church at all times:

> It is not for you to know the times or dates the Father has set by his own authority. But you will receive power when the Holy Spirit comes on you: and you will be my witnesses in Jerusalem, and in all Judea and Samaria, and to the ends of the earth (Acts 1:6-8, cp. Mt. 24:36; 1 Thess. 5:1-3).

Mission to the ends of the earth is the main task of the church between the first and second coming of Christ. When the missionary task is finished, the end will come. When people ask why the second coming has not yet occurred, we should bear in mind that "with the Lord a day is like a thousand years, and a thousand years are like a day" (2 Pet. 3:8). God's timing is different from ours. The reason why Christ has not yet come, is not that he is slow in keeping his promises, but he is patient because he does not want "anyone to perish, but everyone to come to repentance" (2 Pet. 3:9). The mission of God has not yet been completed.

Since we do not know the exact time of his coming, it is our calling to use our spiritual gifts (1 Cor. 1:7) and faithfully serve the Lord while we are waiting for his return (Mt. 24:45). The Bible urges us to be prepared and ready for the coming of Christ at any time (Mt. 24:42-44; 25:1-13; 1 Thess. 5:4-11).

Some Christians have in anticipation of Christ's imminent return neglected their duties as Christians and stewards of God's creation, and passively waited for his coming. Some have also taken the word about the destruction of the present world and the creation of "a new heaven and a new earth, the home of righteousness" (2 Pet. 3:10-13: Rev. 21:1-5), to mean that we may neglect the present creation and only be concerned about "saving souls for eternity". This is, however, a serious misunderstanding. God's command to human beings to "work and take care of" his creation as his stewards (Gen. 2:14, "the cultural commission") has not been revoked.

A comparison may be helpful: although we know that our perishable body will die and be transformed into a spiritual body (1 Cor. 15:42-44), we still take care of and try to heal both our own mortal body and the bodies of others. And although we know that our present families and the societies in which we live will be dissolved and disappear, we still want to protect and serve them as long and well as we can. In the same way, we are also called to protect, take care of and heal the whole created world – with its animals, plants and other resources – and be good stewards who use it responsibly.

It is said that Luther's answer to the question, "What would you do if you knew that the Lord would come back tomorrow?" was "I would plant my apple tree today!" The point is, of course, that we should go on with our duties as usual, at the same time as we are prepared and ready for his coming. Luther's answer has become relevant also in a new way since planting of trees and other measures to protect and restore nature are a high priority in our time. Ignorance, carelessness, and greed threaten to destroy God's creation and thereby also the world of human beings. The love that God pours out in our hearts by the Holy Spirit (Rom. 5:5) should also include the created world. The evangelical *Cape Town Commitment* says:

> We love the world of God's creation. This love […] is the logical outworking of our love for God by caring for what belongs to him […] Such love for God's creation demands that we repent of our part in the destruction, waste and pollution of the earth's resources and our collusion in the toxic idolatry of consumerism. Instead, we commit ourselves to urgent and prophetic ecological responsibility […] The gospel is God's good news, through the cross and resurrection of Jesus Christ, for individual persons, and for society, and for creation. All three are broken and suffering because of sin: all three are included in the redeeming love and mission of God; all three must be part of the comprehensive mission of God's people.[2]

When the hope of the coming of Christ and his kingdom in power has been obscured – and that has happened all too often – the church has not lived, loved, witnessed, served, and suffered, in anticipation of the return of Christ. On the contrary, it has often resigned itself to an existence in this world,

[2] *The Cape Town Commitment*, pp. 19-20.

sought to make its home in it, been influenced by it and entered into alliances with it. It has lost its *identity as a pilgrim people on the way to its future home.*

Until the last moment of the present age, the hope of the return of Christ will remind the church of the mission and service that the Lord sets before us. Have we been faithful stewards of God's grace (1 Pet. 4:10-11), of the talents God has given each of us (Mt. 25:14-30)? We will be called to give account of the grace that God has given us and the time in which to work, and to demonstrate that we did not, like the unfaithful steward, bury our talents.

Some Fresh Impetus to Eschatological Hope in the Charismatic Renewal

What kind of practical experience in the Charismatic renewal has given fresh impetus to the eschatological hope? We recognise such things as these:

- Through a living, Spirit-led involvement with the *Word of God*, people's lives are established more on the basis of the *promises of Scripture* than on the basis merely of human feelings and ideas.
- Through the *indwelling of the Spirit*, healings of illness and other infirmities, deliverance from evil, and various manifestations by the Spirit of the love and power of God, Christians are given a *guarantee and foretaste of the coming kingdom that give hope* (Gal. 3:5; 2 Cor. 1:1:22; 5:5; Eph. 1:14).
- The *spiritual gift* of encouragement or admonition (Rom. 12:8) comes to greater expression in a Spirit-equipped congregation. Persons in need, maybe teetering on the brink of despair, are caught hold of by fellow Christians and receive help and *hope through counselling and intercession.*
- The fundamental *confession* that "Jesus is Lord" is particularly granted by the Holy Spirit in the context of spiritual conflict, for example, in pastoral counselling. Jesus shares his victory concretely with those who stand firm in discipleship, believing the promise that *God will make them overcomers* (1 Cor. 12:3; 1 Jn 4:1-4; Rom. 16:20; 12:21).
- Consistent, Spirit-prompted *praise and worship* of God teach one to focus attention more on the character and acts of God and less on one's own strengths or weaknesses. In personal and corporate life, this brings *encouragement, comfort and hope* (Heb. 12:2-3; Rom. 15:4-6; 2 Cor. 1:3-5).

Hope and Inheritance

Hope reminds the church of its *inheritance*. We are called to share in the glory of Christ and the victory of the kingdom of God. We look to the future, when that hope will be fully revealed. We shall reign together with Christ, as the Father has promised. That is our glorious hope.

But the Father has also called us to already living out of our inheritance; already demonstrating the life of the kingdom, already manifesting the powers of the age to come, already discipling all the nations unto Jesus. That is our humanly impossible, yet divinely possible, calling.

If we stood alone in the light of that glorious hope, faced with that calling, we could only despair. But we hear again the words of the Lord, "I am going to send you what my Father has promised" (Lk. 24:49). "You will receive power when the Holy Spirit comes on you" (Acts 1:8)

And we are given the grace to say, "Welcome, Holy Spirit!"

Appendix: Participants in the International Lutheran Charismatic Theological Consultation that Produced the First Edition in 1987

Austria:
Gerhard Grosse
Denmark:
Jan Bjerregaard
Svend Boysen
Ole Skjerbæk Madsen
Per Mollerup
Federal Republic of Germany:
Lorenz Hein
Gerhard Kelber
Wolfram Kopfermann
German Democratic Republic (DDR, The former East-Germany)
Gottfried Rebner
Paul Toaspern
Finland:
Kirsti Löytty
Seppo Löytty
Gunnar Weckström
Norway:
Tormod Engelsviken
Jens-Petter Jørgensen
Johan Østerhus
Asbjørn Simonnes
Pakistan:
Ame Rudvin
Geir Valle
Sweden:
Fredrik Brosché
Per Eckerdal
Helge Fosseus
Bengt Holmberg
Per-Olof Söderpalm
Carl Gustav Stenbäck
United States of America:
Larry Christenson
Theodore Jungkuntz

Herbert Mirly
W. Dennis Pederson
Morris Vaagenes
Arthur Vincent

Background and Ministry of the Participants in the Consultation[1]

Jan Bjerregaard, cand. theol., *University of Copenhagen*; parish pastor in Hjerring, Denmark; member of the *Charismatic Lutheran Pastors' Committee* in western Denmark.

Svend Boysen, parish pastor in Jutland, Denmark; co-ordinator of *Dialogue and Renewal*, an international mission headquartered in Aarhus, Denmark; author and publisher of books on Charismatic renewal.

Fredrik Brosché, doctor of theology from *Uppsala University*, Sweden, with a dissertation on *Luther and Predestination*; docent of theology at the *University of Uppsala*; chaplain in the *Diocese of Gothenburg*.

Larry Christenson, parish pastor of *Trinity Lutheran Church* (ALC) in San Pedro, California, USA, for 22 years; on the pastoral staff of *North Heights Lutheran Church*, St. Paul, Minnesota; director of the *International Lutheran Renewal Center;* author of *The Charismatic Renewal Among Lutherans* (1976), *Speaking in Tongues* (1968), and other books and articles on spiritual renewal; worldwide teaching and preaching ministry promoting the Charismatic renewal; editor of *Welcome, Holy Spirit;* recognised as the leading spokesman for the worldwide Lutheran charismatic renewal for many years.

Per Eckerdal, parish pastor in the *Diocese of Gothenburg*, Sweden.

Tormod Engelsviken, professor emeritus; Ph.D. from *Aquinas Institute of Theology* in Dubuque, Iowa, USA with the dissertation, *The Gift of the Spirit: An Analysis and Evaluation of the Charismatic Renewal from a Lutheran Theological Perspective* (1981); teacher at *Mekane Yesus Theological Seminary* in Addis Ababa, Ethiopia; teacher at *Fjellhaug University College*, Oslo, Norway; professor of mission studies at *MF – School of Theology, Religion and Society*, Oslo; visiting professor at *Central University for Nationalities* (*Minda*) in Beijing, China; professor II at *NLA University College, Gimlekollen*, Kristiansand, Norway; member/ chairman of the leadership group of the *Oasis Renewal Movement* in Norway; member of the *Theology Working Group* of the international *Lausanne Committee;* member/chair of the *Norwegian*

[1] The information given by the participants was updated in 1987. The information on Tormod Engelsviken, Jens-Petter Jørgensen, Trond Løberg and Asbjørn Simonnes was updated in 2022. It should also be noted that some of the participants have passed on to be with the Lord during the intervening 35 years. Larry Christenson died in 2017.

Lausanne Committee; moderator of the *Church of Norway Council on Ecumenical and International Relations;* member of the *Commission on World mission and Evangelism* of the *World Council of Churches;* editor of *Norwegian Journal of Missiology;* teaching and research in the Nordic countries, USA, Ethiopia, Malaysia and China; author of books and articles on biblical interpretation, mission, spiritual conflict, ethics and the Pentecostal/Charismatic renewal.

Helge Fosseus, Lutheran missionary and bishop in *southern Africa,* during the 1970s; after retirement, co-ordinator of charismatic conferences in *Stockholm*, Sweden.

Gerhard Grosse, parish pastor in *Peggau*, Austria.

Lorenz Hein, doctor of theology in church history; parish pastor in *Oldenburg, Holstein;* professor of church history at the *University of Kiel*, Germany; author of theological articles.

Bengt Holmberg, doctor of theology from *Lund University*, Sweden, with an interdisciplinary (exegesis/sociology) dissertation, *Paul and Power*, 1978; teacher at the *Lutheran Theological College at Makumira*, Tanzania; assistant to the bishop for continuing education of church workers in the *Diocese of Gothenburg*, Sweden; docent in New Testament Exegesis at the *University of Lund.*

Jens-Petter Jørgensen, assistant professor emeritus at *Ansgar School of Theology in Kristiansand*, Norway, co-founder and executive director of the *Oasis Renewal Movement,* Norway; staff member of *Inter – Varsity Fellowship, Norway*; teacher at *Norwegian Home Mission Bible College* in Oslo, pastor at *Lørenskog Evangelical Lutheran Free Church.* Preaching, teaching and counselling ministry to churches and pastors in the Scandinavian countries and Greenland; author of books on Christian growth and ministry, including *Mulighetenes Gud* (The God of Possibilities, 1986) and *Sterk nok til å være svak* (Strong Enough to be Weak, 1999).

Theodore Jungkuntz, doctor of theology from *Erlangen University*, Germany, with a dissertation dealing with the Lutheran church orders of the 16th century; professor of theology at *Valparaiso University* in Indiana, USA; pastor of *Cross and Resurrection Lutheran Church*, a congregation associated with the *Word of God* ecumenical community in *Ann Arbor*, Michigan.

Gerhard Kelber, parish pastor in *Schweinfurt*, Germany; member of the co-ordination committee for *Charismatic Congregational Renewal in the Protestant churches of West Germany*.

Wolfram Kopfermann, parish pastor in *Hamburg,* Germany; chairman of the co-ordination committee for *Charismatic Congregational Renewal in the Protestant Churches of West Germany.*

Kirsti Löytty, master of theology, Finland; missionary in Namibia; teacher at the *Lutheran Theological College* at Makumira, Tanzania.

Seppo Löytty, doctor of theology from *Helsinki University*, Finland; missionary in Namibia as teacher in theology; Dean of the *Cathedral in Mikkeli*, Finland; chairman of the *Working Committee of Spiritual Renewal* within the *Lutheran Church in Finland*; teacher of systematic theology in the *Lutheran Theological College* at Makumira, Tanzania.

Ole Skjerbæk Madsen, parish pastor at *Bethlehemskirken*, Copenhagen; member of the steering committee for the Danish branch of the *Fellowship of St. Alban and St. Sergius*; member of *Charismatic Service Committee* for eastern Denmark; author of a research project on eucharistic prayer in the *Coptic Orthodox church* and of several articles on spiritual renewal with special attention to liturgical questions

Herbert Mirly, senior pastor of *Resurrection Lutheran Church* (LCMS), *Charlotte*, North Carolina, USA; leader of seminars and counselling ministry for pastors and their families.

Per Mollerup, parish pastor in *Böslunde*, Denmark.

W. Dennis Pederson, doctor of ministry from the *Jesuit School of Theology* in Berkeley, California, USA; administrative assistant to the governor of Minnesota; chairman of the *Parish Renewal Council*, a confederation of Protestant groups working for parish renewal in the United States; on the pastoral staff of *North Heights Lutheran Church*, St. Paul, Minnesota, and co-ordinator of international ministries for the *International Lutheran Renewal Center.*

Gottfried Rebner, parish pastor in Lauter, Germany; chairman of the *Committee for Spiritual Congregational Renewal* in the Lutheran Church in the German Democratic Republic (DDR); member of the steering committee of the *Volksmissionskreis in Saxony.*

Arne Rudvin, Norwegian missionary to Pakistan, bishop of the *Karachi diocese* in *the United Church of Pakistan.*

Asbjørn Simonnes, professor emeritus at *Volda University College;* D. Min. and Ph.D. from *Fuller Theological Seminary*, California, USA, with the D. Min. dissertation *Features of the Charismatic Movement from a Historical, Sociological and Anthropological Perspective*, 1996; member/chairman/director of the leadership group of the *Oasis Renewal Movement, Norway*, co-ordinator of a number of renewal events in Norway and Scandinavia; ordained pastor in the Church of Norway; preaching, teaching and counselling ministry in Norway and India; author of books and articles on the Charismatic renewal.

Per-Olof Söderpalm, parish pastor in *Gothenburg*, Sweden; assistant to the bishop in the *Diocese of Gothenburg*.

Carl Gustaf Stenbäck, parish pastor in *St. Lundby,* Sweden: missionary to Malaysia; leader of the *Reference Group for Spiritual Renewal* within the *Church of Sweden* and the equivalent group in the *Diocese of Gothenburg;* author of training manuals for evangelism.

Paul Toaspern, doctor of theology, parish pastor; *Hauptabteilungsleiter im Diakonischen Werk der Evangelischen Kirchen* in the German Democratic Republic (DDR); *Geschäftsführer der "Arbeitsgemeinschaft Missionarische Dienste"* in the DDR; author of numerous books and articles on devotional life and spiritual renewal.

Morris Vaagenes, doctor of ministry from *Luther Northwestern Theological Seminary* in St. Paul, Minnesota, USA; studies in anthropology at the *University of Minnesota* and in French civilisation at the *Sorbonne University,* Paris; senior pastor at *North Heights Lutheran Church* (ALC), St. Paul, Minnesota.

Geir Valle, evangelist and District Superintendent of *Mardan Deanery, Peshawar Diocese, Church of Pakistan*; missionary from the *Norwegian Missionary Society.*

Arthur Vincent, doctor of ministry from *Eden Seminary*, St. Louis, Missouri, USA; professor of practical theology at *Concordia Seminary* and *Christ Seminary (Seminex)*, St. Louis, Missouri; founder/director of *Advancing Renewal Ministries*.

Gunnar Weckström, parish pastor in the *Lutheran Church in Finland.*

Johan Østerhus, parish pastor at *Strømsø church* in Drammen, Norway; university chaplain for *Inter-Varsity Fellowship* in Norway; committee member for the *Oasis Summer Conference* in Norway.

In addition to the 31 participants in the consultation, nine other people contributed material, or read the manuscript at different stages of development, and offered helpful suggestions.

Advisory Group for the New, Revised, Updated and Expanded Edition

Jan Gossner, senior pastor emeritus; co-founder of the *Oasis Renewal Movement, Norway;* student pastor in *Inter-Varsity Fellowship, Norway;* parish pastor in *Halden;* principal of the *Norwegian Deaconal College* in Oslo; senior pastor in the *Lutheran Free Church* in Kristiansand; principal of the *Evangelical Lutheran College in Staffeldtsgate,* Oslo (now NLA Oslo); board member of the *Norwegian Mission to the Santals* (now *Normisjon*) and the *Norwegian Lausanne Committee;* president of the *Stefanus Alliance, Norway*. Preaching, teaching and counselling ministry to churches and missionaries in Norway, India, Bangladesh, Nepal, Ecuador, Madagascar, Myanmar and Mali.

Jens-Petter Jørgensen (see information above).

Trond Løberg, senior pastor in a Church of Norway Lutheran congregation in *Oslo, Norway*, and vice chairman of the *Oasis Renewal Movement, Norway*: senior pastor of *Storsalen Congregation* in Oslo, chairman of the Oasis Movement, board member of the *Stefanus Alliance Norway* and the *Sandom Foundation*. Preaching, teaching, counselling and music ministry in Lutheran Churches and renewal movements in Norway, Sweden and India.

Asbjørn Simonnes (see information above).

Abbreviations

A. Luther's Works

AE = *Luther's Works*. 55 vols., Jaroslav Pelikan and Helmut T. Lehmann, general editors. St. Louis: Concordia Publishing House; Philadelphia: Fortress Press, 1955-1986. Example: Vol. 12, p. 92 would be cited as AE 12, 92.

WA = *D. Martin Luthers Werke. Kritische Gesamtausgabe*. 61 vols. Weimar, 1883ff. Example: vol. 18, p. 606 would be cited as WA 18, 606.

WABr = *D. Martin Luthers Werke. Briefwechsel.* 18 vols. Weimar, 1930-

WADB = *D. Martin Luthers Werke. Deutsche Bibel*. 12 vols. Weimar, 1906-1961.

WATr = *D. Martin Luthers Werke. Tischreden*. 6 vols. Weimar, 1912-1921.

B. Lutheran Confessional Documents

CA = *The Augsburg Confession*
Apol. = *Apology of the Augsburg Confession*
SA = *Smalcald Articles*
Treatise = *Treatise on the Power and Primacy of the Pope*
SC = *Small Catechism*
LC = *Large Catechism*
FC = *Formula of Concord*
FCEpit. = Epitome of the *Formula of Concord*
FC SD = Solid Declaration of the *Formula of Concord*

Roman numerals refer to the major sections of a document. Where paragraph and page numbers are cited, they refer to the "Tappert Edition": *The Book of Concord*, translated and edited by Theodore G. Tappert (Philadelphia: Fortress Press, 1959). Example: the Solid Declaration of the *Formula of Concord*, section XI, paragraph 76, pp. 628-629 would be cited as FC SD XI, 76, pp. 628-629.

Bibliography

Aalen, Leiv. *Testimonium Spiritus Sancti Internum som teologisk prinsipp* (The Inner Testimony of the Holy Spirit as Theological Principle). Oslo: Lutherstiftelsens forlag, 1938.

Aarflot, Andreas. *Tro og lydighet. Hans Nielsen Hauges kristendomsforståelse* (Faith and Obedience. Hans Nielsen Hauge's Understanding of Christianity). Oslo: Universitetsforlaget, 1969.

Adrianasolo, Jaona and Yvonne Randrianmanantena. "The Prophet Nenilava and the Development of the Ankaramalaza Revival Movement", in Cynthia Holder Rich, Ed. *The Fifohazana: Madagascar's Indigenous Christian Movement.* Amherst, NY: Cambria Press, 2008.

Altaner, Berthold. *Patrologie.* Freiburg im Breisgau: Herder, 1955.

Althaus, Paul. *The Theology of Martin Luther*, trans. Robert C. Shultz. Philadelphia, PA: Fortress Press, 1966.

The American Lutheran Church. "Order of Confirmation", in *Service Book and Hymnal.* Minneapolis, MN: Augsburg, 1958.

Anderson, Paul. "Finding the Balance in Worship", *Loaves and Fishes*, No. 183. San Pedro, CA: Trinity Lutheran Church, 1983.

Anderson, Paul. "The Nature of Grace", *Loaves and Fishes*, No. 153. San Pedro, CA: Trinity Lutheran Church, 1982.

Antola, Markku. *The Experience of Christ's Real Presence in Faith: An Analysis of the Christ-Presence Motif in the Lutheran Charismatic Renewal.* Helsinki: Luther Agricola seura, 1998.

Arén, Gustav. *Evangelical Pioneers in Ethiopia.* Stockholm: EFS-förlaget, 1978.

Arles, Siga. "India: Religious Polarisation in a Hindu Context", in Hans Aage Gravaas *et al.,* Eds. *Freedom of Belief and Christian Mission.* Oxford: Regnum, 2015.

Arndt, William F. and Wilbur Gingrich. *A Greek-English Lexicon of the New Testament and Other Early Christian Literature.* Chicago, IL: University of Chicago Press, 1957.

Austnaberg, Hans. *Shepherds and Demons: A Study of Exorcism as Practiced and Understood by Shepherds in the Malagasy Lutheran Church.* New York: Peter Lang, 2008.

Barrett, David. "Annual Statistical Table on Global Mission", *International Bulletin of Missionary Research* 10(1), (January 1986): 22-23.

Bartsch, Hans Werner, Ed. *Kerygma and Myth.* London: SPCK, 1953.

Bays, Daniel. "Marie Monsen", in Gerald H. Anderson, Ed. *Biographical Dictionary of Christian Mission.* New York: Macmillan Reference USA, 1998.

Becker, Ernest. *The Denial of Death.* New York: Free Press, 1973.

Bennett, Dennis. *Nine O'Clock in the Morning.* Newberry, FL: Bridge Publishing, 1970.

Benz, Ernst, Ed. *Die Vision: Erfahrungsformen und Bilderwelt.* Stuttgart: Ernst Klett, 1969.

Betz, Hans Dieter. *Galatians*. Philadelphia, PA: Fortress Press, 1979.

Bittlinger, Arnold, Ed. *The Church is Charismatic: The World Council of Churches and the Charismatic Movement.* Geneva: World Council of Churches, 1981.

Bittlinger, Arnold. "Der Oekumenische Rat der Kirchen und die Charismatische Gemeinde-Erneuerung", *Erneuerung in Kirche und Gesellschaft, ökumenische Zeitschrift*, 7, (1980).

—. *Epistle of Joy.* Minneapolis, MN: Bethany Fellowship, 1975.

—. *Gifts and Ministries.* Grand Rapids, MI: Eerdmans, 1970.

—. *Gifts and Graces.* Grand Rapids, MI: Eerdmans, 1968.

Bloesch, Donald G. *The Battle for the Trinity: The Debate over Inclusive God Language.* Ann Arbor, MI: Servant, 1985.

Blumhardt, Johann Christoph. *Seelsorge.* Munich and Hamburg: Siebenstern, 1949.

Bosch, David. *Transforming Mission: Paradigm Shifts in Theology of Mission.* Maryknoll, NY: Orbis, 1991.

Bouley, Allan. *From Freedom to Formula: The Evolution of the Eucharistic Prayer from Oral Improvisation to Written Texts.* Washington D.C.: Catholic University of America Press, 1981.

Bouyer, Louis. *Eucharist: Theology and Spirituality of the Eucharistic Prayer.* Notre Dame, IN: University of Notre Dame Press, 1968.

Bright, John. *The Kingdom of God.* Nashville, TN: Abingdon, 1953.

Brown, Dale W. *Understanding Pietism.* Grand Rapids, MI: Eerdmans, 1978.

Brown, William and Asbjørn Simonnes. "Hans Nielsen Hauge (1771-1824): Offering a Prescription for Social Change", in R.H. Wood and N.K. Wood, Eds. *In Words and Witnesses: Communication Studies in Christian Thought from Athanasius to Desmond Tutu.* Peabody, MA: Hendrickson Publishers, 2018.

Bruner, Frederick D. *A Theology of the Holy Spirit.* Grand Rapids, MI: Eerdmans, 1971.

Bruner, Frederick D. and William Hordern. *The Holy Spirit – Shy Member of the Trinity.* Minneapolis, MN: Augsburg, 1984.

Brunner, Emil. *Dogmatik III: Die christliche Lehre von der Kirche, vom Glauben und von der Vollendung.* Zürich: Theologischer Verlag Zürich, 1960.

—. *The Misunderstanding of the Church*, trans. Harold Knight. London: Lutterworth, 1952.

Bultmann, Rudolf. *Jesus Christ and Mythology.* New York: Charles Scribner's Sons, 1958.

Burgess, Stanley and Eduard M. van der Maas, Eds. *The New International Dictionary of Pentecostal and Charismatic Movements*, revised and expanded edition. Grand Rapids, MI: Zondervan, 2010.

Burrows, Robert J.L. "Americans Get Religion in the New Age", *Christianity Today*, 16th May 1986.

Calvin, John. *Commentary on the Epistle of Paul the Apostle to the Romans*, translated and edited by John Owen. Grand Rapids, MI: Eerdmans, 1955.

Von Campenhausen, Hans. *Ecclesiastical Authority and Spiritual Power in the Church of The First Three Centuries*, trans. J.A. Baker. Stanford, CA: Stanford University Press, 1969.

Carothers, Merlin. *Prison to Praise.* Plainfield, NJ: Logos, 1969.

The Catholic Catechism, Second Edition. Citta del Vaticano: Libreria Editrice Vaticana, 2019.

Christenson, Larry. "Receiving the Holy Spirit", *Practical Christianity.* Wheaton, IL: Tyndale, 1987.

Christenson, Larry, Ed. *Welcome Holy Spirit: A Study of Charismatic Renewal in the Church,* Minneapolis, MN: Augsburg, 1987.

——. *What About Baptism*? Minneapolis, MN: Augsburg, 1986.

——. *The Charismatic Renewal Among Lutherans.* Minneapolis, MN: International Lutheran Renewal Center, 1976, rev. ed., 1985.

——. "God is Speaking – Are You Listening?" *International Lutheran Renewal*, No. 49, December 1983.

——. *Back to Square One*. Minneapolis, MN: Bethany Fellowship, 1979.

——. "Pentecostalism's Forgotten Forerunner", in Vinson Synan, Ed. *Aspects of Pentecostal-Charismatic Origins.* Plainfield, NJ: Logos, 1975.

——. "The Holy Spirit in the Charismatic Life and Renewal of the Church Today in Evangelization Report", in J. D. Douglas, Ed. *Let the Earth Hear His Voice.* Minneapolis, MN: World Wide Publications, 1975.

——. *The Renewed Mind.* Minneapolis, MN: Bethany Fellowship, 1974.

——. "The Pastoral Ministry in Relation to the Charismatic Movement", in Walter Wietzke and Jack Hustad, Eds. *Towards a Mutual Understanding of Neo-Pentecostalism.* Minneapolis, MN: Augsburg, 1973.

——. *A Message to the Charismatic Movement.* Minneapolis, MN: Bethany Fellowship, 1972.

——. *The Christian Family*. Minneapolis, MN: Bethany Fellowship, 1970.

——. *Speaking in Tongues and Its Significance for the Church.* Minneapolis, MN: Bethany Fellowship, 1968.

——. *The Gift of Tongues*. Minneapolis, MN: Bethany Fellowship, 1963.

Christenson, Larry, Asbjørn Simonnes and Tormod Engelsviken, Eds. *Velkommen, Hellige Ånd – karismatisk fornyelse i kirken.* Ottestad: Proklamedia, 2018.

Clark, Stephen B. *Baptized in the Spirit and Spiritual Gifts*. Ann Arbor, MI: Servant, 1976.

Daunton-Fear, Andrew. *Healing in the Early Church. The Church's Ministry of Healing and Exorcism from the First to the Fifth Century.* Milton Keynes: Paternoster, 2009.

Dorman, David A. "The Purpose of Empowerment in the Christian Life", in J. Rodman Williams, Ed. *Toward a Pentecostal/Charismatic Theology of Baptism in the Holy Spirit.* Bound Volume of Papers from the Fourteenth Annual Meeting of the Society for Pentecostal Studies, 1984.

Dorpat, David. "Hindrances to Faith", *International Lutheran Renewal* 57, (August 1984).

Douglas, J.D., Ed. *Let the Earth Hear His Voice,* International Congress on World Evangelization at Lausanne, Official Reference Volume. Minneapolis, MN: World Wide Publications, 1975.

Droege, Thomas A. *Self-Realization and Faith.* Chicago, IL: Lutheran Education Society, 1978.

Dunn, James D.G. *Baptism in the Holy Spirit.* Philadelphia, PA: Westminster, 1970.

Ebeling, Gerhard. *Luther: An Introduction to His Thought*, trans. R.A. Wilson. London: Collins, 1979.

Engelsviken, Tormod. "Misjonsteologi og misjonal teologi", in Jeppe Bach Nikolajsen *et al.*, Eds. *Missiologi: En innføring* (Missiology: An Introduction). Oslo: Cappelen-Damm, 2021.

—. "Mission and Reconciliation", *International Review of Mission* 109(2), (November 2020): 163-179.

—. "Deliver Us From Evil: Evangelism, Spiritual Conflict, 'Signs and Wonders'", in Younghoon Lee and Wonsuk Ma, Eds. *Pentecostal Mission and Global Christianity.* Oxford: Regnum, 2018.

—. "Mission, Pentecostalism and Ethiopian Identity: The Beginnings Of the Mulu Wongel Believers' Church", *Norwegian Journal of Missiology* 68(4), 2014: 195-215.

—. "Missional Church: Theory and Practice and a Malaysian Case Study", in Gillian Mary Bediako *et al.*, Eds. *Seeing New Facets of the Diamond: Christianity as a Universal Faith. Essays in Honour of Kwame Bediako.* Oxford: Regnum Africa, 2014: 144-161.

—. "Spiritual Conflict: A Challenge for the Church in the West with a View to the Future", in Charles Van Engen *et al.*, Eds. *Paradigm Shifts in Christian Witness: Insights from Anthropology, Communication, and Spiritual Power. Essays in Honor of Charles H. Kraft.* Maryknoll, NY: Orbis Books, 2008.

—. "Church/Ecclesiology", in John Corrie, Ed. *Dictionary of Mission Theology: Evangelical Foundations*. Downers Grove, IL: InterVarsity Press, 2007: 51-55.

—. "Missio Dei: The Understanding and Misunderstanding of a Theological Concept in European Churches and Missiology", *International Review of Mission* 92(367), (2003).

——. *Spiritual Conflict in Today's Mission.* Lausanne Occasional Paper No. 29. Monrovia, CA: MARC, 2001.

——. "Exorcism and Healing in the Evangelical Churches in Ethiopia", *Journal of Mission Theology* 1(1), (1991).

——. *The Gift of the Spirit: An Analysis and Evaluation of the Charismatic Movement from a Lutheran Theological Perspective*, Unpublished Ph.D. dissertation, Dubuque, IA: Aquinas Institute of Theology, 1981 (available from Ann Arbor, MI: University Microfilms International). See also *Dissertation Abstracts International,* A. Humanities and Social Sciences, 43(1), (July 1982).

——. *Mulu Wongel: A Documentary Report on the Life and History of the Independent Pentecostal Movement in Ethiopia 1960-1975,* Unpublished manuscript. Oslo: The Free Faculty of Theology (now: MF-Norwegian School of Theology, Religion and Society), 1975.

Engelsviken, Tormod, Notto R. Thelle and Knut Edvard Larsen, Eds. *A Passion for China. Norwegian Mission to China until 1949.* Oxford: Regnum, 2015.

Engelsviken, Tormod, Ove Conrad Hanssen and Kjell Olav Sannes. *Den Hellige Ånd in kirkens liv* (The Holy Spirit in the Life of the Church). Oslo: Luther Forlag, 1981.

Ensley, Eddie. *Sounds of Wonder.* New York: Paulist Press, 1977.

Erdahl, Lowell. "Viewpoint", *The Lutheran Standard,* November 1983.

Eshete, Tibebe. "Marxism and Church Growth: The Paradox of Church Growth in Ethiopia 1974-1991", in Hans Aage Gravaas *et al.*, Eds. *Freedom of Belief and Christian Mission.* Oxford: Regnum, 2015.

Fagerberg, Holsten. *A New Look at the Lutheran Confessions*, trans. Gene J. Lund. St Louis, MO: Concordia, 1972.

Fee, Gordon. "Baptism in the Holy Spirit: The Issue of Separability and Sequence", in J. Rodman Williams, Ed. *Toward a Pentecostal/Charismatic Theology of Baptism in the Holy Spirit.* Bound Volume of Papers from the Fourteenth Annual Meeting of the Society for Pentecostal Studies, 1984.

Fisher, J.D.C. *Confirmation Then and Now.* London: SPCK, 1978.

Fiske, Edward. "Pentecostals Gain Among Catholics", *The New York Times*, 3rd November 1970.

Forell, George W. and James F. McCue, Eds. *Confessing One Faith: A Joint Commentary on the Augsburg Confession by Lutheran and Catholic Theologians.* Minneapolis, MN: Augsburg Publishing House, 1982.

Francke, Hermann August. *Of Useful Preaching: A Guide to the Reading and Study of the Holy Scriptures.* Philadelphia, PA: David Hogan, 1823.

Froelich, Karlfried. "Charismatic Manifestations and the Lutheran Incarnational Stance", in Paul Opsahl, Ed. *The Holy Spirit in the Life of the Church.* Minneapolis, MN: Augsburg, 1978.

Gehlhar, Philip. *"Are Charismatic Lutherans Confused in Their Theological Understanding of Salvation by Grace through Faith?"*

Summary of a Survey of Lutheran Congregations with Charismatic Pastors, Unpublished paper. Westminster, CA: St. Luke's Church, 1979.

Gerlach, Luther P. and Virginia H. Hine. *People, Power, Change – Movements of Social Transformation*, Indianapolis, IN: Bobbs-Merrill, 1970.

Gesenius. *Hebrew and Chaldee Lexicon of the Old Testament Scriptures*, trans. Samuel P. Tregelles. Grand Rapids, MI: Eerdmans, 1954.

Goheen, Michael W. *Introducing Christian Mission Today*. Downers Grove, IL: IVP Academic, 2014.

Goppelt, Leonhard. *Theologie des Neuen Testaments: Part 1: Jesu Wirken in seiner theologischen Bedeutung*. Göttingen: Vandenhoeck & Ruprecht, 1975.

Gravaas, Hans Aage, Christof Sauer, Tormod Engelsviken, Maqsood Kamil and Knud Jørgensen, Eds. *Freedom of Belief and Christian Mission*. Oxford: Regnum, 2015.

Grim, Brian. "Global Challenges and Opportunities in Religious Liberty", in Hans Aage Gravaas *et al*., Eds. *Freedom of Belief and Christian Mission*. Oxford: Regnum, 2015.

Gritsch, Eric. "Lutheranism and Born Againism", *Academy* 40(1 & 2), (1984).

Gross, Don H. *The Case for Spiritual Healing*. New York: Thomas Nelson, 1958.

Guder, Darrell. *Called to Witness: Doing Missional Theology*. Grand Rapids, MI: Eerdmans, 2015.

—, Ed. *Missional Church – A Vision for the Sending of the Church in North America*. Grand Rapids, MI: Eerdmans, 1998.

Gudstjänstordning för Svenska Kyrkan. Älvsjö: Skeab/Verbum, 1982.

Hallesby, Ole. *Prayer*. Minneapolis, MN: Augsburg, 1994 [*Fra bønnens verden*, 1927].

—. *Daglig fornyelse* (Daily Renewal). Oslo: Luther Forlag, 1979 [1932].

Hamilton, Michael P., Ed. *The Charismatic Movement*. Grand Rapids, MI: Eerdmans, 1975.

Hemingway, Ernest. *For Whom the Bell Tolls*. New York: Scribner's, 1968 [1940].

Hein, Lorenz. "Philipp Jacob Spener, ein Theologe des Heiligen Geistes und Prophet der Kirche", in Lorenz Hein, Ed. *Festgabe für Peter Meinhold*. Wiesbaden: Franz Steiner, 1977.

Hiebert, Paul G. *Missiological Implications of Epistemological Shifts: Affirming Truth in a Modern/Postmodern World*. Harrisburg, PA: Trinity Press International, 1999.

—. *Anthropological Insights for Missionaries*. Grand Rapids, MI: Baker, 1985.

—. "The Flaw of the Excluded Middle", *Missiology* X(1), (January 1982).

Hoffman, Bengt. *Luther and the Mystics*. Minneapolis, MN: Augsburg, 1976.

Hunt, Robert *et al.*, Eds. *Christianity in Malaysia: A Denominational History*. Petaling Jaya: Pelanduk, 1992.
Hunter, Harold D. *Spirit-Baptism. A Pentecostal Alternative*. Lanham, MD: University Press of America, 1983.
Hutcheson, Richard G. Jr. *Mainline Churches and the Evangelicals*. Atlanta, GA: John Knox, 1981.
Hwa Yung. *Mangoes or Bananas? The Quest for an Authentic Asian Christian Theology*. Oxford: Regnum, 1997.
Ising, Dieter. *Johann Christoph Blumhardt – Life and Work*. Eugene, OR: Cascade, 2009.
Jenkins, Philip. *The Next Christendom: The Coming of Global Christianity*. Oxford: Oxford University Press, 2002.
Jensen, Richard A. *Touched by the Spirit*. Minneapolis, MN: Augsburg, 1975.
Jeremias, Joachim. *Neutestamentliche Theologie*. Gütersloh: Gütersloher Verlagshaus Gerd Mohn, 1973.
Johnson, Ben. "The Authority of the Bible: Its World View", *Trinity Seminary Review* 2(2), n.d.
Johnson, Larry, Ed. *Institutions and Movements: Two Structures within One Church*, Unpublished paper. St. Paul, MN: Luther Northwestern Theological Seminary, n.d.
Johnson, Todd M., Gina A. Zurlo, Albert W. Hickman and Peter F. Crossing. "Christianity 2017: Five Hundred Years of Protestant Christianity", *International Bulletin of Mission Research* 41(1), (January 2017).
Johnson, Todd M, and Gina A. Zurlo, Eds. *World Christian Encyclopedia*, Third Edition, Edinburgh: Edinburgh University Press, 2020.
Jorstad, Erling. *Bold in the Spirit*. Minneapolis, MN: Augsburg, 1974.
Jung, C.G. *Modern Man in Search of a Soul*. New York: Marcourt Brace, 1933.
Jungkuntz, Theodore. "The Charismatic Renewal in Light of the Reformation", *Academy* 40(3 & 4), 1984.
——. *Confirmation and the Charismata*. Lanham, MD: University Press of America, 1983.
——. "Secularization Theology, Charismatic Renewal, and Luther's Theology of the Cross", *Concordia Theological Monthly* 62(11), (January 1971).
Jørgensen, Jens-Petter. *Sterk nok til å være svak* (Strong Enough to Be Weak). Oslo: Luther Forlag, 1999.
——. *Mulighetenes Gud* (The God of Opportunities). Oslo: Luther Forlag, 1986.
Jørgensen, Knud. "Spiritual Conflict in Socio-Political Context", in Moreau *et al.*, Eds. *Deliver Us From Evil: An Uneasy Frontier in Christian Mission*. Monrovia, CA: MARC, 2002.
Kallas, James. *The Satanward View*. Philadelphia, PA: Westminster, 1966.

Kantzer, Kenneth S. "The Charismatics among Us", *Christianity Today*, 11th February 1980.

Kärkkäinen, Veli-Matti. *Pneumatology: The Holy Spirit in Ecumenical, International, and Contextual Perspective*, 2nd Edition. Grand Rapids, MI: Baker Academic, 2018.

—. *Spirit and Salvation: A Constructive Christian Theology for a Pluralistic World.* Grand Rapids, MI: Eerdmans, 2016.

Keener, Craig S. *Christobiography: Memory, History and the Reliability of the Gospels.* Grand Rapids, MI: Eerdmans, 2019.

—. *Acts: An Exegetical Commentary*, 4 Vols. Grand Rapids, MI: Baker Academic, 2013-2014.

—. *Miracles. The Credibility of the New Testament Accounts,* Vols. 1 & 2. Grand Rapids, MI: Baker Academic, 2011.

Kelsey, Morton. *Encounter with God.* Minneapolis, MN: Bethany Fellowship, 1972.

—. "The Healing Ministry within the Church", *Journal of Religion and Health* 9(2), (April 1970).

—. *Tongue Speaking.* New York: Crossroad, 1964, rev. ed. 1981.

Kevorkian, Raymond. *The Armenian Genocide: A Complete History.* London: I.B. Tauris, 2011.

Kim, Sebastian and Kirsteen Kim. *Christianity as a World Religion.* London: Continuum, 2008.

Kirchner, Hubert *et al.*, Eds. *Charismatische Erneuerung und Kirche.* Berlin: Evangelische Verlagsanstalt, 1983.

Kittel, Gerhard, Ed. *Theological Dictionary of the New Testament*, Vol. 1, Grand Rapids, MI: Eerdmans, 1964.

Kohls, Ernst Wilhelm. *Luther oder Erasmus.* Basel: Friedrich Reinhardt, 1972.

Köberle, Alfred. *The Quest for Holiness*. Minneapolis, MN: Augsburg, 1938.

Kvalbein, Hans, *Fortolkning til Matteusevangeliet* (Commentary on the Gospel of Matthew), Bind 1, 2. Utgave. Oslo: Luther Forlag, 2009.

Kvalbein, Hans. "The Kingdom of God in the Ethics of Jesus", *Studia Theologica* 51(1), (1997): 60-84.

Land, Stephen. *Pentecostal Spirituality: A Passion for the Kingdom.* Cleveland, TN: CPT Press, 2010.

Lausanne Committee. *The Cape Town Commitment*. The Lausanne Committee for World Evangelization, 2011.

Lee, Younghoon. "Pentecostal Mission in the Third Christian Millennium: An Introduction", in Younghoon Lee and Wonsuk Ma, Eds. *Pentecostal Mission and Global Christianity: An Edinburgh Centenary Reader.* Oxford: Regnum, 2018.

Lee, Younghoon and Wonsuk Ma, Eds. *Pentecostal Mission and Global Christianity: An Edinburgh Centenary Reader.* Oxford: Regnum, 2018.

Lehmann, Martin E. *Luther and Prayer*. Milwaukee, WI: Northwestern, 1985.

Lenker, John N., Ed. *The Precious and Sacred Writings of Martin Luther.* Minneapolis, MN: Lutherans in All Lands Company, 1904.
Lewis, C.S. *Christian Reflections*. Grand Rapids, MI: Eerdmans, 1971.
Lindberg, Carter. *The Third Reformation? Charismatic Movements and the Lutheran Tradition*, Macon, GA: Mercer University Press, 1983.
Lovekin, Arthur Adams. *Glossolalia: Behavioral Science Perspectives on Speaking in Tongues.* New York: Oxford University Press, 1985.
—. *Glossolalia: A Critical Study of Alleged Origins, the New Testament and the Early Church.* Sewanee, TN: American Theological Library Association Microtext Project, 1962.
The Lutheran, "Lutheran Evangelism a Joke", *The Lutheran,* 17th September 1986.
Luther, Martin. *Commentary on Galatians*, edited by Philip Watson. Westwood, NJ: Fleming H. Revell, n.d.
—. *The Small Catechism, in Contemporary English.* Minneapolis, MN: Augsburg, 1979.
—. *Reformation Writings of Martin Luther*, trans. Bertram Lee Wolf. New York: Philosophical Library, 1956.
—. *Luthers Evangelien-Auslegung, ein Kommentar zu den vier Evangelien*, edited by Christian Gustav Eberle. Stuttgart: Verlag der evangelischen Bücherstiftung, 1877.
Ma, Wonsuk. "The Theological Motivation for Mission", in Younghoon Lee and Wonsuk Ma, Eds. *Pentecostal Mission and Global Christianity.* Oxford: Regnum, 2018.
Madsen, Ole Skjerbæk. "The Authority of Scripture", *Ånd og Liv,* December 1982.
Marsden, George M. *Fundamentalism and American Culture.* Oxford: Oxford University Press, 1980.
Marshall, Howard I. *Luke: Historian and Theologian.* Grand Rapids, MI: Zondervan, 1970.
Marty, Martin E. *Health and Medicine in the Lutheran Tradition.* New York: Crossroad, 1983.
McDonnell, Kilian. *The Other Hand of God: The Holy Spirit as the Universal Touch and Goal.* Collegeville, MN: Liturgical Press, 2003.
—. "Towards a Critique of the Churches and the Charismatic Renewal", *One in Christ* 16(4), (1981).
—, Ed. *Presence, Power, Praise – Documents of the Charismatic Renewal*, Vols. 1-3. Collegeville, MN: Liturgical Press, 1980.
—. *The Baptism with the Holy Spirit as an Ecumenical Problem.* Notre Dame, IN: Charismatic Renewal Services, 1972.
McDonnell, Kilian and George T. Montague. *Christian Initiation and Baptism in the Holy Spirit. Evidence from the First Eight Centuries.* Collegeville, MN: Liturgical Press, 1991.
McGavran, Donald A. "The Total Picture", *Christian Life*, October 1982.
McLean, Mark D. "Toward a Pentecostal Hermeneutic", in J. Rodman Williams, Ed. *Toward a Pentecostal/Charismatic Theology of Baptism*

in the Holy Spirit. Bound Volume of Papers from the Fourteenth Annual Meeting of the Society for Pentecostal Studies, 1984.

McNutt, Francis. *Healing.* Notre Dame, IN: Ave Maria Press, 1991/2001.

Meinhold, Peter. *Studien zu Ignatius von Antiochien.* Wiesbaden: Franz Steiner, 1979.

—. *Geschichte der kirchlichen Historiographie*, Vol. 1. Freiburg/Munich: Karl Alber, 1967.

Michaelsson, Lisbeth. "Marie Monsen's Achievement", in Tormod Engelsviken *et al.*, Eds. *A Passion for China.* Oxford: Regnum, 2015.

Moeller, Bernd. *Geschichte des Christentums.* Göttingen: Vandenhoeck & Ruprecht, 1965.

Montague, George T. *First Corinthians.* Catholic Commentary on Sacred Scripture, Grand Rapids, MI: Baker Academic, 2011.

Montgomery, John Warwick, Ed. *Principalities and Powers: A New Look at the World of the Occult.* Minneapolis, MN: Bethany Fellowship, 1973.

Moreau, A. Scott *et al.*, Eds. *Deliver Us From Evil: An Uneasy Frontier in Christian Mission.* Monrovia, CA: MARC, 2002.

Moreau, A. Scott. "Gaining Perspective on Territorial Spirits", in Moreau *et al.*, Eds. *Deliver Us From Evil: An Uneasy Frontier in Christian Mission.* Monrovia, CA; MARC, 2002.

Mumper, Sharon E. "Where in the World is the Church Growing?" *Christianity Today*, 11th July 1986.

Mungadze, Jerry. "Spiritual Conflict in Light of Psychology and Medicine", in Moreau *et al.*, Eds. *Deliver Us From Evil: An Uneasy Frontier in Christian Mission.* Monrovia, CA; MARC, 2002.

Neuhaus, Richard John. *The Religion and Society Report* 3(4), (April 1986).

Noesgen, D.K.F. *Geschichte der Lehre vom Heiligen Geist.* Gütersloh: Druck und Verlag von C. Bartelsmann, 1899.

Olsen, Peder. *Healing Through Prayer*, trans. John Jensen. Minneapolis, MN: Augsburg, 1962.

Opsahl, Paul, Ed. *The Holy Spirit in the Life of the Church.* Minneapolis, MN: Augsburg, 1978.

Owojaije, Moses. "The Problem of False Prophets in Africa", *Lausanne Global Analysis* 8(6), (20th November 2019).

Padgett, John G. "'I Am the Truth': An Understanding of Truth from Christology for Scripture", in Alan G. Padgett and Patrick R. Keifert, Eds. *But Is It All True? The Bible and the Question of Truth.* Grand Rapids, MI: Eerdmans, 2006.

Pederson, Dennis W. *A Letter Home for Family and Friends from an Itinerant Renewal Teacher and Evangelist,* unpublished report, International Lutheran Renewal Center, n.d.

Pelikan, Jaroslav and Helmut T. Lehmann, Eds. *Luther's Works*, 55 volumes. St. Louis, MO: Concordia; Philadelphia, PA: Fortress, 1957.

Porterfield, Amanda. *Healing in the History of Christianity.* Oxford: Oxford University Press, 2005.

Prange, Erwin. *The Gift Is Already Yours*. Plainfield, NJ: Logos, 1973.

Prenter, Regin. "Taler Gud direkte i dag? Profeti – åpenbaring – kall – ledelse", in Lars Østnor, Ed. *Jeg tror på Den hellige Ånd.* Oslo: Land og kirke/Gyldendal Norsk Forlag, 1982.

——. *Spiritus Creator*, trans. John M. Jensen. Philadelphia, PA: Fortress, 1953.

Quebedeaux, Richard. *The New Charismatics*. New York: Doubleday, 1976.

Rakotojoelinandrasana, Daniel. "Holistic and Integrated Care for Spirit, Mind, and Body as Practiced by the Fifohanzana", in Cynthia Holder Rich, Ed. *The Fifohanzana: Madagascar's Indigenous Christian Movement.* Amherst, NY: Cambria, 2008.

Klauser, Theodor, Ed. *Reallexikon für Antike und Christentum*. Stuttgart: Anton Hirsemann, 1955-57.

Rich, Cynthia Holder, Ed. *The Fifohanzana: Madagascar's Indigenous Christian Movement.* Amherst, NY: Cambria, 2008.

Richard, Marie E. *Philipp Jacob Spener and His Work, August Hermann Francke and His Work*. Philadelphia, PA: Lutheran Publication Society, 1897.

Rienecker, Fritz. *Sprachlicher Sclüssel zum Griechischen Neuen Testament*. Giessen-Basel: Brunnen Verlag, 1952.

Roberson, Jim. "Radical Evangelism! What Is It?" *International Lutheran Renewal* 85, (December 1986).

Rossteuscher, Ernst Adolph. *Der Aufbau der Kirche Christi auf den ursprünglichen Grundlagen: Eine geschichtliche Darstellung seiner Anfänge.* Siegen: Hermann Neier Nachf., 1871, reprinted 1969.

Ruhbach, G. "Das Charisma-Verständnis des Neuen Testaments", *Monatshefte für Pastoraltheologie*, (October 1964).

Sandnes, Karl Olav. *New Family: Conversion and Ecclesiology in the Early Church with Cross-Cultural Comparisons.* Pieterlen, Switzerland: Peter Lang, 1994.

Sanford, Agnes. *The Healing Light*. St. Paul, MN: Macalaster Park, 1947.

Santala, Risto. *Armolahjoista armon tasolta.* Helsinki: Karas-Sana Oy, 1978.

Sauer, Christof. "Christian Solidarity in the Face of Discrimination and Persecution", in Hans Aage Gravaas *et al.*, Eds., *Freedom of Belief and Christian Mission*, Oxford: Regnum, 2015.

Schaff, Philip. *History of the Christian Church*, Vol. 1. New York: Scribner's, 1882-1910.

Schlink, Edmund. *The Doctrine of Baptism*, trans. Herbert J.A. Bouman. St. Louis, MO: Concordia, 1972.

——. *Der kommende Christus und die kirchlichen Traditionen; Beiträge zum Gespräch zwischen den getrennten Kirchen.* Göttingen: Vandenhoeck & Ruprecht, 1961.

——. *Theology of the Lutheran Confessions*, trans. Paul F. Koehneke and Herbert J.A. Bouman. Philadelphia, PA: Fortress, 1961.

Schmidt, Martin. *Pietismus*, 3. Ausgabe. Stuttgart: Kohlhammar Verlag, 2008.

Schreiter, Robert. "The Emergence of Reconciliation as a Paradigm of Mission: Dimensions, Levels and Characteristics", in Knud Jørgensen and Robert Schreiter, Eds. *Mission as Ministry of Reconciliation.* Oxford: Regnum, 2013.

Schweizer, Eduard. "Pneuma", in Gerhard Friedrich Kittel, Ed. *Theologisches Wörterbuch zum Neuen Testament,* Vol. 6. Stuttgart: W. Kohlhammar Verlag, 1960.

Seeberg, Erich. *Luthers Theologie in ihren Grundzügen.* Stuttgart: W. Kohlhammar Verlag, 1950.

Seeberg, Reinhold. *Lehrbuch der Dogmengeschichte*, 1(4). Leipzig and Erlangen: A. Deichert, 1895.

Shakarian, Demos. *The Happiest People on Earth.* Old Tappan, NJ: Chosen, 1975.

Simonnes, Asbjørn. *Features of the Charismatic Movement from a Historical, Sociological and Anthropological Perspective*, unpublished D. Min. Dissertation. Pasadena, CA: Fuller Theological Seminary, 1996.

Skarsaune, Oskar and Tormod Engelsviken. "Possession and Exorcism in the History of The Church", in A. Scott Moreau *et al.*, Eds. *Deliver Us From Evil: An Uneasy Frontier in Christian Mission.* Monrovia, CA: MARC, 2002.

Skarsaune, Oskar. *Proof from Prophecy.* Leiden: Brill, 1987.

Spener, Philip Jacob. *Pia Desideria*, edited by Theodore G. Tappert. Philadelphia, PA: Fortress, 1964.

Stamoolis, James S. "Mission, Persecution and Martyrdom in the Early Church", in Hans Aage Gravaas *et al.,* Eds. *Freedom of Belief and Christian Mission.* Oxford: Regnum, 2015.

Stang, Tone Haugeto. *Ringer i vann. Historien om Ungdom i Oppdrag gjennom 50 år.* Ottestad: Proklamedia, 2021.

Staudenmaier, Franz Anton. *Der Pragmatismus der Geistesgaben oder das Wirken des göttlichen Geistes im Menschen und in der Menschheit.* Tübingen: Heinrich Laupp, 1835.

Stendahl, Krister. *Paul Among Jews and Gentiles, and Other Essays.* Philadelphia, PA: Fortress, 1976.

—. "Glossolalia – The New Testament Evidence", in Michael P. Hamilton, Ed. *The Charismatic Movement.* Grand Rapids, MI: Eerdmans, 1975.

—. *The Bible and the Role of Women.* Philadelphia, PA: Fortress, 1966.

Stone, Glenn C. and Charles LaFontaine, Eds. *Exploring the Faith We Share.* New York: Paulist Press, 1980.

Stott, John R., Ed. *Making Christ Known: Historic Mission Documents from the Lausanne Movement 1974-1989.* Carlisle: Paternoster Press, 1996.

——. *For the Lord We Love: Your Study Guide to the Lausanne Covenant.* The Lausanne Movement, 2009, first published in 1975.

——. *The Baptism and Fullness of the Holy Spirit.* Downers Grove, IL: Inter-Varsity, 1964.

Strommen, Merton P. *et al. A Study of Generations.* Minneapolis, MN: Augsburg, 1972.

Stronstad, Roger. *Spirit, Scripture and Theology: A Pentecostal Perspective*, 2nd Edition. Eugene, OR: Wipf and Stock, 2019.

——. *The Charismatic Theology of St. Luke.* Peabody, MA: Hendrickson, 1984.

——. "'Filled with the Holy Spirit': Terminology in Luke-Acts", in J. Rodman Williams, Ed. *Toward a Pentecostal/Charismatic Theology of Baptism in the Holy Spirit*, Bound volume of papers from the Fourteenth Annual Meeting of the Society for Pentecostal Studies, 15th-17th November 1984.

Sullivan, Francis. *Baptism in the Holy Spirit: A Catholic Interpretation of the Charismatic Experience.* Rome: Gregorian University, 1974.

Sundkler, Bengt and Christopher Steed. *A History of the Church in Africa.* Cambridge: Cambridge University Press, 2000.

Synan, Vinson. *The Holiness-Pentecostal Tradition: Charismatic Movements in the 20th Century,* 2nd edition. Grand Rapids, MI: Eerdmans, 1997, [first published under the title *The Holiness-Pentecostal Movement in the United* States, 1971].

——. *In the Latter Days.* Ann Arbor, MI: Servant, 1984.

Synan, Vinson, Ed. *Aspects of Pentecostal-Charismatic Origins.* Plainfield, NJ: Logos, 1975.

Tappert, Theodore G., Ed. *The Book of Concord.* Philadelphia, PA: Fortress, 1959.

Taylor, George Aiken. *A Sober Faith.* New York: Macmillan, 1953.

Taylor, Vincent. *The Gospel According to St. Mark.* London: Macmillan, 1955.

Thielicke, Helmut. *I Believe: The Christian's Creed.* Philadelphia, PA: Fortress, 1968.

Thomas, J.C. "Spiritual Conflict in Illness and Affliction", in A. Scott Moreau *et al.*, Eds. *Deliver Us From Evil: An Uneasy Frontier in Christian Mission.* Monrovia, CA: MARC, 2002.

——. "The Devil, Disease and Deliverance: Origins of Illness in New Testament Thought", *Journal of Pentecostal Theology*, Supplement Series 13. Sheffield: Sheffield Academic Press, 1998.

Thorvaldsen, Steinar. *A Prophet Behind the Plough: Hans Nielsen Hauge and His Ministry.* Tromsø: Tromsø University, Eureka Digital 1-2010.

Till, W.C. *Koptische Heiligen und Märtyrerlegenden II.* Roma: Orientalia Christiana Analecta, 1935-1936.

Van Engen, Charles. *The Growth of the True Church: An Analysis of the Ecclesiology of the Church Growth Theory.* Amsterdam: Rodopi, 1981.

Vasvig, William. *I Prayed. He Answered.* Minneapolis, MN: Augsburg, 1977.

Veerman, Frans. "Religious Persecution and Violence in the 21st Century: A Global Survey Based on the World Watch List", in Hans Aage Gravaas *et al.*, Eds. *Freedom of Belief and Christian Mission.* Oxford: Regnum, 2015.

Verkuyl, Johannes. *Contemporary Missiology: An Introduction.* Grand Rapids, MI: Eerdmans, 1978.

Walker, Williston. *A History of the Christian Church.* New York: Scribner's, 1959.

Webster, Noah. *Webster's New Collegiate Dictionary.* Springfield, MA: G & C. Merriam, 1949.

Wells, David. *Turning to God: Biblical Conversion in the Modern World.* Exeter: The Paternoster Press, 1989.

—. *God the Evangelist: How the Holy Spirit Works to Bring Men and Women to Faith.* Grand Rapids, MI: Eerdmans, 1987.

Whitaker, E.C. *Documents of the Baptismal Liturgy.* London: SPCK, 1977.

Wietzke, Walter and Jack Hustad, Eds. *Towards a Mutual Understanding of Neo-Pentecostalism.* Minneapolis, MN: Augsburg, 1973.

Williams, J. Rodman, Ed. *Toward a Pentecostal/Charismatic Theology of Baptism in the Holy Spirit*, Bound volume of papers from the Fourteenth Annual Meeting of the Society for Pentecostal Studies, 15th-17th November 1984.

Wimber, John and Kevin Springer. *Power Evangelism*. Revised and updated edition. Grand Rapids, MI: Baker, 2009.

Wimber, John. *Power Healing.* San Francisco, CA: Harper, 1991.

—. "Zip to 3000 in 5 Years", *Christian Life*, October 1982.

Wink, Walter. *Engaging the Powers: Discernment and Resistance in a World of Dominion*. Philadelphia, PA: Fortress, 1992.

Winkler, Gabriele. "Confirmation or Chrismation? A Study in Comparative Liturgy", *Worship* 58(1), (1974).

Winter, Ralph D. "The Two Structures of God's Redemptive Mission", *Missiology: An International Review* (January 1974).

Winter, Ralph D. and P. Beaver, *The Warp and the Woof: Organising Christian Mission.* Pasadena, CA: William Carey Library, 1970.

Wogen, Norris, Ed. *Jesus, Where Are You Taking Us*? Carol Stream, IL: Creation House, 1973.

Wood, Wayne. *The Lutheran Charismatic Movement in the United States*, unpublished D.Min. dissertation. Nashville, TN: Divinity School of Vanderbilt University, 1983.

World Council of Churches. *The Gift of Being: Called to Be a Church of All and for All.* Geneva: The World Council of Churches, 2016.

World Council of Churches. *Baptism, Eucharist and Ministry.* Faith and Order Paper, no. 111, the "Lima Text". Geneva: The World Council of Churches, 1982.

Yokum, Bruce. *Prophecy.* Ann Arbor, MI: Servant, 1976.

Yong, Amos. *Renewing Christian Theology: Systematics for a Global Christianity.* Waco, TX: Baylor University Press, 2014.

—. *Spirit of Love: A Trinitarian Theology*. Waco, TX: Baylor University Press, 2012.

—. *The Spirit Poured Out on All Flesh: Pentecostalism and the Possibility of a Global Theology.* Grand Rapids, MI: Baker Academic, 2005.

Zuendel, Fridrich. *Johann Christof Blumhardt: A Biography,* New edition. Walden, NY: Plough, 2019.